"Only a free and unrestrained ... expose deception in government ... among the responsibilities of a free press is the duty to prevent any part of the Government from deceiving the people and sending them off to distant lands to die of foreign fevers and foreign shot and shell. In my view, far from deserving condemnation for their courageous reporting, The New York Times, The Washington Post and other newspapers should be commended for serving the purpose that the Founding Fathers saw so clearly. In revealing the workings of government that led to the Vietnam war, the newspapers nobly did precisely that which the founders hoped and trusted they would do."

—From Justice Hugo L. Black's concurring opinion in the Supreme Court's historic decision in favor of The New York Times.

THE PENTAGON PAPERS

as published by

The New York Times

Based on investigative reporting by Neil Sheehan

Written by Neil Sheehan, Hedrick Smith,
E. W. Kenworthy and Fox Butterfield

Articles and documents edited by
Gerald Gold, Allan M. Siegal and Samuel Abt

BANTAM BOOKS, INC.
TORONTO • NEW YORK • LONDON
A NATIONAL GENERAL COMPANY

This book is available in a cloth edition
from Quadrangle Books, Inc., 12 E. Delaware Place,
Chicago, Illinois 60611.

THE PENTAGON PAPERS
A Bantam Book / published July 1971
2nd printing
3rd printing

Photographs in the insert were researched by
THE NEW YORK TIMES *and are not an integral
part of the Pentagon Papers nor were they included
in the official Government documents.*

Published simultaneously in the United States and Canada

*Bantam Books are published by Bantam Books, Inc., a National
General company. Its trade-mark, consisting of the words "Bantam
Books" and the portrayal of a bantam, is registered in the United
States Patent Office and in other countries. Marca Registrada.
Bantam Books, Inc., 666 Fifth Avenue, New York, N.Y. 10019.*

PRINTED IN THE UNITED STATES OF AMERICA

Contents

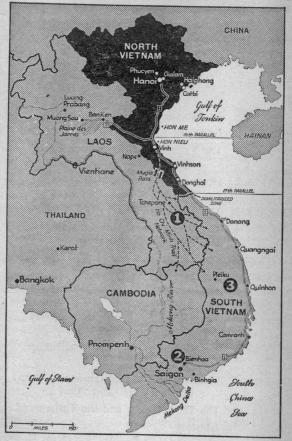

The New York Times

June 14, 1971

U.S. bombing of foe's Laotian trails (1) began in October, 1964. Enemy attack on Bienhoa (2) in December spurred study of U.S. options. Air war on North Vietnam followed guerrilla blows at Pleiku and Quinhon (3) in February, 1965.

Introduction

For the most of the past 20 years, directly or by proxy, the United States has been waging war in Indochina. Forty-five thousand Americans have died in the fighting, 95,000 men of various nationalities in the former French colonial army, and no one knows how many Indochinese—the guesses run from one to two million. Only a very small number of men have known the inner story of how and why four succeeding Administrations, those of Presidents Truman, Eisenhower, Kennedy and Johnson, helped to maintain this semipermanent war in Indochina—a conflict that the Administration of President Nixon has continued.

In the middle of 1967, Robert S. McNamara, who was then Secretary of Defense, made what may turn out to be one of the most important decisions in his seven years at the Pentagon. He commissioned what has since become known as the Pentagon papers—a massive top-secret history of the United States role in Indochina. The work took a year and a half. The result was approximately 3,000 pages of narrative history and more than 4,000 pages of appended documents —an estimated total of 2.5 million words. The 47 volumes cover American involvement in Indochina from World War II to May, 1968, the month the peace talks began in Paris after President Johnson had set a limit on further military commitments and revealed his intention to retire.

The New York Times obtained most of the narrative history and documents and began publishing a series of articles based on them on Sunday, June 13, 1971. After the first three daily installments appeared, the Justice Department obtained a temporary restraining order against further publication from the Federal District Court for the Southern District of New York. The Government, contending that if public dissemination of the history continued "the national defense interests of the United States and the nation's security will suffer immediate and irreparable harm," argued for a permanent injunction. The issue was fought through the courts for 15 days, as *The Times* and *The Washington Post,* which had subsequently begun publishing articles on the history, along with other newspapers, argued that the Pentagon papers belonged in the public domain and that no danger to the nation's security was involved.

On June 30, 1971, the Supreme Court of the United States freed the newspapers to continue publication of their articles. By a vote of 6 to 3, the justices held that the right to a free press under the First Amendment to the Constitution overrode any subsidiary legal considerations that would block publication by the news media.

Though far from a complete history, despite their bulk, the Pentagon papers form a great archive of government decision-making on Indochina over three decades. The papers tell what decisions were made, how and why they were made and who made them. The story is told in the written words of the principal actors themselves—in their memorandums, their cablegrams and their orders—and in narrative-analyses of these documents written by the 36 authors of the history.

These authors functioned as anonymous government historians. The majority were careerists, experienced State and Defense Department civilian officials and military officers, as well as defense-oriented intellectuals from government-financed research institutes. They were promised anonymity when they were recruited for the project so that they would be free to make judgments in the course of their writing. The anonymity was designed to protect their careers if the judgments later displeased higher authority.

The anonymous character of the history was also preserved by having several authors collaborate on each of the various chronological and thematic sections. The process gave the history a fragmented character and it does not reflect consistent themes throughout, as would a history written by one author or a group of authors who shared a similar overview of events.

Nevertheless, the history as a whole demonstrates that the four Administrations progressively developed a sense of commitment to a non-Communist Vietnam, a readiness to fight the North to protect the South, and an ultimate frustration with this effort—to a much greater extent than their public statements acknowledged at the time. The historians were led to many broad conclusions and specific findings, including the following:

• That the Truman Administration's decision to give military aid to France in her colonial war against the Communist-led Vietminh "directly involved" the United States in Vietnam and "set" the course of American policy.

• That the Eisenhower Administration's decision to rescue a fledgling South Vietnam from a Communist takeover and the Administration's attempt to undermine the new Communist regime of North Vietnam gave the Administration a "direct role in the ultimate breakdown of the Geneva settlement" for Indochina in 1954.

• That the Kennedy Administration, though ultimately spared from major escalation decisions by the death of its leader, transformed a policy of "limited-risk gamble," which it inherited, into a "broad commitment" that left President Johnson with a choice between more war and withdrawal.

• That the Johnson Administration, though the President was reluctant and hesitant to take the final decisions, intensified the covert warfare against North Vietnam and began planning in the spring of 1964 to wage overt war, a full year before it publicly revealed the depth of its involvement and its fear of defeat.

• That this campaign of growing clandestine military pressure through 1964 and the expanding program of bombing North Vietnam in 1965 were begun despite the judgment of the Government's intelligence community that the measures would not cause Hanoi to cease its support of the Vietcong insurgency in the South, and that the bombing was deemed militarily ineffective within a few months.

• That these four succeeding administrations built up the American political, military and psychological stakes in Indochina, often more deeply than they realized at the time, with large-scale shipments of military equipment to the French in 1950; with acts of sabotage and terror warfare against North Vietnam beginning in 1954; with moves that encouraged and abetted the overthrow of President Ngo Dinh Diem of South Vietnam in 1963; with plans, pledges and threats of further action that sprang to life in the Tonkin Gulf clashes in August, 1964; with the careful preparation of public opinion for the years of open warfare that were to follow; and with the calculation in 1965, as the planes and troops were openly committed to sustained combat, that neither accommodation inside South Vietnam nor early negotiations with North Vietnam would achieve the desired result.

In these disclosures and analyses of the origins and course of the war lie the immediate significance of the Pentagon papers.

But the documents and the narrative histories have a greater significance beyond the war in Indochina and its traumatic effects upon the United States and the countries of Southeast Asia. For this archive represents the first good look since the end of World War II at the inner workings of the machinery of the Executive Branch that has grown up under the American Presidency. The most recent body of policy documents to come into the public domain is dated 1946, the last year for which the State Department has released any of its archives. The Pentagon papers also contain documents, such as the reports on clandestine warfare, of a kind that generally are excluded from the State Department's policy of releasing documents after 25 years.

Clandestine warfare, as this collection of *New York Times* articles on the Pentagon papers will illustrate, naturally has an important effect on public events. Covert operations also occasionally violate treaties and contradict open policy pronouncements. No matter what vintage, therefore, documents related to clandestine war are, in the bureaucratic phrase, "excluded from downgrading" under the classification regulations, in order to avoid embarrassing the Executive Branch and the men responsible.

The instances are also rare in which a collection of documents akin to the Pentagon papers has come to light in modern history. The last examples were the release of the secret Czarist archives after the Russian Revolution in 1917, the publication of imperial Germany's records by the Weimar Republic following World War I, and the capture of the Nazi archives by the Allies at the climax of World War II.

The internal functioning of the machinery of the post-World War II Executive Branch has been much theorized about, but only intermittently perceived in authentic detail. Usually these perceptions have come in the personal memoirs of the policy-makers, whose version of history has been understandably selective.

To read the Pentagon papers in their vast detail is to step through the looking glass into a new and different world. This world has a set of values, a dynamic, a language and a perspective quite distinct from the public world of the ordinary citizen and of the other two branches of the Republic—Congress and the judiciary.

Clandestine warfare against North Vietnam, for example,

is not seen, either in the written words of the senior decision-makers in the Executive Branch or by the anonymous authors of the study, as violating the Geneva Accords of 1954, which ended the French Indochina War, or as conflicting with the public policy pronouncements of the various administrations. Clandestine warfare, because it is covert, does not exist as far as treaties and public posture are concerned. Further, secret commitments to other nations are not sensed as infringing on the treaty-making powers of the Senate, because they are not publicly acknowledged.

The guarded world of the government insider and the public world are like two intersecting circles. Only a small portion of the government circle is perceived from the public domain, however. Vigorous internal policy debates are only dimly heard and high-level intelligence analyses that contradict policy are not read outside. But, as the Pentagon papers demonstrate, knowledge of these policy debates and the dissents from the intelligence agencies might have given Congress and the public a different attitude toward the publicly announced decisions of the successive administrations.

The segments of the public world—Congress, the news media, the citizenry, even international opinion as a whole—are regarded from within the world of the government insider as elements to be influenced. The policy memorandums repeatedly discuss ways to move these outside "audiences" in the desired direction, through such techniques as the controlled release of information and appeals to patriotic stereotypes. The Pentagon papers are replete with examples of the power the Executive Branch has acquired to make its influence felt in the public domain.

The papers also make clear the deep-felt need of the government insider for secrecy in order to keep the machinery of state functioning smoothly and to maintain a maximum ability to affect the public world. And even within the inner world, only a small number of men at the top know what is really happening. During the five-day bombing pause in May, 1965, for instance, Secretary McNamara, in order to guard against leaks, sent a top-secret but misleading order through the entire military command structure stating that the purpose was to permit reconnaissance aircraft to conduct "a thorough study of [North Vietnamese] lines of communication."

The real purpose of the pause, the history says, was to provide an opportunity to secretly deliver what amounted to "a 'cease and desist' order" to Hanoi to call off the insurgency in the South. When this "demand for their surrender" was rejected, the history continues, the seemingly peaceful gesture of the pause would provide political credit for an escalation of the air war against North Vietnam afterwards. As President Johnson explained in a personal cable directly to General Maxwell D. Taylor, then the American Ambassador in Saigon, he wanted a pause "which I could use to good effect with world opinion."

"You should understand that my purpose in this plan is to begin to clear a path either toward restoration of peace or toward increased military action, depending upon the reaction of the Communists," the President said. "We have amply demonstrated our determination and our commitment in the last two months, and I now wish to gain some flexibility."

Such sharp and fresh detail in the Pentagon papers on the hitherto gray workings of the Executive Branch poses broad questions, for all spectrums of American political opinion, about the process of governing.

The principal actors in this history, the leading decision-makers, emerge as confident men—confident of place, of education and of accomplishment. They are problem-solvers, who seem rarely to doubt their ability to prevail. In a memorandum to President Johnson on Feb. 7, 1965, recommending a full-scale bombing campaign against North Vietnam, McGeorge Bundy, the former Harvard dean who was now the special presidential assistant for national security affairs, remarked in self-assured tones that "measured against the costs of defeat in Vietnam, this program seems cheap. And even if it fails to turn the tide—as it may—the value of the effort seems to us to exceed its cost." In the same memorandum, Mr. Bundy assured the President that General Taylor and the other senior members of the United States Mission in Saigon were "outstanding men, and United States policy within Vietnam is mainly right and well directed."

"None of the special solutions or criticisms put forward with zeal by individual reformers in Government or in the press is of major importance, and many of them are flatly wrong," Mr. Bundy told the President. "No man is perfect, and not every tactical step of recent months has been perfectly chosen, but when you described the Americans in Vietnam as your first team, you were right."

Of the generals, like William C. Westmoreland, the military commander in Vietnam, and Earle G. Wheeler, the Chairman of the Joint Chiefs of Staff, the history remarks that they were "men accustomed to winning."

The written language of these men, and that of a number of the Pentagon authors, is the dry, sparse language of problem-solving. There are the options, "Option A, Option B and Option C," and the "scenarios" for war planning, and the phrases like "wider action" and "overt military pressures" to describe open warfare. The conflict in Indochina is approached as a practical matter that will yield to the unfettered application of well-trained minds, and of the bountiful resources in men, weapons and money that a great power can command.

The restraints, the limits of action perceived, are what the body politic at home will tolerate and the fear of clashing with another major power—the Soviet Union or China. There is an absence of emotional anguish or moral questioning of action in the memorandums and cablegrams and records of the high-level policy discussions. Only once in the history do two of the leading participants, Secretary McNamara and the late John T. McNaughton, the head of the Pentagon's politico-military operations as the Assistant Secretary of Defense for International Affairs, express emotional and moral qualms. The occasion, recounted in Chapter 9, was a personal letter from Mr. McNaughton to Mr. McNamara, his friend as well as superior, in May, 1967, and a subsequent memorandum both men drafted for President Johnson later that month, unsuccessfully recommending a cutback in the bombing of the North to the 20th Parallel as a gesture toward peace. The letter and the related memorandum stand out as lonely cries against the magnitude of the human cost of the war.

One of the major limitations of the Pentagon papers is that the narrative-analyses were based solely upon the documents. To preserve the secrecy of the project, the historians were forbidden to interview the decision-makers, a number of whom had left government by the time the history was being written. Thus, the history lacks the motives and the considerations that were never committed to paper. The historians could not fill in the breaks in the documentary trail or always be certain of the precise context of a document.

This limitation, however, conversely gives the Pentagon papers a validity of their own. For it is a commonplace among journalists and historians that the memories of men, particularly men who have participated in an ill-fated venture, change with time.

For example, in an "eyes only" cable to President Kennedy after a crucial fact-finding mission to South Vietnam in the fall of 1961, General Taylor recommended sending an 8,000-man American combat task force under the cover of a flood relief mission. The majority of the troops should consist of "logistical-type units," General Taylor said, but "after acquiring experience in operating in SVN [South Vietnam], this initial force will require reorganization and adjustment to the local scene." Among the missions of the task force would be to act as "an emergency reserve" for the Saigon government army and as "an advance party of such additional [American] forces as may be introduced if . . . contingency plans are invoked."

"As a general reserve," General Taylor continued, the task force "might be thrown into action (with U.S. agreement) against large, formed guerrilla bands which have abandoned the forests for attacks on major targets."

"I am presently inclined to favor a dual mission, initially help to the flood area and subsequently use in any other area of SVN where its [the task force's] resources can be used effectively to give tangible support in the struggle against the VC [Vietcong]. However, the possibility of emphasizing the humanitarian mission will wane if we wait long in moving in our forces or in linking our stated purpose with the emergency conditions created by the flood." Without the combat task force, General Taylor warned, "I do not believe that our program to save SVN will succeed . . ."

Nearly 10 years later, in a television program recorded in the early spring of 1971 and broadcast on Sunday, June 27, 1971, General Taylor was asked about this recommendation, the gist of which has been publicly known.

"I did not recommend combat forces," he said. "I stressed we would bring in engineer forces, logistics forces, that could work on logistics and help in the very serious flood problem in 1961. So this was not a combat force."

"But you also described it as a military task force which might become the base for a further military expansion into combat forces," the television interviewer persisted.

"That is right, that's correct," the general said. "But I did not recommend anything other than three battalions of infantry. Pardon me, three battalions of engineers."

The Pentagon papers are beyond the reach of memory. The documents are the written words of the men who set the armies in motion and launched the warplanes. These written words undoubtedly contain factual errors and omissions by the decision-makers themselves, and the documents will have to be explained and elaborated upon for a complete historical account. But the written words are immutable, engraved now in the history of the nation for all to examine. This is the strength of the Pentagon papers.

The Times perceived several choices in deciding how to report the Pentagon history.

One choice was to disregard the narrative-analyses of the Pentagon historians, for whatever individual or institutional biases these might contain, and to report solely on the documents. This approach, however, would have forced *The Times* reporter to interpret the documents and made him the historian, and so it was rejected.

A second choice was to go beyond the narrative-analyses and the documents by interviewing the leading decision-makers and by seeking alternative interpretations of major events from published histories of the war. This approach would also have meant that *The Times* was, in effect, writing its own history of the war, and so it, too, was rejected.

The third approach, and the one adopted, was to keep the articles within the general limits set by the narrative-analyses and the documents as a whole. Material was brought in from the public record only where it seemed necessary to put the papers into context for the general reader. When the need to interpret events arose, *The Times* sought to confine itself to the interpretations in the Pentagon history. Where the Pentagon historians noted gaps in the documentary record, *The Times* so indicated.

The purpose was to report as accurately as possible on the corporate body of history that the narrative-analyses and the documents form, but the very selection and arrangement of facts, whether in a history or in a newspaper article, inevitably mirrors a point of view or state of mind. The articles that follow thus undoubtedly reflect some of the conceptions of *The Times* reporters who wrote them. But the hope has been to provide a fair reflection of the Pentagon papers and the desire has been to move them into the public domain as quickly as possible, so that the average citizen and the professional historian can judge the papers on their own merits.

NEIL SHEEHAN

July 2, 1971
New York City

Foreword

On June 17, 1967, at a time of great personal disenchantment with the Indochina war and rising frustration among his colleagues at the Pentagon, Secretary of Defense Robert S. McNamara commissioned a major study of how and why the United States had become so deeply involved in Vietnam.

According to Mr. McNamara's instructions, the report was to be "encyclopedic and objective." The final results were so candid and sensitive that only 15 copies of the report were produced and an effort by Mr. McNamara to have it declassified at the end of the Johnson Administration was reportedly rejected by the President.

The history project took a year and one-half to complete and yielded a highly unusual study of Government self-analysis. It was compiled by a team of 36 government authors, the majority civilian and military officials who had helped to develop or to carry out the policies they were asked to evaluate and some of whom were simultaneously active in the debates that changed the course of those policies.

While Mr. McNamara turned over his job to Clark M. Clifford, while the war reached a military peak in the 1968 Tet, or Lunar New Year, Offensive, while President Johnson cut back the bombing of North Vietnam and announced his plan to retire, and while the peace talks began in Paris, the study group burrowed through top-secret government files.

Its members sought to probe American policy toward Southeast Asia from the World War II pronouncements of President Franklin D. Roosevelt into the opening phase of the Vietnam peace talks in the summer of 1968. They wrote 42 book-length volumes, backed up by annexes of cablegrams, memorandums, draft proposals, dissents and other documents —47 volumes in all.

Their report, officially entitled, "History of U.S. Decision-Making Process on Vietnam Policy," runs to more than 7,000 pages—1.5 million words of historical narratives plus a mililon words of documents—enough to fill a small crate.

Even so, it is not a complete or polished history, as its participants knew. It displays many inconsistencies and it lacks a single all-embracing summary. It is an extended internal critique based on the documentary record, which the researchers did not supplement with interviews, because, in the words of the Pentagon project's director, Leslie H. Gelb, "Our guidance prohibited personal interviews with any of the principal participants."

The study emerged as a middle-echelon and official view of the war, incorporating material from the personal files of Secretary McNamara and those of other top-level officials in the Defense Department, into which flowed papers from the White House, the State Department, the Central Intelligence Agency and the Joint Chiefs of Staff.

Some important gaps appear in the study. The researchers did not have access to the complete files of Presidents or to all of the memorandums of Presidential policy discussions and decisions, nor to the full files of the State Department or the Central Intelligence Agency, though they had many documents from all three.

Moreover, there is another important gap in the copy of the Pentagon study obtained by *The New York Times:* it lacks the four volumes on the secret diplomacy of the Johnson period.

But whatever its limitations, the Pentagon's study discloses a vast amount of new information about the unfolding American commitment to South Vietnam and the way in which the United States engaged itself in that conflict. It is also rich in insights into the workings of government and the reasoning of the men who ran it.

The Pentagon account and its accompanying documents reveal that once the basic objective of policy was set, the internal debate on Vietnam from 1950 until mid-1967 dealt almost entirely with how to reach those objectives rather than with the basic direction of policy.

The study relates that American governments from the Truman Administration onward felt it necessary to take action to prevent Communist control over all of Vietnam. As a rationale for policy, the domino theory—that if South Vietnam fell, other countries would inevitably follow—was repeated in endless variations for nearly two decades.

Especially during the nineteen-sixties, the Pentagon study discloses, the Government was confident that American power—or even the threat of its use—would bring the war under control.

But the study reveals that high officials in the Johnson Administration were troubled by the potential dangers of Chinese Communist intervention and felt the need for self-restraint to avoid provoking Peking, or the Soviet Union, into combat involvement.

As some top policy-makers came to question the effectiveness of the American effort in mid-1967, the report shows, their policy papers began not only to seek to limit the military strategies on the ground and in the air but also to worry about the impact of the war on American society.

"A feeling is widely and strongly held that 'the Establishment' is out of its mind," wrote John T. McNaughton, Assistant Secretary of Defense, in a note to Secretary McNamara in early May, 1967. Mr. McNaughton, who three years earlier had been one of the principal planners of the air war against North Vietnam, went on to say:

"The feeling is that we are trying to impose some U.S. image on distant peoples we cannot understand (any more than we can the younger generation here at home), and that we are carrying the thing to absurd lengths. Related to this feeling is the increased polarization that is taking place in the United States with seeds of the worst split in our people in more than a century."

Late that June, Mr. McNamara—deeply disillusioned with the war—decided to commission the Pentagon study of Vietnam policy that Mr. McNaughton and other high officials had encouraged him to undertake.

Mr. McNamara's instructions, conveyed orally and evidently in writing as well, were for the researchers to pull together the Pentagon's documentary record of the American involvement.

The Pentagon researchers aimed at the broadest possible interpretation of events. They examined not only the policies and motives of American administrations, but also the effectiveness of intelligence, the mechanics and consequences of bureaucratic compromises, the difficulties of imposing American tactics on the South Vietnamese, the governmental uses of the American press, and many other tributaries of their main story.

The authors reveal, for example, that the American intelligence community repeatedly provided the policy makers with what proved to be accurate warnings that desired goals were either unattainable or likely to provoke costly reactions from the enemy. They cite some lapses in the accuracy of reporting and intelligence, but give a generally favorable assessment of the C.I.A. and other intelligence units.

The Pentagon researchers relate many examples of bureaucratic compromise forged by Presidents from the conflicting proposals of their advisers.

In the mid-fifties, they found, the Joint Chiefs of Staff were a restraining force, warning that a successful defense of South Vietnam could not be guaranteed under the limits imposed by the 1954 Geneva Accords and agreeing to send in American military advisers only on the insistence of Secretary of State John Foster Dulles.

In the nineteen-sixties, the report found, both Presidents Kennedy and Johnson chose partial measures, overriding advice that some military proposals were valid only as packages and could not be adopted piecemeal.

In examining Washington's constant difficulties with the governments in Saigon, the study found the United States so heavily committed to the regime of the moment and so fearful of instability that it was unable to persuade the South Vietnamese to make the political and economic reforms that Americans deemed necessary to win the allegiance of the people.

Though it ranges widely to explain events, the Pentagon report makes no effort to put the blame for the war on any single administration or to find fault with individual officials.

The writers appear to have stood at the political and bureaucratic center of the period, directing their criticisms toward both left and right.

In one section, Senator Eugene J. McCarthy, the antiwar candidate for the 1968 Democratic Presidential nomination, is characterized as "impudnet and dovish," and as an "upstart challenger." At another point in the same section the demands of Adm. U. S. Grant Sharp, commander of Pacific forces, for all-out bombing of North Vietnam, are characterized as "fulminations."

For the most part, the writers assumed a calm and unemotional tone, dissecting their materials in detached and academic manner. They ventured to answer key questions only when the evidence was at hand. They found no conclusive answers to some of the most widely asked questions about the war, including these:

• Precisely how was Ngo Dinh Diem returned to South Vietnam in 1954 from exile and helped to power?

• Who took the lead in preventing the 1956 Vietnam-wide

elections provided for in the Geneva Accords of 1954—Mr. Diem or the Americans?

• If President Kennedy had lived, would he have led the United States into a full-scale ground war in South Vietnam and an air war against North Vietnam as President Johnson did?

• Was Secretary of Defense McNamara dismissed for opposing the Johnson strategy in mid-1967 or did he ask to be relieved because of disenchantment with Administration policy?

• Did President Johnson's cutback of the bombing to the 20th Parallel on March 31, 1968, signal a lowering of American objectives for the war or was it merely an effort to buy more time and patience from a war-weary American public?

The research project was organized in the Pentagon's office of International Security Affairs—I.S.A., as it is known to government insiders—the politico-military affairs branch, whose head is the third ranking official in the Defense Department. This was Assistant Secretary McNaughton when the study was commissioned and Assistant Secretary Paul C. Warnke when the study was completed.

On Jan. 15, 1959, Mr. Gelb, head of I.S.A.'s Office of Policy Planning, who had acted as director of the Vietnam history task force, forwarded a letter to the then Secretary of Defense Clark Clifford informing him that the work was completed. Mr. Warnke reportedly "signed off" on the letter of transmittal to Mr. Clifford. Former officials say this meant that, while forwarding the history to the Secretary, Mr. Warnke acknowledged the completion of the work without endorsing its contents.

Although the project was completed after Mr. McNamara had left the Pentagon, "in everyone's mind it always remained Mr. McNamara's study," one official explained.

Three of the 15 copies that were eventually produced were hand delivered by Mr. Gelb to Mr. McNamara, then president of the World Bank. He is reported to have said since that he was satisfied with the study, though more than one other former policy maker is known to have been displeased by the results.

Other copies were said to have been provided to President Johnson, the State Department and President Nixon's staff, as well as to have been kept for Pentagon files.

The authors, mostly working part-time over several months, were middle-level officials drawn from I.S.A., Systems Analysis, and from the military staffs in the Pentagon, or lent by the State Department or the White House Staff. Probably two-thirds of the group had worked on Vietnam for the Government at one time or another.

"The people who worked on the task force were superb—uniformly bright and interested, although not always versed in the art of research," Mr. Gelb wrote in his letter to Mr. Clifford.

"We had a sense of doing something important and of the need to do it right. Of course, we all had our prejudices and axes to grind and these shine through clearly at all times, but we tried, we think, to suppress or compensate for them."

The result, he said, was not so much a documentary history, as a history based solely on documents that were sometimes contradictory, and "not immediately self-revealing or self-explanatory." For this reason, the project director explained, the documents were "checked and rechecked with ant-like diligence" by the research team.

Both the writing and editing were described as group efforts, though individuals with academic qualifications, such as historians, political scientists and the like, were in charge of various sections.

For their research, the Pentagon team depended primarily on the files of Secretary McNamara and Mr. McNaughton. William P. Bundy, former Assistant Secretary of State for Far Eastern Affairs, provided some State Department files.

For extended periods, probably the most serious limitation of the Pentagon study is the lack of access to White House archives. The researchers did possess the Presidential decision papers that normally circulated to high Pentagon officials, plus White House messages to commanders or ambassadors in Saigon. These provide insight into Presidential moods and motives, but only intermittently.

An equally important handicap is that the Pentagon researchers generally lacked records of the oral discussions of the National Security Council or the most intimate gatherings of Presidents with their closest advisers, where decisions were often reached.

As the authors themselves remark, it is common practice for the final recommendations, drafted before a key Presidential decision is made, to be written to the President's spoken specifications on the basis of his reactions to earlier proposals. The missing link is often the meeting of the Administration's inner circle.

Also, because the Pentagon study draws almost entirely on internal Government papers, and primarily papers that circulated through the Defense Department, the picture of so important a figure as Secretary of State Dean Rusk remains shadowy. Mr. Rusk was known as a man who rarely committed himself to paper and who, especially during the Johnson Administration, saved his most sensitive advice for solitary talks with the President.

In the late months of the Johnson Administration, the lack of records of such meetings is a considerable weakness because, as the survey comments, Mr. Johnson operated a split-level government. Only his most intimate advisers were aware of the policy moves he was contemplating, and some of the most important officials at the second level of government—Assistant Secretaries of State and Defense—were late to learn the drift of the President's thinking.

The Pentagon account notes that at times the highest Administration officials not only kept information about their real intentions from the press and Congress but also kept secret from the government bureaucracy the real motives for their written recommendations or actions.

"The lesson in this," one Pentagon analyst observes, "is that the rationales given in such pieces of paper (intended for fairly wide circulation among the bureaucracy, as opposed to tightly held memoranda limited to those closest to the decision maker), do not reliably indicate why recommendations were made the way they were." The words in parentheses are the analyst's.

Another omission is the absence of any extended discussion of military or political responsibility for such matters as civilian casualties or the restraints imposed by the rules of land warfare and the Geneva and Hague Conventions.

The approach of the writers varies markedly from section to section. Some of the writers are analytical and incisive. Others offer narrative compendiums of the most important available documents for their periods, with little comment or interpretation.

As a bureaucratic history, this account is necessarily fragmented. The writers either lacked time or did not choose to provide a coherent, integrated summary-analysis for each of the four Administrations that became involved in Vietnam from 1950 to 1968.

The Pentagon account divides the Kennedy period, for example, into five sections—dealing with the key decisions of 1961, the strategic-hamlet programs, the buildup of the American advisory mission in Vietnam, the development of plans for phased American withdrawal, and the coup d'etat that ousted President Diem.

In the Johnson era, four simultaneous stories are told in separate sections—the land war in South Vietnam, the air war against the North, political relations with successive South Vietnamese governments, and the secret diplomatic search for negotiations. There is some overlapping, but no single section tries to summarize or draw together the various strands.

The weaknesses were recognized by the authors themselves. "Writing history, especially where it blends into current events, especially where the current event is Vietnam, is a treacherous exercise," Mr. Gelb remarked in his letter to Mr. Clifford.

Although necessarily incomplete and inconsistent at points, the over-all effect of the history, however, is to provide the American public with a vast storehouse of new information —the most complete and informative central archive thus far on the Vietnam era.

HEDRICK SMITH

Chapter 1

The Truman and Eisenhower Years: 1945–1960

—BY FOX BUTTERFIELD

The secret Pentagon study of the Vietnam war discloses that a few days after the Geneva accords of 1954, the Eisenhower Administration's National Security Council decided that the accords were a "disaster" and approved actions to prevent further Communist expansion in Vietnam.

These National Security Council decisions, the Pentagon account concludes, meant that the United States had "a direct role in the ultimate breakdown of the Geneva settlement."

That judgment contradicts the repeated assertion of several American administrations that North Vietnam alone was to blame for the undermining of the Geneva accords.

According to the Pentagon writer, the National Security Council, at a meeting on Aug. 3, 1954, just after the Geneva conference, ordered an urgent program of economic and military aid—substituting American advisers for French advisers —to the new South Vietnamese Government of Ngo Dinh Diem.

The objectives set by the Council were "to maintain a friendly non-Communist South Vietnam" and "to prevent a Communist victory through all-Vietnam elections."

Under the Geneva settlement, Vietnam was to be temporarily divided into two zones pending reunification through elections scheduled for 1956. The introduction of foreign troops or bases and the use of Vietnamese territory for military purposes were forbidden. The United States, which did not join with the nations that endorsed the accords, issued a declaration taking note of the provisions and promising not to disturb them.

1

Highlights of the Period

South Vietnam, the secret Pentagon account contends, is essentially the creation of the United States, and the formative years were those of the Truman and—in particular—the Eisenhower Administrations.

Here, in chronological order, are key events—actions, decisions, policy formulations—of this period.

1945-6

Ho Chi Minh writes series of appeals for U.S. support to President Truman, Secretary of State; no indication, account says, of any reply.

1950

National Security Council study urges U.S. to "scrutinize closely the development of threats from Communist aggression" in Asia and to aid "directly concerned" governments; urges "particular attention" to French Indochina.

U.S. recognizes Bao Dai regime, not Ho; French ask military aid; Secretary of State Dean Acheson says alternative is "extension of Communism" throughout Southeast Asia "and possibly westward." Aid decision, account says, meant U.S. was "thereafter" directly involved "in the developing tragedy in Vietnam."

1953

National Security Council says loss of Indochina to Communism "would be critical to the security of the U.S." and "any negotiated settlement" would mean losing Indochina and "whole of Southeast Asia."

1954

National Security Council urges President Eisenhower to warn that "French acquiescence" in negotiated settlement would end U.S. aid to France. Suggests U.S. might continue war to "military victory."

French ask U.S. air strike with disguised planes. President's nonintervention decision still tentative. Secretary of State John Foster Dulles says he will give "broad hint" to French that U.S. intervention is possible with preconditions. Eisenhower orders draft Congressional resolution Defense Department prepares memo on required U.S. forces.

Joint Chiefs of Staff memo says Indochina is "devoid of decisive military objectives."

June—Col. Edward G. Lansdale of C.I.A. arrives Saigon to head team of agents for "paramilitary operations" and "political-psychological warfare" against North.

August—National intelligence estimate terms chances for strong regime in South poor. National Security Council finds Geneva accords "disaster" completing "major forward stride of Communism," study says. Joint Chiefs' memo says "strong, stable civil government" is "absolutely essential" basis for U.S. military-training aid. But Mr. Dulles feels military-training program is "one of the most efficient means" of stabilizing regime. With President's approval of Council recommendations for direct economic, military aid to South Vietnam, "American policy toward post-Geneva Vietnam was drawn," account says.

October—Lansdale team in "delayed sabotage" of Hanoi railroad; contaminates oil supply for city's buses for "gradual wreckage" of motors, distributes fake Vietminh leaflets; recruits, trains, equips two teams Vietnamese agents.

December—Gen. J. Lawton Collins, U.S. special representative, urges removal and replacement of Ngo Dinh Diem as leader or "re-evaluation of our plans" for area aid. Mr. Dulles replies he has "no other choice but to continue our aid to Vietnam and support of Diem."

1955

April—Mr. Dulles, after meeting with General Collins, cables embassy in Saigon to seek Diem alternative.

May—Mr. Diem, with Lansdale aid, quashes sect uprising, Saigon. Mr. Dulles cancels cable. National Security Council draft statement—its "main features" conveyed to Mr. Diem—suggests he insist on free elections by secret ballot with strict supervision. Communists in Germany had rejected those conditions; "hopefully the Vietminh would follow suit," account says.

December—Mr. Dulles, in cable to embassy, says U.S. should not act "to speed up present process of decay of Geneva accords" but not make "slightest effort to infuse life into them."

1956

U.S. sends 350 additional military men to Saigon; account says this "example of the U.S. ignoring" Geneva accords.

1960

National intelligence estimate predicts "dissatisfaction and discontent with the Government will probably continue to rise" and these "adverse trends," unchecked, "will almost certainly in time cause the collapse of Diem's regime."

But a lengthy report, accompanying the Pentagon study, describes in detail how the Eisenhower Administration sent a team of agents to carry out clandestine warfare against North Vietnam from the minute the Geneva conference closed.

The team, headed by the legendary intelligence operative Col. Edward G. Lansdale, gave a graphic account of the actions just before evacuating Hanoi in October 1954. [See Document #15.]

The report says the team "spent the last days of Hanoi in contaminating the oil supply of the bus company for a gradual wreckage of engines in the buses, in taking actions for delayed sabotage of the railroad (which required teamwork with a C.I.A. special technical team in Japan who performed their part brilliantly), and in writing detailed notes of potential targets for future para-military operations."

"U. S. adherence to the Geneva agreement," the authors of the report said, "prevented [the American team] from carrying out the active sabotage it desired to do against the power plant, water facilities, harbor and bridge."

"The team had a bad moment when contaminating the oil. They had to work quickly at night, in an enclosed storage room. Fumes from the contaminant came close to knocking them out. Dizzy and weak-kneed, they masked their faces with handkerchiefs and completed the job."

The report is attributed to a hastily assembled group identified as the Saigon Military Mission. Its authors do not explain why they believed sabotage of buses and the railroad was allowed under the Geneva accords if sabotage of the power plant and harbor was forbidden.

The Pentagon study, which was commissioned by Secretary of Defense Robert S. McNamara to determine how the United States became involved in the Vietnam war, devotes nine lengthy sections to the nineteen-forties and fifties.

At key points during these years, the Pentagon study says, the Truman and Eisenhower Administrations made far-reaching decisions on Vietnam policy that the public knew little about or misunderstood. And by the time John F. Kennedy became President in 1961, the writers recount, the American Government already felt itself heavily committed to the defense of South Vietnam.

One of the earliest disclosures in the account is that in late 1945 and early 1946, Ho Chi Minh wrote at least eight letters to President Truman and the State Department requesting American help in winning Vietnam's independence from France. [See Document #1.]

The analyst says he could find no record that the United States ever answered Ho Chi Minh's letters. Nor has Washington ever revealed that it received the letters.

A key point came in the winter of 1949-50 when the United States made what the account describes as a watershed decision affecting American policy in Vietnam for the next two decades: After the fall of mainland China to the Chinese Communists, the Truman Administration moved to support Emperor Bao Dai and provide military aid to the French against the Communist-led Vietminh.

This decision, which was made amid growing concern in the United States over the expansion of Communism in Eastern Europe and Asia, reversed Washington's long-standing reluctance to become involved with French colonialism in Indochina.

With this action, the account says, "the course of U. S. policy was set to block further Communist expansion in Asia." And "the United States thereafter was directly involved in the developing tragedy in Vietnam."

Another key point came in the spring of 1954, the writer discloses, when the Eisenhower Administration strongly hinted to France twice that it was willing to intervene with American military forces to prevent French defeat in Indochina.

While some information has been made public about these proposals, the Pentagon study says that the public has not understood how seriously the Eisenhower Administration debated intervention.

It adds that during the second episode, which occurred in May and June, 1954, while the Geneva conference was in session, President Dwight D. Eisenhower had aides draft a resolution requesting Congressional authority to commit American troops in Indochina.

The National Security Council was so opposed to France's negotiating an end to the war, the analyst relates, that "the President was urged to inform Paris that French acquiescence in a Communist take-over of Indochina would bear on its status as one of the Big Three" and that "U.S. aid to France would automatically cease."

Then in August, 1954, came the decision that the Pentagon account says determined United States policy toward Vietnam for the rest of the decade: The National Security Council launched its program of economic and military aid to Mr. Diem, then Premier and later President, though its action was not made public for months. [See Document #4.]

5

The Pentagon account discloses that most of these major decisions from 1950 on were made against the advice of the American intelligence community.

Intelligence analysts in the Central Intelligence Agency, the State Department and sometimes the Pentagon repeatedly warned that the French, Emporer Bao Dai and Premier Diem were weak and unpopular and that the Communists were strong.

In early August, 1954, for example, just before the National Security Council decided to commit the United States to propping up Premier Diem, a national intelligence estimate warned:

"Although it is possible that the French and Vietnamese, even with firm support from the U.S. and other powers, may be able to establish a strong regime in South Vietnam, we believe that the chances for this development are poor and moreover, that the situation is more likely to continue to deteriorate progressively over the next year."

"Given the generally bleak appraisals of Diem's prospects, they who made U.S. policy could only have done so by assuming a significant measure of risk," the study says of the Eisenhower commitments.

The Pentagon study does not deal at length with a major question: Why did the policy-makers go ahead despite the intelligence estimates prepared by their most senior intelligence officials?

The most important reason advanced by the Pentagon study is that after the fall of China to the Communists in 1949 and the hardening of American anti-Communist attitudes, "Indochina's importance to U.S. security interests in the Far East was taken for granted."

The basic rationale for American involvement—what later came to be called the domino theory—was first clearly enunciated by the National Security Council in February, 1950, when it decided to extend military aid to the French in Indochina.

"It is important to U.S. security interests," the Council said, "that all practicable measures be taken to prevent further Communist expansion in Southeast Asia. Indochina is a key area and is under immediate threat.

"The neighboring countries of Thailand and Burma could be expected to fall under Communist domination if Indochina is controlled by a Communist government. The balance of Southeast Asia would then be in grave hazard."

Subsequent Council decision papers throughout the nineteen-fifties repeated this formulation with ever-increasing sweep.

A Council paper approved by President Eisenhower in January, 1954, predicted that the "loss of any single country" in Southeast Asia would ultimately lead to the loss of all Southeast Asia, then India and Japan, and finally "endanger the stability and security of Europe."

"The domino theory and the assumptions behind it were never questioned," the Pentagon account says of the Eisenhower years. The result was that the Government's internal debate usually centered more on matters of military feasibility than on questions of basic national interests.

U.S. Policy in "Disarray"

The Pentagon study, which begins its account of American involvement in Vietnam with World War II, says that American policy from 1940 to 1950 has been a subject of "significant misunderstanding."

American policy toward Vietnam during these years, the study says, was "Less purposeful" than most people have assumed, and more characterized by "ambivalence and indecision."

President Franklin D. Roosevelt, the writer relates, never made up his mind whether to support the French desire to reclaim their Indochina colonies from the Japanese at the end of the war.

And at his death, American policy toward Indochina was in "disarray," the writer says.

He recounts that at first the Truman Administration had no clear-cut reaction to the conflict that broke out in 1945 and 1946 between the French and the Vietminh and eventually led to full-scale war. American policy, he adds, remained "ambivalent."

In a cablegram still kept secret in State Department files, Secretary of State George C. Marshall described the Government's quandary to the embassy in Paris:

"We have fully recognized France's sovereign position and we do not wish to have it appear that we are in any way endeavoring undermine that position.

"At same time we cannot shut our eyes to fact there are two sides this problem and that our reports indicate both a

7

lack of French understanding other side and continued existence dangerously outmoded colonial outlook and method in areas.

"On other hand we do not lose sight fact that Ho Chi Minh has direct Communist connections and it should be obvious that we are not interested in seeing colonial empire administrations supplanted by philosophy and political organization directed from and controlled by Kremlin.

"Frankly we have no solution of problem to suggest."

On this reasoning, the Truman Government refused French requests for American planes and ships to transport French troops to Indochina and similarly turned down appeals for American arms to help fight the Vietminh.

But the Truman Administration also rebuffed the appeals from Ho Chi Minh. In August and September, 1945, the account relates, while his forces were in control of Hanoi, he sent a request to President Truman through the Office of Strategic Services, precursor of the C.I.A., asking that Vietnam be accorded "the same status as the Philippines" for a period of tutelage pending independence.

From October, 1945, until the following February, the account continues, Ho Chi Minh wrote at least eight letters to President Truman or to the Secretary of State, formally appealing for United States and United Nations intervention against French colonialism.

There is no record, the analyst says, that any of the appeals were answered.

"Nonintervention by the United States on behalf of the Vietnamese was tantamount to acceptance of the French," the Pentagon account declares.

In 1948 and 1949, as concern about the Soviet Union's expansion in Eastern Europe grew in the United States, Washington became increasingly anxious about Ho Chi Minh's Communist affiliations. Nevertheless, the account discloses, a survey by the State Department's Office of Intelligence and Research in the fall of 1948 concluded that it could not find any hard evidence that Ho Chi Minh actually took his orders from Moscow.

"If there is a Moscow-directed conspiracy in Southeast Asia, Indochina is an anomaly so far," the study reported in its evaluation section.

With its growing concern about Communism, Washington began to press Paris harder to give more independence to the Indochina states. The American Government thus hoped to encourage Vietnamese popular support for Bao Dai as a non-Communist alternative to Ho Chi Minh and his Vietminh.

Yet, the narrative relates, even when in March, 1949, France did agree with Emperor Bao Dai to grant Vietnam independence within the French Union, the Truman Administration continued to withhold its backing, fearful that Bao Dai was still weak and tainted with French colonialism.

In a cablegram to the Paris embassy, the State Department outlined its concern:

"We cannot at this time irretrievably commit the U.S. to support of a native government which by failing to develop appeal among Vietnamese might become virtually a puppet government separated from the people and existing only by the presence of French military forces."

But when Mao Tse-tung's armies drove Generalissimo Chiang Kai-shek out of China in late 1949, Washington's ambivalence ended dramatically.

On Dec. 30 President Truman approved a key National Security Council study on Asia, designated N.S.C. 48/2. With it, the Pentagon study says, "The course of U. S. policy was set to block further Communist expansion in Asia."

"The United States on its own initiative," the document declared, should now scrutinize closely the development of threats from Communist aggression, direct or indirect, and be prepared to help within our means to meet such threats by providing political, economic and military assistance and advice where clearly needed to supplement the resistance of other governments in and out of the area which are more directly concerned."

The Council document concluded that "particular attention should be given to the problem of French Indochina."

The basic policy decisions having been made, the Pentagon account relates, developments followed swiftly.

When Peking and Moscow recognized Ho Chi Minh's Democratic Republic of Vietnam in January, 1950, Washington followed by recognizing Bao Dai that Feb. 7.

Nine days later, the French requested military aid for the war in Indochina. Secretary of State Dean Acheson, in recommending a favorable reply, wrote in a memorandum to President Truman:

"The choice confronting the U. S. is to support the legal governments in Indochina or to face the extension of Communism over the remainder of the continental area of Southeast Asia and possibly westward."

On May 8, Washington announced that it would provide

economic and military aid to the French in Indochina, beginning with a grant of $10-million.

The first step had been taken. "The U.S. thereafter was directly involved in the developing tragedy in Vietnam," the account says.

Ultimately, the American military aid program reached $1.1-billion in 1954, paying for 78 per cent of the French war burden.

Brink of Intervention

In the spring of 1954, as the French military position in Indochina deteriorated rapidly and the date for the Geneva conference approached, the Eisenhower Administration twice hinted to France that it was ready to intervene with American forces.

The Pentagon study contends that while some information about these two episodes has become public, the American people have never been told how seriously the Eisenhower inner circle debated intervening.

"The record shows plainly," the analyst says, "that the U.S. did seriously consider intervention and advocated it to the U.K. and other allies."

The first of these episodes, during March and April before the fall of the French fortress at Dienbienphu, was disclosed not long afterward by American journalists. But the story of the second, in May and early June while the Geneva conference was in session, has never been fully revealed. Mr. Eisenhower himself, in his 1963 book "Mandate for Change," mentioned the second debate over intervention but gave only a sketchy account and did not report asking Secretary Dulles to draft a Congressional resolution.

The Eisenhower Administration felt intervention might be necessary, the study says, because without American help the French were likely to negotiate a "sellout" at Geneva to escape an unpopular war.

As early as August, 1953, the National Security Council decided that American policy should be that "under present conditions any negotiated settlement would mean the eventual loss to Communism not only of Indochina but of the whole of Southeast Asia. The loss of Indochina would be critical to the security of the U.S."

The Eisenhower Administration stated its opposition to a

negotiated settlement most fully in an N.S.C. paper, "United States Position on Indochina to be Taken at Geneva," late in April in the week the conference opened.

It was at this point, according to the study, that the Council urged President Eisenhower "to inform Paris that French acquiescence in a Communist take-over of Indochina would bear on its status as one of the Big Three" and that "U.S. aid to France would automatically cease."

In addition, the Council's policy paper said that the United States should consider continuing the war itself, with the Indochina states, if France negotiated an unsatisfactory settlement. America's goal should be nothing short of a "military victory," the Council said.

The Government's internal record shows, the study says, that while Secretary of State John Foster Dulles and Adm. Arthur W. Radford, Chairman of the Joint Chiefs of Staff, pushed hard for intervention, other service chiefs, particularly Gen. Matthew B. Ridgway of the Army, were more cautious. They remembered the bitter and protracted experience in Korea and were not eager to repeat it.

President Eisenhower finally reached a decision against intervention on April 4 after a meeting of Mr. Dulles and Admiral Radford with Congressional leaders the previous day showed that the Congress would not support American action without allied help.

As journalists wrote, at the time, the President felt he must have Congressional approval before he committed American troops, and the Congressional leaders insisted on allied participation, especially by Britain.

At the very time the President was reaching this conclusion, Ambassador Douglas Dillon in Paris was cabling that the French had requested the "immediate armed intervention of U.S. carrier aircraft at Dienbienphu." [See Document #5.]

Mr. Dillon noted that the French had been prompted to make the request because they had been told by Admiral Radford that "he would do his best to obtain such help from the U.S. Government."

Moreover, the President's decision of April 4, contrary to what was written at the time, was only tentative. The debate on intervention was still very much alive, the Pentagon account says.

In fact, the following day, April 5, the National Security Council, in an action paper, concluded:

"On balance, it appears that the U.S. should now reach a decision whether or not to intervene with combat forces if that is necessary to save Indochina from Communist control, and tentatively the form and conditions of any such intervention."

On May 7, with the news that Dienbienphu had just fallen and with the delegates already in Geneva, President Eisenhower met with Mr. Dulles in the White House to again consider intervention.

According to a memorandum by Robert Cutler, the President's executive assistant, they discussed how "the U.S. should (as a last act to save Indochina) propose to France" that if certain conditions were met "the U.S. will go to Congress for authority to intervene with combat forces." The words in parentheses appeared in the memorandum. [See Document #8.]

Mr. Cutler noted that he explained to the President that some members of the Council's Planning Board "felt that it had never been made clear to the French that the United States was willing to ask for Congressional authority" if the preconditions were met.

Mr. Dulles said he would mention the subject to the French Ambassador, Henry Bonnet, that afternoon, "perhaps making a more broad hint than heretofore."

The preconditions included a call for the French to grant "genuine freedom" to the Indochina states—Laos, Cambodia and Vietnam.

They also stipulated that American advisers in Vietnam should "take major responsibility for training indigenous forces" and "share responsibility for military planning." American officers in Vietnam had long chafed under the limits on the role the French allowed them, the study says.

Participation by the British, who had shown themselves extremely reluctant to get involved, was no longer cited as a condition.

The French picked up Mr. Dulles's hint, and on May 10 Premier Joseph Laniel told Ambassador Dillon that France needed American intervention to save Indochina. That evening the President again met with Mr. Dulles, along with Admiral Radford and Secretary of Defense Charles E. Wilson, to discuss the French appeal.

During the meeting President Eisenhower directed Secretary Dulles to prepare a resolution that he could take before a joint meeting of Congress, requesting authority to commit American troops in Indochina.

From a document included in the Pentagon chronicle— the partial text of a legal commentary by a Pentagon official

12

on the draft Congressional resolution—it is clear that such a Congressional resolution was prepared and circulated in the State Department, the Justice Department and the Defense Department.

Both the State Department and the Defense Department then undertook what the account describes as "contingency planning" for possible intervention—the State Department drawing up a hypothetical timetable of diplomatic moves and the Defense Department preparing a memorandum on the U.S. forces that would be required.

The Joint Chiefs of Staff, in a memorandum to Secretary of Defense Wilson on May 20, recommended that the United States limit its involvement to "air and naval support directed from outside Indochina."

"From the point of view of the United States," the Joint Chiefs said, "Indochina is devoid of decisive military objectives and the allocation of more than token U.S. armed forces to that area would be a serious diversion of limited U.S. capabilities."

In the debates over intervention, the study says, advocates of American action advanced several novel ideas. Admiral Radford proposed to the French, for example, that the United States help create an "International Volunteer Air Corps" for Indochina. The French in April had suggested an American air strike with the planes painted with French markings. And late in May the French suggested that the President might be able to get around Congress if he sent just a division of marines—some 15,000 men.

But all the arguments in favor of intervention came to naught. The French Cabinet felt that the war-weary National Assembly would balk at any further military action.

And the military situation in the Red River Delta near Hanoi deteriorated so badly in late May and early June that Washington felt intervention would now be useless. On June 15 Secretary Dulles informed Ambassador Bonnet that the time for intervention had run out.

The Geneva "Disaster"

When the Geneva agreements were concluded on July 21, 1954 the account says, "except for the United States, the major powers were satisfied with their handiwork."

13

France, Britain, the Soviet Union, Communist China and to some extent North Vietnam believed that they had ended the war and had transferred the conflict to the political realm.

And, the study says, most of the governments involved "anticipated that France would remain in Vietnam." They expected that Paris would retain a major influence over the Diem regime, train Premier Diem's army and insure that the 1956 elections specified by the Geneva accords were carried out.

But the Eisenhower Administration took a different view, the Pentagon account relates.

In meetings Aug. 8 and 12, the National Security Council concluded that the Geneva settlement was a "disaster" that "completed a major forward stride of Communism which may lead to the loss of Southeast Asia."

The Council's thinking appeared consistent with its decision in April before the conference began, that the United States would not associate itself with an unsatisfactory settlement. Secretary Dulles had announced this publicly on several occasions, and in the end the United States had only taken note of the agreements.

But before the Council reached a final decision in August on exactly what programs to initiate in Indochina, several dissenting voices rose inside the Government.

The national intelligence estimate of Aug. 3 warned that even with American support it was unlikely that the French or Vietnamese would be able to establish a strong government. And the National Intelligence Board predicted that the situation would probably continue to deteriorate.

The Joint Chiefs of Staff had also objected to proposals that the United States train and equip the South Vietnamese Army.

In a memorandum to the Secretary of Defense on Aug. 4, the Joint Chiefs listed their preconditions for U.S. military aid to the Diem regime:

"It is absolutely essential that there be a reasonably strong, stable civil government in control. It is hopeless to expect a U. S. military training mission to achieve success unless the nation concerned is able effectively to perform those governmental functions essential to the successful raising and maintenance of armed forces."

The Joint Chiefs also called for the complete "withdrawal of French forces, French officials and French advisers from Indochina in order to provide motivation and a sound basis for the establishment of national armed forces."

Finally the Joint Chiefs expressed concern about the limits placed on American forces in Vietnam by the Geneva accords—they were restricted to 342 men, the number of American military personnel present in Vietnam when the armistice was signed.

Despite these arguments, the study says, Secretary of State Dulles felt that the need to stop Communism in Vietnam made action imperative.

In a letter to Secretary of Defense Wilson, he said that while the Diem regime "is far from strong or stable," a military training program would be "one of the most efficient means of enabling the Vietnamese Government to become strong."

In the end, the study recounts, Secretary Dulles's views were persuasive.

On Aug. 20 the President approved a National Security Council paper titled "Review of U.S. Policy in the Far East." It outlined a threefold program:

• Militarily, the United States would "work with France only so far as necessary to build up indigenous forces able to provide internal security."

• Economically, the United States would begin giving aid directly to the Vietnamese, not as before through the French. The French were to be dissociated from the levers of command."

• Politically, the United States would work with Premier Diem, but would encourage him to broaden his Government and establish more democratic institutions.

With these decisions, the account says "American policy toward post-Geneva Vietnam was drawn." The commitment for the United States to assume the burden of defending South Vietnam had been made.

"The available record does not indicate any rebuttal" to the warnings of the National Intelligence Board or the Joint Chiefs of Staff, the account reports. "What it does indicate is that the U.S. decided to gamble with very limited resources because the potential gains seemed well worth a limited risk."

Although this major decision for direct American involvement in Vietnam was made in August, the Pentagon account shows that the Eisenhower Administration had already sent a team of Americans to begin secret operations against the Vietminh in June, while the Geneva conference was still in session.

The team was headed by Colonel Lansdale, the C.I.A.

agent who had established a reputation as America's leading expert in counterguerrilla warfare in the Philippines, where he had helped President Ramon Magsaysay suppress the Communist-led Hukbalahap insurgents.

So extensive were his subsequent exploits in Vietnam in the nineteen-fifties that Colonel Landsdale was widely known as the model for the leading characters in two novels of Asian intrigue—"The Quiet American," by Graham Greene, and "The Ugly American," by William J. Lederer and Eugene Burdick.

A carefully detailed 21,000-word report by members of Colonel Lansdale's team, the Saigon Military Mission, is appended to the Pentagon chronicle. [See Document #15.]

According to that report, in the form of a diary from June, 1954, to August, 1955, the team was originally instructed "to undertake paramilitary operations against the enemy and to wage political-psychological warfare."

"Later," it adds, "after Geneva, the mission was modified to prepare the means for undertaking paramilitary operations in Communist areas rather than to wage unconventional warfare."

One of Colonel Lansdale's first worries was to get his team members into Vietnam before the Aug. 11 deadline set by the Geneva agreements for a freeze on the number of foreign military personnel. As the deadline approached, the report says, it appeared that the Saigon Military Mission "might have only two members present unless action was taken."

It adds that Lieut. Gen. John W. O'Daniel, chief of the United States Military Assistance Advisory Group, "agreed to the addition of 10 S.M.M. members under MAAG cover, plus any others in the Defense pipeline who arrived before the deadline. A call for help went out. Ten officers in Korea, Japan and Okinawa were selected and rushed to Vietnam."

While the report says that the team members were given cover by being listed as members of MAAG, the report also points out that they communicated with Washington through the C.I.A. station in Saigon.

Colonel Lansdale himself is identified as a member of the C.I.A. in a memorandum on the actions of the President's Special Committee on Indochina, written Jan. 30, 1954, by Maj. Gen. Charles H. Bonesteel 3d. [See Document #3.]

The memorandum, which is appended to the Pentagon study, lists Colonel Lansdale as one of the C.I.A. representatives present at the meeting. Allen W. Dulles, Director of Central Intelligence, also attended the meeting.

In the fall of 1954, after all the members had arrived in Vietnam, the report says, the team's activities increased.

Under Colonel Lansdale, "a small English-language class [was] conducted for mistresses of important personages at their request."

This class provided valuable contacts for Colonel Lansdale, enabling him to get to know such people as the "favorite mistress" of the army Chief of Staff, Gen. Nguyen Van Hinh, the report recounts.

When the Oct. 9 deadline for the French evacuation of Hanoi approached, the team sought to sabotage some of Hanoi's key facilities.

"It was learned that the largest printing establishment in the north intended to remain in Hanoi and do business with the Vietminh," the report relates. "An attempt was made by S.M.M. to destroy the modern presses, but Vietminh security agents already had moved into the plant and frustrated the attempt."

It was the mission's team in Hanoi that spent several nights pouring contaminant in the engines of the Hanoi bus company so the buses would gradually be wrecked after the Vietminh took over the city.

At the same time, the mission's team carried out what the report calls "black psywar strikes"—that is, psychological warfare with materials falsely attributed to the other side. The team printed what appeared to be "leaflets signed by the Vietminh instructing Tonkinese on how to behave for the Vietminh takeover of the Hanoi region in early October, including items about property, money reform and a three-day holiday of workers upon take-over." The attempt to scare the people worked.

"The day following the distribution of these leaflets," the report adds, "refugee registration [of those wishing to flee North Vietnam] tripled. Two days later Vietminh currency was worth half the value prior to the leaflets.

"The Vietminh took to the radio to denounce the leaflets; the leaflets were so authentic in appearance that even most of the rank-and-file Vietminh were sure that the radio denunciations were a French trick."

In the South, the team hired Vietnamese astrologers—in whose art many Asians place great trust—to compile almanacs bearing dire predictions for the Vietminh and good omens for the new Government of Premier Diem.

To carry out clandestine operations in North Vietnam after the team evacuated Hanoi, the report adds, Maj. Lucien Conein, an officer of S.M.M., recruited a group of Vietnamese agents under the code name of Binh.

"The group was to be trained and supported by the U.S. as patriotic Vietnamese," the report says, "to come eventually under Government control when the Government was ready for such activities. Thirteen Binhs were quietly exfiltrated through the port of Haiphong . . . and taken on the first stage of the journey to their training area by a U.S. Navy ship."

Until Haiphong was finally evacuated in May, 1955, Civil Air Transport, the Taiwan-based airline run by Gen. Claire Chennault, smuggled arms for the Binh team from Saigon to Haiphong.

In exchange, the report says, the Lansdale Mission got C.A.T. the lucrative contract for flying the thousands of refugees out of North Vietnam.

As the report describes the team's actions, "Haiphong was reminiscent of our own pioneer days as it was swamped with people whom it couldn't shelter. Living space and food were at a premium, nervous tension grew. It was a wild time for our northern team."

Another team of 21 agents, code-named the Hao group, were recruited in Saigon, smuggled out on a U.S. Navy ship while disguised as coolies, and taken to a "secret site" for training, the report goes on.

Arms for the Haos were smuggled into Saigon by the United States Air Force, the report says, adding that S.M.M. brought in eight and a half tons of equipment. This included 14 radios, 300 carbines, 50 pistols, 300 pounds of explosives and 100,000 rounds of ammunition.

The Lansdale team's report does not tell what kinds of intelligence or sabotage activities the Binh and Hao groups carried out in North Vietnam. But it does recount that one Binh agent was mistakenly picked up by Premier Diem's troops on his return to South Vietnam.

"He was interrogated by being handcuffed to a leper, both beaten with the same stick to draw blood, told he would now have leprosy, and both locked up in a tiny cell together," it says "S.M.M. was able to have him released."

For fiscal year 1955, the report shows, expenses for the Saigon Military Mission ran to $228,000. This did not include salary for the American officers or costs of weapons drawn from American stocks.

The largest item, $123,980, was listed as payment for operations, including pay and expenses for agents, safe-houses and transportation.

Lansdale in the Breach

While Colonel Lansdale's team carried out its covert operations, the major policy decisions made by the National Security Council in August, 1954, were being put into practice.

In December, Gen. J. Lawton Collins, who had been chosen by President Eisenhower as his personal representative to Vietnam, signed an agreement with the French providing for the United States to take over all military training duties from them.

The agreement was put into effect in February, 1955, the account says, and the French, under American pressure, began their unexpected withdrawal from South Vietnam.

Despite the decision in August, 1954, to back Premier Diem, there was still widespread uneasiness in the American Government over his lack of support and the fragile political situation in Saigon, the Pentagon account goes on.

General Collins, who had been given the rank of Ambassador, felt that Premier Diem was unequal to the task and urged that he be removed.

If the United States was unwilling to replace Mr. Diem, General Collins wrote to Washington in December, 1954, then "I recommend re-evaluation of our plans for assisting Southeast Asia." This is the "least desirable but in all honesty and in view of what I have observed here to date this may be the only sound solution," he said.

Still Secretary Dulles remained convinced, as he cabled in reply to General Collins's message, that "we have no other choice but continue our aid to Vietnam and support of Diem." And he told Assistant Secretary of State Walter Robertson several days later that the United States must "take the plunge" with Mr. Diem, the narrative adds.

In the spring of 1955 the crisis in Saigon worsened. The Hoa Hao and Cao Dai armed sects formed a united front with the Binh Xuyen, a group of gangsters who controlled Saigon's police against Premier Diem, and sporadic fighting broke out in the city. The French told Washington they thought Premier Diem was "hopeless" and "mad."

General Collins, now adamant that Mr. Diem must go, flew back to Washington in late April to press his case personally with the Secretary of State.

On April 27, after a meeting with General Collins, Secretary Dulles reluctantly agreed to the replacing of Premier Diem. He cabled the embassy in Saigon to find an alternative.

But Colonel Lansdale was working hard to support his friend Mr. Diem. In October the colonel had foiled a coup against Mr. Diem by Gen. Nguyen Van Hinh, the army Chief of Staff, by inviting General Hinh's two key aides to visit the Philippines for a tour of secret projects.

The authors of the Lansdale group's report do not specifically state that the team's instructions included supporting Mr. Diem against internal non-Communist opposition. But it is apparent from Colonel Lansdale's actions that he considered this an important part of his mission.

During the fall of 1954 Colonel Lansdale helped Mr. Diem recruit, pay and train reliable bodyguards. He had been shocked to discover when he visited Mr. Diem at the palace during a coup attempt that the official bodyguards had all deserted. "Not a guard was left on the grounds," the report says. "President Diem was alone upstairs, calmly getting his work done."

With permission from the embassy, the Saigon Military Mission then began secretly paying funds to a Cao Dai leader, Gen. Trinh Minh The, who offered his services to Premier Diem.

Colonel Lansdale also brought from the Philippines President Magsaysay's senior military aide and three assistants to train a battalion of Vietnamese palace guards.

When the sect crisis broke out in the spring of 1955 Colonel Lansdale visited Mr. Diem nearly every day, the S.M.M. report says. "At President Diem's request, we had been seeing him almost nightly as tensions increased, our sessions with him lasting for hours at a time."

During the sect armies' uprising, the Saigon Military Mission helped Premier Diem plan measures against the Binh Xuyen, and Colonel Lansdale repeatedly pressed the embassy to support the Premier.

With the acting C.I.A. station chief, Colonel Lansdale formed a team to help take action against the Binh Xuyen. The S.M.M. report recounts that "all measures possible under the narrow limits permitted by U.S. policy were taken."

Uncharacteristically, the report adds, "These will not be described here, but there were a number of successful actions."

On what proved to be the crucial day, April 28, the Pentagon study reports, Premier Diem summoned Colonel Lansdale to the palace and outlined his troubles. He had just received word from his embassy in Washington that the U.S. appeared to be about to stop supporting him."

This was probably a reference to Secretary Dulles's decision of the previous day.

Premier Diem also reported that Binh Xuyen units had begun firing on his troops.

Colonel Lansdale sought to reassure him. "We told him that it looked as though Vietnam still needed a leader," the report says, "that Diem was still President, that the U.S. was still supporting him."

That afternoon Premier Diem ordered a counterattack against the Binh Xuyen, and within nine hours achieved a major victory.

"Washington responded with alacrity to Diem's success, superficial though it was," the narrative says. Saigon was told to forget Secretary Dulles's order to drop Diem. The embassy then burned the April 27 message.

Thereafter Mr. Diem had full American backing, the study reports, and moved with more confidence. The next October he organized a referendum to choose between himself and Bao Dai.

After winning what the Pentagon narrative describes as a "too resounding" 98.2 per cent of the vote, Premier Diem proclaimed himself President.

Elections Balked

In July, 1955, under the provisions of the Geneva agreements, the two zones of Vietnam were to begin consultations on the elections scheduled for the next year.

But Premier Diem refused to talk with the Communists. And in July, 1956, he refused to hold elections for reunification. He asserted that the South Vietnamese Government

had not signed the Geneva accords and therefore was no
bound by them.

American scholars and government officials have lon
argued over whether the United States was responsible fo
Mr. Diem's refusal to hold the elections and therefore, in
sense, whether Americans had a role in turning the Com
munists from politics back to warfare.

The Pentagon study contends that the "United States di
not—as it is often alleged—connive with Diem to ignore th
elections. U.S. State Department records indicate tha
Diem's refusal to be bound by the Geneva accords and hi
opposition to pre-election consultations were at his ow
initiative."

But the Pentagon account also cites State Departmen
cables and National Security Council memorandums indicat
ing that the Eisenhower Administration wished to postpon
the elections as long as possible and communicated its feel
ings to Mr. Diem.

As early as July 7, 1954, during the Geneva conference
Secretary Dulles suggested that the United States ought t
seek to delay the elections and to require guarantees tha
the Communists could be expected to reject.

In a secret cablegram to Under Secretary of State Walte
Bedell Smith, who filled in for him after he withdrew fron
the Geneva conference, Secretary Dulles wrote:

"Since undoubtedly true that elections might eventuall
mean unification Vietnam under Ho Chi Minh, this makes
all more important they should be only held as long afte
cease-fire agreement as possible and in conditions free fron
intimidation to give democratic elements best chance."

Following similar reasoning the National Security Counci
in May, 1955, shortly before consultations on the election
were supposed to begin, produced a draft statement, "U.S
Policy on All-Vietnam Elections."

According to the Pentagon study, it "held that to give n
impression of blocking elections while avoiding the possi
bility of losing them, Diem should insist on free elections b
secret ballot with strict supervision. Communists in Kore
and Germany had rejected these conditions; hopefully th
Vietminh would follow suit."

But on June 9, the account says, the Council "decided t
shelve the draft statement. Its main features had already bee
conveyed to Diem."

Secretary Dulles's ambivalent attitude toward the Geneva
accords is also reflected in a cablegram he sent to th

United States Embassy in Saigon on Dec. 11, 1955, outlining Washington's position toward the International Control Commission.

"While we should certainly take no positive step to speed up present process of decay of Geneva accords," it said "neither should we make the slightest effort to infuse life into them."

In May, 1956, in what the Pentagon account says is an "example of the U.S. ignoring" the Geneva accords, 350 additional military men were sent to Saigon under the pretext of helping the Vietnamese recover and redistribute equipment abandoned by the French.

This was "a thinly veiled device to increase the number of Americans in Vietnam," the Pentagon account says.

These men, who were officially designated the Temporary Equipment Recovery Mission or TERM, stayed on as a permanent part of the Military Assistance Advisory Group, the narrative says, to help in intelligence and administrative work.

Washington dispatched the TERM group, the Pentagon study discloses, "when it was learned informally that the Indian Government would instruct its representative on the I.C.C. to interpose no objection."

The I.C.C. is composed of representatives from Poland, India and Canada, with the Indian usually considered the neutral representative.

After the crisis with the sects in the spring of 1955 and the uneventful passing of the date for elections in 1956, American officials were hopeful that President Diem had succeeded.

"It seemed for a while that the gamble against long odds had succeeded," the Pentagon account says. "The Vietminh were quiescent; the Republic of Vietnam armed forces were markedly better armed and trained than they were when the U.S. effort began; and President Diem showed a remarkable ability to put down factions threatening the GVN [Government of Vietnam] and to maintain himself in office."

The American aid effort, the study reports, was focused almost entirely on security. Eight out of every 10 dollars went to security, and much of what was intended for agriculture, education, or transportation actually went to security-directed programs.

For example, the account says, a 20-mile stretch of highway, built between Saigon and Bienhoa at the insistence of the MAAG commander, Gen. Samuel T. Williams, received more aid money than all the funds provided for labor, community development, social welfare, health and education from 1954 to 1961.

But despite American hopes and the aid effort, the insurgency in the countryside began to pick up again in 1957 and particularly in 1959. The number of terrorist murders and kidnappings of local officials rose dramatically, and enemy units began to attack in ever-increasing size.

As the insurgency grew, the small American intelligence network "correctly and consistently estimated" the nature of the opposition to President Diem and his own weaknesses, the Pentagon study says. The American intelligence estimates "were remarkably sound," it adds.

A special national intelligence estimate in August, 1960, for example, said that:

"In the absence of more effective Government measures to protect the peasants and to win their positive cooperation, the prospect is for expansion of the areas of Vietcong control in the countryside, particularly in the southwestern provinces.

"Dissatisfaction and discontent with the Government will probably continue to rise.

"These adverse trends are not irreversible, but if they remain unchecked, they will almost certainly in time cause the collapse of Diem's regime."

However, the study relates, "the national intelligence estimates re Diem do not appear to have restrained the N.S.C. in its major reviews of U.S. policy" toward Vietnam.

The basic Eisenhower Administration policy papers on Southeast Asia in 1956, 1958 and 1960 repeated American objectives in "virtually identical" language, the Pentagon account reports.

According to the 1956 paper by the National Security Council, these were among the goals of American policy toward Vietnam:

• "Assist Free Vietnam to develop a strong, stable and constitutional government to enable Free Vietnam to assert an increasingly attractive contrast to conditions in the present Communist zone."

• "Work toward the weakening of the Communists in North and South Vietnam in order to bring about the eventual peaceful reunification of a free and independent Vietnam under anti-Communist leadership."

• "Support the position of the Government of Free Vietnam that all-Vietnam elections may take place only after it is satisfied that genuinely free elections can be held throughout both zones of Vietnam."

During the late nineteen-fifties, the study relates, United States officials in Saigon were also optimistic in their public comments about the situation, despite the pessimistic secret reports they forwarded to Washington.

"While classified policy paper thus dealt with risks," the account says, "public statements of U.S. officials did not refer to the jeopardy. To the contrary, the picture presented the public and Congress by Ambassador Durbrow, General Williams and other Administration spokesmen was of continuing progress, virtually miraculous improvement, year in and year out."

Ambassador Elbridge Durbrow and General Williams for example, told the Senate Foreign Relations Committee in the summer of 1959 that Vietnam's internal security was "in no serious danger" and that South Vietnam was in a better position that ever before to cope with an invasion from the North.

The next spring General Williams wrote to Senator Mike Mansfield that President Diem was doing so well that the United States could begin a "phased withdrawal" of American advisers in 1961.

That was the situation that confronted President Kennedy when he took office early in 1961.

"The U.S. had gradually developed a special commitment in South Vietnam," writes the Pentagon analyst charged with explaining the problems facing President Kennedy. "It was certainly not absolutely binding—but the commitment was there . . ."

"Without U.S. support," the analyst says, "Diem almost certainly could not have consolidated his hold on the South during 1955 and 1956.

"Without the threat of U.S. intervention, South Vietnam could not have refused to even discuss the elections called for in 1956 under the Geneva settlement without being immediately overrun by the Vietminh armies.

"Without U.S. aid in the years following, the Diem regime certainly, and an independent South Vietnam almost as certainly, could not have survived . . ."

In brief, the analyst concludes, "South Vietnam was essentially the creation of the United States."

KEY DOCUMENTS

Following are the texts of key documents accompanying the Pentagon's study of the Vietnam war, covering events in the Truman and Eisenhower Administrations. Except where excerpting is specified, the documents appear verbatim, with only unmistakable typographical errors corrected.

1

Report of Ho's Appeals to U.S. in '46 to Support Independence

Cablegram from an American diplomat in Hanoi, identified as Landon, to State Department, Feb. 27, 1946, as provided in the body of the Pentagon study.

Ho Chi Minh handed me 2 letters addressed to President of USA, China, Russia, and Britain identical copies of which were stated to have been forwarded to other governments named. In 2 letters to Ho Chi Minh request USA as one of United Nations to support idea of Annamese independence according to Philippines example, to examine the case of the Annamese, and to take steps necessary to maintenance of world peace which is being endangered by French efforts to reconquer Indochina. He asserts that Annamese will fight until United Nations interfered in support of Annamese independence. The petition addressed to major United Nations contains:

A. Review of French relations with Japanese where French Indochina allegedly aided Japs:

B. Statement of establishment on 2 September 1945 of PENW Democratic Republic of Viet Minh:

C. Summary of French conquest of Cochin China began 23 Sept 1945 and still incomplete:

D. Outline of accomplishments of Annamese Government in Tonkin including popular elections, abolition of undesirable taxes, expansion of education and resumption as far as possible of normal economic activities:

E. Request to 4 powers: (1) to intervene and stop the war in Indochina in order to mediate fair settlement and (2) to bring the Indochinese issue before the United Nations organization.

The petition ends with the statement that Annamese ask for full independence in fact and that in interim while awaiting UNO decision the Annamese will continue to fight the reestablishment of French imperialism. Letters and petition will be transmitted to Department soonest.

2

1952 Policy Statement by U.S. on Goals in Southeast Asia

Statement of Policy by the National Security Council, early 1952, on "United States Objectives and Courses of Action With Respect to Southeast Asia." According to a footnote, the document defined Southeast Asia as "the area embracing Burma, Thailand, Indochina, Malaya and Indonesia."

OBJECTIVE

1. To prevent the countries of Southeast Asia from passing into the communist orbit, and to assist them to develop will and ability to resist communism from within and without and to contribute to the strengthening of the free world.

GENERAL CONSIDERATIONS

2. Communist domination, by whatever means, of all Southeast Asia would seriously endanger in the short term, and critically endanger in the longer term, United States security interests.

a. The loss of any of the countries of Southeast Asia to communist aggression would have critical psychological, political and economic consequences. In the absence of effective and timely counteraction, the loss of any single country would probably lead to relatively swift submission to or an alignment with communism by the remaining countries of this group. Furthermore, an alignment with communism of the rest of Southeast Asia and India, and in the longer term, of the Middle East (with the probable exceptions of at least Pakistan and Turkey) would in all probability progressively follow: Such widespread alignment would endanger the stability and security of Europe.

b. Communist control of all of Southeast Asia would render the U.S. position in the Pacific offshore island chain precarious and would seriously jeopardize fundamental U.S. security interests in the Far East.

c. Southeast Asia, especially Malaya and Indonesia, is the principal world source of natural rubber and tin, and a producer of petroleum and other strategically important commodities. The rice exports of Burma and Thailand are critically important to

Malaya, Ceylon and Hong Kong and are of considerable significance to Japan and India, all important areas of free Asia.

d. The loss of Southeast Asia, especially of Malaya and Indonesia, could result in such economic and political pressures in Japan as to make it extremely difficult to prevent Japan's eventual accommodation to communism.

3. It is therefore imperative that an overt attack on Southeast Asia by the Chinese Communists be vigorously opposed. In order to pursue the military courses of action envisaged in this paper to a favorable conclusion within a reasonable period, it will be necessary to divert military strength from other areas thus reducing our military capability in those areas, with the recognized increased risks involved therein, or to increase our military forces in being, or both.

4. The danger of an overt military attack against Southeast Asia is inherent in the existence of a hostile and aggressive Communist China, but such an attack is less probable than continued communist efforts to achieve domination through subversion. The primary threat to Southeast Asia accordingly arises from the possibility that the situation in Indochina may deteriorate as a result of the weakening of the resolve of, or as a result of the inability of the governments of France and of the Associated States to continue to oppose the Viet Minh rebellion, the military strength of which is being steadily increased by virtue of aid furnished by the Chinese Communist regime and its allies.

5. The successful defense of Tonkin is critical to the retention in non-Communist hands of mainland Southeast Asia. However, should Burma come under communist domination, a communist military advance through Thailand might make Indochina, including Tonkin, militarily indefensible. The execution of the following U.S. courses of action with respect to individual countries of the area may vary depending upon the route of communist advance into Southeast Asia.

6. Actions designed to achieve our objectives in Southeast Asia require sensitive selection and application, on the one hand to assure the optimum efficiency through coordination of measures for the general area, and on the other, to accommodate to the greatest practicable extent to the individual sensibilities of the several governments, social classes and minorities of the area.

COURSES OF ACTION

Southeast Asia

7. With respect to Southeast Asia, the United States should:

a. Strengthen propaganda and cultural activities, as appropriate, in relation to the area to foster increased alignment of the people with the free world.

b. Continue, as appropriate, programs of economic and technical assistance designed to strengthen the indigenous non-communist governments of the area.

c. Encourage the countries of Southeast Asia to restore and expand their commerce with each other and with the rest of the free world, and stimulate the flow of the raw material resources of the area to the free world.

d. Seek agreement with other nations, including at least France, the UK, Australia and New Zealand, for a joint warning to Communist China regarding the grave consequences of Chinese aggression against Southeast Asia, the issuance of such a warning to be contingent upon the prior agreement of France and the UK to participate in the courses of action set forth in paragraphs 10 c, 12, 14 f (1) and (2) and 15 c (1) and (2), and such others as are determined as a result of prior trilateral consultation, in the event such a warning is ignored.

e. Seek UK and French agreement in principle that a naval blockade of Communist China should be included in the minimum courses of action set forth in paragraph 10c below.

f. Continue to encourage and support closer cooperation among the countries of Southeast Asia, and between those countries and the United States, Great Britain, France, the Philippines, Australia, New Zealand, South Asia and Japan.

g. Strengthen, as appropriate, covert operations designed to assist in the achievement of U.S. objectives in Southeast Asia.

h. Continue activities and operations designed to encourage the overseas Chinese communities in Southeast Asia to organize and activate anti-communist groups and activities within their own communities, to resist the effects of parallel pro-communist groups and activities and, generally, to increase their orientation toward the free world.

i. Take measures to promote the coordinated defense of the area, and encourage and support the spirit of resistance among the peoples of Southeast Asia to Chinese Communist aggression and to the encroachments of local communists.

j. Make clear to the American people the importance of Southeast Asia to the security of the United States so that they may be prepared for any of the courses of action proposed herein.

Indochina

8. With respect to Indochina the United States should:

a. Continue to promote international support for the three Associated States.

b. Continue to assure the French that the U.S. regards the French effort in Indochina as one of great strategic importance in the general international interest rather than in the purely French interest, and as essential to the security of the free world, not only in the Far East but in the Middle East and Europe as well.

c. Continue to assure the French that we are cognizant of the sacrifices entailed for France in carrying out her effort in Indo-

29

china and that, without overlooking the principle that France has the primary responsibility in Indochina, we will recommend to the Congress appropriate military, economic and financial aid to France and the Associated States.

d. Continue to cultivate friendly and increasingly cooperative relations with the Governments of France and the Associated States at all levels with a view to maintaining and, if possible, increasing the degree of influence the U.S. can bring to bear on the policies and actions of the French and Indochinese authorities to the end of directing the course of events toward the objectives we seek. Our influence with the French and Associated States should be designed to further those constructive political, economic and social measures which will tend to increase the stability of the Associated States and thus make it possible for the French to reduce the degree of their participation in the military, economic and political affairs of the Associated States.

e. Specifically we should use our influence with France and the Associated States to promote positive political, military, economic and social policies, among which the following are considered essential elements:

(1) Continued recognition and carrying out by France of its primary responsibility for the defense of Indochina.

(2) Further steps by France and the Associated States toward the evolutionary development of the Associated States.

(3) Such reorganization of French administration and representation in Indochina as will be conducive to an increased feeling of responsibility on the part of the Associated States.

(4) Intensive efforts to develop the armies of the Associated States, including independent logistical and administrative services.

(5) The development of more effective and stable Governments in the Associated States.

(6) Land reform, agrarian and industrial credit, sound rice marketing systems, labor development, foreign trade and capital formation.

(7) An aggressive military, political, and psychological program to defeat or seriously reduce the Viet Minh forces.

(8) U.S.-French cooperation in publicizing progressive developments in the foregoing policies in Indochina.

(9) In the absence of large scale Chinese Communist intervention in Indochina, the United States should:

a. Provide increased aid on a high priority basis for the French Union forces without relieving French authorities of their basic military responsibility for the defense of the Associated States in order to:

(1) Assist in developing indigenous armed forces which will eventually be capable of maintaining internal security without assistance from French units.

(2) Assist the French Union forces to maintain progress in the restoration of internal security against the Viet Minh.

(3) Assist the forces of France and the Associated States to defend Indochina against Chinese Communist aggression.

b. In view of the immediate urgency of the situation, involving possible large-scale Chinese Communist intervention, and in order that the United States may be prepared to take whatever action may be appropriate in such circumstances, make the plans necessary to carry out the courses of action indicated in paragraph 10 below.

c. In the event that information and circumstances point to the conclusion that France is no longer prepared to carry the burden in Indochina, or if France presses for an increased sharing of the responsibility for Indochina, whether in the UN or directly with the U.S. Government, oppose a French withdrawal and consult with the French and British concerning further measures to be taken to safeguard the area from communist domination.

10. In the event that it is determined, in consultation with France, that Chinese Communist forces (including volunteers) have overtly intervened in the conflict in Indochina, or are covertly participating to such an extent as to jeopardize retention of the Tonkin Delta area by French Union forces, the United States should take the following measures to assist these forces in preventing the loss of Indochina, to repel the aggression and to restore peace and security in Indochina:

a. Support a request by France or the Associated States for immediate action by the United Nations which would include a UN resolution declaring that Communist China has committed an aggression, recommending that member states take whatever action may be necessary, without geographic limitation, to assist France and the Associated States in meeting the aggression.

b. Whether or not UN action is immediately forthcoming, seek the maximum possible international support for, and participation in, the minimum courses of military action agreed upon by the parties to the joint warning. These minimum courses of action are set forth in subparagraph c immediately below.

c. Carry out the following minimum courses of military action, either under the auspices of the UN or in conjunction with France and the United Kingdom and any other friendly governments:

(1) A resolute defense of Indochina itself to which the United States would provide such air and naval assistance as might be practicable.

(2) Interdiction of Chinese Communist communication lines including those in China.

(3) The United States would expect to provide the major forces for task (2) above; but would expect the UK and France to provide at least token forces therefor and to render such other assistance as is normal between allies, and France to carry the burden of providing, in conjunction with the Associated States, the ground forces for the defense of Indochina.

11. In addition to the courses of action set forth in paragraph 10 above, the United States should take the following military actions as appropriate to the situation:

a. If agreement is reached pursuant to paragraph 7-e, establishment in conjunction with the UK and France of a naval blockade of Communist China.

b. Intensification of covert operations to aid anti-communist guerrilla forces operating against Communist China and to interfere with and disrupt Chinese Communist lines of communication and military supply areas.

c. Utilization, as desirable and feasible, of anti-communist Chinese forces, including Chinese Nationalist forces in military operations in Southeast Asia, Korea, or China proper.

d. Assistance to the British to cover an evacuation from Hong Kong, if required.

e. Evacuation of French Union civil and military personnel from the Tonkin delta, if required.

12. If, subsequent to aggression against Indochina and execution of the minimum necessary courses of action listed in paragraph 10-c above, the United States determines jointly with the UK and France that expanded military action against Communist China is rendered necessary by the situation, the United States should take air and naval action in conjunction with at least France and the U.K. against all suitable military targets in China, avoiding insofar as practicable those targets in areas near the boundaries of the USSR in order not to increase the risk of direct Soviet involvement.

13. In the event the concurrence of the United Kingdom and France to expanded military action against Communist China is not obtained, the United States should consider taking unilateral action.

3

Eisenhower Committee's Memo on
French Requests for Aid

Excerpts from memorandum for the record, Jan. 30, 1954, by Brig. Gen. Charles H. Bonesteel 3d on meeting of President's Special Committee on Indochina.

1. The Special Committee met in Mr. Kyes' office at 3:30 p.m. 29 January 1954. . . .

3. Admiral Radford said he had been in touch with General Ely, French Chief of Staff, through General Valluy. Ten B-26 aircraft are on the way to Indochina this week. These would contribute to filling the French request for aircraft to bring two B-26 squadrons up to a strength of 25 operational aircraft each. However, an additional 12 are needed to fill the full requirement

because a total of 22 are needed (12 to fill the annual attrition plus 10 to fill the additional French request). There was some discussion on the seeming differences in requests reaching Washington via Paris and those coming through the MAAG. Subsequently in the meeting it was agreed that the French should be informed that the U.S. would act only on requests which had been approved by General O'Daniel after General O'Daniel was set up in Indochina.

4. Admiral Radford indicated that to fill the entire requirement for 22 B-26's on an urgent basis would mean taking some of them from U.S. operational squadrons in the Far East, but this could be done. The aircraft would not all have "zero" maintenance time on them.

5. As to the additional French request for 25 B-26's to equip a third squadron, it was decided that final decision to furnish them should await the return of General O'Daniel. However, the Air Force has been alerted that they may have to be furnished on short notice.

6. As to the provision of a small "dirigible," it was decided to inform the French that this could not be furnished.

7. Regarding the French request for 400 mechanics trained in maintenance of B-26 and C-47 aircraft, there was considerable discussion. Admiral Radford said he had informed General Ely, through General Valluy, that the U.S. does not believe the French have exhausted all efforts to get French civilian maintenance crews. He suggested the French try to find them through "Air France" Mr. Kyes mentioned the possibility of obtaining French personnel from their eight aircraft factories or from the big Chateauroux maintenance base where the U.S. employed French mechanics. General Smith inquired about the possibility of lowering French NATO commitments to enable transfer of French military mechanics. Admiral Radford said General Valluy had informed him the French Staff have carefully considered the idea but the French Air Force does not have enough military mechanics trained in B-26 or C-47 maintenance to fill the requirement. Therefore, there would be such a delay while their military mechanics were being trained on these aircraft that the urgent requirement could not be met. He had also said that the employment of French civilian mechanics presented a difficult problem in security clearance.

8. General Smith recommended that the U.S. send 200 U.S. Air Force mechanics to MAAG, Indochina, and tell the French to provide the rest. Admiral Radford said this could be done and that the Air Force is, somewhat reluctantly, making plans to this end. He had let the French know that if American mechanics were sent they must be used only on air bases which were entirely secure from capture. General Smith wondered, in light of additional French requests, if the Committee should not consider sending the full 400 mechanics.

9. Mr. Kyes questioned if sending 200 military mechanics would

not so commit the U.S. to support the French that we must be prepared eventually for complete intervention, including use of U.S. combat forces. General Smith said he did not think this would result—we were sending maintenance forces not ground forces. He felt, however, that the importance of winning in Indochina was so great that if worst came to the worst he personally would favor intervention with U.S. air and naval forces—not ground forces. Admiral Radford agreed. Mr. Kyes felt this consideration was so important that it should be put to the highest level. The President himself should decide. General Smith agreed. Mr. Allen Dulles wondered if our preoccupation with helping to win the battle at Dien Bien Phu was so great that we were not going to bargain with the French as we supplied their most urgent needs. Mr. Kyes said this was an aspect of the question he was resisting. Admiral Radford read from a cable just received from General O'Daniel, which indicated General Navarre had been most cordial to General O'Daniel at their meeting and had indicated he was pleased with the concept of U.S. liaison officers being assigned to his general headquarters and to the training command. General Navarre and General O'Daniel agreed to try to work out a maximum of collaboration at the military level.

10. Later in the meeting, Mr. Allen Dulles raised the question as to sending the CAP pilots the French had once requested. It was agreed that the French apparently wanted them now, that they should be sent, and CIA should arrange for the necessary negotiations with the French in Indochina to take care of it.

11. Mr. Kyes said that if we meet the French urgent demands they should be tied to two things: first, the achievement of maximum collaboration with the French in training and strategy, and secondly, the strengthening of General O'Daniel's hand in every way possible. General Smith agreed and felt we should reinforce General O'Daniel's position not only with the French in Indochina but also at the highest level in Paris. . . .

12. **Summary of Action Agreed Regarding Urgent French Requests**

It was agreed:

a. To provide 200 uniformed U.S. Air Force mechanics who would be assigned as an augmentation to MAAG, Indochina, these mechanics to be provided only on the understanding that they would be used at bases where they would be secure from capture and would not be exposed to combat.

c. To send the CAP pilots, with CIA arranging necessary negotiations.

d. Not to provide a "dirigible."

e. To await General O'Daniel's return to Washington before making a decision on the other French requests. Efforts should continue to get the French to contribute a maximum number of mechanics.

It was further agreed that General Smith would clear these recommended actions with the President.

13. The next item discussed was the status of General O'Daniel. Mr. Kyes said General Trapnell, the present Chief of MAAG, is being replaced at the normal expiration of his tour. General Dabney had been chosen to replace General Trapnell and is about to leave for Indochina. Admiral Radford pointed out that General O'Daniel could be made Chief of MAAG without any further clearance with the French Government. General Smith said this would be all right but should not preclude further action to increase the position of General O'Daniel. General Erskine pointed out that the MAAG in Indochina is not a "military mission" but only an administrative group concerned with the provision of MDAP equipment. He thought the MAAG status should be raised to that of a mission which could help in training. It was agreed that General O'Daniel should probably be first assigned as Chief of MAAG and that, for this reason, General Dabney's departure for Indochina should be temporarily held up. General Dabney should, however, go to Indochina to assist General O'Daniel by heading up the present MAAG functions. Admiral Davis was requested to assure that General Dabney did not depart until further instructions were given.

20. Mr. Allen Dulles inquired if an unconventional warfare officer, specifically Colonel Lansdale, could not be added to the group of five liaison officers to which General Navarre had agreed. Admiral Radford thought this might be done and at any rate Colonel Lansdale could immediately be attached to the MAAG, but he wondered if it would not be best for Colonel Lansdale to await General O'Daniel's return before going to Indochina. In this way, Colonel Lansdale could help the working group in its revision of General Erskine's paper. This was agreeable to Mr. Allen Dulles. . . .

4

'54 Report by Special Committee on the Threat of Communism

Excerpts from memorandum for the record, Jan. 30, on Southeast Asia, April 5, 1954. Part I was not made available with it.

IV CONCLUSIONS

A. The special Committee considers that these factors reinforce the necessity of assuring that Indo-China remain in the non-Communist bloc, and believes that defeat of the Viet Minh in Indo-China is essential if the spread of Communist influence in Southeast Asia is to be halted.

B. Regardless of the outcome of military operations in Indo-China and without compromising in any way the overwhelming strategic importance of the Associated States to the Western position in the area, the U.S. should take all affirmative and practical steps, with or without its European allies, to provide tangible evidence of Western strength and determination to defeat Communism; to demonstrate that ultimate victory will be won by the free world; and to secure the affirmative association of Southeast Asian states with these purposes.

C. That for these purposes the Western position in Indo-China must be maintained and improved by a military victory.

D. That without compromise to C, above, the U.S. should in all prudence reinforce the remainder of Southeast Asia, including the land areas of Malaya, Burma, Thailand, Indonesia and the Philippines.

RECOMMENDED COURSES OF ACTION*

A. The Special Committee wishes to reaffirm the following recommendations which are made in NCS 5405, the Special Committee Report concerning military operations in Indo-China, and the position paper of the Special Committee, concurred in by the Department of Defense, concerning U.S. courses of action and policies with respect to the Geneva Conference:

(1) It be U.S. policy to accept nothing short of a military victory in Indo-China.

(2) It be the U.S. position to obtain French support of this position; and that failing this, the U.S. actively oppose any negotiated settlement in Indo-China at Geneva.

(3) It be the U.S. position in event of failure of (2) above to initiate immediate steps with the governments of the Associated States aimed toward the continuation of the war in Indo-China, to include active U.S. participation and without French support should that be necessary.

(4) Regardless of whether or not the U.S. is successful in obtaining French support for the active U.S. participation called for in (3) above, every effort should be made to undertake this active participation in concert with other interested nations.

B. The Special Committee also considers that all possible political and economic pressure on France must be exerted as the obvious initial course of action to reinforce the French will to continue operatings [sic] in Indo-China. The Special Committee recognizes that this course of action will jeopardize the existing French Cabinet, may be unpopular among the French public, and may be considered as endangering present U. S. policy with respect to EDC. The Committee nevertheless considers that the free world strategic position, not only in Southeast Asia but in Europe and the Middle East as well, is such as to require the most extraordinary efforts to prevent Communist domination of South-

---

*The Department of State representative recommends the deletion of paragraphs A and B hereunder as being redundant and included in other documents.

ast Asia. The Committee considers that firm and resolute action now in this regard may well be the key to a solution of the entire problem posed by France in the free world community of nations.

C. In order to make the maximum contribution to the free world strength in Southeast Asia, and regardless of the outcome of military operations currently in progress in Indo-China, the U. S. should, in all prudence, take the following courses of action in addition to those set forth in NSC 5405 and in Part I of the Special Committee Report:

Political and Military:

(1) Ensure that there be initiated no cease-fire in Indo-China prior to victory whether that be by successful military action or clear concession of defeat by the Communists.

Action: State, CIA

(2) Extraordinary and unilateral, as well as multi-national, efforts should be undertaken to give vitality in Southeast Asia to the concept that Communist imperialism is a transcending threat to each of the Southeast Asian states. These efforts should be so undertaken as to appear through local initiative rather than as a result of U.S. or UK, or French instigation.

ACTION: USIA, State, CIA

(3) It should be U.S. policy to develop within the UN Charter a Far Eastern regional arrangement subscribed and underwritten by the major European powers with interests in the Pacific.

a. Full accomplishment of such an arrangement can only be developed in the long term and should therefore be preceded by the development, through indigenous sources, or regional economic and cultural agreements between the several Southeast Asian countries and later with Japan. Such agreements might take a form similar to that of OEEC in Europe.

Action: State, CIA, FOA

b. Upon the basis of such agreements, the U.S. should actively but unobtrusively seek their expansion into mutual defense agreements and should for this purpose be prepared to underwrite such agreements with military and economic aid and should [rest unavailable].

D. The courses of action outlined above are considered as mandatory regardless of the outcome of military operations in Indo-China.

(1) If Indo-China is held they are needed to build up strength and resistance to Communism in the entire area.

(2) If Indo-China is lost they are essential as partial steps:

a. To delay as long as possible the extension of Communist domination throughout the Far East, or

b. In conjunction with offensive operations to retake Indo-China from the Communists.

(3) Should Indo-China be lost it is clear to the Special Committee that the involvement of U. S. resources either in an attempt to stop the further spread of Communism in the Far East,

(which is bound, except in terms of the most extensive military and political effort, to be futile) or to initiate offensive operations to retake and reorient Indo-China, (which would involve a major military campaign), will greatly exceed those needed to hold Indo-China before it falls.

(4) Furthermore, either of these undertakings (in the light of the major setback to U.S. national policy involved in the loss of Indo-China) would entail as an urgent prerequisite the restoration of Asian morale and confidence in U.S. policy which will have reached an unprecedentedly low level in the area.

(5) Each of these courses of action would involve greater risk of war with Communist China, and possibly the Soviet Union, than timely preventive action taken under more favorable circumstances before Indo-China is lost.

5

Dillon Cable to Dulles on Appeal for Air Support at Dienbienphu

Cablegram from Douglas Dillon, United States Ambassador to France, to Secretary of State John Foster Dulles on April 5, 1954.

URGENT. I was called at 11 o'clock Sunday night and asked to come immediately to Matignon where a restricted Cabinet meeting was in progress. On arrival Bidault received me in Laniel's office and was joined in a few minutes by Laniel. They said that immediate armed intervention of U.S. carrier aircraft at Dien Bien Phu is now necessary to save the situation.

Navarre reports situation there now in state of precarious equilibrium and that both sides are doing best to reinforce—Viet Minh are bringing up last available reinforcements which will way outnumber any reinforcing French can do by parachute drops. Renewal of assault by reinforced Viet Minh probable by middle or end of week. Without help by then fate of Dien Bien Phu will probably be sealed.

Ely brought back report from Washington that Radford gave him his personal (repeat personal) assurance that if situation at Dien Bien Phu required U.S. naval air support he would do his best to obtain such help from U.S. Government. Because of this information from Radford as reported by Ely, French Government now asking for U.S. carrier aircraft support at Dien Bien Phu. Navarre feels that a relatively minor U.S. effort could turn the tide but naturally hopes for as much help as possible. French report Chinese intervention in Indochina already fully established as follows:

First. Fourteen technical advisors at Giap headquarters plus numerous others at division level. All under command of Chinese Communist General Ly Chen-hou who is stationed at Giap headquarters.

Second. Special telephone lines installed maintained and operated by Chinese personnel.

Third. Forty 37 mm. anti-aircraft guns radar-controlled at Dien Bien Phu. These guns operated by Chinese and evidently are from Korea. These AA guns are now shooting through clouds to bring down French aircraft.

Fourth. One thousand supply trucks of which 500 have arrived since 1 March, all driven by Chinese army personnel.

Fifth. Substantial material help in guns, shells, etc., as is well known.

Bidault said that French Chief of Air Staff wished U.S. be informed that U.S. air intervention at Dien Bien Phu could lead to Chinese Communist air attack on delta airfields. Nevertheless, government was making request for aid.

Bidault closed by saying that for good or evil the fate of Southeast Asia now rested on Dien Bien Phu. He said that Geneva would be won or lost depending on outcome at Dien Bien Phu. This was reason for French request for this very serious action on our part.

He then emphasized necessity for speed in view of renewed attack which is expected before end of week. He thanked U.S. for prompt action on airlift for French paratroops. He then said that he had received Dulles' proposal for Southeast Asian coalition, and that he would answer as soon as possible later in week as restricted Cabinet session not competent to make this decision.

New Subject. I passed on Norstad's concern that news of airlift (DEPTEL 3470, April 3) might leak as planes assembled. Pleven was called into room. He expressed extreme concern as any leak would lead to earlier Viet Minh attack. He said at all costs operation must be camouflaged as training exercise until troops have arrived. He is preparing them as rapidly as possible and they will be ready to leave in a week. Bidault and Laniel pressed him to hurry up departure date of troops and he said he would do his utmost.

6

Dulles Cable Barring Intervention

Cablegram from Secretary Dulles to Ambassador Dillon in Paris, April 5, 1954.

As I personally explained to Ely in presence of Radford, it is not (rpt not) possible for U.S. to commit belligerent acts in Indochina without full political understanding with France and other countries. In addition, Congressional action would be required. After conference at highest level, I must confirm this position. U.S. is doing everything possible as indicated my 5175 to prepare public, Congressional and Constitutional basis for united action in Indochina. However, such action is impossible except on coalition basis with active British Commonwealth participation. Meanwhile U.S. prepared, as has been demonstrated, to do everything short of belligerency.

FYI U.S. cannot and will not be put in position of alone salvaging British Commonwealth interests in Malaya, Australia and New Zealand. This matter now under discussion with UK at highest level.

7

Dillon Reply on French Reaction

Cablegram from Ambassador Dillon to Secretary Dulles, April 5, 1594.

I delivered message DEPTEL 3482 to Bidault Monday evening. He asked me to tell Secretary that he personally could well understand position US Government and would pass on your answer to Laniel.

He asked me to say once more that unfortunately the time for formulating coalitions has passed as the fate of Indochina will be decided in the next ten days at Dien-Bien-Phu. As I left he said that even though French must fight alone they would continue fighting and he prayed God they would be successful.

8

Memo of Eisenhower-Dulles Talk on the French Cease-Fire Plan

Memorandum by Robert Cutler, special assistant to President Dwight D. Eisenhower, May 7, 1954.

At a meeting in the President's office this morning with Dulles, three topics were discussed.

1. Whether the President should approve paragraph 1b of the tentative Record of Action of the 5/6/54 NSC meeting, which covers the proposed answer to the Eden proposal. The Secretary of State thought the text was correct. Wilson and Radford preferred the draft message to Smith for Eden prepared yesterday by MacArthur and Captain Anderson, and cleared by the JCS, which included in the Five Power Staff Agency Thailand and the Philippines. Radford thinks that the Agency (which has hitherto been not disclosed in SEA) has really completed its military

planning; that if it is enlarged by top level personnel, its actions will be necessarily open to the world; that therefore some Southeast Asian countries should be included in it, and he fears Eden's proposal as an intended delaying action.

The President approved the text of paragraph 1b but suggested that Smith's reply to Eden's proposal should make clear the following:

1. Five Power Staff Agency, alone or with other nations, is not to the United States a satisfactory substitute for a broad political coalition which will include the Southeast Asian countries which are to be defended.

2. Five Power Staff Agency examination is acceptable to see how these nations can give military aid to the Southeast Asian countries in the cooperative defense effort.

3. The United States will not agree to a "white man's party" to determine the problems of the Southeast Asian nations.

I was instructed to advise Wilson and Radford of the above, and have done so.

2. The President went over the draft of the speech which Dulles is going to make tonight, making quite a few suggestions and changes in text. He thought additionally the speech should include some easy to understand slogans, such as "The U.S. will never start a war," "The U.S. will not go to war without Congressional authority," "The U.S., as always, is trying to organize cooperative efforts to sustain the peace."

3. With reference to the cease-fire proposal transmitted by Bidault to the French cabinet, I read the following, as views principally of military members of the Planning Board, expressed in their yesterday afternoon meeting:

1. U.S. should not support the Bidault proposal.

2. Reasons for this position:

a. The mere proposal of the cease-fire at the Geneva Conference would destroy the will to fight of French forces and make fencesitters jump to Vietminh side.

b. The Communists would evade covertly cease-fire controls.

3. The U.S. should (as a last act to save IndoChina) propose to France that if the following 5 conditions are met, the U.S. will go to Congress for authority to intervene with combat forces:

a. grant of genuine freedom for Associated States

b. U.S. take major responsibility for training indigenous forces

c. U.S. share responsibility for military planning

d. French forces to stay in the fight and no requirement of replacement of U.S. forces

(e. Action under UN auspices?)

This offer to be made known simultaneously to the other members of the proposed regional grouping (UK, Australia, NZ, Thailand, Associated States, Philippines) in order to enlist their participation.

I then summarized possible objections to making the above proposal to the French:

a. No French Government is now competent to act in a lasting way.

b. There is no indication France wants to "internationalize" the conflict.

c. The U.S. proposal would be made without the prior assurance of a regional grouping of SEA states, a precondition of Congress; although this point might be added as another condition to the proposal.

d. U.S. would be "bailing out colonial France" in the eyes of the world.

e. U.S. cannot undertake *alone* to save every situation of trouble.

I concluded that some PB members felt that it had never been made clear to the French that the U.S. was willing to ask for Congressional authority, if certain fundamental preconditions were met; that these matters had only been hinted at, and that the record of history should be clear as to the U.S. position. Dulles was interested to know the President's views, because he is talking with Ambassador Bonnet this afternoon. He indicated that he would mention these matters to Bonnet, perhaps making a more broad hint than heretofore. He would not circulate any formal paper to Bonnet, or to anyone else.

The President referred to the proposition advanced by Governor Stassen at the April 29 Council Meeting as not having been thoroughly thought out. He said that he had been trying to get France to "internationalize" matters for a long time, and they are not willing to do so. If it were thought advisable at this time to point out to the French the essential preconditions to the U.S. asking for Congressional authority to intervene, then it should also be made clear to the French as an additional precondition that the U.S. would never intervene alone, that there must be an invitation by the indigenous people, and that there must be some kind of regional and collective action.

I understand that Dulles will decide the extent to which he cares to follow this line with Ambassador Bonnet. This discussion may afford Dulles guidance in replying to Smith's request about a U.S. alternative to support the Bidault proposal, but there really was no decision as to the U.S. attitude toward the cease-fire proposal itself.

9

Eisenhower's Instructions to U.S.
Envoy at Geneva Talks

Cablegram from Secretary of State Dulles to Under Secretary Walter Bedell Smith, May 12, 1594.

The following basic instructions, which have been approved by the President, and which are in confirmation of those already

42

given you orally, will guide you, as head of the United States Delegation, in your participation in the Indochina phase of the Geneva Conference.

1. The presence of a United States representative during the discussion at the Geneva Conference of "the problem of restoring peace in Indochina" rests on the Berlin Agreement of February 18, 1954. Under that agreement the U.S., UK, France, and USSR agreed that the four of them plus other interested states should be invited to a conference at Geneva on April 26 "for the purpose of reaching a peaceful settlement of the Korean question" and agreed further, that "the problem of restoring peace in Indochina" would also be discussed at Geneva by the four powers represented at Berlin, and Communist China and other interested states.

2. You will not deal with the delegates of the Chinese Communist regime, or any other regime not now diplomatically recognized by the United States, on any terms which imply political recognition or which concede to that regime any status other than that of a regime with which it is necessary to deal on a de facto basis in order to end aggression or the threat of aggression, and to obtain peace.

3. The position of the United States in the Indochina phase of the Geneva Conference is that of an interested nation which, however, is neither a belligerent nor a principal in the negotiation.

4. The United States is participating in the Indochina phase of the Conference in order thereby to assist in arriving at decisions which will help the nations of that area peacefully to enjoy territorial integrity and political independence under stable and free governments with the opportunity to expand their economies, to realize their legitimate national aspirations, and to develop security through individual and collective defense against aggression, from within or without. This implies that these people should not be amalgamated into the Communist bloc of imperialistic dictatorship.

5. The United States is not prepared to give its express or implied approval to any cease-fire, armistice, or other settlement which would have the effect of subverting the existing lawful governments of the three aforementioned states or of permanently impairing their territorial integrity or of placing in jeopardy the forces of the French Union in Indochina, or which otherwise contravened the principles stated in (4) above.

6. You should, insofar as is compatible with these instructions, cooperate with the Delegation of France and with the Delegations of other friendly participants in this phase of the Conference.

7. If in your judgment continued participation in the Indochina phase of the Conference appears likely to involve the United States in a result inconsistent with its policy, as stated above, you should immediately so inform your Government, recommending either withdrawal or the limitation of the U.S. role to that of an

observer. If the situation develops such that, in your opinion, either of such actions is essential under the circumstances and time is lacking for consultation with Washington, you may act in your discretion.

8. You are authorized to inform other delegations at Geneva of these instructions.

10

1954 Study by the Joint Chiefs on Possible U.S. Intervention

Excerpts from memorandum from Admiral Arthur W. Radford, Chairman of the Joint Chiefs of Staff, to Secretary of Defense Charles E. Wilson, May 26, 1954, on "Studies With Respect to Possible U.S. Action Regarding Indochina."

1. Reference is made to the memorandum by the Acting Secretary of Defense, dated 18 May 1954, subject as above, wherein the Joint Chiefs of Staff were requested to prepare certain studies, and agreed outline answers to certain questions relating thereto, for discussion with the Acting Secretary of Defense on or before 24 May, and for subsequent submission to the National Security Council (NSC).

2 a. The Studies requested by the Acting Secretary of Defense were developed within the parameters prescribed in the memorandum by the Executive Secretary, NSC, dated 18 May 1954, subject as above. This memorandum is interpreted as assuming no concurrent involvement in Korea. This assumption may be quite unrealistic and lead to malemployment of available forces. The Joint Chiefs of Staff desire to point out their belief that, from the point of view of the United States, with reference to the Far East as a whole, *Indochina is devoid of decisive military objectives and the allocation of more than token U.S. armed forces in Indochina would be a serious diversion of* limited U.S. capabilities. The principal sources of Viet Minh military supply lie outside Indochina. The destruction or neutralization of these sources in China proper would materially reduce the French military problems in Indochina.

b. In connection with the above, it may be readily anticipated that, upon Chinese Communist intervention in Indochina, the French would promptly request the immediate deployment of U.S. ground and air forces, additional naval forces, and a considerable increase in MDAF armament and equipment. The Joint Chiefs of Staff have stated their belief that committing to the Indochina conflict naval forces in excess of a Fast Carrier Task Force and supporting forces as necessary in accordance with the developments in the situation, of basing substantial air forces in Indochina, will involve maldeployment of forces and reduce readiness to meet probable Chinese Communist reaction elsewhere in the Far East. Simultaneously, it is necessary to keep in mind the considerable Allied military potential available in the Korea-Japan-Okinawa area.

c. In light of the above, it is clear that the denial of these forces to Indochina could result in a schism between the United States and France unless they were employed elsewhere. However, it should be noted that the Joint Chiefs of Staff have plans, both approved and under consideration, which provide for the employment of these forces in combat operations outside Indochina. Nevertheless, it is desired to repeat that this particular report is responsive to the question of U.S. intervention in Indochina only.

ASSUMING THE CHINESE COMMUNISTS INTERVENE

3. Strategic Concept and Plan of Operation

Seek to create conditions through the destruction of effective Communist forces and their means for support in the Indochina action and by reducing Chinese Communist capability for further aggression, under which Associated States forces could assume responsibility for the defense of Indochina. In the light of this concept the major courses of action would be as follows:

a. Employing atomic weapons, whenever advantageous, as well as other weapons, *conduct offensive air* operations against *selected military targets in Indochina and against* those *military targets in China, Hainan,* and other Communist-held offshore islands which are being used by the Communists in *direct support of their operations,* or which threaten the security of U.S. and allied forces in the area.

b. Simultaneously, French Union Forces, augmented by U.S. naval, and air forces, would exploit by coordinated ground, naval, and air action such successes as may be gained as a result of the aforementioned air operations in order to destroy enemy forces in Indochina.

c. Conduct coordinated ground, naval, and air action to destroy enemy forces in Indochina.

d. In the light of circumstances prevailing at the time, and subject to an evaluation of the results of operations conducted under subparagraphs *a* and *b* above, be prepared to take further action against Communist China to reduce its war-making capability, such as:

(1) Destruction of additional selected military targets. In connection with these additional targets, such action requires an enlarged but highly selective atomic offensive in addition to attacks employing other weapons systems.

(2) Blockade of the China coast. This might be instituted progressively from the outset.

(3) Seizure or neutralization of Hainan Island.

(4) Operations against the Chinese mainland by Chinese Nationalist forces. . . .

ASSUMING CHINESE COMMUNISTS
DO NOT INTERVENE

9. Strategic Concept and Plan of Action

Seek to create conditions by destroying effective Communist forces in Indochina, under which the Associated States Forces could assume responsibility for the defense of Indochina. In the light of this concept, the major courses of action which would be undertaken are as follows:

a. *Conduct air operations* in support of allied forces in *Indochina*. The employment of atomic weapons is contemplated in the event that such course appears militarily advantageous.

b. Simultaneously, French Union Forces augmented by such armed forces of the Philippines and Thailand as may be committed would, in coordination with U.S. naval and Air Force forces, conduct coordinated ground, naval and air action to destroy enemy forces in Indochina. . . .

11

Cable by Dulles on Negotiations at Geneva
on Vietnam Elections

Cablegram by Secretary Dulles to United States Embassy in Paris with copies to the United States Embassies in London and Saigon and to the United States Consul General in Geneva for Under Secretary Bedell Smith, July 7, 1954.

We see no real conflict between paragraphs 4 and 5 U.S.-UK terms. We realize of course that even agreement which appears to meet all seven points cannot constitute guarantee that Indochina will not one day pass into Communist hands. Seven points are intended provide best chance that this shall not happen. This will require observance of criteria not merely in the letter but in the spirit. Thus since undoubtedly true that elections might eventually mean unification Vietnam under Ho Chi Minh this makes it all more important they should be only held as long after cease-fire agreement as possible and in conditions free from intimidation to give democratic elements best chance. We believe important that no date should be set now and especially that no conditions should be accepted by French which would have direct or indirect effect of preventing effective international supervision of agreement ensuring political as well as military guarantees. Also note paragraph 3 of President and Prime Minister joint declaration of June 29 regarding QTE unity through free elections supervised by the UN UNQTE.

Our interpretation of willingness QTE respect UNQTE agreement which might be reached is that we would not (repeat not) oppose a settlement which conformed to seven points contained Deptel 4853. It does not (repeat not) of course mean we would guarantee such settlement or that we would necessarily support it publicly. We consider QTE respect UNQTE as strong a word as we can possibly employ in the circumstances to indicate our position with respect to such arrangements as French may evolve along lines points contained DEPTEL 4853. QTE respect UNQTE would also mean that we would not seek directly or indirectly to upset settlement by force.

You may convey substance above to French.

12

Chinese Communists' Position on a Neutralized Indochina

*Cablegram from Under Secretary of State Bedell Smith
At Geneva to Secretary Dulles, July 18, 1954.*

Following despatch given us in advance by Topping of Associated Press apparently represents official Chinese Communist position and was given Topping in order that we would become aware of it. It begins:

QUOTE

The Communist bloc has demanded that the United States guarantee the partition peace plan for Indochina and join in an agreement to neutralize the whole country, a responsible Chinese Communist informant said today.

The informant, who reflects the views of Red China Premier Chou En-lai, said the Communists are hopeful of a cease-fire agreement by next Tuesday's deadline if the Western powers agree to 'bar all foreign military bases from Indochina and keep the three member states out of any military bloc.'

The informant said the Communists are pressing for the stamp of American approval on the armistice agreement—already okayed in principle by Britain and France—which would divide Vietnam between Communists leader Ho Chi Minh's Viet Minh and Bao Dai's pro-Western regime.

'We believe that the U.S. as a member of the conference should and is obligated to subscribe to and guarantee any settlement. Morally, there is no reason for the U.S. to avoid this obligation.'

But the informant did not (repeat not) rule out the chance of an Indochina cease-fire even if the U.S. refuses to okay the armistice agreement.

The Eisenhower administration has told France and Britain that they can go ahead with their plan for an Indochina settlement based on partition of Vietnam. But Washington has made it clear that it is not (repeat not) ready to associate itself formally with the plan which would sanction putting millions of Vietnamese under Red rule.

The Communist informant said the 'crucial issue' now in the Geneva peace negotiations revolves around whether the Western powers will agree effectively to neutralize Indochina.

'Refusal to join in such a guarantee,' the informant said, 'could seriously deter a final settlement. On other important points in the negotiations we are in agreement or close to it. We are hopeful and we believe that there is time to reach a settlement by July 20.'

French Premier Pierre Mendes-France has promised to resign with his Cabinet if he fails to end the bloody eight-year-old war by next Tuesday. Fall of the French Government probably would doom the Geneva negotiations. The informant declared that American efforts to organize a Southeast Asia Treaty organization (SEATO) is a 'threat to any possible Indochina agreement.'

'Success or failure of the Geneva Conference may depend on the attitude of the American delegation in this regard,' he added.

END QUOTE

The above seems to me extremely significant, particularly in view of the fact that in my discussion with Eden last night he expressed pessimism, which he said was now shared for the first time by Krishna Menon. Latter had begun to feel, as I do, that Molotov wishes to force Mendes-France's resignation. Eden remarked that Molotov had now become the most difficult and intransigent member of Communist delegation. You will note obvious intention to place on shoulders of U.S. responsibility for failure of Geneva Conference and fall of French Government if this occurs.

Molotov is insisting on a meeting this afternoon which French and British are trying to make highly restricted as they are apprehensive of what may occur. If such a meeting is held and if demands are made for U.S. association in any agreement, I will simply say that in the event a reasonable settlement is arrived at which U.S. could "respect", U.S. will probably issue a unilateral statement of its own position. If question of participation Laos, Cambodia and Vietnam in security pact is raised, I will reply that this depends on outcome of conference.

Eden has already told Molotov that security pact is inevitable, that he himself favored it some time ago and that he would not (repeat not) withdraw from that position, but he made the mistake of saying that no consideration had been given to inclusion of Laos and Cambodia.

This final gambit is going to be extremely difficult to play and I do not (repeat not) now see the moves clearly. However, my opinion as expressed to you before leaving, i.e., that Molotov will gain more by bringing down Mendes Government than by a settlement, has grown stronger.

13

Details on Chinese Informant

Cablegram from Under Secretary Bedell Smith at Geneva to Secretary Dulles, July 19, 1954.

Topping has supplied in confidence following background information concerning his story on views of Chinese Communist delegation.

He stated his informant was Huang Hua, whom he has known for many years. Interview was at Huang's initiative, was called on short notice, and was conducted in extremely serious manner without propaganda harangues.

Topping said he had reported Huang's statement fully in his story but had obtained number of "visual impressions" during interview. When Huang spoke of possibility American bases in Indochina or anti-Communist pact in Southeast Asia, he became very agitated, his hands shook, and his usually excellent English broke down, forcing him to work through interpreter. Huang also spoke seriously and with apparent sincerity concerning his belief that I have returned to Geneva to prevent settlement. Topping believes Chinese Communists convinced Americans made deal with French during Paris talks on basis of which Mendes-France has raised price of settlement.

14

"Final Declaration" at Geneva Conference and U.S. Statement Renouncing Use of Force

Following are the texts of the "final declaration" signed by France and the Vietminh at the end of the Geneva conference in July, 1954, and of the statement of United States policy delivered at the concluding session by Under Secretary of State Walter Bedell Smith. The "final declaration," agreement also signed by France and the Vietminh, constitutes the Geneva accords on Vietnam.

THE 'FINAL DECLARATION'

FINAL DECLARATION, dated the 21st July, 1954, of the Geneva Conference on the problem of restoring peace in Indo-

China, in which the representatives of Cambodia, the Democratic Republic of Viet-Nam, France, Laos, the People's Republic of China, the State of Viet-Nam, the Union of Soviet Socialist Republics, the United Kingdom, and the United States of America took part.

1. The Conference takes note of the agreements ending hostilities in Cambodia, Laos and Viet-Nam and organizing international control and the supervision of the execution of the provisions of these agreements.

2. The Conference expresses satisfaction at the ending of hostilities in Cambodia, Laos and Viet-Nam; the Conference expresses its conviction that the execution of the provisions set out in the present declaration and in the agreements on the cessation of hostilities will permit Cambodia, Laos, and Viet-Nam henceforth to play their part, in full independence and sovereignty, in the peaceful community of nations.

3. The Conference takes note of the declarations made by the Governments of Cambodia and of Laos of their intention to adopt measures permitting all citizens to take their place in the national community, in particular by participating in the next general elections, which, in conformity with the constitution of each of these countries, shall take place in the course of the year 1955, by secret ballot and in conditions of respect for fundamental freedoms.

4. The Conference takes note of the clauses in the agreement on the cessation of hostilities in Viet-Nam prohibiting the introduction into Viet-Nam of foreign troops and military personnel as well as of all kinds of arms and munitions. The Conference also takes note of the declarations made by the Governments of Cambodia and Laos of their resolution not to request foreign aid, whether in war material, in personnel or in instructors except for the purpose of the effective defense of their territory and, in the case of Laos, to the extent defined by the agreements on the cessation of hostilities in Laos.

5. The Conference takes note of the clauses in the agreement on the cessation of hostilities in Viet-Nam to the effect that no military base under the control of a foreign State may be established in the regrouping zones of the two parties, the latter having the obligation to see that the zones allotted to them shall not constitute part of any military alliance and shall not be utilized for the resumption of hostilities or in the service of an aggressive policy. The Conference also takes note of the declarations of the Governments of Cambodia and Laos to the effect that they will not join in any agreement with other States if this agreement includes the obligation to participate in a military alliance not in conformity with the principles of the Charter of the United Nations or, in the case of Laos, with the principles of the agreement on the cessation of hostilities in Laos or, so long as their security is not threatened, the obligation not to establish

bases on Cambodia or Laotian territory for the military forces of foreign powers.

6. The Conference recognizes that the essential purpose of the agreement relating to Viet-Nam is to settle military questions with a view to ending hostilities and that the military demarcation line is provisional and should not in any way be interpreted as constituting a political or territorial boundary. The Conference expresses its conviction that the execution of the provisions set out in the present declaration and in the agreement on the cessation of hostilities creates the necessary basis for the achievement in the near future of a political settlement in Viet-Nam.

7. The Conference declares that, so far as Viet-Nam is concerned, the settlement of political problems, effected on the basis of respect for the principles of independence, unity and territorial integrity, shall permit the Viet-Namese people to enjoy the fundamental freedoms, guaranteed by democratic institutions established as a result of free general elections by secret ballot. In order to ensure that sufficient progress in the restoration of peace has been made, and that all the necessary conditions obtain for free expression of the national will, general elections shall be held in July 1956, under the supervision of an international commission composed of representatives of the Member States of the International Supervisory Commission, referred to in the agreement on the cessation of hostilities. Consultations will be held on this subject between the competent representative authorities of the two zones from 20 July 1955 onwards.

8. The provisions of the agreements on the cessation of hostilities intended to ensure the protection of individuals and of property must be most strictly applied and must, in particular, allow everyone in Viet-Nam to decide freely in which zone he wishes to live.

9. The competent representative authorities of the Northern and Southern zones of Viet-Nam, as well as the authorities of Laos and Cambodia, must not permit any individual or collective reprisals against persons who have collaborated in any way with one of the parties during the war, or against members of such persons' families.

10. The Conference takes note of the declaration of the Government of the French Republic to the effect that it is ready to withdraw its troops from the territory of Cambodia, Laos, and Viet-Nam, at the requests of the Governments concerned and within periods which shall be fixed by agreement between the parties except in the cases where, by agreement between the two parties, a certain number of French troops shall remain at specified points and for a specified time.

11. The Conference takes note of the declaration of the French Government to the effect that for the settlement of all the problems connected with the re-establishment and consolidation of peace in Cambodia, Laos and Viet-Nam, the French Government will proceed from the principle of respect for the inde-

pendence and sovereignty, unity, and territorial integrity of Cambodia, Laos and Viet-Nam.

12. In their relations with Cambodia, Laos and Viet-Nam, each member of the Geneva Conference undertakes to respect the sovereignty, the independence, the unity and the territorial integrity of the above-mentioned states, and to refrain from any interference in their internal affairs.

13. The members of the Conference agree to consult one another on any question which may be referred to them by the International Supervisory Commission, in order to study such measures as may prove necessary to ensure that the agreements on the cessation of hostilities in Cambodia, Laos and Viet-Nam are respected.

THE AMERICAN STATEMENT

As I stated on July 18, my Government is not prepared to join in a declaration by the Conference such as is submitted. However, the United States makes this unilateral declaration of its position in these matters:

"The Government of the United States being resolved to devote its efforts to the strengthening of peace in accordance with the principles and purposes of the United Nations takes note of the agreements concluded at Geneva on July 20 and 21, 1954 between (a) The Franco-Laotian Command and the Command of the Peoples Army of Viet-Nam; (b) the Royal Khmer Army Command and the Command of the Peoples Army of Viet-Nam; (c) Franco-Vietnamese Command and the Command of the Peoples Army of Viet-Nam and of paragraphs 1 to 12 inclusive of the declaration presented to the Geneva Conference on July 21, 1954 declares with regard to the aforesaid agreements and paragraphs that (i) it will refrain from the threat or the use of force to disturb them, in accordance with Article 2 (4) of the Charter of the United Nations dealing with the obligation of members to refrain in their international relations from the threat or use of force; and (ii) it would view any renewal of the aggression in violation of the aforesaid agreements with grave concern and as seriously threatening international peace and security.

"In connection with the statement in the declaration concerning free elections in Viet-Nam my Government wishes to make clear its position which it has expressed in a declaration made in Washington on June 29, 1954, as follows:

" 'In the case of nations now divided against their will, we shall continue to seek to achieve unity through free elections supervised by the United Nations to insure that they are conducted fairly.'

"With respect to the statement made by the representative of the State of Viet-Nam, the United States reiterates its traditional position that peoples are entitled to determine their own future and that it will not join in an arrangement which would hinder

52

this. Nothing in its declaration just made is intended to or does indicate any departure from this traditional position.

"We share the hope that the agreements will permit Cambodia, Laos and Viet-Nam to play their part, in full independence and sovereignty, in the peaceful community of nations, and will enable the peoples of that area to determine their own future."

15

Lansdale Team's Report on Covert Saigon Mission in '54 and '55

Following are excerpts from the report of the Saigon Military Mission, an American team headed by Edward G. Lansdale, covering its activities in the 1954-55 period. The report accompanies the Pentagon's study of the Vietnam war, which cites it without identifying the author or date. The excerpts appear verbatim, with only unmistakable typographical errors corrected.

I. FOREWORD

. . . This is the condensed account of one year in the operations of a "cold war" combat team, written by the team itself in the field, little by little in moments taken as the members could. The team is known as the Saigon Military Mission. The field is Vietnam. There are other teams in the field, American, French, British, Chinese, Vietnamese, Vietminh, and others. Each has its own story to tell. This is ours.

The Saigon Military Mission entered Vietnam on 1 June 1954 when its Chief arrived. However, this is the story of a team, and it wasn't until August 1954 that sufficient members arrived to constitute a team. So, this is mainly an account of the team's first year, from August 1954 to August 1955.

It was often a frustrating and perplexing year, up close. The Geneva Agreements signed on 21 July 1954 imposed restrictive rules upon all official Americans, including the Saigon Military Mission. An active and intelligent enemy made full use of legal rights to screen his activities in establishing his stay-behind organizations south of the 17th Parallel and in obtaining quick security north of that Parallel. The nation's economy and communications system were crippled by eight years of open war. The government, including its Army and other security forces, was in a painful transition from colonial to self rule, making it a year of hot-tempered incidents. Internal problems arose quickly to points where armed conflict was sought as the only solution. The enemy was frequently forgotten in the heavy atmosphere of suspicion, hatred, and jealousy.

The Saigon Military Mission received some blows from allies and the enemy in this atmosphere, as we worked to help stabilize the government and to beat the Geneva time-table of Communist takeover in the north. However, we did beat the time-table. The government did become stabilized. The Free Vietnamese are now becoming unified and learning how to cope with the Communist enemy. We are thankful that we had a chance to help in this work in a critical area of the world, to be positive and constructive in a year of doubt.

II. MISSION

The Saigon Military Mission (SMM) was born in a Washington policy meeting early in 1954, when Dien Bien Phu was still holding out against the encircling Vietminh. The SMM was to enter into Vietnam quietly and assist the Vietnamese, rather than the French, in unconventional warfare. The French were to be kept as friendly allies in the process, as far as possible.

The broad mission for the team was to undertake paramilitary operations against the enemy and to wage political-psychological warfare. Later, after Geneva, the mission was modified to prepare the means for undertaking paramilitary operations in Communist areas rather than to wage unconventional warfare. ...

III. HIGHLIGHTS OF THE YEAR

a. Early Days

The Saigon Military Mission (SMM) started on 1 June 1954, when its Chief, Colonel Edward G. Lansdale, USAF, arrived in Saigon with a small box of files and clothes and a borrowed typewriter, courtesy of an SA-16 flight set up for him by the 13th Air Force at Clark AFB. Lt-General John O'Daniel and Embassy Charge Rob McClintock had arranged for his appointment as Assistant Air Attache, since it was improper for U.S. officers at MAAG at that time to have advisory conferences with Vietnamese officers. Ambassador Heath had concurred already. There was no desk space for an office, no vehicle, no safe for files. He roomed with General O'Daniel, later moved to a small house rented by MAAG. Secret communications with Washington were provided through the Saigon station of CIA.

There was deepening gloom in Vietnam. Dien Bien Phu had fallen. The French were capitulating to the Vietminh at Geneva. The first night in Saigon, Vietminh saboteurs blew up large ammunition dumps at the airport, rocking Saigon throughout the night. General O'Daniel and Charge McClintock agreed that it was time to start taking positive action. O'Daniel paved the way for a quick first-hand survey of the situation throughout the country. McClintock paved the way for contacts with Vietnamese political leaders. Our Chief's reputation from the Philippines had preceded him. Hundreds of Vietnamese acquaintanceships were made quickly.

Working in close cooperation with George Hellyer, USIS Chief, a new psychological warfare campaign was devised for the Vietnamese Army and for the government in Hanoi. Shortly after, a refresher course in combat psywar was constructed and Vietnamese Army personnel were rushed through it. A similar course was initiated for the Ministry of Information. Rumor campaigns were added to the tactics and tried out in Hanoi. It was almost too late.

The first rumor campaign was to be a carefully planted story of a Chinese Communist regiment in Tonkin taking reprisals against a Vietminh village whose girls the Chinese had raped, recalling Chinese Nationalist troop behavior in 1945 and confirming Vietnamese fears of Chinese occupation under Vietminh rule; the story was to be planted by soldiers of the Vietnamese Armed Psywar Company in Hanoi dressed in civilian clothes. The troops received their instructions silently, dressed in civilian clothes, went on the mission, and failed to return. They had deserted to the Vietminh. Weeks later, Tonkinese told an excited story of the misbehavior of the Chinese Divisions in Vietminh territory. Investigated, it turned out to be the old rumor campaign, with Vietnamese embellishments.

There was political chaos. Prince Buu Loc no longer headed the government. Government ministries all but closed. The more volatile leaders of political groups were proposing a revolution, which included armed attacks on the French. Col. Jean Carbonel of the French Army proposed establishing a regime with Vietnamese (Nungs and others) known to him close to the Chinese border and asked for our backing. Our reply was that this was a policy decision to be made between the FEC top command and U.S. authorities.

Oscar Arellano, Junior Chamber International vice-president for Southeast Asia, stopped by for a visit with our Chief; an idea in this visit later grew into "Operation Brotherhood."

On 1 July, Major Lucien Conein arrived, as the second member of the team. He is a paramilitary specialist, well-known to the French for his help with French-operated maquis in Tonkin against the Japanese in 1945, the one American guerrilla fighter who had not been a member of the Patti Mission. He was assigned to MAAG for cover purposes. Arranged by Lt-Col William Rosson, a meeting was held with Col Carbonel, Col Nguyen Van Vy, and the two SMM officers; Vy had seen his first combat in 1945 under Conein. Carbonel proposed establishing a maquis, to be kept as a secret between the four officers. SMM refused, learned later that Carbonel had kept the FEC Deuxieme Bureau informed. Shortly afterwards, at a Defense conference with General O'Daniel, our Chief had a chance to suggest Vy for a command in the North, making him a general. Secretary of

State for Defense Le Ngoc Chan did so, Vy was grateful and remained so.

Ngo Dinh Diem arrived on 7 July, and within hours was in despair as the French forces withdrew from the Catholic provinces of Phat Diem and Nam Dinh in Tonkin. Catholic militia streamed north to Hanoi and Haiphong, their hearts filled with anger at French abandonment. The two SMM officers stopped a planned grenade attack by militia girls against French troops guarding a warehouse; the girls stated they had not eaten for three days; arrangements were made for Chinese merchants in Haiphong to feed them. Other militia attacks were stopped, including one against a withdrawing French artillery unit; the militia wanted the guns to stand and fight the Vietminh. The Tonkinese had hopes of American friendship and listened to the advice given them. Governor [name illegible] died, reportedly by poison. Tonkin's government changed as despair grew. On 21 July, the Geneva Agreement was signed. Tonkin was given to the Communists. Anti-Communists turned to SMM for help in establishing a resistance movement and several tentative initial arrangements were made.

Diem himself had reached a nadir of frustration, as his country disintegrated after the conference of foreigners. With the approval of Ambassador Heath and General O'Daniel, our Chief drew up a plan of overall governmental action and presented it to Diem, with Hellyer as interpreter. It called for fast constructive action and dynamic leadership. Although the plan was not adopted, it laid the foundation for a friendship which has lasted.

Oscar Areliano visited Saigon again. Major Charles T. R. Bohanan, a former team-mate in Philippine days, was in town. At an SMM conference with these two, "Operation Brotherhood" was born: volunteer medical teams of Free Asians to aid the Free Vietnamese who have few doctors of their own. Washington responded warmly to the idea. President Diem was visited; he issued an appeal to the Free World for help. The Junior Chamber International adopted the idea. SMM would monitor the operation quietly in the background.

President Diem had organized a Committee of Cabinet Ministers to handle the problem of refugees from the Communist North. The Committee system was a failure. No real plans had been made by the French or the Americans. After conferences with USOM (FOA) officials and with General O'Daniel, our Chief suggested to Ambassador Heath that he call a U.S. meeting to plan a single Vietnamese agency, under a Commissioner of Refugees to be appointed by President Diem, to run the Vietnamese refugee program and to provide a channel through which help could be given by the U.S., France, and other free nations. The meeting was called and the plan adopted, with MAAG under General O'Daniel in the coordinating role. Diem adopted the plan. The French pitched in enthusiastically to help. CAT asked SMM for help in obtaining a French contract for the refugee airlift, and got it. In return, CAT provided SMM with the means for secret air travel between the North and Saigon. . . .

b. August 1954

An agreement had been reached that the personnel ceiling of U.S. military personnel with MAAG would be frozen at the number present in Vietnam on the date of the cease-fire, under the terms of the Geneva Agreement. In South Vietnam this deadline was to be 11 August. It meant that SMM might have only two members present, unless action were taken. General O'Daniel agreed to the addition of ten SMM men under MAAG cover, plus any others in the Defense pipeline who arrived before the deadline. A call for help went out. Ten officers in Korea, Japan, and Okinawa were selected and were rushed to Vietnam.

SMM had one small MAAG house. Negotiations were started for other housing, but the new members of the team arrived before housing was ready and were crammed three and four to a hotel room for the first days. Meetings were held to assess the new members' abilities. None had had political-psychological warfare experience. Most were experienced in paramilitary and clandestine intelligence operations. Plans were made quickly, for time was running out in the north; already the Vietminh had started taking over secret control of Hanoi and other areas of Tonkin still held by French forces.

Major Conein was given responsibility for developing a paramilitary organization in the north, to be in position when the Vietminh took over. . . . [His] . . . team was moved north immediately as part of the MAAG staff working on the refugee problem. The team had headquarters in Hanoi, with a branch in Haiphong. Among cover duties, this team supervised the refugee flow for the Hanoi airlift organized by the French. One day, as a CAT C-46 finished loading, they saw a small child standing on the ground below the loading door. They shouted for the pilot to wait, picked the child up and shoved him into the aircraft, which then promptly taxied out for its takeoff in the constant air shuttle. A Vietnamese man and woman ran up to the team, asking what they had done with their small boy, whom they'd brought out to say goodbye to relatives. The chagrined team explained, finally talked the parents into going south to Free Vietnam, put them in the next aircraft to catch up with their son in Saigon. . . .

A second paramilitary team was formed to explore possibilities of organizing resistance against the Vietminh from bases in the south. This team consisted of Army Lt-Col Raymond Wittmayer, Army Major Fred Allen, and Army Lt Edward Williams. The latter was our only experienced counter-espionage officer and undertook double duties, including working with revolutionary political groups. Major Allen eventually was able to mount a Vietnamese paramilitary effort in Tonkin from the south, barely beating the Vietminh shutdown in Haiphong as his teams went in, trained and equipped for their assigned missions.

Navy Lt Edward Bain and Marine Captain Richard Smith were assigned as the support group for SMM. Actually, support for an effort such as SMM is a major operation in itself, running the gamut from the usual administrative and personnel functions to the intricate business of clandestine air, maritime, and land supply of paramilitary materiel. In effect, they became our official smugglers as well as paymasters, housing officers, transportation officers, warehousemen, file clerks, and mess officers. The work load was such that other team members frequently pitched in and helped.

c. September 1954

Highly-placed officials from Washington visited Saigon and, in private conversations, indicated that current estimates led to the conclusion that Vietnam probably would have to be written off as a loss. We admitted that prospects were gloomy, but were positive that there was still a fighting chance.

On 8 September, SMM officers visited Secretary of State for Defense Chan and walked into a tense situation in his office. Chan had just arrested Lt-Col Lan (G-6 of the Vietnamese Army) and Capt Giai (G-5 of the Army). Armed guards filled the room. We were told what had happened and assured that everything was all right by all three principals. Later, we discovered that Chan was alone and that the guards were Lt-Col Lan's commandos. Lan was charged with political terrorism (by his "action" squads) and Giai with anti-Diem propaganda (using G-5 leaflet, rumor, and broadcast facilities).

The arrest of Lan and Giai, who simply refused to consider themselves arrested, and of Lt Minh, officer in charge of the Army radio station which was guarded by Army troops, brought into the open a plot by the Army Chief of Staff, General Hinh, to overthrow the government. Hinh had hinted at such a plot to his American friends, using a silver cigarette box given him by Egypt's Naguib to carry the hint. SMM became thoroughly involved in the tense controversy which followed, due to our Chief's closeness to both President Diem and General Hinh. He had met the latter in the Philippines in 1952, was a friend of both Hinh's wife and favorite mistress. (The mistress was a pupil in a small English class conducted for mistresses of important personages, at their request. . . .

While various U.S. officials including General O'Daniel and Foreign Service Officer Frank [name illegible] participated in U.S. attempts to heal the split between the President and his Army, Ambassador Heath asked us to make a major effort to end the controversy. This effort strained relations with Diem and never was successful, but did dampen Army enthusiasm for the plot. At one moment, when there was likelihood of an attack by armored vehicles on the Presidential Palace, SMM told Hinh bluntly that U.S. support most probably would stop in such an event. At the same time a group from the Presidential Guards asked for tactical advice on how to stop armored vehicles with the only weapons available to the Guards: carbines, rifles, and hand grenades. The advice, on tank traps and destruction with improvised weapons, must have sounded grim. The following morning, when the attack was to take place, we visited the Palace; not a guard was left on the grounds; President Diem was alone upstairs, calmly getting his work done.

As a result of the Hinh trouble, Diem started looking around for troops upon whom he could count. Some Tonkinese militia, refugees from the north, were assembled in Saigon close to the Palace. But they were insufficient for what he needed. Diem made an agreement with General Trinh Minh The, leader of some 3,000 Cao Dai dissidents in the vicinity of Tayninh, to give General The some needed financial support; The was to give armed support to the government if necessary and to provide a safe haven for the government if it had to flee. The's guerrillas, known as the Lien Minh, were strongly nationalist and were still fighting the Vietminh and the French. At Ambassador Heath's request, the U.S. secretly furnished Diem with funds for The, through the SMM. Shortly afterwards, an invitation came from The to visit him. Ambassador Heath approved the visit. . . .

The northern SMM team under Conein had organized a paramilitary group, (which we will disguise by the Vietnamese name of Binh) through the Northern Dai Viets, a political party with loyalties to Bao Dai. The group was to be trained and supported by the U.S. as patriotic Vietnamese, to come eventually under government control when the government was ready for such activities. Thirteen Binhs were quietly exfiltrated through the port of Haiphong, under the direction of Lt Andrews, and taken on the first stage of the journey to their training area by a U.S. Navy ship. This was the first of a series of helpful actions by Task Force 98, commanded by Admiral Sabin.

Another paramilitary group for Tonkin operations was being developed in Saigon through General Nguyen Van Vy. In September this group started shaping up fast, and the project was given to Major Allen. (We will give this group the Vietnamese name of Hao). . . .

Towards the end of the month, it was learned that the largest printing establishment in the north intended to remain in Hanoi and do business with the Vietminh. An attempt was made by SMM to destroy the modern presses, but Vietminh security agents already had moved into the plant and frustrated the attempt. This operation was under a Vietnamese patriot whom we shall call Trieu; his case officer was Capt Arundel. Earlier in the month they had engineered a black psywar strike in Hanoi: leaflets signed by the Vietminh instructing Tonkinese on how to behave for the Vietminh takeover of the Hanoi region in early October, including items about property, money reform, and a three-day holiday of workers upon takeover. The day following the distribution of these leaflets, refugee registration tripled. Two days later Vietminh currency was worth half the value prior to the leaflets. The Vietminh took to the radio to denounce the leaflets; the leaflets were so authentic in appearance that even most of the rank and file Vietminh were sure that the radio denunciations were a French trick.

The Hanoi psywar strike had other consequences. Binh had enlisted a high police official of Hanoi as part of his team, to effect the release from jail of any team members if arrested. The official at the last moment decided to assist in the leaflet distribution personally. Police officers spotted him, chased his vehicle through the empty Hanoi streets of early morning, finally opened fire on him and caught him. He was the only member of the group caught. He was held in prison as a Vietminh agent.

d. October 1954

Hanoi was evacuated on 9 October. The northern SMM team left with the last French troops, disturbed by what they had seen of the grim efficiency of the Vietminh in their takeover, the contrast between the silent march of the victorious Vietminh troops in their tennis shoes and the clanking armor of the well-equipped French whose Western tactics and equipment had failed against the Communist military-political-economic campaign.

The northern team had spent the last days of Hanoi in contaminating the oil supply of the bus company for a gradual wreckage of engines in the buses, in taking the first actions for delayed sabotage of the railroad (which required teamwork with a CIA special technical team in Japan who performed their part brilliantly), and in writing detailed notes of potential targets for future paramilitary operations (U.S. adherence to the Geneva Agreement prevented SMM from carrying out the active sabotage it desired to do against the power plant, water facilities, harbor, and bridge). The team had a bad moment when contaminating the oil. They had to work quickly at night, in an enclosed storage room. Fumes from the contaminant came close to knocking them out. Dizzy and weak-kneed, they masked their faces with handkerchiefs and completed the job.

Meanwhile, Polish and Russian ships had arrived in the south to transport southern Vietminh to Tonkin under the Geneva Agreement. This offered the opportunity for another black psywar strike. A leaflet was developed by Binh with the help of Capt Arundel, attributed to the Vietminh Resistance Committee. Among other items, it reassured the Vietminh they would be kept safe below decks from imperialist air and submarine attacks, and requested that warm clothing be brought; the warm clothing item would be coupled with a verbal rumor campaign that Vietminh were being sent into China as railroad laborers.

SMM had been busily developing G-5 of the Vietnamese Army

for such psywar efforts. Under Arundel's direction, the First Armed Propaganda Company printed the leaflets and distributed them, by soldiers in civilian clothes who penetrated into southern Vietminh zones on foot. (Distribution in Camau was made while columnist Joseph Alsop was on his visit there which led to his sensational, gloomy articles later; our soldier "Vietminh" failed in an attempt to get the leaflet into Alsop's hands in Camau; Alsop was never told this story). Intelligence reports and other later reports revealed that village and delegation committees complained about "deportation" to the north, after distribution of the leaflet. . . .

Contention between Diem and Hinh had become murderous. . . . Finally, we learned that Hinh was close to action; he had selected 26 October as the morning for an attack on the Presidential Palace. Hinh was counting heavily on Lt-Col Lan's special forces and on Captain Giai who was running Hinh's secret headquarters at Hinh's home. We invited these two officers to visit the Philippines, on the pretext that we were making an official trip, could take them along and open the way for them to see some inner workings of the fight against Filipino Communists which they probably would never see otherwise. Hinh reluctantly turned down his own invitation; he had had a memorable time of it on his last visit to Manila in 1952. Lt-Col Lan was a French agent and the temptation to see behind-the-scenes was too much. He and Giai accompanied SMM officers on the MAAG C-47 which General O'Daniel instantly made available for the operation. 26 October was spent in the Philippines. The attack on the palace didn't come off.

e. November 1954

General Lawton Collins arrived as Ambassador on 8 November. . . .

Collins, in his first press conference, made it plain that the U.S. was supporting President Diem. The new Ambassador applied pressure on General Hinh and on 29 November Hinh left for Paris. His other key conspirators followed.

Part of the SMM team became involved in staff work to back up the energetic campaign to save Vietnam which Collins pushed forward. Some SMM members were scattered around the Pacific, accompanying Vietnamese for secret training, obtaining and shipping supplies to be smuggled into north Vietnam and hidden there. In the Philippines, more support was being constructed to help SMM, in expediting the flow of supplies, and in creating Freedom Company, a non-profit Philippines corporation backed by President Magsaysay, which would supply Filipinos experienced in fighting the Communist Huks to help in Vietnam (or elsewhere). . . .

On 23 November, twenty-one selected Vietnamese agents and two cooks of our Hao paramilitary group were put aboard a Navy ship in the Saigon River, in daylight. They appeared as coolies, joined the coolie and refugee throng moving on and off ship, and disappeared one by one. It was brilliantly planned and executed, agents being picked up from unobtrusive assembly points throughout the metropolis. Lt Andrews made the plans and carried out the movement under the supervision of Major Allen. The ship took the Hao agents, in compartmented groups, to an overseas point, the first stage in a movement to a secret training area.

f. December 1954

. . . discussions between the U.S., Vietnamese and French had reached a point where it appeared that a military training mission using U.S. officers was in the immediate offing. General O'Daniel had a U.S.-French planning group working on the problem, under Col. Rosson. One paper they were developing was a plan for pacification of Vietminh and dissident areas; this paper was passed to SMM for its assistance with the drafting. SMM wrote much of the paper, changing the concept from the old rigid police controls of all areas to some of our concepts of winning over the population and instituting a classification of areas by the amount of trouble in each, the amount of control required, and fixing responsibilities between civil and military authorities. With a few changes, this was issued by President Diem on 31 December as the National Security Action (Pacification) Directive. . . .

There was still much disquiet in Vietnam, particularly among anti-Communist political groups who were not included in the government. SMM officers were contacted by a number of such groups who felt that they "would have to commit suicide in 1956" (the 1956 plebiscite promised in the 1954 Geneva agreement), when the Vietminh would surely take over against so weak a government. One group of farmers and milita in the south was talked out of migrating to Madagascar by SMM and staying on their farms. A number of these groups asked SMM for help in training personnel for eventual guerrilla warfare if the Vietminh won. Persons such as the then Minister of Defense and Trinh Minh The were among those loyal to the government who also requested such help. It was decided that a more basic guerrilla training program might be undertaken for such groups than was available at the secret training site to which we had sent the Binh and Hao groups. Plans were made with Major Bohanan and Mr. John C. Wachtel in the Philippines for a solution of this problem; the United States backed the development, through them, of a small Freedom Company training camp in a hidden valley on the Clark AFB reservation.

Till and Peg Durdin of the N. Y. Times, Hank Lieberman of the N. Y. Times, Homer Bigart of the N. Y. Herald-Tribune, John Mecklin of Life-Time, and John Roderick of Associated Press, have been warm friends of SMM and worked hard to penetrate the fabric of French propaganda and give the U.S. an objective account of events in Vietnam. The group met with us at times to analyze objectives and motives of propaganda known to them, meeting at their own request as U.S. citizens. These mature and responsible news correspondents performed a valuable service for their country. . . .

g. January 1955

The Vietminh long ago had adopted the Chinese Communist thought that the people are the water and the army is the fish. Vietminh relations with the mass of the population during the fighting had been exemplary, with a few exceptions; in contrast, the Vietnamese National Army had been like too many Asian armies, adept at cowing a population into feeding them, providing them with girls. SMM had been working on this problem from the beginning. Since the National Army was the only unit of government with a strong organization throughout the country and with good communications, it was the key to stabilizing the situation quickly on a nation-wide basis. If Army and people could be brought together into a team, the first strong weapon against Communism could be forged.

The Vietminh were aware of this. We later learned that months before the signing of the Geneva Agreement they had been planning for action in the post-Geneva period; the National Army was to be the primary target for subversion efforts, it was given top priority by the Central Committee for operations against its enemy, and about 100 superior cadres were retrained for the operations and placed in the [words illegible] organization for the work, which commenced even before the agreement was signed. We didn't know it at the time, but this was SMM's major opponent, in a secret struggle for the National Army. . . .

General O'Daniel was anticipating the culmination of long negotiations to permit U.S. training of the Vietnamese Armed Forces, against some resistance on the part of French groups. In January, negotiations were proceeding so well that General O'Daniel informally organized a combined U.S.-French training mission which eventually became known as the Training Relations & Instruction Mission (TRIM) under his command, but under the overall command of the top French commander, General Paul Ely.

The French had asked for top command of half the divisions in the TRIM staff. Their first priority was for command of the division supervising National Security Action by the Vietnamese, which could be developed into a continuation of strong French control of key elements of both Army and population. In conferences with Ambassador Collins and General O'Daniel, it was decided to transfer Colonel Lansdale from the Ambassador's staff to TRIM, to head the National Security division. Colonel Lansdale requested authority to coordinate all U.S. civil and military efforts in this National Security work. On 11 January, Ambassador

Collins announced the change to the country team, and gave him authority to coordinate this work among all U.S. agencies in Vietnam. . . .

President Diem had continued requesting SMM help with the guard battalion for the Presidential Palace. We made arrangements with President Magsaysay in the Philippines and borrowed his senior aide and military advisor, Col. Napoleon Valeriano, who had a fine combat record against the Communist Huks and also had reorganized the Presidential Guard Battalion for Magsaysay. Valeriano, with three junior officers, arrived in January and went to work on Diem's guard battalion. Later, selected Vietnamese officers were trained with the Presidential Guards in Manila. An efficient unit gradually emerged. Diem was warmly grateful for this help by Filipinos who also continuously taught our concept of loyalty and freedom.

The patriot we've named Trieu Dinh had been working on an almanac for popular sale, particularly in the northern cities and towns we could still reach. Noted Vietnamese astrologers were hired to write predictions about coming disasters to certain Vietminh leaders and undertakings, and to predict unity in the south. The work was carried out under the direction of Lt Phillips, based on our concept of the use of astrology for psywar in Southeast Asia. Copies of the almanac were shipped by air to Haiphong and then smuggled into Vietminh territory.

Dinh also had produced a Thomas Paine type series of essays on Vietnamese patriotism against the Communist Vietminh, under the guidance of Capt. Arundel. These essays were circulated among influential groups in Vietnam, earned front-page editorials in the leading daily newspaper in Saigon. Circulation increased with the publication of these essays. The publisher is known to SMM as The Dragon Lady and is a fine Vietnamese girl who has been the mistress of an anti-American French civilian. Despite anti-American remarks by her boy friend, we had helped her keep her paper from being closed by the government . . . and she found it profitable to heed our advice on the editorial content of her paper.

Arms and equipment for the Binh paramilitary team were being cached in the north in areas still free from the Vietminh. Personnel movements were covered by the flow of refugees. Haiphong was reminiscent of our own pioneer days as it was swamped with people whom it couldn't shelter. Living space and food were at a premium, nervous tension grew. It was a wild time for our northern team.

First supplies for the Hao paramilitary group started to arrive in Saigon. These shipments and the earlier ones for the Binh group were part of an efficient and effective air smuggling effort by the 581st [word illegible] Wing, U.S. Air Force, to support SMM, with help by CIA and Air Force personnel in both Okinawa and the Philippines. SMM officers frequently did coolie labor in manhandling tons of cargo, at times working throughout the night. . . . All . . . officers pitched in to help, as part of our "blood, sweat and tears". . . .

By 31 January, all operational equipment of the Binh paramilitary group had been trans-shipped to Haiphong from Saigon, mostly with the help of CAT, and the northern SMM team had it cached in operational sites. Security measures were tightened at the Haiphong airport and plans for bringing in the Hao equipment were changed from the air route to sea. Task Force 98, now 98.7 under command of Captain Frank, again was asked to give a helping hand and did so. . . .

. . . . Major Conein had briefed the members of the Binh paramilitary team and started them infiltrating into the north as individuals. The infiltration was carried out in careful stages over a 30 day period, a successful operation. The Binhs became normal citizens, carrying out every day civil pursuits, on the surface.

We had smuggled into Vietnam about eight and a half tons of supplies for the Hao paramilitary group. They included fourteen agent radios, 300 carbines, 90,000 rounds of carbine ammunition, 50 pistols, 10,000 rounds of pistol ammunition, and 300 pounds of explosives. Two and a half tons were delivered to the Hao agents in Tonkin, while the remainder was cached along the Red River by SMM, with the help of the Navy. . . .

j. April 1955

. . . the Hao paramilitary team had finished its training at the secret training site and been flown by the Air Force to a holding site in the Philippines, where Major Allen and his officers briefed the paramilitary team. In mid-April, they were taken by the Navy to Haiphong, where they were gradually slipped ashore. Meanwhile, arms and other equipment including explosives were being flown into Saigon via our smuggling route, being readied for shipment north by the Navy task force handling refugees. The White team office gradually became an imposing munitions depot. Nightly shootings and bombings in restless Saigon caused us to give them dispersed storage behind thick walls as far as this one big house would permit. SMM personnel guarded the house night and day, for it also contained our major files other than the working file at our Command Post. All files were fixed for instant destruction, automatic weapons and hand grenades distributed to all personnel. It was a strange scene for new personnel just arriving. . . .

Haiphong was taken over by the Vietminh on 16 May. Our Binh and northern Hao teams were in place, completely equipped. It had taken a tremendous amount of hard work to beat the Geneva deadline, to locate, select, exfiltrate, train, infiltrate, equip the men of these two teams and have them in place, ready for actions required against the enemy. It would be a hard task to do openly, but this had to be kept secret from the Vietminh, the International Commission with its suspicious French and Poles and Indians, and even friendly Vietnamese. Movements of personnel and supplies had had to be over thousands of miles. . . .

Chapter 2

Origins of the Insurgency in South Vietnam

The Pentagon's study analyzes the Vietcong movement and its role in the development of the war. The following article, by Fox Butterfield, describes the analysts' findings.

The secret Pentagon study of the Vietnam war says the United States Government's official view that the war was imposed on South Vietnam by aggression from Hanoi is "not wholly compelling."

Successive administrations in Washington, from President John F. Kennedy to President Richard M. Nixon, have used this interpretation of the origins of the war to justify American intervention in Vietnam. But American intellilgence estimates during the nineteen-fifties show, the Pentagon account says, that the war began largely as a rebellion in the South against the increasingly oppressive and corrupt regime of Ngo Dinh Diem.

"Most of those who took up arms were South Vietnamese and the causes for which they fought were by no means contrived in North Vietnam," the Pentagon account says of the years from 1956 to 1959, when the insurgency began.

The study also disputes many critics of American policy in Vietnam who have contended that North Vietnam became involved in the South only after 1965 in response to large-scale American intervention.

"It is equally clear that North Vietnamese Communists operated some form of subordinate apparatus in the South in the years 1954-1960," the Pentagon study says.

And in 1959, the account continues, Hanoi made a clear decision to assert its control over the growing insurgency and to increase its infiltration of trained cadres from the North.

67

Other Events of the Period

April 12, 1945—Roosevelt dies.
May 8, 1945—War in Europe ends.
Aug. 6, 1945—Atom bomb dropped on Hiroshima.
Aug. 14, 1945—Japan surrenders.
Jan. 10, 1946—First U.N. General Assembly opens.
Nov. 2, 1948—Truman elected.
Dec. 7, 1949—Communists complete take-over of China.
June 25, 1950—North Korean troops invade South Korea.
Nov. 1, 1952—First U.S. hydrogen bomb explosion.
Nov. 4, 1952—Eisenhower elected.
March 5, 1953—Stalin dies.
July 27, 1953—Korean war armistice.
Aug. 12, 1953—Soviet Union explodes first H-bomb.
Sept. 8, 1954—SEATO Pact signed.
July 18-23, 1955—Summit meeting, Geneva.
Oct. 23, 1956—Hungarian uprising begins.
Oct. 29, 1956—Suez invasion.
Nov. 6, 1956—Eisenhower re-elected.
Oct. 4, 1957—Soviet Union launches Sputnik I.
July 15, 1958—U.S. Marines in Lebanon.
Jan. 1, 1959—Castro takes power in Cuba.
Sept. 15-27, 1959—Khrushchev visits U.S.
Nov. 8, 1960—Kennedy elected.

Thereafter, the study says, "Hanoi's involvement in the developing strife became evident."

Developments related to the origins of the war that are disclosed by the Pentagon history include the following:

• American officials in Saigon, including those in the embassy, the Central Intelligence Agency and the military command were fully aware of President Diem's shortcomings. They regularly reported to Washington that he was "authoritarian, inflexible and remote," that he entrusted power only to his own family and that he had alienated all elements of the population by his oppressive policies.

• From 1954 to 1958 North Vietnam concentrated on its internal development, apparently hoping to achieve reunification either through the elections provided for in the Geneva settlement or through the natural collapse of the weak Diem regime. The Communists left behind a skeletal apparatus in the South when they regrouped to North Vietnam in 1954 after the war with the French ended, but the cadre members were ordered to engage only in "political struggle."

• In the years before 1959 the Diem regime was nearly successful in wiping out the agents, who felt constrained by their orders not to fight back. Their fear and anger at being caught in this predicament, however, apparently led them to begin the insurgency against Mr. Diem, despite their orders, sometime during 1956-57.

North Vietnam's leaders formally decided in May, 1959, at the 15th meeting of the Lao Dong (Communist) party's Central Committee, to take control of the growing insurgency. Captured Vietcong personnel and documents report that as a result of the decision the Ho Chi Minh Trail of supply lines was prepared, southern cadre members who had been taken North were infiltrated back to the South and the tempo of the war suddenly speeded up.

The Pentagon account says that both American intelligence and Vietcong prisoners attributed the Vietcong's rapid success after 1959 to the Diem regime's mistakes.

In a report prepared by the Rand Corporation of Santa Monica, Calif., on the interrogation of 23 Vietcong cadre members, one southern member said of the Communists' success:

"The explanation is not that the cadre were exceptionally gifted but the people they talked to were ready for rebellion. The people were like a mound of straw, ready to be ignited.

"If at that time the Government in the South had been a

good one, if it had not been dictatorial, then launching the movement would have been difficult."

A United States intelligence estimate of August, 1960, on the rapidly deteriorating situation in South Vietnam concluded:

"The indications of increasing dissatisfaction with the Diem government have probably encouraged the Hanoi regime to take stronger action at this time."

To emphasize how the Diem regime's oppressive and corrupt policies helped prepare the way for the insurgency in South Vietnam, the Pentagon study devotes a lengthy section to Mr. Diem's rule—as Premier from 1954 until late 1955 and then as President until he was overthrown in 1963.

When Mr. Diem took office in 1954, the account notes, it seemed for a while that he "did accomplish miracles," as his supporters contended.

To the surprise of most observers, he put down the Binh Xuyen gangster sect in Saigon and the Cao Dai and the Hoa Hao, armed sects in the countryside. He created a stable government and a loyal army where there had been only chaos. And he won diplomatic recognition for South Vietnam from many foreign governments.

But from the beginning, the account says, President Diem's personality and political concepts tended to decrease his Government's effectiveness.

The product of a family that was both zealously Roman Catholic and a member of the traditional Mandarin ruling class, Mr. Diem was authoritarian, moralistic, inflexible, bureaucratic and suspicious. His mentality is described in the account as like that of a "Spanish Inquisitor."

His political machine was a "rigidly organized, overcentralized family oligarchy." He trusted only his family members, particularly his brother Ngo Dinh Nhu, who had organized the semi-secret Can Lao party.

An American intelligence estimate of May, 1959, described the situation as follows:

"President Diem continues to be the undisputed ruler of South Vietnam; all important and many minor decisions are referred to him.

"Although he professes to believe in representative government and democracy, Diem is convinced that the Vietnamese are not ready for such a political system and that he must rule with a firm hand, at least so long as national security is threatened.

"He also believes that the country cannot afford a political opposition which could obstruct or dilute the Government's efforts to establish a strong rule. He remains a somewhat austere and remote figure to most Vietnamese and has not generated widespread popular enthusiasm.

"Diem's regime reflects his ideas. A facade of representative government is maintained, but the Government is in fact essentially authoritarian.

"The legislative powers of the National Assembly are strictly circumscribed; the judiciary is undeveloped and subordinate to the executive; and the members of the executive branch are little more than the personal agents of Diem.

"No organized opposition, loyal or otherwise, is tolerated, and critics of the regime are often repressed."

To make matters worse, according to the account, Mr. Diem's programs designed to increase security in the countryside were carried out so badly that they "drove a wedge not between the insurgents and the farmers, but between the farmers and the Government, and eventuated in less rather than more security."

The Civic Action program, designed to help the Government in Saigon establish communication with the peasants, went astray when President Diem used northern refugees and Catholics almost exclusively to go into the villages. To the peasants these Civic Action team members were outsiders.

The Diem land-reform program, instead of redistributing land to the poor, ended up taking back what the peasants had been given by the Vietminh and returning it to the landlords. In 1960, 75 percent of the land was still owned by 15 percent of the people.

Mr. Diem abolished the traditional elected village councils out of fear that Communists might gain power in them. Then he replaced these popular bodies with appointed outsiders, northern refugees and Catholics loyal to him.

In the so-called anti-Communist denunciation campaign, which was begun in the summer of 1955, from 50,000 to 100,000 people were put in detention camps. But, the account says, many of the detainees were not Communists at all.

President Diem also ordered a number of population-relocation programs to increase security, but these too backfired, it says.

Montagnard tribesmen who were forced to leave their traditional homelands in the Central Highlands for more settled and secure areas made easy recruits for the Vietcong, the chronicle relates, and peasants who were forced to move out

71

of their ancestral villages and build new ones in the so-called agroville program resented the Saigon Government.

Despite "Diem's preoccupation with security," the account says, "he poorly provided for police and intelligence in the countryside"; the Self-Defense Corps and Civil Guard—both militia groups—were "poorly trained and equipped, miserably led."

"Their brutality, petty thievery and disorderliness induced innumerable villagers to join in open revolt against Diem," the account continues.

By curbing freedom of speech and jailing dissidents, the history says, Mr. Diem alienated the intellectuals; by promoting officers on the basis of loyalty to his family rather than on the basis of ability, he alienated large segments of the armed forces.

Looking at the Diem Government's growing problems in January, 1960, the United States Embassy concluded in a "Special Report on the Internal Security Situation in Vietnam":

"The situation may be summed up in the fact that the Government has tended to treat the population with suspicion or to coerce it and has been rewarded with an attitude of apathy and resentment.

"The basic factor which has been lacking is a feeling of rapport between the Government and the population. The people have not identified themselves with the Government."

The report pointed to this "growth of apathy and considerable dissatisfaction among the rural populace" as a major cause of the insurgency.

"Political Struggle"

The Pentagon study divides the development of the insurgency in South Vietnam into roughly three periods:

From 1954 to 1956 the country enjoyed relative quiet as Communist cadres left behind in the South devoted themselves to "political struggle." From 1956 to 1958, after President Diem's rejection of the scheduled elections, dissident cadres in the South began the insurgency. With Hanoi's decision to take over the insurgency in 1959, the third period, that of full-scale war, began.

When Ho Chi Minh established his capital in Hanoi after

the Geneva conference in 1954, American intelligence reported that North Vietnam's new leaders could be expected to concentrate on building their war-ravaged and primitive economy.

According to the American information, the Communists had taken with them 90,000 armed men from the South, leaving 5,000 to 10,000 armed men behind as a "skeletal apparatus."

From captured documents, American intelligence officials believed that the "stay-behind cadres" had the main task of preparing for the elections scheduled for 1956 to reunify the country. The cadre members were ordered to carry out only "political struggle," which meant largely propaganda activity and infiltration of the Saigon Government.

A document captured early in 1955 from a Communist field organizer and sent to Washington by the Central Intelligence Agency warned that "it is not the time to meet the enemy." The Communists apparently believed, the study says, that they would get control of the country either through the elections or by the collapse of the Diem regime through its own weakness.

In 1966 the confidential Rand Corporation study of captured southern cadre members who originally went to the North in 1954 showed that most of them had expected that the Communists would win in the 1956 elections.

"Our political officer explained that we were granted Vietnam north of the 17th Parallel now, but in 1956 there would be a general election and we would regain the South and be reunited with our families," one captive reported.

"I was a political officer," another explained. "I went to the North just like all the other combatants in my unit. I believed, at the time, that regroupment was only temporary, because from the study sessions on the Geneva agreement we drew the conclusion that we could return to the South after the general election."

While there were some incidents of murder or kidnapping in the southern countryside from 1954 to 1956, they were not directly attributable to the Communist "stay-behinds," the account says.

A United States intelligence estimate of July, 1956, noted:

"During the past year the Communists in South Vietnam have remained generally quiescent. They have passed by a number of opportunities to embarrass the Diem regime.

"Although some cadres and supplies are being infiltrated across the 17th Parallel, the D.R.V. [Democratic Republic of

North Vietnam] probably has not sent any large-scale reinforcement or supply to the South."

The American intelligence network in South Vietnam, though limited in size, was well informed of the Communists' attitudes and actions during this period, the study explains. An intelligence estimate in May, 1957, noted:

"Because the countrywide elections envisaged by the Geneva agreements have not been held and because military action has been prevented, the D.R.V. has been frustrated in its hopes of gaining control of SVN. This has caused some discontent among cadres evacuated from the South in the expectation that they would soon return."

Intelligence gathered from Communist agents and documents captured in the nineteen-sixties, when the American intelligence network had expanded, filled out this picture of frustration and disillusionment among the cadre members.

A captured Communist who had been in charge of propaganda in Saigon testified: "The period from the armistice of 1954 until 1958 was the darkest time for the Vietcong in South Vietnam. The political agitation policy proposed by the Communist party could not be carried out due to the arrest of a number of party members."

Another cadre member reported: "The cadres who had remained behind in the South had almost all been arrested. Only one or two cadres were left in every three to five villages."

A document that appears to be a party history, captured in 1966 by the United States First Infantry Division during a sweep through the area called the Iron Triangle near Saigon, described the cadres' predicament. Noting that the Diem Government's harsh security policies had "truly and efficiently destroyed our party," the document referring to the scheduled date for the elections said:

"Particularly after 20 July 1956, the key cadres and party members in South Vietnam asked questions which demanded answers:

"Can we still continue the struggle to demand the implementation of the Geneva agreement given the existing regime in South Vietnam? If not, what must be done? A mood of skepticism and nonconfidence in the orientation of the struggle began to seep into the party apparatus and among some of the masses."

For some cadres, the documents said the answer was "armed struggle" despite their orders. It continued:

"The situation truly ripened for an armed movement

74

against the enemy. But the leadership of the Nam Bo Regional Committee [then the Vietcong's headquarters for the southern part of South Vietnam] at that time still hesitated for many reasons, but the principal reason was the fear of violating the party line.

"The majority of party members and cadres felt that it was necessary to immediately launch an armed struggle in order to preserve the movement and protect the forces. In several areas the party members on their own initiative had organized armed struggle against the enemy."

According to the Pentagon account, the result of the cadres' decision to begin armed struggle was soon apparent in Saigon.

American intelligence officers in Saigon estimated that 30 armed terrorist incidents were initiated in the last quarter of 1957, with at least 75 local officials assassinated or kidnapped. On Oct. 22, 13 Americans were wounded in three bombings in Saigon.

But, the account says, "there is only sparse evidence that North Vietnam was directing, or was capable of directing, that violence."

During this period, from 1956 to 1958, the party leaders in Hanoi were engaged in "a serious reconsideration" of their policy, the account says.

Sometime early in 1957 Le Duan, a southerner who had led the fight in the South during the French Indochina war, returned to Hanoi from a two-year stay in the South, carrying news that the struggle there was going badly. According to American intelligence reports, he told the Politburo that it was wasting time with its orders for "political struggle." He was said to have urged military pressure.

Mr. Duan, the study notes, was named a member of the Politburo later that same year, and in September, 1960, he became the First Secretary of the party.

The futility of their policy must have been brought home to the leaders in Hanoi according to the study, when on Jan. 24, 1957, the Soviet Union proposed the admission of both North and South Vietnam to the United Nations.

But until 1958 North Vietnam was still primarily concerned with its internal development, the account says, especially during 1956, when there was a peasant revolt against the Communists' harsh land-reform program.

In December, 1958, or January, 1959, the study continues, "Hanoi apparently decided that the time had come to intensify its efforts."

American intelligence quickly picked up clues about this decision.

The C.I.A. came into possession of a directive from Hanoi to its headquarters for the Central Highlands during December, 1958, stating that the Lao Dong party's Central Committee had decided to "open a new stage of the struggle."

And in January, 1959, the C.I.A. received a copy of an order directing the establishment of two guerrilla operations bases, one in Tayninh Province near the Cambodian border and another in the western Central Highlands.

The C.I.A. also learned at this time that Mr. Duan was making a secret visit to the South.

The decision that had been made privately by the Politburo was formally ratified by the Central Committee at its 15th meeting in May, 1959. All available evidence suggests that this was "the point of departure for D.R.V. intervention," the narrative says.

Scholars and journalists who have studied the origins of the insurgency, but who have not had access to American intelligence reports, have not attached such significance to that 15th session.

The United States Embassy in Saigon, reporting to Washington on the Central Committee decision, noted that a resolution had been passed saying that the struggle for reunification would have to be carried out by "all appropriate measures other than peaceful," the embassy reported.

The document captured by the First Infantry Division recalled the 1959 decision:

"After the resolution of the 15th plenum of the Central Committee was issued, all of South Vietnam possessed a clear and correct strategic policy and orientation.

"The directive of the Politburo in May, 1959, stated that the time had come to push the armed struggle. Thanks to this we closely followed the actual situation in order to formulate a program, and in October, 1959, the armed struggle was launched."

A rapid build-up of Hanoi's potential for infiltration followed the party's decision to take a more active role in the insurgency, the analyst says.

Infiltration from North Vietnam had actually begun as early as 1955, United States intelligence reports show, but only in 1959 did the C.I.A. pick up evidence of large-scale infiltration.

To operate the infiltration trails, a group of montagnard

tribesmen from Quangtri and Thuathien Provinces were given special training in North Vietnam in 1958 and 1959.

Early in 1959 also, the C.I.A. reported, Hanoi formed "special border crossing teams" composed of southerners who went to the North in 1954. Their mission was to carry food, drugs and other supplies down the trail network.

And in April, 1959, the C.I.A. learned, the 559th Transportation Group was established directly under the party's Central Committee as a headquarters in charge of infiltration.

Large training centers for infiltrators were reportedly established early in 1960 at Xuanmai and Sontay, near Hanoi. During 1959 and 1960, United States intelligence officials estimated, 26 groups of infiltrators, totaling 4,500 people, made the trip south.

From later interrogation of captured infiltrators, United States intelligence officers learned that until 1964 almost all the infiltrators were native southerners who went to the North in 1954.

A Rand Corporation study of 71 of the infiltrators showed that two out of three were members of the Lao Dong party; that they had all undergone extensive periods of training in North Vietnam before being sent south; and that most of them were officers, senior noncommissioned officers or party cadre members.

Hanoi's decision to switch from "political struggle" to "armed struggle" was rapidly reflected in a rise in terrorist attacks in South Vietnam during the second half of 1959, the Pentagon study says.

The United States Embassy, in a Special Report on the Internal Security Situation in Vietnam in January, 1960, noted that while there were 193 assassinations in all of 1958, there were 119 assassinations in the last four months of 1959 alone.

Even more alarming, the embassy said, were Vietcong attacks for the first time on large South Vietnamese Army units. A Vietcong ambush of two companies of Saigon's 23d Division on Sept. 26, 1959, with the killing of 12 Government soldiers and the loss of most of their weapons, brought home "the full impact of the seriousness of the present situation."

The stepped-up insurgency led to the first American casualties of the war in South Vietnam. On July 8, 1959, a terrorist bomb inside the Bienhoa base compound killed two United States servicemen.

In its January, 1960, report on the deteriorating situation, the embassy also passed on to Washington two comments made by the North Vietnamese Premier, Pham Van Dong, which it considered significant:

First: " 'You must remember we will be in Saigon tomorrow, we will be in Saigon tomorrow.' These words were spoken by Premier Pham Van Dong in a conversation with French Consul Georges-Picot on Sept. 12, 1959."

And second: "In November, Pham Van Dong twice told Canadian Commissioner Erichsen-Brown that 'We will drive the Americans into the sea.' " The Canadian, a representative on the International Control Commission, was stationed in Hanoi.

The National Liberation Front for South Vietnam was officially founded on Dec. 20, 1960, the study relates, and within a year its membership had quadrupled to 300,000. By then the insurgency had taken root.

Chapter 3

The Kennedy Years: 1961–1963

—BY HEDRICK SMITH

The Pentagon's study of the Vietnam war concludes that President John F. Kennedy transformed the "limited-risk gamble" of the Eisenhower Administration into a "broad commitment" to prevent Communist domination of South Vietnam.

Although Mr. Kennedy resisted pressures for putting American ground-combat units into South Vietnam, the Pentagon analysts say, he took a series of actions that significantly expanded the American military and political involvement in Vietnam but nonetheless left President Lyndon B. Johnson with as bad a situation as Mr. Kennedy inherited.

"The dilemma of the U.S. involvement dating from the Kennedy era," the Pentagon study observes, was to use "only limited means to achieve excessive ends."

Moreover, according to the study, prepared in 1967-68 by Government analysts, the Kennedy tactics deepened the American involvement in Vietnam piecemeal, with each step minimizing public recognition that the American role was growing.

President Kennedy made his first fresh commitments to Vietnam secretly. The Pentagon study discloses that in the spring of 1961 the President ordered 400 Special Forces troops and 100 other American military advisers sent to South Vietnam. No publicity was given to either move.

Small as the numbers seem in retrospect, the Pentagon study comments that even the first such expansion "signaled a willingness to go beyond the 685-man limit on the size of the U.S. [military] mission in Saigon, which, if it were done openly, would be the first formal breach of the Geneva agreement." Under the interpretation of that agreeemnt in effect

Highlights of the Period

The Pentagon study reaches no conclusion as to how the course of the Vietnam war might have changed if John F. Kennedy had lived—but it sums up the Kennedy years as a time of significantly deepening United States involvement.

Here, arranged chronologically, are highlights of those two and a half years:

1961

National intelligence estimate reports "extremely critical" period" for South Vietnam and Saigon regime is "immediately ahead." Says President Ngo Dinh Diem's "reliance on virtual one-man rule" and a "toleration of corruption" lead many in military and government to "question Diem's ability to lead in this period."

President orders 400 Special Forces soldiers and 100 other military advisers to South Vietnam, study says. Also orders clandestine campaign of "sabotage and light harassment" in North by South Vietnamese agents trained by United States.

Task force headed by Roswell W. Gilpatric proposes discussion with President Diem on "possibility of a defensive security Alliance" despite violation of Geneva accords. President approves.

Vice President Lyndon B. Johnson, in report on mission to Saigon, says United States must decide "whether to help these countries" or to "throw in the towel" and "pull back our defenses to San Francisco."

President Diem, in letter to President Kennedy, asks "considerable" build-up United States forces and 100,000-man increase in South Vietnamese Army. Uses "inflated infiltration figures" to support threat of Communism, study says.

White House agrees to finance 30,000-man increase in South Vietnam's Army.

U. Alexis Johnson, Deputy Under Secretary of State, in draft paper, urges President Kennedy to accept "defeat of the Vietcong" as "real and ultimate" objective.

Joint Chiefs of Staff esimate 40,000 United States servicemen will be needed to "clean up the Vietcong threat."

William P. Bundy note to Mr. McNamara urges "early and hard-hitting" United States intervention. Gives this 70 per cent chance of "arresting things": estimates 30 per cent chance "we would wind up like the French in 1954: white men can't win this kind of fight."

National intelligence estimate reports "little evidence" that Vietcong rely on external supplies, Pentagon account says. Ambassador Frederick E. Nolting Jr. reports that Saigon is considering asking Nationalist China for "one division of combat troops" and wants United States "combat-trainer units."

General Taylor meets with President Diem. Recommends

80

Mekong Delta flood "relief task force, largely military in composition," including "combat troops" for protection. Recommends 6,000-8,000-man U.S. force, warns they "may expect to take casualties" but can be removed or phased into "other activities."

He discounts risk of "major Asian war," says North is "extremely vulnerable to conventional bombing."

Secretary of Defense McNamara says he and Joint Chiefs are "inclined to recommend" General Taylor's proposal although "struggle may be prolonged." Estimates maximum United States ground-force requirement "will not exceed six divisions."

Secretary of State Rusk cables Washington stressing importance of political reforms, reluctance for United States prestige tie with a "losing horse."

General Taylor, in message to President Kennedy, says "U.S. military task force is essential."

Mr. McNamara and Mr. Rusk, in joint memo, back General Taylor's recommendations. Say losing South Vietnam "would make pointless any further discussion about the importance of Southeast Asia to the Free World." Recommend initially "U.S. units of modest size" for "direct support" "as speedily as possible"; insist on government reform as precondition.

National Security Council meeting. Notes say President asks importance of South Vietnam and Laos. Gen. Lyman L. Lemnitzer, Chairman of Joint Chiefs: "We would lose Asia all the way Singapore."

President approves major recommendations. President Diem said to be upset by United States response. Demands for reforms softened, insistence on American participation in decision-making withdrawn.

1962

Military briefing paper for President reports 948 United States servicemen were in South Vietnam by end of November; 2,646 by Jan. 9. Also helicopter combat-support missions, Navy minesweepers sailing along coast, United States aircraft in surveillance, reconnaissance missions.

Mr. McNamara orders planning for United States withdrawal, partly on basis of what he calls "tremendous progress," also difficulty in holding public support for American operations "indefinitely."

1963

Michael V. Forrestal, White House aide, reports to Kennedy, that long, costly conflict should be expected. Says Vietcong ecruiting is so effective that guerrillas could do without infiltration.

United States by October, has 16,732 men in Vietnam. Planning for withdrawal continues, study says, on "the most Micawberesque predictions" of progress.

since 1956, the United States was limited to 685 military advisers in Vietnam. Washington, while it did not sign the accord, pledged not to undermine it.

On May 11, 1961, the day on which President Kennedy decided to send the Special Forces, he also ordered the start of a campaign of clandestine warfare against North Vietnam, to be conducted by South Vietnamese agents directed and trained by the Central Intelligence Agency and some American Special Forces troops. [See Document #20.]

The President's instructions, as quoted in the documents, were, "In North Vietnam . . . [to] form networks of resistance, covert bases and teams for sabotage and light harassment. The American military mission in Saigon was also instructed to prepare South Vietnamese Army units "to conduct ranger raids and similar military actions in North Vietnam as might prove necessary or appropriate."

The Pentagon study reports that the primary target of the clandestine campaign against North Vietnam, and Laos as well, was to be "lines of communication"—railroads, highways, bridges, train depots and trucks.

The study does not report how many agents were actually sent north, though documents accompanying it described some of the build-up and training of the First Observation Group, the main South Vietnamese unit conducting the covert campaign.

Within weeks of President Kennedy's May 11 decision, moreover, the North Vietnamese Government made repeated protests to the International Control Commission that its airspace and territory were being violated by foreign aircraft and South Vietnamese ground raids thrusting into the demilitarized zone along the border between the two Vietnams.

In July, 1961, Hanoi announced publicly that it had captured and was putting on trial three South Vietnamese participants in undercover operations who had survived the crash of a plane that was shot down, Hanoi said, while preparing to drop them into North Vietnam. The North Vietnamese, protesting formally to Britain and the Soviet Union—the co-chairmen of the 1954 Geneva conference on Vietnam—described in detail what they said the survivors had disclosed about their American training and equipment.

Mr. Kennedy's May 11 orders, the study discloses, also called for infiltration of South Vietnamese forces into southeastern Laos to find and attack Communist bases and supply lines.

On Oct. 13, moreover, the President reportedly gave additional secret orders for allied forces to "initiate ground action, including the use of U.S. advisers if necessary," against Communist aerial resupply missions in the vicinity of Tchepone, in the southern Laotian panhandle.

The Pentagon study does not analyze these covert operations in detail, but it shows Mr. Kennedy's decisions as part of an unbroken sequence that built up to much more ambitious covert warfare against North Vietnam under President Johnson in 1964.

The analysts handling the Kennedy period put more stress, however, on the evolution of President Kennedy's decision in November, 1961, to expand greatly the American military advisory mission in Vietnam and, for the first time, to put American servicemen in combat-support roles that involved them increasingly in actual fighting.

In a cablegram to Washington on Nov. 18, cited in the study, Frederick E. Nolting Jr., the United States Ambassador in Saigon, described the significance attached to those moves.

He said he had explained to President Ngo Dinh Diem of South Vietnam that the new roles of American servicemen "could expose them to enemy action."

"In response to Diem's question," Mr. Nolting continued, "[I] said that in my personal opinion these personnel would be authorized to defend themselves if attacked. I pointed out that this was one reason why the decisions were very grave from U.S. standpoints."

Questions for Kennedy

The Pentagon study shows President Kennedy facing three main questions on Vietnam during his term of office: whether to make an irrevocable commitment to prevent a Communist victory; whether to commit ground combat units to achieve his ends; whether to give top priority to the military battle against the Vietcong or to the political reforms necessary for winning popular support.

President Kennedy's response during 34 months in office, as the Pentagon account tells it, was to increase American advisers from the internationally accepted level of 685 to roughly 16,000 to put Americans into combat situations—resulting in a tenfold increase in American combat casualties in one year—and eventually to inject the United States into the internal South Vietnamese maneuvering that finally toppled the Diem regime.

The judgment of the Pentagon study is that while President Kennedy's actions stopped short of the fundamental decision to commit ground troops, nonetheless, "the limited-risk gamble undertaken by Eisenhower had been transformed into an unlimited commitment under Kennedy." Later, more cautiously, the study says that Mr. Kennedy's policies produced a "broad commitment" to Vietnam's defense, giving priority to the military aspects of the war over political reforms.

The study also observes that the pervasive assumption in the Kennedy Administration was that "the Diem regime's own evident weaknesses—from the 'famous problem of Diem as administrator' to the Army's lack of offensive spirit—could be cured if enough dedicated Americans, civilians and military, became involved in South Vietnam to show the South Vietnamese, at all levels, how to get on and win the war."

President Kennedy and his senior advisers are described in the study as considering defeat unthinkable and assuming that the mere introduction of Americans would provide the South Vietnamese with what the authors call "the élan and style needed to win."

The description of the debates in the Kennedy Administration presented in the study are revealing—particularly when the President decides against committing ground troops—because they emerge, in effect, as a rehearsal for the planning in the Johnson era that led to outright war in 1965. Many of the same officials advanced many of the same arguments and the intelligence communitiy offered some of the same ominous forewarnings.

President Kennedy was told that sending ground troops would be a "shot in the arm" that would "spark real transformation" of the Southern Vietnamese Army. The Joint Chiefs of Staff calculated that, at worst, no more than 205,000 American soldiers would be required to cope not only with the Vietcong but also with North Vietnam and Communist China if they should intervene. Both military and civilian advisers contended that American bombing of the North—even the mere threat of it—would hold Hanoi and the other Communist nations at bay.

In secretly urging the first commitment of American ground troops to Vietnam in November, 1961, Gen. Maxwell D. Taylor, then the President's personal military adviser, discounted the risks of a major land war. In a private message to the President from the Philippines, on his way home from Saigon on Nov. 1, he said:

"The risks of backing into a major Asian war by way of SVN are present but are not impressive. NVN is extremely vulnerable to conventional bombing, a weakness which should be exploited diplomatically in convincing Hanoi to lay off SVN.

"Both the D.R.V. [Democratic Republic of (North) Vietnam] and the Chicoms would face severe logistical difficulties in trying to maintain strong forces in the field in SEA [Southeast Asia], difficulties which we share but by no means to the same degree. There is no case for fearing a mass onslaught of Communist manpower into SVN and its neighboring states, particularly if our airpower is allowed a free hand against logistical targets."

In General Taylor's recommendations for an initial commitment of 6,000 to 8,000 American ground troops, the account relates, he had a co-author, Walt W. Rostow, then the senior White House aide working on Southeast Asia.

On Nov. 5 Secretary of Defense Robert S. McNamara sent President Kennedy a memorandum stating that he and the Joint Chiefs of Staff were "inclined to recommend" General Taylor's proposal—but with the significant warning that much greater troop commitments were likely in the future. [See Document #29.]

"The struggle may be prolonged and Hanoi and Peiping may intervene overtly," the McNamara memorandum told the President. It estimated that even so, "the maximum U.S. forces required on the ground in Southeast Asia will not exceed six divisions, or about 205,000 men."

The President eventually rejected this approach. But the Pentagon study comments that the ground-troop issue so dominated the discussions that Mr. Kennedy's ultimate decisions to approve the advisory build-up and the introduction of combat-support troops was made "without a careful examination" of precisely what it was expected to produce and how.

The study concludes that the Kennedy strategy was fatally flawed from the outset for political as much as for military reasons. It depended, the study notes, on successfully prodding President Diem to undertake the kind of political, economic and social reforms that would, in the slogan of that day, "win the hearts and minds of the people."

"The U.S. over-all plan to end the insurgency was on shaky ground on the GVN side," the study comments. "Diem needed the U.S. and the U.S. needed a reformed Diem."

It also says: "If he could not [reform], the U.S. plan to end the insurgency was foredoomed from its inception, for it depended on Vietnamese initiatives to solve a Vietnamese problem."

And in the end, the Pentagon account relates, the Kennedy Administration concluded that President Diem could not reform sufficiently and in 1963 abandoned him.

Abandoning President Diem was what Ambassador Eldridge Durbrow had suggested in September, 1960, [see Document #16.] and again that December, shortly before Mr. Kennedy took office as President. Drawing on the Ambassador's reports, among others, a national intelligence estimate provided for Mr. Kennedy on March 28, 1961, gave a bleak appraisal of the situation in Vietnam:

"An extremely critical period for President Ngo Dinh Diem and the Republic of Vietnam lies immediately ahead. During the past six months the internal security situation has continued to deteriorate and has now reached serious proportions . . .

"More than one-half of the entire rural region south and southwest of Saigon, as well as some areas to the north, are under considerable Communist control. Some of these areas are in effect denied to all government authority not immediately backed by substantial armed force. The Vietcong's strength encircles Saigon and has reecntly begun to move closer in on the city . . . .

"The deterioration in the position of the Diem Government reached a new extreme in November when army paratroop officers joined forces with a number of civilian oppositionsts in a narrowly defeated attempt to overthrow Diem. On the surface, Diem's position appears to have improved somewhat since then. . . .

"However, the facts which gave rise to the coup attempt have not been seriously dealt with and still exist. Discontent with the Diem Government continues to be prevalent among intellectual circles and, to a lesser degree, among labor and business groups. There has been an increasing disposition within official circles and the Army to question Diem's ability to lead in this period. Many feel that he is unable to rally the people in the fight against the Communists because of his reliance on virtual one-man rule, his toleration of corruption extending even to his immediate entourage, and his refusal to relax a rigid system of public controls."

This assessment, the Pentagon study relates, echoed the themes and even some of the language of Ambassador Durbrow's cablegrams. One of these, on Sept. 24, 1960, suggested that if President Diem was unable to regain support through political and social reforms, "it may become necessary for U.S. Government to begin consideration alternative courses of action and leaders."

A Challenge for the U.S.

However serious the problem in South Vietnam, the situation in Laos was far more critical. "The Western position was in the process of falling apart as Kennedy took office," the Pentagon account says.

And during the spring of 1961, when President Kennedy made his first series of Vietnam decisions, Laos—not Vietnam —was the dominant issue and largely determined how Vietnam should be handled, according to the Pentagon account.

The Eisenhower Administration had chosen to back right-wing elements in Laos, and by early 1961 they were reeling under Communist and neutralist attacks. President Kennedy chose to seek a political compromise and a military cease-fire rather than to continue to support the Laotian rightists.

Because of this shift in strategy in Laos, the Pentagon study says, the Kennedy Administration felt impelled to show strength in Vietnam to reassure America's allies in Asia.

In what the Administration saw as a global power competition with the Soviet Union, the account notes, Washington thought it dangerous to give ground too often. Summing up the Administration's reasoning, the author writes: "After the U.S. stepped back in Laos, it might be hard to persuade the Russians that we intended to stand firm anywhere if we then gave up on Vietnam."

Moreover, the Kennedy Administration sensed a particular challenge in the declaration by the Soviet Premier, Nikita S. Khrushchev, on Jan. 6, 1961, that Moscow intended to back "wars on national liberation" around the world. In response, counterinsurgency—as strategy against guerrilla war became known—grew to be a primary preoccupation of the Kennedy White House, as a steady flow of Presidential decision papers testifies.

"Vietnam was the only place in the world where the Administration faced a well-developed Communist effort to topple a pro-Western government with an externally aided pro-Communist insurgency," the Pentagon study comments. "It was a challenge that could hardly be ignored."

On April 12 Mr. Rostow, the senior White House specialist on Southeast Asia and a principal architect of counterinsurgency doctrine, put Vietnam directly before President Kennedy with a memorandum [see Document #22.] asserting that the time had come for "gearing up the whole Vietnam operation." He proposed a series of moves that the study calls "pretty close to an agenda" for the Kennedy Administration's first high-level review of Vietnam. Among other things Mr. Rostow proposed these measures:

• "The appointment of a full-time first-rate backstop man in Washington."

• "A possible visit to Vietnam in the near future by the Vice President."

• "The raising of the MAAG [Military Assistance Advisory Group] ceiling, which involves some diplomacy, unless we can find an alternative way of introducing into the Vietnam operation a substantial number of Special Forces types."

• "Setting the question of extra funds for Diem."

• "The tactics of persuading Diem to move more rapidly to broaden the base of his Government, as well as to decrease its centralization and improve its efficiency."

Virtually all the Rostow proposals eventually became policy except his suggestion for a "first-rate backstop man." His candidate, the study notes, was Brig. Gen. Edward G. Lansdale, a long-time Central Intelligence Agency operative who was close to President Diem and who in 1961 was in charge of "special operations" for the Pentagon. The State Department blocked his appointment, the study reports.

On April 20—the day after the collapse of the Bay of Pigs invasion of Cuba—President Kennedy ordered a quick review of the Vietnam situation. As quoted by Secretary McNamara, the President's instructions were to "appraise . . . the Communist drive to dominate South Vietnam" and "recommend a series of actions (military, political and/or economic, overt and/or covert) which, in your opinion, will prevent Communist domination of that country."

The task force, headed by Roswell L. Gilpatric, Deputy Secretary of Defense, turned in its report on April 27.

The report, quoted in the Pentagon study, recommended a 100-man increase in the American military advisory mission in Saigon, more American arms and aid for the Vietnamese regional forces known as the Civil Guard, the release of funds for a previously approved expansion of the South

Vietnamese Army and the dropping of earlier conditions that President Diem undertake political and social reforms in return. Allied efforts, the report said, should be infused with a sense of urgency to impress friends and foes alike that "come what may, the U.S. intends to *win* this battle." The emphasis was in the original report.

Even before the report was submitted, it was overtaken by events: The Laotian crisis was at its peak. President Kennedy met with the National Security Council on April 26 to decide whether to send troops into Laos. Late that night the Joint Chiefs of Staff alerted the commander in chief of Pacific forces, Adm. Harry D. Felt, "to be prepared to undertake air strikes against North Vietnam, and possibly southern China," the account reports.

Overnight the Vietnam recommendations changed. "As insurance against a conventional invasion of South Vietnam" through the eastern, mountainous portions of Laos, the Gilpatric task force recommended quick expansion of the South Vietnamese Army by two divisions—40,000 men—plus the first major input of American troops, as training forces, according to the Pentagon study.

The April 28 "Laos annex," the narrative recounts, called for "a 1,600-man [American] training team for each of the two new [South Vietnamese] divisions, plus a 400-man Special Forces contingent to speed up counterinsurgency forces: a total of 3,600 men."

On April 29—described in the narrative as a day of "prolonged crisis meetings at the White House"—Admiral Felt was alerted to prepare to move one American combat brigade of 5,000 men with air elements to northeastern Thailand and another to Danang, on the South Vietnamese coast, as a threat to intervene in Laos. "Decision to make these deployments not firm," the Joint Chiefs of Staff cabled Admiral Felt. The tactics were directly related to the Laos crisis.

Acting on Vietnam that day, the study reports, President Kennedy approved the modest 100-man increase in the American advisory mission and a few other steps suggested in the first Gilpatric task force's report.

"The only substantial significance that can be read into these April 29 decisions," the analyst writes, "is that they signaled a willingness to go beyond the 685-man limit of the U.S. military mission in Saigon." Publicity would have entailed "the first formal breach of the Geneva agreements," the study says, so the move was kept quiet.

By May 1 the acute fever of the Laos crisis had eased, the

account goes on, and there was a "strong sense . . . that the U.S. would not go into Laos: that if the cease-fire failed, we would make a strong stand, instead, in Thailand and Vietnam."

Vietnam planning was directly affected. The State Department drafted the first of several revisions to tone down the Gilpatric task force's recommendations. When the task-force report finally went before the National Security Council on May 9, the study recounts, the State Department had largely prevailed. Shortly before that the White House announced that Vice President Johnson was leaving within days for a trip to Saigon and other Asian capitals.

The final task-force report, quoted in the Pentagon account, recommended the deployment of 400 Special Forces soldiers and an immediate Pentagon study of a further build-up "in preparation for possible commitment of U.S. forces to Vietnam, which might result from an N.S.C. decision following discussions between Vice President Johnson and President Diem." The idea of sending 3,200 other soldiers right away was dropped.

In place of a Pentagon proposal made on May 1 for unilateral American intervention in Vietnam if that became necessary to "save the country from Communism," the final report by the Gilpatric task force proposed a new "bilateral arrangement with Vietnam."

"On the grounds that the Geneva accords have placed inhibitions upon Free World action while at the same time placing no restrictions upon the Communists," the report said, "Ambassador Nolting should be instructed to enter into preliminary discussions with Diem regarding the possibility of a defensive security alliance despite the inconsistency of such action with the Geneva accords . . . . Communist violations, therefore, justify the establishment of the security arrangements herein recommended."

A Sterner Objective

On May 11, two days after Vice President Johnson's departure for Saigon, President Kennedy made his decisions. As recorded in National Security Action Memorandum 52, a copy of which accompanies the Pentagon study, the American objective was stated more bluntly and more ambitiously than in typical public pronouncements. The memorandum said the American objective was "to prevent Communist domination of South Vietnam," whereas six days earlier President Kennedy himself spoke at a news conference of a vaguer desire "to assist Vietnam to obtain its independence."

The memorandum also specified measures that were not disclosed to the public: Presidential approval for the deployment of 400 Special Forces troops, for Ambassador Nolting to start negotiations on "a new bilateral arrangement with Vietnam" and for the initiation of a covert-warfare campaign against North Vietnam.

The one step, in the Pentagon analyst's view, that involved the United States more than the President's public statements suggested was the decision to send Special Forces. "Obviously the President was sold on their going," the study comments, "and since the Vietnamese Special Forces were themselves supported by C.I.A. rather than the regular military-aid program, it was possible to handle these troops covertly."

According to the documentary record, President Kennedy's specific orders on covert warfare called for these steps:

• "Dispatch . . . agents to North Vietnam" for intelligence gathering.

• "Infiltrate teams under light civilian cover to southeast Laos to locate and attack Vietnamese Communist bases and lines of communications."

• "In North Vietnam, using the foundation established by intelligence operations, from networks of resistance, covert bases and teams for sabotage and light harassment."

• "Conduct overflights for dropping of leaflets to harass the Communists and to maintain morale of North Vietnamese population, and increase gray [unidentified-source] broadcasts to North Vietnam for the same purposes."

• Train "the South Vietnamese Army to conduct ranger raids and similar military actions in North Vietnam as might prove necessary or appropriate."

The documents also show that Mr. Kennedy approved plans "for the use in North Vietnam operations of civilian air crews of American and other nationality, as appropriate, in addition to Vietnamese." The plans, quoted in full in the final report of the Gilpatric task force, designate the South Vietnamese Army's First Observation Group, stationed at Nhatrang, as the main unit for carrying on unconventional warfare in Laos, South Vietnam and North Vietnam.

In July, 1961, General Lansdale submitted to General Taylor, the President's military adviser, a preliminary report on preparations for this clandestine warfare. By that time, the report said, the First Observation Group had "some limited operations in North Vietnam and some shallow penetrations into Laos." [See Document #22.]

The Lansdale report stated, however, that most of the unit's operations had been directed against the Vietcong in South Vietnam and that this was being changed to focus it entirely on North Vietnam and Laos—"denied areas," in official terminology.

"The plan is to relieve the group from these combat assignments [against the Vietcong] to ready its full strength for denied-areas missions," General Lansdale said. As of July 6, the unit was to be expanded to 805 men from 340. "Personnel are volunteers who have been carefully screened by security organizations," General Lansdale said. "Many are from North Vietnam. They have ben trained for guerrilla operations at the group's training center at Nhatrang."

In addition, the Lansdale report said, 400 selected South Vietnamese soldiers, 60 montagnard tribesmen and 70 civilians were being formed into "additional volunteer groups, apart from the First Observation Group, for similar operations." The general listed 50 Americans—35 from the Defense Department and 15 from the C.I.A.—engaged in training these groups and preparing other South Vietnamese intelligence and psychological-warfare operations. According to the Pentagon study, these were to be augmented by some of the 400 Special Forces soldiers President Kennedy ordered to the field on May 11.

The study does not report on the actual operations of the units during the Kennedy years.

Bernard Fall, in his history "The Two Vietnams," published in 1963, described the organization of the First Observation Group into 15-man combat teams and 24-man support teams. "One such unit was captured near Ninhbinh (180 miles north of the 17th Parallel) in July, 1961, when its aircraft developed engine trouble," Mr. Fall reported.

In July the Hanoi radio, as monitored by the United States Government, carried several English-language broadcasts on the incident, saying that North Vietnam had shot down a plane encroaching on its airspace and describing a number of American-made items to try to authenticate the plane's origin. According to the broadcasts, the plane was marked in red letters "C-47," the oil tank "Douglas Aircraft" and the radio apparatus "Bendix Radio, Baltimore, U.S.A.," and some of the 10 men aboard carried "Colt" automatics. The generator was marked "Signal Corps U.S. Army," one broadcast said.

The North Vietnamese Government announced plans to try three survivors on charges of sabotage and espionage, saying that they confessed to having been trained by Americans who gave them a map and traced out their flight route over North Vietnam. Hanoi protested the incident formally to Britain and the Soviet Union, as co-chairmen of the 1954 Geneva conference on Vietnam, asserting that since May 13, 1961— two days after President Kennedy's orders were issued—the "U.S.-Diem regime" had "continuously carried out espionage and provocative acts against the North."

The North Vietnamese Foreign Minister described the C-47 incident as "an extremely impudent violation of the Geneva agreements." During July and August the North Vietnamese also broadcast descriptions of the build-up of the First Observation Group and the American organization and training of that unit, with details that corresponded almost exactly with the Lansdale report.

The North Vietnamese Government also formally protested several times to the International Control Commission that South Vietnamese units had conducted raids into the demilitarized zone separating the two Vietnams.

On Nov. 1 The New York Times carried a dispatch from Saigon quoting informants as reporting disaffection in North Vietnam and citing as evidence the sabotaging of an industrial plant at Vinh on Aug. 11 and other similar incidents.

Diem at the Fulcrum

President Kennedy's decision in May deferred—but did not settle—the issue of combat troops for South Vietnam. Throughout the summer and fall of 1961 the Administration's debate on that crucial matter was significantly affected by the attitude of President Diem, according to the Pentagon account. Initially, it relates, Vice President Johnson found the South Vietnamese leader reluctant; in midsummer he warmed to the idea somewhat; by fall he was appealing to the United States to become a co-belligerent.

The Vietnam troop decisions were also affected by the confrontation with the Soviet Union over Berlin. At his meeting in Vienna with Premier Khrushchev in June, President Kennedy managed to strike a general bargain to seek neutralization in Laos. But the Soviet leader applied pressure on the Berlin issue by threatening to sign a peace treaty with East Germany, making Western access to West Berlin extremely vulnerable. The tension on this issue mounted—and overshadowed developments in Southeast Asia—until, on Oct. 17, Premier Khrushchev dropped the idea of the peace treaty with East Germany.

Vice President Johnson, on his whirlwind mission through Asia to bolster the confidence of America's allies, met with President Diem on May 12. According to an embassy report of their meeting, when Mr. Johnson raised the possibility of sending America combat units to Vietnam or working out a bilateral defense treaty, he found Mr. Diem uninterested. The embassy report quoted President Diem as saying he wanted American combat troops only in the event of an open invasion.

In his private report to President Kennedy on May 23, the Vice President painted American alternatives in Asia in blacks and whites, giving Thailand and Vietnam pivotal significance. "We must decide whether to help these countries to the best of our ability," he declared, "or throw in the towel in the area and pull back our defenses to San Francisco and a "Fortress America" concept." [See Document #21.]

Nonetheless, alluding to President Diem's response on the troop question, Mr. Johnson told Mr. Kennedy: "Asian leaders—at this time—do not want American troops involved in Southeast Asia other than on training missions. . . . This does not minimize or disregard the probability that open attack would bring calls for U.S. combat troops."

If this seemed to close the issue for President Kennedy, as the study indicates, it was not the last word from President Diem. Responding to a suggestion from Vice President Johnson, the South Vietnamese leader spelled out his military proposals in a letter to President Kennedy on June 9.

The letter, quoted extensively in the Pentagon account, urged a major expansion of the South Vietnamese Army, from 170,000 to 270,000 men, accompanied by "considerable" United States build-up with "selected elements of the American armed forces." President Diem said that the increases were needed "to counter the ominous threat" of Communist domination—a threat that he documented by what the study calls "inflated infiltration figures."

The plea for "selected elements of the American armed forces," according to the Pentagon narrative, sounded "very much like" a request for the kind of forces that the Defense

Department had proposed in April and that the American advisory mission in Saigon was urging in midsummer.

The real interest of the Joint Chiefs and other military officers, the account says, was "in getting U.S. combat units into Vietnam, with the training mission a possible device for getting this accepted by Diem" and by civilian leaders in Washington.

The White House, preoccupied by Berlin, sidestepped the issue by agreeing in August to finance a much more modest increase in the Vietnamese Army—30,000 men—and by postponing any build-up of American advisers, according to the study.

Moreover, the writer suggests that the White House was already developing other ideas about Southeast Asia. During the summer discussions, Mr. Rostow once again produced proposals that, in the study's words, were a "quite exact" prescription for President Kennedy's decisions in the fall. In what is described in the account as a handwritten note to Secretary McNamara on a piece of scratch paper, probably passed by hand during a meeting about June 5, Mr. Rostow said:

"Bob:

"We must think of the kind of forces and missions for Thailand now, Vietnam later.

"We need a guerrilla *deterrence* operation in Thailand's northeast.

"We shall need forces to support a counterguerrilla war in Vietnam:

"aircraft

"helicopters

"communications men

"special forces

"militia teachers

"etc.

"WWR"

The emphasis on deterrence was Mr. Rostow's.

In late fall President Diem jolted the Kennedy Administration into its most urgent consideration of the troop issue—and its most significant military decisions—with a sudden, secret request for the bilateral defense treaty he previously spurned.

On Sept. 29 the study recounts, Mr. Diem had a gloomy meeting with American officials, and Ambassador Nolting sent Washington this cablegram:

"Diem asked for bilateral defense treaty. Large and unexplained request. Serious. Put forward as result of Diem's fear of outcome of Laos situation, SVN vulnerability to increased infiltration, feelings that SEATO action would be inhibited by U.K. and France in the case of SVN as in Laos. . . .

"Our reaction is that the request should be seriously and carefully treated to prevent feeling that U.S. is not serious in intention to support SVN. But see major issues including overriding Article 19, Geneva accords, possible ratification problems as well as effect on SEATO.

"Diem's request arises from feeling that U.S. policy on Laos will expose his flank [to] infiltration and lead to large-scale hostilities in SVN. So seeking a stronger commitment than he thinks he has now through SEATO."

Admiral Felt, the Pacific commander, who was also present at the Sept. 29 meeting, cabled a fuller report several days later saying that President Diem wanted not only a treaty but also an accelerated American "military build-up." Specifically, Admiral Felt said, the President pressed for a "large increase in advisers of all types" and American tactical air squadrons to help break up the larger Vietcong units that had recently been massing for attacks.

The Felt message explained that the stepped-up scale of combat in Vietnam was worrying President Diem as much as the threat of infiltration or attack from the Laotian side, if not more. It added: "Diem said VC now able to assemble large units, had extensive radio net, operating in one or more battalions with heavy arms capable of raiding principle cities in provinces. . . . Could enter a city, burn out stores, attack leaders, withdraw."

The Pentagon narrative explains that the Vietcong, now believed to be 17,000 strong, had nearly tripled the level of their attacks to 450 a month in September.

"The most spectacular attack, which seems to have had a shattering effect in Saigon," the writer goes on, "was the seizure of Phuocthanh, a provincial capital only 55 miles from Saigon," where the Vietcong held the town most of the day and publicly beheaded the province chief, departing before the South Vietnamese Army arrived.

For Washington the situation had become more alarming than it was in the spring. Then Laos was the primary cause of Vietnam's jitters. "This time," the study comments, "the problem was not directly Laos, but strong indications of moderate deterioration of Diem's military position and very substantial deterioration of morale in Saigon."

Even before President Diem's request for a treaty, momentum for American intervention in Southeast Asia had been mounting.

By early October the Pentagon papers recount, several proposals had emerged: The Joint Chiefs of Staff advocated allied intervention to seize and hold major portions of Laos, mainly to protect the borders of South Vietnam and Thailand; the "Rostow proposal" urged sending a force of about 25,000 men from the Southeast Asia Treaty Organization into Vietnam to try to guard the border with Laos; and several other plans suggested putting American forces into the Vietnamese Central Highlands or the port of Danang, with or without a training mission.

In the bureaucratic maneuvering that led up to the important National Security Council meeting of Oct. 11, a significant new element was injected.

For the first time, the study notes, a proposal was put before President Kennedy urging that the United States accept "as our real and ultimate objective the defeat of the Vietcong." The analyst says this was suggested in a compromise paper drafted hastily by U. Alexis Johnson, Deputy Under Secretary of State. The paper said that "three divisions would be a guess" on the number of American troops needed but that a more precise estimate would be forthcoming from the Joint Chiefs of Staff.

The study describes this as a "somewhat confusing" blend of earlier proposals by Mr. Rostow and the Joint Chiefs of Staff, put together on Oct. 10. "It was pretty clear," the account continues, "that the main idea was to get some American combat troops into Vietnam, with the nominal excuse for doing so quite secondary."

The Joint Chief's provided a supplemental note estimating "that 40,000 U.S. forces will be needed to clean up the Vietcong threat" and that 128,000 additional soldiers would be sufficient to cope with possible North Vietnamese or Chinese Communist intervention. The note, which accompanies the historical study, cited the Berlin crisis as another strain on American military manpower and urged "a step-up in the present mobilization, possibly of major proportions."

A third paper, which the narrative terms notable for its candor, also advocated "early and hard-hitting" intervention in Vietnam. This paper, a note to Secretary McNamara from

William P. Bundy, Acting Assistant Secretary of Defense, said:

"It *is* really now or never if we are to arrest the gains being made by the Vietcong. Walt Rostow made the point yesterday that the Vietcong are about to move, by every indication, from the small-unit basis to a moderate battalion-size basis. Intelligence also suggests that they may try to set up a provisional government' . . . in the very Kontum area into which the present initial plan would move SEATO forces. If the Vietcong movement 'blooms' in this way, it will almost certainly attack all the back-the-winner sentiment that understandably prevails in such cases and that beat the French in early 1954 and came within an ace of beating Diem in early 1955."

Mr. Bundy bluntly put the odds as he saw them:

"An early and hard-hitting operation has a good chance (70 per cent would be my guess) of *arresting* things and giving Diem a chance to do better and clean up . . . It all depends on Diem's effectiveness, which is very problematical. The 30 per cent chance is that we would wind up like the French in 1954; white men can't win this kind of fight.

"On a 70-30 basis, I would myself favor going in. But if we let, say, a month go by before we move, the odds will slide . . . down to 60-40, 50-50 and so on."

The italics are Mr. Bundy's.

The intelligence community provided what the study calls a "conspicuously more pessimistic (and more realistic)" assessment than the formal recommendations of the Pentagon or Mr. Rostow. In spite of all the American worry about infiltration into South Vietnam through Laos, a special national intelligence estimate on Oct. 5 reported "that 80-90 per cent of the estimated 17,000 VC had been locally recruited, and that there was little evidence that the VC relied on external supplies," according to the Pentagon account.

The intelligence estimate also included a warning about the kind of enemy shrewdness and tenacity that became reality. The estimate, drafted while the Administration was thinking primarily of SEATO—rather than unilateral American—intervention, forecast:

"The Communists would expect worthwhile political and psychological rewards from successful harassment and guerrilla operations against SEATO forces. The D.R.V. would probably not relax its Vietcong campaign against the GVN [Government of (South) Vietnam] to any significant extent. Meanwhile, Communist strength in south Laos would probably be increased by forces from North Vietnam to guard against an effort to partition Laos. . . . The Soviet airlift would probably be increased with a heavier flow of military supply into south Laos. . . ."

Confronted with such conflicting advice, President Kennedy decided to send General Taylor to Saigon. According to minutes of the National Security Council meeting on Oct. 11, quoted in the Pentagon account, the general was instructed to consider three strategies:

• Bold intervention to "defeat the Vietcong," using up to three divisions of American troops.

• Sending "fewer U.S. combat forces" to Vietnam, not to crush the insurgency but "for the purpose of establishing a U.S. 'presence' in Vietnam."

• "Stepping up U.S. assistance and training of Vietnam units, furnishing of more U.S. equipment, particularly helicopters and other light aircraft, trucks and other ground transport"—short of using American combat forces.

The minutes said President Kennedy was to announce the Taylor mission, at an afternoon news conference, "as an economic survey." But, the account says, the President did "not make the hardly credible claim that he was sending his personal military adviser to Vietnam to do an economic survey." After a vaguely worded announcement, the narrative relates, President Kennedy was "noncommittal when asked whether Taylor was going to consider the need for combat troops."

Even before General Taylor and his party could leave Washington, the Diem Government had sent new and urgent requests for American combat troops. Ambassador Nolting reported to Washington on Oct. 13 that Nguyen Dinh Thuan, the Vietnamese Acting Defense Minister, had requested: "U.S. combat units or units to be introduced into SVN as 'combat trainer units' . . . Wanted a symbolic U.S. strength near the 17th [Parallel] to prevent attacks there, free own forces there. Similar purpose station U.S. units in several provincial seats in Central Highlands. . . . Thuan said first step quicker than [defense] treaty and time was of the essence. Thuan said token forces would satisfy SVN and would be better than treaty." [See Document #25.]

The South Vietnamese Government's state of alarm was communicated by Mr. Nolting's additional report that Saigon was considering asking Nationalist China "to send one division of combat troops in the southwest." Ambassador Nolting said he had tried to discourage this approach.

The Pentagon study goes on to report that Administration officials effectively squelched press speculation about the troop question with carefully managed news leaks at this point.

It cites a dispatch on Oct. 14 in The New York Times reporting that military leaders, including General Taylor, were reluctant to send combat units to Vietnam and that this question was "near the bottom of the list" of things the general would consider.

From the way the dispatch was handled, the acount says, it clearly "came from a source authorized to speak for the President, and probably from the President himself." He adds that "in the light of the recommendations quoted throughout this paper, and particularly most of the staff papers . . . that led up to the Taylor mission, most of this was simply untrue." But he concludes: "The Times story had the apparently desired effect. Speculation about combat troops almost disappeared from news stories."

State of Emergency

The Taylor mission arrived in Saigon on Oct. 18 and was greeted by what the Pentagon study calls a "spectacular opening shot": President Diem's formal declaration of a state of emergency. Within the next week General Taylor met twice with the chief of state.

According to an embassy message to Washington on Oct. 20, President Diem told General Taylor at their first meeting that he wanted a bilateral defense treaty, American support for another expansion of the South Vietnamese Army and a list of combat-support items very close to those suggested in June by Mr. Rostow in his handwritten note to Secretary McNamara.

"He asked specifically for tactical aviation, helicopter companies, coastal patrol forces and logistic support (ground transport)," the embassy report said. He did not, however, repeat the earlier request for actual American ground combat units.

By the second Diem-Taylor meeting, on Oct. 24, American and South Vietnamese officials had discussed the disastrous flooding in the Mekong River Delta, where the American military advisory mission, headed by Lieut. Gen. Lionel C. McGarr, thought American troops mights be of some help.

General Taylor had incorporated this idea in a series of recommendations, which he put before President Diem at the second meeting. Item E, the study reports, was headed "Introduction of U.S. Combat Troops," and it proposed "a flood-relief task force, largely military in composition, to work with GVN over an extended period for rehabilitation of area. Such a force might contain engineer, medical, signal and transportation elements as well as combat troops for the protection of relief operations."

The general directed two messages to Washington after that meeting, both quoted in the Pentagon account. The first, sent through regular channels, reported that President Diem's reaction to all of General Taylor's recommendations —including the flood-relief task force—"was favorable."

In his second message, sent privately to President Kennedy and the President's most senior advisers, General Taylor was more specific. He proposed a force of 6,000 to 8,000 American soldiers not only to cope with the flooding but significantly, as the narrative points out, to assure "Diem of our readiness to join him in a military showdown with Vietcong or Vietminh." [See Documents #26 and #27.]

General Taylor said that he envisioned mostly logistics forces but that "some combat troops" would be necessary to defend the American engineer troops and their encampments. He warned that "any troops coming to VN may expect to take casualties."

The general underscored the propaganda advantage of relating the introduction of American ground troops to the need for flood relief as "offering considerable advantages in VN and abroad" and leaving President Kennedy his choice on further action. "As the task is a specific one," he explained, "we can extricate our troops when it is done if we so desire. Alternatively, we can phase them into other activities if we wish to remain longer."

He acknowledged, in conclusion: "This kind of task force will exercise little direct influence on the campaign against the VC. It will, however, give a much needed shot in the arm to national morale."

General Taylor's proposals engendered State Department opposition. His messages, evidently relayed to Secretary of State Dean Rusk, who was in Japan for a conference, prompted Mr. Rusk to cable Washington, warning about the risks of making a military commitment without reciprocal political reforms by President Diem.

According to his Nov. 1 message, which is appended to the Pentagon study, Mr. Rusk said that if, as previously, the South Vietnamese leader was not willing to trust his military commanders more and to take steps to bring more non-Communist elements into influential roles, it was "difficult to see how handful of American troops can have decisive influence." While attaching the "greatest possible importance" to the security of Southeast Asia, Mr. Rusk expressed reluctance to see American prestige committed too deeply for the sake of "a losing horse."

Similar reservations were already reflected by reports from two middle-level State Department members of General Taylor's mission. Sterling J. Cottrell and William J. Jorden submitted separate dissents to General Taylor on their way home by way of Bangkok and the Philippines.

Mr. Cottrell, head of the interagency Vietnam task force in Washington, asserted in a memorandum dated Oct. 27 that "since U.S. combat troops of division size cannot be employed effectively, they should not be introduced at this stage" despite the "favorable psychological lift" it would give the Vietnamese.

"Since it is an open question whether the GVN can succeed even with U.S. assistance," he went on, "it would be a mistake for the U.S. to commit itself irrevocably to the defeat of the Communists in SVN." But if combined American and Vietnamese efforts failed in the South, he recommended moving "to the 'Rostow plan' of applying graduated punitive measures on the D.R.V. with weapons of our choosing."

Mr. Jorden reported finding explosive pressures for political and administrative change in South Vietnam as well as "near paralysis" in parts of the Government because so many decisions had to await personal approval by President Diem. Many Government officials and military officers, he said, "have lost confidence in President Diem and his leadership." He urged that the United States not identify itself "with a man or a regime."

Quite contrary pressures were being exerted on Washington, however, by the American mission in Saigon. On Oct. 31, the study says, the embassy reported to Washington the Vietnamese people's "virtually unanimous desire" for the introduction of American troops.

From Baguio, in the Philippines, where he had stopped to draft his formal report with Mr. Rostow and his other aides, General Taylor sent two more messages to President Kennedy on Nov. 1, urging a commitment of a "U.S. military task force" to Vietnam.

But, the messages show, he now listed the flood-relief mission as secondary to the objective of providing a "U.S. military presence capable of raising national morale and of showing to Southeast Asia the seriousness of the U.S. intent to resist a Communist take-over."

Writing in more sweeping language than he used in Saigon a week before, the general now advocated a "massive joint effort" with the South Vietnamese "to cope with both the Vietcong and the ravages of the flood." The presence of American ground units, he said, was "essential" to "reverse the present downward trend of events."

His second message discounted the risks of sliding into a major Asian land war accidentally and sought to assure President Kennedy that the American troops would not be aggressively hunting down the Vietcong guerrillas though they would be involved in some combat. He wrote:

"This force is not proposed to clear the jungles and forests of Vietcong guerrillas. That should be the primary task of the armed forces of Vietnam for which they should be specifically organized, trained and stiffened with ample U.S. advisers down to combat battalion levels.

"However, the U.S. troops may be called upon to engage in combat to protect themselves, their working parties and the area in which they live. As a general reserve, they might be thrown into action (with U.S. agreement) against large, formed guerrilla bands which have abandoned the forests for attacks on major targets."

The parenthetical matter was in General Taylor's original cablegram.

The message also repeated the theme, attributed by the analyst and by Mr. Cottrell to Mr. Rostow, that bombing of North Vietnam could be used as a diplomatic threat to hold Hanoi at bay.

The language of all of General Taylor's messages, the Pentagon study comments, suggests that the support forces —helicopter companies, the expanded advisory mission, tactical air support—"were essentially already agreed to by the President before Taylor left Washington."

The general's interest, the study explains, was in getting a commitment of "ground forces (not necessarily all or even mainly infantrymen, but ground soldiers who would be out in the countryside where they could be shot at and shoot back)."

His argument for ground troops, the study observes, was based more on "psychological than military reasons."

The formal report by the Taylor mission, submitted on Nov. 3, incorporated the proposal for what the analyst calls a "hard commitment on the ground" and other measures, all under the over-all concept of a new American role in Vietnam: "limited partnership." The drift of the report, which the Pentagon narrative says was probably written with Mr. Rostow, was reflected in the proposal that the American military advisory mission in Saigon not only should be "radically increased" but also should undertake more active direction of the war by becoming "something nearer [to] —but not quite—an operational headquarters in a theater of war."

The main evaluation section, the study comments, "puts Saigon's weakness in the best light and avoids suggesting that perhaps the U.S. should consider limiting rather than increasing commitments to the Diem regime."

The dissents of Mr. Cottrell and Mr. Jorden were submitted, along with a military annex, which said: "The performance of ARVN [the Army of South Vietnam] is disappointing and generally is characterized by a lack of aggressiveness and at most levels is devoid of a sense of urgency."

The Taylor report, the Pentagon account notes, proposed solving this type of problem through administrative reforms in the army and the infusion of Americans. The writer comments that there was no serious demand for pressing President Diem to make the kind of reforms that Secretary Rusk felt necessary.

Moreover, the Pentagon study notes two important underlying assumptions for the report. The first was that South Vietnamese problems—whether the Army's lack of spirit or President Diem's bottlenecks—"could be cured if enough dedicated Americans become involved." There was great implicit faith, the study goes on, that Americans could provide the South Vietnamese "with the élan and style needed to win."

The second major assumption, the analyst notes, was that "if worse comes to worst, the U.S. could probably save its position in Vietnam by bombing the North."

Both these assumptions, as the Pentagon narrative recounts in later sections, were essential ingredients of the advice given to President Johnson in late 1964 and 1965, as he made the decisions to move forcefully into the war.

As the Taylor recommendations were submitted to President Kennedy, he also received a special national intelligence estimate forecasting that American escalation would be matched by Hanoi. According to the Pentagon account, the Nov. 5 estimate considered four possibilities—expanding the American advisory mission, plus an American airlift for Vietnamese troops; sending an 8,000-to-10,000-man flood-relief task force; sending a 25,000-to-40,000-man combat force, and warning Hanoi, in conjunction with any of those steps, that the United States "would launch air attacks against North Vietnam" unles Hanoi stopped supporting the Vietcong.

"The gist" of the intelligence estimate, the Pentagon account says, "was that the North Vietnamese would respond to an increased U.S. commitment with an offsetting increase in infiltrated support for the Vietcong." The greater the American involvement, the intelligence estimate prophesied, the stronger the North Vietnamese reaction. The estimate also implied, the narrative goes on, that "threats to bomb would not cause Hanoi to stop its support for the Vietcong, and . . . actual attacks on the North would bring a strong response from Moscow and Peiping. . . ."

Nonetheless, the Taylor recommendations received backing from Secretary McNamara, Deputy Secretary Gilpatric and the Joint Chiefs of Staff. In a memo on Nov. 8 to President Kennedy, reprinted in the study, Mr. McNamara summarized their position:

"We are inclined to recommend that we do commit the U.S. to the clear objective of preventing the fall of South Vietnam to Communism and that we support this commitment by the necessary military actions.

"If such a commitment is agreed upon, we support the recommendations of General Taylor as the first steps toward its fulfillment."

But the memorandum warned President Kennedy that the 8,000-man task force "probably will not tip the scales decisively," meaning that "we would be almost certain to get increasingly mired down in an inconclusive struggle."

"In short," the study comments, "the President was being told that the issue was not whether to send an 8,000-man task force, but whether or not to embark on a course that, without some extraordinary good luck, would lead to combat involvement in Southeast Asia on a very substantial scale."

The Pentagon narrative says that while the Joint Chiefs' position was clear, Mr. McNamara's position "remains a little ambiguous," especially in view of his qualified phrase "inclined to recommend" sending ground troops. The implication seems to be that Secretary McNamara was willing to go along with the Joint Chiefs to this extent to draw them out for President Kennedy on the full, long-term meaning of their recommendations.

Moreover, as the study records, three days later Mr. McNamara joined Mr. Rusk in a quite different recommendation and, the analyst says, "one obviously more to the President's liking (and, in the nature of such things, quite possibly drawn up to the President's specifications)." [See Document #30.]

This memorandum, almost totally adopted by President Kennedy as policy, contained stronger rhetoric than the earlier McNamara note but milder recommendations. The memorandum, quoted nearly in full in the Pentagon account, began wth a strong exposition of the domino theory:

"The loss of South Vietnam would make pointless any further discussion about the importance of Southeast Asia to the Free World; we would have to face the near certainty that the remainder of Southeast Asia and Indonesia would move to a complete accommodation with Communism, if not formal incorporation within the Communist bloc."

The language on the troop issue, omitting any mention of the flood-relief task force, seems carefully drafted:

"The commitment of United States forces to South Vietnam involves two different categories: (A) units of modest size required for the direct support of South Vietnamese military effort, such as communications, helicopter and other forms of airlift, reconnaisance aircraft, naval patrols, intelligence units, etc., and (B) larger organized units with actual or potential direct military missions. *Category (A) should be introduced as speedily as possible.* Category (B) units pose a more serious problem. . . ."

The italicized emphasis is in the original document.

The two Secretaries recommended that the United States "now take the decision to commit ourselves to the objective of preventing the fall of South Vietnam to Communism and that, in doing so, we recognize that the introduction of United States and other SEATO forces may be necessary to achieve this objective." But for the present it said only that the Pentagon should prepare plans for ground combat forces.

Three lines of reasoning for opposing a commitment of ground combat troops emerge from this document.

The first and possibly the most significant, the Pentagon study suggests, is that such a move "prior to a Laotian settlement would run a considerable risk of stimulating a Communist breach of the cease-fire and a resumption of hostilities in Laos," leaving the President the unattractive choice of "the use of combat forces in Laos or an abandonment of that country to full Communist control." The second reason was the need "to involve forces from other nations" as well; otherwise it would be "difficult to explain to our own people why no effort had been made to invoke SEATO or why the United States undertook to carry this burden unilaterally." The third was the dilemma underlying the troop proposals— that "if there is a strong South Vietnamese effort, they may not be needed [but] if there is not such an effort, United States forces could not accomplish their mission in the midst of an apathetic or hostile population."

The Rusk-McNamara memorandum fully acknowledged that even sending support troops and more advisers would mean openly exceeding military ceilings imposed by the 1954 Geneva accords. The memorandum proposed an exchange of letters with President Diem in which President Kennedy would assert "the necessity now of exceeding some provisions of the accords in view of the D.R.V. violations." It also called for the release of a white paper, "A Threat to Peace," reporting on infiltration from North Vietnam and on Vietcong terrorism.

Embracing the essence of Mr. Rusk's message from Japan, the joint memorandum added a demand for reform from President Diem before the United States build-up would be put in motion.

The President accepted all major recommendations, according to the study, except for the unqualified commitment to the goal of saving South Vietnam from Communism. His decisions were formally embodied on Nov. 22 in a national security action memorandum, No. 111, entitled "First Phase of Vietnam Program."

But on Nov. 14 Washington sent a summary of the President's decisions—evidently made the day before—to Ambassador Nolting. The message demanded "concrete demonstration by Diem that he is now prepared to work in an orderly way [with] his subordinates and broaden the political base of his regime." For the first time it sought to inject the United States more deeply into managing the war by asserting: "We would expect to share in the decision-making process in the political, economic and military fields as they affect the security situation."

Possibly to assuage President Diem's expected disappointment, it noted that the decision on combat-support troops and many more advisers "will sharply increase the commitment of our prestige to save SVN." It concluded by asserting that while the Pentagon was preparing contingency plans for ground combat forces, the "objective of our policy is to do all possible to accomplish [our] purpose without use of U.S. combat forces."

No Presidential paper in the Pentagon record clearly details Mr. Kennedy's thinking, but two documents shed light: the Nov. 14 message and some unsigned notes of a National Security Council meeting that, according to the Pentagon account, took place on Nov. 15.

The notes included these entries: "Pres expressed concern over 2-front war. Another bother him, no overt Chicom aggression in SVN, unlike Korea. These Diem's own people; difficult operating area. If go beyond advisers need other nations with us . . . Pres receiving static from Congress; they against using U.S. troops."

At another point, Mr. Kennedy reportedly asked why it was important to retain South Vietnam and Laos. The notes record the reply from Gen. Lyman L. Lemnitzer, Chairman of the Joint Chiefs of Staff: "We would lose Asia all the way Singapore. Serious setback to U.S. and F.W. [free world]."

President Kennedy was also reportedly concerned about the lack of support from the British and worried about the proposed letter acknowledging that the United States would be breaking the Geneva accords. "Pres asked Rusk," the notes say, "why do we take onus, saying we are going to break Geneva accords (in letter to Diem). Why not remain silent. Don't say this ourselves. Directed State to reword letter." The parentheses were in the original notes.

The Nov. 14 message reflects similar reasoning. The implication is that one important consideration for President Kennedy was fear that sending ground combat forces to South Vietnam, in the language of the message, "might wreck chances for agreement" in Laos and lead to a breakdown of the cease-fire there.

A second drawback cited in the message was the risk of provoking confrontations with the Soviet Union elsewhere—the "two front" problem—especially in Berlin where the acute crisis had eased less than a month before.

The decision disappointed President Diem who, according to the Pentagon study, was seeking a firm U.S. commitment to him. The account reports that Ambassador Nolting cabled Washington on Nov. 18 to say that the South Vietnamese leader had immediately inquired about ground combat units. After hearing Mr. Nolting's response, the Ambassador said, President Diem "took our proposals rather better than I expected." Two days later the Ambassador said he was getting high-level reports that President Diem was upset and brooding.

If this was a bargaining tactic to get the United States to back down on its demands for reform, the study says, it worked. On Dec. 7 Washington sent the embassy new instructions, the account goes on, softening demands for reforms and settling for "close partnership" and frequent consultation with the South Vietnamese Government rather than insisting, as before, on taking part in decision-making.

Whether intentionally or not, the Pentagon study contends, the over-all effect of these actions was to give the military side of the war higher priority than the political side.

"To continue to support Diem without reform," the study comments, "meant quite simply that he, not we, would determine the course of the counterinsurgent effort and that the steps he took to assure his continuance in power would continue to take priority over all else." The account says that this emphasis came to plague the Kennedy Administration when South Vietnamese disaffection with the Diem regime boiled over in 1963.

Copters and Casualties

Even before the American decisions on the troop build-up were announced formally on Dec. 14 with a public exchange of letters between Presidents Kennedy and Diem, the first two American helicopter companies had arrived—400 men with 33 H-21C helicopters. On Feb. 5 the press reported that the first helicopter had been shot down by the enemy.

Despite the Administration's efforts to draw a careful bureaucratic distinction between support troops ("Category A") and combat troops ("Category B"), this was hard to maintain in the field. The study records without comment that by mid-February President Kennedy was asked at a news conference if the Administration was being "less than candid" about American involvement in Vietnam. He acknowledged that American troops were "firing back" to protect themselves although he contended that these were not combat troops "in the generally understood sense of the word."

The Pentagon study goes on to record that on April 11, two days after two American soldiers were killed in a Vietcong ambush while on a combat operation with Vietnamese troops, President Kennedy was asked at a news conference: "Sir, what are you going to do about the American soldiers getting killed in Vietnam?"

In reply, the President said: "We are attempting to help Vietnam maintain its independence and not fall under the domination of the Communists . . . We cannot desist in Vietnam." Months later, he admitted to increased casualties along with the build-up he ordered.

According to Pentagon records, nearly 10 times as many Americans were killed or wounded in action in 1962 as in 1961—figures closely paralleling the tenfold build-up in American forces to 11,000 men by the end of 1962. The Pentagon statistics show that the number of killed and wounded in combat increased from 14 in 1961 to 109 in 1962 and to 489 in 1963.

Although the Pentagon study describes the Kennedy years as a period of new commitments, it does not indicate whether in this case President Kennedy—by putting American airmen in position to fly tactical air missions and ground advisers to take part in combat operations with South Vietnamese units—crossed an important firebreak in the American involvement in Vietnam.

Documents accompanying the Pentagon study amply recount the rapid tempo of the American build-up—rapid by standards of the previous seven years. A military briefing paper for the President on Jan. 9, 1962 cited in the Pentagon account reported:

• The number of American servicemen in Vietnam jumped from 948 at the end of November to 2,646 by Jan. 9 and would reach 5,576 by June 30.

• Two Army helicopter companies were flying combat support missions and an air commando unit code-named Jungle Jim was "instructing the Vietnamese Air Force in combat air support tactics and techniques."

• United States Navy Mine Division 73, with a tender and five minesweepers, was sailing from Danang along the coastline.

• American aircraft from Thailand and from the Seventh Fleet aircraft carriers off Vietnam were flying surveillance and reconnaissance missions over Vietnam.

• Six C-123 spray-equipped aircraft "for support of defoliant operations" had "received diplomatic clearance" to enter South Vietnam.

At a news conference on March 18, 1962, Secretary McNamara acknowledeged under questioning that American "training" of the South Vietnamese "occasionally takes place under combat conditions." He added that "there has been sporadic fire aimed at U.S. personnel, and in a few minor instances they have returned the fire in self-defense." News reports in the spring of 1962 told of American pilots flying in the front, or action, seats of "trainer" aircraft while Vietnamese trainees rode behind.

A Spurt of Optimism

Whatever public uneasiness was expressed in the news-conference questions, the Pentagon study notes, official American assessments on the war in the spring and summer of 1962 took on an increasingly favorable tenor.

One special object of praise and of American official confidence, the account notes, was the development of the strategic-hamlet program as an all-embracing counterguerrilla strategy in rural Vietnam. But the Pentagon study comments that the optimism proved misplaced.

Government documents available in the Pentagon records describe this strategy as a program to regroup the Vietnamese population into fortified hamlets in which the Government was to undertake political, social and economic measures designed both to weed out Vietcong sympathizers and to gain popular allegiance through improved local services and better security.

President Diem formally adopted the strategy for the Mekong Delta in mid-March, 1962, and made it nationwide in August. By Sept. 30, according to the study, the Diem Government was stating that more than a third of the total rural population was living in completed hamlets.

One flaw inherent in this strategy, the Pentagon study asserts, was that Saigon and Washington had different objectives for it: President Diem saw it as a means of controlling his population, non-Communist as well as Communist, while Washington saw it as a means of winning greater allegiance and thereby squeezing out the Vietcong.

Moreover, the account goes on, popular allegiance was so difficult to assess that even American officials turned increasingly to physical aspects of the program for statistical evaluations of progress. It left them vulnerable, the study notes, to exaggerated Vietnamese reports, which they did not uncover until after the Diem Government had been overthrown in 1963.

Fundamentally, the Pentagon analysts assert, the strategic hamlets "failed dismally," like previous programs tried by the French and the Vietnamese, "because they ran into resentment if not active resistance" from peasants who objected to being moved forcibly from their fields and their ancestral homes.

The Pentagon study lays "a principal responsibility for the unfounded optimism of U.S. policy" in 1962 and early 1963 on inadequate and relatively uninformed American intelligence and reporting systems. The official optimism, the Pentagon account discloses, reached its peak in the plans for an American military "phase-out" in Vietnam on the assumption that the war against the Vietcong would be won by the end of 1965.

The tone was set, the analyst writes at a Honolulu conference on Vietnam strategy. On July 23, 1962, the same day that the Laotian peace agreement was signed in Geneva, Secretary McNamara ordered the start of planning for American withdrawal from Vietnam and long-term projections for reducing American financial aid to the Saigon Government.

Mr. McNamara is depicted in the study as repeatedly pressing the somewhat reluctant military command to come up with a long-range plan for an American phase-out, in part because of satisfaction with what he called the "tremendous progress" in early 1962.

But Mr. McNamara's orders also reflected domestic political problems. At the Honolulu conference, the account says, "he observed that it might be difficult to retain public support for U.S. operations indefinitely."

"Political pressures would build up as losses continued," it added.

The Pentagon account gives no indication that this planning was personally originated by President Kennedy or that it was ever presented to him in completed form. For roughly 18 months, with little urgency, documents flowed back and forth between Mr. McNamara and the American military mission in Saigon through Pentagon channels, with Mr. McNamara constantly urging lower budget figures and reduction to 1,500 American troops by late 1968. Even so, the President was told in February, 1963, by a senior White House aide, Michael V. Forrestal, to expect a long and costly war.

"No one really knows," Mr. Forrestal wrote in a report to Mr. Kennedy on Feb. 11, "how many of the 20,000 'Vietcong' killed last year were only innocent, or at least persuadable, villagers, whether the strategic hamlet program is providing enough govt. services to counteract the sacrifices it requires, or how the mute mass of villagers react to the charges against Diem of dictatorship and nepotism." The report, which accompanies the Pentagon study, went on to say that Vietcong recruitment inside South Vietnam was so effective that the war could be continued even without infiltration from the North.

Moreover, while the phase-out planning continued, the American involvement grew to 16,732 men in October, 1963. And the analyst comments that once the political struggle began in earnest against President Diem in May, 1963, this planning took on an "absurd quality" based on "the most Micawberesque predictions" of progress.

"Strangely," the Pentagon study continues, "as a result of the public White House promise in October and the power of the wheels set in motion, the U.S. did effect a 1,000-man withdrawal in December of 1963." But the study discounts this as "essentially an accounting exercise" offset in part by troop rotations.

Because of the complete political upheaval against the Diem regime in 1963, the situation deteriorated so profoundly in the final five months of the Kennedy Administration, according to a private report from Secretary McNamara quoted in the study, that the entire phase-out had to be formally dropped in early 1964.

Thus, the Pentagon study relates, in spite of the military build-up under the Kennedy Administration, President Kennedy left President Johnson a Vietnamese legacy of crisis, of political instability and of military deterioration at least as alarming to policy makers as the situation he had inherited from the Eisenhower Administration.

The decision to build up the combat support and advisory missions, the Pentagon study comments, was made "almost by default" because the Kennedy Administration was focused so heavily in the fall of 1961 on the question of sending ground combat units to Vietnam. That decision, the analyst writes, was reached "without extended study or debate" or precise expectation of what it would achieve.

Despite the tens of thousands of words in the Pentagon account of the Kennedy Administration, backed by scores of documents, the study does not provide a conclusive answer to the most vigorously debated question about President Kennedy's Vietnam policy since his death in November, 1963: If President Kennedy had lived until 1965, would he have felt compelled by events, as President Johnson was, to undertake full-scale land war in South Vietnam and an air war against the North?

The situation, as the Pentagon account discloses, had changed significantly between 1961 and 1965. In 1961 President Kennedy was confronted by other crises—Berlin, Cuba, Laos—while he faced his harshest decisions on Vietnam, and these acted as restraints; President Johnson did not have quite the same distractions elsewhere. Too, President Diem never pushed so aggressively for American escalation as did Gen. Nguyen Khanh, the South Vietnamese leader in 1964 and 1965. Nor, as the analysts note, had other measures short of full-scale air and ground combat been exhausted, without producing success.

The Pentagon account, moreover, presents the picture of an unbroken chain of decision-making from the final months of the Kennedy Administration into the early months of the Johnson Administration, whether in terms of the political view of the American stakes in Vietnam, the advisory build-up or the hidden growth of covert warfare against North Vietnam.

"No reliable inference can be drawn," the Pentagon study concludes, "about how Kennedy would have behaved in 1965 and beyond had he lived. (One of those who had advised retaining freedom of action on the issue of sending U.S. combat troops was Lyndon Johnson.) It does not prove that Kennedy behaved soundly in 1961. Many people will think so; but others will argue that the most difficult problem of recent years might have been avoided if the U.S. had made a hard commitment on the ground in South Vietnam in 1961."

114

KEY DOCUMENTS

Following are texts of key documents accompanying the Pentagon's study of the Vietnam war, dealing with the Administration of President John F. Kennedy up to the events that brought the overthrow of President Ngo Dinh Diem in 1963. Except where excerpting is specified, the documents are printed verbatim, with only unmistakable typographical errors corrected.

16

U.S. Ambassador's '60 Analysis of Threats to Saigon Regime

Cablegram from Elbridge Durbrow, United States Ambassador in Saigon, to Secretary of State Christian A. Herter, Sept. 16, 1960.

As indicated our 495 and 538 Diem regime confronted by two separate but related dangers. Danger from demonstrations or coup attempt in Saigon could occur earlier; likely to be predominantly non-Communistic in origin but Communists can be expected to endeavor infiltrate and exploit any such attempt. Even more serious danger is gradual Viet Cong extension of control over countryside which, if current Communist progress continues, would mean loss free Viet-nam to Communists. These two dangers are related because Communist successes in rural areas embolden them to extend their activities to Saigon and because non-Communist temptation to engage in demonstrations or coup is partly motivated by sincere desire prevent Communist take-over in Viet-nam.

Essentially [word illegible] sets of measures required to meet these two dangers. For Saigon danger essentially political and psychological measures required. For countryside danger security measures as well as political, psychological and economic measures needed. However both sets measures should be carried out simultaneously and to some extent individual steps will be aimed at both dangers.

Security recommendations have been made in our 539 and other messages, including formation internal security council, centralized intelligence, etc. This message therefore deals with our political and economic recommendations. I realize some measures I am recommending are drastic and would be most [word illegible] for an ambassador to make under normal circumstances. But conditions here are by no means normal. Diem government is in quite serious danger. Therefore, in my opinion prompt and even drastic action is called for. I am well aware that Diem has in past demonstrated astute judgment and has survived other serious crises. Possibly his judgment will prove superior to ours this time, but I believe nevertheless we have no alternative but to give him our best judgment of what we believe is required to preserve his government. While Diem obviously resented my frank talks earlier this year and will probably resent even more suggestions outlined below, he has apparently acted on some of our earlier suggestions and might act on at least some of the following:

1. I would propose have frank and friendly talk with Diem and explain our serious concern about present situation and his political position. I would tell him that, while matters I am raising deal primarily with internal affairs, I would like to talk to him frankly and try to be as helpful as I can be giving him the considered judgment of myself and some of his friends in Washington on appropriate measures to assist him in present serious situation. (Believe it best not indicate talking under instructions.) I would particularly stress desirability of actions to broaden and increase his [word illegible] support prior to 1961 presidential elections required by constitution before end April. I would propose following actions to President:

2. Psychological shock effect is required to take initiative from Communist propagandists as well as non-Communist oppositionists and convince population government taking effective measures to deal with present situation, otherwise we fear matters could get out of hand. To achieve that effect following suggested:

(A) Because of Vice President Tho's knowledge of south where Communist guerrilla infiltration is increasing so rapidly would suggest that he be shifted from ministry national economy to ministry interior. (Diem has already made this suggestion but Vice President most reluctant take job.)

(B) It is important to remove any feeling within armed forces that favoritism and political considerations motivate promotions and assignments. Also vital in order deal effectively with Viet Cong threat that channels of command be followed both down and up. To assist in bringing about these changes in armed forces, I would suggest appointment of full-time minister national defense. (Thuan has indicated Diem has been thinking of giving Thuan defense job.)

(C) Rumors about Mr. and Mrs. Nhu are creating growing dissension within country and seriously damage political position of Diem government. Whether rumors true or false, politically important fact is that more and more people believe them to be true. Therefore, becoming increasingly clear that in interest Diem government some action should be taken. In analagous situation in other countries including U.S. important, useful government personalities have had to be sacrificed for political reasons. I would suggest therefore that President might appoint Nhu to ambassadorship abroad.

(D) Similarly Tran Kim Tuyen, Nhu's henchman and head of secret intelligence service, should be sent abroad in diplomatic capacity because of his growing identification in public mind with alleged secret police methods of repression and control.

(E) One or two cabinet ministers from opposition should be appointed to demonstrate Diem's desire to establish government of national union in fight against VC.

3. Make public announcement of disbandment of Can Lao party or at least its surfacing, with names and positions of all members made known publicly. Purpose this step would be to eliminate atmosphere of fear and suspicion and reduce public belief in favoritism and corruption, all of which party's semi-covert status has given rise to.

4. Permit National Assembly wider legislative initiative and area of genuine debate and bestow on it authority to conduct, with appropriate publicity, public investigations of any department of government with right to question any official except President himself. This step would have three-fold purpose: (A) find some mechanism for dispelling through public investigation constantly generated rumors about government and its personalities; (B) provide people with avenue recourse against arbitrary actions by some government officials, (C) assuage some of intellectual opposition to government.

5. Require all government officials to declare publicly their property and financial holdings and give National Assembly authority to make public investigation of these declarations in effort dispel rumors of corruption.

6. [Words illegible] of [word illegible] control over content of the Vietnamese publication [word illegible] magazines, radio, so that the [words illegible] to closing the gap between government and [words illegible] ideas from one to the other. To insure that the press would reflect, as well as lead, public opinion without becoming a means of upsetting the entire GVN [word illegible], it should be held responsible to a self-imposed code of ethics or "canon" of press-conduct.

7. [Words illegible] to propaganda campaign about new 3-year development plan in effort convince people that government genuinely aims at [word illegible] their welfare. (This suggestion [word illegible] of course upon assessment of soundness of development plan, which has just reached us.)

8. Adopt following measures for immediate enhancement of peasant support of government: (A) establish mechanism for increasing price peasant will receive for paddy crop beginning to come on market in December, either by direct subsidization

117

or establishment of state purchasing mechanism; (B) institute modest payment for all corvee labor; (C) subsidize agroville families along same lines as land resettlement families until former on feet economically; (D) increase compensation paid to youth corps. If Diem asks how these measures are to be financed I shall suggest through increased taxes or increased deficit financing, and shall note that under certain circumstances reasonable deficit financing becomes a politically necessary measure for governments. I should add that using revenues for these fundamental and worthy purposes would be more effective than spending larger and larger sums on security forces, which, while they are essential and some additional funds for existing security forces may be required, are not complete answer to current problems.

9. Propose suggest to Diem that appropriate steps outlined above be announced dramatically in his annual state of union message to National Assembly in early October. Since Diem usually [word illegible] message in person this would have maximum effect, and I would recommend that it be broadcast live to country.

10. At [words illegible] on occasion fifth anniversary establishment Republic of Vietnam on October 26, it may become highly desirable for President Eisenhower to address a letter of continued support to Diem. Diem has undoubtedly noticed that Eisenhower letter recently delivered to Sihanouk. Not only for this reason, but also because it may become very important for us to give Diem continued reassurance of our support. Presidential letter which could be published here may prove to be very valuable.

Request any additional suggestions department may have and its approval for approach to Diem along lines paras 1 to 9.

We believe U.S. should at this time support Diem as best available Vietnamese leader, but should recognize that overriding U.S. objective is strongly anti-Communist Vietnamese government which can command loyal and enthusiastic support of widest possible segments of Vietnamese people, and is able to carry on effective fight against Communist guerrillas. If Diem's position in country continues deteriorate as result failure adopt proper political, psychological, economic and security measures, it may become necessary for U.S. government to begin consideration alternative courses of action and leaders in order achieve our objective.

17

Memo from Rostow to Kennedy with Nine Proposals for Action

Memorandum from Walt W. Rostow, deputy Presidential assistant for national security, to President Kennedy, April 12, 1961.

Now that the Viet-Nam election is over, I believe we must turn to gearing up the whole Viet-Nam operation. Among the possible lines of action that might be considered at an early high level meeting are the following:

1. The appointment of a full time first-rate back-stop man in Washington. McNamara, as well as your staff, believes this to be essential.

2. The briefing of our new Ambassador, Fritz Nolting, including sufficient talk with yourself so that he fully understands the priority you attach to the Viet-Nam problem.

3. A possible visit to Viet-Nam in the near future by the Vice President.

4. A possible visit to the United States of Mr. Thuan, acting Defense Minister, and one of the few men around Diem with operational capacity and vigor.

5. The sending to Viet-Nam of a research and development and military hardware team which would explore with General McGarr which of the various techniques and gadgets now available or being explored might be relevant and useful in the Viet-Nam operation.

6. The raising of the MAAG ceiling, which involves some diplomacy, unless we can find an alternative way of introducing into Viet-Nam operation a substantial number of Special Forces types.

7. The question of replacing the present ICA Chief in Viet-Nam, who, by all accounts, has expanded his capital. We need a vigorous man who can work well with the military, since some of the rural development problems relate closely to guerilla operations.

8. Sending the question of the extra funds for Diem.

9. The tactics of persuading Diem to move more rapidly to broaden the base of his government, as well as to decrease its centralization and improve its efficiency.

Against the background of decisions we should urgently take on these matters, you may wish to prepare a letter to Diem which would not only congratulate him, reaffirm our support, and specify new initiatives we are prepared to take, but would make clear to him the urgency you attach to a more effective political and morale setting for his military operation, now that the elections are successfully behind him.

18

Vietnam "Program of Action" by Kennedy's Task Force

Excerpts from "A Program of Action for South Viet-nam," May 8, 1961, presented to President Kennedy by an interdepartmental task force comprising representatives from the Departments of State and Defense, the Central

Intelligence Agency, the International Cooperation Administration, the United States Information Agency and the Office of the President.

. . . 2. MILITARY:

a. The following military actions were approved by the President at the NSC meeting of 29 April 1961:

(1) Increase the MAAG as necessary to insure the effective implementation of the military portion of the program including the training of a 20,000-man addition to the present G.V.N. armed forces of 150,000. Initial appraisal of new tasks assigned CHMAAG indicate that approximately 100 additional military personnel will be required immediately in addition to the present complement of 685.

(2) Expand MAAG responsibilities to include authority to provide support and advice to the Self-Defense Corps with a strength of approximately 40,000.

(3) Authorize MAP support for the entire Civil Guard force of 68,000. MAP support is now authorized for 32,000; the remaining 36,000 are not now adequately trained and equipped.

(4) Install as a matter of priority a radar surveillance capability which will enable the G.V.N. to obtain warning of Communist overflights being conducted for intelligence or clandestine air supply purposes. Initially, this capability should be provided from U.S. mobile radar capability.

(5) Provide MAP support for the Vietnamese Junk Force as a means of preventing Viet Cong clandestine supply and infiltration into South Vietnam by water. MAP support, which was not provided in the Counter-Insurgency Plan, will include training of junk crews in Vietnam or at U.S. bases by U.S. Navy personnel.

b. The following additional actions are considered necessary to assist the G.V.N. in meeting the increased security threat resulting from the new situation along the Laos-G.V.N. frontier:

(1) Assist the G.V.N. armed forces to increase their border patrol and insurgency suppression capabilities by establishing an effective border intelligence and patrol system, by instituting regular aerial surveillance over the entire frontier area, and by applying modern technological area-denial techniques to control the roads and trails along Vietnam's borders. A special staff element (approximately 6 U.S. personnel), to concentrate upon solutions to the unique problems of Vietnam's borders, will be activated in MAAG, Vietnam, to assist a similar special unit in the RVNAF which the G.V.N. will be encouraged to establish; these two elements working as an integrated team will help the G.V.N. gain the support of nomadic tribes and other border inhabitants, as well as introduce advanced techniques and equipment to strengthen the security of South Vietnam's frontiers.

(2) Assist the G.V.N. to establish a Combat Development and Test Center in South Vietnam to develop, with the help of modern

technology, new techniques for use against the Viet Cong forces. (Approximately 4 U.S. personnel.)

(3) Assist the G.V.N. forces with health, welfare and public work projects by providing U.S. Army civic action mobile training teams, coordinated with the similar civilian effort. (Approximately 14 U.S. personnel.)

(4) Deploy a Special Forces Group (approximately 400 personnel) to Nha Trang in order to accelerate G.V.N. Special Forces training. The first increment, for immediate deployment in Vietnam, should be a Special Forces company (52 personnel).

(5) Instruct JCS, CINCPAC, and MAAG to undertake an assessment of the military utility of a further increase in the G.V.N. forces from 170,000 to 200,000 in order to create two new division equivalents for deployment to the northwest border region. The parallel political and fiscal implications should be assessed. . . .

4. ECONOMIC:

1. Objective: Undertake economic programs having both a short-term immediate impact as well as ones which contribute to the longer range economic viability of the country.

a. Undertake a series of economic projects designed to accompany the counter-insurgency effort, by the following action:

(1) Grant to ICA the authority and funds to move into a rural development-civic action program. Such a program would include short-range, simple, impact projects which would be undertaken by teams working in cooperation with local communities. This might cost roughly $3 to $5 million, mostly in local currency. Directors of field teams should be given authority with respect to the expenditure of funds including use of dollar instruments to purchase local currency on the spot.

b. Assist Vietnam to make the best use of all available economic resources, by the following action:

(1) Having in mind that our chief objective is obtaining a full and enthusiastic support by the G.V.N. in its fight against the Communists, a high level team preferably headed by Assistant Secretary of the Treasury John Leddy, with State and ICA members, should be dispatched to Saigon to work out in conjunction with the Ambassador a plan whereby combined U.S. and Vietnamese financial resources can best be utilized. This group's terms of reference should cover the broad range of fiscal and economic problems. Authority should be given to make concessions necessary to achieve our objectives and to soften the blow of monetary reform. Ambassador Nolting and perhaps the Vice President should notify Diem of the proposed visit of this group stressing that their objective is clearly to maximize the joint effort rather than to force the Vietnamese into inequitable and unpalatable actions.

(2) As a part of the foregoing effort, an assessment should be

undertaken of the fiscal and other economic implications of a further force increase from 170,000 to 200,000 (as noted in the Military section above).

c. Undertake the development of a long-range economic development program as a means of demonstrating U.S. confidence in the economic and political future of the country by the following action:

(1) Authorize Ambassador Nolting to inform the G.V.N. that the U.S. is prepared to discuss a long-range joint five-year development program which would involve contributions and undertakings by both parties. . . .

5. PSYCHOLOGICAL:

a. Assist the G.V.N. to accelerate its public information program to help develop a broad public understanding of the actions required to combat the Communist insurgents and to build public confidence in the G.V.N.'s determination and ability to deal with the Communist threat.

b. The U.S. Country Team, in coordination with the G.V.N. Ministry of Defense, should compile and declassify for use of media representatives in South Vietnam and throughout the world, documented facts concerning Communist infiltration and terrorists' activities and the measures being taken by the G.V.N. to counter such attacks.

c. In coordination with CIA and the appropriate G.V.N. Ministry, USIS will increase the flow of information about unfavorable conditions in North Vietnam to media representatives.

d. Develop agricultural pilot-projects throughout the country, with a view toward exploiting their beneficial psychological effects. This project would be accomplished by combined teams of Vietnamese Civic Action personnel, Americans in the Peace Corps, Filipinos in Operation Brotherhood, and other Free World nationals.

e. Exploit as a part of a planned psychological campaign and rehabilitation of Communist Viet Cong prisoners now held in South Vietnam. Testimony of rehabilitated prisoners, stressing the errors of Communism, should be broadcast to Communist-held areas, including North Vietnam, to induce defections. This rehabilitation program would be assisted by a team of U.S. personnel including U.S. Army (Civil Affairs, Psychological Warfare and Counter-Intelligence), USIS, and USOM experts.

f. Provide adequate funds for an impressive U.S. participation in the Saigon Trade Fair of 1962.

6. COVERT ACTIONS:

a. Expand present operations in the field of intelligence, unconventional warfare, and political-psychological activities to support the U.S. objective as stated.

b. Initiate the communications intelligence actions, CIA and ASA personnel increases, and funding which were approved by the President at the NSC meeting of 29 April 1961.

c. Expand the communications intelligence actions by inclusion of 15 additional Army Security Agency personnel to train the Vietnamese Army in tactical COMINT operations. . . .

7. FUNDING:

a. As spelled out in the funding annex, the funding of the counter-insurgency plan and the other actions recommended in this program might necessitate increases in U.S. support of the G.V.N. budget for FY 61 of as much as $58 million, making up to a total of $192 million compared to $155 million for FY 60. The U.S. contribution for the G.V.N. Defense budget in FY 62 as presently estimated would total $161 million plus any deficiency in that Budget which the G.V.N. might be unable to finance. The exact amount of U.S. contributions to the G.V.N. Defense budgets for FY 61 and FY 62 are subject to negotiation between the U.S. and the G.V.N.

b. U.S. military assistance to G.V.N., in order to provide the support contemplated by the proposed program would total $140 million, or $71 million more than now programmed for Vietnam in the U.S. current MAP budget for FY 62. . . .

ANNEX 6

Covert Actions

a. Intelligence: Expand current positive and counter-intelligence operations against Communist forces in South Vietnam and against North Vietnam. These include penetration of the Vietnamese Communist mechanism, dispatch of agents to North Vietnam and strengthening Vietnamese internal security services. Authorization should be given, subject to existing procedures, for the use in North Vietnam operations of civilian air crews of American and other nationality, as appropriate, in addition to Vietnamese. Consideration should be given for overflights of North Vietnam for photographic intelligence coverage, using American or Chinese Nationalists crews and equipment as necessary.

b. Communications Intelligence: Expand the current program of interception and direction-finding covering Vietnamese Communist communications activities in South Vietnam, as well as North Vietnam targets. Obtain further USIB authority to conduct these operations on a fully joint basis, permitting the sharing of results of interception, direction finding, traffic analysis and cryptographic analysis by American agencies with the Vietnamese to the extent needed to launch rapid attacks on Vietnamese Communist communications and command installations.

This program should be supplemented by a program, duly coordinated, of training additional Vietnamese Army units in intercept and direction-finding by the U.S. Army Security Agency. Also, U.S. Army Security Agency teams could be sent to Vietnam for direct operations, coordinated in the same manner—Approved by the President at the NSC meeting of 29 April 1961.

c. Unconventional Warfare: Expand present operations of the First Observation Battalion in guerrilla areas of South Vietnam, under joint MAAG-CIA sponsorhip and direction. This should be in full operational collaboration with the Vietnamese, using Vietnamese civilians recruited with CIA aid.

In Laos, infiltrate teams under light civilian cover to Southeast Laos to locate and attack Vietnamese Communist bases and lines of communications. These teams should be supported by assault units of 100 to 150 Vietnamese for use on targets beyond capability of teams. Training of teams could be a combined operation by CIA and U.S. Army Special Forces.

In North Vietnam, using the foundation established by intelligence operations, form networks of resistance, covert bases and teams for sabotage and light harassment. A capability should be created by MAAG in the South Vietnamese Army to conduct Ranger raids and similar military actions in North Vietnam as might prove necessary or appropriate. Such actions should try to avoid any outbreak of extensive resistance or insurrection which could not be supported to the extent necessary to stave off repression.

Conduct overflights for dropping of leaflets to harass the Communists and to maintain morale of North Vietnamese population, and increase gray broadcasts to North Vietnam for the same purposes.

d. Internal South Vietnam: Effect operations to penetrate political forces, government, armed services and opposition elements to measure support of government, provide warning of any coup plans and identify individuals with potentiality of providing leadership in event of disappearance of President Diem.

Build up an increase in the population's participation in and loyalty to free government in Vietnam, through improved communication between the government and the people, and by strengthening independent or quasi-independent organizations of political, syndical or professional character. Support covertly the GVN in allied and neutral countries, with special emphasis on bringing out GVN accomplishments, to counteract tendencies toward a "political solution" while the Communists are attacking GVN. Effect, in support, a psychological program in Vietnam and elsewhere exploiting Communist brutality and aggression in North Vietnam.

e. The expanded program outlined above was estimated to require an additional 40 personnel for the CIA station and an increase in the CIA outlay for Vietnam of approximately $1.5 million for FY 62, partly compensated by the withdrawal of personnel from other areas. The U.S. Army Security Agency actions to supplement communications intelligence will require 78 personnel and approximately $1.2 million in equipment. The personnel and fund augmentations in this paragraph were approved by the President at the NSC meeting of 29 April 1961.

f. In order adequately to train the Vietnamese Army in tactical COMIT operations, the Army Security Agency estimates that an additional 15 personnel are required. This action has been approved by the U.S. Intelligence Board.

19

'61 Memo from the Joint Chiefs on Commitment of U.S. Forces

Memorandum on "U.S. Forces in South Vietnam" from the Joint Chiefs of Staff to Secretary of Defense Robert S. McNamara, May 10, 1961.

1. In considering the possible commitment of U.S. forces to South Vietnam, the Joint Chiefs of Staff have reviewed the overall critical situation in Southeast Asia with particular emphasis upon the present highly flammable situation in South Vietnam. In this connection the question, however, of South Vietnam should not be considered in isolation but rather in conjunction with Thailand and their over-all relationship to the security of Southeast Asia. The views of the Joint Chiefs of Staff on the question regarding the deployment of U.S. forces into Thailand were provided to you by JCSM-311-61, dated 9 May 1961. The current potentially dangerous military and political situation in Laos, of course, is the focal point in this area. Assuming that the political decision is to hold Southeast Asia outside the Communist sphere, the Joint Chiefs of Staff are of the opinion that U.S. forces should be deployed immediately to South Vietnam; such action should be taken primarily to prevent the Vietnamese from being subjected to the same situation as presently exists in Laos, which would then require deployment of U.S. forces into an already existing combat situation.

2. In view of the foregoing, the Joint Chiefs of Staff recommend that the decision be made now to deploy suitable U.S. forces to South Vietnam. Sufficient forces should be deployed to accomplish the following purposes:

a. Provide a visible deterrent to potential North Vietnam and/or Chinese Communist action;

b. Release Vietnamese forces from advanced and static defense positions to permit their fuller commitment to counter-insurgency actions;

125

c. Assist in training the Vietnamese forces to the maximum extent possible consistent with their mission;

d. Provide a nucleus for the support of any additional U.S. or SEATO military operation in Southeast Asia; and

e. Indicate the firmness of our intent to all Asian nations.

3. In order to maintain U.S. flexibility in the Pacific, it is envisioned that some or all of the forces deployed to South Vietnam would come from the United States. The movement of these troops could be accomplished in an administrative manner and thus not tax the limited lift capabilities of CINCPAC.

4. In order to accomplish the foregoing, the Joint Chiefs of Staff recommend that:

a. President Diem be encouraged to request that the United States fulfill its SEATO obligation, in view of the new threat now posed by the Laotian situation, by the immediate deployment of appropriate U.S. forces to South Vietnam;

b. Upon receipt of this request, suitable forces could be immediately deployed to South Vietnam in order to accomplish the above-mentioned purposes. Details of size and composition of these forces must include the views of both CINCPAC and CHMAAG which are not yet available.

20

U.S. Approval, in 1961, of Steps to Strengthen South Vietnam

National Security Action Memorandum 52, signed by McGeorge Bundy, Presidential adviser on national security, May 11, 1961.

1. The U.S. objective and concept of operations stated in report are approved: to prevent Communist domination of South Vietnam; to create in that country a viable and increasingly democratic society, and to initiate, on an accelerated basis, a series of mutually supporting actions of a military, political, economic, psychological and covert character designed to achieve this objective.

2. The approval given for specific military actions by the President at the National Security Council meeting on April 29, 1961, is confirmed.

3. Additional actions listed at pages 4 and 5 of the Task Force Report are authorized, with the objective of meeting the increased security threat resulting from the new situation along the frontier between Laos and Vietnam. In particular, the President directs an assessment of the military utility of a further increase in G.V.N. forces from 170,000 to 200,000, together with an assessment of the parallel political and fiscal implications.

4. The President directs full examination by the Defense Department, under the guidance of the Director of the continuing Task Force on Vietnam, of the size and composition of forces which would be desirable in the case of a possible commitment of U.S. forces to Vietnam. The diplomatic setting within which this action might be taken should also be examined.

5. The U.S. will seek to increase the confidence of President Diem and his Government in the United States by a series of actions and messages relating to the trip of Vice President Johnson. The U.S. will attempt to strengthen President Diem's popular support within Vietnam by reappraisal and negotiation, under the direction of Ambassador Nolting. Ambassador Nolting is also requested to recommend any necessary reorganization of the Country Team for these purposes.

6. The U.S. will negotiate in appropriate ways to improve Vietnam's relationship with other countries, especially Cambodia, and its standing in world opinion.

7. The Ambassador is authorized to begin negotiations looking toward a new bilateral arrangement with Vietnam, but no firm commitment will be made to such an arrangement without further review by the President.

8. The U.S. will undertake economic programs in Vietnam with a view to both short-term immediate impact and a contribution to the longer-range economic viability of the country, and the specific actions proposed on pages 12 and 13 of the Task Force Report are authorized.

9. The U.S. will strengthen its efforts in the psychological field as recommended on pages 14 and 15 of the Task Force Report.

10. The program for covert actions outlined on page 15 of the Task Force Report is approved.

11. These decisions will be supported by appropriate budgetary action, but the President reserves judgment on the levels of funding proposed on pages 15 and 16 of the Task Force Report and in the funding annex.

12. Finally, the President approves the continuation of a special Task Force on Vietnam, established in and directed by the Department of State under Sterling J. Cottrell as Director, and Chalmers B. Wood as Executive Officer.

21

Report by Vice President Johnson on His Visit to Asian Countries

Excerpts from memorandum, "Mission to Southeast Asia, India and Pakistan," from Vice President Lyndon B. Johnson to President Kennedy, May 23, 1961.

. . . I took to Southeast Asia some basic convictions about the problems faced there. I have come away from the mission there—and to India and Pakistan—with many of those convictions sharpened and deepened by what I saw and learned. I have also reached certain other conclusions which I believe may be of value as guidance for those responsible in formulating policies.

These conclusions are as follows:

1. The battle against Communism must be joined in Southeast Asia with strength and determination to achieve success there—or the United States, inevitably, must surrender the Pacific and take up our defenses on our own shores. Asian Communism is compromised and contained by the maintenance of free nations on the subcontinent. Without this inhibitory influence, the island outposts—Philippines, Japan, Taiwan—have no security and the vast Pacific becomes a Red Sea.

2. The struggle is far from lost in Southeast Asia and it is by no means inevitable that it must be lost. In each country it is possible to build a sound structure capable of withstanding and turning the Communist surge. The will to resist—while now the target of subversive attack—is there. The key to what is done by Asians in defense of Southeast Asia freedom is confidence in the United States.

3. There is no alternative to United States leadership in Southeast Asia. Leadership in individual countries—or the regional leadership and cooperation so appealing to Asians—rests on the knowledge and faith in United States power, will and understanding.

4. SEATO is not now and probably never will be the answer because of British and French unwillingness to support decisive action. Asian distrust of the British and French is outspoken. Success at Geneva would prolong SEATO's role. Failure at Geneva would terminate SEATO's meaningfulness. In the latter event, we must be ready with a new approach to collective security in the area.

We should consider an alliance of all the free nations of the Pacific and Asia who are willing to join forces in defense of their freedom. Such an organization should:

a) have a clear-cut command authority

b) also devote attention to measures and programs of social justice, housing, land reform, etc.

5. Asian leaders—at this time—do not want American troops involved in Southeast Asia other than on training missions. American combat troop involvement is not only not required, it is not desirable. Possibly Americans fail to appreciate fully the subtlety that recently-colonial peoples would not look with favor upon governments which invited or accepted the return this soon of Western troops. To the extent that fear of ground troop involvement dominates our political responses to Asia in Congress or elsewhere, it seems most desirable to me to allay those paralyzing fears in confidence, on the strength of the individual statements

made by leaders consulted on this trip. This does not minimize or disregard the probability that open attack would bring calls for U.S. combat troops. But the present probability of open attack seems scant, and we might gain much needed flexibility in our policies if the spectre of combat troop commitment could be lessened domestically.

6. Any help—economic as well as military—we give less developed nations to secure and maintain their freedom must be a part of a mutual effort. These nations cannot be saved by United States help alone. To the extent the Southeast Asian nations are prepared to take the necessary measures to make our aid effective, we can be—and must be—unstinting in our assistance. It would be useful to enunciate more clearly than we have—for the guidance of these young and unsophisticated nations—what we expect or require of them.

7. In large measure, the greatest danger Southeast Asia offers to nations like the United States is not the momentary threat of Communism itself, rather that danger stems from hunger, ignorance, poverty and disease. We must—whatever strategies we evolve—keep these enemies the point of our attack, and make imaginative use of our scientific and technological capability in such enterprises.

8. Vietnam and Thailand are the immediate—and most important—trouble spots, critical to the U.S. These areas require the attention of our very best talents—under the very closest Washington direction—on matters economic, military and political.

The basic decision in Southeast Asia is here. We must decide whether to help these countries to the best of our ability or throw in the towel in the area and pull back our defenses to San Francisco and a "Fortress America" concept. More important, we would say to the world in this case that we don't live up to treaties and don't stand by our friends. This is not my concept. I recommend that we move forward promptly with a major effort to help these countries defend themselves. I consider the key here is to get our best MAAG people to control, plan, direct and exact results from our military aid program. In Vietnam and Thailand, we must move forward together.

a. In Vietnam, Diem is a complex figure beset by many problems. He has admirable qualities, but he is remote from the people, is surrounded by persons less admirable and capable than he. The country can be saved—if we move quickly and wisely. We must decide whether to support Diem—or let Vietnam fall. We must have coordination of purpose in our country team, diplomatic and military. The Saigon Embassy, USIS, MAAG and related operations leave much to be desired. They should be brought up to maximum efficiency. The most important thing is imaginative, creative, American management of our military aid program. The Vietnamese and our MAAG estimate that $50 million of U.S. military and economic assistance will be needed if we decide to support Vietnam. This is the best information available to us at the present time and if it is confirmed by the best Washington military judgment it should be supported. Since you proposed and Diem agreed to a joint economic mission, it should be appointed and proceed forthwith.

b. In Thailand, the Thais and our own MAAG estimate probably as much is needed as in Vietnam—about $50 million of military and economic assistance. Again, should our best military judgment concur, I believe we should support such a program. Sarit is more strongly and staunchly pro-Western than many of his people. He is and must be deeply concerned at the consequence to his country of a communist-controlled Laos. If Sarit is to stand firm against neutralism, he must have—soon—concrete evidence to show his people of United States military and economic support. He believes that his armed forces should be increased to 150,000. His Defense Minister is coming to Washington to discuss aid matters.

The fundamental decision required of the United States—and time is of the greatest importance—is whether we are to attempt to meet the challenge of Communist expansion now in Southeast Asia by a major effort in support of the forces of freedom in the area or throw in the towel. This decision must be made in a full realization of the very heavy and continuing costs involved in terms of money, of effort and of United States prestige. It must be made with the knowledge that at some point we may be faced with the further decision of whether we commit major United States forces to the area or cut our losses and withdraw should our other efforts fail. We must remain master in this decision. What we do in Southeast Asia should be part of a rational program to meet the threat we face in the region as a whole. It should include a clear-cut pattern of specific contributions to be expected by each partner according to his ability and resources. I recommend we proceed with a clear-cut and strong program of action.

I believe that the mission—as you conceived it—was a success. I am grateful to the many who labored to make it so.

22

Lansdale Memo for Taylor on Unconventional Warfare

Excerpts from memorandum from Brig. Gen. Edward G. Lansdale, Pentagon expert on guerrilla warfare, to Gen. Maxwell D. Taylor, President Kennedy's military adviser, on "Resources for Unconventional Warfare, S.E. Asia," undated but apparently from July, 1961. Copies were sent to Secretary of Defense Robert S. McNamara, Deputy Secretary of Defense Roswell L. Gilpatric, Secretary of State

Dean Rusk, Allen W. Dulles, Director of Central Intelligence, and Gen. C. P. Cabell, Deputy Director of Central Intelligence.

This memo is in response to your desire for early information on unconventional-warfare resources in Southeast Asia. The information was compiled within Defense and CIA.

A. SOUTH VIETNAM

1. Vietnamese

a. First Observation Group

This is a Special Forces type of unit, with the mission of operating in denied (enemy) areas. It currently has some limited operations in North Vietnam and some shallow penetrations into Laos. Most of the unit has been committed to operations against Viet Cong guerillas in South Vietnam.

Strength, as of 6 July, was 340. The First Observation Group had an authorized strength of 305 and now is being increased by 500, for a total of 805, under the 20,000-man force increase. Personnel are volunteers who have been carefully screened by security organizations. Many are from North Vietnam. They have been trained for guerrilla operations, at the Group's training center at Nha Trang. The unit is MAP-supported, as a TO&E unit of the RVNAF (Republic of Vietnam Armed Forces). It receives special equipment and training from CIA and U.S. control is by CIA/MAAG.

The Group and its activities are highly classified by the Government of Vietnam. Only a select few senior RVNMAF officers have access to it. Operations require the approval of President Diem, on much the same approval basis as certain U.S. special operations. The unit is separate from normal RVNAF command channels.

The Group was organized in February, 1956, with the initial mission of preparing stay-behind organizations in South Vietnam just below the 17th Parallel, for guerrilla warfare in the event of an overt invasion by North Vietnamese forces. It was given combat missions against Viet Cong guerrillas in South Vietnam last year, when these Communist guerrillas increased their activities. The plan is to relieve the Group from these combat assignments, to ready its full strength for denied area missions, as RVNAF force increases permit relief. It is currently being organized into twenty teams of 15 men each, with two RS-1 radios per team, for future operations.

b. Other RVNAF

MAAG-Vietnam has reported the formation of additional volunteer groups, apart from the First Observation Group, for similar operations to augment the missions of the Group. As of 6 July, the additional volunteers were reported as:

131

1). 60 Mois (Montagnard tribesmen) recruited, being security screened, to receive Special Forces training.

2). 400 military (RVNAF), to receive Special Forces training. 80 will be formed into small teams, to augment operations of the First Operations Group. 320 will be formed into two Ranger (Airborne) companies.

3). 70 civilians, being organized and trained for stay-behind operations, penetration teams, and communicators.

Other special units of the RVNAF, now committed to operations against the Viet Cong and with Special Forces/Ranger training, are:

9,096 Rangers, in 65 companies.

2,772 more Rangers being activated, part of 20,000-man increase

4,786 Paratroopers

2,300 Marines

673 men in Psychological Warfare Bn.

In addition, cadres from all other combat elements of the RVNAF have received Special Forces/Ranger training.

2. U.S.

a. Defense

1). There are approximately 6 officers and 6 enlisted men from the 1st Special Group on Okinawa currently attached to the MAAG to assist with Ranger-type training.

2). There are three 4-man intelligence training teams present —Combat Intelligence, Counter-Intelligence, Photo-Interpretation and Foreign Operations Intelligence (clandestine collection) in addtion to eight officers and two enlisted intelligence advisors on the MAAG staff.

3). There are two Psychological Warfare staff officers on the MAAG staff and a 4-man Civil Affairs mobile training team (3 officers—1 enlisted man) advising the G-5 staff of the Vietnamese Army in the psy/ops-civic action fields.

b. CIA

1). There are 9 CIA officers working with the First Observation Group in addition to one MAAG advisor.

2). CIA also has five officers working with the Vietnamese Military Intelligence Service and one officer working with the covert [one word illegible] of the Army Psychological Warfare Directorate.

B. THAILAND

1. Thai

a. Royal Thai Army Ranger Battalion (Airborne)

A Special Forces type unit, its stated mission is to organize and conduct guerrilla warfare in areas of Thailand overrun by the enemy in case of an open invasion of Thailand. It currently has the mission of supplying the Palace Guard for the Prime Minister.

Based at Lopburi, the Ranger Battalion has a MAP authorized strength of 580. It is organized into a Headquarters and Headquarters company, a Service company, and four Ranger companies. The Battalion has 4 command detachments and 26 operations detachments, trained and organized along the lines of U.S. Special Forces in strength, equipment, and rank structure.

The Ranger Battalion is loosely attached to the 1st Division. In reality, it is an independent unit of the Royal Thai Army, under the direct control of Field Marshal Sarit, the Commander in Chief, and receives preferential treatment.

Each ranger company has been assigned a region of Thailand, in which it is to be prepared to undertake guerrilla warfare in case of enemy occupation. Field training is conducted in these assigned regions, to acquaint the detachments with the people, facilities and terrain.

b. Police Aerial Resupply Unit (PARU)

The PARU has a mission of undertaking clandestine operations in denied areas. 99 PARU personnel have been introduced covertly to assist the Meos in operations in Laos, where their combat performance has been outstanding.

This is a special police unit, supported by CIA (CIA control in the Meo operations has been reported as excellent), with a current strength of 300 being increased to 550 as rapidly as possible. All personnel are specially selected and screened, and have been rated as of high quality. Officers are selected from the ranks.

Training consists of 10 weeks' basic training, 3 weeks' jumping, 3 weeks' jungle operations, 4 weeks' police law and 3 months of refresher training yearly. Forty individuals have been trained as W/T communicators.

All personnel have adequate personal gear to be self-sustaining in the jungle. Weapons are M-1 rifles, M-3 submachine guns and BAR. In addition, personnel are trained to use other automatic weapons, 2.34 rocket launchers, and 60-mm. mortars.

There are presently 13 PARU teams, totaling 99 men, operating with the Meo guerillas in Laos. Combat reports of these operations have included exceptionally heroic and meritorious actions by PARU personnel. The PARU teams have provided timely intelligence and have worked effectively with local tribes.

c. Thai Border Patrol (BPP)

The mission of the BPP is to counter infiltration and subversion during peace-time, in addition to normal police duties, in the event of an armed invasion of Thailand, the BPP will operate as guerrilla forces in enemy-held areas, in support of regular Thai armed forces.

The BPP has a current strength of 4,500. It was organized in 1955 as a gendarmerie patrol force (name changed to BPP in 1959), composed of 71 active and 23 reserve platoons, from existing police units. It is an element of the Thai National Police, subordinate to the Ministry of the Interior.

Although technically a police organization, the BPP is armed with infantry weapons, including light machine guns, rocket launchers and light mortars. It is trained in small-unit infantry tactics and counter-guerrilla operations. Training is currently being conducted by a 10-man U.S. Army Special Forces team from Okinawa, under ICA auspices.

This unusual police unit was created initially to cope with problems posed by foreign guerrilla elements using Thailand as a safehaven: the Vietminh in eastern Thailand and the Chinese Communists along the Malayan border in the south. There has been some tactical liaison with Burmese Army units.

2. U.S.

a. Defense

1). A Special Forces qualified officer is assigned to advise the RTA Ranger Battalion.

2). A ten-man Special Forces team from the 1st Special Forces Group in Okinawa is currently conducting training for the Thai Border Patrol Police under ICA auspices.

3). There are 5 officers and 1 enlisted man attached to MAAG as advisers to J-2 and the Thai Armed Forces Security Center.

b. CIA

1). 2 advisers with PARU.

2). 3 officers who work with the Border Patrol Police providing advice, guidance and limited training in the collection and processing of intelligence in addition to management of their communications system.

C. LAOS

1. Lao

a. Commandos

According to CINCPAC, there are two special commando companies in the Lao Armed Forces (FAL), with a total strength of 256. These commandos have received Special Forces training.

b. Meo Guerillas

About 9,000 Meo tribesmen have been equipped for guerrilla operations, which they are now conducting with considerable effectiveness in Communist-dominated territory in Laos. They have been organized into Auto-Defense Choc units of the FAL, of varying sizes. Estimates on how many more of these splendid fighting men could be recruited vary, but a realistic figure would be around 4,000 more, although the total manpower pool is larger.

Political leadership of the Meos is in the hands of Touby Lyfoung, who now operates mostly out of Vientiane. The military leader is Lt-Col Vang Pao, who is the field commander. Command control of Meo operations is exercised by the Chief CIA Vientiane with the advice of Chief MAAG Laos. The same CIA paramilitary and U.S. military teamwork is in existence for advisory activities (9 CIA operations officers, 9 LTAG/Army Special Forces personnel, in addition to the 99 Thai PARU under CIA control) and aerial resupply.

As Meo villages are over-run by Communist forces and as men leave food-raising duties to serve as guerrillas, a problem is growing over the care and feeding of non-combat Meos. CIA has given some rice and clothing to relieve this problem. Consideration needs to be given to organized relief, a mission of an ICA nature, to the handling of Meo refugees and their rehabilitation.

c. National Directorate of Coordination

This is the Intelligence arm of the RLG. Its operations are mainly in the Vientiane area at present. It has an armed unit consisting of two battalions and is under the command of Lt-Col Siho, a FAL officer. In addition to intelligence operations this force has a capability for sabotage, kidnapping, commando-type raids, etc.

d. There is also a local veteran's organization and a grass-roots political organization in Laos, both of which are subject to CIA direction and control and are capable of carrying out propaganda, sabotage and harrassment operations. Both are located (in varying degrees of strength and reliability) throughout Laos.

2. U.S.

a. Defense

1). There are 154 Special Forces personnel (12 teams) from the 7th Special Forces Group at Fort Bragg, N. C., attached to the MAAG and providing tactical advice to FAL commanders and conducting basic training when the situation permits.

2). A 10-man intelligence training team is assisting the FAL in establishing a military intelligence system.

3). An 8-man psychological warfare team is assisting the FAL with psy war operations and operation of its radio transmitters.

b. CIA

1). Nine CIA officers are working in the field with the Meo guerrillas, backstopped by two additional officers in Vientiane.

2). Three CIA officers plus 2-3 Vietnamese are working with the National Directorate of Coordination.

D. OTHERS

1. Asian

a. Eastern Construction Company [Filipinos]

This is a private, Filipino-run public service organization, similar to an employment agency, with an almost untapped potential for unconventional warfare (which was its original mission). It now furnishes about 500 trained, experienced Filipino technicians to the Governments of Vietnam and Laos, under the auspices of MAAGs (MAP) and USOMs (ICA activities). Most of these Filipinos are currently augmenting U.S. military logistics programs with the Vietnamese Army and Lao Army. They instruct local military personnel in ordnance, quartermaster, etc. maintenance, storage, and supply procedures. MAAG Chiefs in both Vietnam and Laos have rated this service as highly effective. CIA has influence and some continuing interest with individuals.

The head of Eastern Construction is "Frisco" Johnny San Juan, former National Commander, Philippines Veterans Legion, and former close staff assistant to President Magsaysay of the Philippines (serving as Presidential Complaints and Action Commissioner directly under the President). Its cadre are mostly either former guerrillas against the Japanese in WW II or former Philippine Army personnel. Most of the cadre had extensive combat experience against the Communist Huk guerrillas in the Philippines. This cadre can be expanded into a wide range of counter-Communist activities, having sufficient stature in the Philippines to be able to draw on a very large segment of its trained, experienced, and well-motivated manpower pool.

Eastern Construction was started in 1954 as Freedom Company of the Philippines, a non-profit organization, with President Magsaysay as its honorary president. Its charter stated plainly that it was "to serve the cause of freedom." It actually was a mechanism to permit the deployment of Filipino personnel in other Asian countries, for unconventional operations, under cover of a public service organization having a contract with the host government. Philippine Armed Forces and government personnel were "sheep-dipped" and served abroad. Its personnel helped write the Constitution of the Republic of Vietnam, trained Vietnam's Presidential Guard Battalion, and were instrumental in founding and organizing the Vietnamese Veterans Legion.

When U.S. personnel instrumental in the organization and operational use of Freedom Company departed from the Asian area, direct U.S. support of the organization (on a clandestine basis) was largely terminated. The Filipino leaders in it then decided to carry on its mission privately, as a commercial undertaking. They changed the name to Eastern Construction Company. The organization survived some months of very hard times financially. Its leaders remain as a highly-motivated, experienced, anti-Communist "hard core."

b. Operation Brotherhood (Filipino)

There is another private Filipino public-service organization, capable of considerable expansion in socio-economic-medical operations to support counter-guerilla actions. It is now operating teams in Laos, under ICA auspices. It has a measure of CIA control.

Operation Brotherhood (OB) was started in 1954 by the International Jaycees, under the inspiration and guidance of Oscar Arellano, a Filipino architect who was Vice President for Asia of the International Jaycees. The concept was to provide medical service to refugees and provincial farmers in South Vietnam, as part of the 1955 pacification and refugee program. Initially Filipino teams, later other Asian and European teams, served in OB in Vietnam. Their work was closely coordinated with Vietnamese Army operations which cleaned up Vietminh stay-behinds and started stabilizing rural areas. . . .

c. The Security Training Center (STC)

This is a counter-subversion, counter-guerrilla and psychological warfare school overtly operated by the Philippine Government and covertly sponsored by the U.S. Government through CIA as the instrument of the Country Team. It is located at Fort McKinley on the outskirts of Manila. Its stated mission is: "To counter the forces of subversion in Southeast Asia through more adequate training of security personnel, greater cooperation, better understanding and maximum initiative among the countries of the area." . . .

The training capability of the STC includes a staff of approximately 12 instructors in the subjects of unconventional and counter-guerrilla warfare. . . .

d. CAT. Civil Air Transport (Chinese Nationalist)

CAT is a commercial air line engaged in scheduled and non-scheduled air operations throughout the Far East, with headquarters and large maintenance facilities located in Taiwan. CAT, a CIA proprietary, provides air logistical support under commercial cover to most CIA and other U.S. Government agencies' requirements. CAT supports covert and clandestine air operations by providing trained and experienced personnel, procurement of supplies and equipment through overt commercial channels, and the maintenance of a fairly large inventory of transport and other type aircraft under both Chinat and U.S. registry.

CAT has demonstrated its capability on numerous occasions to meet all types of contingency or long-term covert air requirements in support of U.S. objectives. During the past ten years, it has had some notable achievements, including support of the Chinese Nationalist withdrawal from the mainland, air drop support to the French at Dien Bien Phu, complete logistical and tactical air support for the Indonesian operation, air lifts of refugees from North Vietnam, more than 200 overflights of Mainland China and Tibet, and extensive air support in Laos during the current crisis. . . .

2. U.S.

b. CIA

1) Okinawa—Support Base

Okinawa Station is in itself a para-military support asset and, in critical situations calling for extensive support of UW activity in the Far East, could be devoted in its entirety to this mission. Located at Camp Chinen, it comprises a self-contained base under Army cover with facilities of all types necessary to the storage, testing, packaging, procurement and delivery of supplies—ranging from weapons and explosives to medical and clothing. Because of its being a controlled area, it can accommodate admirably the holding of black bodies in singletons or small groups, as well as small groups of trainees. . . .

4). Saipan Training Station.

CIA maintains a field training station on the island of Saipan located approximately 160 miles northeast of Guam in the Marianas Islands. The installation is under Navy cover and is known as the Naval Technical Training Unit. The primary mission of the Saipan Training Station is to provide physical facilities and competent instructor personnel to fulfill a variety of training requirements including intelligence tradecraft, communications, counter-intelligence and psychological warfare techniques. Training is performed in support of CIA activities conducted throughout the Far East area.

In addition to the facilities described above, CIA maintains a small ship of approximately 500 tons' displacement and 140 feet in length. This vessel is used presently to provide surface transportation between Guam and Saipan. It has an American Captain and First Mate and a Philippine crew, and is operated under the cover of a commercial corporation with home offices in Baltimore, Maryland. Both the ship and the corporation have a potentially wider paramilitary application both in the Far East area and elsewhere.

23

Cable on Diem's Treaty Request

Cablegram from the United States Embassy in Saigon to the State Department, Oct. 1, 1961. A copy of the message was sent to the commander in chief of Pacific forces.

Discussion with Felt and party, McGarr, Nolting yesterday Diem asked for bilateral defense treaty. Large and unexplained request. Serious. Put forward as result of Diem's fear of outcome of Laos situation, SVN vulnerability to increased infiltration, feelings that SEATO action would be inhibited by UK and France in the case of SVN as in Laos.

Nolting told Diem question had important angle and effect on SEATO. Major repeated to Thuan and believe he understands better than Diem some of thorny problems.

Fuller report of conversation with Diem will follow but would like to get quick preliminary reaction from Washington on this request.

Our reaction is that the request should be seriously and carefully treated to prevent feeling that U.S. is not serious in intention to support SVN. But see major issues including overriding Article 19, Geneva Accords, possible ratification problems as well as effect on SEATO.

Diem's request arises from feeling that U.S. policy on Laos will expose his flank in infiltration and lead to large-scale hostilities in SVN. So seeking a stronger commitment than he thinks he has now through SEATO. Changing U.S. policy on Laos, especially SEATO decision to use force if necessary to protect SVN and Thailand, would relieve pressure for bilateral treaty.

24

Note on a Plan for Intervention

Supplemental note to a paper entitled "Concept for Intervention in Viet-Nam," Oct. 11, 1961. According to the Pentagon history, the paper was drafted mainly by U. Alexis Johnson, Deputy Under Secretary of State for Political Affairs, and was either a "talking paper" for a meeting that included Secretary of State Dean Rusk and Secretary of Defense McNamara "or a revision put together later in the day, after the meeting."

As the basic paper indicates, the likelihood of massive DRV and Chicom intervention cannot be estimated with precision. The SNIE covers only the initial phase when action might be limited to 20-25,000 men. At later stages, when the JCS estimate that 40,000 U.S. forces will be needed to clean up the Viet Cong threat, the chances of such massive intervention might well become substantial, with the Soviets finding it a good opportunity to tie down major U.S. forces in a long action, perhaps as part of a multiprong action involving Berlin and such additional areas as Korea and Iran.

Because of this possibility of major Bloc intervention, the maximum possible force-needs must be frankly faced. Assuming present estimates of about 40,000 U.S. forces for the stated military objective in South Vietnam, plus 128,000 U.S. forces for meeting North Vietnam and Chicom intervention, the drain on U.S.-based reserve forces could be on the order of 3 or 4 divisions and other forces as well. The impact on naval capabilities for blockade plans (to meet Berlin) would also be major. In light of present Berlin contingency plans, and combat attrition, including scarce items of equipment, the initiation of the Vietnam action in itself should indicate a step-up in the present mobilization, possibly of major proportions.

25

1961 Request by South Vietnam for U.S. Combat Forces

Cablegram from United State Embassy in Saigon to the State Department, Oct. 13, 1961, on requests by Nguyen Dinh Thuan, Defense Minister of South Vietnam. Copies of this message were sent to Commander in Chief of Pacific forces and to the United States Embassies in Bangkok, Thailand, and Taipei, Taiwan.

Thuan in meeting October 13 made the following requests:

1. Extra squadron of AD-6 in lieu of proposed T-28's and delivery ASAP.

2. U.S. Civilian contract pilots for helicopters and C-47's for "non-combat" operations.

3. U.S. combat units or units to be introduced into SVN as "combat-trainer units". Part to be stationed in North near 17th Parallel to free ARVN forces there for anti-guerrilla action in high plateau. Also perhaps in several provincial seats in the highlands of Central Vietnam.

4. U.S. reaction to proposal to request Nationalist China to send one division of combat troops for operations in the Southwest.

Thuan referred to captured diary of VM officer killed in Central SVN, containing information on VM plans and techniques. Being analyzed, translated and would pass on. Said Diem in light of situation in Laos, infiltration into SVN, and JFK's interest as shown by sending Taylor, requested U.S. to urgently consider requests.

On U.S. combat trainer units, Nolting asked whether Diem's considered request, in view of repeated views opposed. Thuan so confirmed, Diem's views changed in light of worsening situation. Wanted a symbolic U.S. strength near 17th to prevent attacks there, free own forces there. Similar purpose station U.S. units in several provincial seats in central highlands, freeing ARVN ground forces there. Nolting said major requests on heels of Diem request for bilateral treaty. Nolting asked if in lieu of treaty. Thuan said first step quicker than treaty and time was of the essence. Thuan said token forces would satisfy SVN and would be better than treaty (Had evidently not thought through nor discussed with Diem).

Discussed ICC angle. Nolting mentioned value SVN previously attached to ICC presence. Thuan agreed, felt case could be made for introduction of U.S. units for guard duty not combat unless attacked. Could be put in such a way to preserve ICC in SVN. Nolting said doubted if compatable but could be explored (McGarr and I call attention to two points: in view of proposed units, training function more a cover than reality; if send U.S. units should be sufficient strength, since VC attack likely).

On Chinat force, Thuan said Chiang had earlier given some indication (not too precise I gathered) of willingness. Thuan said GVN did not want to follow-up without getting U.S. reaction. Idea to use about 10,000 men in southwest as far from 17th as possible. Also intended to draft eligibles of Chinese origin into forces. Thuan thought perhaps Chinats could be introduced covertly, but on analyses gave this up. Nolting said he thought Chinats would want something out of deal, maybe political lift from introducing Chinat forces on Asia mainland (Nolting thinks trial balloon only).

Questions will undoubtedly be raised with Taylor. Obvious GVN losing no opportunity to ask for more support as a result of our greater interest and concern. But situation militarily and psychologically has moved to a point where serious and prompt consideration should be given.

(Note: Will be meeting on this in Admiral Heinz's office, 1330, 16 October to get reply out today. Applicable CINCPAC 140333, 140346)

26

Cable from Taylor to Kennedy on Introduction of U.S. Troops

Cablegram from Baguio, the Philippines, by General Taylor to President Kennedy, Nov. 1, 1961.

This message is for the purpose of presenting my reasons for recommending the introduction of a U.S. military force into SVN. I have reached the conclusion that this is an essential action if we are to reverse the present downward trend of events in spite of a full recognition of the following disadvantages:

a. The strategic reserve of U.S. forces is presently so weak that we can ill afford any detachment of forces to a peripheral area of the Communist bloc where they will be pinned down for an uncertain duration.

b. Although U.S. prestige is already engaged in SVN, it will become more so by the sending of troops.

c. If the first contingent is not enough to accomplish the necessary results, it will be difficult to resist the pressure to reinforce. If the ultimate result sought is the closing of the frontiers and the clean-up of the insurgents within SVN, there is no limit to our possible commitment (unless we attack the source in Hanoi).

d. The introduction of U.S. forces may increase tensions and risk escalation into a major war in Asia.

On the other side of the argument, there can be no action so convincing of U.S. seriousness of purpose and hence so reassuring to the people and Government of SVN and to our other friends and allies in SEA as the introduction of U.S. forces into SVN. The views of indigenous and U.S. officials consulted on our trip were unanimous on this point. I have just seen Saigon 575 to State and suggest that it be read in connection with this message.

The size of the U.S. force introduced need not be great to provide the military presence necessary to produce the desired effect on national morale in SVN and on international opinion. A bare token, however, will not suffice; it must have a significant value. The kinds of tasks which it might undertake which would have a significant value are suggested in Baguio 0005. They are:

(a) Provide a U.S. military presence capable of raising national morale and of showing to SEA the seriousness of the U.S. intent to resist a Communist takeover.

(b) Conduct logistical operations in support of military and flood relief operations.

(c) Conduct such combat operations as are necessary for self-defense and for the security of the area in which they are stationed.

(d) Provide an emergency reserve to back up the Armed Forces of the GVN in the case of a heightened military crisis.

(e) Act as an advance party of such additional forces as may be introduced if CINCPAC or SEATO contingency plans are invoked.

It is noteworthy that this force is not proposed to clear the jungles and forests of VC guerrillas. That should be the primary task of the Armed Forces of Vietnam for which they should be specifically organized, trained and stiffened with ample U.S. advisors down to combat battalion levels. However, the U.S. troops may be called upon to engage in combat to protect themselves, their working parties, and the area in which they live. As a general reserve, they might be thrown into action (with U.S. agreement) against large, formed guerrilla bands which have abandoned the forests for attacks on major targets. But in general, our forces should not engage in small-scale guerrilla operations in the jungle.

As an area for the operations of U.S. troops, SVN is not an excessively difficult or unpleasant place to operate. While the border areas are rugged and heavily forested, the terrain is comparable to parts of Korea where U.S. troops learned to live and work without too much effort. However, these border areas, for reasons stated above, are not the places to engage our forces. In the High Plateau and in the coastal plain where U.S. troops would probably be stationed, these jungle-forest conditions do not exist to any great extent. The most unpleasant feature in the coastal areas would be the heat and, in the Delta, the mud left behind by the flood. The High Plateau offers no particular obstacle to the stationing of U.S. troops.

The extent to which the Task Force would engage in flood relief activities in the Delta will depend upon further study of the problem there. As reported in Saigon 537, I see considerable advantages in playing up this aspect of the TF mission. I am presently inclined to favor a dual mission, initially help to the flood area and subsequently use in any other area of SVN where its resources can be used effectively to give tangible support in the struggle against the VC. However, the possibility of emphasizing the humanitarian mission will wane if we wait long in moving in our forces or in linking our stated purpose with the emergency conditions created by the flood.

The risks of backing into a major Asian war by way of SVN are present but are not impressive. NVN is extremely vulnerable to conventional bombing, a weakness which should be exploited diplomatically in convincing Hanoi to lay off SVN. Both the D.R.V. and the Chicoms would face severe logistical difficulties in trying to maintain strong forces in the field in SEA, difficulties which we share but by no means to the same degree. There is no case for fearing a mass onslaught of Communist manpower into SVN and its neighboring states, particularly if our airpower is allowed a free hand against logistical targets. Finally, the starvation conditions in China should discourage Communist leaders there from being militarily venturesome for some time to come.

By the foregoing line of reasoning, I have reached the conclusion that the introduction of [word illegible] military Task Force without delay offers definitely more advantage than it creates risks and difficulties. In fact, I do not believe that our program to save SVN will succeed without it. If the concept is approved, the exact size and composition of the force should be determined by Sec Def in consultation with the JCS, the Chief MAAG and CINCPAC. My own feeling is that the initial size should not exceed about 8000, of which a preponderant number would be in logistical-type units. After acquiring experience in operating in SVN, this initial force will require reorganization and adjustment to the local scene.

As CINCPAC will point out, any forces committed to SVN will need to be replaced by additional forces to his area from the strategic reserve in the U.S. Also, any troops to SVN are in addition to those which may be required to execute SEATO Plan 5 in Laos. Both facts should be taken into account in current considerations of the FY 1963 budget which bear upon the permanent increase which should be made in the U.S. military establishment to maintain our strategic position for the long pull.

27

Taylor's Summary of Findings on His Mission to South Vietnam

Cablegram from Baguio, the Philippines, by Gen. Maxwell D. Taylor, Presidential military adviser, to Mr. Kennedy, Nov. 1, 1961.

1. Transmitted herewith are a summary of the fundamental conclusions of my group and my personal recommendations in response to the letter of the President to me dated 13 October 1961. At our meeting next Friday I hope to be allowed to explain the thinking which lies behind them. At that time I shall transmit our entire report which will provide detailed support for the recommendations and will serve as a working paper for the interested departments and agencies.

2. It is concluded that:

a. Communist strategy aims to gain control of Southeast Asia by methods of subversion and guerrilla war which by-pass conventional U.S. and indigenous strength on the ground. The interim Communist goal—en route to total take-over—appears to be a neutral Sutheast Asia, detached from U.S. protection. This strategy is well on the way to success in Vietnam.

b. In Vietnam "and Southeast Asia" there is a double crisis in confidence: doubt that U.S. is determined to save Southeast Asia; doubt that Diem's methods can frustrate and defeat Communist purposes and methods. The Vietnamese (and Southeast Asians) will undoubtedly draw—rightly or wrongly—definitive conclusions in coming weeks and months concerning the probable outcome and will adjust their behavior accordingly. What the U.S. does or fails to do will be decisive to the end result.

c. Aside from the morale factor, the Vietnamese Government is caught in interlocking circles of bad tactics and bad administrative arrangements which pin their forces on the defensive in ways which permit a relatively small Viet-Cong force (about one-tenth the size of the GVN regulars) to create conditions of frustration and terror certain to lead to a political crisis, if a positive turning point is not soon achieved. The following recommendations are designed to achieve that favorable turn, to avoid a further deterioration in the situation in South Vietnam, and eventually to contain and eliminate the threat to its independence.

3. It is recommended:

GENERAL

a. That upon request from the Government of Vietnam (GVN) to come to its aid in resisting the increasing aggressions of the Viet-Cong and in repairing the ravages of the Delta flood which, in combination, threaten the lives of its citizens and the security

144

of the country, the U.S. Government offer to join the GVN in a massive joint effort as a part of a total mobilization of GVN resources to cope with both the Viet-Cong (VC) and the ravages of the flood. The U.S. representatives will participate actively in this effort, particularly in the fields of government administration, military plans and operations, intelligence, and flood relief, going beyond the advisory role which they have observed in the past.

SPECIFIC

b. That in support of the foregoing broad commitment to a joint effort with Diem, the following specific measures be undertaken:

(1) The U.S. Government will be prepared to provide individual administrators for insertion into the governmental machinery of South Vietnam in types and numbers to be worked out with President Diem.

(2) A joint effort will be made to improve the military-political intelligence system beginning at the provincial level extending upward through the government and armed forces to the Central Intelligence Organization.

(3) The U.S. Government will engage in a joint survey of the conditions in the provinces to assess the social, political, intelligence, and military factors bearing on the prosecution of the counter-insurgency in order to reach a common estimate of these factors and a common determination of how to deal with them. As this survey will consume time, it should not hold back the immediate actions which are clearly needed regardless of its outcome.

(4) A joint effort will be made to free the Army for mobile, offensive operations. This effort will be based upon improving the training and equipping of the Civil Guard and the Self-Defense Corps, relieving the regular Army of static missions, raising the level of the mobility of Army forces by the provision of considerably more helicopters and light aviation, and organizing a Border Ranger Force for a long-term campaign on the Laotian border against the Viet-Cong infiltrators. The U.S. Government will support this effort with equipment and with military units and personnel to do those tasks which the Armed Forces of Vietnam cannot perform in time. Such tasks include air reconnaissance and photography, airlift (beyond the present capacity of SVN forces), special intelligence, and air-ground support techniques.

(5) The U.S. Government will assist the GVN in effecting surveillance and control over the coastal waters and inland waterways, furnishing such advisors, operating personnel and small craft as may be necessary for quick and effective operations.

(6) The MAAG, Vietnam, will be reorganized and increased in size as may be necessary by the implementation of these recommendations.

(7) The U.S. Government will offer to introduce into South Vietnam a military Task Force to operate under U.S. control for the following purposes:

(a) Provide a U.S. military presence capable of raising national morale and of showing to Southeast Asia the seriousness of the U.S. intent to resist a Communist take-over.

(b) Conduct logistical operations in support of military and flood relief operations.

(c) Conduct such combat operations as are necessary for self-defense and for the security of the area in which they are stationed.

(d) Provide an emergency reserve to back up the Armed Forces of the GVN in the case of a heightened military crisis.

(e) Act as an advance party of such additional forces as may be introduced if CINCPAC or SEATO contingency plans are invoked.

(8) The U.S. Government will review its economic aid program to take into account the needs of flood relief and to give priority to those projects in support of the expanded counter-insurgency program.

28

Evaluation and Conclusions of Taylor's Report on Vietnam

Excerpts from General Taylor's report, Nov. 3, 1961, on his mission to South Vietnam for President Kennedy.

. . . LIMITED PARTNERSHIP

. . . Following are the specific categories where the introduction of U.S. working advisors or working military units are suggested . . . an asterisk indicating where such operations are, to some degree, under way.

—A high-level government advisor or advisors. General Lansdale has been requested by Diem; and it may be wise to envisage a limited number of Americans—acceptable to Diem as well as to us—in key ministries. . . .

—A Joint U.S.-Vietnamese Military Survey, down to the provincial level, in each of three corps areas, to make recommendations with respect to intelligence, command and control, more economical and effective passive defense, the build-up of a reserve for offensive purposes, military-province-chief relations, etc. . . .

—Joint planning of offensive operations, including border control operations.* . . .

—Intimate liaison with the Vietnamese Central Intelligence Organizations (C.I.O.) with each of the seven intelligence [rest of sentence illegible].

—Jungle Jim. . . .

—Counter infiltration operations in Laos.* . . .

—Increased covert offensive operations in North as well as in Laos and South Vietnam.* . . .

—The introduction, under MAAG operational control, of three helicopter squadrons—one for each corps area—and the provision of more light aircraft, as the need may be established. . . .

—A radical increase in U.S. trainers at every level from the staff colleges, where teachers are short—to the Civil Guard and Self-Defense Corps, where a sharp expansion in competence may prove the key to mobilizing a reserve for offensive operations. . . .

—The introduction of engineering and logistical elements within the proposed U.S. military task force to work in the flood area within the Vietnamese plan, on both emergency and longer term reconstruction tasks. . . .

—A radical increase in U.S. special force teams in Vietnam: to work with the Vietnamese Ranger Force proposed for the border area . . . ; to assist in unit training, including training of Clandestine Action Service. . . .

—Increase the MAAG support for the Vietnamese Navy.* . . .

—Introduction of U.S. Naval and/or Coast Guard personnel to assist in coastal and river surveillance and control, until Vietnamese naval capabilities can be improved. . . .

—Reconsideration of the role of air power, leading to more effective utilization of assets now available, including release from political control of the 14 D-6 aircraft, institution of close-support techniques, and better employment of available weapons. . . .

To execute this program of limited partnership requires a change in the charter, the spirit, and the organization of the MAAG in South Vietnam. It must be shifted from an advisory group to something nearer—but not quite—an operational headquarters in a theater of war. . . . The U.S. should become a limited partner in the war, avoiding formalized advice on the one hand, trying to run the war, on the other. Such a transition from advice to partnership has been made in recent months, on a smaller scale, by the MAAG in Laos.

Among the many consequences of this shift would be the rapid build-up of an intelligence capability both to identify operational targets for the Vietnamese and to assist Washington in making a sensitive and reliable assessment of the progress of the war. The basis for such a unit already exists in Saigon in the Intelligence Evaluation Center. It must be quickly expanded. . . .

In Washington, as well, intelligence and back-up operations must be put on a quasi-wartime footing. . . .

CONTINGENCIES

The U.S. action proposed in this report—involving as it does the overt lifting of the MAAG ceiling, substantial encadrement and the introduction of limited U.S. forces—requires that the United

States also prepare for contingencies that might arise from the enemy's reaction. The initiative proposed here should not be undertaken unless we are prepared to deal with any escalation the communists might choose to impose. Specifically we must be prepared to act swiftly under these three circumstances: an attempt to seize and to hold the Pleiku-Kontum area; a political crisis in which the communists might attempt to use their forces around Saigon to capture the city in the midst of local confusion; an undertaking of overt major hostilities by North Vietnam.

As noted earlier, the present contingency plans of CINCPAC must embrace the possibility both of a resumption of the communist offensive in Laos and these Vietnamese contingency situations. Taken together, the contingencies in Southeast Asia which we would presently choose to meet without the use of nuclear weapons appear to require somewhat more balanced ground, naval, and air strength in reserve in the U.S. than we now have available, so long as we maintain the allocation of the six divisions for the Berlin crisis.

Therefore, one of the major issues raised by this report is the need to develop the reserve strength in the U.S. establishment required to cover action in Southeast Asia up to the nuclear threshold in that area, as it is now envisaged. The call up of additional support forces may be required.

In our view, nothing is more calculated to sober the enemy and to discourage escalation in the face of the limited initiatives proposed here than the knowledge that the United States has prepared itself soundly to deal with aggression in Southeast Asia at any level.

29

Conclusions of McNamara on Report by General Taylor

Memorandum for the President from Secretary of Defense McNamara, Nov. 8, 1961, as provided in the Pentagon analysts' narrative.

The basic issue framed by the Taylor Report is whether the U.S. shall:

a. Commit itself to the clear objective of preventing the fall of South Vietnam to Communism, and

b. Support this commitment by necessary immediate military actions and preparations for possible later actions.

The Joint Chiefs, Mr. Gilpatric and I have reached the following conclusions:

1. The fall of South Vietnam to Communism would lead to the fairly rapid extension of Communist control, or complete accom-

148

modation to Communism, in the rest of mainland Southeast Asia and in Indonesia. The strategic implications worldwide, particularly in the Orient, would be extremely serious.

2. The chances are against, probably sharply against, preventing that fall by any measures short of the introduction of U.S. forces on a substantial scale. We accept General Taylor's judgment that the various measures proposed by him short of this are useful but will not in themselves do the job of restoring confidence and setting Diem on the way to winning his fight.

3. The introduction of a U.S. force of the magnitude of an initial 8,000 men in a flood relief context will be of great help to Diem. However, it will not convince the other side (whether the shots are called from Moscow, Peiping, or Hanoi) that we mean business. Moreover, it probably will not tip the scales decisively. We would be almost certain to get increasingly mired down in an inconclusive struggle.

4. The other side can be convinced we mean business only if we accompany the initial force introduction by a clear commitment to the full objective stated above, accompanied by a warning through some channel to Hanoi that continued support of the Viet Cong will lead to punitive retaliation against North Vietnam.

5. If we act in this way, the ultimate possible extent of our military commitment must be faced. The struggle may be prolonged and Hanoi and Peiping may intervene overtly. In view of the logistic difficulties faced by the other side, I believe we can assume that the maximum U.S. forces required on the ground in Southeast Asia will not exceed 6 divisions, or about 205,000 men (CINCPAC Plan 32-59, Phase IV). Our military posture is, or with the addition of more National Guard or regular Army divisions, can be made, adequate to furnish these forces without serious interference with our present Berlin plans.

6. To accept the stated objective is of course a most serious decision. Military force is not the only element of what must be a most carefully coordinated set of actions. Success will depend on factors many of which are not within our control—notably the conduct of Diem himself and other leaders in the area. Laos will remain a major problem. The domestic political implications of accepting the objective are also grave, although it is our feeling that the country will respond better to a firm initial position than to courses of action that lead us in only gradually, and that in the meantime are sure to involve casualties. The overall effect on Moscow and Peiping will need careful weighing and may well be mixed; however, permitting South Vietnam to fall can only strengthen and encourage them greatly.

7. In sum:

a. We do not believe major units of U.S. forces should be introduced in South Vietnam unless we are willing to make an affirmative decision on the issue stated at the start of this memorandum.

b. We are inclined to recommend that we do commit the U.S.

to the clear objective of preventing the fall of South Vietnam to Communism and that we support this commitment by the necessary military actions.

c. If such a commitment is agreed upon, we support the recommendations of General Taylor as the first steps toward its fulfillment.

30

1961 Rusk-McNamara Report to Kennedy on South Vietnam

Excerpts from memorandum for President Kennedy from Secretary of State Rusk and Secretary of Defense Mc-Namara, Nov. 11, 1961, as provided by the Pentagon study.

1. United States National Interests in South Viet-Nam.

The deteriorating situation in South Viet-Nam requires attention to the nature and scope of United States national interests in that country. The loss of South Viet-Nam to Communism would involve the transfer of a nation of 20 million people from the free world to the Communist bloc. The loss of South Viet-Nam would make pointless any further discussion about the importance of Southeast Asia to the free world; we would have to face the near certainty that the remainder of Southeast Asia and Indonesia would move to a complete accommodation with Communism, if not formal incorporation with the Communist bloc. The United States, as a member of SEATO, has commitments with respect to South Viet-Nam under the Protocol to the SEATO Treaty. Additionally, in a formal statement at the conclusion session of the 1954 Geneva Conference, the United States representative stated that the United States "would view any renewal of the aggression . . . with grave concern and seriously threatening international peace and security."

The loss of South Viet-Nam to Communism would not only destroy SEATO but would undermine the credibility of American commitments elsewhere. Further, loss of South Viet-Nam would stimulate bitter domestic controversies in the United States and would be seized upon by extreme elements to divide the country and harass the Administration. . . .

3. The United States' Objective in South Viet-Nam.

The United States should commit itself to the clear objective of preventing the fall of South Viet-Nam to Communist [sic]. *The basic means for accomplishing this objective must be to put the Government of South Viet-Nam into a position to win its own war against the Guerillas. We must insist that that Government* itself take the measures necessary for that purpose in exchange for large-scale United States assistance in the military, economic and political fields. At the same time we must recognize that it will probably not be possible for the GVN to win this war as long as the flow of men and supplies from North Viet-Nam continues unchecked and the guerillas enjoy a safe sanctuary in neighboring territory.

We should be prepared to introduce United States combat forces if that should become necessary for success. Dependent upon the circumstances, it may also be necessary for United States forces to strike at the source of the aggression in North Viet-Nam.

4. The Use of United States Forces in South Viet-Nam.

The commitment of United States forces to South Viet-Nam involves two different categories: (A) Units of modest size required for the direct support of South Viet-Namese military effort, such as communications, helicopter and other forms of airlift, reconnaissance aircraft, naval patrols, intelligence units, etc., and (B) larger organized units with actual or potential direct military mission. *Category (A) should be introduced as speedily as possible.* Category (B) units pose a more serious problem in that they are much more significant from the point of view of domestic and international political factors and greatly increase the probabilities of Communist bloc escalation. Further, the employment of United States combat forces (in the absence of Communist bloc escalation) involves a certain dilemma: if there is a strong South-Vietnamese effort, they may not be needed; if there is not such an effort, United States forces could not accomplish their mission in the midst of an apathetic or hostile population. Under present circumstances, therefore, the question of injecting United States and SEATO combat forces should in large part be considered as a contribution to the morale of the South Vietnamese in their own effort to do the principal job themselves.

5. Probable Extent of the Commitment of United States Forces.

If we commit Category (B) forces to South Viet-Nam, the ultimate possible extent of our military commitment in Southeast Asia must be faced. The struggle may be prolonged, and Hanoi and Peiping may overtly intervene. It is the view of the Secretary of Defense and the Joint Chiefs of Staff that, in the light of the logistic difficulties faced by the other side, we can assume that the maximum United States forces required on the ground in Southeast Asia would not exceed six divisions, or about 205,000 men (CINCPAC Plan 32/59 PHASE IV). This would be in addition to local forces and such SEATO forces as may be engaged. It is also the view of the Secretary of Defense and the Joint Chiefs of Staff that our military posture is, or, with the addition of more National Guard or regular Army divisions, can be made, adequate to furnish these forces and support them in action without serious interference with our present Berlin plans. . . .

In the light of the foregoing, the Secretary of State and the Secretary of Defense recommend that:

1. We now take the decision to commit ourselves to the objective of preventing the fall of South Viet-Nam to Communism and that, in doing so, we recognize that the introduction of United States and other SEATO forces may be necessary to achieve this objective. (However, if it is necessary to commit outside forces to achieve the foregoing objective our decision to introduce United States forces should not be contingent upon unanimous SEATO agreement thereto.)

2. The Department of Defense be prepared with plans for the use of United States forces in South Viet-Nam under one or more of the following purposes:

(a) Use of a significant number of United States forces to signify United States determination to defend Viet-Nam and to boost South Viet-Nam morale.

(b) Use of substantial United States forces to assist in suppressing Viet Cong insurgency short of engaging in detailed counter-guerrilla operations but including relevant operations in North Viet-Nam.

(c) Use of United States forces to deal with the situation if there is organized Communist military intervention.

3. We immediately undertake the following actions in support of the GVN:

. . . (c) Provide the GVN with small craft, including such United States uniformed advisers and operating personnel as may be necessary for quick and effective operations in effecting surveillance and control over coastal waters and inland waterways. . . .

(e) Provide such personnel and equipment as may be necessary to improve the military-political intelligence system beginning at the provincial level and extending upward through the Government and the armed forces to the Central Intelligence Organization.

(f) Provide such new terms of reference, reorganization and additional personnel for United States military forces as are required for increased United States participation in the direction and control of GVN military operations and to carry out the other increased responsibilities which accrue to MAAG under these recommendations. . . .

(i) Provide individual administrators and advisers for insertion into the Governmental machinery of South Viet-Nam in types and numbers to be agreed upon by the two Governments. . . .

5. Very shortly before the arrival in South Viet-Nam of the first increments of United States military personnel and equipment proposed under 3., above, that would exceed the Geneva Accord ceilings, publish the "Jorden report" as a United States "white paper," transmitting it as simultaneously as possible to the Governments of all countries with which we have diplomatic relations, including the Communist states.

6. Simultaneous with the publication of the "Jorden report," release an exchange of letters between Diem and the President.

(a) Diem's letter would include: reference to the DRV violations of Geneva Accords as set forth in the October 24 GVN letter to the ICC and other documents; pertinent references to GVN statements with respect to its intent to observe the Geneva Accords; reference to its need for flood relief and rehabilitation; reference to previous United States aid and the compliance hitherto by both countries with the Geneva Accords; reference to the USG statement at the time the Geneva Accords were signed; the necessity of now exceeding some provisions of the Accords in view of the DRV violations thereof; the lack of aggressive intent with respect to the DRV; GVN intent to return to strict compliance with the Geneva Accords as soon as the DRV violations ceased; and request for additional United States assistance in framework foregoing policy. The letter should also set forth in appropriate general terms steps Diem has taken and is taking to reform Governmental structure.

(b) The President's reply would be responsive to Diem's request for additional assistance and acknowledge and agree to Diem's statements on the intent promptly to return to strict compliance with the Geneva Accords as soon as DRV violations have ceased. . . .

31

Memo from Joint Chiefs Urging a Greater Role in South Vietnam

Excerpts from memorandum from the Joint Chiefs of Staff to Secretary of Defense McNamara, Jan. 13, 1962. On Jan. 27, 1962, Mr. McNamara sent the memorandum to President Kennedy with a covering letter that said in part: "The Joint Chiefs of Staff have asked that the attached memorandum . . . be brought to your attention. The memorandum requires no action by you at this time. I am not prepared to endorse the experience with our present program in South Vietnam."

3. Military Considerations. . . .

a. Early Eventualities—Loss of the Southeast Asian Mainland would have an adverse impact on our military strategy and would markedly reduce our ability in limited war by denying us air, land and sea bases, by forcing greater intelligence effort with lesser results, by complicating military lines of communication and by the introduction of more formidable enemy forces in the area. Air access and access to 5,300 miles of mainland coastline would be outflanked, the last significant United Kingdom military

153

strength in Asia would be eliminated with the loss of Singapore and Malaya and U.S. military influence in that area, short of war, would be difficult to exert.

b. Possible Eventualities—Of equal importance to the immediate losses are the eventualities which could follow the loss of the Southeast Asian mainland. All of the Indonesian archipelago could come under the domination and control of the USSR and would become a communist base posing a threat against Australia and New Zealand. The Sino-Soviet Bloc would have control of the eastern access to the Indian Ocean. The Philippines and Japan could be pressured to assume at best, a neutralist role, thus eliminating two of our major bases in the Western Pacific. Our lines of defense then would be pulled north to Korea, Okinawa and Taiwan resulting in the subsequent overtaking of our lines of communications in a limited war. India's ability to remain neutral would be jeopardized and, as the Bloc meets success, its concurrent stepped-up activities to move into and control Africa can be expected. . . .

. . . 13. Three salient factors are of the greatest importance if the eventual introduction of U.S. forces is required.

a. Any war in the Southeast Asian Mainland will be a peninsula and island-type of campaign—a mode of warfare in which all elements of the Armed Forces of the United States have gained a wealth of experience and in which we have excelled both in World War II and Korea.

b. Study of the problem clearly indicates that the Communists are limited in the forces they can sustain in war in that area because of natural logistic and transportation problems.

c. Our present world military posture is such that we now have effective forces capable of implementing existing contingency plans for Southeast Asia without affecting to an unacceptable degree our capability to conduct planned operations in Europe relating to Berlin or otherwise.

14. The Joint Chiefs of Staff recommend that in any consideration of further action which may be required because of possible unacceptable results obtained despite Diem's full cooperation and the effective employment of South Vietnam armed forces, you again consider the recommendation provided you by JCSM-320-61, dated 10 May 1961, that a decision be made to deploy suitable U.S. forces to South Vietnam sufficient to accomplish the following:

a. Provide a visible deterrent to potential North Vietnam and/or Chinese Communist action;

b. Release Vietnamese forces from advanced and static defense positions to permit their future commitment to counterinsurgency actions;

c. Assist in training the Vietnamese forces;

d. Provide a nucleus for the support of any additional U.S. or SEATO military operations in Southeast Asia; and

e. Indicate the firmness of our intent to all Asian nations.

We are of the opinion that failure to do so under such circumstances will merely extend the date when such action must be taken and will make our ultimate task proportionately more difficult.

32

State Department Study in Late '62 on Prospects in South Vietnam

Excerpts from research memorandum from Roger Hilsman, director of the State Department Bureau of Intelligence and Research, to Secretary of State Rusk, Dec. 3, 1962. The memorandum bore the title "The Situation and Short-Term Prospects in South Vietnam" and a footnote said that the report was based on information available through Nov. 12, 1962.

. . . President Ngo Dinh Diem and other leading Vietnamese as well as many U.S. officials in South Vietnam apparently believe that the tide is now turning in the struggle against Vietnamese Communist (Viet Cong) insurgency and subversion. This degree of optimism is premature. At best, it appears that the rate of deterioration has decelerated with improvement, principally in the security sector, reflecting substantially increased U.S. assistance and GVN implementation of a broad counterinsurgency program.

The GVN has given priority to implementing a basic strategic concept featuring the strategic hamlet and systematic pacification programs. It has paid more attention to political, economic, and social counterinsurgency measures and their coordination with purely military measures. Vietnamese military and security forces —now enlarged and of higher quality—are significantly more offensive-minded and their counterguerilla tactical capabilities are greatly improved. Effective GVN control of the countryside has been extended slightly. In some areas where security has improved peasant attitudes toward the government appear also to have improved.

As a result, the Viet Cong has had to modify its tactics and perhaps set back its timetable. But the "national liberation war" has not abated nor has the Viet Cong been weakened. On the contrary, the Viet Cong has expanded the size and enhanced the capability and organization of its guerilla force—now estimated at about 23,000 in elite fighting personnel, plus some 100,000 irregulars and sympathizers. It still controls about 20 percent of the villages and about 9 percent of the rural population, and has varying degrees of influence among additional 47 percent of the villages. Viet Cong control and communication lines to the peasant have not been seriously weakened and the guerillas have thus been able to maintain good intelligence and a high degree of initiative, mobility, and striking power. Viet Cong influence has almost certainly improved in urban areas not only through subversion and terrorism but also because of its propaganda appeal to the increasingly frustrated non-Communist anti-Diem elements.

The internal political situation is considerably more difficult to assess. Diem has strengthened his control of the bureaucracy and the military establishment. He has delegated a little more authority than in the past, and has become increasingly aware of the importance of the peasantry to the counterinsurgency effort. Nevertheless, although there are fewer reports of discontent with Diem's leadership within official circles and the civilian elite, there are still many indications of continuing serious concern, particularly with Diem's direction of the counterinsurgency effort. There are also reports that important military and civilian officials continue to participate in coup plots. Oppositionists, critics, and dissenters outside the government appear to be increasingly susceptible to neutralist, pro-Communist, and possibly anti-U.S. sentiments. They are apparently placing increased reliance on clandestine activities.

The Viet Cong is obviously prepared for a long struggle and can be expected to maintain the present pace and diversity of its insurgent-subversive effort. During the next month or so, it may step up its military effort in reaction to the growing GVN-U.S. response. Hanoi can also be expected to increase its efforts to legitimatize its "National Front for the Liberation of South Vietnam" (NFLSV) and to prepare further groundwork for a "liberation government" in South Vietnam. On the present evidence, the Communists are not actively moving toward neutralization of South Vietnam in the Laos pattern, although they could seek to do so later. Elimination, even significant reduction, of the Communist insurgency will almost certainly require several years. In either case, a considerably greater effort by the GVN, as well as continuing U.S. assistance, is crucial. If there is continuing improvement in security conditions, Diem should be able to alleviate concern and boost morale within the bureaucracy and the military establishment. But the GVN will not be able to consolidate its military successes into permanent political gains and to evoke the positive support of the peasantry unless it gives more emphasis to non-military aspects of the counterinsurgency program, integrates the strategic hamlet program with an expanded systematic pacification program, and appreciably modified military tactics (particularly those relating to large-unit actions and tactical use of air-power and artillery). Failure to do so might increase militant opposition among the peasants and their positive identification with the Viet Cong.

A coup could occur at any time, but would be more likely if the fight against the Communists goes badly, if the Viet Cong launches a series of successful and dramatic operations, or if Vietnamese army casualties increase appreciably over a protracted period. The coup most likely to succeed would be one with non-Communist leadership and support, involving middle and top echelon military and civilian officials. For a time at least, the serious disruption of government leadership resulting from a coup would probably halt and possibly reverse the momentum of the government's counterinsurgency effort. The role of the U.S. can be extremely important in restoring this momentum and in averting widespread fighting and a serious internal power struggle. . . .

Chapter 4

The Overthrow of Ngo Dinh Diem: May–November, 1963

—BY HEDRICK SMITH

The Pentagon's secret study of the Vietnam war discloses that President Kennedy knew and approved of plans for the military coup d'état that overthrew President Ngo Dinh Diem in 1963.

"Our complicity in his overthrow heightened our responsibilities and our commitment" in Vietnam, the study finds.

In August and October of 1963, the narrative recounts, the United States gave its support to a cabal of army generals bent on removing the controversial leader, whose rise to power Mr. Kennedy had backed in speeches in the middle nineteen-fifties and who had been the anchor of American policy in Vietnam for nine years.

The coup, one of the most dramatic episodes in the history of the American involvement in Vietnam, was a watershed. As the Pentagon study observes, it was a time when Washington—with the Diem regime gone—could have reconsidered its entire commitment to South Vietnam and decided to disengage.

At least two Administration officials advocated disengagement but, according to the Pentagon study, it "was never seriously considered a policy alternative because of the assumption that an independent, non-Communist SVN was too important a strategic interest to abandon."

The effect, according to this account, was that the United States, discovering after the coup that the war against the Vietcong had been going much worse than officials previously thought, felt compelled to do more—rather than less—for Saigon. By supporting the anti-Diem coup, the analyst asserts,

158

"the U.S. inadvertently deepened its involvement. The inadvertence is the key factor."

According to the Pentagon account of the 1963 events in Saigon, Washington did not originate the anti-Diem coup, nor did American forces intervene in any way, even to try to prevent the assassinations of Mr. Diem and his brother Ngo Dinh Nhu, who, as the chief Diem political adviser, had accumulated immense power. Popular discontent with the Diem regime focused on Mr. Nhu and his wife.

But for weeks—and with the White House informed every step of the way—the American mission in Saigon maintained secret contacts with the plotting generals through one of the Central Intelligence Agency's most experienced and versatile operatives, an Indochina veteran, Lieut. Col. Lucien Conein. He first landed in Vietnam in 1944 by parachute for the Office of Strategic Services, the wartime forerunner of the C.I.A.

So trusted by the Vietnamese generals was Colonel Conein that he was in their midst at Vietnamese General Staff headquarters as they launched the coup. Indeed, on Oct. 25, a week earlier, in a cable to McGeorge Bundy, the President's special assistant for national security, Ambassador Lodge had occasion to describe Colonel Conein of the C.I.A.—referring to the agency, in code terminology, as C.A.S.—as the indispensable man:

"C.A.S. has been punctilious in carrying out my instructions. I have personally approved each meeting between General Don [one of three main plotters] and Conein who has carried out my orders in each instance explicitly. . . .

"Conein, as you know, is a friend of some 18 years' standing with General Don, and General Don has expressed extreme reluctance to deal with anyone else. I do not believe the involvement of another American in close contact with the generals would be productive." [See Document #52.]

So closely did the C.I.A. work with the generals, official documents reveal, that it provided them with vital intelligence about the arms and encampments of pro-Diem military forces after Mr. Lodge had authorized C.I.A. participation in tactical planning of the coup.

So intimately tied to the conspiracy did the Ambassador himself become that he offered refuge to the families of the generals if their plot failed—and he obtained Washington's approval. Near the end, he also sent a message to Washington seeking authority to put up the money for bribes to win over officers still loyal to President Diem. [See Document #57.]

159

Highlights of the Period

The Kennedy Administration's "complicity" in the 1963 overthrow of President Ngo Dinh Diem is documented in the Pentagon study, which says that this episode "inadvertently deepened" United States involvement in the Vietnam conflict.

Here, in chronological order, are highlights of this period:

MAY-JUNE, 1963

Buddhist protests against Diem Government flare into violence after Government troops attack demonstrators in Hue. Crisis worsens as confrontations become focus for widespread political disaffection with Diem's regime and Ngo Dinh Nhu, his brother.

AUGUST, 1963

Saigon regime, violating pledge to U.S. that it will seek to conciliate Buddhists, stages midnight raids on Buddhist pagodas. Many arrests and beatings.

First request for U.S. support of coup plot made to C.I.A. agent.

George W. Ball, Acting Secretary of State, tells Henry Cabot Lodge, new U.S. Ambassador, that Diem must "remove" Nhus or "we can no longer support Diem." Says "appropriate military commanders" can be pledged "direct support in any interim period of breakdown central government mechanism." Authorizes Ambassador to threaten aid cut-off unless jailed Buddhists are released.

Lodge replies chances of "Diem's meeting our demands are virtually nil." Says "by making them, we give Nhu chance to forestall" coup. Suggests "we go straight to generals with our demands."

C.I.A. agents make contact with two plotters.

Col. Lucien Conein, a top C.I.A. agent, meets with Lieut Gen. Duong Van Minh, plot leader. Minh asks U.S. to suspend economic aid to Diem regime as signal of support. It is indicated that C.I.A. gave plotters sensitive information about loyalist forces.

Lodge, replying to query from President Kennedy, says "U.S. prestige" is publicly committed; "there is no turning back. . . ."

National Security Council meeting "reaffirmed basic course." U.S. "will support a coup which has a good chance of succeeding." Gen. Paul D. Harkins, U.S. military commander, Saigon, told to state "he is prepared to establish liaison" with plotters. Lodge authorized to "announce suspension of aid" at will.

Private Kennedy message to Lodge pledges "everything possible to help you conclude this operation successfully," but asks continuing reports to allow possible "reverse" signal. Says "we must go to win, but it will be better to change our minds than fail."

Ambassador reports breakdown in conspiracy.

National Security Council meets. Paul M. Kattenburg, head of Vietnam Interdepartmental Working Group, urges U.S. disengagement. Secretary of State Dean Rusk says U.S. will not pull out "until the war is won," and "will not run a coup."

OCTOBER, 1963

Robert S. McNamara, Secretary of Defense, and Gen. Maxwell D. Taylor, Chairman of Joint Chiefs, propose after Diem meeting that U.S. "work with the Diem regime but not support it." Urge economic pressure.

Conein, and other C.I.A. agents renew contact with Minh and other plotters. Lodge urges assurances U.S. will not "thwart" coup.

President accepts McNamara-Taylor proposals, series of economic cut-offs. Study says this "leaves ambiguous" question whether aid suspension is meant as "green light for coup."

Aid cut-offs start.

White House messages to Ambassador stress "surveillance and readiness," not "active promotion" of coup. Study says they stress desire for "plausibility of denial" of U.S. involvement.

Coup canceled. Leader cites Harkins's attitude as reason. Harkins denies "trying to thwart" coup but "would not discuss coups that were not my business."

Doubts about coup revived in Washington, study says. White House wants "option of judging and warning on any plan with poor prospects of success."

Lodge opposes any move to "pour cold water" on plot.

Lodge and Diem have "fruitless, frustrating" meeting. Ambassador says Diem "gave me a blank look and changed the subject" when asked for "some one thing" to "favorably impress" U.S. opinion.

White House tells Lodge to "discourage" plot if quick success is unlikely. Lodge replies U.S. is unable to "delay or discourage a coup."

NOVEMBER

Coup proceeds on schedule. Diem, on telephone with Lodge, asks "attitude of the U.S." Lodge replies he is not "well enough informed" to say, tells him: "If I can do anything for your personal safety, please call me."

Pentagon study says Diem finally accepts Generals' offer of safe-conduct out of country; he and brother are shot to death by armored units.

The fear of failure—fed by bitterly conflicting advice from Ambassador Lodge and Gen. Paul D. Harkins, chief of the American Military Assistance Command in Saigon—dogged President Kennedy to the end.

In late August, with a coup by the generals expected any hour, President Kennedy sent a private message to Ambassador Lodge. Possibly thinking back to the collapse of the Bay of Pigs invasion of Cuba he said: "I know from experience that failure is more destructive than an appearance of indecision. . . . When we go, we must go to win, but it will be better to change our minds than fail."

In his Aug. 30 cablegram, obtained by The New York Times along with the Pentagon study, the President also pledged "We will do all that we can to help you conclude this operation successfully."

On Oct. 30, after the plot had been postponed and later revived, the White House cabled Mr. Lodge with instructions to delay further any coup that did not have "a high prospect of success." But it left the ultimate judgment up to the Ambassador and asserted that once a coup "under responsible leadership" had begun, "it is in the interest of the U.S. Government that it should succeed." [See Document #56.]

The conclusions of the Pentagon study run contrary to the denial of American involvement by Ambassador Lodge in a press interview on June 29, 1964, and the impression given by the more carefully worded disavowals of American responsibility published in the memoirs of some Kennedy Administration officials.

"For the military coup d'état against Ngo Dinh Diem, the U.S. must accept its full share of responsibility," the Pentagon account asserts.

"Beginning in August of 1963 we variously authorized, sanctioned and encouraged the coup efforts of the Vietnamese generals and offered full support for a successor government. In October we cut off aid to Diem in a direct rebuff, giving a green light to the generals. We maintained clandestine contact with them throughout the planning and execution of the coup and sought to review their operational plans and proposed new government."

The intrigues of the Vietnamese generals and of Mr. Nhu have largely been recounted before. Two added elements emerge from the Pentagon study: the step-by-step American collusion with the conspiracy, revealed previously only in shadowy outline; and the feud inside the American Government that brought it close to paralysis at decisive moments.

For if the Diem regime was a house divided against itself, so was the Kennedy Administration.

In Saigon, the two chief antagonists were Ambassador Lodge, considered even by admirers an aloof, shrewd Massachusetts Brahmin politician; and General Harkins, an affable, athletic cavalry officer who had been a protégé of the World War II tank commander, Maj. Gen. George S. Patton, 3d.

As the Pentagon study recounts it, the Ambassador quickly became a partisan of the anti-Diem plot, while General Harkins resented what he felt would be shabby treatment of President Diem. "I would suggest we try not to change horses too quickly," the general declared in a cable to Gen. Maxwell D. Taylor, Chairman of the Joint Chiefs of Staff, on Oct. 30, less than 48 hours before the coup. [See Document #54.]

"After all, rightly or wrongly, we have backed Diem for eight long hard years. To me it seems incongruous now to get him down, kick him around and get rid of him. The U.S. has been his mother superior and father confessor since he's been in office and he leaned on us heavily."

The Ambassador and the general clashed at almost every juncture on almost every major issue and their controversy reverberated at the highest levels of government in Washington.

At one point, the study relates, the two men even relayed contradictory messages to the plotters. Subsequently, Ambassador Lodge held such tight control over the conspiratorial maneuvering that General Harkins protested to Washington that he was being kept in the dark.

Ultimately, the Pentagon narrative shows, it was Mr. Lodge—a supremely self-confident ambassador, a former Republican vice-presidential nominee with independent political power, firm in his views, jealous of his ambassadorial prerogatives, intent on asserting his full authority—who exerted critical influence on the Government.

"Political Decay"

Until the eruption of Buddhist demonstrations against the Diem regime in May, 1963, much of the American public was oblivious to the "political decay" in Vietnam described in the Pentagon account: the atmosphere of suspicion, the pervasive but latent disaffection with the autocratic Diem regime, the taint of corruption, the suppressed discontent in the Army.

In America, the early months of 1963 were a season of bullish public pronouncements about the war. In his State of the Union address on Jan. 14, President Kennedy declared that the "spearpoint of aggression has been blunted in Vietnam" while Adm. Harry D. Felt, commander in chief of Pacific forces, predicted victory within three years.

Although this reflected the view prevailing among policy-makers, a national intelligence estimate on April 17 offered a less glowing picture. Provided that outside help to the Vietcong was not increased, the intelligence paper estimated that the guerrillas could be "contained militarily" but added that there was still no persuasive evidence that the enemy had been "grievously hurt" by the allied war efforts. Conclusion: "The situation remains fragile."

Moreover, as the Pentagon account recalls, military officers had twice tried to kill President Diem—in November, 1960, and again in February, 1962. Deeply distrustful of the army, the South Vietnamese President had placed loyal favorites in sensitive posts commanding troops around Saigon, established a trusted network of military chiefs in all provinces and stripped potential challengers and malcontents of troop commands.

Over the years, secret intelligence reports had told of the corrosive effect of such methods on military morale. Periodically, they also described the gulf between the mandarin ruler and the apathetic peasantry, or the alienation of an urban middle class resentful of overbearing political controls and of its lack of real political voice.

At times even Washington felt exasperated with its chosen ally for failing to strive for greater popular allegiance through political, military and economic reforms. But the United States had become accustomed to having President Diem reject its advice and, early in 1963, found itself somewhat on the defensive before his complaint that there were too many prying Americans roaming his land.

"As the U.S. commitment and involvement deepened," the Pentagon chronicle relates, "frictions between American advisers and Vietnamese counterparts at all levels increased. Diem, under the influence of Nhu, complained about the quantity and zeal of U.S. advisers. They were creating a colonial impression among the people, he said."

Despite such frictions, the Kennedy Administration was content to continue the general policy that, the Pentagon analyst observes, was aptly captured in a journalistic aphorism: "Sink or swim with Ngo Dinh Diem."

As the Pentagon study recounts the 1963 political crisis, the spark of revolt was struck in the central Vietnamese city of Hue on May 8, when Government troops fired into a crowd of Buddhists displaying religious banners in defiance of a Government decree. Nine persons were killed and 14 injured, when they were crushed by armored vehicles.

The regime blamed a Vietcong provocateur. The Buddhists demanded that the Government admit it was the guilty party and pay indemnities to families of the victims. President Diem refused and, despite superficial compromises, the deadlock was never broken. The two sides slid into a series of increasingly violent confrontations.

The Buddhist protests—mass demonstrations and the immolations of yellow-robed monks—were met by police truncheons and growing arrests. Mrs. Nhu, the bachelor President's outspoken sister-in-law, angered the opposition by ridiculing the fiery Buddhist suicides as "barbecues." There was an outcry of shock abroad, especially in America, which brought the Kennedy Administration under strong public criticism for the United States' policy of backing President Diem.

The original May incident was hardly enough to shake the foundations of power. The Pentagon account blames the regime's mandarin rigidity for fueling the crisis. The Buddhist protests became a lightning rod for accumulated political frustrations. For the first time, the protests exposed the American public to the depth of Vietnamese disaffection with the Government.

By early July C.I.A. agents were tipped off to two rapidly developing coup plots. And a special national intelligence estimate on July 10 forecast that unless President Diem satisfied the Buddhists, "disorders will probably flare again and the chances of a coup or assassination attempts against him will become better than ever." [See Document #34.]

The very next day, Mr. Nhu daringly faced down some senior generals and the plotting subsided temporarily.

Throughout May and June the United States Embassy tried to prod President Diem into meeting Buddhist demands by alternately soft and hard tactics. Ambassador Frederick E. Nolting, a soft-spoken Virginian who, the Pentagon narrative notes, considered it his duty to get along with President Diem, tried gentle persuasion. When he left on vacation, his deputy, William C. Trueheart, took a tougher line, warning Mr. Diem on June 12 that unless the Buddhist crisis was solved, the United States would be forced to dissociate itself from him.

Cutting short his vacation, Ambassador Nolting rushed to Washington early in July to urge the Administration not to abandon President Diem yet, arguing that his overthrow would plunge Vietnam into religious civil war. Although President Kennedy had already decided to send Mr. Lodge to Saigon as Ambassador late in August, he granted Mr. Nolting a last chance to try to talk President Diem into conciliating the Buddhists.

The Pentagon study relates that on Aug. 14, the eve of his departure, Ambassador Nolting extracted such a promise. As a final gesture to the departing American envoy, President Diem gave a press interview on Aug. 15 saying that conciliation had always been his policy toward the Buddhists and, contradicting Mrs. Nhu's earlier criticism, asserted that his family was pleased with the Lodge appointment.

Shock for Washington

Six days later the dam broke. South Vietnamese Special Forces troops in white helmets carried out midnight raids against Buddhist pagodas throughout the country. More than 1,400 people, mostly monks, were arrested and many of them beaten. Two days later, the army generals conspiring against President Diem first sought official American support.

The pagoda raids stunned Washington.

"In their brutality and their blunt repudiation of Diem's solemn word to Nolting, they were a direct, impudent slap in the face for the U.S.," the narrative asserts. "For better or worse, the Aug. 21 pagoda raids decided the issue for us."

American officials found them particularly galling because the raiding parties were led by Vietnamese Special Forces, which were largely financed by the C.I.A. for covert war operations, but which had in effect become the private army of Mr. Nhu.

The Pentagon account describes how Mr. Nhu had telephone lines to the United States Embassy cut to keep American officials ignorant and how he fooled them into believing the army had carried out the crackdown.

Because the army had declared martial law the day before and because some of those raiding parties wore borrowed paratroop uniforms, the embassy initially put the blame on Saigon's army in reporting to Washington.

Actually, the study explains, Mr. Nhu had bypassed the regular army chain of command and had ordered the raids personally. This version does not make it clear whether President Diem had approved in advance or merely accepted after the fact.

Both in Washington and Saigon, the United States denounced the raids and dissociated itself from such repressive policies. Mr. Lodge, in Honolulu for final briefings, was told to fly at once to Saigon where he landed on the morning of Aug. 22. Significantly, the next section of the Pentagon narrative is entitled "Lodge vs. Diem."

What the study terms the "first requests for support" came from the acting chief of staff of the armed forces, Maj. Gen. Tran Van Don, a French-trained Vietnamese aristocrat, and one of his deputies, Maj. Gen. Le Van Kim, reputed to be the real brains behind the coup. Despite their high positions, neither general had direct command over troops because Mr. Nhu had become suspicious of them.

Drawing on a C.I.A. information report, the study recounts that on Aug. 23, General Don told an American agent that the Voice of America should retract its broadcasts blaming the army for the pagoda raids and put out an accurate version in order to help the army. It was time, he said, for the United States to make its position known on internal Vietnamese affairs.

General Kim was more explicit. The pagoda raids, he told another agent, showed the lengths to which Mr. Nhu would go, and a firm American stand now in favor of his removal would unify the army and permit it to take action against both Mr. Nhu and his wife.

Significantly, the embassy reported that high civilian officials were also telling American diplomats that the Nhus' removal was vital. Nguyen Dinh Thuan, President Diem's Defense Minister, gave the blunt advice that "under no circumstances should the United States acquiesce in what the Nhus had done." Foreign Minister Vu Van Mau resigned and shaved his head like a Buddhist monk in protest.

Less than 48 hours after his arrival in Saigon, Ambassador Lodge cabled the State Department to report the coup feelers but cautioned that the most pivotal commanders around Saigon were still loyal to the Ngo brothers. Other officers' loyalties were unknown. Those circumstances, Mr. Lodge reckoned, would make American support of a coup d'état a "shot in the dark."

His message reached Washington Saturday morning, Aug. 24, setting off what became one of the most controversial actions in the Kennedy Administration. The State Department, over the signature of Acting Secretary George W. Ball, sent Ambassador Lodge a reply that served as the initial American sanction for the coup.

It began by saying that the United States could not tolerate the powerful role of Mr. Nhu and his wife any longer. The key passage went on to declare in the stuttering language of cables:

"We wish give Diem reasonable opportunity to remove Nhus, but if he remains obdurate, then we are prepared to accept the obvious implication that we can no longer support Diem. You may also tell appropriate military commanders we will give them direct support in any interim period of breakdown central government mechanism." [See Document #35.]

Moreover, the message gave Ambassador Lodge broad leeway on how to proceed, and pledged to "back you to the hilt on actions you take to achieve our objectives."

This crucial message also cleared the way for public retractions of the earlier Voice of America broadcasts and instructed Mr. Lodge to pass the word that Washington could not provide further military and economic support to South Vietnam unless "prompt dramatic actions" were taken to release the jailed Buddhists and fulfill their demands.

The Pentagon study, drawing upon Roger Hilsman's book "To Move a Nation," published in 1964, explains that the controversial message was drafted by Mr. Hilsman, Assistant Secretary of State; W. Averell Harriman, Under Secretary of State for Political Affairs; Michael V. Forrestal, White House specialist on Vietnam and Southeast Asia, and Mr. Ball. The prime movers were said to be Mr. Hilsman and Mr. Harriman.

The necessary top-level approval of the cablegram was complicated by the fact that President Kennedy was in Hyannisport, Mass., for the weekend, Secretary of State Dean Rusk was in New York and Secretary of Defense Robert S. McNamara and John A. McCone, Director of Central Intelligence, were on vacation.

According to the Hilsman account, both the President and Mr. Rusk were furnished early drafts of the cable and, through several telephone conversations, participated in revising the message before it was sent. Roswell L. Gilpatric,

Acting Secretary of Defense, approved it for the civilian side of the Pentagon. Gen. Maxwell D. Taylor, Chairman of the Joint Chiefs of Staff, was given a belated check by telephone while out to dinner and, upon being told the President had approved the message, accepted on behalf of the military.

The Pentagon study reports that on Monday, when all the principal officers of government returned to Washington, several, especially General Taylor, had second thoughts. But by then it was too late.

In Saigon, the State Department's message had set a new chain of events in motion. The cablegram arrived in Saigon at midday Sunday, Aug. 25, and according to the Pentagon account, Ambassador Lodge immediately summoned General Harkins and John H. Richardson, the C.I.A. station chief. After their strategy session, Mr. Lodge urgently cabled the State Department, proposing a change in tactics:

"Believe that chances of Diem's meeting our demands are virtually nil. At same time, by making them we give Nhu chance to forestall or block action by military. Risk, we believe, is not worth taking, with Nhu in control combat forces Saigon.

"Therefore, propose we go straight to generals with our demands, without informing Diem. Would tell them we prepared have Diem without Nhus but it is in effect up to them whether we keep him. Would insist generals take steps to release Buddhist leaders and carry out June 16 agreement. Request immediate modification instructions." [See Document #36.]

The Ambassador said that General Harkins concurred, and a separate report from Mr. Richardson to C.I.A. headquarters fully endorsed Mr. Lodge's approach.

The immediate reply, obtained by The New York Times though not cited in the Pentagon narrative, was from Mr. Hilsman and Mr. Ball: "Agree to modification proposed."

It is not known whether this was cleared with President Kennedy and other senior officials, but under normal bureaucratic practice Mr. Hilsman would have initiated it.

When that cable reached Saigon, the Pentagon account reports, Mr. Lodge called another strategy session Monday morning. His inner circle decided that the "American official hand should not show," meaning that General Harkins would not talk to the generals. The contact men would be Colonel Conein, an old acquaintance of several of the generals, and another C.I.A. officer; the second agent's contacts petered out eventually.

The C.I.A. men were not only to tell the generals the gist of Washington's Aug. 24 message but also, as Mr. Richardson advised headquarters on Aug. 26, to convey the following message: "We cannot be of any help during initial action of assuming power of the state. Entirely their own action, win or lose. Don't expect to be bailed out." The plotters, moreover, were to be informed that the United States "hoped bloodshed can be avoided or reduced to absolute minimum." [See Document #37.]

In Washington on that same Monday, President Kennedy, informed of the misgivings of General Taylor and others, called together the National Security Council.

The Pentagon study, with very limited direct access to written records of Council meetings and none for these crucial days, accepts the Hilsman book's recollection that the principal doubters were Secretary McNamara, Mr. McCone and General Taylor, opposed by the senior State Department officials.

The Council met again on Tuesday. The Hilsman book reports that at that session Mr. Nolting, the former Ambassador, was doubtful that President Diem could be separated from his brother, as the Pentagon leaders proposed, but he also spoke with prophetic doubt about the capacity of the generals to lead the country.

The upshot, the Pentagon study continues, was that Saigon was asked on Aug. 27 to give more details about the plot and to assess the effect of delaying the coup.

This opened the breach between Ambassador Lodge and General Harkins, in turn worsening the rift in Washington.

The documentary record indicates that Washington's message reached Saigon after the two C.I.A. agents had made separate contacts with two additional members of the army cabal to convey the American position. Significantly, they learned that the plot leader was Lieut. Gen. Duong Van Minh, military adviser to the Presidency, a good combat commander and the general with the strongest following among the officer corps.

His supporters included not only Generals Don and Kim but also Maj. Gen. Tran Thien Khiem, executive officer of the Joint General Staff; Maj. Gen. Nguyen Khanh, commander of the II Corps region stretching northward from Saigon, and Col. Nguyen Van Thieu, commander of the Fifth Division just north of the capital. But Saigon itself and the Mekong Delta to the south were in the hands of supporters of President Diem.

From this balance of force, the Pentagon study recounts, Ambassador Lodge sized up the coup's prospects favorably, arguing that "chances of success would be diminished by delay."

General Harkins sent a separate message that he saw no clear-cut advantage for the coup plotters and no reason for "crash approval" of the plot. He doubted that the coup would be launched until the United States gave the word. His cablegram pledged full support to the Ambassador in carrying out the earlier instructions but, the analyst notes, it cryptically implied that his earlier concurrence had "been volunteered," evidently meaning that Mr. Lodge had overstated his views. But the incident is left unexplained.

A third message from Mr. Richardson, the C.I.A. chief, backed Ambassador Lodge. "Situation here has reached point of no return," he told the agency's headquarters. "Saigon is armed camp. Current indications are the Ngo family have dug in for last ditch battle. . . . There may be widespread fighting in Saigon and serious loss of life." [See Document #38.]

But Mr. Richardson warned that even if the Ngo brothers prevailed, "They and Vietnam will stagger on to final defeat at the hands of their own people and the VC."

Meanwhile, the Vietnamese generals, accustomed over the years to being warned by Americans not to engage in conspiracies against their own government, were having their own worries about the Americans.

On Aug. 29, the Pentagon study says, General Minh himself met Colonel Conein and asked for clear evidence that the United States would not betray the conspiracy to Mr. Nhu. As a clear sign of American support, he asked that Washington suspend economic aid to the Diem regime.

A second general made another check with the result that, according to the Pentagon study, the Ambassador authorized the C.I.A. to "assist in tactical planning" of the coup d'état. A subsequent C.I.A. message, on Oct. 5, discloses that in August the American agents provided the coup organizers with sensitive information including a detailed plan and an armaments inventory for Camp Longthanh, a secret installation of the loyalist Special Forces commanded by Col. Le Quang Tung.

The Americans in Saigon were well ahead of the policy makers in Washington. The top-level debate there, the Pentagon study relates, had become so heated and testy that President Kennedy personally cabled Ambassador Lodge and

General Harkins asking each man again for his "independent judgment."

The Ambassador's reply to the President was an ardent case for the coup:

"We are launched on a course from which there is no respectable turning back: the overthrow of the Diem Government. There is no turning back in part because U.S. prestige is already publicly committed to this end in large measure and will become more so as facts leak out. In a more fundamental sense, there is no turning back because there is no possibility, in my view, that the war can be won under a Diem administration. . . ." [See Document #39.]

Rejecting the idea of seeing President Diem, Mr. Lodge suggested instead that General Harkins be authorized personally to repeat earlier C.I.A. messages to the generals to ease their doubts. If that proved inadequate, the Ambassador wanted to suspend American aid as General Minh had requested.

The study recounts that General Harkins, for his part, stuck to his position that there was still time, without endangering the plotters, for a final approach to President Diem with an ultimatum to drop Mr. Nhu.

With tension high in both Saigon and Washington, the National Security Council held a climactic meeting on Aug. 29. A State Department message to Saigon that night indicated that President Kennedy leaned more on Ambassador Lodge's advice than on General Harkins's. [See Document #40.]

The N.S.C., the cablegram said, had "reaffirmed basic course" and, specifically authorized General Harkins to repeat earlier C.I.A. messages to the plotters. It told him to stress American support for the move "to eliminate the Nhus from the government" but it did not mention President Diem one way or the other.

Nonetheless, it reflected the prevailing acceptance of Ambassador Lodge's view that there was no turning back. "The U.S.G. will support a coup which has good chance of succeeding but plans no direct involvement of U.S. armed forces," it said. "Harkins should state that he is prepared to establish liaison with the coup planners and to review their plans, but will not engage directly in joint coup planning."

Moreover, the message authorized Mr. Lodge "to announce suspension of aid" to the Diem regime whenever and however he chose. But with an eye to the Administration's public image, it cautioned him to "manage" such an announcement

172

so as to "minimize appearance of collusion" with the generals.

The State Department cablegram explained that the question of a "last approach" to President Diem—advocated by General Harkins—"remains undecided." Secretary Rusk, possibly reflecting some personal doubts, raised this issue in a separate message to Mr. Lodge. But the Ambassador rejected the idea out of hand.

At this point Mr. Kennedy sent his totally private message to Ambassador Lodge. The President said he had given his "full support" to the earlier message and promised that Washington would do everything possible "to help you conclude this operation successfully."

He asked the Ambassador to provide him with a running assessment of the coup's prospects right up to the "go signal" to permit him to "reverse previous instructions," if necessary.

The Ambassador's brief reply, on Aug. 30, acknowledged the President's right to change directions but warned him that, since "the operation" had to be Vietnamese-run, the American President might not be able to control it.

As matters turned out, Washington's agonizing had been to no avail. For, according to the study, General Harkins's first direct contact with the conspirators brought news that General Minh had called off the coup for the time being, fearing a bloody standoff in Saigon.

According to the Pentagon account, General Harkins was also told that Mr. Richardson's careful cultivation of Mr. Nhu had aroused suspicions among the generals that the C.I.A. chief might be undercutting them and that the President's brother was on the C.I.A. payroll. Later this would become an important issue and would lead to Mr. Richardson's replacement.

But on Aug. 31, Ambassador Lodge reported to Washington the collapse of the conspiracy and the end of the coup phase. He told Secretary Rusk—who had worried in a cable only the day before about the lack of "bone and muscle" among the conspirators—that there was "neither the will nor the organization among the generals to accomplish anything."

Mr. Lodge also reported hearing that Mr. Nhu was secretly dealing with Hanoi and the Vietcong through the French and Polish ambassadors, both of whose governments favored a neutralist solution between North and South Vietnam.

Washington was in a quandary. It had finally taken the risk of seeking an alternative to the Diem regime only to see the attempt dissolve. As the Pentagon narrative says: "The

173

U.S. found itself at the end of August, 1963, without a policy and with most of its bridges burned."

The members of the National Security Council—minus the President—held a "where do we go from here?" meeting on Aug. 31. That session was revealing, the author comments, because of the "rambling inability to focus on the problem"— the sense of an administration adrift.

The most controversial position was advanced by Paul M. Kattenburg, a 39-year-old diplomat who headed the Vietnam Interdepartmental Working Group. He proposed disengagement—thereby, according to the Pentagon version, becoming the first official on record in a high-level Vietnam policy meeting to pursue to its logical conclusion the analysis that the war effort was irretrievable, either with or without President Diem.

Until he spoke, the trend of the discussion seemed to favor reluctantly sliding back toward some workable relationship with the Diem regime since there seemed no alternative. Secretary Rusk commented that it was "unrealistic" to insist that Mr. Nhu "must go" and Secretary McNamara pushed for reopening high-level contact with the Presidential Palace. [See Document #44.]

In rebuttal, Assistant Secretary of State Hilsman reminded the group of the crippling malaise within the Vietnamese Government and the impact on the American image and policy elsewhere if Washington acquiesced "to a strong Nhu-dominated government."

According to the minutes of the meeting, Mr. Kattenburg pushed this argument a step further by asserting that if the United States tried to "live with" the Diem regime, it would be "thrown out of the country in six months." In the next six months to a year, he argued the war effort would go steadily downhill to the point where the Vietnamese people "will gradually go to the other side and we will be obliged to leave."

His analysis was immediately dismissed by Vice President Johnson, Secretary Rusk and Secretary McNamara. Mr. Rusk was reported in the minutes as insisting that American policy be based on two points—"than we will not pull out of Vietnam until the war is won, and that we will not run a coup." Mr. McNamara endorsed this view.

Vice President Johnson said he agreed completely, reportedly declaring that "we should stop playing cops and robbers and get back to talking straight to the [Saigon Government] . . . and once again go about winning the war."

It was more easily said than done. As the Pentagon study recounts, the Kennedy Administration passed through the next five weeks without any real policy but with three general notions in mind: first, the compulsion to send special missions to reassess the situation in Vietnam; second, the attempt to coerce the Diem regime into moderation through economic and propaganda pressures; and third, Ambassador Lodge's efforts to persuade the Nhus to leave the country while giving the cold shoulder to President Diem.

President Kennedy, in a television interview Sept. 2, applied his personal pressure on the Diem regime for the first time. The South Vietnamese Government, he said, would have to "take steps to bring back popular support" after the Buddhist repressions, otherwise the war could not be won. Success was possible, he said "with changes in policy and perhaps with personnel." But he did not specify whom he meant.

At another inconclusive National Security Council meeting four days later, Attorney General Robert F. Kennedy returned to the question of disengagement. The Pentagon account reports him as reasoning that if the war was unwinnable by any foreseeable South Vietnamese regime, it was time to get out of Vietnam. But, if the Diem regime was the obstacle, he contended, then Ambassador Lodge should be given the power to bring about the necessary changes.

But the Administration's immediate response to its dilemma was—at Secretary McNamara's suggestion—to send a fact-finding mission to Vietnam for a fresh look: Maj. Gen. Victor H. Krulak, the Pentagon's top-ranking expert in counterguerrilla warfare, and Joseph A. Mendenhall, the former political counselor in the Saigon Embassy.

The two men came back after an exhausting four-day tour with such diametrically opposed assessments that President Kennedy was moved to ask, "You two did visit the same country, didn't you?"

Dissatisfied, President Kennedy dispatched Secretary McNamara and General Taylor on a new fact-finding mission on Sept. 23. They met with President Diem on Sept. 29 and although Mr. McNamara had the authority to press the South Vietnamese ruler to remove his brother from power, he did not raise the issue. No explanation is given for this significant omission.

The Pentagon analyst comments that the report of their mission, submitted on Oct. 2, tried to bridge the Lodge-Harkins gap, and in the process reflected for the first time serious doubts in Mr. McNamara's mind.

The military assessment—which the Secretary of Defense radically revised in retrospect after the successful Nov. 1 coup—was generally optimistic. It reported "great progress" in the last year with no ill effects on the conduct of the war from the prolonged political crisis, and asserted that the "bulk" of American troops could be withdrawn by the end of 1965. The two men proposed and—with the President's approval—announced that 1,000 Americans would be pulled out by the end of 1963. [See Document #47.]

Their political analysis found discontent with the Diem-Nhu regime a "seething problem" that could boil over at any time. Unaware of the revived plotting, they discounted prospects for an early coup on grounds that the generals appeared to have "little stomach" for it and proposed that in the meantime, "we should work with the Diem regime but not support it." The study notes that they recommended a series of economic pressures, including an aid cutoff, without indicating whether they remembered that this was the "go" signal that the generals had previously requested.

The Kennedy Administration was already engaged in a pressure campaign that, whatever its intent, was bound to encourage the army generals to try again, as the narrative notes.

The President's televised remark on the need for possible changes in personnel was the first shot. Next, on Sept. 14, Washington informed the embassy that it was deferring decisions on an $18.5-million program to finance commercial imports to South Vietnam. Three days later the White House instructed Ambassador Lodge to make new efforts to achieve a "visible reduction" in the influence of the Nhus—preferably by arranging their departure from Vietnam "at least for an extended vacation." [See Document #45.]

It gave him broad authority to use aid as leverage in this venture, "bearing in mind that it is not our current policy to cut off aid entirely." In particular, it was suggested, Mr. Lodge might want to limit or reroute aid now going "to or through Nhu" or his collaborators. It also urged him—without ordering him—to resume contact with President Diem. But Mr. Lodge demurred.

Washington's high-level messages to the Ambassador throughout the fall of 1963 are notable for the unusual-deference they show him. President Kennedy himself proceeded with delicacy on those rare occasions when he overruled the Ambassador. Once, in a personal cablegram to Mr. Lodge in mid-September, he commented that, as the son of a former Ambassador, "I am well trained in the importance of protecting the effectiveness of the man-on-the-spot." The record shows that the President understood, too, how firm and explicit he had to be to overrule the Ambassador—and, significantly, he did not do so in the final days before the coup.

Death Knell for Diem

In October, the tempo of events quickened. In Saigon on Oct. 2, the analyst writes, Colonel Conein "accidentally" ran into General Don, who proposed a date that evening in Nhatrang. That night, the C.I.A. man learned that the conspiracy was on the track again and that General Minh, its leader, wanted to discuss the details. Ambassador Lodge approved the meeting.

Oct. 5 was a fateful day both in Saigon and in Washington. For the first time in weeks, another Buddhist monk burned himself to death in the central marketplace in Saigon. Mr. Richardson, the C.I.A. chief whose links to Mr. Nhu had aroused suspicions among the Army generals, left South Vietnam after what are described as behind-the-scenes efforts by Ambassador Lodge to have him transferred. And President Kennedy took far-reaching decisions to apply major economic sanctions against the Diem regime.

At 8:30 A.M. that same day Colonel Conein went to General Minh's headquarters for a 70-minute meeting. According to the C.I.A. account of the meeting, the two men talked in French. The South Vietnamese general, nicknamed Big Minh by his colleagues because of his burly build, disclaimed any personal political ambition.

But he said that the army commanders felt the war would be lost unless the government was changed soon and that he "must know" the American Government's position on a change of regime "within the very near future." The general said he did not expect "any specific American support" for the coup d'état but did need assurances that the Americans would not block it. He did not press for an on-the-spot commitment, but asked for another date with Colonel Conein.

General Minh outlined several possible tactics. The two main ones called for retaining President Diem but assassinating his two powerful and feared brothers Mr. Nhu and Ngo Dinh Can, the regime's proconsul in Central Vietnam; or, a head-on military battle for control of Saigon and the government against roughly 5,500 loyalist troops in the capital.

Because of the abortive plot in August, Ambassador Lodge reacted warily. In a special message to Secretary Rusk, he commented that neither he nor General Harkins had "great faith in Big Minh." [See Document #49.] Nonetheless, he recommended giving the generals assurance that the United States would not "thwart" their coup, that it would review their plans—"other than assassination plans"—and that it would continue aid to any future government that gave promise of gaining popular support and winning the war. He said General Harkins concurred in these recommendations.

In Washington, too, events were gaining momentum. On Oct. 2, President Kennedy had received the recommendations of the McNamara-Taylor mission (drafted before the new Saigon contacts) urging tight new pressures on the regime in the hopes of gaining some reforms and simultaneously advocating covert contacts with "possible alternative leadership" without actively promoting a coup.

The President accepted all the report's proposals. According to the Pentagon account, he specifically authorized suspension of economic subsidies for South Vietnam's commercial imports, a freeze on loans to enable Saigon to build a waterworks and an electric-power plant for the capital region, and, significantly, a cut-off of financial support for the Vietnamese Special Forces—controlled by Mr. Nhu—unless they were put under the Joint General Staff, headed by the plotting generals.

There were to be no public announcements, and the various steps were to be unrolled consecutively at Mr. Lodge's discretion. But in a city as keyed-up and alert to every nuance in American policy as Saigon, the Pentagon study notes, these steps were bound to be read in many quarters as the death knell for the Diem regime. Only a month before, he recalls, the cut-offs had been discussed—and approved—as a signal of American support to the generals, if necessary.

The analyst comments that the documentary record in early October "leaves ambiguous" whether the White House intended the aid suspensions to be a "green light" for the coup. But he says that they were interpreted that way by the generals. The Diem regime reacted furiously. Its press outlets publicized the freeze on import subsidies on Oct. 7 and accused Washington of sabotaging the war effort.

In a White House message—sent on Oct. 5 through C.I.A. channels for tight security within the American Government—

Washington gave Ambassador Lodge careful coaching. It instructed him that "no initiative should now be taken to give any active covert encouragement to a coup." But he was to organize an "urgent covert effort . . . to identify and build up contacts with possible alternative leadership as and when it appears." [See Document #50.]

The Washington message emphasized that the objectives should be "surveillance and readiness" rather than "active promotion of a coup." It told Mr. Lodge that "you alone" should manage the operation, through the C.I.A. chief in Saigon.

These instructions were transmitted before Washington had received the report of the Minh-Conein contact, the Pentagon study observes. For, on the very next day, with time to digest that report, Washington took a considerably more flexible approach.

The C.I.A. relayed new White House instructions on Oct. 6. In a passage that Ambassador Lodge interpreted as signaling a desire for a change of regime—though General Harkins later disputed him vigorously on this point—Washington said that while it did not wish to "stimulate" a coup, it also did not want "to leave the impression that the U.S. would thwart a change of government." Nor would it withhold aid from a new regime. [See Document #51.]

In view of General Minh's modest request for American acquiescence, the generals could interpret this as a go ahead.

The Oct. 6 message also ordered the C.I.A. man to obtain "detailed information" to help Washington assess the plot's chances. Yet it cautioned against "being drawn into reviewing or advising on operational plans or other actions" that might eventually "tend to identify U.S. too closely" with a coup. In the language of the Oct. 5 cable, Washington wanted to preserve "plausibility of denial."

The new American position was conveyed to General Minh by his C.I.A. contact about Oct. 10.

On Oct. 18, with the cut-off of commercial import subsidies already causing financial scares in Saigon, the Pentagon study reports that General Harkins informed President Diem that American funds were being cut off from the Special Forces. The narrative notes that by then, the coup plans were well advanced and the American move against what amounted to a Presidential Palace guard was an obvious spur to the conspirators.

By mid-October the Administration was hearing very disturbing intelligence estimates on the war. On Oct. 19 the

C.I.A. reported that the tempo of Vietcong attacks was rising, Government troops "missing in action" were increasing and other military indicators were "turning sour," as the Pentagon account puts it. In a controversial report on Oct. 22, the State Department's Bureau of Intelligence and Research contested the military optimism of recent months. It concluded that there had been "an unfavorable shift in the military balance" since July and that the Government would have been in trouble even without the Buddhist crisis.

Against this background, the conspiracy in Saigon hit a snag.

The narrative recounts that General Don, in a state of agitation, told Colonel Conein on Oct. 23 that the coup had been scheduled for Oct. 26—and then called off because General Harkins had discouraged it on Oct. 22. General Don's account was that General Harkins complained to him that a Vietnamese colonel had discussed the coup plans with an American officer, asking for support—all without sanction from the senior generals.

General Harkins, he said, had insisted that American officers should not be approached about a coup because it distracted them from the war. He implied that General Harkins might have leaked word of the plot to the palace. He demanded reassurance of American support—and got it from Colonel Conein.

The Pentagon study quotes a message from Ambassador Lodge on Oct. 23 saying that he had talked with General Harkins who said he had misunderstood Washington's policy guidance. The Ambassador quoted the general as saying he hoped he had not upset the delicate arrangements and would tell General Don that his previous remarks did not reflect American policy. That very night, the Pentagon version says, General Harkins saw General Don to retract his earlier statements.

On Oct. 24, however, in a message to General Taylor, the Chairman of the Joint Chiefs, General Harkins disputed Mr. Lodge's version of the events. He denied having violated Washington's policy guidance, saying he had merely rebuffed General Don's suggestion that they meet again to discuss coup plans.

"I told Don that I would not discuss coups that were not my business though I had heard rumors of many," General Harkins told Washington. Insisting that he was "not trying to thwart a change in government," he did, however, voice the prophetic fear that if the Diem regime was toppled, its fall might touch off factional warfare within the army that would eventually "interfere with the war effort."

General Taylor's immediate reply was: "View here is that your actions in disengaging from the coup discussions were correct and that you should continue to avoid any involvement." This evidently reflected Washington's earlier instructions that Mr. Lodge alone should manage the coup contacts through the C.I.A.

The incident once again opened the breach between the Ambassador and the general. It underscored not only their differences in views but also, the Pentagon analyst says, their total lack of coordination.

Moreover, it deepened the Vietnamese generals' suspicion of General Harkins, whom they had always mistrusted because of his closeness to President Diem. Not only did they subsequently refuse to talk to him about the coup out of fear of leaks to the palace, the account says, but they consistently refused to show any Americans their detailed plans despite repeated promises to do so—a point that bedeviled Washington.

Nonetheless, Colonel Conein's reassurances had sufficiently emboldened them that, according to a C.I.A. information report, they passed the word to Ambassador Lodge on Oct. 24 that the coup would occur before Nov. 2. President Diem also chose Oct. 24 finally to break the ice with Mr. Lodge by inviting him to spend Sunday, Oct. 27, with him at the presidential villa in the mountain resort of Dalat.

But in Washington General Harkins's reports had revived doubts about the coup, and it was now Mr. Lodge's turn to be on the defensive.

The Pentagon study recounts that Mr. McCone, the C.I.A. director, and McGeorge Bundy, the President's special assistant for national security, sent out cablegrams expressing worry that General Don might be a double-agent from the Diem-Nhu regime trying to entrap the United States. Mr. Bundy also suggested replacing Colonel Conein as the C.I.A. contact man.

On Oct. 25 Ambassador Lodge tried to put Washington's mind at ease. In a message to Mr. Bundy, he discounted the likelihood that General Don was engaged in a "provocation" and stoutly defended Colonel Conein.

The Ambassador also argued against any temptation to "pour cold water" on the plot. While he acknowledged that struggles among successors of the Diem regime could damage the war effort, he contended that it was "at least an even bet that the next government would not bungle and stumble as much as the present one has." [See Document #52.]

The White House reply, on Oct. 25, endorsed his view that the United States "should not be in position of thwarting coup" but urged him to give the White House "the option of judging and warning on any plan with poor prospects of success." [See Document #53.]

It indicated that President Kennedy's main worries, as in August, were failure and the appearance of complicity. "We are particularly concerned," the White House cablegram said, "about hazard that an unsuccessful coup, however carefully we avoid direct engagement, will be laid at our door by public opinion almost everywhere."

What neither the Ambassador nor the White House knew, the Pentagon narratives notes, was that the coup plotters were even then manipulating the balance of military forces around Saigon in their favor, double-dealing with Mr. Nhu and outwitting him.

The pivotal figure was Maj. Gen. Ton That Dinh, the military governor of Saigon and commander of the III Corps—all the regular army troops in the capital region. The Pentagon account describes how General Don played upon General Dinh's vanity to maneuver him into a clash with Mr. Nhu, thereby enlisting his cooperation for the coup plot.

Through another channel, however, Mr. Nhu learned of the conspiracy and, confronting General Dinh with that news, told him to help lay a trap for the other generals. This maneuver called for starting a false coup to lure the anti-Diemists into the open and then using General Dinh's forces to crush the real plot.

The young general informed the other conspirators of Mr. Nhu's counterplot. To be on the safe side, in case he was really loyal to Mr. Nhu, they recruited troop commanders under him.

In Saigon, the atmosphere had become one of impending violence. So intense was the maneuvering, according to the Pentagon study, that it was "virtually impossible to keep track of all the plots against the regime." The United States Embassy in one cable to Washington identified 10 dissident groups in addition to the generals' plot.

Nonetheless President Diem, at his Oct. 27 meeting with Mr. Lodge, seemed unprepared to yield an inch—a "fruitless, frustrating" exchange, according to the Pentagon version.

Paraphrasing the Ambassador's report, the study recounts that President Diem inquired about the suspension of American aid and in reply Mr. Lodge asked about the release of hundreds of arrested Buddhists and student demonstrators, and about reopening schools shut by the regime in fear of further turbulence. President Diem, the analyst says, "offered excuses and complaints."

Finally, Ambassador Lodge said: "Mr. President, every single specific suggestion which I have made, you have rejected. Isn't there some one thing you may think of that is within your capabilities to do and that would favorably impress U.S. opinion?"

The Ambassador reported that President Diem "gave me a blank look and changed the subject."

At Saigon airport the next morning, as President Diem and Mr. Lodge were about to go to a ceremony dedicating a Vietnamese power plant, General Don daringly took the Ambassador aside.

The Pentagon account says General Don "asked [Mr. Lodge] if Conein was authorized to speak for him."

"Lodge assured Don that he was," the account continues. "Don said that the coup must be thoroughly Vietnamese and that the U.S. must not interfere. Lodge agreed, adding that the U.S. wanted no satellites but would not thwart a coup. When Lodge asked about the timing of the coup, Don replied the generals were not yet ready.

Later that day, General Don met with Colonel Conein and urged that Mr. Lodge make no change in his previously announced plans to leave on a trip to Washington on Oct. 31 for fear that postponement might tip off the Presidential Palace. General Don also disclosed that General Dinh, the III Corps commander, had been neutralized, shifting the military balance in the coup's favor.

By Oct. 29, the analyst comments, Ambassador Lodge clearly felt that the United States was "committed" to the coup and that it was too late for second thoughts, and he communicated those views forcefully to Washington.

After reporting the support of prominent leaders, including Vice President Nguyen Ngoc Tho, for the coup, the Ambassador said he felt an attempt was "imminent."

"Whether this coup fails or succeeds," Mr. Lodge said, "the U.S.G. must be prepared to accept the fact that we will be blamed, however unjustifiably; and finally that no positive action by the U.S.G. can prevent a coup attempt—short of informing Diem and Nhu with all the opprobrium that such an action would entail."

With the first Vietnamese troop movements preparatory to

the coup already under way, the Pentagon gave orders to have a naval task force stand off the Vietnamese coast "if events required," as the account puts it. When Mr. Lodge was informed of this, he urged discretion lest the Diem regime be alerted.

Events now had an ineluctable momentum. But, in Washington, the study reports, Secretary McNamara and the Joint Chiefs of Staff were vacillating over the continuing differences between Ambassador Lodge and General Harkins.

They put their anxieties before a National Security Council meeting on Oct. 29, and the White House then instructed Ambassador Lodge to show General Harkins, who had been away in Bangkok briefly, the relevant messages to be sure that he would be fully aware of the coup arrangements. If Mr. Lodge was to go through with his trip home as scheduled, Washington felt that General Harkins—rather than the Ambassador's deputy, as would have been customary—should be in charge of the American mission.

Belatedly apprised of the continuing Don-Conein contacts and the Ambassador's latest recommendations to Washington, General Harkins sent off three angry cables to General Taylor on Oct. 30.

He was "irate," the analyst remarks, not only at having been excluded by Mr. Lodge from information about the coup but also at reading the Ambassador's gloomy assessments of how the war was going, which diametrically opposed his own views. He protested to Washington that the Ambassador was keeping him in the dark.

More important, he declared, in a message cited by the study, there was a "basic" difference between them in interpreting Washington's instructions.

Since receiving the Oct. 5 guidance from the White House, General Harkins said, he had been operating in the belief that the basic American policy line was that "no initiative" should be taken to encourage a coup. But he said Mr. Lodge took the position that the Oct. 6 message—"not to thwart" a coup—modified the policy line and indicated that "a change of government is desired and . . . the only way to bring about such a change is by a coup."

Moreover, General Harkins sought to undermine confidence in the conspiracy by accusing General Don of lying or serving as a double agent. Overlooking his own earlier refusal to talk about the coup, General Harkins told Washington:

"What he [Don] told me is diametrically opposed to what he told Colonel Conein. He told Conein the coup would be before Nov. 2. He told me he was not planning a coup when I sat with Don and Big Minh for two hours during the parade last Saturday. No one mentioned coups." [See Document [#54.]

The Harkins messages shook Washington's confidence severely and the White House conveyed its anxieties to Ambassador Lodge on Oct. 30. It reckoned the military balance of forces as "approximately equal," raising the danger of prolonged fighting or even defeat. If the coup group could not show prospects for quick success, the White House said, "we should discourage them from proceeding since a miscalculation could result in jeopardizing the U.S. position in Southeast Asia." [See Document #56.]

Contrary to Mr. Lodge's position, the White House also felt that a word from the Americans could delay the coup but it refrained from ordering him to halt the conspiracy.

That same night, the documentary record discloses, Mr. Lodge replied, suggesting an even deeper involvement. In answer to Washington's worries, he held to the view that the Americans did not "have the power to delay or discourage a coup." [See Document #57.]

At this late hour, he urged that the United States keep "hands off," not only because he believed "Vietnam's best generals are involved" but also because he shared their expectation that some wavering units would join the coup.

"If we were convinced that the coup was going to fail, we would, of course do everything we could to stop it," he pledged. But that was not his expectation.

Mr. Lodge dismissed the suggestion of opening up a second channel to the generals. Instead, he suggested that the cabal might need "funds at the last moment with which to buy off potential opposition. To the extent that these funds can be passed discreetly, I believe we should furnish them."

The Ambassador took a considerably less apocalyptic view of failure than did Washington. "We will have to pick up the pieces as best we can at that time," he said. "We have a commitment to the generals from the August episode to attempt to help in the evacuation of their dependents. We should try to live up to this if conditions will permit."

He predicted that once the coup was under way, the Diem regime "will request me or General Harkins to use our influence to call it off." His response, he said, would be that "our influence could not be superior to [President Diem's] and if he is unable to call it off, we would certainly be unable to do so."

In the event of a deadlock or some negotiations that required the "removal of key personalities," he suggested Saipan as a good destination because "the absence of press, communications, etc., would allow us some leeway to make further decision as to their ultimate disposition."

And he said that if asked to provide political asylum for senior officials, presumably meaning not only President Diem but such opponents as Vice President Tho, "We would probably have to grant it."

In addition, the Ambassador responded to General Harkins's attacks on his operating methods by objecting vigorously to the Administration's plans to put the general in charge of the American mission if the Ambassador left Saigon. He thought it wrong, he said, to put a military man in control during such a politically charged time.

"This is said impersonally," the Ambassador commented, "since General Harkins is a splended general and an old friend of mine to whom I would gladly entrust anything I have."

His message ended by saying: "General Harkins has read this and does not concur."

The final White House message to Ambassador Lodge, which went out later that night, was stern in tone and refused to accept his contention that the United States was powerless to stop a coup without betraying it to the Diem regime.

"If you should conclude that there is not clearly a high prospect of success," the White House told Mr. Lodge, "you should communicate this doubt to generals in a way calculated to persuade them to desist at least until chances are better." [See Document #58.]

But once again Washington left the matter in Mr. Lodge's hands by allowing him to make the final judgment on the prospects for the coup's success. It asserted, more over, that once a coup was under way, "it is in the interest of the U.S. Government that it should succeed."

The message also set out guidelines for the American mission in the event of a coup—to reject appeals for direct intervention from either side; if necessary, to be ready to play some intermediary role but to maintain strict neutrality without the appearance of pressure on either side; and if the coup failed, to "afford asylum . . . to those to whom there is any expressed or implied obligation" with the hope that they would use other countries' embassies as well.

The White House urged the Ambassador not to feel committed to this scheduled visit home on Oct. 31. But it insisted that if he left and the coup did occur, General Harkins would be put in charge. Mr. Lodge, of course, was forced to cancel his trip to Washington, and the coup was launched on Nov. 1.

That morning the Ambassador called on President Diem with Adm. Harry D. Felt, commander in chief of American forces in the Pacific. At noon, Admiral Felt went to the airport, unaware that the military forces were already gathering for the final assault on the Diem regime.

The coup unrolled like clockwork. At 1:30 P.M., coup forces seized the police headquarters, radio stations, the airport and other installations and began their attacks on the Presidential Palace and the Special Forces barracks.

When loyal officers alerted Mr. Nhu to the first crucial moves, he thought it all part of his devious counterplot with General Dinh and he told the loyal commanders not to intervene. But later, when the attack on the palace began, he tried to call General Dinh to order the counterattack only to be told that the general was unavailable.

Within three hours all resistance had been crushed except at the Presidential Palace, and the generals broadcast demands for the Ngo brothers to resign. President Diem replied by asking them to come to the palace for consultations—a tactic used in 1960 to delay the coup long enough for loyal troops to reach the city. But the generals refused.

Not long afterward, President Diem telephoned Ambassador Lodge to ask where the United States stood. Their conversation was recorded by the Embassy:

DIEM: Some units have made a rebellion, and I want to know what is the attitude of the U.S.

LODGE: I do not feel well enough informed to be able to tell you. I have heard the shooting, but am not acquainted with all the facts. Also it is 4:30 A.M. in Washington and the U.S. Government cannot possibly have a view.

DIEM: But you must have general ideas. After all, I am a chief of state. I have tried to do my duty. I want to do now what duty and good sense require. I believe in duty above all.

LODGE: You have certainly done your duty. As I told you only this morning, I admire your courage and your great contributions to your country. No one can take away from you the credit for all you have done. Now I am worried about your physical safety. I have a report that those in charge of the current activity offer

you and your brother safe conduct out of the country
if you resign. Have you heard this?

LODGE: [sic] DIEM: No. [And then, after a pause] You have my
telephone number.

LODGE: Yes. If I can do anything for your physical safety, please call me.

DIEM: I am trying to re-establish order.

While fighting continued at the palace, President Diem and
his brother escaped through a secret tunnel and hid in Cholon,
the Chinese section of the capital. Shortly after dawn, the
last palace stronghold surrendered.

Throughout the night the Pentagon study recounts, President Diem kept contact by phone with the generals who,
urging him to surrender, offered a guarantee of safe conduct
to the airport to permit him to leave South Vietnam. At 6:20
A.M. the President finally agreed, but did not tell General
Minh his whereabouts.

According to the account, the Ngo brothers were tracked
down by some armored units commanded by a long-time
enemy of the President, and, after their capture, they were
shot to death inside an armored car carrying them to the
Joint General Staff headquarters.

Washington delayed immediate recognition of the new
regime because, the study says, Secretary Rusk felt that a delay
would reduce the appearance of American complicity in the
coup and would make the generals look less like American
stooges. Mr. Rusk also discouraged any large delegations of
generals from calling on Ambassador Lodge as if they were
"reporting in."

The Kennedy Administration is described as shocked and
dismayed by the murders of the two leaders but says it had
been "reluctant to intervene on behalf of Diem and Nhu for
fear of appearing to offer support to them or reneging on our
pledges of noninterference to the generals."

The Americans had also reportedly counted on the coup
committee's offer of safe conduct to the Ngo brothers which,
until the very last moment—when the armored units were
just about to seize them—President Diem had repeatedly
rejected.

New Omens of Peril

In what the analyst calls the first of self-satisfaction, Ambassador Lodge cabled Washington on Nov. 4 predicting that the change of regime would shorten the war against the Vietcong because of the improved morale in the South Vietnamese Army.

But the Pentagon study recounts a number of immediate and disturbing omens. Vietcong activity jumped dramatically immediately after the coup. The fall of the Diem regime, as Mr. Lodge reported, also exposed the inflated South Vietnamese reports of success for the strategic-hamlet program.

Equally significant, when Mr. Lodge first met General Minh, the new chief of state, he reported to Washington that the general seemed "tired and somewhat frazzled" though "obviously a good, well-intentioned man."

"Will he be strong enough to get on top of things?" Mr. Lodge wondered.

It was a prophetic comment, for within three months one of the coup group, Maj. Gen. Nguyen Khanh, seized power for himself, starting a round of intramural power struggles that plagued Washington for the next two years drawing it ever deeper into the Vietnam war in an effort to prop up successive South Vietnamese regimes.

Just before President Kennedy's assassination, his top aides held a Vietnam strategy conference at Honolulu. Within four days of that meeting, President Johnson issued a new Vietnam policy paper to demonstrate that there would be no break from the Kennedy policies.

Particularly in the sphere of covert operations against North Vietnam, which became a prelude to the Tonkin Gulf clashes in 1964, the Pentagon narrative describes a smooth transition in the decision-making process. The Honolulu conference, set up under President Kennedy, ordered planning for a stepped-up program of what the account calls "non-attributable hit-and-run" raids against North Vietnam. In his first Vietnam policy document, on Nov. 26, President Johnson gave his personal sanction to the planning for these operations.

In confident language, President Johnson set an objective in South Vietnam that was to stand unchallenged within the Administration for three and a half years: to assist "the people and Government of that country to win their contest against the externally directed and supported Communist conspiracy." He reaffirmed the goal of concluding the war by the end of 1965. [See Document #60.]

But a harbinger of events was a report to President Johnson from Secretary McNamara—"laden with gloom" as the analyst puts it—a month later.

After a trip to Vietnam, the Secretary of Defense reported on Dec. 21, 1963, that the new regime was "indecisive and drifting."

"Vietcong progress," Mr. McNamara said, in a major shift of his own thinking, "has been great during the period since the coup, with my best guess being that the situation has in fact been deteriorating in the countryside since July to a far greater extent than we realize because of our undue dependence on distorted Vietnamese reporting."

In conclusion, he felt compelled to say: "The situation is very disturbing. Current trends, unless reversed in the next two-three months, would lead to a neutralization at best and more likely to a Communist-controlled state."

His assessment laid the ground work for decisions in early 1964 to step up the covert war against North Vietnam, and increase American aid to the South.

KEY DOCUMENTS

Following are texts of key documents accompanying the Pentagon's study of the Vietnam war, for the period of the 1963 coup d'état against President Ngo Dinh Diem, the events leading up to it and its aftermath. Except where excerpting is specified, the documents are printed verbatim, with only unmistakable typographical errors corrected.

33

Notes on Kennedy Meeting on Diem Regime in July, 1963

Memorandum by Roger Hilsman, Assistant Secretary of State for Far Eastern Affairs, on a meeting held at the White House July 4, 1963. Besides President Kennedy and Mr. Hilsman, participants were Under Secretary of State George Ball; Under Secretary of State Averell Harriman; McGeorge Bundy, Presidential assistant for national security, and Michael V. Forrestal, Southeast Asia specialist on the White House staff.

The President was briefed on developments in Indonesia, Laos and Viet-Nam. The portion on Viet-Nam follows:

A joint agreement was signed on June 16 in which the Government met the Buddhists' five demands. The Buddhists and the Government then worked together on the funeral arrangements for the bonze who burned himself to death so that incidents could be avoided. The funeral came off without trouble.

Since then there have been rumors circulating in Saigon that the Government does not intend to live up to the agreement. These rumors were given credence by an article appearing in the English-language "Times" of Viet-Nam, which is dominated by the Nhus. The article contained a veiled attack on the U.S. and on the Buddhists. There was a suggestion that the monk who burned himself to death was drugged and a provocative challenge to the Buddhists that, if no further demonstrations occurred on July 2, this would amount to an admission by the Buddhists that they were satisfied with the Government's action. (The President injected questions on the possibility of drugging, to which Mr. Hils-

191

man replied that religious fervor was an adequate explanation.)

At this point there was a discussion of the possibility of getting rid of the Nhus in which the combined judgment was that it would not be possible.

Continuing the briefing, Mr. Hilsman said that the Buddhists contained an activist element which undoubtedly favored increasing demands as well as charging the Government with dragging its feet. There was thus an element of truth in Diem's view that the Buddhists might push their demands so far as to make his fall inevitable.

During these events the U.S. had put extremely heavy pressure on Diem to take political actions. Most recently we had urged Diem to make a speech which would include announcements that he intended to meet with Buddhist leaders, permit Buddhist chaplains in the army and so on. If Diem did not make such a speech and there were further demonstrations, the U.S. would be compelled publicly to dissassociate itself from the GVN's Buddhist policy. Mr. Hilsman reported that Diem had received this approach with what seemed to be excessive politeness but had said he would consider making such a speech.

Our estimate was that no matter what Diem did there will be coup attempts over the next four months. Whether or not any of these attempts will be successful is impossible to say.

Mr. Hilsman said that everyone agreed that the chances of chaos in the wake of a coup are considerably less than they were a year ago. An encouraging sign relative to this point is that the war between the Vietnamese forces and the Viet Cong has been pursued throughout the Buddhist crisis without noticeable let-up.

At this point Mr. Forrestal reported on General Krulak's views that, even if there were chaos in Saigon, the military units in the field would continue to confront the Communists.

Mr. Hilsman went on to say that Ambassador Nolting believes that the most likely result of a coup attempt that succeeded in killing Diem was civil war. Mr. Hilsman disagreed with this view slightly in that he thought civil war was not the most likely result but that it was certainly a possible result.

The timing of Ambassador Nolting's return and Ambassador Lodge's assumption of duty was then discussed. The President's initial view was that Ambassador Nolting should return immediately and that Ambassador Lodge should assume his duties as soon thereafter as possible. The President volunteered that Ambassador Nolting had done an outstanding job, that it was almost miraculous the way he had succeeded in turning the war around from the disastrously low point in relations between Diem and ourselves that existed when Ambassador Nolting took over. Mr. Hilsman pointed out the personal sacrifices that Ambassador Nolting had been forced to make during this period, and the President said that he hoped a way could be found to commend Ambassador Nolting publicly so as to make clear the fine job he had done and that he hoped an appropriate position could be found for him in Washington so that he could give his children a suitable home in the years immediately ahead.

The President's decision was to delegate the authority to decide on the timing of Ambassador Nolting's return to the Assistant Secretary for Far Eastern Affairs; that Ambassador Lodge should report to Washington no later than July 15 so that he could take the Counterinsurgency Course simultaneously with the normal briefings for an ambassador; and that Ambassador Lodge should arrive in Saigon as soon as possible following completion of the CI Course on August 14. Arrangements were made for Ambassador Nolting to see the President at 4:00 p.m. on Monday, July 8.

34

Intelligence Estimate on '63 Unrest

Excerpts from Special National Intelligence Estimate 53-2-63, "The Situation in South Vietnam," July 10, 1963.

CONCLUSIONS

A. The Buddhist crisis in South Vietnam has highlighted and intensified a widespread and long-standing dissatisfaction with the Diem regime and its style of government. If—as is likely—Diem fails to carry out truly and promptly the commitments he has made to the Buddhists, disorders will probably flare again and the chances of a coup or assassination attempts against him will become better than ever . . .

B. The Diem regime's underlying uneasiness about the extent of the U.S. involvement in South Vietnam has been sharpened by the Buddhist affair and the firm line taken by the U.S. This attitude will almost certainly persist and further pressure to reduce the U.S. presence in the country is likely. . . .

C. Thus far, the Buddhist issue has not been effectively exploited by the Communists, nor does it appear to have had any appreciable effect on the counterinsurgency effort. We do not think Diem is likely to be overthrown by a Communist coup. Nor do we think the Communists would necessarily profit if he were overthrown by some combination of his non-Communist opponents. A non-Communist successor regime might be initially less effective against the Viet Cong, but, given continued support from the U.S. could provide reasonably effective leadership for the government and the war effort. . . .

35

Washington Message to Lodge on
Need to Remove Nhus

*Cablegram from the State Department to Ambassador
Henry Cabot Lodge in Saigon, Aug. 24, 1963.*

It is now clear that whether military proposed martial law or
whether Nhu tricked them into it, Nhu took advantage of its
imposition to smash pagodas with police and Tung's Special
Forces loyal to him, thus placing onus on military in eyes of world
and Vietnamese people. Also clear that Nhu has maneuvered himself into commanding position.

U.S. Government cannot tolerate situation in which power lies
in Nhu's hands. Diem must be given chance to rid himself of
Nhu and his coterie and replace them with best military and
political personalities available.

If, in spite of all of your efforts, Diem remains obdurate and
refuses, then we must face the possibility that Diem himself
cannot be preserved.

We now believe immediate action must be taken to prevent
Nhu from consolidating his position further. Therefore, unless you
in consultation with Harkins perceive overriding objections you
are authorized to proceed along following lines:

(1) First we must press on appropriate levels of GVN following line:

(a) USG cannot accept actions against Buddhists taken by Nhu
and his collaborators under cover martial law.

(b) Prompt dramatic actions redress situation must be taken,
including repeal of decree 10, release of arrested monks, nuns, etc.

(2) We must at same time also tell key military leaders that
U.S. would find it impossible to continue support GVN militarily
and economically unless above steps are taken immediately which
we recognize requires removal of Nhus from the scene. We wish
give Diem reasonable opportunity to remove Nhus, but if he
remains obdurate, then we are prepared to accept the obvious
implication that we can no longer support Diem. You may also
tell appropriate military commanders we will give them direct
support in any interim period of breakdown central government
mechanism.

(3) We recognize the necessity of removing taint on military
for pagoda raids and placing blame squarely on Nhu. You are
authorized to have such statements made in Saigon as you consider desirable to achieve this objective. We are prepared to take
same line here and to have Voice of America make statement
along lines contained in next numbered telegram whenever you
give the word, preferably as soon as possible.

Concurrently, with above, Ambassador and country team should urgently examine all possible alternative leadership and make detailed plans as to how we might bring about Diem's replacement if this should become necessary.

Assume you will consult with General Harkins re any precautions necessary protect American personnel during crisis period.

You will understand that we cannot from Washington give you detailed instructions as to how this operation should proceed, but you will also know we will back you to the hilt on actions you take to achieve our objectives.

Needless to say we have held knowledge of this telegram to minimum essential people and assume you will take similar precautions to prevent premature leaks.

36
Lodge's Reply to Washington

Cablegram from Ambassador Lodge to Secretary of State Dean Rusk and Assistant Secretary of State Roger Hilsman, Aug. 25, 1963.

Believe that chances of Diem's meeting our demands are virtually nil. At same time, by making them we give Nhu chance to forestall or block action by military. Risk, we believe, is not worth taking, with Nhu in control combat forces Saigon.

Therefore, propose we go straight to Generals with our demands, without informing Diem. Would tell them we prepared have Diem without Nhus but it is in effect up to them whether to keep him. Would also insist generals take steps to release Buddhist leaders and carry out June 16 agreement.

Request immediate modification instructions. However, do not propose move until we are satisfied with E and E plans. Harkins concurs. I present credentials President Diem tomorrow 11 A.M.

37
C.I.A. Aide's Cable to Chief on Contact with Saigon Generals

Cablegram from John Richardson, the Central Intelligence Agency's Saigon station chief, to John A. McCone, Director of Central Intelligence, Aug. 26, 1963.

During meeting with Harkins, Trueheart, Mecklin and COS on morning 26 Aug Lodge made decision that American official hand should not show. Consequently, Harkins will take no initiative with VNese generals. (Conein to convey points below to Gen. Khiem; Spera to Khanh; if Khiem agrees on Conein talking to Don, he will).

(A) Solicitation of further elaboration of action aspects of present thinking and planning. What should be done?

(B) We in agreement Nhus must go.

(C) Question of retaining Diem or not up to them.

(D) Bonzes and other arrestees must be released immediately and five-point agreement of 16 June fully carried out.

(E) We will provide direct support during any interim period of breakdown central gov mechanism.

(F) We cannot be of any help during initial action of assuming power of state. Entirely their own action, win or lose. Don't expect be bailed out.

(G) If Nhus do not go and if Buddhists situation is not redressed as indicated, we would find it impossible continue military and economic support.

(H) It hoped bloodshed can be avoided or reduced to absolute minimum.

(I) It hoped that during process and after, developments conducted in such manner as to retain and increase the necessary relations between VNese and Americans which will allow for progress of country and successful prosecution of the war.

38

C.I.A. Station Chief's Cable on Coup Prospects in Saigon

Cablegram from Mr. Richardson to Mr. McCone, Aug. 28, 1963.

Situation here has reached point of no return. Saigon is armed camp. Current indications are that Ngo family have dug in for last ditch battle. It is our considered estimate that General officers cannot retreat now. Conein's meeting with Gen. Khiem (Saigon 0346) reveals that overwhelming majority of general officers, excepting Dinh and Cao, are united, have conducted prior planning, realize that they must proceed quickly, and understand that they have no alternative but to go forward. Unless the generals are neutralized before being able to launch their operation, we believe they will act and that they have good chance to win. If General Dinh primarily and Tung secondly cannot be neutralized at outset, there may be widespread fighting in Saigon and serious loss of life.

We recognize the crucial stakes and involved and have no doubt that the generals do also. Situation has changed drastically since 21 August. If the Ngo family wins now, they and Vietnam will stagger on to final defeat at the hands of their own people and the VC. Should a generals' revolt occur and be put down, GVN will sharply reduce American presence in SVN. Even if they did not do so, it seems clear that American public opinion and Congress, as well as world opinion, would force withdrawal or reduction of American support for VN under the Ngo administration.

Bloodshed can be avoided if the Ngo family would step down before the coming armed action. . . . It is obviously preferable that the generals conduct this effort without apparent American assistance. Otherwise, for a long time in the future, they will be vulnerable to charges of being American puppets, which they are not in any sense. Nevertheless, we all understand that the effort must succeed and that whatever needs to be done on our part must be done. If this attempt by the generals does not take place or if it fails, we believe it no exaggeration to say that VN runs serious risk of being lost over the course of time.

39

Lodge Cable to Secretary Rusk on U.S. Policy Toward a Coup

Cablegram from Ambassador Lodge to Secretary Rusk, Aug. 29, 1963.

We are launched on a course from which there is no respectable turning back: the overthrow of the Diem government. There is no turning back in part because U.S. prestige is already publicly committed to this end in large measure and will become more so as the facts leak out. In a more fundamental sense, there is no turning back because there is no possibility, in my view, that the war can be won under a Diem administration, still less that Diem or any member of the family can govern the country in a way to gain the support of the people who count, i.e., the educated class in and out of government service, civil and military—not to mention the American people. In the last few months (and especially days) they have in fact positively alienated these people to an incalculable degree. So that I am personally in full agreement with the policy which I was instructed to carry out by last Sunday's telegram.

2. The chance of bringing off a Generals' coup depends on them to some extent; but it depends at least as much on us.

3. We should proceed to make all-out effort to get Generals to move promptly. To do so we should have authority to do following:

(a) That Gen. Harkins repeat to Generals personally message previously transmitted by CAS officers. This should establish their authenticity. Gen. Harkins should have order on this.

(b) If nevertheless Generals insist on public statement that all U.S. aid to VN through Diem regime has been stopped, we would agree, on express understanding that Generals will have started at same time. (We would seek persuade Generals that it would be better to hold this card for use in event of stalemate. We hope it will not be necessary to do this at all.)

(c) VNese Generals doubt that we have the will power, courage, and determination to see this thing through. They are haunted by the idea that we will run out on them even though we have told them pursuant to instructions, that the game had started.

5. We must press on for many reasons. Some of these are:

(a) Explosiveness of the present situation which may well lead to riots and violence if issue of discontent with regime is not met. Out of this could come a pro-Communist or at best a neutralist set of politicians.

(b) The fact that war cannot be won with the present regime.

(c) Our own reputation for steadfastness and our unwillingness to stultify ourselves.

(d) If proposed action is suspended, I believe a body blow will be dealt to respect for us by VNese Generals. Also, all those who expect U.S. to straighten out this situation will feel let down. Our help to the regime in past years inescapably gives a responsibility which we cannot avoid.

6. I realize that this course involves a very substantial risk of losing VN. It also involves some additional risk to American lives. I would never propose it if I felt there was a reasonable chance of holding VN with Diem.

[Point 7 unavailable.]

8. . . . Gen. Harkins thinks that I should ask Diem to get rid of the Nhus before starting the Generals' action. But I believe that such a step has no chance of getting the desired result and would have the very serious effect of being regarded by the Generals as a sign of American indecision and delay. I believe this is a risk which we should not run. The Generals distrust us too much already. Another point is that Diem would certainly ask for time to consider such a far-reaching request. This would give the ball to Nhu.

9. With the exception of par. 8 above Gen. Harkins concurs in this telegram.

40

Rusk Cable to Lodge on Views of National Security Council

Cablegram from Secretary Rusk to Ambassador Lodge, Aug. 29, 1963. The Pentagon study says the message followed a meeting of the National Security Council.

1. Highest level meeting noon today reviewed your 375 and reaffirmed basic course. Specific decisions follow:

2. In response to your recommendation, General Harkins is hereby authorized to repeat to such Generals as you indicate the messages previously transmitted by CAS officers. He should stress that the USG supports the movement to eliminate the Nhus from the government, but that before arriving at specific understandings with the generals, General Harkins must know who are involved, resources available to them and overall plan for coup. The USG will support a coup which has good chance of succeeding but plans no direct involvement of U.S. armed forces. Harkins should state that he is prepared to establish liaison with the coup planners and to review plans, but will not engage directly in joint coup planning.

3. Question of last approach to Diem remains undecided and separate personal message from Secretary to you develops our concern and asks your comment.

4. On movement of U.S. forces, we do not expect to make any announcement or leak at present and believe that any later decision to publicize such movements should be closely connected to developing events on your side. We cannot of course prevent unauthorized disclosures or speculation, but we will in any event knock down any reports of evacuation.

5. You are hereby authorized to announce suspension of aid through Diem government at a time and under conditions of your choice. In deciding upon the use of this authority, you should consider importance of timing and managing announcement so as to minimize appearance of collusion with Generals and also to minimize danger of unpredictable and disruptive reaction by existing government. We also assume that you will not in fact use this authority unless you think it essential, and we see it as possible that Harkins' approach and increasing process of cooperation may provide assurance Generals desire. Our own view is that it will be best to hold this authority for use in close conjunction with coup, and not for present encouragement of Generals, but decision is yours.

41

Further Rusk Cable to Lodge on Diem-Nhu Relationship

Cablegram from Secretary Rusk to Ambassador Lodge, Aug. 29, 1963.

Deeply appreciate your 375 which was a most helpful clarification. We fully understand enormous stakes at issue and the heavy responsibilities which you and Harkins will be carrying in the days ahead and we want to do everything possible from our end to help.

Purpose of this message is to explore further question of possible attempt to separate Diem and the Nhus. In your telegram you appear to treat Diem and the Nhus as a single package whereas we had indicated earlier to the Generals that if the Nhus were removed the question of retaining Diem would be up to them. My own personal assessment is (and this is not an instruction) that the Nhus are by all odds the greater part of the problem in Vietnam, internally, internationally and for American public opinion. Perhaps it is inconceivable that the Nhus could be removed without taking Diem with them or without Diem's abandoning his post. In any event, I would appreciate your comment on whether any distinction can or should be drawn as between Diem and Counselor and Madame Nhu.

The only point on which you and General Harkins have different views is whether an attempt should be made with Diem to eliminate the Nhus and presumably take other steps to consolidate the country behind a winning effort against the Viet Cong. My own hunch, based in part on the report of Kattenburg's conversations with Diem is that such an approach could not succeed if it were cast purely in terms of persuasion. Unless such a talk included a real sanction such as a threatened withdrawal of our support, it is unlikely that it would be taken completely seriously by a man who may feel that we are inescapably committed to an anti-Communist Vietnam. But if a sanction were used in such a conversation, there would be a high risk that this would be taken by Diem as a sign that action against him and the Nhus was imminent and he might as a minimum move against the Generals or even take some quite fantastic action such as calling on North Vietnam for assistance in expelling the Americans.

It occurs to me, therefore, that if such an approach were to be made it might properly await the time when others were ready to move immediately to constitute a new government. If this be so, the question then arises as to whether an approach to insist upon the expulsion of the Nhus should come from Americans rather than from the Generals themselves. This might be the means by which the Generals could indicate that they were prepared to distinguish between Diem and the Nhus. In any event, were the Generals to take this action it would tend to protect succeeding Vietnam administrations from the charge of being wholly American puppets subjected to whatever anti-American sentiment is inherent in so complex a situation.

I would be glad to have your further thoughts on these points as well as your views on whether further talks with Diem are contemplated to continue your opening discussions with him. You will have received formal instructions on other matters through other messages. Good luck.

Lodge's Response to Rusk on Diem's Closeness to Brother

Cablegram from Ambassador Lodge to Secretary Rusk, Aug. 30, 1963.

I agree that getting the Nhus out is the prime objective and that they are "the greater part . . ."

This surely cannot be done by working through Diem. In fact Diem will oppose it. He wishes he had more Nhus, not less.

The best chance of doing it is by the Generals taking over the government lock, stock and barrel.

After this has been done, it can then be decided whether to put Diem back in again or go on without him. I am rather inclined to put him back, but I would not favor putting heavy pressure on the Generals if they don't want him. My greatest single difficulty in carrying out the instructions of last Sunday is inertia. The days come and go and nothing happens. It is, of course, natural for the Generals to want assurances and the U.S. Government has certainly been prompt in its reactions. But here it is Friday and, while in one way much has been done, there is not yet enough to show for the hours which we have all put in.

If I call on Diem to demand the removal of the Nhus, he will surely not agree. But before turning me down, he will pretend to consider it and involve us in prolonged delays. This will make the Generals suspicious of us and add to the inertia.

Such a call by me would look to the Nhus like an ultimatum and would result in their taking steps to thwart any operation dealing with them.

I agree with you that if a sanction were used, it could provoke an even more fantastic reaction. In fact I greatly dislike the idea of cutting off aid in connection with the Generals' operation and while I thank you for giving me the authority to make an announcement, I hope I will never have to use it.

It is possible, as you suggested . . . for the Generals when, as and if their operation gets rolling to demand the removal of the Nhus before bringing their operation to fruition. But I am afraid they will get talked out of their operation which will then disintegrate, still leaving the Nhus in office.

If the Generals' operation does get rolling, I would not want to stop it until they were in full control. They could then get rid of the Nhus and decide whether they wanted to keep Diem.

It is better for them and for us for them to throw out the Nhus than for us to get involved in it.

I am sure that the best way to handle this matter is by a truly VNese movement even if it puts me rather in the position of pushing a piece of spaghetti.

I am contemplating no further talks with Diem at this time.

43

Cable by U.S. General in Saigon to Taylor on End of August Plot

Cablegram from Gen. Paul D. Harkins, United States commander in Saigon, to Gen. Maxwell D. Taylor, Chairman of the Joint Chiefs of Staff, Aug. 31, 1963.

(saw Khiem: he stated Big Minh had stopped planning at this time, and was working on other methods; others had called off planning also, himself and Khanh, following Minh. He knew Thao was making plans—but that few of military trusted him because of his VC background—and that he might still be working for the VC. The Generals were not ready as they did not have enough forces under their control compared to those under President and now in Saigon. He indicated they, the Generals, did not want to start anything they could not successfully finish.

. . . At a meeting yesterday, Mr. Nhu said he now went along with everything the U.S. wants to do, and even had the backing of Pres. Kennedy. I said this was news to me. Khiem said he wondered if Nhu was again trying to flush out the generals. He intimated the generals do not have too much trust in Nhu and that he's such a friend of Mr. Richardson the generals wonder if Mr. Nhu and Mme. Nhu were on the CIA payroll. . . .

. . . I asked if someone couldn't confront the Nhus with the fact that their absence from the scene was the key to the overall solution. He replied that for anyone to do that would be self-immolation—he also went on to say he doubted if the Nhus and Diem could be split.

. . . So we see we have an "organisation de confusion" with everyone suspicious of everyone else and none desiring to take any positive action as of right now. You can't hurry the East. . . .

44

Memo on Washington Meeting in Aftermath of August Plot

Memorandum by Maj. Gen. Victor H. Krulak, special assistant to the Joint Chiefs of Staff for counterinsurgency and special activities, on a meeting at the State Department Aug. 31, 1963. Besides General Krulak, participants were Vice President Johnson; Secretary Rusk; Secretary McNamara; Deputy Secretary of Defense Roswell L. Gilpatric; McGeorge Bundy; General Taylor; Edward R. Murrow, director of the United States Information Agency; Lieut.

Gen. Marshall S. Carter, Deputy Director of the Central Intelligence Agency. Richard Helms and William E. Colby of the C.I.A.; Frederick E. Nolting Jr., former Ambassador in Saigon; Assistant Secretary Hilsman, and Paul M. Kattenburg of the State Department, head of the Interdepartmental Working Group on Vietnam.

1. Secretary Rusk stated that, in his judgment, we were back to where we were about Wednesday of last week, and this causes him to go back to the original problem and ask what in the situation led us to think well of a coup. Ruling out hatred of the Nhus, he said, there would appear to be three things:

a. The things that the Nhus had done or supported, which tended to upset the GVN internally.

b. The things that they had done which had an adverse external effect.

c. The great pressures of U.S. public opinion.

2. Mr. Rusk then asked if we should not pick up Ambassador Lodge's suggestion in his message of today (Saigon 391) and determine what steps are required to re-gird solidarity in South Vietnam—such as improvement in conditions concerning students and Buddhists and the possible departure of Madame Nhu. He said that we should determine what additional measures are needed to improve the international situation—such as problems affecting Cambodia—and to improve the Vietnamese position wherein U.S. public opinion is concerned. He then said that he is reluctant to start off by saying now that Nhu has to go; that it is unrealistic.

3. Mr. McNamara stated that he favored the above proposals of the Secretary of State, with one additional step—that is to establish quickly and firmly our line of communication between Lodge, Harkins and the GVN. He pointed out that at the moment our channels of communication are essentially broken and that they should be reinstituted at all costs.

4. Mr. Rusk added that we must do our best not to permit Diem to decapitate his military command in light of its obviously adverse effect on the prosecution of the war. At this point he asked if anyone present had any doubt in his mind but that the coup was off.

5. Mr. Kattenburg said that he had some remaining doubt; that we have not yet sent the generals a strong enough message; that the BOA statement regarding the withdrawal of aid was most important, but that we repudiated it too soon. He stated further that the group should take note of the fact that General Harkins did not carry out his instructions with respect to communication with the generals. Mr. Rusk interrupted Kattenburg to state that, to the contrary, he believed Harkins' conduct was exactly correct in light of the initial response which he received from General Khiem (they were referring to Harkins' report in MACV 1583).

6. Mr. Hilsman commented that, in his view, the generals are not now going to move unless they are pressed by a revolt from below. In this connection Ambassador Nolting warned that in the uncoordinated Vietnamese structure anything can happen, and that while an organized successful coup is out, there might be small flurries by irresponsible dissidents at any time.

7. Mr. Hilsman undertook to present four basic factors which bear directly on the problem confronting the U.S. now. They are, in his view:

a. The mood of the people, particularly the middle level officers, non-commissioned officers and middle level bureaucrats, who are most restive. Mr. McNamara interrupted to state that he had seen no evidence of this and General Taylor commented that he had seen none either, but would like to see such evidence as Hilsman could produce. Mr. Kattenburg commented that the middle level officers and bureaucrats are uniformly critical of the government, to which Mr. McNamara commented that if this indeed be the fact we should know about it.

b. The second basic factor, as outlined by Hilsman, was what effect will be felt on our programs elsewhere in Asia if we acquiesce to a strong Nhu-dominated government. In this connection, he reported that there is a Korean study now underway on just how much repression the United States will tolerate before pulling out her aid. Mr. McNamara stated that he had not seen this study and would be anxious to have it.

c. The third basic factor is Mr. Nhu, his personality and his policy. Hilsman recalled that Nhu has once already launched an effort aimed at withdrawal of our province advisors and stated that he is sure he is in conversation with the French. He gave, as supporting evidence, the content of an intercepted message, which Mr. Bundy asked to see. Ambassador Nolting expressed the opinion that Nhu will not make a deal with Ho Chi Minh on Ho's terms.

d. The fourth point is the matter of U.S. and world opinion, Hilsman stated that this problem was moving to a political and diplomatic plane. Part of the problem, he said, is the press, which concludes incorrectly that we have the ability to change the things in Vietnam of which they are critical. To this Mr. Murrow added that this problem of press condemnation is now worldwide.

8. Mr. Kattenburg stated that as recently as last Thursday it was the belief of Ambassador Lodge that, if we undertake to live with this repressive regime, with its bayonets at every street corner and its transparent negotiations with puppet bonzes, we are going to be thrown out of the country in six months. He stated that at this juncture it would be better for us to make the decision to get out honorably. He went on to say that, having been acquainted with Diem for ten years, he was deeply disappointed in him, saying that he will not separate from his brother. It was Kattenburg's view that Diem will get very little

support from the military and, as time goes on, he will get less and less support and the country will go steadily down hill.

9. General Taylor asked what Kattenburg meant when he said that we would be forced out of Vietnam within six months. Kattenburg replied that in from six months to a year, as the people see we are losing the war, they will gradually go to the other side and we will be obliged to leave. Ambassador Nolting expressed general disagreement with Mr. Kattenburg. He said that the unfavorable activity which motivated Kattenburg's remarks was confined to the city and, while city support of Diem is doubtless less now, it is not greatly so. He said that it is improper to overlook the fact that we have done a tremendous job toward winning the Vietnam war, working with this same imperfect, annoying government.

10. Mr. Kattenburg added that there is one new factor—the population, which was in high hopes of expelling the Nhus after the VOA announcement regarding cessation of aid; now, under the heel of Nhu's military repression, they would quickly lose heart.

11. Secretary Rusk commented that Kattenburg's recital was largely speculative; that it would be far better for us to start on the firm basis of two things—that we will not pull out of Vietnam until the war is won, and that we will not run a coup. Mr. McNamara expressed agreement with this view.

12. Mr. Rusk then said that we should present questions to Lodge which fall within these parameters. He added that he believes we have good proof that we have been winning the war, particularly the contrast between the first six months of 1962 and the first six months of 1963. He then asked the Vice President if he had any contribution to make.

13. The Vice President stated that he agreed with Secretary Rusk's conclusions completely; that he had great reservations himself with respect to a coup, particularly so because he had never really seen a genuine alternative to Diem. He stated that from both a practical and a political viewpoint, it would be a disaster to pull out; that we should stop playing cops and robbers and get back to talking straight to the GVN, and that we should once again go about winning the war. He stated that after our communications with them are genuinely reestablished, it may be necessary for someone to talk rough to them—perhaps General Taylor. He said further that he had been greatly impressed with Ambassador Nolting's views and agreed with Mr. McNamara's conclusions.

14. General Taylor raised the question of whether we should change the disposition of the forces which had been set in motion as a result of the crisis. It was agreed that there should be no change in the existing disposition for the time being.

45

White House Cable to Lodge on Pressure for Saigon Reforms

Cablegram from White House to Ambassador Lodge, Sept. 17, 1963. The Pentagon study says this message followed a meeting of the National Security Council but adds, "There is no evidence on the degree of consensus of the principals in this decision."

1. Highest level meeting today has approved broad outline of an action proposals program designed to obtain from GVN, if possible, reforms and changes in personnel necessary to maintain support of Vietnamese and US opinion in war against Viet Cong. This cable reports this program and our thinking for your comment before a final decision. Your comment requested soonest.

2. We see no good opportunity for action to remove present government in immediate future; therefore, as your most recent messages suggest, we must for the present apply such pressures as are available to secure whatever modest improvements on the scene may be possible. We think it likely that such improvements can make a difference, at least in the short run. Such a course, moreover, is consistent with more drastic effort as and when means become available, and we will be in touch on other channels on this problem.

3. We share view in your 523 that best available reinforcement to your bargaining position in this interim period is clear evidence that all U.S. assistance is granted only on your say-so. Separate telegram discusses details of this problem, but in this message we specifically authorize you to apply any controls you think helpful for this purpose. You are authorized to delay any delivery of supplies or transfer of funds by any agency until you are satisfied that delivery is in U.S. interest, bearing in mind that it is not our current policy to cut off aid, entirely. In other words, we share your view that it will be helpful for GVN to understand that your personal approval is a necessary part of all U.S. assistance. We think it may be particularly desirable for you to use this authority in limiting or rerouting any and all forms of assistance and support which now go to or through Nhu or individuals like Tung who are associated with him. This authorization specifically includes aid actions currently held in abeyance and you are authorized to set those in train or hold them up further in your discretion. We leave entirely in your hands decisions on the degree of privacy or publicity you wish to give to this process.

4. Subject to your comment and amendment our own list of possible helpful action by government runs as follows in approximate order of importance:

A. Clear the air—Diem should get everyone back to work and

get them to focus on winning the war. He should be broadminded and compassionate in his attitude toward those who have, for understandable reasons, found it difficult under recent circumstances fully to support him. A real spirit of reconciliation could work wonders on the people he leads; a punitive, harsh or autocratic attitude could only lead to further resistance.

B. Buddhists and students—Let them out and leave them unmolested. This more than anything else would demonstrate the return of a better day and the refocusing on the main job at hand, the war.

C. Press—The press should be allowed full latitude of expression. Diem will be criticized, but leniency and cooperation with the domestic and foreign press at this time would bring praise for his leadership in due course. While tendentious reporting is irritating, suppression of news leads to much more serious trouble.

D. Secret and combat police—Confine its role to operations against the VC and abandon operations against non-Communist opposition groups thereby indicating clearly that a period of reconciliation and political stability has returned.

E. Cabinet changes to inject new untainted blood, remove targets of popular discontent.

F. Elections—These should be held, should be free, and should be widely observed.

G. Assembly—Assembly should be convoked soon after the elections. The Government should submit its policies to it and should receive its confidence. An assembly resolution would be most useful for external image purposes.

H. Party—Can Lao party should not be covert or semi-covert but a broad association of supporters engaged in a common, winning cause. This could perhaps be best accomplished by

I. Repeal or suitable amendment Decree 10.

J. Rehabilitation by ARVN of pagodas.

K. Establishment of Ministry of Religious Affairs.

L. Liberation of passport issuances and currency restrictions enabling all to leave who wish to.

M. Acceptance of Buddhist Inquiry Mission from World Federation to report true facts of situation to world.

5. You may wish to add or subtract from the above list, but need to set psychological tone and image is paramount. Diem has taken positive actions in past of greater or less scope than those listed, but they have had little practical political effect since they were carried out in such a way as to make them hollow or, even if real, unbelievable (e.g., martial law already nominally lifted, Assembly elections scheduled, and puppet bonzes established).

6. Specific "reforms" are apt to have little impact without dramatic, symbolic move which convinces Vietnamese that reforms are real. As practical matter we share your views that this can best be achieved by some visible reduction in influence of Nhus, who are symbol to disaffected of all that they dislike in

GVN. This we think would require Nhus' departure from Saigon and preferably Vietnam at least for extended vacation. We recognize the strong possibility that these and other pressures may not produce this result, but we are convinced that it is necssary to try.

7. In Washington, in this phase, we would plan to maintain a posture of disapproval of recent GVN actions, but we would not expect to make public our specific requests of Diem. Your comment on public aspects of this phase is particularly needed.

8. We note your reluctance to continue dialogue with Diem until you have more to say, but we continue to believe that discussions with him are at a minimum an important source of intelligence and may conceivably be a means of exerting some persuasive effect even in his present state of mind. If you believe that full control of U.S. assistance provides you with means of resuming dialogue, we hope you will do so. We ourselves can see much virtue in effort to reason even with an unreasonable man when he is on a collision course. We repeat, however, that this is a matter for your judgment.

9. Meanwhile, there is increasing concern here with strictly military aspects of the problem, both in terms of actual progress of operations and of need to make effective case with Congress for continued prosecution of the effort. To meet these needs President has decided to send Secretary of Defense and General Taylor to Vietnam, arriving early next week. It will be emphasized here that it is a military mission and that all political decisions are being handled through you as President's Senior Representative.

10. We repeat that political program outlined above awaits your comment before final decision. President particularly emphasizes that it is fully open to your criticism and amendment. It is obviously an interim plan and further decisions may become necessary very soon.

46

Lodge Cable to Kennedy on Means of Bringing Reforms

Cablegram from Ambassador Lodge to State Department "for President only," Sept. 19, 1963.

1. Agree that no good opportunity for action to remove present government in immediate future is apparent and that we should therefore, do whatever we can as an interim measure pending such an eventuality.

2. Virtually all the topics under paragraph 4, letters A to M have been taken up with Diem and Nhu at one time or another

most of them by me personally. They think that most of them would either involve destroying the political structure on which they rest or loss of face or both. We, therefore, could *not* realistically hope for more than lip service. Frankly, I see no opportunity at all for substantive changes. Detailed comments on items A to M are contained in separate telegram.

3. There are signs that Diem-Nhu are somewhat bothered by my silence. According to one well placed source, they are guessing and off-balance and "desperately anxious" to know what U.S. posture is to be. They may be preparing some kind of a public relations package, possibly to be opened after the elections. I believe that for me to press Diem on things which are *not* in the cards and to repeat what we have said several times already would be a little shrill and would make us look weak, particularly in view of my talk with Nhu last night at a dinner where I had a golden opportunity to make the main points of your CAP 63516 as reported in 541.

4. Also, I doubt that a public relations package will meet needs of situation which seems particularly grave to me, notably in the light of General Big Minh's opinion expressed very privately yesterday that the Viet Cong are steadily gaining in strength; have more of the population on their side than has the GVN; that arrests are continuing and that the prisons are full; that more and more students are going over to the Viet Cong; that there is great graft and corruption in the Vietnamese administration of our aid; and that the "Heart of the Army is *not* in the war." All this by Vietnamese No. 1 General is now echoed by Secretary of Defense Thuan (See my 542), who wants to leave the country.

5. As regards your paragraph 3 on withholding of aid, I still hope that I may be informed of methods, as requested in my 478, September 11, which will enable us to apply sanctions in a way which will really affect Diem and Nhu without precipitating an economic collapse and without impeding the war effort. We are studying this here and have not yet found a solution. If a way to do this were to be found, it would be one of the greatest discoveries since the enactment of the Marshall Plan in 1947 because, so far as I know, the U.S. had never yet been able to control any of the very unsatisfactory governments through which we have had to work in our many very successful attempts to make these countries strong enough to stand alone.

6. I also believe that whatever sanctions we may discover should be directly tied to a promising coup d'etat and should *not* be applied without such a coup being in prospect. In this connection, I believe that we should pursue contact with Big Minh and urge him along if he looks like acting. I particularly think that the idea of supporting a Vietnamese Army independent of the government should be energetically studied.

7. I will, of course, give instructions that programs which one [sic] can be effectively held up should be held up and not released without my approval provided that this can be done without

serious harmful effect to the people and to the war effort. Techni
cal assistance and (omission) support to communications suppor
programs may be one way. This would be a fly-speck in the
present situation and would have *no* immediate effect, but I hope
that U.S. (omission) may get Vietnamese officials into the habi
of asking me to release items which are held up and that, ove
a long period of time, it might create opportunities for us to
get little things done.

8. But it is not even within the realm of possibility that such
a technique could lead them to do anything which causes los
of face or weakening of their political organization. In fact, to
threaten them with suppression of aid might well defeat our
purposes and might make a bad situation very much worse.

9. There should in any event be no publicity whatever about
this procedure. If it is possible (ommission) a program, I intend
to (omission).

10. As regards your paragraph 6 and "dramatic symbolic
moves," I really do not think they could understand this even
if Thao wanted to, although I have talked about it to Diem, and
to Nhu last night (See my 541). They have scant comprehension
of what it is to appeal to public opinion as they have really n
interest in any other opinion than their own. I have repeatedly
brought up the question of Nhu's departure and have stressed tha
if he would just stay away until after Christmas, it might help
get the Appropriation Bill through. This seems like a small thing
to us but to them it seems tremendous as they are quite sure
that the Army would take over if he even stepped out of the
country.

11. Your paragraph 8. I have, of course, no objection to seeing
Diem at any time that it would be helpful. But I would rather
let him sweat for awhile and not go to see him unless I have
something really new to bring up. I would much prefer to wai
until I find some part of the AID program to hold up in which
he is interested and then have him ask me to come and see him
For example, last night's dinner which I suspect Nhu of stimulat
ing is infinitely better than for me to take the initiative for an
appointment and to call at the office. Perhaps my silence had
something to do with it.

47

McNamara-Taylor Report on Mission to
South Vietnam

*Excerpts from memorandum for President Kennedy from
Secretary McNamara and General Taylor, dated Oct. 2,
1963, and headed "Report of McNamara-Taylor Mission
to South Vietnam."*

A. CONCLUSIONS.

1. The military campaign has made great progress and continues to progress.

2. There are serious political tensions in Saigon (and perhaps elsewhere in South Vietnam) where the Diem-Nhu government is becoming increasingly unpopular.

3. There is no solid evidence of the possibility of a successful coup, although assassination of Diem or Nhu is always a possibility.

4. Although some, and perhaps an increasing number, of GVN military officers are becoming hostile to the government, they are more hostile to the Viet Cong than to the government and at least for the near future they will continue to perform their military duties.

5. Further repressive actions by Diem and Nhu could change the present favorable military trends. On the other hand, a return to more moderate methods of control and administration, unlikely though it may be, would substantially mitigate the political crisis.

6. It is not clear that pressures exerted by the U.S. will move Diem and Nhu toward moderation. Indeed, pressures may increase their obduracy. But unless such pressures are exerted, they are almost certain to continue past patterns of behavior.

B. RECOMMENDATIONS.

We recommend that:

1. General Harkins review with Diem the military changes necessary to complete the military campaign in the Northern and Central areas (I, II, and III Corps) by the end of 1954, and in the Delta (IV Corps) by the end of 1965. This review would consider the need for such changes as:

a. A further shift of military emphasis and strength to the Delta (IV Corps).

b. An increase in the military tempo in all corps areas, so that all combat troops are in the Field an average of 20 days out of 30 and static missions are ended.

c. Emphasis on "clear and hold operations" instead of terrain sweeps which have little permanent value.

d. The expansion of personnel in combat units to full authorized strength.

e. The training and arming of hamlet militia at an accelerated rate, especially in the Delta.

f. A consolidation of the strategic hamlet program, especially in the Delta, and action to insure that future strategic hamlets are not built until they can be protected, and until civic action programs can be introduced.

2. A program be established to train Vietnamese so that essential functions now performed by U.S. military personnel can be carried out by Vietnamese by the end of 1965. It should be possible to withdraw the bulk of U.S. personnel by that time.

3. In accordance with the program to train progressively Vietnamese to take over military functions, the Defense Department should announce in the very near future presently prepared plans to withdraw 1000 U.S. military personnel by the end of 1963. This action should be explained in low key as an initial step in a long-term program to replace U.S. personnel with trained Vietnamese without impairment of the war effort.

4. The following actions be taken to impress upon Diem our disapproval of his political program.

a. Continue to withhold commitment of funds in the commodity import program, but avoid a formal announcement. The potential significance of the withholding of commitments for the 1964 military budget should be brought home to the top military officers in working level contacts between USOM and MAVC and the Joint General Staff; up to now we have stated $95 million may be used by the Vietnamese as a planning level for the commodity import program for 1964. Henceforth we could make clear that this is uncertain both because of lack of final appropriation action by the Congress and because of executive policy.

b. Suspend approval of the pending AID loans for the Saigon-Cholon Waterworks and Saigon Electric Power Project. We should state clearly that we are doing so as a matter of policy.

c. Advise Diem that MAP and CIA support for designated units, now under Colonel Tung's control (mostly held in or near the Saigon area for political reasons) and will be cut off unless these units are promptly assigned to the full authority of the Joint General Staff and transferred to the field.

d. Maintain the present purely "correct" relations with the top GVN, and specifically between the Ambassador and Diem. Contact between General Harkins and Diem and Defense Secretary Thuan on military matters should not, however, be suspended, as this remains an important channel of advice. USOM and USIA should also seek to maintain contacts where these are needed to push forward programs in support of the effort in the field, while taking care not to cut across the basic picture of U.S. disapproval and uncertainty of U.S. aid intentions. We should work with the Diem government but not support it. . . .

As we pursue these courses of action, the situation must be closely watched to see what steps Diem is taking to reduce repressive practices and to improve the effectiveness of the military effort. We should set no fixed criteria, but recognize that we would have to decide in 2 - 4 months whether to move to more drastic action or try to carry on with Diem even if he had not taken significant steps.

5. At this time, no initiative should be taken to encourage actively a change in government. Our policy should be to seek urgently to identify and build contacts with an alternative leadership if and when it appears.

6. The following statement be approved as current U.S. policy toward South Vietnam and constitute the substance of the govern-

ment position to be presented both in Congressional testimony and in public statements.

a. The security of South Vietnam remains vital to United States security. For this reason, we adhere to the overriding objective of denying this country to Communism and of suppressing the Viet Cong insurgency as promptly as possible. (By suppressing the insurgency we mean reducing it to proportions manageable by the national security forces of the GVN, unassisted by the presence of U.S. military forces.) We believe the U.S. part of the task can be completed by the end of 1965, the terminal date which we are taking as the time objective of our counterinsurgency programs.

b. The military program in Vietnam has made progress and is sound in principle.

c. The political situation in Vietnam remains deeply serious. It has not yet significantly affected the military effort, but could do so at some time in the future. If the result is a GVN ineffective in the conduct of the war, the U.S. will review its attitude toward support for the government. Although we are deeply concerned by repressive practices, effective performance in the conduct of the war should be the determining factor in our relations with the GVN.

d. The U.S. has expressed its disapproval of certain actions of the Diem-Nhu regime will do so again if required. Our policy is to seek to bring about the abandonment of repression because of its effect on the popular will to resist. Our means consist of expressions of disapproval and the withholding of support from the GVN activities that are not clearly contributing to the war effort. We will use these means as required to assure an effective military program. . . .

48

Lodge Message on Meeting of C.I.A. Agent with Gen. Minh

Cablegram from Ambassador Lodge to the State Department, Oct. 5, 1963.

1. Lt. Col. Conein met with Gen Duong Van Minh at Gen. Minh's Headquarters on Le Van Duyet for one hour and ten minutes morning of 5 Oct 63. This meeting was at the initiative of Gen Minh and has been specifically cleared in advance by Ambassador Lodge. No other persons were present. The conversation was conducted in French.

2. Gen. Minh stated that he must know American Government's position with respect to a change in the Government of Vietnam within the very near future. Gen. Minh added the Generals were aware of the situation is deteriorating rapidly and that action to change the Government must be taken or the war will be lost to

the Viet Cong because the Government no longer has the suppor
of the people. Gen. Minh identified among the other General
participating with him in this plan:

Maj. Gen. Tran Van Don

Brig. Gen. Tran Thien Khiem

Maj. Gen. Tran Van Kim

3. Gen. Minh made it clear that he did not expect any specifi
American support for an effort on the part of himself and hi
colleagues to change the Government but he states he does nee
American assurances that the USG will not rpt not attempt t
thwart this plan.

4. Gen. Minh also stated that he himself has no political amb
tions nor do any of the other General Officers except perhaps, h
said laughingly, Gen. Ton That Dinh. Gen. Minh insisted that h
only purpose is to win the war. He added emphatically that to d
this continuation of American Military and Economic Aid at th
present level (he said one and one half million dollars per day)
necessary.

5. Gen. Minh outlined three possible plans for the accomplis
ment of the change of Government:

a. Assassination of Ngo Dinh Nhu and Ngo Dinh Can keepin
President Diem in Office. Gen Minh said this was the easiest pla
to accomplish.

b. The encirclement of Saigon by various military units particu
larly the unit at Ben Cat.

c. Direct confrontation between military units involved in th
coup and loyalist military units in Saigon. In effect, dividing th
city of Saigon into sectors and cleaning it out pocket by pocke
Gen. Minh claims under the circumstances Diem and Nhu coul
count on the loyalty of 5,500 troops within the city of Saigon.

6. Conein replied to Gen. Minh that he could not answe
specific questions as to USG non-interference nor could he giv
any advice with respect to tactical planning. He added that h
could not advise concerning the best of the three plans.

7. Gen. Minh went on to explain that the most dangerous me
in South Viet-Nam are Ngo Dinh Nhu, Ngo Dinh Can and Ng
Trong Hieu. Minh stated that Hieu was formerly a Communist an
still has Communist sympathies. When Col. Conein remarked tha
he had considered Col. Tung as one of the more dangerous in
dividuals, Gen. Minh stated 'if I get rid of Nhu, Can and Hiev
Col. Tung will be on his knees before me."

8. Gen. Minh also stated that he was worried as to the role o
Gen. Tran Thien Khiem since Khiem may have played a doub
role in August. Gen. Minh asked that copies of the documen
previously passed to Gen. Khiem (plan of Camp Long Thanh an
munitions inventory at that camp) be passed to Gen. Minh pe
sonally for comparison with papers passed by Khiem to Minh pu
portedly from CAS.

9. Minh further stated that one of the reasons they are havin
to act quickly was the fact that many regimental, battalion an

company commanders are working on coup plans of their own which could be abortive and a "catastrophe."

10. Minh appeared to understand Conein's position of being unable to comment at the present moment but asked that Conein again meet with Gen. Minh to discuss the specific plan of operations which Gen. Minh hopes to put into action. No specific date was given for this next meeting. Conein was again noncommittal in his reply. Gen. Minh once again indicated his understanding and stated that he would arrange to contact Conein in the near future and hoped that Conein would be able to meet with him and give the assurance outlined above.

49

Further Lodge Comments to Rusk

Cablegram from Ambassador Lodge to Secretary Rusk, Oct. 5, 1963.

Reference Big Minh-Conein meeting (CAS Saigon 1455). While neither General Harkins nor I have great faith in Big Minh, we need instructions on his approach. My recommendation, in which General Harkins concurs, is that Conein when next approached by Minh should:

1. Assure him that U.S. will not attempt to thwart his plans.
2. Offer to review his plans, other than assassination plans.
3. Assure Minh that U.S. aid will be continued to Vietnam under Government which gives promise of gaining support of people and winning the war against the Communists. Point out that it is our view that this is most likely to be the case if Government includes good proportion of well qualified civilian leaders in key positions. (Conein should press Minh for details his thinking Re composition future Government). I suggest the above be discussed with Secretary McNamara and General Taylor who contacted Minh in recent visit.

50

Kennedy Position on Coup Plots

Cablegram from White House to Ambassador Lodge, transmitted on Central Intelligence Agency channel, Oct. 5, 1963. The Pentagon study says this message emanated from a meeting of the National Security Council.

In conjunction with decisions and recommendations in separate EPTEL, President today approved recommendation that no intiative should now be taken to give any active covert encouragement to a coup. There should, however, be urgent covert effort with closest security, under broad guidance of Ambassador to identify and build contacts with possible alternative leadership as and when it appears. Essential that this effort be totally secure and fully deniable and separated entirely from normal political analysis and reporting and other activities of country team. We repeat that this effort is not repeat not to be aimed at active promotion of coup but only at surveillance and readiness. In order to provide plausibility to denial suggest you and no one else in Embassy issue these instructions orally to Acting Station Chief and hold him responsible to you alone for making appropriate contacts and reporting to you alone.

All reports to Washington on this subject should be on this channel.

51

White House Cable for Lodge on Response to Gen. Minh

Cablegram from White House to Ambasador Lodge, Oct. 6, 1963.

1. Believe CAP 63560 gives general guidance requested REFTEL. We have following additional general thoughts which have been discussed with President. While we do not wish to stimulate coup, we also do not wish to leave impression that U.S. would thwart a change of government or deny economic and military assistance to a new regime if it appeared capable of increasing effectiveness of military effort, ensuring popular suport to win war and improving working relations with U.S. We would like to be informed on what is being contemplated but we should avoid being drawn into reviewing or advising on operational plans or any other act which might tend to identify U.S. too closely with change in government. We would, however, welcome information which would help us assess character of any alternate leadership.

2. With reference to specific problem of General Minh you should seriously consider having contact take position that in present state his knowledge he is unable present Minh's case to responsible policy officials with any degree of seriousness. In order to get responsible officials even to consider Minh's problem, contact would have to have detailed information clearly indicating that Minh's plans offer a high prospect of success. At present contact sees no such prospect in the information so far provided.

3. You should also consider with Acting Station Chief whether it would be desirable in order to preserve security and deniability in this as well as similar approaches to others whether appropriate arrangements could be made for follow-up contacts by individuals

brought in especially from outside Vietnam. As we indicated in CAP 63560 we are most concerned about security problem and we are confining knowledge these sensitive matters in Washington to extremely limited group, high officials in White House, State, Defense and CIA with whom this message cleared.

52

Lodge Message to Bundy on Dealings with Generals

Cablegram from Ambassador Lodge to McGeorge Bundy, Oct. 25, 1963.

1. I appreciate the concern expressed by you in ref. a relative to the Gen. Don/Conein relationship, and also the present lack of firm intelligence on the details of the general's plot. I hope that ref. b will assist in clearing up some of the doubts relative to general's plans, and I am hopeful that the detailed plans promised for two days before the coup attempt will clear up any remaining doubts.

2. CAS has been punctilious in carrying out my instructions. I have personally approved each meeting between Gen. Don and Conein who has carried out my orders in each instance explicitly. While I share your concern about the continued involvement of Conein in this matter, a suitable substitute for Conein as the principal contact is not presently available. Conein, as you know, is a friend of some eighteen years' standing with Gen. Don, and General Don has expressed extreme reluctance to deal with anyone else. I do not believe the involvement of another American in close contact with the generals would be productive. We are, however, considering the feasibility of a plan for the introduction of an additional officer as a cut-out between Conein and a designee of Gen. Don for communication purposes only. This officer is completely unwitting of any details of past or present coup activities and will remain so.

3. With reference to Gen. Harkins' comment to Gen. Don which Don reports to have referred to a presidential directive and the proposal for a meeting with me, this may have served the useful purpose of allaying the General's fears as to our interest. If this were a provocation, the GVN could have assumed and manufactured any variations of the same theme. As a precautionary measure, however, I of course refused to see Gen. Don. As to the lack of information as to General Don's real backing, and the lack of evidence that any real capabilities for action have been developed, ref. b provides only part of the answer. I feel sure that the reluctance of the generals to provide the U.S. with full details of their plans at this time, is a reflection of their own

sense of security and a lack of confidence that in the large American community present in Saigon their plans will not be prematurely revealed.

4. The best evidence available to the Embassy, which I grant you is not as complete as we would like it, is that Gen. Don and the other generals involved with him are seriously attempting to effect a change in the government. I do not believe that this is a provocation by Ngo Dinh Nhu, although we shall continue to assess the planning as well as possible. In the event that the coup aborts, or in the event that Nhu has masterminded a provocation, I believe that our involvement to date through Conein is still within the realm of plausible denial. CAS is perfectly prepared to have me disavow Conein at any time it may serve the national interest.

5. I welcome your reaffirming instructions contained in CAS Washington 74228. It is vital that we neither thwart a coup nor that we are even in a position where we do not know what is going on.

6. We should not thwart a coup for two reasons. First, it seems at least an even bet that the next government would not bungle and stumble as much as the present one has. Secondly, it is extremely unwise in the long range for us to pour cold water on attempts at a coup, particularly when they are just in their beginning stages. We should remember that this is the only way in which the people in Vietnam can possibly get a change of government. Whenever we thwart attempts at a coup, as we have done in the past, we are incurring very long lasting resentments, we are assuming an undue responsibility for keeping the incumbents in office, and in general are setting ourselves in judgment over the affairs of Vietnam. Merely to keep in touch with this situation and a policy merely limited to "not thwarting" are courses both of which entail some risks but these are lesser risks than either thwarting all coups while they are stillborn or our not being informed of what is happening. All the above is totally distinct from not wanting U.S. military advisors to be distracted by matters which are not in their domain, with which I heartily agree. But obviously this does not conflict with a policy of not thwarting. In judging proposed coups, we must consider the effect on the war effort. Certainly a succession of fights for control of the Government of Vietnam would interfere with the war effort. It must also be said that the war effort has been interfered with already by the incompetence of the present government and the uproar which this has caused.

7. Gen. Don's intention to have no religious discrimination in a future government is commendable and I applaud his desire not to be "a vassal" of the U.S. But I do not think his promise of a democratic election is realistic. This country simply is not ready for that procedure. I would add two other requirements. First, that there be no wholesale purges of personnel in the government. Individuals who were particularly reprehensible could be dealt with later by the regular legal process. Then I would be im-

practical, but I am thinking of a government which might include Tri Quang and which certainly should include men of the stature of Mr. Buu, the labor leader.

8. Copy to Gen. Harkins.

53

Bundy's Reply on Coup Hazards

Cablegram from McGeorge Bundy to Ambassador Lodge, Oct. 25, 1963.

Your 1964 most helpful.

We will continue to be grateful for all additional information giving increased clarity to prospects of action by Don or others, and we look forward to discussing with you the whole question of control and cut-out on your return, always assuming that one of these D-Days does not turn out to be real. We are particularly concerned about hazard that an unsuccessful coup, however carefully we avoid direct engagement, will be laid at our door by public opinion almost everywhere. Therefore, while sharing your view that we should not be in position of thwarting coup, we would like to have option of judging and warning on any plan with poor prospects of success. We recognize that this is a large order, but President wants you to know of our concern.

54

Harkins Message to Taylor Voicing Doubts on Plot

Cablegram from General Harkins in Saigon to General Taylor, Oct. 30, 1963.

Your JCS 4188-63 arrived as I was in the process of drafting one for you along the same lines. I share your concern. I have not as yet seen Saigon 768. I sent to the Embassy for a copy at 0830 this morning—as of now 1100—the Embassy has not released it. Also CINCPAC 0-300040Z infor JCS came as a surprise to me as I am unaware of any change in local situation which indicates necessity for actions directed. Perhaps I'll find the answer in Saigon 768. Or perhaps actions directed in CINCPAC 300040Z are precautionary in light of Gen. Don's statement reported in CAS 1925 that a coup would take place in any case not later than 2 November. It might be noted Don also is supposed to have said CAS Saigon 1956—that though the coup committee would not release the details, the Ambassador would receive the complete plan for study two days prior to the scheduled times for the coup.

I have not been informed by the Ambassador that he has received any such plan. I talked to him yesterday on my return from Bangkok and he offered no additional information. He has agreed to keep me completely informed if anything new turns up.

Incidentally he leaves for Washington tomorrow (31st) afternoon. If the coup [one word illegible] to happen before the second he's hardly going to get two days notice.

One thing I have found out, Don is either lying or playing both ends against the middle. What he told me is diametrically opposed to what he told Col. Conein. He [word illegible] Conein the coup will be before November 2nd. He told me he was not planning a coup. I sat with Don and Big Minh for 2 hours during the parade last Saturday. No one mentioned coups. To go on:

Both CAS Saigon 1896 and 1925 were sent first and delivered to me after dispatch. My 1991 was discussed with the Ambassador prior to dispatch. My 1993 was not, basically because I had not seen CAS Saigon 1925 before dispatch and I just wanted to get the record straight from my side and where my name was involved.

The Ambassador and I are certainly in touch with each other but whether the communications between us are effective is something else. I will say Cabot's methods of operations are entirely different from Amb Nolting's as far as reporting in the [word illegible] is concerned.

Fritz would always clear messages concerning the military with me or my staff prior to dispatch. So would John Richardson if MACV was concerned. This is not [word illegible] today. Cite CAS 1896 and 1925 for examples. Also you will recall I was not the recipient of several messages you held when you were here.

CINCPAC brought this matter up again when I saw him in Bangkok, this past [word illegible] end. He is going to make a check when he returns to see if he holds messages I [word illegible] not received. Have just received Saigon 768. I will have to report you are correct in believing that the Ambassador is forwarding military reports and evaluation [word illegible] consulting me. For his weekly report to the President, at his request, I furnish [word illegible] a short military statement. For preparation of 768 I made no mention of the [word illegible] I will answer 768 separately today.

There is a basic difference apparently between the Ambassador's thinking and mine on the interpretation of the guidance contained in CAP 63560 dated 6 October and the additional thoughts, I repeat, thoughts expressed in CAS Washington 74228 dated 9 October. I interpret CAP 63560 as our basic guidance and that CAS 74228 being additional thoughts did not change the basic guidance in that no initiative should now be taken to give any active covert encouragement to a coup. The Ambassador feels that 74228 does change 63560 and that a change of government is desired and feels as stated in CAS Saigon 1964 that the only way to bring about such a change is by a coup.

I'm not opposed to a change in government, no indeed, but I'm inclined to feel that at this time the change should be in methods of governing rather than complete change of personnel. I have seen no batting order proposed by any of the coup groups. I think we should take a hard look at any proposed list before we make any decisions. In my contacts here I have seen no one with the strength of character of Diem, at least in fighting Communists. Certainly there are no Generals qualified to take over in my opinion.

I am not a Diem man per se. I certainly see the faults in his character. I am here to back 14 million SVN people in their fight against communism and it just happens that Diem is their leader at this time. Most of the Generals I have talked to agree they can go along with Diem, all say it's the Nhu family they are opposed to.

Perhaps the pressures we have begun to apply will cause Diem and Nhu to change their ways. This apparently not evident as yet. I'm sure the pressures we have begun to apply if continued will affect the war effort. To date they have not. I am watching this closely and will report when I think they have.

I do not agree with the Ambassador's assessment in 768 that we are just holding our own. The GVN is a way ahead in the I, II and parts of the III Corps and making progress in the Delta. Nothing has happened in October to change the assessment you and Secretary McNamara made after your visit here.

I would suggest we not try to change horses too quickly. That we continue to take persuasive actions that will make the horses change their course and methods of action. That we win the military effort as quickly as possible, then let them make any and all the changes they want.

After all, rightly or wrongly, we have backed Diem for eight long hard years. To me it seems incongruous now to get him down, kick him around and get rid of him. The U.S. has been his mother superior and father confessor since he's been in office and he has leaned on us heavily.

Leaders of other under-developed countries will take a dim view of our assistance if they too were led to believe the same fate lies in store for them.

55

Further Harkins Comments to General Taylor

Cablegram from General Harkins to General Taylor, Oct. 30, 1963.

1. Admiral Felt not addee [sic] this message but will be provided copy upon his arrival Saigon tomorrow.

2. I now hold copy of SAIGON 768 and this amplifies my MAC 2028 which initially responded to your JCS 4188-63.

3. SAIGON 768 was Ambassador Lodge personal report to President in response to DEPTEL 576 which is possible explanation why I had not seen 768 until one week after dispatch and only when I requested a copy so that I might intelligently respond to your JCS 4188-63 which referred to 768.

4. Upon receipt of DEPTEL 576 Ambassador Lodge requested that I provide him brief suggested inputs for responses to questions 1 and 2 (a) 1 of DEPTEL 576 in that they were principally military in nature. I have done this on weekly basis but have had no knowledge as to whether my suggested brief inputs were utilized in his personal report since as indicated abot [sic] these were not opened to me.

5. My suggested brief inputs for para 1 which were provided the Ambassador for use as he saw fit in drafting his personal evaluations for the past three weeks follow:

16 OCT: On balance we are gaining in contest with the VC. There will continue to be minor ups and downs but the general trend has been and continues upward.

23 OCT: While significant changes are, and will be, difficult to identify on a day to day or even weekly comparative basis as regards the contest with the Viet Cong, the general trend continues to be favorable. The tempo of RVN-initiated operations is increasing and recently the tempo of VC-initiated activity has fallen off.

30 OCT: No change from that previously reported. National day affair this past week tended to bring about a slight reduction in the tempo of RVN initiated actions, however VC actions also waned and on balance the trend continues to be favorable.

6. My suggested brief inputs for paragraph 2 (a) which were provided the Ambassador for use as he saw fit in drafting his personal evaluations for the past three weeks follow:

16 OCT: The government has responded at many points when we have cited need for improvement in the campaign against the VC (shift of boundaries; placement of VNSF activities in corps areas under OPCON of corps comdr; reallocation of forces). Additionally Gen Don and Gen Stilwell, my G-3 have spent the last week in the conduct of a Corps by Corps assessment of the present situation with a view to further desirable reallocation of forces. Based on their recommendations I will make further recommendations to Pres. Diem. (for inclusion in ANS to para 2 (a) Ambassador was advised that US/GVN military relations remain good).

23 OCT: Response received from the government in reaction to military areas where we have cited needed improvement has been favorable in some areas, while in other areas no indication of response has been received to date. In no case have they flatly

resisted recommended improvements. Favorable indications are the commitment of nearly half of the general reserve to operations, plans for possible further redistribution of forces, and a recognition of the requirement to effect consolidation in the strategic hamlet program.

30 OCT: No specific responses have been received from the government this past week in reaction to military areas where we have cited need for improvement. This is believed due in great part to their preoccupation with National day affairs.

7. Comparison of my 23 October suggested brief inputs quoted above with SAIGON 678 indicates Ambassador Lodge did not see fit to utilize my suggestions to any significant degree. It also apparent that upon further reflection Ambassador determined that more retailed response was required than he initially felt necessary when he requested brief inputs on principally military items.

8. I believe certain portions SAIGON 768 require specific comment. These follow:

Para F of answer to question 1—View of Vice Pres Tho that there are only 15 to 20 all-around hamlets in the area south of Saigon which are really good is ridiculous and indicates need for him to get out of Saigon and visit countryside so as to really know of progress which is being made. In past two weeks I have visited nine Delta provinces (Tay Ninh, Binh Duong, Hau Nghia, Long An, Kien Phong, Kien Hoa, An Giang, Phong Dinh, Chuong Thien) eight of which are south of Saigon, and I do not find the province chiefs or sector advisors to hold the same views as Vice Pres Tho.

Para H of answer to question 1—I am unable to concur in statement that quote one cannot drive as much around the country as one could two years ago end of quote. I believe it will be some time before, if we ever do, experience mass surrenders of the VC. I am unable to concur in statement that VC is quote in fact, reckoned at a higher figure than it was two years ago end quote. I have not observed the signs that hatred of the government has tended to diminish the Army's vigor, enthusiasm and enterprise. I find it difficult to believe the few rumors one hears regarding Generals being paid off with money and flashy cars. Most cars I see in use by Generals are same they have been using for past two years and few if any qualify as flashy to my mind. I do not concur with the evaluation of the 14 October report of the Delta Subcommittee of the Committee on Province Rehabilitation which states that the VC are gaining. Moreover take exception to the implication that the report represents official country team agency views and is consequently authoritative in the views it presents. Agency representatives on this sub-committee served as individuals in reporting to the COPROR Committee, incidentally there were wide divergencies even among sub-committee members. COPROR Committee received but did not place its stamp of approval or concurrence on report of its Sub-Committee. COPROR Committee returned the report to its Sub-Committee for rework. Consequently this report has not as yet been submitted to country team nor has it been referred to individual country team agencies for review and/or comment. Any views quoted from this Sub-Committee report therefore have no rpt no validity as expressions of country team or individual agency views.

Para J of answer to question 1—With regard to the quote existing political control over troop movement, which prevents optimum use of the Army end quote. I do not deny that political influences enter into this picture however I feel we have made and are making significant strides in this area and do not concur that time is not working for us—so long as political controls remain as at present.

Para J of answer to question 1—As indicated in paras 5 and 6 above and in other reports I have filed my evaluation is that from the military point of view the trend is definitely in RVN favor consequently I cannot concur that quote we at present are not doing much more than holding our own end quote.

Answer under (a) to question 2—I am correctly quoted here but para 6 gives full context of my suggested input.

Answer under (c) to question 2—As indicated para 6 above Ambassador was advised that US/GVN military relations remain good.

56

Bundy Cable to Lodge Voicing
White House Concern

Cablegram from McGeorge Bundy to Ambassador Lodge, Oct. 30, 1963.

1. Your 2023, 2040, 2041 and 2043 examined with care at highest levels here. You should promptly discuss this reply and associated messages with Harkins whose responsibilities toward any coup are very heavy especially after you leave (see para. 7 below). They give much clearer picture group's alleged plans and also indicate chances of action with or without our approval now so significant that we should urgently consider our attitude and contingency plans. We note particularly Don's curiosity your departure and his insistence Conein be available from Wednesday night on, which suggests date might be as early as Thursday.

2. Believe our attitude to coup group can still have decisive effect on its decisions. We believe that what we say to coup group can produce delay of coup and that betrayal of coup plans to Diem is not repeat not our only way of stopping coup. We therefore need urgently our combined assessment with Harkins and CAS (including their separate comments if they desire). We concerned that our line-up of forces in Saigon (being cabled in next

message) indicates approximately equal balance of forces, with substantial possibility serious and prolonged fighting or even defeat. Either of these could be serious or even disastrous for U.S. interests, so that we must have assurance balance of forces clearly favorable.

3. With your assessment in hand, we might feel that we should convey message to Don, whether or not he gives 4 or 48 hours notice that would (A) continue explicit hands-off policy, (B) positively encourage coup, or (C) discourage.

4. In any case, believe Conein should find earliest opportunity express to Don that we do not find presently revealed plans give clear prospect of quick results. This conversation should call attention important Saigon units still apparently loyal to Diem and raise serious issue as to what means coup group has to deal with them.

5. From operational standpoint, we also deeply concerned Don only spokesman for group and possibility cannot be discounted he may not be in good faith. We badly need some corroborative evidence whether Minh, and others directly and completely involved. In view Don's claim he doesn't handle "military planning" could not Conein tell Don that we need better military picture and that Big Minh could communicate this most naturally and easily to Stillwell? We recognize desirability involving MACV to minimum, but believe Stillwell far more desirable this purpose than using Conein both ways.

6. Complexity above actions raises question whether you should adhere to present Thursday schedule. Concur you and other U.S. elements should take no action that could indicate U.S. awareness coup possibility. However, DOD is sending berth-equipped military aircraft that will arrive Saigon Thursday and could take you out thereafter as late as Saturday afternoon in time to meet your presently proposed arrival Washington Sunday. You could explain this being done as convenience and that your Washington arrival is same. A further advantage such aircraft is that it would permit your prompt return from any point en route if necessary. To reduce time in transit, you should use this plane, but we recognize delaying your departure may involve greater risk that you personally would appear involved if any action took place. However, advantages your having extra two days in Saigon may outweigh this and we leave timing of flight to your judgment.

7. Whether you leave Thursday or later, believe it essential that prior your departure there be fullest consultation Harkins and CAS and that there be clear arrangements for handling (A) normal activity, (B) continued coup contacts, (C) action in event a coup starts. We assume you will wish. Truehart as charge to be head of country team in normal situation, but highest authority desires it clearly understood that after your departure Harkins should participate in supervision of all coup contacts and that in event a coup begins, he become head of country team and direct representative of President, with Truehart in effect acting as

POLAD. On coup contacts we will maintain continuous guidance and will expect equally continuous reporting with prompt account of any important divergences in assessments of Harkins and Smith.

8. If coup should start, question of protecting U.S. nationals at once arises. We can move Marine Battalion into Saigon by air from Okinawa within 24 hours if—[sic] available. We are sending instructions to CINCPAC to arrange orderly movement of seaborne Marine Battalion to waters adjacent to South Vietnam in position to close Saigon within approximately 24 hours.

9. We are now examining post-coup contingencies here and request your immediate recommendations on position to be adopted after coup begins, especially with respect to requests for assistance of different sorts from one side or the other also request you forward contingency recommendations for action if coup (A) succeeds, (B) fails, (C) is indecisive.

10. We reiterate burden of proof must be on coup group to show a substantial possibility of quick success; otherwise, we should discourage them from proceeding since a miscalculation could result in jeopardizing U.S. position in Southeast Asia.

57

Lodge Response to Bundy on Letting Coup Plan Proceed

Cablegram from Ambassador Lodge to McGeorge Bundy, Oct. 30, 1963. The Pentagon study identifies this message as a reply to Mr. Bundy's cablegram.

1. We must, of course, get best possible estimate of chance of coup's success and this estimate must color our thinking, but do not think we have the power to delay or discourage a coup. Don has made it clear many times that this is a Vietnamese affair. It is theoretically possible for us to turn over the information which has been given to us in confidence to Diem and this would undoubtedly stop the coup and would make traitors out of us. For practical purposes therefore I would say that we have very little influence on what is essentially a Vietnamese affair. In addition, this would place the heads of the Generals, their civilian supporters, and lower military officers on the spot, thereby sacrificing a significant portion of the civilian and military leadership needed to carry the war against the VC to its successful conclusion. After our efforts not to discourage a coup and this change of heart, we would foreclose any possibility of change of the GVN for the better. Diem/Nhu have displayed no intentions to date of a desire to change the traditional methods of control through police action or take any repeat any actions which would undermine the power position or solidarity of the Ngo family. This, despite our heavy

226

pressures directed DEPTEL 534. If our attempt to thwart this coup were successful, which we doubt, it is our firm estimate that younger officers, small groups of military, would then engage in an abortive action creating chaos ideally suited to VC objectives.

2. While we will attempt a combined assessment in a following message, time has not yet permitted substantive examination of this matter with General Harkins. My general view is that the U.S. is trying to bring this medieval country into the 20th Century and that we have made considerable progress in military and economic ways but to gain victory we must also bring them into the 20th Century politically and that can only be done by either a thoroughgoing change in the behavior of the present government or by another government. The Viet Cong problem is partly military but it is also partly psychological and political.

3. With respect to paragraph 3 Ref., I believe that we should continue our present position of keeping hands off but continue to monitor and press for more detailed information. CAS has been analyzing potential coup forces for some time and it is their estimate that the Generals have probably figured their chances pretty closely and probably also expect that once they begin to move, not only planned units, but other units will join them. We believe that Vietnam's best Generals are involved in directing this effort. If they can't pull it off, it is doubtful other military leadership could do so successfully. It is understandable that the Generals would be reticent to reveal full details of their plan for fear of leaks to the GVN.

4. Re para. 4, Ref., we expect that Conein will meet Don on the night of 30 Oct or early morning 31 Oct. We agree with Para. 4, Ref., that we should continue to press for details and question Don as to his estimate of the relative strengths of opposing forces. We do not believe, however, that we should show any signs of attempting to direct this affair ourselves or of giving the impression of second thoughts on this Vietnamese initiation. In the meantime, we will respond specifically to CAS Washington 79126. Please note that CAS Saigon 2059 corrects CAS Saigon 2023 and two regiments of the 7th Division are included in the coup forces.

5. Apparently Para. 5, Ref., overlooks CAS 1445, 5 Oct 1963 which gave an account of the face to face meeting of General "Big Minh" and Conein at Minh's instigation and through the specific arrangement of Gen Don. Minh specifically identified Gen Don as participating in a plan to change the government. Please note that Minh's remarks parallel in every way the later statements of Gen. Don. We believe that the limitation of contact to Don and Cein [sic] is an appropriate security measure consonant with our urging that the smallest number of persons be aware of these details.

6. We do not believe it wise to ask that "Big Minh" pass his plans to Gen. Stilwell. The Vietnamese believe that there are members of the U.S. military who leak to the Government of Vietnam. I do not doubt that this is an unjust suspicion but it is a

fact that this suspicion exists and there is no use in pretending that it does not.

7. I much appreciate your furnishing the berth-equipped military aircraft which I trust is a jet. I intend to tell Pan American that a jet has been diverted for my use and therefore I will no longer need their services. This will undoubtedly leak to the newspapers and the GVN may study this move with some suspicion. I will answer any inquiries on this score to the effect that I am most pleased by this attention and that this is obviously done as a measure to insure my comfort and save my time. To allay suspicions further, I will offer space on the aircraft to MACV for emergency leave cases, etc., and handle this in as routine fashion as possible. I wish to reserve comment as to my actual time of departure until I have some additional information, hopefully tomorrow.

8. Your para. 7 somewhat perplexes me. It does not seem sensible to have the military in charge of a matter which is so profoundly political as a change of government. In fact, I would say to do this would probably be the end of any hope for a change of government here. This is said impersonally as a general proposition, since Gen. Harkins is a splendid General and an old friend of mine to whom I would gladly entrust anything I have. I assume that the Embassy and MACV are able to handle normal activities under A, that CAS can continue coup contacts under B and as regards C, we must simply do the very best we can in the light of events after the coup has started.

9. We appreciate the steps taken as outlined in para. 8. However, we should remember that the GVN is not totally inept in its foreign soundings and that these moves should be as discreet and security conscious as possible. I would, of course, call for these forces only in case of extreme necessity since my hope coincides with the Generals that this will be an all-Vietnamese affair.

10. We anticipate that at the outset of the coup, unless it moves with lightning swiftness, the GVN will request me or Gen. Harkins to use our influence to call it off. I believe our responsibilities should be that our influence certainly could not be superior to that of the President who is Commander-in-Chief and that if he is unable to call it off, we would certainly be unable to do so and would merely be risking American lives attempting to interfere in this Vietnamese problem. The Government might request aircraft, Helicopters, for the evacuation of key personalities that would have to be studied closely, but we would certainly not commit our planes and pilots between the battle lines of the opposing forces. We should, rather, state that we would be willing to act in this fashion during a truce in which both sides agree to the removal of key personalities. I believe that there would be immediate political problems in attempting to take these personalities to another neighboring country and probably we would be best served in depositing them in Saipan where the absence of press communications, etc., would allow us some leeway to make

rther decision as to their ultimate disposition. If senior Vietnamese personalities and their families requested asylum in the mbassy or other American installations, we would probably have grant it in light of our previous action with respect to Tri uang. This will undoubtedly present later problems but hopefully e new government might feel disposed to help us solve this oblem. Naturally, asylum would be granted on the same basis the Buddhists, i.e., physical presence at the Embassy or other cation.

11. As to requests from the Generals, they may well have need f funds at the last moment with which to buy off potential opposition. To the extent that these funds can be passed discreetly, I elieve we should furnish them, provided we are convinced that e proposed coup is sufficiently well organized to have a good ance of success. If they are successful, they will undoubtedly sk for prompt recognition and some assurance that military and conomic aid will continue at normal level. We should be prepared to make these statements if the issue is clear-cut predicating ur position on the President's stated desire to continue the war gainst the VC to final victory. VOA might be an important eans of disseminating this message. Should the coup fail, we will ave to pick up the pieces as best we can at that time. We have commitment to the Generals from the August episode to attempt help in the evacuation of their dependents. We should try to ve up to this if conditions will permit. American complicity will ndoubtedly be charged and there might be some acts taken gainst specific personalities which we should anticipate and make rovision against as best we can. Should the coup prove indecisive nd a protracted struggle is in progress, we should probably offer ur good offices to help resolve the issue in the interest of the war gainst the VC. This might hold some benefit in terms of concessions by GVN. We will naturally incur some opprobrium from oth sides in our role as mediator. However, this opprobrium ould probably be less distasteful than a deadlock which would pen the door to the VC. We consider such a deadlock as the least kely possibility of the three.

12. As regards your para. 10, I do not know what more proof an be offered than the fact these men are obviously prepared to sk their lives and that they want nothing for themselves. If I am ny judge of human nature, Don's face expressed of sincerity and etermination on the morning that I spoke to him. Heartily agree at a miscalculation could jeopardize position in Southeast Asia. Ve also run tremendous risks by doing nothing.

If we were convinced that the coup was going to fail, we would, f course, do everything we could to stop it.

13. Gen. Harkins has read this and does not concur.

58

Further Bundy Instructions to Lodge on Contingency Plans

Cablegram from McGeorge Bundy to Ambassador Lodge, Oct. 30, 1963.

1. Our reading your thoughtful 2063 leads us to believe a significant difference of shading may exist on one crucial point (see next para.) and on one or two lesser matters easily clarified.

2. We do not accept as a basis for U.S. policy that we have power to delay or discourage a coup. In your paragraph 12 you say that if you were convinced that the coup was going to fail you would of course do everything you could to stop it. We believe that on this same basis you should take action to persuade coup leaders to stop or delay any operation which, in your best judgment, does not clearly give high prospect of success. We have not considered any betrayal of generals to Diem, and our 79109 explicitly reject that course. We recognize the danger of appearing hostile to generals, but we believe that our own position should be on as firm ground as possible, hence we cannot limit ourselves proposition implied in your message that only conviction of certain failure justifies intervention. We believe that your standard for intervention should be that stated above.

3. Therefore, if you should conclude that there is not clearly high prospect of success, you should communicate this doubt generals in a way calculated to persuade them to desist at least until chances are better. In such a communication you should use the weight of U.S. best advice and explicitly reject any implication that we oppose the effort of the generals because of preference for present regime. We recognize need to bear in mind general interpretation of U.S. role in 1960 coup attempt, and your agents should maintain clear distinction between strong and honest advice given as a friend and any opposition to their objectives.

We continue to be deeply interested in up-to-the-minute assessment of prospects and are sending this before reply to our CAS 79126. We want continuous exchange latest assessments on this topic.

5. To clarify our intent, paragraph 7 of our 79109 is rescinded and we restate our desires as follows:

a. While you are in Saigon you will be Chief of Country Team in all circumstances and our only instruction is that we are sure it will help to have Harkins fully informed at all stages and to use advice from both him and Smith in framing guidance for coup contacts and assessment. We continue to be concerned that neither Conein nor any other reporting source is getting the clarity we would like with respect to alignment of forces and level of determination among generals.

b. When you leave Saigon and before there is a coup, Trueha

will be Chief of the Country Team. Our only modification of existing procedures is that in this circumstance we wish all instruction to Conein to be conducted in immediate consultation with Harkins and Smith so that all three know what is sold in Conein. Any disagreement among the three on such instruction should be reported to Washington and held for our resolution, when time permits.

c. If you have left and a coup occurs, we believe that emergency situation requires, pending your return, that direction of country team be vested in most senior officer with experience of military decisions, and the officer in our view is Harkins. We do *not* intend that this switch in final responsibility should be publicized in any way, and Harkins will of course be guided in basic posture by our instructions, which follow in paragraph 6. We do not believe that this switch will have the effect suggested in your paragraph 8.

6. This paragraph contains our present standing instructions for U.S. posture in the event of a coup.

a. U.S. authorities will reject appeals for direct intervention from either side, and U.S.-controlled aircraft and other resources will not be committed between the battle lines or in support of either side, without authorization from Washington.

b. In event of indecisive contest, U.S. authorities may in their discretion agree to perform any acts agreeable to both sides, such as removal of key personalities or relay of information. In such actions, however, U.S. authorities will strenuously avoid appearance of pressure on either side. It is not in the interest of USG to be or appear to be either instrument of existing government or instrument of coup.

c. In the event of imminent or actual failure of coup, U.S. authorities may afford asylum in their discretion to those to whom there is any express or implied obligation of this sort. We believe however that in such a case it would be in our interest and probably in interest of those seeking asylum that they seek protection of other Embassies in addition to our own. This point should be made strongly if need arises.

d. But once a coup under responsible leadership has begun, and within these restrictions, it is in the interest of the U.S. Government that it should succeed.

7. We have your message about return to Washington and we suggest that all public comment be kept as low-key and quiet as possible, and we also urge that if possible you keep open the exact time of your departure. We are strongly sensitive to great disadvantage of having you out of Saigon if this should turn out to be a week of decision, and if it can be avoided we would prefer not to see you pinned to a fixed hour of departure now.

59

Lodge's Last Talk with Diem

Excerpt from cablegram from Ambassador Lodge to State Department, Nov. 1, 1963, as provided in the body of the Pentagon study. According to the narrative, the message says that at 4:30 P.M. on Nov. 1 President Diem telephoned Ambassador Lodge and the following conversation ensued:

DIEM: Some units have made a rebellion and I want to know what is the attitude of the U.S.?

LODGE: I do not feel well enough informed to be able to tell you. I have heard the shooting, but am not acquainted with all the facts. Also it is 4:30 a.m. in Washington and the U.S. Government cannot possibly have a view.

DIEM: But you must have some general ideas. After all, I am a Chief of State. I have tried to do my duty. I want to do now what duty and good sense require. I believe in duty above all.

LODGE: You have certainly done your duty. As I told you only this morning, I admire your courage and your great contributions to your country. No one can take away from you the credit for all you have done. Now I am worried about your physical safety. I have a report that those in charge of the current activity offer you and your brother safe conduct out of the country if you resign. Had you heard this?

DIEM: No. (And then after a pause) You have my telephone number.

LODGE: Yes. If I can do anything for your physical safety, please call me.

DIEM: I am trying to re-establish order.

60

Order by Johnson Reaffirming Kennedy's Policy on Vietnam

Excerpts from National Security Action Memorandum 273, Nov. 26, 1963, four days after the assassination of President Kennedy, as provided in the body of the Pentagon study. Paragraphs in italics are the study's paraphrase.

"A National Security Action Memorandum was drafted to give guidance and direction to our efforts to improve the conduct of the war under the new South Vietnamese leadership. It described the purpose of the American involvement in Vietnam as, "to assist

232

the people and Government of that country to win their contest against the externally directed and supported Communist conspiracy." It defined contribution to that purpose as the test of all U.S. actions in Vietnam. It reiterated the objectives of withdrawing 1,000 U.S. troops by the end of 1963 and ending the insurgency in I, II, and III Corps by the end of 1964, and in the Delta by the end of 1965. U.S. support for the new regime was confirmed and all U.S. efforts were directed to assist it to consolidate itself and expand its popular support. . . .

The objectives of the United States with respect to the withdrawal of U.S. military personnel remain as stated in the White House statement of October 2, 1963. . . .

The President expects that all senior officers of the government will move energetically to insure the full unity of support for established U.S. policy in South Vietnam. Both in Washington and in the field, it is essential that the government be unified. It is of particular importance that express or implied criticism of officers of other branches be assiduously avoided in all contacts with the Vietnamese government and with the press. . . .

We should concentrate our efforts, and insofar as possible we should persuade the government of South Vietnam to concentrate its effort, on the critical situation in the Mekong Delta. This concentration should include not only military but political, economic, turn the tide not only of battle but of belief, and we should seek to turn not only of battle but of belief, and we should seek to increase not only the controlled hamlets but the productivity of this area, especially where the proceeds can be held for the advantage of anti-Communist forces . . .

It is a major interest of the United States government that the present provisional government of South Vietnam should be assisted in consolidating itself in holding and developing increased public support.

. . . And in conclusion, plans were requested for clandestine operations by the GVN against the North and also for operations up to 50 kilometers into Laos; and, as a justification for such measures, State was directed to develop a strong, documented case "to demonstrate to the world the degree to which the Viet Cong is controlled, sustained and supplied from Hanoi, through Laos and other channels." . . .

Chapter 5

The Covert War and Tonkin Gulf: February–August, 1964

—BY NEIL SHEEHAN

This article, the first in the series as published by The Times, appears here in chronological order, with the initial paragraphs revised.

The Covert War

The Pentagon papers disclose that for six months before the Tonkin Gulf incident in August, 1964, the United States had been mounting clandestine military attacks against North Vietnam while planning to obtain a Congressional resolution that the Administration regarded as the equivalent of a declaration of war.

When the incident occurred, the Johnson Administration did not reveal these clandestine attacks and pushed the previously prepared resolution through both houses of Congress on Aug. 7.

Within 72 hours, the Administration, again drawing on a prepared plan, secretly sent a Canadian emissary to Hanoi. He warned Premier Pham Van Dong that the resolution meant North Vietnam must halt the Communist-led insurgencies in South Vietnam and Laos or "suffer the consequences."

The magnitude of this threat to Hanoi, the nature and extent of the covert military operations and the intent of the Administration to use the resolution to commit the nation to open warfare, if this later proved desirable, were all kept secret.

The section of the Pentagon history dealing with the internal debate, planning and action in the Johnson Administration from the beginning of 1964 to the August clashes between North Vietnamese PT boats and American destroyers—portrayed as a critical period when the groundwork was laid for the wider war that followed—also makes the following disclosures:

• The clandestine military operations had become so extensive by August, 1964, that Thai pilots flying American T-28 fighter planes apparently bombed and strafed North Vietnamese villages near the Laotian border on Aug. 1 and 2.

• Although a firm decision to begin sustained bombing of North Vietnam was not made until months later, the Administration was able to order retaliatory air strikes on less than six hours' notice during the Tonkin incident because planning had progressed so far that a list of targets was available for immediate choice.

• The target list had been drawn up in May, along with a draft of the Congressional resolution, also as part of a proposed "scenario" culminating in air raids on North Vietnam.

• During a whirlwind series of Pentagon meetings at which the targets for the Tonkin reprisals were selected, Secretary of Defense Robert S. McNamara and the Joint Chiefs of Staff also arranged for the deployment to Southeast Asia of air strike forces earmarked for the opening phases of the bombing campaign. Within hours of the retaliatory air strikes on Aug. 4, and three days before the passage of the Tonkin resolution, the squadrons began their planned moves.

What the Pentagon papers call "an elaborate program of covert military operations against the state of North Vietnam" began on Feb. 1, 1964, under the code name Operation Plan 34A. President Johnson ordered the program, on the recommendation of Secretary McNamara, in the hope, held very faint by the intelligence community, that "progressively escalating pressure" from the clandestine attacks might eventually force Hanoi to order the Vietcong guerrillas in Vietnam and the Pathet Lao in Laos to halt their insurrections.

In a memorandum to the President on Dec. 21, 1963, after a two-day trip to Vietnam, Mr. McNamara remarked that the plans, drawn up by the Central Intelligence Agency station and the military command in Saigon, were "an excellent job."

"They present a wide variety of sabotage and psychological operations against North Vietnam from which I believe we

Highlights of the Period

Here, in chronological sequence, are highlights of the period covered in this article:

FEBRUARY, 1964

Start of Operation Plan 34A program of clandestine military operations against North Vietnam.

MARCH, 1964

Plans for "new and significant pressures on North Vietnam" urged by Mr. McNamara on return from Vietnam; since new Government of Gen. Nguyen Khanh considered unable to improve South Vietnam outlook.

President Johnson approves; cables Henry Cabot Lodge, United States Ambassador in Saigon, that "our planning for action against the North is on a contingency basis at the present."

APRIL, 1964

Scenarios for escalation reviewed in Saigon by Mr. Lodge, William P. Bundy, Dean Rusk, Gen. Earle G. Wheeler. Plans cover details of stepping up United States military involvement to conform with Administration conviction that Hanoi controls Vietcong. Extent of Hanoi's involvement should be "proven to the satisfaction of our own public, of our allies and of the neutralists," according to Mr. Rusk.

List of 94 potential targets for bombing in North drawn up by Joint Chiefs.

MAY, 1964

General Khanh asks United States attacks on the North, tells Mr. Lodge Saigon wants to declare war on North Vietnam. Mr. McNamara does not "rule out" possibility of bombing, but stresses "such actions must be supplementary to and not a substitute for" success against Vietcong in South. Mr. Lodge cables Mr. Rusk that United States cannot "expect a much better performance" from Saigon Government "unless something" in the way of United States action is forthcoming.

William Bundy sends President 30-day scenario for graduated military pressure against the North that would culminate in full-scale bombing attacks. Includes joint Congressional resolution "authorizing whatever is necessary with respect to Vietnam."

JUNE, 1964

Honolulu strategy meeting. Ambassador Lodge urges "a selective bombing campaign against military targets in the North" to bolster shaky morale in South. He questions need for Congressional resolution; Mr. Rusk, Mr. McNamara, John McCone of C.I.A. support it.

Preparatory military deployments under way in Southeast Asia.

J. Blair Seaborn, Canadian diplomat, meets secretly in Hanoi with Pham Van Dong, North Vietnam's Premier, warns of "the greatest devastation" that would result from escalation by North Vietnam.

President resists pressure to ask for Congressional resolution immediately and to step up the war effort.

Mr. Johnson queries C.I.A. on "domino theory." Agency replies only Cambodia is likely to "quickly succumb to Communism" if Laos and South Vietnam fall, but says U.S. prestige would be damaged.

JULY, 1964

General Khanh announces "March North" propaganda campaign.

South Vietnamese naval commandos raid two North Vietnamese islands in Gulf of Tonkin. Part of "growing operational capabilities" of 34A program, the Pentagon study says.

AUGUST, 1964

Destroyer Maddox, on Gulf of Tonkin intelligence patrol, attacked by North Vietnamese PT boats seeking South Vietnamese raiders. Joined by the C. Turner Joy, attacked again by torpedo boats, history reports.

Less than 12 hours after news of second attack reaches Washington, bombers on way to North Vietnam on reprisal raiders from carrier.

Tonkin Gulf resolution, drafted by Administration, introduced. Administration officials testify; Mr. McNamara disclaims knowledge South Vietnamese attacks on islands. Resolution passes.

What study calls "an important threshold in the war"—U.S. reprisal air strikes against North—crossed with "virtually no domestic criticism."

should aim to select those that provide maximum pressure with minimum risk," Mr. McNamara wrote. [See Document 61.]

President Johnson, in this period, showed a preference for steps that would remain "noncommitting" to combat, the study found. But weakness in South Vietnam and Communist advances kept driving the planning process. This, in turn, caused the Saigon Government and American officials in Saigon to demand ever more action.

Through 1964, the 34A operations ranged from flights over North Vietnam by U-2 spy planes and kidnappings of North Vietnamese citizens for intelligence information, to parachuting sabotage and psychological-warfare teams into the North, commando raids from the sea to blow up rail and highway bridges and the bombardment of North Vietnamese coastal installations by PT boats.

These "destructive undertakings," as they were described in a report to the President on Jan. 2, 1964, from Maj. Gen. Victor H. Krulak of the Marine Corps, were designed "to result in substantial destruction, economic loss and harassment." The tempo and magnitude of the strikes were designed to rise in three phases through 1964 to "targets identified with North Vietnam's economic and industrial well-being."

The clandestine operations were directed for the President by Mr. McNamara through a section of the Joint Chiefs organization called the Office of the Special Assistant for Counterinsurgency and Special Activities. The study says that Mr. McNamara was kept regularly informed of planned and conducted raids by memorandums from General Krulak, who first held the position of special assistant, and then from Maj. Gen. Rollen H. Anthis of the Air Force, who succeeded him in February, 1964. The Joint Chiefs themselves periodically evaluated the operations for Mr. McNamara.

Secretary of State Dean Rusk was also informed, if in less detail.

The attacks were given "interagency clearance" in Washington, the study says, by coordinating them with the State Department and the Central Intelligence Agency, including advance monthly schedules of the raids from General Anthis.

The Pentagon account and the documents show that William P. Bundy, the Assistant Secretary of State for Far Eastern Affairs, and John T. McNaughton, head of the Pentagon's politico-military operations as the Assistant Secretary of Defense for International Security Affairs, were the senior civilian officials who supervised the distribution of the schedules and the other aspects of interagency coordination for Mr. McNamara and Mr. Rusk.

The analyst notes that the 34A program differed in a significant respect from the relatively low-level and unsuccessful intelligence and sabotage operations that the C.I.A. had earlier been carrying out in North Vietnam.

The 34A attacks were a military effort under the control in Saigon of Gen. Paul D. Harkins, chief of the United States Military Assistance Command there. He ran them through a special branch of his command called the Studies and Observations Group. It drew up the advance monthly schedules for approval in Washington. Planning was done jointly with the South Vietnamese and it was they or "hired personnel," apparently Asian mercenaries, who performed the raids, but General Harkins was in charge.

The second major segment of the Administration's covert war against North Vietnam consisted of air operations in Laos. A force of propeller-driven T-28 fighter-bombers, varying from about 25 to 40 aircraft, had been organized there. The planes bore Laotian Air Force markings, but only some belonged to that air force. The rest were manned by pilots of Air America (a pseudo-private airline run by the C.I.A.) and by Thai pilots under the control of Ambassador Leonard Unger. [See Document #74.]

Reconnaissance flights by regular United States Air Force and Navy jets, code-named Yankee Team, gathered photographic intelligence for bombing raids by the T-28's against North Vietnamese and Pathet Lao troops in Laos.

The Johnson Administration gradually stepped up these air operations in Laos through the spring and summer of 1964 in what became a kind of preview of the bombing of the North. The escalation occurred both because of ground advances by the North Vietnamese and the Pathet Lao and because of the Administration's desire to bring more military pressure against North Vietnam.

As the intensity of the T-28 strikes rose, they crept closer to the North Vietnamese border. The United States Yankee Team jets moved from high-altitude reconnaissance at the beginning of the year to low-altitude reconnaissance in May. In June, armed escort jets were added to the reconnaissance missions. The escort jets began to bomb and strafe North Vietnamese and Pathet Lao troops and installations whenever the reconnaissance planes were fired upon.

The destroyer patrols in the Gulf of Tonkin, code-named De Soto patrols, were the third element in the covert military pressures against North Vietnam. While the purpose of the patrols was mainly psychological, as a show of force, the destroyers collected the kind of intelligence on North Vietnamese warning radars and coastal defenses that would be useful to 34A raiding parties or, in the event of a bombing campaign, to pilots. The first patrol was conducted by the destroyer Craig without incident in February and March, in the early days of the 34A operations.

The analyst states that before the August Tonkin incident there was no attempt to involve the destroyers with the 34A attacks or to use the ships as bait for North Vietnamese retaliation. The patrols were run through a separate naval chain of command.

Although the highest levels of the Administration sent the destroyers into the gulf while the 34A raids were taking place, the Pentagon study, as part of its argument that a deliberate provocation was not intended, in effects says that the Administration did not believe that the North Vietnamese would dare to attack the ships.

But the study makes it clear that the physical presence of the destroyers provided the elements for the Tonkin clash. And immediately after the reprisal air strikes, the Joint Chiefs of Staff and Assistant Secretary of Defense McNaughton put forward a "provocation strategy" proposing to repeat the clash as a pretext for bombing the North.

Of the three elements of the covert war, the analyst cites the 34A raids as the most important. The "unequivocal" American responsibility for them "carried with it an implicit symbolic and psychological intensification of the U.S. commitment," he writes. "A firebreak had been crossed."

The fact that the intelligence community and even the Joint Chiefs gave the program little chance of compelling Hanoi to stop the Vietcong and the Pathet Lao, he asserts, meant that "a demand for more was stimulated and an expectation of more was aroused."

On Jan. 22, 1964, a week before the 34A raids started, the Joint Chiefs warned Mr. McNamara in a memorandum signed by the Chairman, Gen. Maxwell D. Taylor, that while "we are wholly in favor of executing the covert actions against North Vietnam . . . it would be idle to conclude that these efforts will have a decisive effect" on Hanoi's will to support the Vietcong. [See Document #62.]

The Joint Chiefs said the Administration "must make ready to conduct increasingly bolder actions," including "aerial bombing of key North Vietnam targets, using United States resources under Vietnamese cover," sending American ground troops to South Vietnam and employing "United States forces as necessary in direct actions against North Vietnam."

And after a White House strategy meeting on Feb. 20, President Johnson ordered that "contingency planning for pressures against North Vietnam should be speeded up."

"Particular attention should be given to shaping such pressures so as to produce the maximum credible deterrent effect on Hanoi," the order said.

The impelling force behind the Administration's desire to step up the action during this period was its recognition of the steady deterioration in the positions of the pro-American governments in Laos and South Vietnam, and the corresponding weakening of the United States hold on both countries. North Vietnamese and Pathet Lao advances in Laos were seen as having a direct impact on the morale of the anti-Communist forces in South Vietnam, the primary American concern.

This deterioration was also concealed from Congress and the public as much as possible to provide the Administration with maximum flexibility to determine its moves as it chose from behind the scenes.

The United States found itself particularly unable to cope with the Vietcong insurgency, first through the Saigon military regime of Gen. Duong Van Minh and later through that of Gen. Nguyen Khanh, who seized power in a coup d'état on Jan. 30, 1964. Accordingly, attention focused more and more on North Vietnam as "the root of the problem," in the words of the Joint Chiefs.

Walt W. Rostow, the dominant intellectual of the Administration, had given currency to this idea and provided the theoretical framework for escalation. His concept, first enunciated in a speech at Fort Bragg, N.C., in 1961, was that a revolution could be dried up by cutting off external sources of support and supply.

Where North Vietnam was concerned, Mr. Rostow had evolved another theory—that a credible threat to bomb the industry Hanoi had so painstakingly constructed out of the ruins of the French Indochina War would be enough to frighten the country's leaders into ordering the Vietcong to halt their activities in the South.

In a memorandum on Feb. 13, 1964, Mr. Rostow told Secretary of State Rusk that President Ho Chi Minh "has an industrial complex to protect: he is no longer a guerrilla fighter with nothing to lose."

The Administration was firmly convinced from interceptions of radio traffic between North Vietnam and the guerrillas in the South that Hanoi controlled and directed the Vietcong. Intelligence analyses of the time stated, however, that "the primary sources of Communist strength in South Vietnam are indigenous," arising out of the revolutionary social aims of the Communists and their identification with the nationalist cause during the independence struggle against France in the nineteen-fifties.

The study shows that President Johnson and most of his key advisers would not accept this intelligence analysis that bombing the North would have no lasting effect on the situation in the South, although there was division—even among those who favored a bombing campaign if necessary—over the extent to which Vietcong fortunes were dependent on the infiltration of men and arms from North Vietnam.

William Bundy and Mr. Rusk mentioned on several occasions the need to obtain more evidence of this infiltration to build a case publicly for stronger actions against North Vietnam.

Focus Turns to Bombing

As the Vietcong rebellion gathered strength, so did interest in bombing the North as a substitute for successful prosecution of the counterinsurgency campaign in the South, or at least as an effort to force Hanoi to reduce guerrilla activity to a level where the feeble Saigon Government could handle it.

This progression in Administration thinking was reflected in Mr. McNamara's reports to President Johnson after the Secretary's trips to Vietnam in December and March.

In his December memorandum recommending initiation of the covert 34A raids, Mr. McNamara painted a "gloomy picture" of South Vietnam, with the Vietcong controlling most of the rice and population heartland of the Mekong Delta south and west of Saigon. "We should watch the situation very carefully," he concluded, "running scared, hoping for the best, but preparing for more forceful moves if the situation does not show early signs of improvement."

Then, in his memorandum of March 16 on his latest trip, Mr. McNamara reported that "the situation has unquestionably been growing worse" and recommended military planning for two programs of "new and significant pressures upon North Vietnam."

The first, to be launched on 72 hours' notice, was described as "Border Control and Retaliatory Actions." These would include assaults by Saigon's army against infiltration routes along the Ho Chi Minh Trail network of supply lines through southeastern Laos, "hot pursuit" of the guerrillas into Cambodia, "retaliatory bombing strikes" into North Vietnam by the South Vietnamese Air Force "on a tit-for-tat basis" in response to guerrilla attacks, and "aerial mining . . . (possibly with United States assistance) of the major . . . ports in North Vietnam." The words in parentheses are Mr. Mc-Namara's.

The second program, called "Graduated Overt Military Pressure," was to be readied to begin on 30 days' notice. "This program would go beyond reacting on a tit-for-tat basis," Mr. McNamara told the President. "It would include air attacks against military and possibly industrial targets." The raids would be carried out by Saigon's air force and by an American air commando squadron code-named Farmgate, then operating in South Vietnam with planes carrying South Vietnamese markings. To conduct the air strikes, they would be reinforced by three squadrons of United States Air Force B-57 jet bombers flown in from Japan.

President Johnson approved Mr. McNamara's recommendations at a National Security Council meeting on March 17, 1964, directing that planning "proceed energetically."

Mr. McNamara had advocated trying a number of measures to improve the Saigon Government's performance first, before resorting to overt escalation. "There would be the problem of marshaling the case to justify such action, the problem of Communist escalation and the problem of dealing with pressures for premature or 'stacked' negotiations," he remarked in his March memorandum.

His description of negotiations echoed a belief in the Administration that the Government of General Khanh was incapable of competing politically with the Communists. Therefore, any attempt to negotiate a compromise political settlement of the war between the Vietnamese themselves was to be avoided because it would result in a Communist take-over and the destruction of the American position in South Vietnam.

Similarly, any internal accommodation between the opposing Vietnamese forces under the vague "neutralization" formula for Vietnam that had been proposed by President de Gaulle of France that June was seen as tantamount to the same thing, a Communist victory. In his March memorandum, Mr. McNamara mentioned the dangerous growth of "neutralist sentiment" in Saigon and the possibility of a coup by neutralist forces who might form a coalition government with the Communists and invite the United States to leave.

William Bundy would later refer to this possibility as a "Vietnam solution" that must be prevented.

In a glimpse into the President's thoughts at this time, the study shows he was concerned with the problem. Mr. Johnson told Ambassador Henry Cabot Lodge in a cablegram to Saigon on March 20, 1964, that he was intent on "knocking down the idea of neutralization wherever it rears its ugly head, and on this point I think nothing is more important than to stop neutralist talk wherever we can by whatever means we can." [See Document #65.]

Mr. Lodge was opposed to planning for "massive destruction actions" before trying what he described as "an essentially diplomatic carrot and stick approach, backed by covert military means."

This plan, which Mr. Lodge had been proposing since the previous October, involved sending a secret non-American envoy to Hanoi with an offer of economic aid, such as food imports to relieve the rice shortages in North Vietnam, in return for calling off the Vietcong. If the North Vietnamese did not respond favorably, the stick—unpublicized and unacknowledged air strikes, apparently with unmarked planes—would be applied until they did.

The President's message of March 20 shared Mr. Lodge's opinion that it was still too early for open assaults on the North.

"As we agreed in our previous messages to each other," Mr. Johnson cabled, "judgment is reserved for the present on overt military action in view of the consensus from Saigon conversations of McNamara mission with General Khanh and you on judgment that movement against the North at the present would be premature. We . . . share General Khanh's judgment that the immediate and essential task is to strengthen the southern base. For this reason, our planning for action against the North is on a contingency basis at present, and immediate problem in this area is to develop the strongest possible military and political base for possible later action."

Mr. Johnson added that the Administration also expected

a "showdown" soon in the Chinese-Soviet dispute "and action against the North will be more practicable" then.

This and the other sporadic insights the study gives into Mr. Johnson's thoughts and motivations during these months leading up to the Tonkin Gulf incident in August indicate a President who was, on the one hand, pushing his Administration to plan energetically for escalation while, on the other, continually hesitating to translate these plans into military action.

The glimpses are of a Chief Executive who was determined to achieve the goal of an "independent, non-Communist South Vietnam" he had enunciated in a national security action memorandum in March, yet who was holding back on actions to achieve that goal until he believed they were absolutely necessary.

Above all, the narrative indicates a President who was carefully calculating international and domestic political conditions before making any of his moves in public.

By the latter half of April, 1964, accordingly, planning for further attacks against the North had matured sufficiently through several scenarios for Secretary Rusk, William Bundy and Gen. Earle G. Wheeler, the Army Chief of Staff, to review the plans with Ambassador Lodge at a Saigon strategy meeting on April 19 and 20.

The scenario envisioned escalation in three stages from intensification of the current clandestine 34A raids, to "covert U.S. support of overt . . . aerial mining and air strike operations" by Saigon to "overt joint . . . aerial reconnaissance, naval displays, naval bombardments and air attacks" by the United States and South Vietnam.

The analyst does not mention any provision in the April planning scenario for a Congressional resolution that would constitute authority to wage war; he refers instead to "Presidential consultations with key Congressional leaders." But the idea of a resolution was already current by then. The author reports its first emergence in discussions in the State Department in mid-February, 1964, "on the desirability of the President's requesting a Congressional resolution, drawing a line at the borders of South Vietnam." He cites a Feb. 13 letter to Secretary Rusk to this effect from Mr. Rostow, then chairman of the State Department's Policy Planning Council.

At the April Saigon meeting and in the weeks immediately afterward, the author says, "a deliberate, cautious pacing of our actions" prevailed over a near-term escalation approach being pressed by the Joint Chiefs and Mr. Rostow.

One reason for this, the study explains, was that the Administration recognized that it "lacked adequate information concerning the nature and magnitude" of infiltration of trained guerrilla leaders and arms from the North and was beginning a major effort to try to gather enough concrete evidence to justify escalation if this became necessary.

"For example," the study reports, "citing the 'lack of clarity' on the 'role of external intrusion' in South Vietnam, Walt Rostow urged William Sullivan [chairman of the interagency Vietnam coordinating committee] on the eve of [a] March visit to attempt to 'come back from Saigon with as lucid and agreed a picture' as possible on the extent of the infiltration and its influence on the Vietcong."

The direct outcome of Mr. Rusk's April visit to Saigon was his agreement to try Ambassador Lodge's carrot-and-stick approach. On April 30, 1964, the Secretary flew to Ottawa and arranged with the Canadian Government for J. Blair Seaborn, Canada's new representative on the International Control Commission, to convey the offer of United States economic aid to Premier Dong when Mr. Seaborn visited Hanoi in June.

On May 4 General Khanh, sensing a decline in his fortunes and beginning to abandon the idea of strengthening his government to the point where it could defeat the Vietcong in the South, told Ambassador Lodge that he wanted to declare war quickly on North Vietnam, have the United States start bombing and send 10,000 Special Forces troops of the United States Army into the South "to cover the whole Cambodian-Laotian border." Mr. Lodge deflected the suggestions.

Secretary McNamara, on a visit to Saigon May 13, was instructed to tell General Khanh that while the United States did not "rule out" bombing the North, "such actions must be supplementary to and not a substitute for successful counter-insurgency in the South" and that "we do not intend to provide military support nor undertake the military objective of 'rolling back' Communist control in North Vietnam."

But on May 17, when the Pathet Lao launched an offensive on the Plaine des Jarres that threatened to collapse the pro-American Government of Premier Souvanna Phouma and with it "the political underpinning of United States-Laotian policy," the study declares, this "deliberate, cautious approach" to escalation planning was suddenly thrown into "crisis management."

The Administration immediately turned the Laotian air operations up a notch by intensifying the T-28 strikes and, on May 21, by starting low-altitude target reconnaissance by United States Navy and Air Force jets over areas held by the Pathet Lao and the North Vietnamese.

In Washington, the chief planner, William Bundy, assisted by Mr. McNaughton and Mr. Sullivan, worked up a 30-day program culminating in full-scale bombing of the North. He submitted it as a formal draft Presidential memorandum for consideration by an executive committee of the National Security Council.

For a number of reasons, this May 23 scenario was never carried out as written. The President, in fact, delayed another nine months the scenario's dénouement in an air war.

But the document is important because it reveals how far the Administration had progressed in its planning by this point and because a number of the steps in the scenario were carried out piecemeal through June and July and then very rapidly under the political climate of the Tonkin Gulf clash.

For the military side of the scenario, the President's order of March 17 to plan for retaliatory air strikes on 72 hours' notice and for full-scale air raids on 30 days' notice had borne fruit in Operation Plan 37-64.

This plan had been prepared in the Honolulu headquarters of Adm. Harry D. Felt, commander in chief of Pacific forces, or CINCPAC, and had been approved by the Joint Chiefs on April 17. It tabulated how many planes and what bomb tonnages would be required for each phase of the strikes, listed the targets in North Vietnam with damage to be achieved, and programed the necessary positioning of air forces for the raids. A follow-up operation plan, designated 32-64, calculated the possible reactions of China and North Vietnam and the American ground forces that might be necessary to meet them.

The Joint Staff had refined the bombing plan with more target studies. These estimated that an initial category of targets associated with infiltration, such as bridges and depots of ammunition and petroleum, could be destroyed in only 12 days if all the air power in the western Pacific were used.

For the political side of the scenario, recommendations from William Bundy and Mr. Rusk had produced more evidence of infiltration by the North for public release to justify escalation. William J. Jorden, a former corespondent of The New York Times who had become a State Department official, had gone to South Vietnam and had pulled together the data available there for a possible new State Department white paper.

Here is the scenario as the Pentagon analyst quotes it. The words in parentheses—and the numbers designating the length of time to "D-Day"—were in the original scenario and the words in brackets were inserted by the analyst for clarification:

"1. Stall off any 'conference [Laos or] Vietnam until D-Day.'

"2. Intermediary (Canadian?) tell North Vietnam in general terms that U.S. does not want to destroy the North Vietnam regime (and indeed is willing 'to provide a carrot') but is determined to protect South Vietnam from North Vietnam.

"3. (D-30) Presidential speech in general terms launching Joint Resolution.

"4. (D-20) Obtain joint resolution approving past actions and authorizing whatever is necessary with respect to Vietnam.

"Concurrently: An effort should be made to strengthen the posture in South Vietnam. Integrating (interlarding in a single chain of command) the South Vietnamese and U.S. military and civilian elements critical to pacification, down at least to the district level, might be undertaken.

"5. (D-16) Direct CINCPAC to take all prepositioning and logistic actions that can be taken 'quietly' for the D-Day forces. . . .

"6. (D-15) Get Khanh's agreement to start overt South Vietnamese air attacks against targets in the North (see D-Day item 15 below), and inform him of U.S. guarantee to protect South Vietnam in the event of North Vietnamese and/or Chinese retaliation.

"7. (D-14) Consult with Thailand and the Philippines to get permission for U.S. deployments; and consult with them plus U.K., Australia, New Zealand and Pakistan, asking for their open political support for the undertaking and for their participation in the re-enforcing action to be undertaken in anticipation of North Vietnamese and/or Chinese retaliation.

"8. (D-13) Release an expanded 'Jorden Report,' including recent photography and evidence of the communication nets, giving full documentation of North Vietnamese supply and direction of the Vietcong.

"9. (D-12) Direct CINCPAC to begin moving forces and making specific plans on the assumption that strikes will be made on D-Day (see Attachment B* in backup materials for deployments).

"10. (D-10) Khanh makes speech demanding that North Vietnam stop aggression, threatening unspecified military action if he does not. (He could refer to a 'carrot.')

"11. (D-3) Discussions with allies not covered in Item above.

"12. (D-3) President informs U.S. public (and thereby North Vietnam) that action may come, referring to Khanh speech (Item 10 above) and declaring support for South Vietnam.

"13. (D-1) Khanh announces that all efforts have failed and that attacks are imminent. (Again he refers to limited goal and possibly to 'carrot.')

"14. (D-Day) Remove U.S. dependents.

"15. (D-Day) Launch first strikes. . . . Initially, mine their ports and strike North Vietnam's transport and related ability (bridge, trains) to move south; and then against targets which have maximum psychological effect on the North's willingness to stop insurgency—POL (petroleum, oil and lubricants) storage, selected airfields, barracks/training areas, bridges, railroad yards, port facilities, communications, and industries. Initially, these strikes would be by South Vietnamese aircraft; they could then be expanded by adding Farmgate, or U.S. aircraft, or any combination of them.

"16. (D-Day) Call for conference on Vietnam (and go to U.N.). State the limited objective: Not to overthrow the North Vietnam regime nor to destroy the country, but to stop D.R.V.-directed efforts in the South. Essential that it be made clear that attacks on the North will continue (i.e., no cease-fire) until (a) terrorism, armed attacks, and armed resistance to pacification efforts in the South stop, and (b) communications on the networks out of the North are conducted entirely in uncoded form."

The last paragraph was to provide a capsule definition of what the Administration meant when it later spoke publicly about "negotiations," a definition the analyst describes as "tantamount to unconditional surrender" for the other side.

The covering memorandum on the scenario pointed out that military action would not begin until after "favorable action" on the joint Congressional resolution. William Bundy drafted the resolution on May 25.

Attached to the scenario were assessments of possible Soviet, Chinese and North Vietnamese reactions. These included a provision for reinforcing the South Vietnamese Army "by U.S. ground forces prepositioned in South Vietnam or on board ship nearby" if Hanoi reacted by intensifying Vietcong activity in the South.

After meetings on May 24 and 25, the Executive Committee of the National Security Council—including Secretaries Rusk and McNamara, John A. McCone, Director of Central Intelligence, and McGeorge Bundy, Presidential assistant for national security—decided to recommend to the President only piecemeal elements of the scenario. Among these were the sending of the Canadian emissary to Hanoi and the move for a joint Congressional resolution.

The documents do not provide a clear explanation for their decision, the analyst says, although an important factor seems to have been concern that "our limited objectives might have been obscured" if the Administration had begun a chain of actions to step up the war at this point.

Whether political considerations in an election year also prompted the President to limit the proposed escalation is a question that is not addressed by the study here. The narrative does attribute such motives to Mr. Johnson's similar hesitation to take major overt actions in the following month, June.

In any case, the account explains, the urgency was taken out of the Laos crisis by a Polish diplomatic initiative on May 27 for a new Laos conference that would not include discussions of Vietnam, a major fear of the Administration. The President instructed his senior advisers to convene another strategy conference in Honolulu at the beginning of June "to review for . . . final approval a series of plans for effective action."

On his way to the conference, after attending the funeral of Prime Minister Jawaharlal Nehru in New Delhi, Secretary Rusk stopped off in Saigon for conversations with General Khanh and Ambassador Lodge.

The Ambassador and Gen. William C. Westmoreland, who was replacing General Harkins as chief of the Military Assistance Command in Saigon, flew to Honolulu with Secretary Rusk for the strategy session at Admiral Felt's headquarters there on June 1 and 2, 1964. They were joined by William Bundy, Mr. McNamara, General Taylor, Mr. McCone and Mr. Sullivan.

While he had previously counseled patience, Mr. Lodge's chief recommendation at Honolulu reflected his growing nervousness over the shakiness of the Saigon regime. He argued for bombing the North soon.

The analyst writes: "In answer to Secretary Rusk's query about South Vietnamese popular attitudes, which supported Hanoi's revolutionary aims, the Ambassador stated his conviction that most support for the VC would fade as soon as some 'counterterrorism measures' were begun against the D.R.V."—the Democratic Republic of (North) Vietnam.

Admiral Felt's record of the first day's session quotes Mr.

Lodge as predicting that "a selective bombing campaign against military targets in the North" would "bolster morale and give the population in the South a feeling of unity."

The Honolulu discussions concentrated on an air war, ranging over its entire implications, down to such details as the kind of antiaircraft guns North Vietnam had and how difficult these defenses might make attacks on particular targets. By now the Joint Chiefs had improved on Admiral Felt's Operation Plan 37-64 to the point of producing the first version of a comprehensive list of 94 targets, from bridges to industries, that Mr. McNamara and President Johnson would use to select the actual sites to be struck when sustained air raids began in the coming year.

Obtaining a Congressional resolution "prior to wider U.S. action in Southeast Asia" was a major topic. The analyst paraphrases and quotes from William Bundy's memorandum of record on the second day's talks to summarize the discussion concerning the resolution:

"Ambassador Lodge questioned the need for it if we were to confine our actions to 'tit-for-tat' air attacks against North Vietnam. However, Secretaries McNamara and Rusk and C.I.A. Director McCone all argued in favor of the resolution. In support, McNamara pointed to the need to guarantee South Vietnam's defense against retaliatory air attacks and against more drastic reactions by North Vietnam and Communist China. He added that it might be necessary, as the action unfolded . . . to deploy as many as seven divisions. Rusk noted that some of the military requirements might involve the calling up of reserves, always a touchy Congressional issue. He also stated that public opinion on our Southeast Asia policy was badly divided in the United States at the moment and that, therefore, the President needed an affirmation of support.

"General Taylor noted that there was a danger of reasoning ourselves into inaction," the memorandum goes on. "From a military point of view, he said the U.S. could function in Southeast Asia about as well as anywhere in the world except Cuba."

The upshot of the conference, however, was that major actions "should be delayed for some time yet," the historian says. A separate briefing paper that William Bundy prepared for Secretary Rusk to use in communicating the conference's findings to the President at a White House meeting late on the afternoon of June 3 counseled more time "to refine our plans and estimates." Mr. Bundy emphasized the need for an "urgent" public relations campaign at home to "get at the basic doubts of the value of Southeast Asia and the importance of our stake there."

Secretary McNamara, General Taylor and Mr. McCone joined Secretary Rusk in making the June 3 report to the President on the Honolulu conference. A documentary record of this White House meeting is not available, but the study deduces the President's reaction and decisions from the subsequent actions taken by his senior advisers.

Where decisive military actions were concerned, "the President apparently recognized the need for more and better information, but did not convey a sense of urgency regarding its acquisition," the analyst says. He notes that on the same day as the White House meeting, "possibly just following," Secretary McNamara told the Joint Chiefs that he wanted to meet with them on June 8, five days later, "to discuss North Vietnamese targets and troop movement capabilities."

But one element of the May 23 scenario, the positioning of forces for later action, began to fall into place right after the White House meeting. The Pentagon study says that "noncommitting military actions . . . were given immediate approval."

On June 4 Mr. McNamara directed the Army to take "immediate action . . . to improve the effectiveness and readiness status of its matériel prestocked for possible use in Southeast Asia."

The Secretary's directive specifically ordered the Army to augment stocks previously placed with Thailand's agreement at Korat, a town south of the Laotian border, to support potential combat operations by a United States Army infantry brigade and to give "first priority at the Okinawa Army Forward Depot to stocking non-air-transportable equipment" that would be required by another Army infantry brigade flown to the island staging base on sudden notice.

The President also "apparently encouraged" the intensified public-relations campaign recommended by William Bundy and the other Honolulu conference participants, the study asserts.

"In June, State and Defense Department sources made repeated leaks to the press affirming U.S. intentions to support its allies and uphold its treaty commitments in Southeast Asia," the analyst explains, citing several articles that month in The New York Times. The Administration also focuses publicity through June and into July on its military prepositioning moves. The augmentation of the Army war stocks at Korat in Thailand was given "extensive press coverage," the account says, citing a dispatch in The Times on June 21, 1964.

And what the analyst calls "the broad purpose" of these positioning moves—to serve as steps in the operation plans—was not explained to the public.

The Administration did openly step up its air operations in Laos in mid-June, after the enemy provided it with a rationale of self-defense. On June 6 and 7 two Navy jets on low-altitude target reconnaissance flights were shot down by enemy ground fire. Washington immediately added armed escort jets to the reconnaissance flights and on June 9 the escort jets struck Pathet Lao gun positions and attacked a Pathet Lao headquarters.

A similar escalation of the T-28 operations and the involvement of Thai pilots was unofficially acknowledged in Washington, although the responsibility for these operations was laid to the Laotian Government. And subsequent strikes by the American escort jets against enemy positions were not made public.

At the end of June the Royal Laotian Air Force was secretly strengthened with more T-28's, and American planes began conducting troop transport operations and night reconnaissance flights for a successful counteroffensive by the Laotian Army to protect the key position of Muong Soui.

Firmness, but Restraint

President Johnson was projecting an image of firmness but moderation, the study notes. In early June, he first requested and then rejected a draft from Mr. Rostow for a major policy speech on Southeast Asia that took an "aggressive approach," and instead relied "on news conferences and speeches by other officials to state the official view," the account continues. "In contrast to the Rostow approach, [the President's] news conference on 23 June and Secretary Rusk's speech at Williams College, 14 June, emphasized the U.S. determination to support its Southeast Asian allies, but avoided any direct challenge to Hanoi and Peking or any hint of intent to increase our military commitment."

A formal question the President submitted to the C.I.A. in June also indicated what was on his mind. "Would the rest of Southeast Asia necessarily fall if Laos and South Vietnam came under North Vietnamese control?" he asked. The agency's reply on June 9 challenged the domino theory, widely believed in one form or another within the Administration.

"With the possible exception of Cambodia," the C.I.A. memorandum said, "it is likely that no nation in the area would quickly succumb to Communism as a result of the fall of Laos and South Vietnam. Furthermore, a continuation of the spread of Communism in the area would not be inexorable, and any spread which did occur would take time—time in which the total situation might change in any number of ways unfavorable to the Communist cause."

The C.I.A. analysis conceded that the loss of South Vietnam and Laos "would be profoundly damaging to the U.S. position in the Far East" and would raise the prestige of China "as a leader of world Communism" at the expense of a more moderate Soviet Union. But the analysis argued that so long as the United States could retain its island bases, such as those on Okinawa, Guam, the Philippines and Japan, it could wield enough military power in Asia to deter China and North Vietnam from overt military aggression against Southeast Asia in general.

Even in the "worst case," if South Vietnam and Laos were to fall through "a clear-cut Communist victory," the United States would still retain some leverage to affect the final outcome in Southeast Asia, according to the analysis.

It said that "the extent to which individual countries would move away from the U.S. towards the Communists would be significantly affected by the substance and manner of U.S. policy in the period following the loss of Laos and South Vietnam."

As in the case of the earlier C.I.A. analysis stating that the real roots of Vietcong strength lay in South Vietnam, the study shows that the President and his senior officials were not inclined to adjust policy along the lines of this analysis challenging the domino theory.

Only the Joint Chiefs, Mr. Rostow and General Taylor appear to have accepted the domino theory in its literal sense—that all of the countries of Southeast Asia, from Cambodia to Malaysia, would tumble automatically into the Communist camp if the linchpin, South Vietnam, were knocked out, and that the United States position in the rest of the Far East, from Indonesia through the Philippines to Japan and Korea, would also be irrevocably harmed.

Yet the President and most of his closest civilian advisers—Mr. Rusk, Mr. McNamara and McGeorge Bundy—seem to have regarded the struggle over South Vietnam in more or less these terms. [See Document #63.]

In 1964, the Administration also feared an outbreak of other "wars of national liberation" in the Asian, African and Latin American countries, and, Mr. McNamara wrote in his March 16 memorandum to the President, "the South Vietnam conflict is regarded as a test case."

The struggle in South Vietnam was likewise bound up with the idea of "containing China," whose potential shadow over Southeast Asia was viewed as a palpable threat by Mr. Rusk because of his World War II experience in Asia and the victory of Mao Tse-tung's revolution in China.

But behind these foreign-policy axioms about domino effects, wars of liberation and the containment of China, the study reveals a deeper perception among the President and his aides that the United States was now the most powerful nation in the world and that the outcome in South Vietnam would demonstrate the will and the ability of the United States to have its way in world affairs.

The study conveys an impression that the war was thus considered less important for what it meant to the South Vietnamese people than for what it meant to the position of the United States in the world.

Mr. McNaughton would later capsulize this perception in a memorandum to Mr. McNamara seeking to apportion American aims in South Vietnam:

"70 pct.—To avoid a humiliating U.S. defeat (to our reputation as a guarantor).

"20 pct.—To keep SVN (and then adjacent) territory from Chinese hands.

"10 pct.—To permit the people of SVN to enjoy a better, freer way of life.

"Also—To emerge from crisis without unacceptable taint from methods used.

"NOT—To 'help a friend,' although it would be hard to stay in if asked out."

The words in parentheses are Mr. McNaughton's.

Thus, he had reasoned in another memorandum, even if bombing North Vietnam did not force Hanoi to call off the Vietcong, "it would demonstrate that U.S. was a 'good doctor' willing to keep promises, be tough, take risks, get bloodied and hurt the enemy badly."

And while the study shows doubt and worry in the Administration, it also reveals an underlying confidence among the decision makers at the top, whose attitude would count, that if this mightiest nation resolved to use its vast power, the other side would buckle.

Mr. Rostow would articulate this confidence in a memorandum to Secretary Rusk that fall: "I know well the anxieties and complications on our side of the line. But there may be a tendency to underestimate both the anxieties and complications on the other side and also to underestimate that limited but real margin of influence on the outcome that flows from the simple fact that we are the greatest power in the world—if we behave like it."

Accordingly, in mid-June, the Administration carried out another element of the May 23 scenario, the element that had first been formulated by Ambassador Lodge as his "carrot and stick." On June 18, at the Administration's request, Mr. Seaborn, the new Canadian representative on the International Control Commission, paid the first of his two secret calls on Premier Dong in Hanoi.

Washington sought to convey to North Vietnam through Mr. Seaborn the more precise and threatening meaning of the preparatory military deployments to Southeast Asia that it was publicizing on a vaguer level in public. Back in May, Mr. Lodge had urged an unacknowledged air strike on some target in the North "as a prelude to his [Mr. Seaborn's] arrival" if the Vietcong had recently committed some terrorist act "of the proper magnitude" in the South, but the President apparently did not see fit to act on the suggestion by June.

The analyst says Mr. Seaborn stressed to Premier Dong that while the United States' ambition in Southeast Asia was limited and its intentions "essentially peaceful," its patience was not limitless. The United States was fully aware of the degree to which Hanoi controlled the Vietcong, Mr. Seaborn said, and "in the event of escalation the greatest devastation would of course result for the D.R.V. itself."

The North Vietnamese Premier, the study relates, "fully understood the seriousness and import of the warning conveyed by Seaborn." Whether Mr. Seaborn also profferred the "carrot" of food and other economic aid is not reported.

At the June 3 meeting at the White House, the President had also apparently approved continued work for the Congressional resolution, the historian says, because planning for it continued apace. "Its intended purpose," the historian comments, "was to dramatize and make clear to other nations the firm resolve of the United States Government in an election year to support the President in taking whatever action was necessary to resist Communist aggression in Southeast Asia."

By June 10, there was "firm support" from most of the foreign-policy-making machinery of the Government for obtaining the resolution, although the account notes that at an interagency meeting that day "five basic 'disagreeable questions' were identified for which the Administration would have to provide convincing answers to assure public support.

"These included: (1) Does this imply a blank check for the President to go to war in Southeast Asia? (2) What kinds of force could he employ under this authorization? (3) What change in the situation (if any) requires the resolution now? (4) Can't our objectives be attained by means other than U.S. military force? (5) Does Southeast Asia mean enough to U.S. national interests?"

Despite the prospect of having to answer these questions publicly, William Bundy wrote in a memorandum for a second interagency meeting on June 12, the Administration required a Congressional resolution immediately as "a continuing demonstration of U.S. firmness and for complete flexibility in the hands of the executive in the coming political months." While the United States did not expect "to move in the near future to military action against North Vietnam," he said, events in South Vietnam or Laos might force it to reconsider this position.

But in the opinion of the analyst, the President in June, 1964, already felt "the political conventions just around the corner and the election issues regarding Vietnam clearly drawn," and so he recoiled at this time from the repercussions of major escalation and of seeking a Congressional resolution. At a high-level meeting on both subjects June 15, McGeorge Bundy, the historian says, brought Presidential guidance to Secretaries Rusk and McNamara in the form of a White House memorandum that postponed a decision for the present.

Washington's efforts to achieve some political stability in Saigon and to hold the line militarily against the guerrillas were coming to naught, however, under the blows of the Vietcong. In his fear and nervousness, General Khanh broke a promise he had made to Ambassador Lodge and Secretary Rusk in their May meeting to consult with Washington before publicly announcing any intention to declare war on the North and to start a bombing campaign.

On July 19, he started a "March North" campaign of militant slogans and oratory at a "unification rally" in Saigon.

The same day, as the analyst puts it, Air Marshal Nguyen Cao Ky, then chief of the South Vietnamese Air Force, "spilled the beans to reporters" on joint planning that the United States and the Saigon Government had secretly been conducting since June, with President Johnson's approval, for ground and air assaults in Laos.

In an emotional meeting on July 23 with General Taylor, who had just replaced Mr. Lodge as Ambassador, General Khanh asserted that North Vietnamese draftees had been taken prisoner with Vietcong guerrillas in fighting in the northern provinces. The United States should realize, he said, that the war had entered a new phase that called for new measures.

During another heated meeting on July 24, General Khanh asked Ambassador Taylor whether to resign. The Ambassador asked him not to do so and cabled Washington urging that the United States undertake covert joint planning with the South Vietnamese for bombing the North.

The State Department, the study says, immediately authorized Ambassador Taylor "to tell Khanh the U.S.G. had considered attacks on North Vietnam that might begin, for example, if the pressure from dissident South Vietnamese factions became too great. He must keep this confidential."

The Pentagon narrative skims over the last few days in July, 1964, but a summary of a command and control study of the Tonkin Gulf incident done by the Defense Department's Weapons System Evaluation Group in 1965, which The Times obtained along with the Pentagon narratives, fills in the events of these few days.

The study discloses that after a National Security Council meeting called on July 25, apparently to discuss these critical developments in Saigon, the Joint Chiefs proposed air strikes by unmarked planes flown by non-American crews against several targets in North Vietnam, including the coastal bases for Hanoi's flotilla of torpedo boats.

Assistant Secretary McNaughton sent the Joint Chiefs' memorandum to Secretary Rusk on July 30, the study reports, the same day that a chain of events was to unfold that would make it unnecessary to carry out the Joint Chiefs' plan, even if the President had wanted to accept it.

The Pentagon narrative now remarks that the clandestine 34A raids against North Vietnam—after getting off to what the Joint Chiefs had called "a slow beginning" in a report to Mr. McNamara on May 19—picked up in tempo and size during the summer, although the analyst provides few details.

The Joint Chiefs had informed Mr. McNamara that trained sabotage teams, electronic intelligence-gathering equipment, C-123 transports for the airdrops and fast PT boats for the coastal raids were giving the program "growing operational capabilities.

At midnight on July 30, South Vietnamese naval commandos under General Westmoreland's command staged an amphibious raid on the North Vietnamese islands of Hon Me and Hon Nieu in the Gulf of Tonkin.

While the assault was occurring, the United States destroyer Maddox was 120 to 130 miles away, heading north into the gulf on the year's second De Soto intelligence-gathering patrol. Her sailing orders said she was not to approach closer than eight nautical miles to the North Vietnamese coast and four nautical miles to North Vietnamese islands in the gulf.

The account does not say whether the captain of the Maddox had been informed about the 34A raid. He does state that the Maddox altered course twice on Aug. 2 to avoid a concentration of three North Vietnamese torpedo boats and a fleet of junks that were still searching the seas around the islands for the raiders.

The destroyer reached the northernmost point of her assigned patrol track the same day and headed south again.

"When the [North Vietnamese] PT boats began their high-speed run at her, at a distance of approximately 10 miles, the destroyer was 23 miles from the coast and heading further into international waters," the study says. "Apparently," it explains, "these boats . . . had mistaken Maddox for a South Vietnamese escort vessel."

In the ensuing engagement, two of the torpedo boats were damaged by planes launched from the aircraft carrier Ticonderoga, stationed to the south for reasons the study does not explain. A third PT boat was knocked dead in the water, sunk by a direct hit from one of the Maddox's five-inch guns.

The next day, Aug. 3, President Johnson ordered the Maddox reinforced by the destroyer C. Turner Joy and directed that both destroyers be sent back into the gulf, this time with instructions not to approach closer than 11 nautical miles to the North Vietnamese coast. A second aircraft carrier, the Constellation, on a visit to Hong Kong, was instructed to make steam and join the Ticonderoga as quickly as possible.

The study terms these reinforcing actions "a normal precaution" in the light of the first attack on the Maddox and not an attempt to use the destroyers as bait for another attack that would provide a pretext for reprisal airstrikes against the North. "Moreover," it comments, "since the augmentation was coupled with a clear [public] statement of intent to continue the patrols and a firm warning to the D.R.V. that a repetition would bring dire consequences, their addition to the patrol could be expected to serve more as a deterrent than a provocation."

The study gives a clear impression that the Administration at this moment did not believe the North Vietnamese would dare to attack the reinforced destroyer patrol.

For on the night of Aug. 3, while the De Soto patrol was resuming, two more clandestine 34A attacks were staged. PT boats manned by South Vietnamese crews bombarded the Rhon River estuary and a radar installation at Vinhson. This time the Maddox and the Turner Joy were definitely warned that the clandestine assaults were going to take place, the documents show.

Apparently expecting the President to order a resumption of the patrol, the admiral commanding the Seventh Fleet asked General Westmoreland on Aug. 2 to furnish him the general location of the planned raids so that the destroyers could steer clear of the 34A force. There was a good deal of cable traffic back and forth between the two commanders through the Pentagon communications center in Washington to modify the patrol's course on Aug. 3 to avoid any interference with the raiders.

On the night of Aug. 4, Tonkin Gulf time, approximately 24 hours after this second 34A assault, North Vietnamese torpedo boats then attacked both the Maddox and the Turner Joy in what was to be the fateful clash in the gulf.

The Pentagon account says that Hanoi's motives for this second attack on the destroyers are still unclear. The narrative ties the attack to the chain of events set off by the 34A raids of July 30, but says that Hanoi's precise motive may have been to recover from the embarrassment of having two torpedo boats damaged and another sunk in the first engagement with the Maddox, without any harm to the American destroyer.

"Perhaps closer to the mark is the narrow purpose of prompt retaliation for an embarrassing and well-publicized rebuff by a much-maligned enemy," the narrative says. "Inexperienced in modern naval operations, D.R.V. leaders may have believed that under the cover of darkness it would be possible to even the score or to provide at least a psychological victory by severely damaging a U.S. ship."

The study does not raise the question whether the second 34A raid on the night of Aug. 3, or the apparent air strikes on North Vietnamese villages just across the Laotian border on Aug. 1. and 2 by T-28 planes, motivated the Hanoi leadership in any way to order the second engagement with the destroyers.

Marshall Green, then the Deputy Assistant Secretary of State for Far Eastern Affairs, mentioned the apparent bombing of the villages in a lengthy memorandum to William Bundy dated Nov. 7, 1964, on United States covert activities in Indochina. [See Document #73.]

Listing complaints that North Vietnam had been making to the International Control Commission over the T-28 operations with Thai pilots, Mr. Green noted charges by Hanoi that "T-28's have violated North Vietnamese airspace and bombed/strafed NVN villages on Aug. 1 and 2, and on Oct. 16 and 17 and again on Oct. 28. The charges are probably accurate with respect to the first two dates (along Route 7) and the last one (Mugia Pass area)." The words in parentheses are Mr. Green's.

The context of the memorandum indicates that the raids on the North Vietnamese villages may have been inadvertent. But neither the narrative nor Mr. Green's memorandum says whether Hanoi thought this at the time the air strikes occurred.

Whatever the North Vietnamese motives for the second clash, President Johnson moved quickly now to carry out what the analyst calls "recommendations made . . . by his principal advisers earlier that summer and subsequently placed on the shelf."

Because of the Pacific time difference, the Pentagon received the first word that an attack on the Maddox and the Turner Joy might be imminent at 9:20 A.M. on the morning of Aug. 4, after the destroyers had intercepted North Vietnamese radio traffic indicating preparations for an assault. The flash message that the destroyers were actually engaged came into the communications center at 11 A.M.

The Joint Chiefs' staff began selecting target options for reprisal air strikes from the 94-target list, the first version of which was drawn up at the end of May. Adm. U.S. Grant Sharp, who had replaced Admiral Felt as commander in chief of Pacific forces, telephoned from Honolulu to suggest bombing the coastal bases for the torpedo boats.

Within 10 minutes, Mr. McNamara convened a meeting with the Joint Chiefs in his conference room on the third floor of the Pentagon to discuss possibilities for retaliation. Secretary Rusk and McGeorge Bundy came over to join them.

Twenty-five minutes later the two secretaries and Mr. Bundy left for a previously scheduled National Security Council meeting at the White House. They would recommend reprisal strikes to the President, while the Joint Chiefs stayed at the Pentagon to decide on specific targets.

At 1:25 P.M., two and a half hours after the flash message of the engagement and possibly while Mr. McNamara, Mr. Rusk, Mr. McCone and McGeorge Bundy were still at lunch with the President, the director of the Joint Staff telephoned Mr. McNamara to say that the Chiefs had unanimously agreed on the targets. Fighter-bombers from the carriers Constellation and Ticonderoga should strike four torpedo boat bases at Hongay, Lochau, Phucloi and Quangkhe, and an oil storage depot near Vinh that held some 10 per cent of North Vietnam's petroleum supply.

At a second National Security Council meeting that afternoon, President Johnson ordered the reprisals, decided to seek the Congressional resolution immediately and discussed with his advisers the swift Southeast Asia deployment of the air strike forces designated in Operation Plan 37-64 for the opening blows in a possible bombing campaign against the North. His approval for these preparatory air deployments, and for the readiness of Marine Corps and Army units planned to meet any Chinese or North Vietnamese retaliation to a bombing campaign, was apparently given later that day, the study shows.

Mr. McNamara returned to the Pentagon at 3 P.M. to approve the details of the reprisal strikes, code-named Pierce Arrow. An execution order was prepared by the Joint Staff, but at 4 P.M. Mr. McNamara learned from Admiral Sharp in a telephone conversation that there was now confusion over whether an attack on the destroyers had actually taken place.

The Secretary told Admiral Sharp that the reprisal order would remain in effect, but that the admiral was to check and make certain that an attack had really occurred before actually launching the planes. At 4:49 P.M., less than six hours after the first message of the attack had flashed into the Pentagon communications center, the formal execution order for the reprisals was transmitted to Honolulu. Admiral Sharp had not yet called back with confirming details of the attack. The order specified that the carriers were to launch their planes within about two and a half hours.

The admiral called back at 5:23 P.M. and again a few minutes after 6 o'clock to say that he was satisfied, on the basis of information from the task group commander of the two destroyers, that the attack had been genuine. The study says that in the meantime Mr. McNamara and the Joint Chiefs had also examined the confirming evidence, including intercepted radio messages from the North Vietnamese saying that their vessels were engaging the destroyers and that two torpedo boats had been sunk.

By now Mr. McNamara and the Chiefs had moved on to discussing the prepositioning of the air strike forces under Operation Plan 37-64.

At 6:45 P.M., President Johnson met with 16 Congressional leaders from both parties whom he had summoned to the White House. He told them that because of the second unprovoked attack on the American destroyers, he had decided to launch reprisal air strikes against the North and to ask for a Congressional resolution, the study says.

The Pentagon study gives no indication that Mr. Johnson informed the Congressional leaders of United States responsibility for and command of the covert 34A raids on July 30 and Aug. 3.

Nor does the history give any indication that Mr. Johnson told the Congressional leaders of what the historian describes as "the broader purpose of the deployments" under Operation Plan 37-64, which Mr. McNamara was to announce at a Pentagon news conference the next day and describe as a precautionary move.

"It is significant," the analyst writes, "that few of these additional units were removed from the western Pacific when the immediate crisis subsided. In late September the fourth attack aircraft carrier was authorized to resume its normal station in the eastern Pacific as soon as the regularly assigned carrier completed repairs. The other forces remained in the vicinity of their August deployment."

At 8:30 P.M. on Aug. 4, Mr. McNamara returned to the Pentagon and at 11:30 P.M., after several telephone calls to Admiral Sharp, he learned that the Ticonderoga had launched her bomb-laden aircraft at 10:43 P.M. They were expected to arrive over their targets in about an hour and 50 minutes.

The carriers had needed more time to get into launching position than the execution order had envisioned. The Constellation, steaming from Hong Kong, was not to launch her planes for another couple of hours.

The President did not wait. Sixteen minutes after Mr. McNamara's last phone call to Admiral Sharp, at 11:36 P.M., he went on television to tell the nation of the reprisal strikes. He characterized his actions as a "limited and fitting" response. "We still seek no wider war," he said.

Almost simultaneously, the air deployments under Operation Plan 37-64 had begun.

The first F-102 Delta Dagger jet fighters were landing at Saigon's airport around the time Mr. McNamara described the deployments at a Pentagon news conference on Aug. 5. He had given a brief post-midnight conference the same day to describe the reprisal strikes. He reported now that 25 North Vietnamese patrol craft had been destroyed or damaged along with 90 per cent of the oil storage tanks near Vinh.

"Last night I announced that moves were under way to reinforce our forces in the Pacific area," he continued. "These moves include the following actions:

"First, an attack carrier group has been transferred from the First Fleet on the Pacific coast to the western Pacific. Secondly, interceptor and fighter-bomber aircraft have been moved into South Vietnam. Thirdly, fighter-bomber aircraft have been moved into Thailand. Fourthly, interceptor and fighter-bomber squadrons have been transferred from the United States into advance bases in the Pacific. Fifthly, an antisubmarine task force group has been moved into the South China Sea. And finally, selected Army and Marine forces have been alerted and readied for movement."

The study notes that the Administration drafted the Congressional resolution for the two men who would sponsor its passage through both houses for the President: Senator J. W. Fulbright of Arkansas, chairman of the Senate Foreign Relations Committee, and Representative Thomas E. Morgan of Pennsylvania, chairman of the House Foreign Affairs Committee.

Precisely who drafted this final version of the resolution is not mentioned. The wording was less precise than that of the resolution drafted by William Bundy for the May 23 scenario, but the key language making the resolution in effect a declaration of war remained:

"Resolved by the Senate and House of Representatives of the United States of America in Congress assembled, That the Congress approve and support the determination of the President, as Commander in Chief, to take all necessary measures to repel any armed attack against the forces of the United States and to prevent further aggression.

"Sec. 2. The United States regards as vital to its national interest and to world peace the maintenance of international peace and security in Southeast Asia. Consonant with the Constitution of the United States and the Charter of the United Nations and in accordance with its obligations under the Southeast Asia Collective Defense Treaty, the United States is, therefore, prepared, as the President determines, to take all necessary steps, including the use of armed force, to assist any member or protocol state of the Southeast Asia Collective Defense Treaty requesting assistance in defense of its freedom."

Mr. McNamara and Secretary Rusk both testified on behalf of the resolution in secret sessions of the Senate and House foreign relations committees on Aug. 6. In his narrative, the Pentagon analyst occasionally quotes from and refers to portions of their testimony that have never been made public by the Pentagon. Along with the study, The Times also obtained more extensive quotations from this portion of the hearing transcript. The following account of the testimony on Aug. 6 thus contains both quotations used by the Pentagon analyst and the fuller quotations obtained by The Times.

Senator Wayne Morse of Oregon had learned that boats manned by South Vietnamese crews had attacked the two North Vietnamese islands on July 30. Mr. Morse, one of two Senators who were to vote against the Tonkin Gulf resolution—the other was Ernest L. Gruening of Alaska—alleged during the secret hearing on Aug. 6 that Mr. McNamara had known about the raids and that the destroyers had been associated with it.

"First," Mr. McNamara replied, "our Navy played absolutely no part in, was not associated with, was not aware of, any South Vietnamese actions, if there were any. . . . The Maddox was operating in international waters, was carrying out a routine patrol of the type we carry out all over the world at all times.

"I did not have knowledge at the time of the attack on the island," he said. "There is no connection between this patrol and any action by South Vietnam."

Mr. McNamara contended that whatever action had taken place against these North Vietnamese islands had been part of an anti-infiltration operation being conducted by a fleet of coastal patrol junks the United States had helped South Vietnam to organize in December, 1961.

"In the first seven months of this year they have searched 149,000 junks, some 570,000 people," he is quoted as telling the committee in this secret session. "This is a tremendous operation endeavoring to close the seacoasts of over 900 miles. In the process of that action, as the junk patrol has increased in strength, they have moved farther and farther north endeavoring to find the source of the infiltration.

"As part of that, as I reported to you earlier this week, [Mr. McNamara had testified before the committee in a secret session on Aug. 3 after the first attack on the Maddox], we understand that the South Vietnamese sea force carried out patrol action around these islands and actually shelled the parts they felt were associated with this infiltration.

"Our ships had absolutely no knowledge of it, were not connected with it; in no sense of the word can be considered to have backstopped the effort," he said.

Senator Frank Church of Idaho then asked Secretary Rusk at the same secret session: "I take it that our government which supplied these boats . . . . did know that the boats would be used for attacks on North Vietnamese targets, and that we acquiesced in that policy, is that correct?"

". . . In the larger sense, that is so, but as far as any particular detail is concerned we don't from Washington follow that in great detail," Mr. Rusk replied.

"They are doing it with our acquiescence and consent, is that correct?" Senator Church continued.

"But within very limited levels as far as North Vietnam is concerned," Mr. Rusk said.

At a Pentagon news conference after his testimony before the committee, Mr. McNamara spoke about the coastal patrol junks again and avoided any specific mention of the July 30 raid:

> Q. Mr. Secretary?
> A. Yes?
> Q. Have there been any incidents that you know involving the South Vietnamese vessels and the North Vietnamese?
> A. No, none that I know of, although I think that I should mention to you the South Vietnamese naval patrol activities that are carried on to prevent in the infiltration of men and matériel from the North into the South.

266

In the last seven months of 1961, for example, about 1,400 men were infiltrated across the 17th Parallel from North Vietnam into South Vietnam. To prevent further infiltration of that kind, the South Vietnamese with our assistance have set up a naval patrol which is very active in that area which continues to inspect and examine junks and their personnel.

In one eight-month period that I can recall they discovered 140 Vietcong infiltrators.

Q. They operate on their own?

A. They operate on their own. They are part of the South Vietnamese Navy, commanded by the South Vietnamese Navy, operating in the coastal waters inspecting suspicious incoming junks, seeking to deter and prevent the infiltration of both men and matériel from North Vietnam into South Vietnam.

Q. Mr. Secretary. Do these junks go north into North Vietnam areas?

A. They have advanced closer and closer to the 17th Parallel and in some cases I think have moved beyond that in an effort to stop the infiltration closer to the point of origin.

Q. Do our naval vessels afford any cover for these operations?

A. Our naval vessels afford no cover whatsoever. Our naval personnel do not participate in the junk operations.

When Senator George S. McGovern of South Dakota subsequently brought up the July 30 attack on the islands during the Senate floor debate on the resolution, Senator Fulbright replied that he had been assured by the Administration that "our boats did not convoy or support or back up any South Vietnamese naval vessels" and that the destroyer patrol "was entirely unconnected or unassociated with any coastal forays the South Vietnamese themselves may have conducted."

The Congressional resolution passed on Aug. 7 by a vote of 88 to 2 in the Senate and 416 to 0 in the House.

The history shows that besides the May 19 progress report from the Joint Chiefs on the 34A Operations, Mr. McNamara had received other memorandums on the clandestine attacks from General Anthis, the special assistant to the Joint Chiefs, on June 13, July 1 and July 28, 1964. General Anthis drew up the advance monthly schedules of the covert operations for approval by William Bundy and Mr. McNaughton.

Where Mr. Rusk is concerned, the study reveals that he was kept reasonably well informed.

The study also makes it clear that there was no connection between the 34A raids and the coastal patrol junk fleet described by Mr. McNamara and referred to by Mr. Rusk.

Thus, in the space of three days, the Administration had put firmly into place two key elements of the May 23 scenario—prepositioning of major air strike forces and Congressional authorization for wider action.

Internal Administration planning for Congressional authorization to escalate also now disappears from the documentary record. The account notes that during the next round of planning "the question of Congressional authority for open acts of war against a sovereign nation was never seriously raised."

There was confusion in Congress, however, over precisely what the resolution meant, the account says, commenting:

"Despite the nearly unanimous votes of support for the resolution, Congressional opinions varied as to the policy implications and the meaning of such support. The central belief seemed to be that the occasion necessitated demonstrating the nation's unity and collective will in support of the President's action and affirming U.S. determination to oppose further aggression. However, beyond that theme, there was a considerable variety of opinion. . . . Several spokesmen stressed that the resolution did not constitute a declaration of war, did not abdicate Congressional responsibility for determining national policy commitments and did not give the President carte blanche to involve the nation in a major Asian war."

The Administration would now communicate the meaning of the resolution to Hanoi by carrying out in a more significant manner an element of the May 23 scenario that Washington had already used once in June when the Canadian emissary had paid his first visit to Hanoi.

On Aug. 10, Mr. Seaborn was sent back with a second message for Premier Dong, which concluded:

"a. That the events of the past few days should add credibility to the statement made last time, that 'U.S. public and official patience with North Vietnamese aggression is growing extremely thin.'

"b. That the U.S. Congressional resolution was passed with near unanimity, strongly reaffirming the unity and determination of the U.S. Government and people not only with respect to any further attacks on U.S. military forces but more broadly to continue to oppose firmly, by all necessary means, D.R.V. efforts to subvert and conquer South Viet-Nam and Laos.

"c. That the U.S. has come to the view that the D.R.V. role in South Vietnam and Laos is critical. If the D.R.V. persists in its present course, it can expect to continue to suffer the consequences. [The word "continue" referred to the reprisal air strikes that followed the Tonkin incident.]

"d. That the D.R.V. knows what it must do if the peace is to be restored.

"e. That the U.S. has ways and means of measuring the D.R.V.'s participation in, and direction and control of, the war on South Vietnam and in Laos and will be carefully watching the D.R.V.'s response to what Mr. Seaborn is telling them." [See Document #68.]

Mr. McNaughton had drafted the message on the day the resolution was passed.

During this, as in his first meeting with Mr. Seaborn in June, the history says, "Pham Van Dong showed himself utterly unintimidated and calmly resolved to pursue the course upon which the D.R.V. was embarked to what he confidently expected would be its successful conclusion."

In the heat of the Tonkin clash, the Administration had also accomplished one of the major recommendations of the June strategy conference at Honolulu—preparing the American public for escalation.

"The Tonkin Gulf reprisal constituted an important firebreak and the Tonkin Gulf resolution set U.S. public support for virtually any action," the study remarks.

Almost none of the "disagreeable questions" the Administration might have to answer about the resolution, which had given the President pause in mid-June, had been asked in the emotional atmosphere of the crisis."

And inside the Administration the planners were moving more quickly now.

On Aug. 10, three days after passage of the resolution, Ambassador Taylor cabled the President a situation report on South Vietnam. It said that the Khanh regime had only "a 50-50 chance of lasting out the year." Therefore, a major objective of the United States Mission in Saigon was to "be prepared to implement contingency plans against North Vietnam with optimum readiness by Jan. 1, 1965."

On Aug. 11, four days after passage of the resolution,

William Bundy drew up a memorandum for a high-level State-Defense Departments policy meeting. The memorandum outlined graduated steps towards a possible full-scale air war against North Vietnam with "a contingency date, as suggested by Ambassador Taylor, of 1 January 1965." But until the end of August, Mr. Bundy said, there should be "a short holding phase, in which we would avoid actions that would in any way take the onus off the Communist side for escalation." [See Documnet #70.]

On Aug. 14, a lengthy summary of Mr. Bundy's memorandum was cabled to Ambassador Taylor, Ambassador Unger in Vientiane, and to Admiral Sharp in Honolulu for comments that would permit "further review and refinement."

The Tonkin Gulf reprisal air strikes, the analyst writes, "marked the crossing of an important threshold in the war, and it was accomplished with virtually no domestic criticism, indeed, with an evident increase in public support for the Administration. The precedent for strikes against the North was thus established and at very little apparent cost.

"There was a real cost, however," he concludes, in that the Administration was psychologically preparing itself for further escalation. "The number of unused measures short of direct military action against the North had been depleted. Greater visible commitment was purchased at the price of reduced flexibility." And "for all these reasons, when a decision to strike the North was faced again, it was much easier to take."

Admiral Sharp, in his cable to Washington on Aug. 17 commenting on Mr. Bundy's memorandum, "candidly" summed up this psychological commitment, the analyst says.

"Pressures against the other side once instituted should not be relaxed by any actions or lack of them which would destroy the benefits of the rewarding steps previously taken," the admiral wrote.

the government of the Cao Dai and Hoa Hao sects, which total three million people and control key areas along the Cambodian border. The Hoa Hao have already made some sort of agreement, and the Cao Dai are expected to do so at the end of this month. However, it is not clear that their influence will be more than neutralized by these agreements, or that they will in fact really pitch in on the government's side.

5. **Infiltration** of men and equipment from North Vietnam continues using (a) land corridors through Laos and Cambodia; (b) the Mekong River waterways from Cambodia; (c) some possible entry from the sea and the tip of the Delta. The best guess is that 1000-1500 Viet Cong cadres entered South Vietnam from Laos in the first nine months of 1963. The Mekong route (and also the possible sea entry) is apparently used for heavier weapons and ammunition and raw materials which have been turning up in increasing numbers in the south and of which we have captured a few shipments.

To counter this infiltration, we reviewed in Saigon various plans providing for cross-border operations into Laos. On the scale proposed, I am quite clear that these would not be politically acceptable or even militarily effective. Our first need would be immediate U-2 mapping of the whole Laos and Cambodian border, and this we are preparing on an urgent basis.

One other step we can take is to expand the existing limited but remarkably effective operations on the Laos side, the so-called Operation HARDNOSE, so that it at least provides reasonable intelligence on movements all the way along the Laos corridor; plans to expand this will be prepared and presented for approval in about two weeks.

As to the waterways, the military plans presented in Saigon were unsatisfactory, and a special naval team is being sent at once from Honolulu to determine what more can be done. The whole waterway system is so vast, however, that effective policing may be impossible.

In general, the infiltration problem, while serious and annoying, is a lower priority than the key problems discussed earlier. However, we should do what we can to reduce it.

6. **Plans for Covert Action into North Vietnam** were prepared as we had requested and were an excellent job. They present a wide variety of sabotage and psychological operations against North Vietnam from which I believe we should aim to select those that provide maximum pressure with minimum risk. In accordance with your direction at the meeting. General Krulak of the JCS is chairing a group that will lay out a program in the next ten days for your consideration.

7. **Possible neutralization of Vietnam** is strongly opposed by Minh, and our attitude is somewhat suspect because of editorials by the New York Times and mention by Walter Lippmann and others. We reassured them as strongly as possible on this—and in somewhat more general terms on the neutralization of Cam-

bodia. I recommend that you convey to Minh a Presidential message for the New Year that would also be a vehicle to stress the necessity of strong central direction by the government and specifically by Minh himself.

8. **U.S. resources and personnel** cannot usefully be substantially increased. I have directed a modest artillery supplement, and also the provision of uniforms for the Self Defense Corps, which is the most exposed force and suffers from low morale. Of greater potential significance, I have directed the Military Departments to review urgently the quality of the people we are sending to Vietnam. It seems to have fallen off considerably from the high standards applied in the original selections in 1962, and the JCS fully agree with me that we must have our best men there.

Conclusion. My appraisal may be overly pessimistic. Lodge, Harkins, and Minh would probably agree with me on specific points, but feel that January should see significant improvement. We should watch the situation very carefully, running scared, hoping for the best, but preparing for more forceful moves if the situation does not show early signs of improvement.

62

'64 Memo by Joint Chiefs of Staff Discussing Widening of the War

Memorandum from Gen. Maxwell D. Taylor, Chairman of the Joint Chiefs of Staff, to Secretary of Defense Mc-Namara, Jan. 22, 1964, "Vietnam and Southeast Asia."

1. National Security Action Memorandum No. 273 makes clear the resolve of the President to ensure victory over the externally directed and supported communist insurgency in South Vietnam. In order to achieve that victory, the Joint Chiefs of Staff are of the opinion that the United States must be prepared to put aside many of the self-imposed restrictions which now limit our efforts, and to undertake bolder actions which may embody greater risks.

2. The Joint Chiefs of Staff are increasingly mindful that our fortunes in South Vietnam are an accurate barometer of our fortunes in all of Southeast Asia. It is our view that if the U.S. program succeeds in South Vietnam it will go far toward stabilizing the total Southeast Asia situation. Conversely, a loss of South Vietnam to the communists will presage an early erosion of the remainder of our position in that subcontinent.

3. Laos, existing on a most fragile foundation now, would not be able to endure the establishment of a communist—or pseudo neutralist—state on its eastern flank. Thailand, less strong today than a month ago by virtue of the loss of Prime Minister Sarit,

would probably be unable to withstand the pressures of infiltration from the north should Laos collapse to the communists in its turn. Cambodia apparently has estimated that our prospects in South Vietnam are not promising and, encouraged by the actions of the French, appears already to be seeking an accommodation with the communists. Should we actually suffer defeat in South Vietnam, there is little reason to believe that Cambodia would maintain even a pretense of neutrality.

4. In a broader sense, the failure of our programs in South Vietnam would have heavy influence on the judgments of Burma, India, Indonesia, Malaysia, Japan, Taiwan, the Republic of Korea, and the Republic of the Philippines with respect to U.S. durability, resolution, and trustworthiness. Finally, this being the first real test of our determination to defeat the communist wars of national liberation formula, it is not unreasonable to conclude that there would be a corresponding unfavorable effect upon our image in Africa and in Latin America.

5. All of this underscores the pivotal position now occupied by South Vietnam in our world-wide confrontation with the communists and the essentiality that the conflict there would be brought to a favorable end as soon as possible. However, it would be unrealistic to believe that a complete suppression of the insurgency can take place in one or even two years. The British effort in Malaya is a recent example of a counterinsurgency effort which required approximately ten years before the bulk of the rural population was brought completely under control of the government, the police were able to maintain order, and the armed forces were able to eliminate the guerrilla strongholds.

6. The Joint Chiefs of Staff are convinced that, in keeping with the guidance in NSAM 273, the United States must make plain to the enemy our determination to see the Vietnam campaign through to a favorable conclusion. To do this, we must prepare for whatever level of activity may be required and, being prepared, must then proceed to take actions as necessary to achieve our purposes surely and promptly.

7. Our considerations, furthermore, cannot be confined entirely to South Vietnam. Our experience in the war thus far leads us to conclude that, in this respect, we are not now giving sufficient attention to the broader area problems of Southeast Asia. The Joint Chiefs of Staff believe that our position in Cambodia, our attitude toward Laos, our actions in Thailand, and our great effort in South Vietnam do not comprise a compatible and integrated U.S. policy for Southeast Asia. U.S. objectives in Southeast Asia cannot be achieved by either economic, political, or military measures alone. All three fields must be integrated into a single, broad U.S. program for Southeast Asia. The measures recommended in this memorandum are a partial contribution to such a program.

8. Currently we and the South Vietnamese are fighting the war on the enemy's terms. He has determined the locale, the timing,

and the tactics of the battle while our actions are essentially re-
active. One reason for this is the fact that we have obliged ourselves to labor under self-imposed restrictions with respect to
impeding external aid to the Viet Cong. These restrictions include keeping the war within the boundaries of South Vietnam,
avoiding the direct use of U.S. combat forces, and limiting U.S.
direction of the campaign to rendering advice to the Government
of Vietnam. These restrictions, while they may make our international position more readily defensible, all tend to make the
task in Vietnam more complex, time-consuming, and in the end,
more costly. In addition to complicating our own problem, these
self-imposed restrictions may well now be conveying signals of
irresolution to our enemies—encouraging them to higher levels of
vigor and greater risks. A reversal of attitude and the adoption
of a more aggressive program would enhance greatly our ability to
control the degree to which escalation will occur. It appears
probable that the economic and agricultural disappointments
suffered by Communist China, plus the current rift with the
Soviets, could cause the communists to think twice about undertaking a large-scale military adventure in Southeast Asia.

9. In adverting to actions outside of South Vietnam, the
Joint Chiefs of Staff are aware that the focus of the counterinsurgency battle lies in South Vietnam itself, and that the war
must certainly be fought and won primarily in the minds of the
Vietnamese people. At the same time, the aid now coming to the
Viet Cong from outside the country in men, resources, advice, and
direction is sufficiently great in the aggregate to be significant—
both as help and as encouragement to the Viet Cong. It is our
conviction that if support of the insurgency from outside South
Vietnam in terms of operational direction, personnel, and material were stopped completely, the character of the war in South
Vietnam would be substantially and favorably altered. Because
of this conviction, we are wholly in favor of executing the covert
actions against North Vietnam which you have recently proposed
to the President. We believe, however, that it would be idle to
conclude that these efforts will have a decisive effect on the communist determination to support the insurgency; and it is our
view that we must therefore be prepared fully to undertake a
much higher level of activity, not only for its beneficial tactical
effect, but to make plain our resolution, both to our friends and
to our enemies.

10. Accordingly, the Joint Chiefs of Staff consider that the
United States must make ready to conduct increasingly bolder
actions in Southeast Asia; specifically as to Vietnam to:

a. Assign to the U.S. military commander responsibilities for
the total U.S. program in Vietnam.

b. Induce the Government of Vietnam to turn over to the
United States military commander, temporarily, the actual tactical direction of the war.

c. Charge the United States military commander with complete responsibility for conduct of the program against North Vietnam.

d. Overfly Laos and Cambodia to whatever extent is necessary for acquisition of operational intelligence.

e. Induce the Government of Vietnam to conduct overt ground operations in Laos of sufficient scope to impede the flow of personnel and material southward.

f. Arm, equip, advise, and support the Government of Vietnam in its conduct of aerial bombing of critical targets in North Vietnam and in mining the sea approaches to that country.

g. Advise and support the Government of Vietnam in its conduct of large-scale commando raids against critical targets in North Vietnam.

h. Conduct aerial bombing of key North Vietnam targets, using U.S. resources under Vietnamese cover, and with the Vietnamese openly assuming responsibility for the actions.

i. Commit additional U.S. forces, as necessary, in support of the combat action within South Vietnam.

j. Commit U.S. forces as necessary in direct actions against North Vietnam.

11. It is our conviction that any or all of the foregoing actions may be required to enhance our position in Southeast Asia. The past few months have disclosed that considerably higher levels of effort are demanded of us if U.S. objectives are to be attained.

12. The governmental reorganization which followed the coup d'etat in Saigon should be completed very soon, giving basis for concluding just how strong the Vietnamese Government is going to be and how much of the load they will be able to bear themselves. Additionally, the five-month dry season, which is just now beginning, will afford the Vietnamese an opportunity to exhibit their ability to reverse the unfavorable situation in the critical Mekong Delta. The Joint Chiefs of Staff will follow these important developments closely and will recommend to you progressively the execution of such of the above actions as are considered militarily required, providing, in each case, their detailed assessment of the risks involved.

13. The Joint Chiefs of Staff consider that the strategic importance of Vietnam and of Southeast Asia warrants preparations for the actions above and recommend that the substance of this memorandum be discussed with the Secretary of State.

63

'64 McNamara Report on Steps to Change the Trend of the War

Excerpts from memorandum, "South Vietnam," from Secretary of Defense McNamara to President Johnson, March 16, 1964.

I. U.S. OBJECTIVES IN SOUTH VIETNAM

We seek an independent non-Communist South Vietnam. We do not require that it serve as a Western base or as a member of a Western Alliance. Vietnam must be free, however, to accept outside assistance as required to maintain its security. This assistance should be able to take the form not only of economic and social pressures but also police and military help to root out and control insurgent elements.

Unless we can achieve this objective in South Vietnam, almost all of Southeast Asia will probably fall under Communist dominance (all of Vietnam, Laos, and Cambodia), accommodate to Communism so as to remove effective U.S. and anti-Communist influence (Burma), or fall under the domination of forces not now explicitly Communist but likely then to become so (Indonesia taking over Malaysia). Thailand might hold for a period with our help, but would be under grave pressure. Even the Philippines would become shaky, and the threat to India to the west, Australia and New Zealand to the south, and Taiwan, Korea, and Japan to the north and east would be greatly increased.

All these consequences would probably have been true even if the U.S. had not since 1954, and especially since 1961, become so heavily engaged in South Vietnam. However, that fact accentuates the impact of a Communist South Vietnam not only in Asia, but in the rest of the world, where the South Vietnam conflict is regarded as a test case of U.S. capacity to help a nation meet a Communist "war of liberation."

Thus, purely in terms of foreign policy, the stakes are high. They are increased by domestic factors.

II. PRESENT U.S. POLICY IN SOUTH VIETNAM

We are now trying to help South Vietnam defeat the Viet Cong, supported from the North, by means short of the unqualified use of U.S. combat forces. We are not acting against North Vietnam except by a very modest "covert" program operated by South Vietnamese (and a few Chinese Nationalists)—a program so limited that it is unlikely to have any significant effect. In Laos, we are still working largely within the framework of the 1962 Geneva Accords. In Cambodia we are still seeking to keep Sihanouk from abandoning whatever neutrality he may still have and fulfilling his threat of reaching an accommodation with Hanoi and Peking. As a consequence of these policies, we and the GVN have had to condone the extensive use of Cambodian and Laotian territory by the Viet Cong, both as a sanctuary and as infiltration routes.

III. THE PRESENT SITUATION IN SOUTH VIETNAM

The key elements in the present situation are as follows:

A. The military tools and concepts of the GVN-US efforts

are generally sound and adequate.* Substantially more can be done in the effective employment of military forces and in the economic and civic action areas. These improvements may require some selective increases in the U.S. presence, but it does not appear likely that major equipment replacement and additions in U.S. personnel are indicated under current policy.

B. The U.S. policy of reducing existing personnel where South Vietnamese are in a position to assume the functions is still sound. Its application will not lead to any major reductions in the near future, but adherence to this policy as such has a sound effect in portraying to the U.S. and the world that we continue to regard the war as a conflict the South Vietnamese must win and take ultimate responsibility for. Substantial reductions in the numbers of U.S. military training personnel should be possible before the end of 1965. However, the U.S. should continue to reiterate that it will provide all the assistance and advice required to do the job regardless of how long it takes.

C. The situation has unquestionably been growing worse, at least since September:

1. In terms of government control of the countryside, about 40% of the territory is under Viet Cong control or predominant influence. In 22 of the 43 provinces, the Viet Cong control 50% or more of the land area, including 80% of Phuoc Tuy; 90% of Binh Duong; 75% of Hau Nghia; 90% of Long An; 90% of Kien Tuong; 90% of Dinh Tuong; 90% of Kien Hoa and 85% of An Xuyen.

2. Large groups of the population are now showing signs of apathy and indifference, and there are some signs of frustration within the U.S. contingent. . . .

a. The ARVN and paramilitary desertion rates, and particularly the latter, are high and increasing.

b. Draft-dodging is high while the Viet Cong are recruiting energetically and effectively.

c. The morale of the hamlet militia and of the Self Defense Corps, on which the security of the hamlets depends, is poor and failing.

3. In the last 90 days the weakening of the government's position has been particularly noticeable. . . .

4. The political control structure extending from Saigon down into the hamlets disappeared following the November coup. . . .

5. North Vietnamese support, always significant, has been increasing. . . .

D. The greatest weakness in the present situation is the uncertain viability of the Khanh government. Khanh himself is a very able man within his experience, but he does not yet have

---

*Mr. McCone emphasizes that the GVN/US program can never be considered completely satisfactory so long as it permits the Viet Cong a sanctuary in Cambodia and a continuing uninterrupted and unmolested source of supply and reinforcement from NVN through Laos.

wide political appeal and his control of the army itself is uncertain. . . .

E. On the positive side, we have found many reasons for encouragement in the performance of the Khanh Government to date. Although its top layer is thin, it is highly responsive to U.S. advice, and with a good grasp of the basic elements of rooting out the Viet Cong. . . .

2. Retaliatory Actions. For example:

a. Overt high and/or low-level reconnaissance flights by U.S. or Farmgate aircraft over North Vietnam to assist in locating and identifying the sources of external aid to the Viet Cong.

b. Retaliatory bombing strikes and commando raids on a tit-for-tat basis by the GVN against NVN targets (communication centers, training camps, infiltration routes, etc.)

c. Aerial mining by the GVN aircraft (possibly with U.S. assistance) of the major NVN ports.

3. Graduated Overt Military Pressure by GVN and U.S. Forces.

This program would go beyond reacting on a tit-for-tat basis. It would include air attacks against military and possibly industrial targets. The program would utilize the combined resources of the GVN Air Force and the U.S. Farmgate Squadron, with the latter reinforced by three squadrons of B-57s presently in Japan. Before this program could be implemented it would be necessary to provide some additional air defense for South Vietnam and to ready U.S. forces in the Pacific for possible escalation.

The analysis of the more serious of these military actions (from 2 (b) upward) revealed the extremely delicate nature of such operations, both from the military and political standpoints. There would be the problem of marshalling the case to justify such action, the problem of communist escalation, and the problem of dealing with the pressures for premature or "stacked" negotiations. We would have to calculate the effect of such military actions against a specified political objective. That objective, while being cast in terms of eliminating North Vietnamese control and direction of the insurgency, would in practical terms be directed toward collapsing the morale and the self-assurance of the Viet Cong cadres now operating in South Vietnam and bolstering the morale of the Khanh regime. We could not, of course, be sure that our objective could be achieved by any means within the practical range of our options. Moreover, and perhaps most importantly, unless and until the Khanh government has established its position and preferably is making significant progress in the South, an overt extension of operations into the North carries the risk of being mounted from an extremely weak base which might at any moment collapse and leave the posture of political confrontation worsened rather than improved.

The other side of the argument is that the young Khanh Government [two words illegible] reinforcement of some significant sources against the North and without [words illegible] the in-country program, even with the expansion discussed in Section [words illegible] may not be sufficient to stem the tide.

[Words illegible] balance, except to the extent suggested in Section V below, I [words illegible] against initiation at this time of overt GVN and/or U.S. military [word illegible] against North Vietnam.

C. Initiate Measures to Improve the Situation in South Vietnam.

There were and are sound reasons for the limits imposed by present policy—the South Vietnamese must win their own fight; U.S. intervention on a larger scale, and/or GVN actions against the North, would disturb key allies and other nations; etc. In any case, it is vital that we continue to take every reasonable measure to assure success in South Vietnam. The policy choice is not an "either/or" between this course of action and possible pressures against the North; the former is essential without regard to our decision with respect to the latter. The latter can, at best, only reinforce the former.

The following are the actions we believe can be taken in order to improve the situation both in the immediate future and over a longer-term period. To emphasize that a new phase has begun, the measures to be taken by the Khanh government should be described by some term such as "South Vietnam's Program for National Mobilization."

Basic U.S. Posture

1. The U.S. at all levels must continue to make it emphatically clear that we are prepared to furnish assistance and support for as long as it takes to bring the insurgency under control.

2. The U.S. at all levels should continue to make it clear that we fully support the Khanh government and are totally opposed to any further coups. The Ambassador should instruct all elements, including the military advisors, to report intelligence information of possible coups promptly, with the decision to be made by the ambassador whether to report such information to Khanh. However, we must recognize that our chances would not be great of detecting and preventing a coup that had major military backing.

3. We should support fully the Pacification Plan now announced by Khanh (described in Annex B), and particularly the basic theory—now fully accepted both on the Vietnamese and U.S. sides—of concentrating on the more secure areas and working out from these through military operations to provide security, followed by necessary civil and economic actions to make the presence of the government felt and to provide economic improvements. . . .

V. POSSIBLE LATER ACTIONS

If the Khanh government takes hold vigorously—inspiring confidence, whether or not noteworthy progress has been made—or if we get hard information of significantly stepped-up VC arms supply from the North, we may wish to mount new and significant pressures against North Vietnam. We should start preparations for such a capability now. (See Annex C for an analysis of the situation in North Vietnam and Communist China.) Specifically, we should develop a capability to initiate within 72 hours the "Border Control"** and "Retaliatory Actions" referred to on pages 5 and 6, and we should achieve a capability to initiate with 30 days' notice the program of "Graduated Overt Military Pressure." The reasoning behind this program of preparations for initiating action against North Vietnam is rooted in the fact that, even with progress in the pacification plan, the Vietnamese Government and the population in the South will still have to face the prospect of a very lengthy campaign based on a war-weary nation and operating against Viet Cong cadres who retain a great measure of motivation and assurance.

In this connection, General Khanh stated that his primary concern is to establish a firm base in the South. He favors continuation of covert activities against North Vietnam, but until such time as "rear-area security" has been established, he does not wish to engage in overt operations against the North.

In order to accelerate the realization of pacification and particularly in order to denigrate the morale of the Viet Cong forces, it may be necessary at some time in the future to put demonstrable retaliatory pressure on the North. Such a course of action might proceed according to the scenario outlined in Annex D. . . .

VII. RECOMMENDATIONS

I recommend that you instruct the appropriate agencies of the U.S. Government:

1. To make it clear that we are prepared to furnish assistance and support to South Vietnam for as long as it takes to bring the insurgency under control.

2. To make it clear that we fully support the Khanh government and are opposed to further coups.

3. To support a Program for National Mobilization (including a national service law) to put South Vietnam on a war footing.

4. To assist the Vietnamese to increase the armed forces (regular plus paramilitary) by at least 50,000 men.

5. To assist the Vietnamese to create a greatly enlarged Civil Administrative Corps for work at province, district and hamlet levels.

6. To assist the Vietnamese to improve and reorganize the paramilitary forces and increase their compensation.

**Authority should be granted immediately for covert Vietnamese operations into Laos, for the purposes of border control and of "hot pursuit" into Laos. Decision on "hot pursuit" into Cambodia should await further study of our relations with that country.

7. To assist the Vietnamese to create an offensive guerrilla force.

8. To provide the Vietnamese Air Force 25 A-1H aircraft in exchange for the present T-28s.

9. To provide the Vietnamese Army additional M-113 armored personnel carriers (withdrawing the M-114s there), additional river boats, and approximately $5-10 million of other additional material.

10. To announce publicly the Fertilizer Program and to expand it with a view within two years to trebling the amount of fertilizer made available.

11. To authorize continued high-level U.S. overflights of South Vietnam's borders and to authorize "hot pursuit" and South Vietnamese ground operations over the Laotian line for the purpose of border control. More ambitious operations into Laos involving units beyond battalion size should be authorized only with the approval of Souvanna Phouma. Operations across the Cambodian border should depend on the state of relations with Cambodia.

12. To prepare immediately to be in a position on 72 hours' notice to initiate the full range of Laotian and Cambodian "Border Control" actions (beyond those authorized in Paragraph 11 above) and the "Retaliatory Actions" against North Vietnam, and to be in a position on 30 days' notice to initiate the program of "Graduated Overt Military Pressure" against North Vietnam.

64

U.S. Order for Preparations for Some Retaliatory Action

Excerpts from National Security Action Memorandum 288, "U.S. Objectives in South Vietnam," March 17, 1964, as provided in the body of the Pentagon study. The words in brackets are the study's. The paragraph in italics is the paraphrase by a writer of the study.

[The United States' policy is] to prepare immediately to be in a position on 72 hours' notice to initiate the full range of Laotian and Cambodian "Border Control actions" . . . and the "Retaliatory Actions" against North Vietnam, and to be in a position on 30 days' notice to initiate the program of "Graduated Overt Military Pressure" against North Vietnam. . . .

We seek an independent non-Communist South Vietnam. We do not require that it serve as a Western base or as a member of a Western Alliance. South Vietnam must be free, however, to accept outside assistance as required to maintain its security. This assistance should be able to take the form not only of economic

283

and social measures but also police and military help to root out and control insurgent elements.

Unless we can achieve this objective in South Vietnam, almost all of Southeast Asia will probably fall under Communist dominance (all of Vietnam, Laos, and Cambodia), accommodate to Communism so as to remove effective U.S. and anti-Communist influence (Burma), or fall under the domination of forces not now explicitly Communist but likely then to become so (Indonesia taking over Malaysia). Thailand might hold for a period without help, but would be under grave pressure. Even the Philippines would become shaky, and the threat to India on the West, Australia and New Zealand to the South, and Taiwan, Korea, and Japan to the North and East would be greatly increased.

All of these consequences would probably have been true even if the U.S. had not since 1954, and especially since 1961, become so heavily engaged in South Vietnam. However, that fact accentuates the impact of a Communist South Vietnam not only in Asia but in the rest of the world, where the South Vietnam conflict is regarded as a test case of U.S. capacity to help a nation to meet the Communist "war of liberation."

Thus, purely in terms of foreign policy, the stakes are high. . . .

We are now trying to help South Vietnam defeat the Viet Cong, supported from the North, by means short of the unqualified use of U.S. combat forces. We are not acting against North Vietnam except by a modest "covert" program operated by South Vietnamese (and a few Chinese Nationalists)—a program so limited that it is unlikely to have any significant effect. . . .

There were and are some sound reasons for the limits imposed by the present policy—the South Vietnamese must win their own fight; U.S. intervention on a larger scale, and/or GVN actions against the North, would disturb key allies and other nations; etc. In any case, it is vital that we continue to take every reasonable measure to assure success in South Vietnam. The policy choice is not an "either/or" between this course of action and possible pressure against the North; the former is essential and without regard to our decision with respect to the latter. The latter can, at best, only reinforce the former. . . .

Many of the actions described in the succeeding paragraphs fit right into the framework of the [pacification] plan as announced by Khanh. Wherever possible, we should tie our urgings of such actions to Khanh's own formulation of them, so that he will be carrying out a Vietnamese plan and not one imposed by the United States. . . .

Among the alternatives considered, but rejected for the time being . . . were overt military pressure on North Vietnam, neutralization, return of U.S. dependents, furnishing of a U.S. combat unit to secure the Saigon area, and a full takeover of the command in South Vietnam by the U.S. With respect to this last proposal, it was said that

. . . the judgment of all senior people in Saigon, with which we concur, was that the possible military advantages of such action would be far outweighed by adverse psychological impact. It would cut across the whole basic picture of the Vietnamese winning their own war and lay us wide open to hostile propaganda both within South Vietnam and outside.

65

Cable from President to Lodge on Escalation Contingencies

Cablegram from President Johnson to Henry Cabot Lodge, United States Ambassador in Saigon, March 20, 1964.

1. We have studied your 1776 and I am asking State to have Bill Bundy make sure that you get out latest planning documents on ways of applying pressure and power against the North. I understand that some of this was ·discussed with you by McNamara mission in Saigon, but as plans are refined it would be helpful to have your detailed comments. As we agreed in our previous messages to each other, judgment is reserved for the present on overt military action in view of the consensus from Saigon conversations of McNamara mission with General Khanh and you on judgment that movement against the North at the present would be premature. We have [sic] share General Khanh's judgment that the immediate and essential task is to strengthen the southern base. For this reason our planning for action against the North is on a contingency basis at present, and immediate problem in this area is to develop the strongest possible military and political base for possible later action. There is additional international reason for avoiding immediate overt action in that we expect a showdown between the Chinese and Soviet Communist parties soon and action against the North will be more practicable after than before a showdown. But if at any time you feel that more immediate action is urgent, I count on you to let me know specifically the reasons for such action, together with your recommendations for its size and shape.

2. On dealing with de Gaulle, I continue to think it may be valuable for you to go to Paris after Bohlen has made his first try. (State is sending you draft instruction to Bohlen, which I have not yet reviewed, for your comment.) It ought to be possible to explain in Saigon that your mission is precisely for the purpose of knocking down the idea of neutralization wherever it rears its ugly head and on this point I think that nothing is more important than to stop neutralist talk wherever we can by whatever means we can. I have made this point myself to Mansfield

and Lippmann and I expect to use every public opportunity to restate our position firmly. You may want to convey our concern on this point to General Khanh and get his ideas on the best possible joint program to stop such talk in Saigon, in Washington, and in Paris. I imagine that you have kept General Khanh abreast of our efforts in Paris. After we see the results of the Bohlen approach you might wish to sound him out on Paris visit by you.

66

Draft Resolution for Congress on Actions in Southeast Asia

Draft Resolution on Southeast Asia, May 25, 1964, as provided in the body of the Pentagon study. The major paragraphs of the resolution as approved by Congress appears.

Whereas the signatories of the Geneva Accords of 1954, including the Soviet Union, the Communist regime in China, and Viet Nam agreed to respect the independence and territorial integrity of South Viet Nam, Laos and Cambodia; and the United States, although not a signatory of the Accords, declared that it would view any renewal of aggression in violation of the Accords with grave concern and as seriously threatening international peace and security;

Whereas the Communist regime in North Viet Nam, with the aid and support of the Communist regime in China, has systematically flouted its obligations under these Accords and has engaged in aggression against the independence and territorial integrity of South Viet Nam by carrying out a systematic plan for the subversion of the Government of South Viet Nam, by furnishing direction, training, personnel and arms for the conduct of guerrilla warfare within South Viet Nam, and by the ruthless use of terror against the peaceful population of that country;

Whereas in the face of this Communist aggression and subversion the Government and people of South Viet Nam have bravely undertaken the defense of their independence and territorial integrity, and at the request of that Government the United States has, in accordance with its Declaration of 1954, provided military advice, economic aid and military equipment;

Whereas in the Geneva Agreements of 1962 the United States, the Soviet Union, the Communist regime in China, North Viet Nam and others solemnly undertook to respect the sovereignty, independence, neutrality, unity and territorial integrity of the Kingdom of Laos;

Whereas in violation of these undertakings the Communist regime in North Viet Nam, with the aid and support of the

Communist regime in China, has engaged in aggression against the independence, unity and territorial integrity of Laos by maintaining forces on Laotian territory, by the use of that territory for the infiltration of arms and equipment into South Viet Nam, and by providing direction, men and equipment for persistent armed attacks against the Government of (words illegible);

Whereas in the face of this Communist aggression the Government of National Unification and the non-Communist elements in Laos have striven to maintain the conditions of unity, independence and neutrality envisioned for their country in the Geneva Agreements of 1962;

Whereas the United States has no territorial, military or political ambitions in Southeast Asia, but desires only that the peoples of South Viet Nam, Laos and Cambodia should be left in peace by their neighbors to work out their own destinies in their own way, and, therefore, its objective is that the status established for these countries in the Geneva Accords of 1954 and the Geneva Agreements of 1962 should be restored with effective means of enforcement;

Whereas it is essential that the world fully understand that the American people are united in their determination to take all steps that may be necessary to assist the peoples of South Viet Nam and Laos to maintain their independence and political integrity.

Now, therefore, be it resolved by the Senate and House of Representatives of the United States of America in Congress assembled:

That the United States regards the preservation of the independence and integrity of the nations of South Viet Nam and Laos as vital to its national interest and to world peace;

Sec. 2. To this end, if the President determines the necessity thereof, the United States is prepared, upon the request of the Government of South Viet Nam or the Government of Laos, to use all measures, including the commitment of armed forces to assist that government in the defense of its independence and territorial integrity against aggression or subversion supported, controlled or directed from any Communist country.

Sec. 3. (a) The President is hereby authorized to use for assistance under this joint resolution not to exceed $_____ during the fiscal year 1964, and not to exceed $_____ during the fiscal year 1965, from any appropriations made available for carrying out the provisions of the Foreign Assistance Act of 1961, as amended, in accordance with the provisions of that Act, except as otherwise provided in this joint resolution. This authorization is in addition to other existing authorizations with respect to the use of such appropriations.

(b) Obligations incurred in carrying out the provisions of this joint resolution may be paid either out of appropriations for military assistance or appropriations for other than military assistance except that appropriations made available for Titles I, III, and VI of Chapter 2, Part I, of the Foreign Assistance Act of 1961, as amended, shall not be available for payment of such obligations.

(c) Notwithstanding any other provision of the Foreign Assistance Act of 1961, as amended, when the President determines it to be important to the security of the United States and in furtherance of the purposes of this joint resolution, he may authorize the use of up to $_____ of funds available under subsection (a) in each of the fiscal years 1964 and 1965 under the authority of section 614 (a) of the Foreign Assistance Act of 1961, as amended, and is authorized to use up to $_____ of such funds in each such year pursuant to his certification that it is inadvisable to specify the nature of the use of such funds, which certification shall be deemed to be a sufficient [words illegible].

(d) Upon determination by the head of any agency making personnel available under authority of section 627 of the Foreign Assistance Act of 1961, as amended, or otherwise under that Act, for purposes of assistance under this joint resolution, any officer or employee so made available may be provided compensation and allowances at rates other than those provided by the Foreign Service Act of 1946, as amended, the Career Compensation Act of 1949, as amended, and the Overseas Differentials and Allowances Act to the extent necessary to carry out the purposes of this joint resolution. The President shall prescribe regulations under which such rates of compensation and allowances may be provided. In addition, the President may utilize such provisions of the Foreign Service Act of 1946, as amended, as he deems appropriate to apply to personnel of any agency carrying out functions under this joint resolution.

67

Cable from Taylor Warning on the "March North" Campaign

Excerpts from cablegram from Ambassador Taylor in Saigon to the State Department, July 25, 1964.

The GVN public campaign for "Marching North" (reported EMBTEL 201) may take several courses. In the face of U.S. coolness and absence of evidence of real grassroots support outside certain military quarters, it may die down for a while although it is hardly likely to disappear completely. On the other hand, the proponents of a "Quick Solution" may be able to keep it alive indefinitely as an active issue, in which case it is likely to forment an increasing amount of dissatisfaction with the U.S. (assuming that we continue to give it no support) to the serious detriment of our working relations with the GVN and hence of the ultimate chances of success of the in-country pacification program. In such a case, Vietnamese leaders in and out of government, unable to find a vent to their frustration in "Marching North" may seek other panaceas in various forms of negotiation formulas. General Khanh may find in the situation an excuse or a requirement to resign.

Finally, this "March North" fever can get out of hand in an act of rashness—one maverick pilot taking off for Hanoi with a load of bombs—which could touch off an extension of hostilities at a time and in a form most disadvantageous to U.S. interests.

Faced with these unattractive possibilities, we propose a course of action designed to do several things.

We would try to avoid head-on collision with the GVN which unqualified U.S. opposition to the "March North" campaign would entail. We could do this by expressing a willingness to engage in joint contingency planning for various forms of extended action against GVN [sic]. Such planning would not only provide an outlet for the martial head of steam now dangerously compressed but would force the generals to look at the hard facts of life which lie behind the neon lights of the "March North" slogans. This planning would also gain time badly needed to stabilize this government and could provide a useful basis for military action if adjudged in our interest at some future time. Finally, it would also afford U.S. an opportunity, for the first time, to have a frank discussion with GVN leaders concerning the political objectives which they would envisage as the purposes inherent in military action against the DRV. . . .

It would be important, however, in initiating such a line of action that we make a clear record that we are not repeat not assuming any commitment to supplement such plans. . . .

68

U.S. Note to Canada on Points for Envoy to Relay to Hanoi

United States note delivered at the Canadian Embassy in Washington, Aug. 8, 1964, for transmission to J. Blair Seaborn, Canadian member of the International Control Commission.

Canadians are urgently asked to have Seaborn during August 10 visit make following points (as having been conveyed to him by U.S. Government since August 6):

A. Re Tonkin Gulf actions, which almost certainly will come up:

1. The DRV has stated that Hon Ngu_ and Hon Me islands

289

were attacked on July 30. It should be noted that the USS MADDOX was all of that day and into the afternoon of the next day, over 100 miles south of those islands, in international waters near the 17th parallel, and that the DRV attack on the MADDOX took place on August 2nd, more than two days later. Neither the MADDOX or any other destroyer was in any way associated with any attack on the DRV islands.

2. Regarding the August 4 attack by the DRV on the two U.S. destroyers, the Americans were and are at a complete loss to understand the DRV motive. They had decided to absorb the August 2 attack on the grounds that it very well might have been the result of some DRV mistake or miscalculation. The August 4 attack, however—from the determined nature of the attack as indicated by the radar, sonar, and eye witness evidence both from the ships and from their protecting aircraft—was, in the American eyes, obviously deliberate and planned and ordered in advance. In addition, premeditation was shown by the evidence that the DRV craft were waiting in ambush for the destroyers. The attack did not seem to be in response to any action by the South Vietnamese nor did it make sense as a tactic to further any diplomatic objective. Since the attack took place at least 60 miles from nearest land, there could have been no question about territorial waters. About the only reasonable hypothesis was that North Vietnam was intent either upon making it appear that the United States was a "paper tiger" or upon provoking the United States.

3. The American response was directed solely to patrol craft and installations acting in direct support of them. As President Johnson stated: "Our response for the present will be limited and fitting."

4. In view of uncertainty aroused by the deliberate and unprovoked DRV attacks this character, U.S. has necessarily carried out precautionary deployments of additional air power to SVN and Thailand.

B. Re basic American position:

5. Mr. Seaborn should again stress that U.S. policy is simply that North Vietnam should contain itself and its ambitions within the territory allocated to its administration by the 1954 Geneva Agreements. He should stress that U.S. policy in South Vietnam is to preserve the integrity of that state's territory against guerrilla subversion.

6. He should reiterate that the U.S. does not seek military bases in the area and that the U.S. is not seeking to overthrow the Communist regime in Hanoi.

7. He should repeat that the U.S. is fully aware of the degree to which Hanoi controls and directs the guerrilla action in South Vietnam and that the U.S. holds Hanoi directly responsible for that action. He should similarly indicate U.S. awareness of North Vietnamese control over the Pathet Lao movement in Laos and the degree of North Vietnamese involvement in that country. He

should specifically indicate U.S. awareness of North Vietnamese violations of Laotian territory along the infiltration route into South Vietnam.

8. Mr. Seaborn can again refer to the many examples of U.S. policy in tolerance of peaceful coexistence with Communist regimes, such as Yugoslavia, Poland, etc. He can hint at the economic and other benefits which have accrued to those countries because their policy of Communism has confirmed itself to the development of their own national territories and has not sought to expand into other areas.

9. Mr. Seaborn should conclude with the following new points:

a. That the events of the past few days should add credibility to the statement made last time, that "U.S. public and official patience with North Vietnamese aggression is growing extremely thin."

b. That the U.S. Congressional Resolution was passed with near unanimity, strongly re-affirming the unity and determination of the U.S. Government and people not only with respect to any further attacks on U.S. military forces but more broadly to continue to oppose firmly, by all necessary means, DRV efforts to subvert and conquer South Vietnam and Laos.

c. That the U.S. has come to the view that the DRV role in South Vietnam and Laos is critical. If the DRV persists in its present course, it can expect to continue to suffer the consequences.

d. That the DRV knows what it must do if the peace is to be restored.

e. That the U.S. has ways and means of measuring the DRV's participation in, and direction and control of, the war on South Vietnam and in Laos and will be carefully watching the DRV's response to what Mr. Seaborn is telling them.

69

Summary of Taylor's Report Sent to McNamara by Joint Chiefs

Excerpts from Summary of Ambassador Taylor's first mission report from Saigon, on Aug. 10, 1964, as transmitted on Aug. 14 by Col. A. R. Brownfield, acting special assistant to the Joint Chiefs of Staff for counterinsurgency and special activities, to Secretary McNamara, through Col. Alfred J. F. Moody, the Secretary's military assistant. Colonel Brownfield's covering memorandum said this summary had also been supplied to Gen. Earle G. Wheeler, Chairman of the Joint Chiefs, and to Deputy Secretary of Defense Cyrus R. Vance, for their appearance before the House Armed Services Committee on Aug. 18.

. . . The basis of this report and monthly reports hereafter are the results of a country-wide canvass of responsible U.S. advisors and observers. The canvass dealt with: Army and public morale, combat effectiveness of military units, U.S./GVN counterpart relationships, and effectiveness of GVN officials.

—In broad terms, the canvass results are surprisingly optimistic at the operational levels of both the civil and military organizations. This feeling of optimism exceeds that of most senior U.S. officials in Saigon. Future reports should determine who is right.

VIET CONG SITUATION:

Strategy:

—The communist strategy as defined by North Vietnam and the puppet National Liberation Front is to seek a political settlement favorable to the communists. This political objective to be achieved by stages, passing first through "neutralism" using the National Liberation Front machinery, and then the technique of a coalition government.

Tactics:

—The VC tactics are to harass, erode and terrorize the VN population and its leadership into a state of demoralization without an attempt to defeat the RVNAF or seize and conquer terrain by military means. U.S./GVN progress should be measured against this strategy and these tactics.

Status:

In terms of equipment and training, the VC are better armed and led today than ever in the past.

—VC infiltration continues from Laos and Cambodia.

—No indication that the VC are experiencing any difficulty in replacing their losses in men and equipment.

—No reason to believe the VC will risk their gains in an overt military confrontation with GVN forces, although they have a sizable force with considerable offensive capability in the central highlands.

GVN SITUATION:

Political:

—The slow pace of the CI campaign and the weakness of his government has caused Khanh to use the March North theme to rally the homefront, and offset the war weariness.

—U.S. observers feel the symptoms of defeatism are more in the minds of the inexperienced and untried leadership in Saigon than in the people and the Army.

—We may face mounting pressure from the GVN to win the war by direct attack on Hanoi which if resisted will cause local politicians to seriously consider negotiation or local soldiers to consider a military adventure without U.S. consent.

—For the present, the Khanh government has the necessary military support to stay in power.

—It is estimated that Khanh has a 50/50 chance of lasting out the year.

—The government is ineffective, beset by inexperienced ministers who are jealous and suspicious of each other.

—Khanh does not have confidence or trust in most of his ministers and is not able to form them into a group with a common loyalty and purpose.

—There is no one in sight to replace Khanh.

—Khanh has, for the moment, allayed the friction between the Buddhists and Catholics.

—Khanh has won the cooperation of the Hoa Hao and Cao Dai.

—Khanh has responded to our suggestions for improved relations between GVN and U.S. Mission.

—The population is confused and apathetic.

—Khanh has not succeeded in building active popular support in Saigon.

—Population support in the countryside is directly proportionate to the degree of GVN protection.

—There are grounds to conclude that no sophisticated psychological approach is necessary to attract the country people to the GVN at this time. The assurance of a reasonably secure life is all that is necessary.

—The success of U.S. attacks on North Vietnam, although furnishing a psychological lift to the GVN, may have whetted their appetite for further moves against the DRV. . . .

Military:

—The regular and paramilitary personnel strengths are slowly rising and by January 1965 should reach 98% of the target strength of 446,000.

—The RVNAF desertion rate has decreased to .572% or ½ the rate of last March.

—Three VNAF squadrons of A-1H aircraft will be combat ready by 30 September 1964 and the fourth by 1 December 1964 with a two to one pilot to cockpit ratio.

—The evaluation of RVNAF units reports the following number combat effective:

28 of 30 regiments

100 of 101 infantry, marine and airborne battalions

17 of 20 ranger battalions

19 of 20 engineer battalions

—The principal defects are low present for duty strengths and weak leadership at the lower levels. Both are receiving corrective treatment.

—Extensive intelligence programs are underway to improve our intelligence capability by the end of the year.

GVN OVERALL OBJECTIVE:

—Increase in percentage of population control represents progress toward stabilizing the in-country situation. Using July figures as a base, the following percentages should be attainable.

	Rural		Urban	
	31 July 64	31 Dec 64	31 July 64	31 Dec 64
GVN control	33%	40%	44%	47%
VC control	20%	16%	18%	14%
Contested	47%	44%	42%	39%

U.S. MISSION OBJECTIVES:

Do everything possible to bolster the Khanh Government.
Improve the in-country pacification campaign against the VC.
Concentrating efforts on strategically important areas such as the provinces around Saigon (The Hop Tac Plan).
Undertake "show-window" social and economic projects in secure urban and rural areas.
Be prepared to implement contingency plans against North Vietnam with optimum readiness by January 1, 1965.
Keep the U.S. public informed of what we are doing and why. . . .

70

William Bundy Memo on Actions Available to U.S. after Tonkin

Excerpts from second draft of a memorandum, "Next Courses of Action in Southeast Asia," by William P. Bundy, Assistant Secretary of State for Far Eastern Affairs, Aug. 11, 1964. A summary was cabled to the Pacific command and the embassies in Saigon and Vientiane on Aug. 14 with requests for comments. According to the Pentagon study, the full draft was edited in the office of Assistant Secretary of Defense John T. McNaughton. Words that were deleted at that time are shown below in double parentheses; words that were inserted at that time are shown in italics. Boldface type denotes underlining in the original document. Also, according to the McNaughton office's editing, the second paragraph, beginning "We have agreed . . .," was to be moved below, to follow the heading "Phase One—'Military Silence' (through August)."

I. INTRODUCTION

This memorandum examines the courses of action the U.S. might pursue, commencing in about two weeks, assuming that the

Communist side does not react further the [sic] the events of last week.

We have agreed that the intervening period will be in effect a short holding phase, in which we would avoid actions that would in any way take the onus off the Communist side for escalation . . .

III. ESSENTIAL ELEMENTS OF U.S. POLICY

A. **South Viet-Nam** is still the main theater. Morale and momentum there must be maintained. This means:

1. We must devise means of action that, *for minimum risks*, get maximum results ((for minimum risks)) *in terms of morale in SVN and pressure on NVN.*

2. We must continue to oppose any Viet-Nam conference, and must play the prospect of a Laos conference very carefully. We must particularly avoid any impression of rushing to a Laos conference, and must show a posture of general firmness into which an eventual Laos conference would fit without serious loss.

3. We particularly need to keep our hands free for at least limited measures against the Laos infiltration areas. . . .

C. *Solution.* Basically, a solution in both South Viet-Nam and Laos will require a combination of *military* pressures and some form of communication under which Hanoi (and Peiping) eventually accept the idea of getting out.* Negotiation without continued pressure, indeed without continued military action will not achieve our objectives in the foreseeable future. But *military* pressure could be accompanied by attempts to communicate with Hanoi and perhaps Peiping—through third-country channels, through side conversations around a Laos conference of any sort—**provided** always that we make it clear both to the Communists and to South Viet-Nam that the pressure will continue until we have achieved our objectives. After, **but only after,** we have ((established a)) *know that North Vietnamese are hurting and that the* clear pattern of pressure *has dispelled suspicions of our motives,* we could ((then)) accept a conference broadened to include the Viet-Nam issue. (The UN now looks to be out as a communication forum, though this could conceivably change.)

---

*We have never defined precisely what we mean by "getting out"—what actions, what proofs, and what future guarantees we would accept. A small group should work on this over the next month. *The actions we want the DRV to take are probably these:*

(a) *Stop training and sending personnel to wage war in SVN and Laos.*

(b) *Stop sending arms and supplies to SVN and Laos.*

(c) *Stop directing and controlling military actions in SVN and Laos.*

(d) *Order the VC and PL to stop their insurgencies and military actions.*

(e) *Remove VM forces and cadres from SVN and Laos.*

(f) *See that VC and PL stop attacks and incidents in SVN and Laos.*

(g) *See that VC and PL cease resistance to government forces.*

(h) *See that VC and PL turn in weapons and relinquish bases.*

(i) *See that VC and PL surrender for amnesty or expatriation.*

IV. TIMING AND SEQUENCE OF ACTIONS

A. PHASE ONE—"Military Silence" (through August) (see p. 1)

(A.) B. PHASE TWO—Limited pressures (September through December)

There are a number of limited actions we could take that would tend to maintain the initiative and the morale of the GVN and Khanh, but that would not involve major risks of escalation. Such actions could be such as to foreshadow stronger measures to come, though they would not in themselves go far to change Hanoi's basic actions.

1. 34A operations could be overtly acknowledged and justified by the GVN. **Marine operations** could be strongly defended on the basis of continued DRV sea infiltration, and successes could be publicized. **Leaflet operations** could also be admitted and defended, again on the grounds of meeting DRV efforts in the South, and their impunity (we hope) would tend to have its own morale value in both Vietnams. **Air-drop operations** are more doubtful; their justification is good and less clear than the other operations, and their successes have been few. With the others admitted, they could be left to speak for themselves—and of course security would forbid any mention of specific operations before they succeeded.

2. Joint planning ** between the US and the GVN already covers possible actions against the DRV and also against the Panhandle. It can be used in itself to maintain the morale of the GVN leadership, as well as to control and inhibit any unilateral GVN moves. With 34A outlined, it could be put right into the same framework. We would not ourselves publicize this planning but it could be leaked (as it probably would anyway) with desirable effects in Hanoi and elsewhere.

3. Stepped-up training of Vietnamese on jet aircraft should now be undertaken in any event in light of the presence of MIG's in North Vietnam. The JCS are preparing a plan, and the existence of training could be publicized both for its morale effect in the GVN and as a signal to Hanoi of possible future action.

4. Cross-border operations into the Panhandle could be conducted on a limited scale. To be successful, **ground operations** would have to be so large in scale as to be beyond what the GVN can spare, and we should not at this time consider major US or Thai ground action from the Thai side. But on the **air side**, there are at least a few worthwhile targets in the infiltration areas, and these could be hit by U.S. *and/or* (([deleted phrase illegible] and by)) GVN air. Probably we should use both (*query if U.S. strike should be under a [word illegible] cover*) U.S. & GVN; probably we should avoid publicity so as not to embarrass Souvanna; the Communist side might squawk, but in the past they

---

** This is in Phase One also

296

have been silent on this area. *The strikes should probably be timed and plotted on the map to bring them to the borders of North Vietnam at the end of December.*

5. DESOTO patrols could be reintroduced at some point. Both for present purposes and to maintain the credibility of our account of the events of last week, they must be clearly dissociated from 34A operations both in fact and in physical appearance. [Sentence deleted here is illegible.] In terms of course patterns, we should probably avoid penetrations of 11 miles or so and stay at least 20 miles off; whatever the importance of asserting our view of territorial waters, it is less than the international drawbacks of appearing to provoke attack unduly. [Previous sentence is marked in handwriting "disagree."]

6. Specific tit-for-tat actions could be undertaken for any *VC or DRV activity suited to the treatment.* [Deleted sentence illegible.] *These would be "actions of opportunity."* As Saigon 377 points out, the VC have "unused dirty tricks" such as mining (or attacks) in the Saigon River, sabotage of major POL stocks, and terrorist attacks on U.S. dependents. The first two, at least, would lend themselves to prompt and precise reprisal, e.g., by mining the Haiphong channel and attacking the Haiphong POL storage. Terrorism against U.S. dependents would be harder to find the right reprisal target, and reprisal has some disadvantages in that it could be asked why this was different from the regular pattern of terrorism against South Vietnamese. However, we should look at possible [deleted word is illegible] *classes of tit-for-tat situations.*

7. The sequence and mix of US and GVN actions needs careful thought. At this point, both the GVN role ((and)) *in the actions and the* rationales directly ((related)) *relating the actions* to what is being done to the GVN should be emphasized. Overt 34A actions should ((certainly)) be the first moves, and the GVN might go first in air attacks on the Panhandle. But there are advantages in other respects to actions related to U.S. forces. If we lost an aircraft in the Panhandle ((or a U-2 over the DRV)) we could act hard and fast, and of course similarly for any attack on the DESOTO patrols. *The loss of a U-2 over NVN does not offer as good a case.* Probably the sequence should be played somewhat by ear.

Summary. The above actions are in general limited and controllable. However, if we accept—as of course we must—the necessity of prompt retaliation especially for attacks on our own forces, they could amount to at least a pretty high noise level that might stimulate some pressures for a conference. The problem is that these actions are not in themselves a truly coherent program of strong enough pressures either to bring Hanoi around or to sustain a pressure posture into some kind of discussions. Hence, while we might communicate privately to Hanoi while all this was going on, we should continue absolutely opposed to any conference.

((B.)) *C. PHASE THREE*—More Serious Pressures. *(January 1965 and following).*

All the above actions would be foreshadowing systematic military action against the DRV, and we might at some point conclude that such action was required either because of incidents arising from the above actions or because of deterioration in the situation in South Viet-Nam, particularly if there were to be clear evidence of greatly increased infiltration from the north. However, in the absence of such major new developments, we should probably be thinking of a contingency date, as suggested by Ambassador Taylor, of 1 January 1965. Possible categories of action ((are)) *beginning at about that time, are:*

1. Action against infiltration routes and facilities is probably the best opening gambit. *It would follow logically the actions in the Sept.-Dec. Phase Two.* It could be justified by evidence that infiltration was continuing and, in all probability, increasing. The family of infiltration-related targets starts with clear military installations near the borders. It can be extended almost at will northward, to inflict progressive damage that would have a meaningful cumulative effect and would always be keyed to one rationale.

2. Action *in the DRV* **against selected military-related targets** would appear to be the next upward move. POL installations and the mining of Haiphong Harbor (to prevent POL import as its rationale) would be spectacular actions, as would action against key bridges and railroads. All of these could probably be designed so as to avoid major civilian casualties.

3. Beyond these points it is probably not useful to think at the present time. . . .

71

Pacific Commander's Evaluation of Washington's Action Scenario

Excerpts from cablegram from Adm. U.S. Grant Sharp, commander of Pacific forces, to Joint Chiefs of Staff, "Next Courses of Action in Southeast Asia," Aug. 17, 1964.

2. Recent U.S. military actions in Laos and North Vietnam demonstrated our intent to move toward our objectives. Our operations and progress in Laos constitute one step along the route. Our directness and rapidity of reaction in bombing North Vietnamese installations and deploying U.S. combat forces to Southeast Asia were others. Each step played a part. Their effect was to interrupt the continually improving Communist posture, catch the imagination of the Southeast Asian peoples, provide some lift to morale, however temporary, and force CHICOM/DRV assessment or reassessment of U.S. intentions. But these were only steps along the way. What we have not done and must do is make plain to Hanoi and Peiping the cost of pursuing their current objectives and impeding ours. An essential element of our military action in this course is to proceed in the development of our physical readiness posture: deploying troops, ships, aircraft, and logistic resources in a manner which accords a maximum freedom of action. This is the thrust we should continue to pursue, one which is intended to provide more than one feasible course for consideration as the changed and changing Southeast Asian situation develops. Remarks in the paragraphs which follow are submitted in light of this assessment and with the view that pressures against the other side once instituted should not be relaxed by any actions or lack of them which would destroy the benefits of the rewarding steps previously taken in Laos and North Vietnam. . . .

3. Para I.

The proposed two weeks suspension of operations is not in consonance with desire to get the message to Hanoi and Peiping. Pierce Arrow showed both force and restraint. Further demonstration of restraint alone could easily be interpreted as period of second thoughts about Pierce Arrow and events leading thereto as well as sign of weakness and lack of resolve. Continuous and effective pressure should be implied to the Communists in both the PDJ and panhandle. Consequently, concur in continued RECCE of DRV, panhandle and PDJ. Concur in attempt to secure Phou Kout and continued T-28 and Triangle operations. Resumption of 34A actions and Desoto Patrols is considered appropriate. Each can be carefully conducted to avoid interference with the other. . . .

7. Para III A 1

Concur that South Vietnam is current hot spot and main concern in S.E. Asia. RVN cannot be reviewed apart from S.E. Asia. It is merely an area in a large theater occupied by the same enemy. Action to produce significant results in terms of pressure on DRV and improvements of morale in RVN must entail risk. Temptation toward zero action and zero risk must be avoided. . . .

11. Para III C

Concur with the thesis set forth that we make clear to all that military pressure will continue until we achieve our objectives. Our actions must keep the Communists apprehensive of what further steps we will take if they continue their aggression. In this regard, we have already taken the large initial step of putting U.S. combat forces into Southeast Asia. We must maintain this posture; to reduce it would have a dangerous impact on the morale and will of all people in Southeast Asia. And we must face up to the fact that these forces will be deployed for some time and to their need for protection from ground or air attack. RVN cannot provide necessary ground security without degraduation of the counterinsurgency effort and has little air defense capability. A conference to include Vietnam, before we have overcome the insurgency, would lose U.S. our allies in Southeast Asia and represent a defeat for the United States.

12. Para IV A 1

Knowledge of success of 34A operations would have a highly beneficial effect morale in the RVN. Suggest that these operations might be leaked to the press rather than overtly acknowledging them. 34A operations should be resumed to keep up external pressure on the DRV....

20. In considering more serious pressure, we must recognize that immediate action is required to protect our present heavy military investment in RVN. We have introduced large amounts of expensive equipment into RVN and a successful attack against Bien Hoa, Tan Son Nhut, Danang, or an installation such as a radar or communication site would be a serious psychological defeat for U.S. MACV reports that inability of GVN to provide requisite degree of security and therefore we must rely on U.S. troops. MACV has requested troops for defense of the three locations mentioned above. My comments on this request are being transmitted by separate message. In addition to the above, consideration should be given to creating a U.S. base in RVN. A U.S. base in RVN would provide one more indication of our intent to remain in S.E. Asia until our objectives are achieved. It could also serve as a U.S. command point or control center in event of the chaos which might follow another coup. By an acknowledged concrete U.S. (as received) commitment, beyond the advisory effort, it informs the Communists that an overt attack on the RVN would be regarded as a threat to U.S. forces. Such a base should be accessible by air and sea, possessed of well developed facilities and installations, and located in an area from which U.S. operations could be launched effectively. Danang meets these criteria....

22. In conclusion, our actions of August 5 have created a momentum which can lead to the attainment of our objectives in S.E. Asia. We have declared ourselves forcefully both by overt acts and by the clear readiness to do more. It is most important that we not lose this momentum.

72

Memo from the Joint Chiefs on September's Covert Raids

Memorandum from Maj. Gen. Rotten H. Anthis, an Air Force aide to the Joint Chiefs of Staff, to Assistant Secretary of State Bundy and Assistant Secretary of Defense

McNaughton, Aug. 27, 1964. The subject of the memorandum was given as "OPLAN 34A—September Schedule."

1. Attached hereto is COMUSMACV'S proposed schedule of 34A actions for September.

2. All of the actions listed have either been specifically approved previously or are similar to such approved actions. For example, Action (3) (d) was specifically approved by consideration of JCSM-426-64 dated 19 May 1964, while Action (3) (b) is similar to a previously approved action against a security post.

3. The method of attack has been changed in some instances from destruction by infiltration of demolition teams to the concept of standoff bombardment from PTFs. These actions are so indicated in the attachment.

———————

The proposed September 34A actions are as follows:

(1) Intelligence Collection Action

(a) 1-30 September—Aerial photography to update selected targets along with pre- and post-strike coverage of approved actions.

(b) 1-30 September—Two junk capture missions; remove captives for 36-48 hours interrogation; booby trap junk with anti-disturbance devices and release; captives returned after interrogation; timing depends upon sea conditions and current intelligence.

(2) Psychological Operations

(a) 1-30 September—In conjunction with approved overflights and maritime operations, delivery of propaganda leaflets, gift kits, and deception devices simulating resupply of phantom teams.

(b) 1-30 September—Approximately 200 letters of various propaganda themes sent through third country mail channels to North Vietnam.

(c) 1-30 September—Black Radio daily 30-minute programs repeated once, purports to be voice of dissident elements in North Vietnam.

(d) 1-30 September—White Radio broadcast of eight-and-one-half hours daily, propaganda "Voice of Freedom."

(3) Maritime Operations

(a) 1-30 September—Demolition of Route 1 bridge by infiltrated team accompanied by fire support teams, place short-delay charges against spans and caissons, place antipersonnel mines on road approaches. (This bridge previously hit but now repaired).

(b) 1-30 September—Bombard Cape Mui Dao observation post with 81 MM mortars and 40 MM guns from two PTFs.

(c) 1-30 September—Demolition of another Route 1 bridge (see map), concept same as (3) (a) above.

(d) 1-30 September—Bombard Sam Son radar, same as (3) (b).

(e) 1-30 September—Bombard Tiger Island barracks, same as (3) (b).

(f) 1-30 September—Bombard Hon Ngu Island, same as (3) (b).

(g) 1-30 September—Bombard Hon Matt Island, same as (3) (b) and run concurrently with (3) (f).

(h) 1-30 September—Destruction of section of Hanoi-Vinh railroad by infiltrated demolition team supported by two VN marine squads, by rubber boats from PTFs, place short-delay charges and antipersonnel mines around area.

(i) 1-30 September—Bombard Hon Me Island in conjunction with (3) (a) above, concept same as (3) (b).

(j) 1-30 September—Bombard Cape Falaise gun positions in conjunction with (3) (h) above, concept same as (3) (b).

(k) 1-30 September—Bombard Cape Mui Ron in conjunction with junk capture mission, concept same as (3) (b).

(4) **Airborne Operations**—Light-of-moon period 16-28 September

(a) Four missions for resupply of in-place teams.

(b) Four missions for reinforcement of in-place teams.

(c) Four missions to airdrop new psyops/sabotage teams depending upon development of drop zone and target information. These are low-key propaganda and intelligence gathering teams with a capability for small-scale sabotage on order after locating suitable targets.

(5) Dates for actual launch of maritime and airborne operations are contingent upon the intelligence situation and weather conditions.

73

State Department Aide's Report on Actions Taken after Tonkin

Part VIII, "Immediate Actions in the Period Prior to Decision," of an outline for Assistant Secretary Bundy, Nov. 7, 1964. Markings indicate that it was drafted by Deputy Assistant Secretary of State Marshall Green.

The U.S., together with the RLG and GVN, are involved in a number of operations—34-A, Yankee Team, Recce, and RLAF T-28 ops—designed to warn and harass North Vietnam and to reduce enemy capabilities to utilize the Lao Panhandle for reinforcing the Vietcong in South Vietnam and to cope with PL/VM pressures in Laos. The U.S. also has under consideration De Soto Patrols and Cross Border Ground Operations. The present status and outlook of these operations are described below, together with a checklist of outstanding problems relating to each of the field of operations.

In general the working group is agreed that our aim should be to maintain present signal strength and level of harassment, showing no signs of lessening of determination but also avoiding actions that would tend to prejudge the basic decision.

A. OPLAN 34-A

Although not all of Oplan 34-A was suspended after the first Tonkin Gulf incident, in effect little was accomplished during the remainder of August and the months of September. Several successful maritime and airborne operations have been conducted under the October schedule. A schedule for November is under discussion and will probably be approved November 7.

1. Maritime Operations

Since the resumption of Marops under the October schedule, the following have been completed:

Recon L Day (Oct. 4) Probe to 12 miles of Vinh Sor.

Recon L + 2 (Oct. 10) Probe to 12 miles of Vinh Sor.

Loki IV L + 5 Junk capture failed

32 & 45 E L 8 (Oct. 28/29) Bombard Vin Son radar and Mui Dai observation post.

The following operation was refused approval:

44c L + 10 Demolition by frog men supported by fire team of bridge on Route 1.

Currently approved is:

34B L + 12 (Nov. 4, on) Bombardment of barracks on Hon Matt and Tiger Island.

The following maritime operations remain on the October schedule and presumably will appear on the November schedule along with some additional similar operations:

L + 13 Capture of prisoner by team from PTF

L + 15 Junk capture

L + 19 Bombard Cap Mui Ron and Tiger Island

L + 25 Bombard Yen Phu and Sam Son radar

L + 28 Blow up Bridge Route 1 and bombard Cap Mui Dao

L + 30 Return any captives from L + 1 15

L + 31 Bombard Hon Ne and Hon Me

L + 36 Blow up pier at Phuc Loi and bombard Hon Ngu

L + 38 Cut Hanoi-Vinh rail line

L + 41 Bombard Dong Hoi and Tiger Island

L + 24 Bombard Nightingale Island.

2. Airborne Operations

Five teams and one singleton agent were in place at the beginning of October. Since then one of the teams has been resupplied and reinforced. The remaining four were scheduled to be resupplied and reinforced but weather prevented flights. These operations, plus the dropping of an additional team, will appear on the November schedule.

Two of the teams carried out successful actions during October. One demolished a bridge, the other ambushed a North Vietnamese patrol. Both teams suffered casualties, the latter sufficient to cast doubt on the wisdom of the action.

3. Psychological Operations

Both black and white radio broadcasts have been made daily.

Black broadcasts have averaged eight to ten hours weekly, white broadcasts sixty hours weekly.

Letters posted through Hong Kong have averaged about from 50 to 100 weekly.

During September and October only one leaflet delivery was made by air. This was done in conjunction with a resupply mission.

The November schedule will call for a large number of leaflet and deception operations.

4. Reconnaissance Flights

An average of four flights per week have covered the bulk of Oplan 34-A targets.

PROBLEMS

1. Surfacing of Marops—The question of whether to surface Marops remains unresolved. While Washington has suggested this be done, General Khanh has been reluctant to do so. It is argued that surfacing the operations would enable the U.S. to offer some protection to them; the counterargument postulates U.S. involvement in North Vietnam and consequent escalation.

2. Security of Operations—The postponement of an operation, whether because of unfavorable weath or failure of Washington to approve at the last moment, jeopardizes the operation. Isolation of teams presents hazards.

3. Base Security—After the Bien Hoa shelling some attention has been given to the security of the Danang base. Perimeter guard has been strengthened, but action remains to be taken for marine security, although a survey is underway.

4. Team welfare—In-place teams Bell and Easy have been in dire need of supplies for several weeks. Weather has prevented resupply, which will be attempted again during the November moon phase.

5. NVN Counteraction—The capability of the North Vietnamese against Marops has improved somewhat, although not yet sufficiently to frustrate these operations.

B. YANKEE TEAM OPERATIONS

For several months now the pattern of Yankee Team Operations has [words illegible] a two-week period and about ten flights during the same time interval [words illegible] for Panhandle coverage. Additionally, we have recently been authorized a maximum of two shallow penetration flights daily to give comprehensive detailed coverage of cross border penetration. We have also recently told MACV that we have a high priority requirement for night photo recce of key motorable routes in Laos. At present about 2 nights recce flights are flown along Route 7 areas within a two-week span.

YT supplies cap for certain T-28 corridor strikes. Cap aircraft are not authorized to participate in strike or to provide suppressive fire.

Pending questions include: (a) whether YT strikes should be made in support of RLAF T-28 corridor operations; (b) whether YT recce should be made of areas north of 20° parallel; (c) YT suppressive attacks against Route 7, especially Ban Ken Bridge; and (d) YT activity in event of large-scale ground offensive by PL (this issue has not arisen but undoubtedly would, should the PL undertake an offensive beyond the capabilities of Lao and sheep-dipped Thai to handle).

C. T-28 OPERATIONS

There are now 27 T-28 (including three RT-28) aircraft in Laos, of which 22 are in operation. CINCPAC has taken action, in response to Ambassador Unger's request to build this inventory back up to 40 aircraft for which a pilot capability, including Thai, is present in Laos.

The T-28's are conducting the following operations:

1. General harassing activities against Pathet Lao military installations and movement, primarily in Xieng Khouang and Sam Neua Provinces. This also includes efforts to interdict Route 7.

2. Tactical support missions for Operation Anniversary Victory No. 2 (Saleumsay), the FAR-Meo clearing operation up Route 4 and north of Tha Thom.

3. Tactical support for Operation Victorious Arrow (Sone Sai), a FAR clearing operations in southern Laos.

4. Strikes on targets of opportunity, including in support of FAR defensive actions such as at Ban Khen northwest Thakhek.

5. Corridor interdiction program. The original targets under this program have been hit and plans are now underway to hit four additional targets (including in the Tchepone area), plus restriking some of the original 13 targets. Ambassador Unger has submitted for approval under this program 6 additional targets.

6. The Ambassador has been authorized to discuss with the RLAF RT-28 reconnaissance in northwest Laos along the area just north of and to the east and west of the line from Veng Phou Kha-Muong Sai.

In recent weeks, the T-28's have been dropping a large number of surrender leaflets on many of their missions. These have already led, in some cases, to PL defections.

U.S. participation in SAR operations for downed T-28's, is authorized.

We are faced by the following problems in connection with the T-28's:

1. Authority for Yankee Team aircraft to engage in suppressive strikes in the corridor area, in support of the T-28 strike program there, has not been given as yet.

2. Also withheld is authorization for YT suppressive fire attack on Ban Ken Bridge on Route 7.

3. We are investigating reports of greatly increased truck movement along Route 7 as well as enemy build-up of tanks and other

equipment just across the border in NVN. Counteraction may be required involving attack on Ban Ken.

4. Thai involvement. Hanoi claims to have shot down a T-28 over DRV territory on August 18 and to have captured the Thai pilot flying the plane. Although the information the North Vietnamese have used in connection with this case seems to be accurate, it is not clear the pilot is alive and can be presented to the ICC. The possibility cannot be excluded, however, nor that other Thai pilots might be captured by the PL.

5. The DRV claims T-28's have violated North Vietnamese airspace and bombed/strafed NVN villages on August 1 and 2, and on October 16 and 17 and again on October 28. The charges are probably accurate with respect to the first two dates (along Route 7) and the last one (Mu Gia Pass area). The October 16 and 17 strikes were actually in disputed territory which was recognized by the 1954 Geneva Agreements as being in Laos.

6. The Pathet Lao has called to the attention of the ICC T-28 strikes in the corridor area and called for the ICC to stop them and inform the Co-Chairmen. The ICC has already agreed to investigate another PL charge concerning alleged U.S./SVN activities in the corridor area in violation of the Geneva Agreements.

D. DeSOTO PATROLS

Further DeSoto Patrols have been held in abeyance pending top-level decision. Ambassador Taylor (Saigon's 1378) sees no advantage in resuming DeSoto Patrols except for essential intelligence purposes. He believes we should tie our actions to Hanoi's support of Viet Cong, not to the defense of purely U.S. interests.

E. CROSS BORDER GROUND OPERATIONS

Earlier in the year several eight-man reconnaissance teams were parachuted into Laos as part of Operation Leaping Lena. All of these teams were located by the enemy and only four survivors returned to RVN. As a result of Leaping Lena, Cross Border Ground Operations have been carefully reviewed and COMUS-MACV has stated that he believes no effective Cross Border Ground Operations can be implemented prior to January 1, 1965 at the earliest.

F. COVERT OPERATIONS IN LAOS

Consideration is being given to improving Hardnose (including greater Thai involvement) and getting Hardnose to operate more effectively in the corridor infiltration areas.

No change in status of Kha.

G. OTHER SENSITIVE INTELLIGENCE OPERATIONS

These include "Queen Bee," "Box Top," "Lucky Dragon" and "Blue Springs."

Chapter 6

The Consensus to Bomb North Vietnam: August, 1964– February, 1965

—BY NEIL SHEEHAN

The Johnson Administration reached a "general consensus" at a White House strategy meeting on Sept. 7, 1964, that air attacks against North Vietnam would probably have to be launched, a Pentagon study of the Vietnam war states. It was expected that "these operations would begin early in the new year."

"It is important to differentiate the consensus of the principals at this September meeting," the study says, "from the views which they had urged on the President in the preceding spring. In the spring the use of force had been clearly contingent on a major reversal—principally in Laos—and had been advanced with the apparent assumption that military actions hopefully would not be required. Now, however, their views were advanced with a sense that such actions were inevitable."

The administration consensus on bombing came at the height of the Presidential election contest between President Johnson and Senator Barry Goldwater, whose advocacy of full-scale air attacks on North Vietnam had become a major issue. That such a consensus had been reached as early as September is a major disclosure of the Pentagon study.

The consensus was reflected, the analysis says, in the final paragraph of a formal national security action memorandum issued by the President three days later, on Sept. 10. This paragraph spoke of "larger decisions" that might be "required at any time."

The last round of detailed planning of various political and

307

Highlights of the Period

Between the Tonkin Gulf resolution of August, 1964, and the start of concentrated United States bombing of North Vietnam in 1965, the details of such an air war were being planned, discussed and debated in the Johnson Administration, according to the secret Pentagon chronicle.

Here, chronologically, are highlights of those months of decision-making.

AUGUST, 1964

Ambassador Maxwell D. Taylor cables agreement with Administration "assumption" that "something must be added in the coming months" to forestall "a collapse of national morale" in Saigon. Suggests "carefully orchestrated bombing attack" on North.

Joint Chiefs of Staff concur, call air war "essential to prevent a complete collapse of the U.S. position in Southeast Asia." Propose what study calls "provocation strategy."

SEPTEMBER, 1964

John T. McNaughton, Assistant Secretary of Defense for International Security Affairs, outlines provocation plan "to provide good grounds for us to escalate if we wished. . . ." Includes South Vietnamese air strikes on Laos infiltration routes; coastal raids on North; resumption U.S. destroyer patrols in Gulf of Tonkin.

White House strategy meeting. Analyst finds "general consensus" on necessity for early 1965 air strikes but says "tactical considerations" require delay. Cites President's "presenting himself as the candidate of reason and restraint," need for "maximum public and Congressional support," fear of "premature negotiations," Saigon weakness.

President orders low-risk interim measures, says William P. Bundy memo, "to assist morale . . . and show the Communists we still mean business. . . ." Coastal raids, destroyer patrols included.

OCTOBER, 1964

Air strikes on Laos infiltration routes start, following delay awaiting outcome Laotian cease-fire talks. U.S. feared new Geneva conference. Analyst says this "not compatible with current perceptions of U.S. interest."

NOVEMBER, 1964

Vietcong attack Bienhoa airfield. Joint Chiefs urge "prompt and strong response" including air strikes on North. Ambassador Taylor urges bombing "selected" targets.

President declines, directs interagency working group under Bundy to consider, recommend Vietnam options, policy.

Group's three recommended options all include bombing

North. Analyst says group's deliberations showed "remarkably little latitude for reopening the basic questions about U.S. involvement."

Option A—reprisal air strikes, covert pressure intensified.

Option B—bomb North "at a fairly rapid pace and without interruption" till all U.S. demands met; U.S. to define negotiating position, chronicle says, "in a way which makes Communist acceptance unlikely" if U.S. pressed to negotiate "before a Communist agreement to comply."

Option C—graduated air war, possible deployment ground troops.

National Security Council select committee meets. George W. Ball, Under Secretary of State, indicates "doubt" about effectiveness bombing North, argues against domino theory, says Bundy memo. Mr. Ball's policy paper suggests diplomatic strategy leading to international Vietnam conference.

DECEMBER, 1964

President approves recommended plan—Option A for 30 days, then Option C. Stresses he feels "pulling the South Vietnamese together" basic to any other action.

Operation Barrel Roll—U.S. air strikes at infiltration routes Laotian panhandle—under way. National Security Council agrees to "no public statements" unless a plane is lost, then "to insist that we were merely escorting reconnaissance flights."

Air Marshal Nguyen Cao Ky and ex-Premier Nguyen Khanh attempt coup. Ambassador Taylor tells them U.S. is "tired of coups," warns that "all the military plans which I know you would like to carry out are dependent on government stability."

JANUARY, 1965

Two U.S. jets lost over Laos. Press reports on "Barrel Roll."

South Vietnam forces trounced at Binhia. Study says Saigon "final collapse" and Vietcong take-over seem "distinct possibility."

Mr. Bundy, in memo, says "shaky" Saigon morale due partly to "widespread feeling that the U.S. is not ready for stronger action" and is "insisting on perfectionism" in Saigon. Urges "stronger action" despite "grave difficulties."

Robert S. McNamara, Secretary of Defense, Mr. McNaughton favor "initiating air strikes"; agree U.S. aim "not to 'help friend' but to contain China," chronicle says.

FEBRUARY, 1965

Vietcong attack U.S. military advisers' compound at Pleiku. Study says this "triggered a swift, though long-contemplated Presidential decision to give an 'appropriate and fitting response'."

Forty-nine U.S. jets in first reprisal strike, raid Donghoi.

Second reprisal strike follows guerrilla attack on U.S. barracks.

Operation Rolling Thunder—sustained air war—ordered.

military strategies for a bombing campaign began "in earnest," the study says, on Nov. 3, 1964, the day that Mr. Johnson was elected President in his own right.

Less than 100 days later, on Feb. 8, 1965, he ordered new reprisal strikes against the North. Then, on Feb. 13, the President gave the order for the sustained bombing of North Vietnam, code-named Rolling Thunder.

This period of evolving decision to attack North Vietnam, openly and directly, is shown in the Pentagon papers to be the second major phase of President Johnson's defense of South Vietnam. The same period forms the second phase of the presentation of those papers by The New York Times.

In its glimpses into Lyndon B. Johnson's personal thoughts and motivations between the fateful September meeting and his decision to embark on an air war, the Pentagon study shows a President moving and being moved toward war, but reluctant and hesitant to act until the end.

But, the analyst explains, "from the September meeting forward, there was little basic disagreement among the principals [the term the study uses for the senior policy makers] on the need for military operations against the North. What prevented action for the time being was a set of tactical considerations."

The first tactical consideration, the analyst says, was that "the President was in the midst of an election campaign in which he was presenting himself as the candidate of reason and restraint as opposed to the quixotic Barry Goldwater," who was publicly advocating full-scale bombing of North Vietnam. The historian also mentions other "temporary reasons of tactics":

• The "shakiness" of the Saigon Government.

• A wish to hold the line militarily and diplomatically in Laos.

• The "need to design whatever actions were taken so as to achieve maximum public and Congressional support . . ."

• The "implicit belief that overt actions at this time might bring pressure for premature negotiations—that is negotiations before the D.R.V. [Democratic Republic of (North) Vietnam] was hurting."

Assistant Secretary of Defense John T. McNaughton, the head of the Pentagon's Office of International Security Affairs, summed up these tactical considerations in the final paragraph of a Sept. 3 memorandum to Secretary of Defense Robert S. McNamara, in preparation for the crucial White House strategy session four days later:

310

"Special considerations during the next two months. The relevant audiences of U.S. actions are the Communists (who must feel strong pressures), the South Vietnamese (whose morale must be buoyed), our allies (who must trust us as underwriters'), and the U.S. public (which must support our risk-taking with U.S. lives and prestige). During the next two months, because of the lack of 'rebuttal time' before election to justify particular actions which may be distorted to the U.S. public, we must act with special care—signaling to the D.R.V. that initiatives are being taken, to the G.V.N. [Government of (South) Vietnam] that we are behaving energetically despite the restraints of our political season, and to the U.S. public that we are behaving with good purpose and restraint." The words in parentheses are Mr. McNaughton's.

"Not to Enlarge the War"

The President was already communicating this sense of restraint to the voters. On the night of Aug. 29, in an address to a crowd at an outdoor barbecue a few miles from his ranch in Texas, when two tons of beef were served in a belated celebration of his 56th bitrhday, he made a statement that he was to repeat in numerous election speeches.

"I have had advice to load our planes with bombs," the President said, "and to drop them on certain areas that I think would enlarge the war and escalate the war, and result in our committing a good many American boys to fighting a war that I think ought to be fought by the boys of Asia to help protect their own land."

The policy of the United States toward Vietnam, the President explained later in his speech, was "to furnish advice, give counsel, express good judgment, give them trained counselors, and help them with equipment to help themselves."

"We are doing that," he said. "We have lost less than 200 men in the last several years, but to each one of those 200 men—and we lost about that many in Texas on accidents on the Fourth of July—to each of those 200 men who have given their life to preserve freedom, it is a war and a big war and we recognize it.

"But we think it is better to lose 200 than to lose 200,000. For that reason we have tried very carefully to restrain ourselves and not to enlarge the war."

Eleven days earlier, on Aug. 18, Ambassador Maxwell D. Taylor had cabled from Saigon that he agreed with an "assumption" now held in the Administration in Washington that the Vietcong guerrillas—the VC, as they were usually termed—could not be defeated and the Saigon Government preserved by a counterguerrilla war confined to South Vietnam itself.

"Something must be added in the coming months," the Ambassador said in his message. What General Taylor proposed to add was "a carefully orchestrated bombing attack on NVN [North Vietnam], directed primarily at infiltration and other military targets" with "Jan. 1, 1965, as a target D-Day."

The bombing should be undertaken under either of two courses of action, the Ambassador said. The first course would entail using the promise of the air attacks as an inducement to persuade the regime of Gen. Nguyen Khanh to achieve some political stability and get on seriously with the pacification program. Under the second course, the United States would bomb the North, regardless of whatever progress General Khanh made, to prevent "a collapse of national morale" in Saigon.

For the Ambassador cautioned that "it is far from clear at the present moment that the Khanh Government can last until Jan. 1, 1965." The Ambassador said that before bombing the North the United States would also have to send Army Hawk antiaircraft missile units to the Saigon and Danang areas to protect the airfields there against retaliatory Communist air attacks—assumed possible from China or North Vietnam—and to land a force of American Marines at Danang to protect the air base there against possible ground assaults.

His cable was designated a joint United States mission message, meaning that Deputy Ambassador U. Alexis Johnson and Gen. William C. Westmoreland, chief of the United States Military Assistance Command, had concurred with the Ambassador's views.

On Aug. 26, three days before the President's speech at the barbecue in Stonewall, Tex., the Joint Chiefs of Staff submitted a memorandum to Secretary McNamara agreeing with Ambassador Taylor. They said that bombing under his second criterion, to stave off a breakdown in Saigon, was "more in accord with the current situation" in their view and added that an air war against the North was now "essential to prevent a complete collapse of the U.S. position in Southeast Asia."

The Joint Chiefs' memorandum was the first appearance, the account says, of a "provocation strategy" that was to be discussed at the Sept. 7 White House session—in the words of the narrative, "deliberate attempts to provoke the D.R.V. into taking actions which could then be answered by a systematic U.S. air campaign."

The memorandum itself is not this explicit, although it does seem to suggest attempting to repeat the Tonkin Gulf clashes as a pretext for escalation.

In a Sept. 3 memorandum to Secretary McNamara, however, Mr. McNaughton was specific. He outlined several means of provocation that could culminate in a sustained air war. In the meantime, they could be employed to conduct reprisal air strikes that would help hold the situation in South Vietnam together and, the analyst notes, permit postponing "probably until November or December any decision as to serious escalation."

This serious escalation Mr. McNaughton defined as "a crescendo of GVN-U.S. military actions against the D.R.V.," such as mining harbors and gradually escalating air raids.

He described his provocation program to Mr. McNamara as "an orchestration of three classes of actions, all designed to meet these five desiderata—(1) From the U.S., GVN and hopefully allied points of view they should be legitimate things to do under the circumstances, (2) they should cause apprehension, ideally increasing apprehension, in the D.R.V., (3) they should be likely at some point to provoke a military D.R.V. response, (4) the provoked response should be likely to provide good grounds for us to escalate if we wished, and (5) the timing and crescendo should be under our control, with the scenario capable of being turned off at any time." [See Document #79.]

The classes of actions were:

• South Vietnamese air strikes at enemy infiltration routes through southeastern Laos that would "begin in Laos near the South Vietnamese border and slowly 'march' up the trails and eventually across the North Vietnamese border."

• A resumption of the covert coastal raids on North Vietnam under Operation Plan 34A, which President Johnson had temporarily suspended since the Tonkin Gulf incident. The South Vietnamese Government would announce them publicly, declaring them "fully justified as necessary to assist in interdiction of infiltration by sea."

• A resumption of patrols in the Gulf of Tonkin by United States destroyers, code-named De Sota patrols, although these would still be physically "disassociated" from the 34A attacks. Mr. McNaughton noted that "the U.S. public is sympathetic to reasonable insistence on the right of the U.S. Navy to ply international waters."

But a majority of the officials at the Sept. 7 White House strategy meeting disagreed. They decided for the present against adopting a provocation strategy for reprisal air attacks, precisely because the Khanh regime was so weak and vulnerable and the morale-lifting benefits of such strikes might be offset by possible Communist retaliation, the analyst says. The meeting was attended by the President; Secretary of State Dean Rusk; Secretary McNamara; Gen. Earle G. Wheeler, the new Chairman of the Joint Chiefs; Ambassador Taylor, who had flown in from Saigon, and John A. McCone, the Director of Central Intelligence.

"We believe such deliberately provocative elements should not be added in the immediate future while the GVN is still struggling to its feet." Assistant Secretary of State William P. Bundy wrote in a memorandum recording the consensus recommendations formally made to the President after the meeting.

"By early October, however, we may recommend such actions depending on GVN progress and Communist reaction in the meantime, especially to U.S. naval patrols." A resumption of the destroyer patrols was one outcome of the Sept. 7 meeting.

The analyst says that a similar reason was given for the decision against beginning a sustained bombing campaign against the North, with or without a provocation strategy, in the near future. "The GVN over the next 2-3 months will be too weak for us to take any major deliberate risks of escalation that would involve a major role for, or threat to, South Vietnam," the Bundy memorandum states.

Ambassador Taylor had acknowledged in his cable of Aug. 18 that bombing the North to prevent a collapse in the South if the Khanh regime continued to decline "increases the likelihood of U.S. involvement in ground action since Khanh will have almost no available ground forces which can be released from pacification employment to mobile resistance of D.R.V. attacks."

The Pentagon account concludes from the Sept. 7 strategy discussions that by now the Saigon regime was being regarded less and less as a government capable of defeating the Vietcong insurgency than "in terms of its suitability as a base for wider action."

Despite the pessimistic analyses of Ambassador Taylor and the Joint Chiefs for future escalation, some of those at the

White House meeting hoped the Khanh regime could be somewhat stabilized. Citing handwritten notes of the meeting in the Pentagon files, the analyst quotes Mr. McNamara as saying that he understood "we are not acting more strongly because there is a clear hope of strengthening the GVN."

"But he went on," the account continues, "to urge that the way be kept open for stronger actions even if the GVN did not improve or in the event the war were widened by the Communists."

The handwritten notes of the meeting quote the President as asking, "Can we really strengthen the GVN?"

And in his memorandum of the consensus, William Bundy wrote: "Khanh will probably stay in control and may make some headway in the next 2-3 months in strengthening the Government (GVN). The best we can expect is that he and the GVN will be able to maintain order, keep the pacification program ticking over (but not progressing markedly), and give the appearance of a valid government."

On Sept. 10, therefore, the President ordered a number of interim measures in National Security Action Memorandum 314, issued over the signature of his special assistant, McGeorge Bundy. These were intended, in the words of William Bundy's memorandum of consensus, "to assist morale in SVN and show the Communists we still mean business, while at the same time seeking to keep the risks low and under our control at each stage."

The most important orders Mr. Johnson gave dealt with covert measures. The final paragraph in the President's memorandum also reflected the consensus, the analyst finds, of the Sept. 7 meeting and other strategy discussions of the time—"the extent to which the new year was anticipated as the occasion for beginning overt military operations against North Vietnam."

This final paragraph read: "These decisions are governed by a prevailing judgment that the first order of business at present is to take actions which will help to strengthen the fabric of the Government of South Vietnam; to the extent that the situation permits, such action should precede larger decisions. If such larger decisions are required at any time by a change in the situation, they will be taken." [See Document #81.]

The interim measures Mr. Johnson ordered included these:

• Resumption of the De Soto patrols by American destroyers in the Tonkin Gulf. They would "operate initially well beyond the 12-mile limit and be clearly disassociated from 34A maritime operations," but the destroyers "would have air cover from carriers."

• Reactivation of the 34A coastal raids, this time after completion of the first De Soto patrol. The directive added that "we should have the GVN ready to admit they are taking place and to justify and legitimize them on the basis of the facts of VC infiltration by sea." The account explains, "It was believed that this step would be useful in establishing a climate of opinion more receptive to expanded (air) operations against North Vietnam when they became necessary." The word in parentheses is the study's.

• An arrangement with the Laotian Government of Premier Souvanna Phouma to permit "limited GVN air and ground operations into the corridor areas of [southeastern] Laos, together with Lao air strikes and possible use of U.S. armed aerial reconnaissance." Armed aerial reconnaissance is a military operation in which the pilot has authority to attack unprogramed targets, such as gun installations or trucks, at his own discretion.

• The United States "should be prepared" to launch "tit for tat" reprisal air strikes like those during the Tonkin Gulf incident "as appropriate against the D.R.V. in the event of any attack on U.S. units or any special D.R.V.-VC action against SVN."

The President also ordered "economic and political actions" in South Vietnam, such as pay raises for Vietnamese civil servants out of American funds, to try to strengthen the Saigon regime.

The United States destroyers Morton and Edwards resumed the De Soto patrols in the Tonkin Gulf on Sept. 12, two days after Mr. Johnson's directive. They were attacked in a third Tonkin incident on the night of Sept. 18, and the President glossed over it.

However, he went ahead with his decision to resume the 34A coastal raids, still covertly, the account says. The order to reactivate them was issued by Mr. Johnson on Oct. 4, with the specification that they were to be conducted under tightened American controls.

Each operation on the monthly schedules now had to be "approved in advance" by Deputy Secretary of Defense Cyrus R. Vance for Secretary McNamara, Llewellyn A. Thompson, acting Deputy Under Secretary of State for Political Affairs, for Secretary Rusk, and McGeorge Bundy at the White House for the President.

During October, a subsequent report to William Bundy on

316

covert activities said, the 34A coastal raids consisted of two shallow probes of North Vietnamese defenses, an attempt to capture a junk, and successfully shellings of the radar station at Vinhson and the observation post at Muidao.

Two of the sabotage teams that had previously been parachuted into the North also "carried out successful actions during October," the report said. "One demolished a bridge, the other ambushed a North Vietnamese patrol. Both teams suffered casualties, the latter sufficient to cast doubt on the wisdom of the action."

The U-2 spy plane flights over North Vietnam and the parachuting of supplies and reinforcements to sabotage and psychological warfare teams in the North continued throughout this period and had not been affected by the President's suspension of the coastal raids after the original Tonkin Gulf incident.

The covert step-up in the air operations in Laos ordered by the President did not take place until mid-October. The Pentagon account says that one reason for the delay was the Administration's need to "await the uncertain outcome" of negotiations then taking place in Paris between the right-wing, neutralist and pro-Communist factions in Laos. The objective of the talks was to arrange a cease-fire that might lead to a new 14-nation Geneva conference to end the Laotian civil war.

"However, a Laotian cease-fire was not compatible with current perceptions of U.S. interest," the analyst writes.

The Administration feared that during an ensuing Geneva conference on Laos, international pressures, particularly from the Communist countries, might force the discussions onto the subject of Vietnam. Negotiations in the present circumstances were considered certain to unravel the shaky anti-Communist regime in Saigon.

The Administration also believed that even the convening of a conference on Laos might create an impression in Saigon that Washington was going to seek a negotiated withdrawal from South Vietnam and set off a political collapse there and the emergence of a neutralist coalition regime that would ask the United States to leave.

The account notes that in his Aug. 11 high-leveled policy memorandum on Southeast Asia, William Bundy had "characterized U.S. strategy" toward the Paris talks with the statement that "we should wish to slow down any progress toward a conference and to hold Souvanna to the firmest possible position." Mr. Bundy had referred to a suggestion

317

by Ambassador Leonard Unger that Prince Souvanna Phouma insist on three-faction administration of the Plaine des Jarres as "a useful delaying gambit."

"Significantly," the analyst says, "this proposal was advanced at Paris by Souvanna Phouma on 1 September—illustrating the fact that Souvanna was carefully advised by U.S. diplomats both prior to and during the Paris meetings. Other features of Souvanna's negotiating posture which apparently were encouraged as likely to have the effect of drawing out the discussions were insistence on Communist acceptance of (1) Souvanna's political status as Premier and (2) unhampered operations by the I.C.C. [International Control Commission]."

"Insistence on Souvanna's position is another point on which he should insist, and there would also be play in the hand on the question of free I.C.C. operations," Mr. Bundy wrote in his Aug. 11 memorandum.

"It will be recalled that the latter point was the issue on which progress toward a cease-fire became stalled," the analyst remarks. The negotiations broke down in Paris late in September.

American mission representatives from Bangkok and Vientiane met in Saigon on Sept. 11 under Ambassador Taylor's auspices, however, and decided that the South Vietnamese Air Force should not participate in the stepped-up air action in Laos authorized by the President in his directive of Sept. 10.

A list of 22 targets in the Laotian panhandle had been drawn up during the summer for the possibility of such raids, including one on a control point at the Mugia Pass, just across the North Vietnamese border.

South Vietnamese air strikes would offend Premier Souvanna Phouma by complicating his political position, the meeting determined, so the air attacks would be confined to clandestine raids by the T-28's in Laos and the United States Navy and Air Force jets—code-named Yankee Team—operating over Laos. Accord was also reached that South Vietnamese troops, possibly accompanied by American advisers, would also make ground forays into Laos up to a depth of 20 kilometers, or 12 miles.

"The mission representatives agreed that, once the [air and ground] operations began, they should not be acknowledged publicly," the analyst writes. "In effect, then, they would supplement the other covert pressures being exerted against North Vietnam. Moreover, while the Lao Government would of course know about the operations of their T-28's, Souvanna was not to be informed of the GVN/U.S. [ground] operations. The unacknowledged nature of these operations would thus be easier to maintain."

On Oct. 6, a joint State and Defense Department message authorized Ambassador Unger in Laos to obtain Premier Souvanna Phouma's approval for the T-28 strikes "as soon as possible."

But as the analyst points out, the message showed that the President had decided to postpone the accompanying strikes by Yankee Team jets, the "U.S. armed aerial reconnaissance" mentioned in Mr. Johnson's National Security Action Memorandum 314.

Five of the targets in the Laotian panhandle, well-defended bridges, had been specifically marked for the American jets, and fire by the Yankee Team planes would also be required against antiaircraft batteries defending the Mugia Pass. The message from Washington excluded these targets from the list of 22.

"You are further authorized to inform Lao that Yankee Team suppressive-fire strikes against certain difficult targets in panhandle, interspersing with further T-28 strikes, are part of the over-all concept and are to be anticipated later, but that such U.S. strikes are not repeat not authorized at this time," the cable said. [Document #83.]

Ambassadors Unger and Taylor both warned that the Laotian Government, without some participation by the American Jets, would not persevere in attacking targets on the Communist infiltration routes. Accordingly, the day before the T-28 strikes began on Oct. 14 with Premier Souvanna Phouma's approval, Washington authorized the Yankee Team jets to fly combat air patrol over the T-28's to raise morale and protect them from any interference by North Vietnamese MIG's.

Ambassador Taylor said in his cable that the combat air patrol missions could be achieved by "a relatively minor extension" of the current rules of engagement for American aircraft in Indochina.

The President also postponed for the present the planned ground forays into Laos by the South Vietnamese. Ambassador Taylor pointed out in a cable on Oct. 9 that these would not be possible "in forseeable future" in any case because the South Vietnamese Army was so tied down fighting the guerrillas in its own country.

Several eight-man South Vietnamese reconnaissance teams were parachuted into Laos in an operation called Leaping

Lena, but the Nov. 7 report to William Bundy on covert operations would note that "all of these teams were located by the enemy and only four survivors returned. . . ."

On Nov. 1, two days before the election, the Vietcong struck with a devastating mortar barrage on American planes and facilities at Bienhoa airfield near Saigon. The attack put the President under great internal pressure, the analyst says, to strike back openly, as he had said in his directive of Sept. 10 that he was prepared to do "in the event of any attack on U.S. units or any special D.R.V./VC action against SVN."

In the enemy's barrage, four Americans were killed, five B-57 bombers were destroyed and eight damaged. These were some of the B-57's that had earlier been sent from Japan to the Philippines at Mr. McNamara's suggestion as part of the preparations for possible bombing of the North. They had since been moved into South Vietnam, however, to try to shore up the Khanh Government's military position by bringing more air power to bear upon the Vietcong.

"As of the end of October (in anticipation of resumed De Soto patrols), elements of our Pacific forces were reported as 'poised and ready' to execute reprisals for any D.R.V. attacks on our naval vessels. Thus, there was a rather large expectancy among Administration officials that the United States would do something in retaliation," the analyst writes. The words in parentheses are his.

The Joint Chiefs told Mr. McNamara that the Bienhoa attack had been "a deliberate act of escalation and a change of the ground rules under which the VC had operated up to now." Asserting that "a prompt and strong response is clearly justified," they proposed, on the same day as the incident, "that the following specific actions be taken" (the words in parentheses are those of the Joint Chiefs; words in brackets have been inserted by The Times for clarification):

"a. Within 24-36 hours Pacific Command (PACOM) forces take initial U.S. military actions as follows:

"(1) Conduct air strikes in Laos against targets No. 3 (Tchepone barracks, northwest), No. 4 (Tchepone military area), No. 19 (Banthay military area), No. 8 (Nape highway bridge), and the Banken bridge on Route 7.

"(2) Conduct low-level air reconnaisance of infiltration routes and of targets in North Vietnam south of Latitude 19 degrees.

"b. Prior to air attacks on the D.R.V. land the Marine special landing forces at Danang and airlift Army or Marine units from Okinawa to the Saigon-Tansonnhut-Bienhoa area, to provide increased security for US personnel and installations.

"c. Use aircraft engaged in airlift (subparagraph b, above) to assist in evacuation of U.S. dependents from Saigon, to commence concurrently with the daylight air strikes against the D.R.V. (subparagraph d, below).

"d. Assemble and prepare necessary forces so that:

"(1) Within 60 to 72 hours, 30 B-52's from Gaum conduct a night strike on D.R.V. target No. 6 (Phucyen airfield). [Phucyen, 13 miles from Hanoi, is the principal North Vietnamese air base].

"(2) Commencing at first light on the day following subparagraph (1) above, PACOM air and naval forces conduct air strikes against D.R.V. targets No. 6 (Phucyen airfield) (daylight follow-up on the above night strike), No. 3 Hanoi Gialam airfield), No. 8 (Haiphong Catbi airfield), No. 48 (Haiphong POL), and No. 49 (Hanoi POL). [POL is a military abbreviation for petroleum, oil and lubricants.]

"(3) Concurrently with subparagraph (2), above the Vietnamese Air Force (VNAF) will strike DRV target No. 36 (Vitthulu barracks).

"(4) Combat air patrols (CAP), flak suppressive fire, strike photographic reconnaissance, and search and rescue operations (S.A.R.) are conducted as appropriate.

"(5) The above actions are followed by:

"(a) Armed reconnaissance on infiltration routes in Laos.

"(b) Air strikes against infiltration routes and targets in the D.R.V.

"(c) Progressive PACOM and SAC [Strategic Air Comand] strikes against the targets listed in 94 Target Study.

"(e) Thai bases be used as necessary in connection with the foregoing, with authority to be obtained through appropriate channels. . . .

"Recognizing that security of this plan is of critical importance, they [the Joint Chiefs] consider that external agencies, such as the VNAF, should be apprised only of those parts of the plan necessary to insure proper and effective coordination. The same limited revelation of plans should govern discussions with the Thais in securing authority for unlimited use of Thai bases."

From Saigon, Ambassador Taylor cabled for a more restrained response consisting of "retaliation bombing attacks on selected D.R.V. targets" using both American and South Vietnamese planes and for a "policy statement that we will act similarly in like cases in the future."

But the President felt otherwise for the moment. "Apparently, the decision was made to do nothing," the analyst says, adding that the documentary evidence does not provide an adequate explanation.

At a White House meeting the same day, the account continued, the President expressed concern that United States retaliatory strikes might bring counterretaliation by North Vietnam or China against American bases and civilian dependents in the South.

In briefing the press, Administration officials, unidentified in the study, drew a contrast "between this incident and the Tonkin Gulf attacks where our destroyers were 'on United States business.'"

"A second [White House] meeting to discuss possible U.S. actions was 'tentatively scheduled' for 2 November, but the available materials contain no evidence that it was held," the account continues. "President Johnson was scheduled to appear in Houston that afternoon, for his final pre-election address, and it may be that the second White House meeting was called off."

"One thing is certain," the writer concludes. "There were no retaliatory strikes authorized following the attack on the U.S. bomber base."

But the President had not altogether declined to act on Nov. 1. He had appointed an interagency working group under William Bundy to draw up various political and military options for direct action against North Vietnam. This was the one "concrete result" of the Nov. 1 mortar raid on Bienhoa, the account reports.

The Bundy working group, as it would be unofficially called in the Government, held its first meeting at 9:30 A.M. on Nov. 3, the day that Mr. Johnson was elected to the Presidency in his own right by a huge landslide.

"Bienhoa may be repeated at any time," Mr. Bundy wrote in a memorandum to the group on Nov. 5. "This would tend to force our hand, but would also give us a good springboard for any decision for stronger action. The President is clearly thinking in terms of maximum use of a Gulf of Tonkin rationale, either for an action that would show toughness and hold the line till we can decide the big issue, or as a basis for starting a clear course of action under the broad options." [See Document #84.]

Ostensibly, the Bundy group had a mandate to re-examine the entire American policy toward Vietnam and to recommend to the National Security Council a broad range of options. Its membership represented the entire foreign-policy-making machine of the Government—Mr. Bundy; Marshall Green; Michael V. Forrestal, head of the interagency Vietnam coordinating committee, and Robert Johnson of the State Department; Mr. McNaughton from the civilian hierarchy of the Pentagon; Vice Adm. Lloyd M. Mustin from the Joint Chiefs' staff and Harold Ford of the Central Intelligence Agency.

But, the account says, 'there appears to have been, in fact, remarkably little latitude for reopening the basic question about U.S. involvement in the Vietnam struggle."

The basic national objective of "an independent, non-Communist South Vietnam," established by the President's National Security Action Memorandum 288 of the previous March, "did not seem open to question."

The Options Harden

The September discussions had established a consensus that bombing of the North "would be required at some proximate future date for a variety of reasons" and individual and institutional pressures all tended to harden the options toward this end as they were finally presented to the National Security Council and then the President.

The analyst gives a number of examples of this stiffening process from the successive draft papers developed by the group during its three weeks of deliberations.

"The extreme withdrawal option was rejected almost without surfacing for consideration" because of its conflict with the policy memorandums. "Fall-back positions outlined in an original working-group draft suffered a similar fate.

The first fallback position, the study says, "would have meant holding the line—placing an immediate, low ceiling on the number of U.S. personnel in SVN, and taking vigorous efforts to build on a stronger base elsewhere, possibly Thailand."

"The second alternative would have been to undertake some spectacular, highly visible supporting action like a limited-duration selective bombing campaign as a last effort to save the South; to have accompanied it with a propaganda campaign about the unwinnability of the war given the GVN's ineptness and, then, to have sought negotiations through compromise and neutralization when the bombing failed."

But because of "forceful objections" by Admiral Mustin, the Joint Chiefs representative, both of these possibilities were downgraded in the final paper presented to the National Security Council on Nov. 21. In effect they were "rejected before they were fully explored," the study says.

Thus all three options, labeled A, B and C, entailed some form of bombing, with "the distinctions between them" tending to blur as they evolved during the group's three weeks of deliberations, the analyst says. Mr. McNaughton and William Bundy collaborated closely on their formulation.

A similar convergence occurred on the question of negotiations.

Here the minimum United States position was defined as forcing Hanoi to halt the insurgency in the South and to agree to the establishment of a secure, non-Communist state there, a position the analyst defines as "acceptance or else." Moreover, talks of any kind with Hanoi were to be avoided until the effects of bombing had put the United States into a position to obtain this minimum goal in negotiations.

"The only option that provided for bargaining in the usual sense of the word was Option C," the study says. Here the United States would be willing to bargain away international supervisory machinery to verify Hanoi's agreement.

"The policy climate in Washington simply was not receptive to any suggestion that U.S. goals might have to be compromised," the study comments.

These are the options in their final form as the study summarizes them:

OPTION A—Conduct U.S. reprisal air strikes on North Vietnam "not only against any recurrence of VC 'spectaculars' such as Bienhoa," intensify the coastal raids of Operation Plan 34A, resume the destroyer patrols in the gulf, step up the air strikes by T-28's against infiltration targets in Laos and seek reforms in South Vietnam.

OPTION B—What Mr. McNaughton called "a fast/full squeeze." Bomb the North "at a fairly rapid pace and without interruption," including early air raids on Phucyen Airfield near Hanoi and key bridges along the road and rail links with China until full American demands are met. "Should pressures for negotiations become too formidable to resist and discussion begin before a Communist agreement to comply," the analyst writes, "it was stressed that the United States should define its negotiating position 'in a way which makes

Communist acceptance unlikely.' In this manner it would be 'very likely that the conference would break up rather rapidly,' thus enabling our military pressures to be resumed."

OPTION C—Mr. McNaughton's "slow squeeze"; the option he and William Bundy favored. Gradually increasing air strikes "against infiltration targets, first in Laos and then in the D.R.V., and then against other targets in North Vietnam" intended to "give the impression of a steady deliberate approach . . . designed to give the United States the option at any time to proceed or not, to escalate or not and to quicken the pace or not." This option also included the possibility of a "significant ground deployment to the northern part of South Vietnam" as an additional bargaining counter.

On Nov. 24, a select committee of the National Security Council met to discuss the option papers formally presented to the council three days earlier. This group comprised Secretaries Rusk and McNamara, Mr. McCone, General Wheeler, McGeorge Bundy and Under Secretary of State George W. Ball. William Bundy attended to keep a record and to represent the working group.

In the account of this meeting, Mr. Ball makes his first appearance in the Pentagon history as the Administration dissenter on Vietnam. William Bundy's memorandum of record says Mr. Ball "indicated doubt" that bombing the North in any fashion would improve the situation in South Vietnam and "argued against" a judgment that a Vietcong victory in South Vietnam would have a falling-domino effect on the rest of Asia.

While the working-group sessions had been in progress, the study discloses, Mr. Ball had been writing a quite different policy paper "suggesting a U.S. diplomatic strategy in the event of an imminent GVN collapse."

"In it, he advocated working through the U.K. [United Kingdom, or Britain] who would in turn seek cooperation from the U.S.S.R., in arranging an international conference (of smaller proportions than those at Geneva) which would work out a compromise political settlement for South Vietnam," the analyst says. The words in parentheses are the analyst's.

Of those present at the November 24 meeting, the memorandum of record indicates, only Mr. Ball favored Option A. The study gives the impression this was conceived as a throwaway option by the Working Group. The group's analysis labeled it "an indefinite course of action" whose "sole advantages" were these:

"(a) Defeat would be clearly due to GVN failure, and we ourselves would be less implicated than if we tried Option B or Option C, *and failed.*

"(b) The most likely result would be a Vietnamese negotiated deal, under which an eventually unified Communist Vietnam would reassert its traditional hostility to Communist China and limit its own ambitions to Loas and Cambodia."

At the Nov. 24 meeting, however, Mr. Rusk said that while he favored bombing North Vietnam, he did not accept an analysis by Mr. McNaughton and William Bundy that if the bombing failed to save South Vietnam "we would obtain international credit merely for trying."

"In his view," the analyst writes, "the harder we tried and then failed, the worse our situation would be."

McGeorge Bundy demurred to some extent, the account goes on, but Mr. Ball "expressed strong agreement with the last Rusk point."

General Wheeler, reflecting the viewpoint of the Joint Chiefs, argued that the hard, fast bombing campaign of Option B actually entailed "less risk of a major conflict before achieving success," in words of the study, than the gradually rising air strikes of Option C.

The study adds that Mr. Bundy and Mr. McNaughton may have deliberately loaded the language of Option B to try to frighten the President out of adopting it lest it create severe international pressure for quick negotiations.

General Wheeler's argument presaged a running controversy between the Joint Chiefs and the civilian leadership after the bombing campaign began in the coming year.

The meeting on Nov. 24 ended without a clear majority decision on which option should be recommended to the President. The principals resumed when Ambassador Taylor reached Washington to join the strategy talks on Nov. 27, 1964.

In a written briefing paper, he told the conferees:

"If, as the evidence shows, we are playing a losing game in South Vietnam . . . it is high time we change and find a better way." He proposed gradually increasing air strikes against the North for a threefold purpose:

"First, establish an adequate government in SVN; second, improve the conduct of the counterinsurgency campaign; finally persuade or force the D.R.V. to stop its aid to the Vietcong and to use its directive powers to make the Vietcong desist from their efforts to overthrow the Government of South Vietnam."

THE PENTAGON PAPERS

A PICTORIAL
DOCUMENTATION

PHOTO RESEARCH
BY RENATO E. PEREZ

Ho Chi Minh, left, in Paris, 1946. Third from left, Gen. Jean de Lattre de Tassigny, later commander of Indochina forces.

Ho planning Dienbienphu attack in 1954. Second from left is Pham Van Dong; at right is Vo Nguyen Giap, chief strategist.

The Vietminh plant their flag on Dienbienphu as the French surrender. The French defeat ended the war in Indochina.

U.S. airlifted French troops from Paris to Saigon in 1954.

In Haiphong, American airmen unload supplies for the French

C-47's given to the French were serviced by U.S. mechanics.

U.S. colonel advises Vietnamese officers at Mytho in 1955.

Pham Van Dong headed Vietminh delegation at 1954 Geneva talks. Next to him are Chou En-lai of People's Republic of China, right, and Andrei Gromyko of Soviet Union.

Chief of U.S. mission in 1955 was Gen. John O'Daniel, left Ambassador Frederick Reinhardt is seated next to Presiden Ngo Dinh Diem. Col. Edward Lansdale, center, doffs his cap

President Truman, Dean Acheson and George Marshall with René Pleven of France. Acheson had counseled Truman to give aid to the French; earlier, Marshall had been ambivalent.

President Eisenhower, John Foster Dulles and Diem in 1957. U.S. vowed to prevent a Communist takeover of South Vietnam, fearing a "domino effect" throughout Southeast Asia.

CORNELL CAPA FROM MAGNUM

President Kennedy, who inherited a policy of "limited-risk gamble," bequeathed to Johnson a broad commitment to war.

Attacks on Vietcong positions were carried out by T-28 fighters piloted by South Vietnamese and American fliers.

In a major policy decision, Kennedy sent the carrier *Core* to Saigon late in 1961, with helicopters and U.S. advisers.

President Kennedy with Dean Rusk and Robert McNamara.
State and Defense Departments coordinated actions closely.

United States advisers in Laos in 1961 and 1962. Their task was to help in the fight against Pathet Lao guerrillas.

Gen. Maxwell Taylor, left, and Walt Rostow with Gen. Duong Van Minh after playing tennis in Saigon in October of 1961.

Minh took part in Diem coup two years later. Taylor's report on this Saigon trip would greatly influence Kennedy's policy.

Buddhist opposition to Diem was
dramatically expressed in the
suicide by fire of Thich Quang
Duc in Saigon in June of 1963.

WIDE WORLD

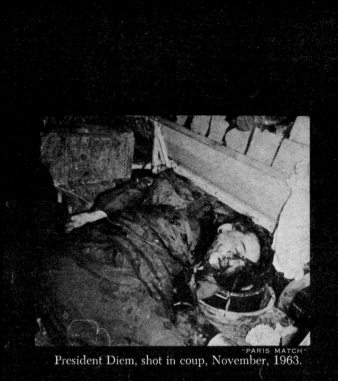

"PARIS MATCH"

President Diem, shot in coup, November, 1963.

Henry Cabot Lodge, U.S. Ambassador, and Diem, Aug., 1963.

Outside the bullet-scarred Presidential Palace in Saigon, soldiers who overthrew Diem display flag found in the rubble.

In the aftermath of the Diem coup, Gen. Duong Van Minh announces the formation of ruling junta. At rear, second from right, is Nguyen Van Thieu, later to become President. Gen. Tran Van Don, below, a leader in plot, is cheered by crowd.

Ngo Dinh Nhu, Diem's brother also died in 1963 coup. Below, Ambassador Lodge, Gen. Paul Harkins and John McCone, who was the Director of Central Intelligence. Lodge and Harkins had often disagreed on the ways to deal with President Diem.

Rusk, McNamara, key men in Kennedy and Johnson cabinets.

Barry Goldwater campaigning for the Presidency in 1964. He was an advocate of full-scale air attacks on North Vietnam

Gen. Maxwell Taylor and Gen. Nguyen Khanh, who seized power early in 1964. With them is Gen. William Westmoreland

TERENCE KHOO—PIX

Khanh wanted to invade North Vietnam. McNamara discouraged the idea but said the U.S. would not rule out bombing.

Taylor, Rusk, McNamara, McCone and Johnson. McCone

dissented on sending U.S. ground troops to South Vietnam.

Adm. Harry Felt, whose headquarters made plans for retaliatory bombing of the North long before Tonkin clash. Walt Rostow and McGeorge Bundy, below, considered the options.

William Bundy wrote 30-day scenario to culminate in bombing.

Photograph taken from the destroyer *Maddox* shows attack

by North Vietnamese PT boat in Gulf of Tonkin, Aug. 2, 1964.

UPI

On Aug. 4, 1964, President Johnson announced the Tonkin Gulf clashes and called for special powers to fight aggression.

Days later he signed the Tonkin Gulf Resolution. Behind him are Everett Dirksen, John McCormack and J. W. Fulbright.

On Aug. 5, McNamara told newsmen of raids on the North in reprisal for Tonkin attacks.

Souvanna Phouma of Laos was urged to hit enemy trails from North Vietnam.

John McNaughton outlined aims and analyzed plans of action against the North.

Air Force Phantom jets bombing North Vietnam

Bombing of Vietcong areas in the South was also stepped up.

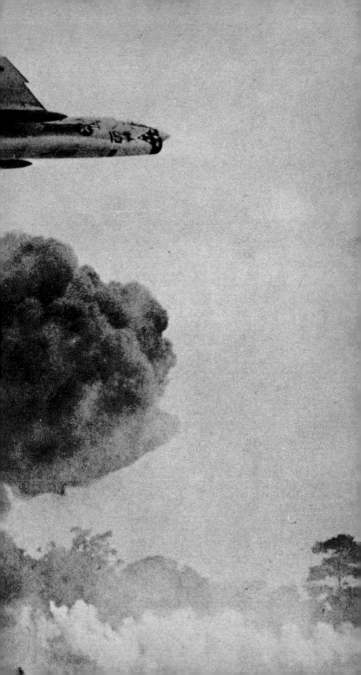

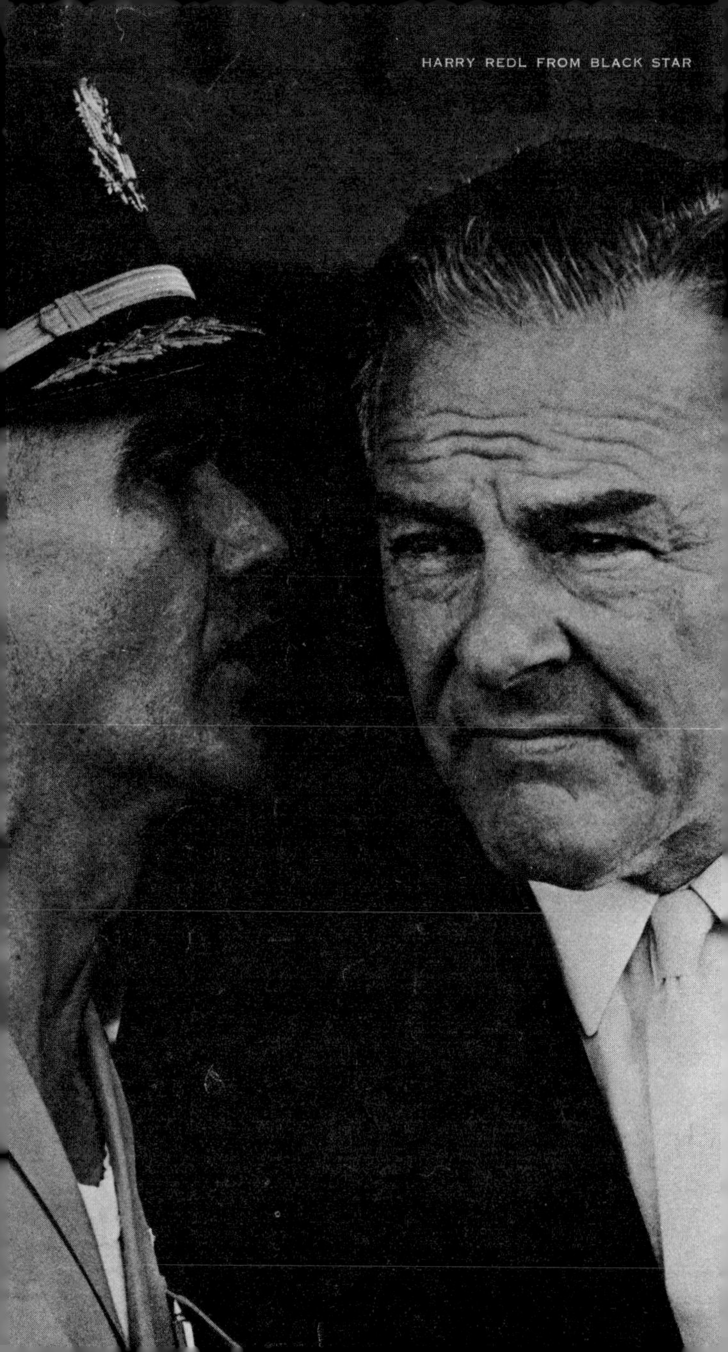

HARRY REDL FROM BLACK STAR

J. Blair Seaborn, Canadian official, delivered warning to Pham Van Dong.

Vestmoreland and Lodge. The Ambassador had proposed the
arrot-and-stick approach to Hanoi made through Seaborn.

"PARIS MATCH"

The landing of marines in Danang bolstered U.S. presence.

Vice Marshal Nguyen Cao Ky became Premier in 1965. Above,
meets with Alexis Johnson, Lodge, Taylor and McNamara.

Honolulu, 1966. McNamara talks with President Nguyen Van

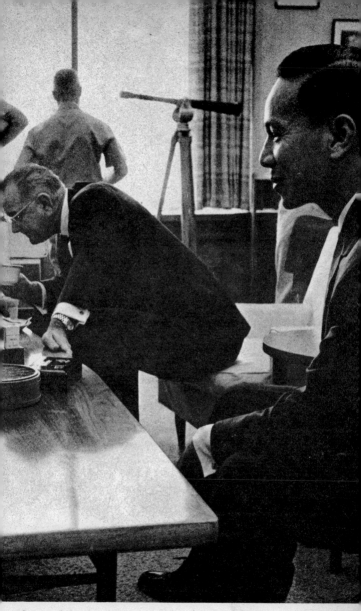

Thieu while President Johnson listens to Vice President Ky.

Aboard Air Force One are Vice President Humphrey, Rusk,

John Gardner, Alexis Johnson, Taylor, Rostow, the President.

Gen. Earle Wheeler briefing the President at the White House.

At left is Gen. John McConnell, at rear Gen. Harold Johnson.

Walt Rostow also counseled the President. At left is George Christian, press aide; at rear is Brig. Gen. Robert Ginsburgh.

CENTRAL PRESS

American bombs explode near an antiaircraft battery outside Hanoi in 1967, the period of greatest pressure on the North.

The Vietcong staged a fierce offensive to mark the Lunar New Year, or Tet, in January of 1968. Here, civilians flee from their homes in Saigon.

WIDE WORLD

The Tet attacks brought
devastation to Cholon,
Chinese area of Saigon.
WIDE WORLD

The Vietcong also struck in the ancient capital of Hue. Marines

fought a house-to-house battle to regain control of the city.

By 1968, McNamara was disenchanted with the war. There were signs Johnson was tired.

Clark Clifford replaced McNamara
as Secretary of Defense in 1968.

Johnson, Westmoreland, Clifford and Rusk. A plea for more troops for Vietnam led Johnson to reconsider his policy.

March, 1968: Johnson preparing speech in which he announced he would limit the bombing and would not seek re-election.

To improve anti-Communist prospects in the South, the Ambassador proposed using the lever of American air strikes against the North to obtain promises from the Saigon leaders that they would achieve political stability, strengthen the army and the police, suppress dissident Buddhist and student factions, replace incompetent officials and get on with the war effort.

The analyst says that the Ambassador had thus revised his earlier view that Washington should bomb the North merely to prevent "a collapse of national morale" in Saigon. He still favored some form of bombing in an emergency, but now he wantedsomething solid from the Saigon leaders in exchange for a coherent program of rising air war.

In the course of discussions on Nov. 27, however, the Ambassador acknowledged that while bombing "would definitely have a favorable effect" in South Vietnam, ". . . he was not sure this would be enough really to improve the situation," the analyst reports, again quoting from William Bundy's memorandum of record.

"Others, including McNamara, agreed with Taylor's evaluation, but the Secretary [Mr. McNamara] added that 'the strengthening effect of Option C could at least buy time, possibly measured in years.' "

Ambassador Taylor proposed that the Administration therefore adopt a two-phase program culminating in the bombing of infiltration facilities south of the 19th Parallel in North Vietnam, in effect Option A plus the first stages of Option C. Phase I would consist of 30 days of the Option A type of actions, such as intensification of the coastal raids on the North, air strikes by American jets at infiltration routes and one or two reprisal raids against the North. Meanwhile, Ambassador Taylor would obtain the promises of improvement from the Saigon leadership.

At the end of the 30 days, with the promises in hand, the United States would then move into Phase II, the air war. The air raids were to last two to six months, during which Hanoi was apparently expected to yield.

The others agreed, and the proposal was redefined further at a meeting on Nov. 28. William Bundy was assigned the task of drawing up a formal policy paper outlining the proposal. The Cabinet-level officials agreed to recommend it to the President at a White House meeting scheduled for Dec. 1, right after Mr. Johnson's Thanksgiving holiday at his ranch.

On Nov. 28, the same day that his closest advisers made

their decision to advise him to bomb North Vietnam, Mr. Johnson was asked at a news conference at the ranch:

"Mr. President, is expansion of the Vietnam war into Laos or North Vietnam a live possibility at this moment?"

"I don't want to give you any particular guide posts as to your conduct in the matter," Mr. Johnson told the newsmen about their articles. "But when you crawl out on a limb, you always have to find another one to crawl back on.

"I have just been sitting here in this serene atmosphere of the Pedernales for the last few days reading about the wars that you [speculating newsmen] have involved us in and the additional undertakings that I have made decisions on or that General Taylor has recommended or that Mr. McNamara plans or Secretary Rusk envisages. I would say, generally speaking, that some people are speculating and taking positions that I think are somewhat premature."

"At the moment," he concluded, "General Taylor will report to us on developments. We will carefully consider these reports. . . . I will meet with him in the early part of the week. I anticipate there will be no dramatic announcement to come out of these meetings except in the form of your speculation."

William Bundy's draft policy paper, written the next day, said the bombing campaign "would consist principally of progressively more serious air strikes, of a weight and tempo adjusted to the situation as it develops (possibly running from two to six months)." The words in parentheses are Mr. Bundy's.

The draft paper added: "Targets in the D.R.V. would start with infiltration targets south of the 19th Parallel and work up to targets north of that point. This could eventually lead to such measures as air strikes on all major military-related targets, aerial mining of D.R.V. ports, and a U.S. naval blockade of the D.R.V. . . .

"Concurrently," it continued, "the U.S. would be alert to any sign of yielding by Hanoi, and would be prepared to explore negotiated solutions that attain U.S. objectives in an acceptable manner." [See Document #88.]

Apparently at Mr. McNamara's suggestion, the analyst says, a final sentence in this paragraph was deleted; it read, "The U.S. would seek to control any negotiations and would oppose any independent South Vietnamese efforts to negotiate." Also removed, possibly during a final meeting of the top officials on Nov. 30 to review the policy paper and "apparently on the advice of McGeorge Bundy," was a proposal that the President make a major speech indicating the new direction that Washington's policy was taking.

Likewise deleted was a provision to brief "available Congressional leaders . . . (no special leadership meeting will be convened for this purpose)" on new evidence being compiled on North Vietnamese infiltration into the South, as a public justification of the bombing.

A separate recommendation from the Joint Chiefs for a series of major raids—like those in their retaliation proposal for the Vietcong mortar strike at Bienhoa air base on Nov. 1— was deleted for unspecified reasons, the analyst says, "in effect, presenting a united front to the President."

The paper that was sent to the President made no mention of American ground troops to provide security for airfields in the South when the bombing began, as General Wheeler had reminded the conferees on Nov. 24 would be necessary.

The writer notes the "gap" between the drastic concessions expected from Hanoi and the relatively modest bombing campaign that was expected to break Hanoi's will. He puts forward "two by no means contradictory explanations of this gap." This is the first:

"There is some reason to believe that the principals thought that carefully calculated doses of force could bring about predictable and desirable responses from Hanoi. Underlying this optimistic view was a significant underestimate of the level of the D.R.V. commitment to victory in the South and an overestimate of the effectiveness of U.S. pressures in weakening that resolve."

A related factor, the account says, "which, no doubt, commended the proposal to the Administration was the relatively low cost—in political terms— of such action." The context here indicates that the Administration thought the public would find an air war less repugnant than a ground war.

The President seems to have shared the view of his chief advisers, the analyst writes, that "the threat implicit in minimum but increasing amounts of force ('slow squeeze') would . . . ultimately bring Hanoi to the table on terms favorable to the U.S."

"McGeorge Bundy, as the President's assistant for national security affairs, was in a position to convey President Johnson's mood to the group," the account goes on. It adds that notes taken at a White House meeting on Dec. 1 when the senior officials met with Mr. Johnson to present the bombing plan "tend to confirm that the President's mood was more closely akin to the measures recommended" than to other, harsher bombing plans.

"A second explanation of the gap between ends and means is a more simple one," the account comments. "In a phrase, we had run out of alternatives other than pressures."

A memorandum by Assistant Secretary McNaughton on Nov. 6, 1964, made the point succinctly: "Action against North Vietnam is to some extent a substitute for strengthening the Government in South Vietnam. That is, a less active VC (on orders from D.R.V.) can be matched by a less efficient GVN. We therefore should consider squeezing North Vietnam." The words in parentheses are Mr. McNaughton's. [See Document #85.]

Doubts at Two Poles

The two dissenters from the view that "calculated doses of force" would bring Hanoi around were, at opposite poles, the Joint Chiefs and the intelligence agencies.

"The J.C.S. differed from this view on the grounds that if we were really interested in affecting Hanoi's will, we would have to hit hard at its capabilities," the account says. The Joint Chiefs wanted the United States to demonstrate a willingness to apply unlimited force.

Their bombing plan, deleted from the position paper before it was presented to the President, asserted that the destruction of all of North Vietnam's major airfields and its petroleum supplies "in the first three days" was intended to "clearly . . . establish the fact that the U.S. intends to use military force to the full limits of what military force can contribute to achieving U.S. objectives in Southeast Asia . . . The follow-on military program—involving armed reconnaissance of infiltration routes in Laos, air strikes on infiltration targets in the D.R.V. and then progressive strikes throughout North Vietnam—could be suspended short of full destruction of the D.R.V. if our objectives were achieved earlier."

The analyst remarks that the Joint Chiefs' plan was "shunted aside because both its risks and costs were too high," but the author does not attempt to evaluate the possible effect of his plan on Hanoi's will.

Like Mr. Ball, the account says, the intelligence community

"tended toward a pessimistic view" of the effect of bombing on the Hanoi leaders.

The intelligence panel within the Bundy working group, composed of representatives from the three leading intelligence agencies—the C.I.A., the State Department's Bureau of Intelligence and Research and the Pentagon's Defense Intelligence Agency—"did not concede very strong chances for breaking the will of Hanoi," the author writes.

"The course of actions the Communists have pursued in South Vietnam over past few years implies a fundamental estimate on their part that the difficulties facing the U.S. are so great that U.S. will and ability to maintain resistance in that area can be gradually eroded—without running high risks that this would wreak heavy destruction on the D.R.V. or Communist China," the panel's report said.

If the United States now began bombing, the panel said, the Hanoi leadership would have to ask itself "a basic question" about how far the United States was willing to step up the war "regardless of the danger of war with Communist China and regardless of the international pressures that could be brought to bear. . . ." The decision of the Hanoi leadership was thus uncertain for a number of reasons, the panel cautioned, and "in any event, comprehension of the others intentions would almost certainly be difficult on both sides, and especially as the scale of hostilities mounted."

The panel then cast doubt on the so-called Rostow thesis of how much Hanoi feared destruction of its industry. This thesis, named for its proponent, Walt W. Rostow, chairman of the State Department's Policy Planning Council, underlay much of the Administration's hope for the success of a bombing campaign.

The panel said: "We have many indications that the Hanoi leadership is acutely and nervously aware of the extent to which North Vietnam's transportation system and industrial plant is vulnerable to attack. On the other hand, North Vietnam's economy is overwhelmingly agricultural and, to a large extent, decentralized in a myriad of more or less economically self-sufficient villages. Interdiction of imports and extensive destruction of transportation facilities and industrial plants would cripple D.R.V. industry. These actions would also seriously restrict D.R.V. military capabilities, and would degrade, though to a lesser extent, Hanoi's capabilities to support guerrilla warfare in South Vietnam and Laos. We do not believe that such actions would have a crucial effect on the daily lives of the overwhelming majority of the North Vietnam population. We do not believe that attacks on industrial targets would so greatly exacerbate current economic difficulties as to create unmanageable control problems. It is reasonable to infer that the D.R.V. leaders have a psychological investment in the work of reconstruction they have accomplished over the last decade. Nevertheless, they would probably be willing to suffer some damage to the country in the course of a test of wills with the U.S. over the course of events in South Vietnam."

As in the case of earlier intelligence findings that contradicted policy intentions, the study indicates no effort on the part of the President or his most trusted advisers to reshape their policy along the lines of this analysis.

One part of the intelligence panel's report that the Administration did accept was a prediction that China would not react in any major way to a bombing campaign unless American or South Vietnamese troops invaded North Vietnam or northern Laos. The study indicates that this analysis eased Administration fears on this point.

Chinese reaction to systematic bombing of North Vietnam was expected to be limited to providing Hanoi with antiaircraft artillery, jet fighters and naval patrol craft. The panel predicted that the Soviet role was "likely to remain a minor one," even where military equipment was concerned. However, the Russians subsequently sent large-scale shipments of formidable antiaircraft equipment to North Vietnam.

"Cautious and Equivocal"

Now that a decision to bomb North Vietnam was drawing near, the study says, Mr. Johnson became "cautious and equivocal" in approaching it. Two analysts of this period, in fact, differ in their characterization of his decision at the two-and-a-half-hour White House meeting on Dec. 1, 1964, a month after the election, when the bombing plan was presented to him.

One analyst says that at this meeting the President "made a tentative decision" to bomb, ordering the preparatory Phase I put into effect and approving Phase II, the air war itself, "in principle."

The second analyst says that while the President approved the entire bombing plan "in general outline at least . . . it is also clear that he gave his approval to implement only the first phase of the concept."

The President tied the actual waging of air war to reforms by the Saigon Government, this analyst says, and left an impression by the end of the meeting that he was "considerably less than certain that future U.S. actions against North Vietnam [the air war] would be taken, or that they would be desirable."

The study notes that "the precise nature of the President's decisions" at the meeting is not known because a national security action memorandum was not issued afterward.

"However," the study continues, "from handwritten notes of the meeting, from instructions issued to action agencies and from later reports of diplomatic and military actions taken, it is possible to reconstruct the approximate nature of the discussion and the decisions reached." The footnotes do not indicate who made the handwritten notes found in the Pentagon files, although the indication is that it was Mr. McNaughton or Mr. McNamara.

After a briefing by Ambassador Taylor on the situation in South Vietnam, the discussion turned to a draft statement, prepared by William Bundy, that the Ambassador was to deliver to the Saigon leaders. The statement explained the two-phase bombing plan and tied Phase II to a serious attempt by the Saigon leadership to achieve some political stability and get on with the war effort against the Vietcong.

In Saigon, General Khanh had nominally surrendered authority to a civilian cabinet headed by Premier Tran Van Huong. The general was intriguing against the Huong Cabinet, however, as the ostensible commander in chief of the armed forces and head of a Military Revolutionary Committee of South Vietnamese generals. Within this council, a group headed by Air Vice Marshall Nguyen Cao Ky, the chief of the air force, was intriguing both with and against General Khanh.

Against this background, the study says of the White House meeting:

"The President made it clear that he considered that pulling the South Vietnamese together was basic to anything else the United States might do. He asked the Ambassador specifically which groups he [Ambassador Taylor] might talk to and what more we might do to help bring unity among South Vietnam's leaders. He asked whether we could not say to them 'we just can't go on' unless they pulled together. To this, Taylor replied that we must temper our insistence somewhat. . . ."

The meeting then moved into a discussion of which allied countries were to be briefed on the proposed air war. The President said he wanted "new, dramatic effective" forms of assistance from several, specifically mentioning Australia, New Zealand, Canada and the Philippines. These briefings by special envoys were included in the draft position paper laying out the bombing plan as the important diplomatic element in Phase I.

"In each case," the study says, "the representative was to explain our concept and proposed actions and request additional contributions by way of forces in the event the second phase of U.S. actions were entered."

The plan made no provision for similar consultations with Congressional leaders and there is no evidence in the study that Mr. Johnson conducted any.

In approving the statement General Taylor was to make to the Saigon leaders, the President also gave his assent to read the military signal that was formally to sound the beginning of the 30 days of Phase I—Operation Barrel Roll, air strikes by United States Air Force and Navy jets of Yankee Team against infiltration routes and facilities in the Laotian panhandle, which was to be the final step-up in the Laos air operations.

At the end of the meeting, the account continues, Ambassador Taylor "slipped out the White House rear entrance" to avoid the press and "only a brief, formal statement" was issued. The analyst, remarks that the White House press statement released immediately afterward "contained only two comments regarding any determinations that had been reached."

One said, "The President instructed Ambassador Taylor to consult urgently with the South Vietnamese Government as to measures that should be taken to improve the situation in all its aspects."

The other, the concluding paragraph, said the President had "reaffirmed the basic U.S. policy of providing all possible and useful assistance to the South Vietnamese people and Government in their struggle to defeat the externally supported insurgency and aggression being conducted against them."

The final sentence in this paragraph, the analyst notes, was one "specifically linking this policy" with Congress's Tonkin Gulf resolution. The sentence read: "It was noted that this policy accords with the terms of the Congressional joint resolution of Aug. 10, 1964, which remains in full force and effect."

Then, on Dec. 3, emerging from a second meeting with Mr. Johnson, "presumably having received the final version of his instructions," the account goes on, Ambassador Taylor told reporters assembled at the White House "that he was going to hold 'across-the-board' discussions with GVN."

"Asserting that U.S. policy for South Vietnam remained the same, he stated that his aim would be to improve the deteriorating situation in South Vietnam. Although he hinted of changes 'in tactics and method,' he quite naturally did not disclose the kind of operations in which the United States was about to engage or any future actions to which immediate activity could lead."

The Administration now moved quickly. William Bundy left for Australia and New Zealand the next day, Dec. 4, to brief their governments on both phases of the bombing plan, the writer says.

Prime Minister Harold Wilson of Britain was "thoroughly briefed on the forthcoming U.S. actions" during a state visit to Washington Dec. 7 to 9, the narrative continues, while other envoys briefed the Canadians and the Asian allies. The writer notes that while Britain, Australia and New Zealand were given "the full picture," the Canadians were "told slightly less" and the Philippines, South Korea and the Chinese Nationalist Government on Taiwan were "briefed on Phase I only." What the Thais and the Laotians were told is not made explicit.

The New Zealand Government "expressed grave doubts" that the bombing would break Hanoi's will, the writer says, and predicted that it might increase infiltration to South Vietnam.

In meetings in Saigon on Dec. 7 and 9 with General Khanh and Premier Huong, Ambassador Taylor exacted the desired promises in exchange for the bombing. At the second meeting, the Ambassador presented them with a draft press release describing the desired improvements, including strengthening of the army and the police, which the Saigon Government released in its own name, at the United States' request, on Dec. 11.

William H. Sullivan, newly appointed as Ambassador to Laos, obtained Premier Souvanna Phouma's agreement on Dec. 10 to the American air strikes at infiltration routes along the Ho Chi Minh Trail supply network through the Laotian panhandle, and Operation Barrel Roll got under way on

Dec. 14 with attacks by American jets on "targets of opportunity"—that is, unprogramed targets sighted by the pilots.

At a meeting of the National Security Council on Dec. 12, when the final details for Barrell Roll were reviewed and approved, the study reports, it was "agreed that there would be no public operations statements about armed reconnaissance in Laos unless a plane were lost."

"In such an event, the principals stated, the Government should continue to insist that we were merely escorting reconnaissance flights as requested by the Laotian Government."

McGeorge Bundy was quoted in the memorandum of record as stating that the agreed plan "fulfilled precisely the President's wishes."

On Dec. 18 Secretary McNamara set the level of Barrell Roll attacks for the 30 days of Phase I—the analyst indicates that he did so at the President's wishes—at two missions of four aircraft apiece each week.

The Administration also stepped up the raids by T-28 fighter planes in Laos with a joint message on Dec. 8 from Secretaries McNamara and Rusk to Ambassador Sullivan. The cable instructed him to have the Laotians intensify bombing "in the corridor areas and close to the D.R.V. border."

The analyst reports that in the three months between the beginning of October and the end of December there were 77 sorties by the T-28's in the panhandle area—a sortie is a strike by a single plane—and that by early December the air raids had "already precipitated several complaints from the D.R.V." to the International Control Commission "alleging U.S.-sponsored air attacks on North Vietnamese territory."

Events in Saigon had meanwhile gone awry. Political turmoil broke out there again with Buddhist and student demonstrations against Premier Huong's Cabinet.

On Dec. 20, in defiance of Ambassador Taylor's wishes, General Khanh, in a temporary alliance with the so-called Young Turks—the young generals led by Marshall Ky—announced the dissolution of the High National Council, a body that was supposed to be functioning as a temporary legislature to draw up a constitution for a permanent civilian government. They also made a large number of political arrests by night, seizing several members of the High National Council.

That day, Ambassador Taylor summoned the Young Turks to the embassy and, in the writer's words, read them "the riot act." They included Gen. Nguyen Van Thieu, now President of South Vietnam.

According to the embassy's cable to Washington, the conversation began like this:

> Ambassador Taylor: Do all of you understand English? (Vietnamese officers indicated they did . . .)
>
> I told you all clearly at General Westmoreland's dinner we Americans were tired of coups. Apparently I wasted my words. Maybe this is because something is wrong with my French because you evidently didn't understand. I made it clear that all the military plans which I know you would like to carry out are dependent on government stability. Now you have made a real mess. We cannot carry you forever if you do things like this.

Marshal Ky and other Vietnamese generals denied that they had staged a coup and said they were trying to achieve unity by getting rid of divisive elements, the account goes on.

The Ambassador tried to persuade them to support the civilian regime of Premier Huong and apparently to restore the High National Council. The Vietnamese officers would not agree.

The embassy cable describes the end of the conversation: "In taking a friendly leave, Ambassador Taylor said: 'You people have broken a lot of dishes and now we have to see how we can straighten out this mess.' " [See Document #89.]

By the end of the month, Ambassador Taylor, Deputy Ambassador Johnson and General Westmoreland had apparently despaired of trading a bombing campaign against the North for a stable Saigon Government that would prosecute the war in the South. On Dec. 31, the account continues, they sent a joint message to Washington saying, in effect, that the United States should go ahead with the air campaign against the North "under any conceivable alliance condition short of complete abandonment of South Vietnam."

The account indicates, however, that the President was reluctant to proceed into Phase II without at least the appearance of a firmer base in Saigon since the turmoil there was making it more difficult for him to justify escalation to the American public.

The writer remarks that at the meeting of the senior National Security Council Members on Dec. 24, Secretary Rusk "raised an issue that was high among Administration concerns—namely that the American public was worried about the chaos in the GVN, and particularly with respect to its viability as an object of increased U.S. commitment."

On Christmas Eve, the Vietcong planted a bomb in the Brinks, an officers billet in Saigon, killing two Americans in the blast and wounding 58 others; the President declined to authorize reprisal air strikes against the North, despite vigorous recommendations from Ambassador Taylor, Admiral Sharp in Honolulu and the Joint Chiefs, who were now pressing hard for escalation.

"Highest levels today reached negative decision on proposal . . . for reprisal action," Mr. Rusk cabled the Ambassador on Dec. 29.

Five days earlier, Mr. Rusk had also instructed Ambassador Taylor to halt, until the turmoil in Saigon subsided, the planned, piecemeal release to the press of evidence of a major increase in infiltration from the North during 1964, the writer says. The Ambassador had first reported the increase to Washington in October, along with a report of the appearance of individual North Vietnamese Army regulars, and the Administration began leaking the information in November through background briefings.

Making a Case in Public

By this time, the Administration felt that it had sufficient information on infiltration to make a public case for bombing the North. The intelligence community had obtained evidence that a minimum of 19,000 and a maximum of 34,000 infiltrators, mostly former southerners who had fought against the French in the Vietminh, had entered the South since 1959. Chester L. Cooper, a former intelligence officer, had put together a major report on Hanoi's support and direction of the guerrillas, but the Administration had decided earlier in December against public disclosure of the document itself because this might create "undesirable speculation," and had instead instructed the Ambassador to continue the piecemeal approach. Now, the analyst says, Mr. Rusk wanted this halted as well for fear that more publicity might create pressure for action prematurely.

The political upheaval in Saigon, the writer continues, was fueling a Vietnam debate in Congress, which, while it did not exhibit much antiwar sentiment, did show considerable confusion and dismay, the writer says.

Secretary Rusk, on television on Jan. 3, 1965, felt it necessary to defend the Administration "in the context of a year-end foreign policy report," the account adds.

Mr. Rusk did not hint at the Administration's plans for possible bombing of the North. "Ruling out either a U.S. withdrawal or a major expansion of the war," the writer says, "Rusk gave assurances that with internal unity, and our aid and persistence the South Vietnamese could themselves defeat the insurgency."

On Jan. 14, however, as a result of the loss of two American jets over Laos in Operation Barrel Roll, "accounts of U.S. air operations against Laotian infiltration routes gained wide circulation for the first time," the writer says. A dispatch from Laos by United Press International, he adds, "in effect blew the lid on the entire Yankee Team operation in Laos since May of 1964."

"Despite official State or Defense refusal to comment on the nature of the Laotian air missions, these disclosures added new fuel to the public policy debate," the writer continues. The disclosures were complicating matters for the President by giving ammunition to the very small minority of antiwar senators who were taking seriously the press speculation that the United States might be getting ready to bomb the North.

In a Senate speech on Jan. 19, the account goes on, Senator Wayne Morse of Oregon charged that the Yankee Team air strikes had ignored the 1962 Geneva accords on Laos and "violated the nation's belief in 'substituting the rule of law for the jungle law of military might.' Broadening his attack, he warned, that 'there is no hope of avoiding a massive war in Asia' if U.S. policy towards Southeast Asia were to continue without change,"

Within the Administration in Washington, key policy makers were coming to the same conclusion that Ambassador Taylor and his colleagues had reached in Saigon—that it was desirable to bomb the North regardless of what state of government existed in the South.

The political turmoil in Saigon, the narrative says, appears "to have been interpreted in Washington as an impending sellout" to the National Liberation Front. Fear increased that a neutralist coalition government would emerge and invite the United States to leave.

Washington's sense of crumbling in the military situation was heightened when Saigon's army suffered a "highly visible" setback in a ferocious battle at Binhgia, southeast of the capital, between Dec. 26 and Jan. 2. Vietcong guerrillas nearly destroyed two South Vietnamese Marine battalions

"All evidence pointed to a situation in which a final collapse of the GVN appeared probable and a victorious consolidation of VC power a distinct possibility," the narrative says.

The Hour Approaches

William Bundy communicated the feeling in a memorandum he wrote to Secretary Rusk on Jan. 6 for a meeting Mr. Rusk was to have with the President that afternoon. Mr. Bundy explained that the memorandum encompassed, besides his own thoughts, those of Mr. Forrestal, head of the interagency committee, and Ambassador Unger, who had recently been transferred back to Washington from Vientiane.

"I think we must accept that Saigon morale in all quarters is now very shaky indeed," he said in part, "and that this relates directly to a widespread feeling that the U.S. is not ready for stronger action and indeed is possibly looking for a way out. We may regard this feeling as irrational and contradicted by our repeated statements, but Bill Sullivan was very vivid in describing the existence of such feelings in October, and we must honestly concede that our actions and statements since the election have not done anything to offset it. The blunt fact is that we have appeared to the Vietnamese (and to wide circles in Asia and even in Europe) to be insisting on a more perfect government than can reasonably be expected, before we consider any additional action—and that we might even pull out our support unless such a government emerges.

"In key parts of the rest of Asia, notably Thailand, our present posture also appears weak. As such key parts of Asia see us, we looked strong in May and early June, weaker in later June and July, and then appeared to be taking a quite firm line in August with the Gulf of Tonkin. Since then we must have seemed to be gradually weakening—and, again, insisting on perfectionism in the Saigon Government before we moved.

"The sum total of the above seems to us to point—together with almost certainly stepped-up Vietcong actions in the current favorable weather—to a prognosis that the situation in Vietnam is now likely to come apart more rapidly than we had anticipated in November. We would still stick to the estimate that the most likely form of coming apart would be a government of key groups starting to negotiate covertly with the Liberation Front or Hanoi, perhaps not asking in the first instance that we get out, but with that necessarily following at a fairly early stage. In one sense this would be a 'Vietnam solution,' with some hope that it would produce a Communist Vietnam that would assert its own degree of independence from Peiping and that would produce a pause in Communist pressure in Southeast Asia. On the other hand, it would still be virtually certain than [sic] Laos would then become untenable and that Cambodia would accommodate in some way. Most seriously, there is grave question whether the Thai in these circumstances would retain any confidence at all in our continued support. In short, the outcome would be regarded in Asia, and particularly among our friends, as just as humiliating a defeat as any other form. As events have developed, the American public would probably not be too sharply critical, but the real question would be whether Thailand and other nations were weakened and taken over thereafter.

"The alternative of stronger action obviously has grave difficulties. It commits the U.S. more deeply, at a time when the picture of South Vietnamese will is extremely weak. To the extent that it included actions against North Vietnam, it would be vigorously attacked by many nations and disapproved initially even by such nations as Japan and India, on present indications. Most basically, its stiffening effect on the Saigon political situation would not be at all sure to bring about a more effective government, nor would limited actions against the southern D.R.V. in fact sharply reduce infiltration or, in present circumstances, be at all likely to induce Hanoi to call it off.

"Nontheless, on balance we believe that such action would have some faint hope of really improving the Vietnamese situation, and, above all, would put us in a much stronger position to hold the next line of defense, namely Thailand. Accepting the present situation—or any negotiation on the basis of it—would be far weaker from this latter key standpoint. If we moved into stronger actions, we should have in mind that negotiations would be likely to emerge from some quarter in any event, and that under existing circumstances, even with the additional element of pressure, we could not expect to get an outcome that would really secure an independent South Vietnam. Yet even on an outcome that pro-

341

duced a progressive deterioration in South Vietnam and an eventual Communist take-over, we would still have appeared to Asians to have done a lot more about it.

"In specific terms, the kinds of action we might take in the near future would be:

"a. A nearly occasion for reprisal action against the D.R.V.

"b. Possibly beginning low-level reconnaissance of the D.R.V. at once.

"Concurrently with a or b, an early orderly withdrawal of our dependents [from Saigon, but only if] stronger action [is contemplated]. If we are to clear our decks in this way— and we are more and more inclined to think we should—it simply must be, for this reason alone, in the context of some stronger action. . . .

"Introduction of limited U.S. ground forces into the northern area of South Vietnam still has great appeal to many of us, concurrently with the first air attacks into the D.R.V. It would have a real stiffening effect in Saigon, and a strong signal effect to Hanoi. On the disadvantage side, such forces would be possible attrition targets for the Vietcong."

Mr. McNaughton, Mr. Bundy's counterpart at the Pentagon, had given Mr. McNamara a similar memorandum three days earlier.

"The impact of these views can be seen in the policy guidance emanating from Washington in mid and late January, 1965," the Pentagon's narrative says.

In a cablegram to Saigon on Jan. 11, the writer goes on, Secretary Rusk instructed Ambassador Taylor "to avoid actions that would further commit the United States to any particular form of political solution" to the turmoil there. If another military regime emerged from the squabbling "we might well have to swallow our pride and work with it," Mr. Rusk said.

Another memorandum to Mr. McNamara from Mr. McNaughton, on Jan. 27, along with Mr. McNamara's penciled comments on it, "adds perspective to this viewpoint," the historian says. Mr. McNaughton stated "and Mr. McNamara agreed" that the United States objective in South Vietnam was "not to 'help friend' but to contain China," and "both favored initiating strikes against North Vietnam."

Paraphrasing the memorandum and Mr. McNamara's comments, the writer says, "At first they believed these [air attacks] should take the form of reprisals; beyond that, the Administration would have to 'feel its way' into stronger, graduated pressures. McNaughton doubted that such strikes would actually help the situation in South Vietnam, but thought they should be carried out anyway. McNamara believed they probably would help the situation, in addition to their broader impacts on the U.S. position in Southeast Asia."

"Clear indication that the Administration was contemplating some kind of increased military activity" had gone out to Saigon two days earlier in another cablegram from Mr. Rusk, the account goes on. "Ambassador Taylor was asked to comment on the 'departmental view' that U.S. dependents should be withdrawn to 'clear the decks' in Saigon and enable better concentration of U.S. efforts on behalf of South Vietnam."

Ever since the original bombing scenario of May 23, 1964, the evacuation of American women and children had been the signal for "D-Day."

"The Rusk cable made specific reference to a current interest in reprisal actions," the analyst says.

The initial blow came in about two weeks. The Vietcong attacked the United States military advisers' compound at Pleiku in the Central Highlands and an Army helicopter base at Camp Holloway, four miles away. Nine Americans were killed and 76 wounded.

"The first flash from Saigon about the assault came on the ticker at the National Military Command Center at the Pentagon at 2:38 P.M. Saturday, Feb. 6, Washington time," the narrative says. "It triggered a swift, though long-contemplated Presidential decision to give an 'appropriate and fitting' response. Within less than 14 hours, by 4 P.M. Sunday, Vietnam time, 49 U.S. Navy jets—A-4 Skyhawks and F-8 Crusaders from the Seventh Fleet carriers U.S.S. Coral Sea and U.S.S. Hancock—had penetrated a heavy layer of monsoon clouds to deliver their bombs and rockets upon North Vietnamese barracks and staging areas at Donghoi, a guerrilla training garrison 40 miles north of the 17th Parallel.

"Though conceived and executed as a limited one-shot tit-for-tat reprisal, the drastic U.S. action, long on the military planners' drawing boards under the operational code name Flaming Dart precipitated a rapidly moving sequence of events that transformed the character of the Vietnam war and the U.S. role in it."

Then the guerrillas attacked an American barracks at Quinhon, on the central coast, and on Feb. 11, the President launched a second and heavier reprisal raid, Flaming Dart II.

Two days later, on Feb. 13, he decided to begin Operation Rolling Thunder, the sustained air war against North Vietnam.

"As is readily apparent," the analyst concludes, "there was no dearth of reasons for striking North. Indeed, one almost has the impression that there were more reasons than were required. But in the end, the decision to go ahead with the strikes seems to have resulted as much from the lack of alternative proposals as from any compelling logic in their favor."

KEY DOCUMENTS

Following are texts of key documents from the Pentagon's history of the Vietnam war, covering events of August, 1964, to February, 1965, the period in which the bombing of North Vietnam was planned. Except where excerpting is specified, the documents are printed verbatim, with only unmistakable typographical errors corrected.

74

Rusk Query to Vientiane Embassy on Desirability of Laos Cease-Fire

Cablegram from Secretary of State Rusk to the United States Embassy in Laos, Aug. 7, 1964. Copies were also sent, with a request for comment, to the American missions in London, Paris, Saigon, Bangkok, Ottawa, New Delhi, Moscow, Pnompenh and Hong Kong, and to the Pacific command and the mission at the United Nations.

1. As pointed out in your 219, our objective in Laos is to stabilize the situation again, if possible within framework of the 1962 Geneva settlement. Essential to stabilization would be establishment of military equilibrium in the country. Moreover, we have some concern that recent RLG successes and reported low PL morale may lead to some escalation from Communist side, which we do not now wish to have to deal with.

2. Until now, Souvanna's and our position has been that military equilibrium would require Pathet Lao withdrawal from areas seized in PDJ since May 15 and that such withdrawal is also basic precondition to convening 14-nation conference. Question now arises whether territorial gains of Operation Triangle, provided they can be consolidated, have in practice brought about a situation of equilibrium and whether, therefore, it is no longer necessary to insist on Pathet Lao withdrawal from PDJ as precondition to 14-nation conference. This is in fact thought which has previously occurred to Souvanna (Vientiane's 191) and is also touched on in Secretary's letter to Butler (Deptel 88 to Vientiane). If Souvanna and we continued to insist on PDJ withdrawal other side would inevitably insist on our yielding Triangle gains, and

345

our judgement is that such arrangement substantially worse tha
present fairly coherent geographical division. If withdrawal pre
condition were to be dropped, it could probably best be done a
tripartite meeting where it might be used by Souvanna as bargain
ing counter in obtaining satisfaction on his other condition tha
he attend conference as head of Laotian Government. Remainin
condition would be cease-fire. While under present condition
cease-fire might not be of net advantage to Souvanna—we ar
thinking primarily of T-28 operations—Pathet Lao would n
doubt insist on it. If so, Souvanna could press for effective ICC
policing of cease-fire. Latter could be of importance in upcomin
period.

3. Above is written with thought in mind that Polish proposal
[one word illegible] effectively collapsed and that pressures con
tinue for Geneva [word illegible] conference and will no doub
be intensified by current crisis brought on by DRV naval attacks
Conference on Laos might be useful safety valve for these gen
eralized pressures while at same time providing some deterren
to escalation of hostilities on that part of the "front." We woul
insist that conference be limited to Laos and believe that it coul
in fact be so limited, if necessary by our withdrawing from th
conference room if any other subject brought up, as we did i
1961-62. Side discussions on other topics could not be avoide
but we see no great difficulty with this; venue for informal cor
ridor discussion with PL, DRV, and Chicoms could be valuabl
at this juncture.

4. In considering this course of action, key initial question is o
course whether Souvanna himself is prepared to drop his with
drawal precondition and whether, if he did, he could maintai
himself in power in Vientiane. We gather that answer to firs
question is probably yes but we are much more dubious abou
the second. Request Vientiane's judgement on these points. View
of other addresses are so requested, including estimated reaction
host governments. It is essential that these estimates take accoun
of recent developments: military successes non-Communist force
in Laos and latest demonstration U.S. determination resist Com
munist aggression in Southeast Asia.

75

Saigon Embassy's Response on Drawbacks
in Laos Talks

*Cablegram from Ambassador Maxwell D. Taylor in
Saigon to Secretary Rusk, Aug. 9, 1964, with copies to the
embassies in Vientiane and Bangkok and the Pacific command.*

From our vantage point we can see positive disadvantages to our position in SEA in pursuing course of action outlined REFTEL.

1. In first place rush to conference table would serve to confirm to Chicoms that U.S. retaliation for destroyed attacks was transient phenomenon and that firm Chicom response in form of commitment to defend NVN has given U.S. "paper tiger" second thoughts. Moreover, much of beneficial effects elsewhere resulting from our strong reaction to events in Gulf of Tonkin would be swiftly dissipated.

2. In Vietnam sudden backdown from previous strongly held U.S. position on PDJ withdrawal prior to conf on Laos would have potentially disastrous effect. Morale and will to fight, particularly willingness to push ahead with arduous pacification task and to enforce stern measure on Khanh's new emergency decree, would be undermined by what would look like evidence that U.S. seeking to take advantage of any slight improvement in non-Communist position as excuse for extricating itself from Indochina via conf route. This would give strength to probable pro-Gaullist contention that GVN should think about following Laotian example by seeking negotiated solution before advantage of temporarily strengthened anti-Communist position recedes.

3. General letdown in Vietnam which would result from softening of our stand in Laos just after we had made great show of firmness vis-a-vis Communists would undoubtedly erode Khanh's personal position with prospects of increased political instability and coup plotting.

4. It should be remembered that our retaliatory action in Gulf of Tonkin is in effect an isolated U.S.-DRV incident. Although this has relation, as Amb. Stevenson has pointed out, to larger problem of DRV aggression by subversion in Vietnam and Laos, we have not rpt not yet come to grips in a forceful way with DRV over the issue of this larger and much more complex problem. Instead, we are engaged, both in Vietnam and Laos, in proxy actions against proxy agents of DRV. If, as both Khanh and Souvanna hope, we are to parlay the consequences of our recent clash with the DRV into actions which specifically direct themselves against DRV violations of the 1954 and 1962 agreements, we must avoid becoming involved in political engagements which will tie our hands and inhibit our action. For example, any effort to undertake credible joint planning operations with GVN re interdictory air strikes upon infiltration network in southern DRV and especially in panhandle would be completely undercut if we were engaged in conf discussing the Laos territory in question.

5. Similarly, it would seem to us that Souvanna's willingness to hold fast on pre-conditions or substantive negotiations bears direct relationship to his assessment of U.S. willingness to meet the problem where it originates—in North Vietnam itself. This

fact shines clearly through his recent brief letter to Pres Johnson. Moreover, it would be folly to assume that Khanh, who is now in fairly euphoric state as result of our Gulf of Tonkin action, would do anything other than slump into deepest funk if we sought to persuade him to send GVN del to conf. [two words illegible] is that he would resign rather than send [two words illegible].

Intensified pressures for Geneva-type conf cited in REFTEL would appear to us to be coming almost entirely from those who are opposed to U.S. policy objectives in SEA (except possibly UK which seems prepared jump on bandwagon). Under circumstances, we see very little hope that results of such conference would be advantageous to U.S. Moreover, prospects of limiting it to consideration of only Laotian problem appear at this time juncture to be dimmer than ever. Even though prior agreement reached to limit conf, we do not see how in actual practice we could limit discussion solely to Laos if others insist on raising other issues. To best our knowledge, we never "withdrew" from room when DRV attempted raise extraneous issues during 1961-1962 conf. Instead, we insisted to chair on point of order and had DRV ruled out of order. Prospect of informal corridor discussions with PL, DRV and Chicoms is just what GVN would fear most and may well increase pressures on GVN to undertake negotiated solution so as to avoid their fear of being faced with "fait accompli" by U.S.

7. Rather than searching for "safety valve" to dissipate current "generalized pressures" SEA, it seems to us we should be looking for means which will channel those pressures against DRV; seems to us "safety valve," if needed (for example by Soviets), exists in current UNSC discussion. We should continue to focus attention in all forms on Communist aggressive actions as root cause of tension in SEA and reinforce our current stance. In the final analysis, this stance would be more valid deterrent to escalation by PL/VM than attempt seek accommodation within context Laos problem alone.

While not rpt not specifically within our province, we would point out that PL/VM appear to have capability of retaking territory regained by RLG in Operation Triangle at any time of their choosing and that therefore "territorial swap" invisaged in DEPTEL may be highly illusory. Moreover, any territorial deal which seems to confirm permanent PL/VM control over corridor as an arrangement acceptable to U.S. would be anathema to GVN and indicate our willingness accept infiltration network as tolerable condition on GVN frontiers. Such situation would in their and U.S. mission opinions vitiate against any hope of successful pacification of GVN territory.

76

U.S. Mission's Recommendations on Further Military Steps

Cablegram from the United States Mission in Saigon to the State Department, Aug. 18, 1964

This is U.S. Mission message.

In preparing our reply, we have found it simpler to produce a new paper which undertakes to state the problem in South Viet Nam as we see it in two possible forms and then to provide course of action responding to each statement of the problem.

Underlying our analysis is the apparent assumption of Deptel 439 (which we believe is correct) that the present in-country pacification plan is not enough in itself to maintain national morale or to offer reasonable hope of eventual success. Something must be added in the coming months.

Statement of the problem—A. The course which US policy in South Viet Nam should take during the coming months can be expressed in terms of four objectives. The first and most important objective is to gain time for the Khanh government to develop a certain stability and to give some firm evidence of viability. Since any of the courses of action considered in this cable carry a considerable measure of risk to the U.S., we should be slow to get too deeply involved in them until we have a better feel of the quality of our ally. In particular, if we can avoid it, we should not get involved militarily with North Viet Nam and possibly with Red China if our base in South Viet Nam is insecure and Khanh's army is tied down everywhere by the VC insurgency. Hence, it is our interest to gain sufficient time not only to allow Khanh to prove that he can govern, but also to free Saigon from the VC threat which presently rigns (as received) it and assure that sufficient GVN ground forces will be available to provide a reasonable measure of defense against any DRV ground reaction which may develop in the execution of our program and thus avoid the possible requirement for a major U.S. ground force commitment.

A second objective in this period is the maintenance of morale in South Viet Nam particularly within the Khanh Government. This should not be difficult in the case of the government if we can give Khanh assurance of our readiness to bring added pressure on Hanoi if he provides evidence of ability to do his part. Thirdly while gaining time for Khanh, we must be able to hold the DRV in check and restrain a further buildup of Viet Cong strength by way of infiltration from the North. Finally, throughout this period, we should be developing a posture of maximum readiness for a deliberate escalation of pressure against North Viet Nam, using January 1, 1965 as a target D-Day. We must always recognize, however, that events may force U.S. to advance D-Day to a considerably earlier date.

[Start of sentence illegible] we then need to design a course of action which will achieve the four objectives enumerated above. Such a course of action would consist of three parts: the first, a series of actions directed at the Khanh Government; the second, actions directed at the Hanoi Government; the third, following a pause of some duration, initiation of an orchestrated air attack against North Viet Nam.

In approaching the Khanh Government, we should express our willingness to Khanh to engage in planning and eventually to exert intense pressure on North Viet Nam, providing certain conditions are met in advance. In the first place before we would agree to go all out against the DRV, he must stabilize his government and make some progress in cleaning up his operational backyard. Specifically, he must execute the initial phases of the Hop Tac Plan successfully to the extent of pushing the Viet Cong from the doors of Saigon. The overall pacification program, including Hop Tac, should progress sufficiently to allow earmarking at least three division equivalents for the defense in I Corps if the DRV step up military operations in that area.

Finally we should reach some fundamental understandings with Khanh and his government concerning war aims. We must make clear that we will engage in actions against North Viet Nam only for the purpose of assuring the security and independence of South Viet Nam within the territory assigned by the 1954 agreements; that we will not (rpt not) join in a crusade to unify the north and south; that we will not (rpt not) even seek to overthrow the Hanoi regime provided the latter will cease its efforts to take over the south by subversive warfare.

With these understandings reached, we would be ready to set in motion the following:

(1) Resume at once 34A (with emphasis on Marine operations) and Desoto patrols. These could start without awaiting outcome of discussions with Khanh.

(2) Resume U-2 overflights over all NVN.

(3) Initiate air and ground strikes in Laos against infiltration targets as soon as joint plans now being worked out with the Khanh Government are ready. Such plans will have to be related to the situation in Laos. It appears to U.S. that Souvanna Phouma should be informed at an appropriate time of the full scope of our plans and one would hope to obtain his acquiescence in the anti-infiltration actions in Laos. In any case we should always seek to preserve our freedom of action in the Laotian corridor.

By means of these actions, Hanoi will get the word that the operational rules with respect to the DRV are changing. We should perhaps consider message to DRV that shooting down of U-2 would result in reprisals. We should now lay public base for justifying such flights and have plans for prompt execution in contingency to shoot down. One might be inclined to consider including at this state tit-for-tat bombing operations in our plans to compensate for VC depredations in SVN. However, the initiation of air attacks from SVN against NVN is likely to release a new order of military reaction from both sides, the outcome of which is impossible to predict. Thus, we do not visualize initiating this form of reprisal as a desirable tactic in the current plan but would reserve the capability as an emergency response if needed.

Before proceeding beyond this point, we should raise the level of precautionary military readiness (if not already done) by taking such visible measures as [word illegible] Hawk units to Danang and Saigon, landing a Marine force at Danang for defense of the airfield and beefing up MACV's support base. By this time (assumed to be late fall) we should have some reading on Khanh's performance.

Assuming that his performance has been satisfactory and that Hanoi has failed to respond favorably, it will be time to embark on the final phase of course of action A, a carefully orchestrated bombing attack on NVN directed primarily at infiltration and other military targets. At some point prior thereto it may be desirable to open direct communications with Hanoi if this not been done before. With all preparations made, political and military, the bombing program would begin, using U.S. reconnaissance planes, VNAF/Farmgate aircraft against those targets which could be attacked safely in spite of the presence of the MIG's and additional U.S. combat aircraft if necessary for the effective execution of the bombing programs.

Pros and cons of course of action—A. If successful course of action A will accomplish the objectives set forth at the outset as essential to the support of U.S. policy in South Viet Nam. I will press the Khanh Government into doing its homework in pacification and will limit the diversion of interest to the out-of-country ventures it gives adequate time for careful preparation estimated at several months, while doing sufficient at once to maintain internal morale. It also provides ample warning to Hanoi and Peking to allow them to adjust their conduct before becoming overcommitted.

On the other hand, course of action A relies heavily upon the durability of the Khanh government. It assumes that there is little danger of its collapse without notice or of its possible replacement by a weaker or more unreliable successor. Also, because of the drawn-out nature of the program it is exposed to the danger of international political pressure to enter into negotiations before NVN is really hurting from the pressure directed against it.

Statement of the Problem—B. It may well be that the problem of U.S. policy in SVN is more urgent than that depicted in the foregoing statement. It is far from clear at the present moment that the Khanh Government can last until January 1, 1965, although the application of course of action A should have the effect of strengthening the government [rest of sentence illegible].

[Start of sentence illegible] we would have to restate the problem in the following terms. Our objective avoid the possible consequences of a collapse of national morale. To accomplish these purposes, we would have to open the campaign against the DRV without delay, seeking to force Hanoi as rapidly as possible to resist from aiding the VC and to convince the DRV that it must cooperate in calling off the VC insurgency.

Course of Action—B. To meet this statement of the problem, we need an accelerated course of action, seeking to obtain results faster than under course of action A. Such an accelerated program would include the following actions:

Again we must inform Khanh of our intentions, this time expressing a willingness to begin military pressures against Hanoi at once, providing that he will undertake to perform as in course of action A. However, U.S. action would not await evidence of performance.

Again we may wish to communicate directly on this subject with Hanoi or awaiting effect of our military actions. The scenario of the ensuing events would be essentially the same as under Course A but the execution would await only the readiness of plans to expedite relying almost exclusively on U.S. military means.

Pros and cons of Course of Action B. This course of action asks virtually nothing from the Khanh Government, primarily because it is assumed that little can be expected from it. It avoids the consequence of the sudden collapse of the Khanh Government and gets underway with minimum delay the punitive actions against Hanoi. Thus, it lessens the chance of an interruption of the program by an international demand for negotiation by presenting a fait accompli to international critics. However, it increases the likelihood of U.S. involvement in ground action since Khanh will have almost no available ground forces which can be released from pacification employment to mobile resistance of DRV attacks.

Conclusion: It is concluded that Course of Action A offers the greater promised achievement of U.S. policy objectives in SVN during the coming months. However, we should always bear in mind the fragility of the Khanh Government and be prepared to shift quickly to Course of Action B if the situation requires. In either case, we must be militarily ready for any response which may be initiated by NVN or by Chicoms.

· **Miscellaneous:** as indicated above, we believe that 34A operations should resume at once at maximum tempo, still on a covert basis; similarily, Desoto patrols should begin advance, operating outside 12-mile limit. We concur that a number of VNAF pilots should be trained on B-57's between now and first of year. There should be no change now with regard to policy on evacuation of U.S. dependents.

Recommendation: It is recommended that USG adopt Course of Action A while maintaining readiness to shift to Course of Action B.

77

Rusk Cable to Embassy in Laos on Search and Rescue Flights

Cablegram from Secretary of State Dean Rusk to the United States Embassy in Vientiane, Laos, Aug. 26, 1964. A copy of this message was sent to the Commander in Chief, Pacific.

We agree with your assessment of importance SAR operations that Air America pilots can play critically important role, and SAR efforts should not discriminate between rescuing Americans, Thais and Lao. You are also hereby granted as requested discretionary authority to use AA pilots in T-28's for SAR operations when you consider this indispensable rpt indispensable to success of operation and with understanding that you will seek advance Washington authorization wherever situation permits.

At same time, we believe time has come to review scope and control arrangements for T-28 operations extending into future. Such a review is especially indicated view fact that these operations more or less automatically impose demands for use of U.S. personnel in SAR operations. Moreover, increased AA capability clearly means possibilities of loss somewhat increased, and each loss with accompanying SAR operations involves chance of escalation from one action to another in ways that may not be desirable in wider picture. On other side, we naturally recognize T-28 operations are vital both for their military and psychological effects in Laos and as negotiating card in support of Souvanna's position. Request your view whether balance of above factors would call for some reduction in scale of operations and-or dropping of some of better-defended targets. (Possible extension T-28 operations to Panhandle would be separate issue and will be covered by septel.)

On central problem our understanding is that Thai pilots fly missions strictly controlled by your Air Command Center with [word illegible] in effective control, but that this not true of Lao pilots. We have impression latter not really under any kind of firm control.

Request your evaluation and recommendations as to future scope T-28 operations and your comments as to whether our impressions present control structure correct and whether steps could be taken to tighten this.

78

Joint Chiefs' Recommendations on Military Courses of Action

Excerpts from memorandum, "Recommended Courses of Action—Southeast Asia," from the Joint Chiefs of Staff to Secretary of Defense Robert S. McNamara, Aug. 26, 1964.

3. The Joint Chiefs of Staff have considered Ambassador Taylor's statements of objectives and courses of action. In recognition of recent events in SVN, however, they consider that his proposed course of action B is more in accord with the current situation and consider that such an accelerated program of actions with respect to the DRV is essential to prevent a complete collapse of the U.S. position in Southeast Asia. Additionally, they do not agree that we should be slow to get deeply involved until we have a better feel for the quality of our ally. The United States is already deeply involved. The Joint Chiefs of Staff consider that only significantly stronger military pressures on the DRV are likely to provide the relief and psychological boost necessary for attainment of the requisite governmental stability and viability.

4. Recent U.S. military actions in Laos and against the DRV have demonstrated our resolve more clearly than any other U.S. actions in some time. These actions showed force and restraint. Failure to resume and maintain a program of pressure through military actions could be misinterpreted to mean we have had second thoughts about Pierce Arrow and the events leading thereto, and could signal a lack of resolve. Accordingly, while maintaining a posture of readiness in the Western Pacific, the Joint Chiefs of Staff believe that the U.S. program should have as concurrent objectives: (1) improvements in South Vietnam, including emphasis on the Pacification Program and the Hop Tac plan to clear Saigon and its surroundings; (2) interdiction of the relatively unmolested VC lines of communication (LOC) through Laos by operations in the Panhandle and of the LOC through Cambodia by strict control of the waterways leading therefrom; (3) denial of Viet Cong (VC) sanctuaries in the Cambodia-South Vietnam border area through the conduct of "hot pursuit" operations into Cambodia, as required; (4) increased pressure on North Vietnam through military actions. As part of the program for increased pressures, the OPLAN 34A operations and the Desoto patrols in the Gulf of Tonkin should be resumed, the former on an intensified but still covert basis.

5. The Joint Chiefs of Staff believe, however, that more direct and forceful actions than these will, in all probability, be required. In anticipation of a pattern of further successful VC and Pathet Lao (PL) actions in RVN and Laos, and in order to increase pressure on the DRV, the U.S. program should also provide for

prompt and calculated responses to such VC/PL actions in the form of air strikes and other operations against appropriate military targets in the DRV.

6. The Joint Chiefs of Staff recognize that defining what might constitute appropriate counteroperations in advance is a most difficult task. We should therefore maintain our prompt readiness to execute a range of selected responses, tailored to the developing circumstances and reflecting the principles in the Gulf of Tonkin actions, that such counteroperations will result in clear military disadvantage to the DRV. These responses, therefore, must be greater than the provocation in degree, and not necessarily limited to response in kind against similar targets. Air strikes in response might be purely VNAF; VNAF with U.S. escort to provide protection from possible employment of MIG's; VNAF with U.S. escort support in the offensive as well as the defensive role; or entirely U.S. The precise combination should be determined by the effect we wish to produce and the assets available. Targets for attack by air or other forces may be selected from appropriate plans including the Target Study for North Vietnam consisting of 94 targets, recently forwarded to you by the Joint Chiefs of Staff. . . .

79

Plan of Action Attributed to McNaughton at Pentagon

Excerpts from memorandum, Sept. 3, 1964, "Plan of Action for South Vietnam," which the Pentagon study indicates was drawn up by Assistant Secretary of Defense John T. McNaughton.

1. **Analysis of the present situation.** The situation in South Vietnam is deteriorating. Even before the government sank into confusion last week, the course of the war in South Vietnam had been downward, with Viet Cong incidents increasing in number and intensity and military actions becoming larger and more successful, and with less and less territory meaningfully under the control of the government. Successful ambushes had demonstrated an unwillingness of the population even in what were thought to be pacified areas to run the risk of informing on the Viet Cong. War weariness was apparent. The crisis of the end of August—especially since the competing forces have left the government largely "faceless" and have damaged the government's ability to manage the pacification program—promises to lead to further and more rapid deterioration. . . . The objective of the United States is to reverse the present downward trend. Failing

that, the alternative objective is to emerge from the situation with as good an image as possible in U.S., allied and enemy eyes.

2. Inside South Vietnam. We must in any event keep hard at work inside South Vietnam. This means, inter alia, immediate action:

(a) to press the presently visible leaders to get a real government in operation;

(b) to prevent extensive personnel changes down the line;

(c) to see that lines of authority for carrying out the pacification program are clear.

New initiatives might include action:

(d) to establish a U.S. naval base, perhaps at Danang;

(e) to embark on a major effort to pacify one province adjacent to Saigon.

A separate analysis is being made of a proposal:

(f) to enlarge significantly the U.S. military role in the pacification program inside South Vietnam—e.g., large numbers of U.S. special forces, divisions of regular combat troops, U.S. air, etc., to "interlard" with or to take over functions of geographical areas from the South Vietnamese armed forces. . . .

3. Outside the borders of South Vietnam. There is a chance that the downward trend can be reversed—or a new situation created offering new opportunities, or at least a convincing demonstration made of the great costs and risks incurred by a country which commits aggression against an ally of ours—if the following course of action is followed. The course of action is made up of actions outside the borders of South Vietnam designed to put increasing pressure on North Vietnam but designed also both to create as little risk as possible of the kind of military action which would be difficult to justify to the American public and to preserve where possible the option to have no U.S. military action at all. . . .

Actions. The actions, in addition to present continuing "extraterritorial" actions (U.S. U-2 recce of DRV, U.S. jet recce of Laos, T-28 activity in Laos), would be by way of an orchestration of three classes of actions, all designed to meet these five desiderata—(1) from the U.S. GVN and hopefully allied points of view, they should be legitimate things to do under the circumstances, (2) they should cause apprehension, ideally increasing apprehension, in the DRV, (3) they should be likely at some point to provoke a military DRV response, (4) the provoked response should be likely to provide good grounds for us to escalate if we wished, and (5) the timing and crescendo should be under our control, with the scenario capable of being turned off at any time. . . .

4. Actions of opportunity. While the above course of action is being pursued, we should watch for other DRV actions which would justify [words illegible]. Among such DRV actions might be the following:

a. Downing of U.S. recce or U.S. rescue aircraft in Laos (likely by AA, unlikely by MIG).

b. MIG action in Laos or South Vietnam (unlikely).

c. Mining of Saigon Harbor (unlikely).

d. VC attacks on South Vietnamese POL storage, RR bridge, etc. (dramatic incident required).

e. VC attacks (e.g., by mortars) on, or take-over of, air fields on which U.S. aircraft are deployed (likely).

f. Some barbaric act of terrorism which inflames U.S. and world opinion (unlikely). . . .

6. Chances to resolve the situation. Throughout the scenario, we should be alert to chances to resolve the situation:

a. To back the DRV down, so South Vietnam can be pacified.

b. To evolve a tolerable settlement:

I. Explicit settlement (e.g., via a bargaining-from-strength conference, etc.).

II. Tacit settlement (e.g., via piecemeal live-and-let-live Vietnamese "settlements," a de facto "writing off" of indefensible portions of SVN, etc.).

c. If worst comes and South Vietnam disintegrates or their behavior becomes abominable, to "disown" South Vietnam, hopefully leaving the image of "a patient who died despite the extraordinary efforts of a good doctor."

7. Special considerations during next two months. The relevant "audiences" of U.S. actions are the Communists (who must feel strong pressures), the South Vietnamese (whose morale must be buoyed), our allies (who must trust us as "underwriters"), and the U.S. public (which must support our risk-taking with U.S. lives and prestige). During the next two months, because of the lack of "rebuttal time" before election to justify particular actions which may be distorted to the U.S. public, we must act with special care—signalling to the DRV that initiatives are being taken, to the GVN that we are behaving energetically despite the restraints of our political season, and to the U.S. public that we are behaving with good purpose and restraint.

80

Top Aides' Proposal to Johnson on Military Steps in Late '64

Memorandum from Assistant Secretary of State for Far Eastern Affairs, William P. Bundy, for President Johnson, Sept. 8, 1964. The memorandum was headed "Courses of Action for South Vietnam."

This memorandum records the consensus reached in discussions between Ambassador Taylor and Secretary Rusk, Secretary

McNamara and General Wheeler, for review and decision by the President.

THE SITUATION

1. Khanh will probably stay in control and may make some headway in the next two-three months in strengthening the Government (GVN). The best we can expect is that he and the GVN will be able to maintain order, keep the pacification program ticking over (but not progressing markedly) and give the appearance of a valid Government.

2. Khanh and the GVN leaders are temporarily too exhausted to be thinking much about moves against the North. However, they do need to be reassured that the U.S. continues to mean business, and as Khanh goes along in his Government efforts, he will probably want more U.S. effort visible, and some GVN role in external actions.

3. The GVN over the next 2-3 months will be too weak for us to take any major deliberate risks of escalation that would involve a major role for, or threat to, South Vietnam. However, escalation arising from and directed against U.S. action would tend to lift GVN morale at least temporarily.

4. The Communist side will probably avoid provocative action against the U.S., and it is uncertain how much they will step up VC activity. They do need to be shown that we and the GVN are not simply sitting back after the Gulf of Tonkin.

COURSES OF ACTION

We recommend in any event:

1. U.S. naval patrols in the Gulf of Tonkin should be resumed immediately (about September 12). They should operate initially beyond the 12-mile limit and be clearly dissociated from 34A maritime operations. The patrols would comprise 2-3 destroyers and would have air cover from carriers; the destroyers would have their own ASW capability.

2. 34A operations by the GVN should be resumed immediately thereafter (next week). The maritime operations are by far the most important. North Vietnam is likely to publicize them, and at this point we should have the GVN ready to admit that they are taking place and to justify and legitimize them on the basis of the facts on VC infiltration by sea. 34A air drop and leaflet operations should also be resumed but are secondary in importance. We should not consider air strikes under 34A for the present.

3. Limited GVN air and ground operations into the corridor areas of Laos should be undertaken in the near future, together with Lao air strikes as soon as we can get Souvanna's permission.

These operations will have only limited effect, however.

4. We should be prepared to respond on a tit-for-tat basis against the DRV in the event of any attack on U.S. units or any

special DRV/VC action against SVN. The response for an attack on U.S. units should be along the lines of the Gulf of Tonkin attacks, against specific and related targets. The response to special action against SVN should likewise be aimed at specific and comparable targets.

The main further question is the extent to which we should add elements to the above actions that would tend deliberately to provoke a DRV reaction, and consequent retaliation by us. Example of actions to be considered would be running U.S. naval patrols increasingly close to the North Vietnamese coast and/or associating them with 34A operations. We believe such deliberately provocative elements should not be added in the immediate future while the GVN is still struggling to its feet. By early October, however, we may recommend such actions depending on GVN progress and Communist reaction in the meantime, especially to U.S. naval patrols.

The aim of the above actions, external to South Vietnam, would be to assist morale in SVN and show the Communists we still mean business, while at the same time seeking to keep the risks low and under our control at each stage.

Further actions within South Vietnam are not covered in this memorandum. We believe that there are a number of immediate-impact actions we can take, such as pay raises for the police and civil administrators and spot projects in the cities and selected rural areas. These actions would be within current policy and will be refined for decision during Ambassador Taylor's visit. We are also considering minor changes in the U.S. air role within South Vietnam, but these would not involve decisions until November.

81

Memo on Johnson's Approval of Renewed Naval Operations

National security action memorandum from McGeorge Bundy, adviser to the President on national security, to Secretary of Defense McNamara and Secretary of State Rusk, Sept. 10, 1964.

The President has now reviewed the situation in South Vietnam with Ambassador Taylor and with other advisers and has approved the following actions:

1. U.S. naval patrols in the Gulf of Tonkin will be resumed promptly after Ambassador Taylor's return. They will operate initially well beyond the 12-mile limit and be clearly dissociated from 34A maritime operations. The patrols will comprise two to three destroyers and would have air cover from carriers; the destroyers will have their own ASW capability.

2. 34A operations by the GVN will be resumed after completion of a first DeSoto patrol. The maritime operations are by far the most important. North Vietnam has already publicized them, and is likely to publicize them even more, and at this point we should have the GVN ready to admit that they are taking place and to justify and legitimize them on the basis of the facts of VC infiltration by sea. 34A air drop and leaflet operations should also be resumed but are secondary in importance. We should not consider air strikes under 34A for the present.

3. We should promptly discuss with the Government of Laos plans for limited GVN air and ground operations into the corridor areas of Laos, together with Lao air strikes and possible use of U.S. armed aerial reconnaissance. On the basis of these discussions a decision on action will be taken, but it should be recognized that these operations will in any case have only limited effect.

4. We should be prepared to respond as appropriate against the DRV in the event of any attack on U.S. units or any special DRV/VC action against SVN.

5. The results of these decisions will be kept under constant review, and recommendations for changes or modifications or additions will be promptly considered.

6. The President reemphasizes the importance of economic and political actions having immediate impact in South Vietnam, such as pay raises for civilian personnel and spot projects in the cities and selected rural areas. The President emphasizes again that no activity of this kind should be delayed in any way by any feeling that our resources for these purposes are restricted. We can find the money which is needed for all worthwhile projects in this field. He expects that Ambassador Taylor and the country team will take most prompt and energetic action in this field.

7. These decisions are governed by a prevailing judgment that the first order of business at present is to take actions which will help to strengthen the fabric of the Government of South Vietnam; to the extent that the situation permits, such action should precede larger decisions. If such larger decisions are required at any time by a change in the situation, they will be taken.

82

Report of Meeting of U.S. Envoys to Review Operations in Laos

Excerpts from cablegram, signed by Ambassador Taylor, from United States Embassy in Saigon to State Department, Defense Department and Commander in Chief, Pacific, Sept. 19, 1964.

Following is a summary, coordinated with Vientiane and Bangkok, of the conclusions of the meeting of the three posts held at Saigon September 11 to review air and limited ground operations of the Lao corridor:

1. Air operations in corridor. This involves attack of 22 targets for which folders available at Vientiane and Saigon. If objective is primarily military, i.e., to inflict maximum damage to targets, to prevent VN/PL dispersal and protective measures, and impede rapid VN/PL riposte, it was agreed that a series of sharp, heavy attacks must be made in a relatively short timespan, which would involve substantial U.S. and/or VNAF/Farmgate attacks. If objective primarily psychological, military disadvantages of attacks over longer time frame would be acceptable and chief reliance could be placed on RLAF T-28s with some Yankee team strikes against harder targets, e.g., five bridges. Estimated sortie requirements for this second option 188 T 28 sorties and 80 USAF sorties. Time required [number illegible] days. Vientiane representatives believe Souvanna would [words illegible] would probably wish [words illegible] such attacks spread out over considerable period of time. Also felt Souvanna would prefer VNAF not conduct air strikes in corridor. It was general consensus that best division of targeting for immediate future would be RLAF/YANKEE team mix.

Vientiane is very reluctant to see VNAF participation such strikes and would hope that by keeping GVN informed of actions being taken by RLAF and U.S. in corridor, psychological needs of GVN could reasonably be met. Saigon will seek to do this, but if there are compelling reasons for covert VNAF participation Vientiane would be given prior info on necessity, timing, and place of such strikes.

Alternatively, it was agreed that, if possible, joint Lao, Thai, RVN, and U.S. participation in a common effort against a common enemy would be desirable but, recognizing that, even if possible, arrangements for such an effort would take some time to achieve. If such negotiations are conducted, however, RLAF/Yankee team strikes should not be precluded. Vientiane has since stated it does not consider that it would be desirable to seek to formalize such four country participation in corridor operations as to do so would raise question of degree of Souvanna Phouma's knowledge and involvement which Vientiane feels would jeopardize success of operations.

2. Ground operations.

A. Although it was agreed that northern Route 9 area offered most profitable targets, conference proceeded on assumption that Vientiane would find operations astride Route 9 politically unacceptable at this time. However, Vientiane's 448 to dept, dispatched after return of conferees, now indicates that "shallow penetration raids (20 kilometers) . . . in Rte 9 area . . . by company-sized units" would be acceptable and would not require clearance by the RLG. . . .

E. It was the view of Saigon group that authority for U.S. advisors to accompany units is a prerequisite to successful operations. Without this U.S. participation probability of success is judged so low that the advisability of conducting cross border operations would be questionable. Vientiane representatives were strongly opposed to presence U.S. advisors because of difficulty with current SAR operations in Laos and political importance of U.S. maintaining credible stance of adhering to provisions Geneva accords.

F. Embassy Vientiane had earlier indicated that they would insist on advanced clearance of cross border operations. All representatives agreed that this requirement would be met by Vientiane having opportunity to comment on all plans submitted to Washington for approval. Once approval to execute is received, Vientiane would be kept informed of day-to-day operations as information addressee on operational traffic between Saigon/Washington/CINCPAC. . . .

83

Cable Authorizing Air Strikes on Laos Infiltration Routes

Cablegram from the State Department and the Defense Department to the United States Embassy in Vientiane, Oct. 6, 1964. Copies of the cablegram were sent to the United States Embassies in Saigon and Bangkok and to the commander in chief of Pacific forces. The embassy in Saigon was asked to relay the message to the United States commander in Vietnam.

You are authorized to urge the RLG to begin air attacks against Viet Cong infiltration routes and facilities in the Laos Panhandle by RLAF T-28 aircraft as soon as possible. Such strikes should be spread out over a period of several weeks, and targets should be limited to those deemed suitable for attack by T-28s and listed Para. 8 Vientiane's 581, excluding Mu Gia pass and any target which Lao will not hit without U.S. air cover or fire support since decision this matter not yet made.

You are further authorized to inform Lao that YANKEE TEAM suppressive fire strikes against certain difficult targets in Panhandle, interspersing with further T-28 strikes, are part of the over-all concept and are to be anticipated later but that such U.S. strikes are not repeat not authorized at this time.

Report soonest proposed schedule of strikes and, upon implementation, all actual commitments of RLG T-28s, including targets attacked, results achieved, and enemy opposition. Also give us any views in addition to those in Vientiane's 581 as to any targets which are deemed too difficult for RLG air strikes and on which U.S. suppressive strikes desired.

FYI: Highest levels have not authorized YANKEE TEAM strikes at this time against Route 7 targets. Since we wish to avoid the impression that we are taking first step in escalation, we inclined defer decision on Route 7 strikes until we have strong evidence Hanoi's preparation for new attack in PDJ, some of which might come from RLAF operations over the Route. END FYI.

You may inform RLG, however, that U.S. will fly additional RECCE over Route 7 to keep current on use being made of the Route by the PL and to identify Route 7 targets and air defenses. The subject of possible decision to conduct strikes on Route 7 being given study in Washington.

FYI: Cross border ground operations not repeat not authorized at this time.

84

William Bundy Draft on Handling World and Public Opinion

Draft section of a paper, "Conditions for Action and Key Actions Surrounding Any Decision," by Assistant Secretary of State Bundy, Nov. 5, 1964.

1. Bien Hoa may be repeated at any time. This would tend to force our hand, but would also give us a good springboard for any decision for stronger action. The President is clearly thinking in terms of maximum use of a Gulf of Tonkin rationale, either for an action that would show toughness and hold the line till we can decide the big issue, or as a basis for starting a clear course of action under the broad options.

2. Congress must be consulted before any major action, perhaps only by notification if we do a reprisal against another Bien Hoa, but preferably by careful talks with such key leaders as Mansfield, Dirksen, the Speaker, Albert, Halleck, Fulbright, Hickenlooper, Morgan, Mrs. Bolton, Russell, Saltonstall, Rivers, (Vinson?), Arends, Ford, etc. He probably should wait till his mind is moving clearly in one direction before such a consultation, which would point to some time next week. Query if it should be combined with other topics (budget?) to lessen the heat.

3. We probably do not need additional Congressional authority, even if we decide on very strong action. A session of this rump Congress might well be the scene of a messy Republican effort.

4. We are on the verge of intelligence agreement that infiltration has in fact mounted, and Saigon is urging that we surface this by the end of the week or early next week. Query how loud we want to make this sound. Actually Grose in the Times had the new estimate on Monday; so the splash and sense of hot new news may be less. We should decide this today if possible. . . . In general, we all feel the problem of proving North Vietnamese participation is less than in the past, but we should have the Jorden Report updated for use as necessary.

5. A Presidential statement with the rationale for action is high on any check list. An intervening fairly strong Presidential noise to prepare a climate for an action statement is probably indicated and would be important in any event to counter any SVN fears of a softening in our policy. We should decide the latter today too if possible.

6. Secretary Rusk is talking today to Dobrynin. For more direct communication Seaborn can be revved up to go up the 15th if we think it wise. He is not going anyway, and we could probably hold him back so that the absence of any message was not itself a signal.

7. Our international soundings appear to divide as follows:

a. We should probably consult with the U.K., Australia, New Zealand, and possibly Thailand before we reach a decision. We would hope for firm moral support from the U.K. and for participation in at least token form from the others.

b. SEATO as a body should be consulted concurrently with stronger action. We should consult the Philippines a day or so before such action but not necessarily before we have made up our minds.

c. The NATO Council should be notified on the Cuban model, i.e., concurrently, by a distinguished representative.

d. For negative reasons, France probably deserves VIP treatment also.

e. In the UN, we must be ready with an immediate affirmative presentation of our rationale to proceed concurrently either with a single reprisal action or with the initiation of a broader course of action.

f. World-wide, we should select reasonably friendly chiefs of state for special treatment seeking their sympathy and support, and should arm all our representatives with the rationale and defense of our action whether individual reprisal or broader.

8. USIA must be brought into the planning process not later than early next week, so that it is getting the right kind of materials ready for all our information media, on a contingency basis. The same [word illegible] true of CIA's outlets.

85

McNaughton's November Draft on Vietnam Aims and Choices

Second draft of a paper, "Action for South Vietnam," by Assistant Secretary of Defense McNaughton, Nov. 6, 1964.

1. U.S. aims:

(a) To protect U.S. reputation as a counter-subversion guarantor.

(b) To avoid domino effect especially in Southeast Asia.

(c) To keep South Vietnamese territory from Red hands.

(d) To emerge from crisis without unacceptable taint from methods.

2. Present situation:

The situation in South Vietnam is deteriorating. Unless new actions are taken, the new government will probably be unstable and ineffectual, and the VC will probably continue to extend their hold over the population and territory. It can be expected that, soon (6 months? two years?), (a) government officials at all levels will adjust their behavior to an eventual VC take-over, (b) defections of significant military forces will take place, (c) whole integrated regions of the country will be totally denied to the GVN, (d) neutral and/or left-wing elements will enter the government, (e) a popular front regime will emerge which will invite the U.S. out, and (f) fundamental concessions to the VC and accommodations to the DRV will put South Vietnam behind the Curtain.

3. Urgency:

"Bien Hoa" having passed, no urgent decision is required regarding military action against the DRV, but (a) such a decision, related to the general deteriorating situation in South Vietnam, should be made soon, and (b) in the event of another VC or DRV "spectacular," a decision (for at least a reprisal) would be urgently needed.

4. Inside South Vietnam:

Progress inside SVN is important, but it is unlikely despite our best ideas and efforts (and progress, if made, will take at least several months). Nevertheless, whatever other actions might be taken, great efforts should be made within South Vietnam: (a) to strengthen the government, its bureaucracy, and its civil-military coordination and planning, (b) to dampen various ethnic, religious, urban and civil-military strife by a broad and positive GVN program designed (with U.S. Team help) to enlist the support of important groups, and (c) to press the pacification program in the countryside.

5. Action against DRV:

Action against North Vietnam is to some extent a substitute

365

for strengthening the government in South Vietnam. That is, a less active VC (on orders from DRV) can be matched by a less efficient GVN. We therefore should consider squeezing North Vietnam.

6. Options open to us:

We have three options open to us (all envision reprisals in the DRV for DRV/VC "spectaculars" against GVN as well as U.S. assets in South Vietnam).

OPTION A. Continue present policies. Maximum assistance within SVN and limited external actions in Laos and by the GVN covertly against North Vietnam. The aim of any reprisal actions would be to deter and punish large VC actions in the South, but not to a degree that would create strong international negotiating pressures. Basic to this option is the continued rejection of negotiating in the hope that the situation will improve.

OPTION B. Fast full squeeze. Present policies plus a systematic program of military pressures against the north, meshing at some point with negotiation, but with pressure actions to be continued at a fairly rapid pace and without interruption until we achieve our central present objectives.

OPTION C. Progressive squeeze-and-talk. Present policies plus an orchestration of communications with Hanoi and a crescendo of additional military moves against infiltration targets, first in Laos and then in the DRV, and then against other targets in North Vietnam. The scenario would be designed to give the U.S. the option at any point to proceed or not, to escalate or not, and to quicken the pace or not. The decision in these regards would be made from time to time in view of all relevant factors.

7. Analysis of OPTION A
(To be provided)

8. Analysis of OPTION B
(To be provided)

9. Analysis of OPTION C

(a) Military actions. Present policy, in addition to providing for reprisals in DRV for DRV actions against the U.S., envisions (1) 34A Airops and Marops, (2) deSoto patrols, for intelligence purposes, (3) South Vietnamese shallow ground actions in Laos when practicable, and (4) T28 strikes against infiltration-associated targets in Laos. Additional actions should be:

PHASE ONE (in addition to reprisals in DRV for VC "spectaculars" in South Vietnam): (5) U.S. strikes against infiltration-associated targets in Laos.

PHASE TWO (in addition to reprisals in DRV against broader range of VC actions): (6) Low-level reconnaissance in southern DRV, (7) U.S./VNAF strikes against infiltration-associated targets in southern DRV.

PHASE THREE: Either continue only the above actions or add one or more of the following, making timely deployment of U.S. forces: (8) Aerial mining of DRV ports, (9) Naval quarantine of DRV, and (10) U.S./VNAF, in "crescendo," strike additional targets on "94 target list."

South Vietnamese forces should play a role in any action taken against the DRV.

(b) Political actions. Establish immediately a channel for bilateral U.S.-DRV communication. This could be in Warsaw or via Seaborn in Hanoi. Hanoi should be told that we do not seek to destroy North Vietnam or to acquire a colony or base, but that North Vietnam must:

(1) Stop training and sending personnel to wage war in SVN and Laos.

(2) Stop sending arms and supplies to SVN and Laos.

(3) Stop directing and controlling military actions in SVN and Laos.

(4) Order the VC and PL to stop their insurgencies and military actions.

(5) Remove VM forces and cadres from SVN and Laos.

(6) Stop propaganda broadcasts to South Vietnam.

[(7) See that VC and PL stop attacks and incidents in SVN and Laos?]

[(8) See that VC and PL cease resistance to government forces?]

[(9) See that VC and PL turn in weapons and relinquish bases?]

[(10) See that VC and PL surrender for amnesty of expatriation?]

U.S. demands should be accompanied by offers (1) to arrange a rice-barter deal between two halves of Vietnam and (2) to withdraw U.S. forces from South Vietnam for so long as the terms are complied with.

We should not seek wider negotiations—in the UN, in Geneva, etc.—but we should evaluate and pass on each negotiating opportunity as it is pressed on us.

(c) Information actions. The start of military actions against the DRV will have to be accompanied by a convincing world-wide public information program. (The information problem will be easier if the first U.S. action against the DRV is related in time and kind to a DRV or VC outrage or "spectacular," preferably against SVN as well as U.S. assets.)

(d) VS/DRV/Chicom-USSR reactions. (To be elaborated later.) The DRV and China will probably not invade South Vietnam, Laos or Burma, nor is it likely that they will conduct air strikes on these countries. The USSR will almost certainly confine herself to political actions. If the DRV or China strike or invade South Vietnam, U.S. forces will be sufficient to handle the problem.

(e) GVN Reactions. Military action against the DRV could be counterproductive in South Vietnam because (1) the VC could step up its activities, (2) the South Vietnamese could panic, (3) they could resent our striking their "brothers," and (4) they could tire of waiting for results. Should South Vietnam disintegrate completely beneath us, we should try to hold it together long enough to permit us to try to evacuate our forces and to convince the world to accept the uniqueness (and congenital impossibility) of the South Vietnamese case.

(f) Allied and neutral reactions. (To be elaborated later.) (1) Even if OPTION C failed, it would, by demonstrating U.S. willingness to go to the mat, tend to bolster allied confidence in the U.S. as an ally. (2) U.S. military action against the DRV will probably prompt military actions elsewhere in the world—e.g., Indonesia against Malaysia or Timor, or Turkey against Cyprus.

86

View of Chiefs' Representative on Options B and C

Memorandum from Vice Adm. Lloyd M. Mustin of the staff of the Joint Chiefs of Staff to Assistant Secretary Bundy as chairman of the Working Group on Southeast Asia, Nov. 14, 1964. The memorandum was headed "Additional Material for Project on Courses of Action in Southeast Asia."

References: a. Your memorandum of 13 November 1964 to the NSC Working Group

b. JCSM 902-64, dated 27 October 1964

c. JCSM 933-64, dated 4 November 1964

d. JCSM 955-64, dated 14 November 1964

1. Reference a requests JCS views spelling out Option "B" as a preferred alternative, with something like Option "C" as a fallback alternative. Because of the way in which formal JCS views in the premises have been developed and expressed, this requires some degree of interpretation.

2. Reference b is the most recent recommendation by the Joint Chiefs of Staff for courses of action with respect to South Vietnam, framed in context of initiation "in cold blood." Various JCS papers, the most recent dated 22 October 1964, identify the corresponding recommendations with respect to Laos. Reference b specifically identifies certain of its listed actions to begin now, with the balance of them "implemented as required, to achieve U.S. objectives in Southeast Asia."

3. Reference c formalized the most recent JCS recommendation for reprisal (hot blood) actions and reference d provided an analysis of DRV/CHICOM reactions to these strikes, and the probable results thereof. The proposed actions are essentially the same as in reference c except for the principal difference that the

"hot blood" actions are initiated at a substantial higher level of military activity.

4. Only in that the courses of action in either of these sets of documents can be completed in minimum time consistent with proper conduct of military operations do they match Option "B" as defined for purposes of the NSC Working Group study. The distinction is that while the Joint Chiefs of Staff offer the capability for pursuing Option "B" as defined, they have not explicitly recommended that the operations be conducted on a basis necessarily that inflexible. All implementing plans do in fact explicity recognize a controlled phase which would permit suspension whenever desired by national authority.

5. I believe my draft cnntribution to PART VI provides a reasonable application of the JCS recommendations to Option "B" as defined for the study, but this does not mean that the Joint Chiefs of Staff have recommended Option "B" as defined in the study.

6. There is in an advanced state of completion a JCS fall-back recommendation for a course of action which, subject to possible further modifications by the Joint Chiefs of Staff, will provide essentially the same military actions listed in my draft input to PART VII. These include the same military actions listed in the above, but without the stress upon starting forthwith, and with more specific emphasis on some extension of the over-all time for execution of the complete list. Thus it imposes what amount to some arbitrary delays, which would provide additional intervals for diplomatic exchanges.

7. Because of the time delays which it reflects, it is specifically the JCS fall-back position.

8. For information, the analysis in reference d develops and supports the conclusion that the United States and its Allies can deal adequately with any course of action the DRV and/or CHI-COMS decide to pursue. You may note that this conclusion is developed in the context of the most intense of all courses of action prepared by the Joint Chiefs of Staff. This reflects a position less pessimistic than some which have appeared in project drafts.

9. A final overall comment by the Joint Staff member of the Working Group:

We recognize quite clearly that any effective military action taken by the United States will generate a hue and cry in various quarters. The influence that this kind of "pressure" may have upon the United States acting in support of its national interests will be no more than what we choose to permit it to be. There are repeated expressions in various project draft materials indicating that this influence will necessarily be great. We do not agree. There are too many current examples of countries acting in what they presumably believe to be their own [word illegible] self-interest, in utter disregard for "world opinion," for us to accept the position that the United States must at all times conduct all its affairs on the basis of a world popularity contest. In short, we believe that certain strong U.S. actions are required in Southeast Asia, that we must take them regardless of opinion in various other quarters, and that results of our failing to take them would be substantially more serious to the United States than would be any results of world opinions if we did take them. And as far as that goes, we do not believe that if we took the necessary actions the adverse pressures from other countries would prove to be very serious after all—at least from countries that matter to us.

87

Taylor's Briefing of Key Officials on Situation in November '64

Excerpts from prepared briefing by Ambassador Taylor, "The Current Situation in South Vietnam—November, 1964," delivered to the "principals"—the senior officials to whom the Southeast Asia working group reported—at a Washington meeting on Nov. 27, 1964.

After a year of changing and ineffective government, the counter-insurgency program country-wide is bogged down and will require heroic treatment to assure revival. Even in the Saigon area, in spite of the planning and the special treatment accorded the Hop Tac plan, this area also is lagging. The northern provinces of South Viet-Nam which a year ago were considered almost free of Viet-Cong are now in deep trouble. In the Quang Ngai-Binh Dinh area, the gains of the Viet-Cong have been so serious that once more we are threatened with a partition of the country by a Viet-Cong salient driven to the sea. The pressure on this area has been accompanied by continuous sabotage of the railroad and of Highway 1 which in combination threaten an economic strangulation of northern provinces.

This deterioration of the pacification program has taken place in spite of the very heavy losses inflicted almost daily on the Viet-Cong and the increase in strength and professional competence of the Armed Forces of South Viet-Nam. Not only have the Viet-Cong apparently made good their losses, but of late, have demonstrated three new or newly expanded tactics: the use of stand-off mortar fire against important targets, as in the attack on the Bien Hoa airfield; economic strangulation on limited areas; finally, the stepped-up infiltration of DRV military personnel moving from the north. These new or improved tactics employed against the background of general deterioration offer a serious threat to the pacification program in general and to the safety of important bases and installations in particular.

Perhaps more serious than the downward trend in the pacification situation, because it is the prime cause, is the continued weakness of the central government. Although the Huong government has been installed after executing faithfully and successfully the program laid out by the Khanh government for its own replacement, the chances for the long life and effective performance of the new line-up appear small. Indeed, in view of the factionalism existing in Saigon and elsewhere throughout the country it is impossible to foresee a stable and effective government under any name in anything like the near future. Nonetheless, we do draw some encouragement from the character and seriousness of purpose of Prime Minister Huong and his cabinet and the apparent intention of General Khanh to keep the Army out of politics, at least for the time being.

As our programs plod along or mark time, we sense the mounting feeling of war weariness and hopelessness which pervade South Viet-Nam, particularly in the urban areas. Although the provinces for the most part appear steadfast, undoubtedly there is chronic discouragement there as well as in the cities. Although the military leaders have not talked recently with much conviction about the need for "marching North," assuredly many of them are convinced that some new and drastic action must be taken to reverse the present trends and to offer hope of ending the insurgency in some finite time.

The causes for the present unsatisfactory situation are not hard to find. It stems from two primary causes, both already mentioned above, the continued ineffectiveness of the central government, and the other, the increasing strength and effectiveness of the Viet-Cong and their ability to replace losses.

While, in view of the historical record of South Viet-Nam, it is not surprising to have these governmental difficulties, this chronic weakness is a critical liability to future plans. Without an effective central government with which to mesh the U.S. effort the latter is a spinning wheel unable to transmit impulsion to the machinery of the GVN. While the most critical governmental weaknesses are in Saigon, they are duplicated to a degree in the provinces. It is most difficult to find adequate provincial chiefs and supporting administrative personnel to carry forward the complex programs which are required in the field for successful pacification. It is true that when one regards the limited background of the provincial chiefs and their associates, one should perhaps be surprised by the results which they have accomplished, but unfortunately, these results are generally not adequate for the complex task at hand or for the time schedule which we would like to establish.

As the past history of this country shows, there seems to be a national attribute which makes for factionalism and limits the development of a truly national spirit. Whether this tendency is innate or a development growing out of the conditions of political suppression under which successive generations have lived is hard to determine. But it is an inescapable fact that there is no national tendency toward team play or mutual loyalty to be found among many of the leaders and political groups within South Viet-Nam. Given time, many of these [words illegible] undoubtedly change for the better, but we are unfortunately pressed for time and unhappily perceive no short term solution for the establishment of stable and sound government.

The ability of the Viet-Cong continuously to rebuild their units and to make good their losses is one of the mysteries of this guerrilla war. We are aware of the recruiting methods by which local boys are induced or compelled to join the Viet-Cong ranks and have some general appreciation of the amount of infiltration personnel from the outside. Yet taking both of these sources into account, we still find no plausible explanation of the continued strength of the Viet-Cong if our data on Viet-Cong losses are even approximately correct. Not only do the Viet-Cong units have the recuperative powers of the phoenix, but they have an amazing ability to maintain morale. Only in rare cases have we found evidences of bad morale among Viet-Cong prisoners or recorded in captured Viet-Cong documents.

Undoubtedly one cause for the growing strength of the Viet-Cong is the increased direction and support of their campaign by the government of North Viet-Nam. This direction and support take the form of endless radioed orders and instructions, and the continuous dispatch to South Viet-Nam of trained cadre and military equipment over infiltration routes by land and by water. While in the aggregate, this contribution to the guerrilla campaign over the years must represent a serious drain on the resources of the DRV, that government shows no sign of relaxing its support of the Viet-Cong. In fact, the evidence points to an increased contribution over the last year, a plausible development, since one would expect the DRV to press hard to exploit the obvious internal weaknesses in the south.

If, as the evidence shows, we are playing a losing game in South Viet-Nam, it is high time we change and find a better way. To change the situation, it is quite clear that we need to do three things: first, establish an adequate government in SVN; second, improve the conduct of the counterinsurgency campaign; and finally, persuade or force the DRV to stop its aid to the Viet-Cong and to use its directive powers to make the Viet-Cong desist from their efforts to overthrow the government of South Viet-Nam. . . .

In bringing military pressure to bear on North Viet-Nam, there are a number of variations which are possible. At the bottom of the ladder of escalation, we have the initiation of intensified covert operations, anti-infiltration attacks in Laos, and reprisal bombings mentioned above as a means for stiffening South Vietnamese morale. From this level of operations, we could begin to escalate progressively by attacking appropriate targets in North Viet-Nam. If we justified our action primarily upon the need to reduce infiltration, it would be natural to direct these attacks on infiltration—related targets such as staging areas, training facilities, communications centers and the like. The tempo and weight of the attacks could be varied according to the effects sought. In its final forms, this kind of attack could extend to the destruction of all important fixed targets in North Viet-Nam and to the interdiction of movement on all lines of communication.

. . . We reach the point where a decision must be taken as to what course or courses of action we should undertake to change the tide which is running against us. It seems perfectly clear that we must work to the maximum to make something out of the present Huong government or any successor thereto. While doing so, we must be thinking constantly of what we would do if our efforts are unsuccessful and the government collapses. Concurrently, we should stay on the present in-country program, intensifying it as possible in proportion to the current capabilities of the government. To bolster the local morale and restrain the Viet-Cong during this period, we should step up the 34-A operations, engage in bombing attacks and armed recce in the Laotian corridor and undertake reprisal bombing as required. It will be important that United States forces take part in the Laotian operations in order to demonstrate to South Viet-Nam our willingness to share in the risks of attacking the North.

If this course of action is inadequate, and the government falls then we must start over again or try a new approach. At this moment, it is premature to say exactly what these new measures should be. In any case, we should be prepared for emergency military action against the North if only to shore up a collapsing situation.

If, on the other hand as we hope, the government maintains and proves itself, then we should be prepared to embark on a methodical program of mounting air attacks in order to accomplish our pressure objectives vis-a-vis the DRV and at the same time do our best to improve in-country pacification program. We will leave negotiation initiatives to Hanoi. Throughout this period, our guard must be up in the Western Pacific, ready for any reaction by the DRV or of Red China. Annex I suggests the train of events which we might set in motion. . . .

88

Final Draft Position Paper Produced by Working Group

"Draft Position Paper on Southeast Asia" circulated to the principal top-level officials concerned, Nov. 29, 1964. The draft was accompanied by a memorandum from William Bundy saying: "I attach a draft action paper for review at the meeting at 1:30 on Monday in Secretary Rusk's conference room. Secretary Rusk has generally approved the

format of these papers, and they have been given a preliminary review for substance by Ambassador Taylor and Messrs. McNaughton and Forrestal. However, I am necessarily responsible for the way they are now drafted." The Pentagon study says this paper was originally a draft national security action memorandum but that it was changed to a draft position paper at the instructions of the principals. Words and phrases that were deleted from the final version are shown in italics. Handwritten interpolations or revisions are shown in double parentheses.

I. CONCEPT

A. U.S. objectives in South Vietnam (SVN) are unchanged. They are to:

1. Get Hanoi and North Vietnam (DRV) support and direction removed from South Vietnam, and, to the extent possible, obtain DRV cooperation in ending Viet Cong (VC) operations in SVN.

2. Re-establish an independent and secure South Vietnam with appropriate international safeguards, including the freedom to accept U.S. and other external assistance as required.

3. Maintain the security of other non-Communist nations in Scutheast Asia including specifically the maintenance and observance of Geneva Accords of 1962 in Laos.

B. We will continue to press the South Vietnamese Government (GVN) in every possible way to make the government itself more effective and to push forward with the pacification program.

C. We will join at once with the South Vietnamese and Lao Governments in a determined action program aimed at DRV activities in both countries and designed to help GVN morale and to increase the costs and strain on Hanoi, foreshadowing still greater pressures to come. Under this program the first phase actions (((see TAB D))) within the next thirty days will be intensified forms of action already under way, plus (1) U.S. armed reconnaissance strikes in Laos, and already under way, plus (1) U.S. armed reconnaissance strikes in Laos, and (2) GVN and possible U.S. air strikes against the DRV, as reprisals against any major or spectacular Viet Cong action in the south, whether against U.S. personnel and installations or not.

D. Beyond the thirty-day period, first phase actions may be continued without change, or additional military measures may be taken including the withdrawal of dependents and the possible initiation of strikes a short distance across the border against the infiltration routes from the DRV. In the later case this would become a transitional phase. ((Be prepared to stop flow of dependents to SVN at [illegible word] time we start air strikes in force.))

E. Thereafter, if the GVN improves its effectiveness to an acceptable degree and Hanoi does not yield on acceptable terms, *or if the GVN can only be kept going by stronger action* the U.S.

374

is prepared—at a time to be determined—to enter into a second phase program, in support of the GVN and RLG, of graduated military pressures directed systematically against the DRV. Such a program would consist principally of progressively more serious air strikes, of a weight and tempo adjusted to the situation as it develops (possibly running from two to six months). Targets in the DRV would start with infiltration targets south of the 19th parallel and work up to targets north of that point. This could eventually lead to such measures as air strikes on all major military-related targets, aerial mining of DRV ports, and a U.S. naval blockade of the DRV. The whole sequence of military actions would be designed to give the impression of a steady, deliberate approach, and to give the U.S. the option at any time (subject to enemy reaction) to proceed or not, to escalate or not, and to quicken the pace or not. Concurrently, the U.S. would be alert to any sign of yielding by Hanoi, and would be prepared to explore negotiated solutions that attain U.S. objectives in an acceptable manner. *The U.S. would seek to control any negotiations and would oppose any independent South Vietnamese efforts to negotiate.*

HEADING ILLEGIBLE

A. **A White House statement** will be issued following the meeting with Ambassador Taylor, with the text as in Tab B, attached.

B. Ambassador Taylor will consult with the GVN promptly on his return, making a general presentation ((in accordance with the draft instructions)) **as stated** in Tab B, attached. He will further press for the adoption of specific measures as listed in the Annex to Tab B.

C. *At the earliest feasible date, we will publicize the evidence of increased DRV infiltration. This action will be coordinated by Mr. Chester Cooper in order to insure that the evidence is sound and that senior government officials who have testified on this subject in the past are in a position to defend and explain the differences between the present estimates and those given in the past. The publicizing will take four forms:*

1. An on-the-record presentation to the press in Washington, concurrently with an on-the-record or background presentation to the press in Saigon.

2. Available Congressional leaders will be given special briefings. (No special leadership meeting will be convened for this purpose.)

3. The Ambassadors of key allied nations will be given special briefiings.

4. A written report will be prepared and published within the next ten days giving greater depth and background to the evidence.

D. **Laos and Thailand**

The US Ambassadors **in** these **countries will** inform the government leaders ((in general terms)) of the concept we propose to follow and of specific actions requiring their concurrence or participation. In the case of Laos, we will obtain RLG approval of an intensified program of ((U.S. armed)) reconnaissance strikes both in the Panhandle area of Laos and along the key infiltration routes in central Laos. These actions will not be publicized except to the degree approved by the RLG. It is important, however, for purposes of morale in SV, that their existence be generally known.

Thailand will be asked to support our program fully, to intensify its own efforts in the north and northeast, and to give further support to operations in Laos, such as additional pilots and possibly artillery teams.

E. Key Allies

We will consult immediately with the UK, ((DC)) **Australia, New Zealand,** ((Bundy)) and the Philippines. ((Humphrey?))

1. UK. The President will explain the concept and proposed actions fully to Prime Minister Wilson, seeking full British support, but without asking for any additional British contribution in view of the British role in Malaysia.

2. Australia and New Zealand will be pressed through their Ambassadors, not only for support but for additional contributions.

3. The Philippines will be particularly pressed for contributions along the lines of the program for approximately 1800 men already submitted to President Macapagal.

F. We will press generally for more third country aid, stressing the gravity of the situation and our deepening concern. A summary of existing third country aid and of the types of aid that might now be obtained is in Tab C, attached.

G. Communist Countries

1. We will convey to Hanoi our unchanged determination ((and)) our objectives, and that we have a growing concern at the DRV role, to see if there is any sign of change in Hanoi's position.

2. We will make no special approaches to Communist China in this period.

3. **We will convey our determination and grave concern to the Soviets, not in the expectation of any change in their position but in effect to warn them to stay out, and with some hope they will pass on the message to Hanoi and Peiping.**

H. Other Countries

1. We will convey our grave concern to key interested governments such as Canada, India, and France, but avoid spelling out the concept fully.

2. In the event of a reprisal action, will explain and defend our action in the UN as at the time of the Gulf of Tonkin incident. We do not plan to raise the issue otherwise in the UN. (The Lao Government may stress the DRV infiltration in Laos in its speech, and we should support this and spread the information.)

I. Intensified Military Actions

1. The GVN maritime operations (MAROPS) will be intensified, *((including U.S. air protection of GVN vessels from attacks by MIGs or DRV surface vessels))* and we will urge the GVN to *surface and defend these as wholly justified in response to the wholly illegal DRV actions.*

2. Lao air operations will be intensified, especially in the corridor areas and close to the DRV border. U.S. air cover and flak suppression *will* ((may)) be supplied *where* ((if)) needed.

3. U.S. high-level reconnaissance over the DRV will be stepped up.

4. U.S. armed ((air)) reconnaissance ((and air)) strikes will be carried out in Laos, first against the corridor area and within a short time against Route 7 and other infiltration routes, *in a major operation to cut key bridges.* (These actions will be publicized only to the degree agreed with Souvanna.) ((At this time we prepare to stop flow of dependents to V.N.))

J. Reprisal Actions.

For any VC provocation similar to the following, a reprisal will be undertaken, preferably with 24 hours, against one or more selected targets in the DRV. GVN forces will be used to the maximum extent, supplemented as necessary by U.S. forces. The exact reprisal will be decided at the time, in accordance with a quick-reaction procedure which will be worked out.

The following may be appropriate occasions for reprisals, but we should be alert for any appropriate occasion.

1. Attacks on airfields.
2. Attack on Saigon.
3. Attacks on provincial or district capitals.
4. Major attacks on U.S. citizens.
5. Attacks on major POL facilities.

((expand))

6. Attacks on bridges and railroad lines after the presently damaged facilities have been restored and warning given.

7. Other "spectaculars" such as earlier attack on a U.S. transport carrier at a pier in Saigon.

In these or similar cases, the reprisal action would be linked as directly as possibly to DRV infiltration, so that we have a common threat of justification.

A flexible list of reprisal targets has been prepared running from infiltration targets in the southern part of the DRV up to airfields, ports, and naval bases also located south of the 19th parallel.

K. US/GVN joint planning will be initiated both for reprisal actions and for possible later air strikes across the border into the DRV.

L. Major statement or speech. Depending on U.S. public reaction, a major statement or speech may be undertaken by the President during this period. This will necessarily be required if a reprisal action is taken, but some other significant action, such as the stopping of the flow of U.S. dependents, might be the occasion.

Such a statement or speech would re-state our objectives and our determination, why we are in South Vietnam, and how gravely we view the situation. It should in any event follow the full publicizing of infiltration evidence.

M. *Dependents. The flow of dependents to South Vietnam will be stopped* [at an early date, probably immediately after Ambassador Taylor has consulted with the GVN] [at the start of the second phase], *and this will be publicly announced.*

N. Deferred Actions. ((See TAB D))

The following actions will not be taken within the thirty-day period, but will be considered for adoption in the transitional or second phases of the program:

1. Major air deployment to the area.

2. *Furnishing U.S. air cover for CVN MAROPS.*

((2)) 3. ((Be required to resume)) Resuming destroyer patrols in the Gulf of Tonkin. If attacked, these would be an alternative basis for reprisals, and should be considered primarily in this light.

((5)) 4. ((Be prepared to evacuate)) Evacuation of U.S. dependents.

((3)) 5. U.S. low-level reconnaissance into the DRV.

((4)) 6. GVN/((LAO/))U.S. air strikes across the border ((s)), initially against the infiltration routes and installations and then against other targets south of the 19th parallel.

NOTE

The Joint Chiefs of Staff recommend immediate initiation of sharply intensified military pressures against the DRV, starting with a sharp and early attack in force on the DRV, subsequent to brief operations in Laos and U.S. low-level reconnaissance north of the boundary to divert DRV attention prior to the attack in force. This program would be designed to destroy in the first three days Phuc Yen airfield near Hanoi, other airfields, and major POL facilities, clearly to establish the fact that the U.S. intends to use military force to the full limits of what military force can contribute to achieving U.S. objectives in Southeast Asia, and to afford the GVN respite by curtailing DRV assistance to and direction of the Viet Cong. The follow-on-military program—involving armed reconnaissance of infiltration routes in Laos, air strikes on infiltration targets in the DRV, and then progressive strikes throughout North Vietnam—could be suspended short of full destruction of the DRV if our objectives were earlier achieved. The military program would be conducted rather swiftly, but the tempo could be adjusted as needed to contribute to achieving our objectives.

89

Account of Taylor's Meeting with Saigon Generals on Unrest

Excerpts from Saigon airgram to the State Department, Dec. 24, 1964, as provided in the body of the Pentagon study. Ambassador Taylor and his deputy, U. Alexis Johnson, met with the so-called Young Turk leaders, among them Generals Nguyen Cao Ky, Nguyen Van Thieu and Nguyen Chanh Thi and an Admiral identified as Cang.

. . . AMBASSADOR TAYLOR: Do all of you understand English? (Vietnamese officers indicated they did, although the understanding of General Thi was known to be weak.) I told you all clearly at General Westmoreland's dinner we Americans were tired of coups. Apparently I wasted my words. Maybe this is because something is wrong with my French because you evidently didn't understand. I made it clear that all the military plans which I know you would like to carry out are dependent on governmental stability. Now you have made a real mess. We cannot carry you forever if you do things like this. Who speaks for this group? Do you have a spokesman?

GENERAL KY: I am not the spokesman for the group but I do speak English. I will explain why the Armed Forces took this action last night.

We understand English very well. We are aware of our responsibilities, we are aware of the sacrifices of our people over twenty years. We know you want stability, but you cannot have stability until you have unity. . . . But still there are rumors of coups and doubts among groups. We think these rumors come from the HNC, not as an organization but from some of its members. Both military and civilian leaders regard the presence of these people in the HNC as divisive of the Armed Forces due to their influence.

Recently the Prime Minister showed us a letter he had received from the Chairman of the HNC. This letter told the Prime Minister to beware of the military, and said that maybe the military would want to come back to power. Also the HNC illegally sought to block the retirement of the generals that the Armed Forces Council unanimously recommended be retired in order to improve unity in the Armed Forces.

GENERAL THIEU: The HNC cannot be bosses because of the Constitution. Its members must prove that they want to fight.

GENERAL KY: It looks as though the HNC does not want unity. It does not want to fight the Communists.

It has been rumored that our action of last night was an intrigue of Khanh against Minh, who must be retired. Why do we seek to retire these generals? Because they had their chance and did badly. . . .

379

Yesterday we met, twenty of us, from 1430 to 2030. We reached agreement that we must take some action. We decided to arrest the bad members of the HNC, bad politicians, bad student leaders, and the leaders of the Committee of National Salvation, which is a Communist organization. We must put the trouble-making organizations out of action and ask the Prime Minister and the Chief of State to stay in office.

After we explain to the people why we did this at a press conference, we would like to return to our fighting units. We have no political ambitions. We seek strong, unified, and stable Armed Forces to support the struggle and a stable government. Chief of State Suu agrees with us. General Khanh saw Huong who also agreed.

We did what we thought was good for this country; we tried to have a civilian government clean house. If we have achieved it, fine. We are now ready to go back to our units.

AMBASSADOR TAYLOR: I respect the sincerity of you gentlemen. Now I would like to talk to you about the consequences of what you have done. But first, would any of the other officers wish to speak?

ADMIRAL CANG: It seems that we are being treated as though we were guilty. What we did was good and we did it only for the good of the country.

AMBASSADOR TAYLOR: Now let me tell you how I feel about it, what I think the consequences are: first of all, this is a military coup that has destroyed the government-making process that, to the admiration of the whole world, was set up last fall largely through the statesman-like acts of the Armed Forces.

You cannot go back to your units, General Ky. You military are now back in power. You are up to your neck in politics.

Your statement makes it clear that you have constituted yourselves again substantially as a Military Revolutionary Committee. The dissolution of the HNC was totally illegal. Your decree recognized the Chief of State and the Huong Government but this recognition is something that you could withdraw. This will be interpreted as a return of the military to power. . . .

AMBASSADOR TAYLOR: Who commands the Armed Forces? General Khanh?

GENERAL KY: Yes, sir . . .

GENERAL THIEU: In spite of what you say, it should be noted that the Vietnamese Commander-in-Chief is in a special situation. He therefore needs advisors. We do not want to force General Khanh; we advise him. We will do what he orders . . .

AMBASSADOR TAYLOR: Would your officers be willing to come into a government if called upon to do so by Huong? I have been impressed by the high quality of many Vietnamese officers. I am sure that many of the most able men in this country are in uniform. Last fall when the HNC and Huong Government was being formed, I suggested to General Khanh there should be some military participation, but my suggestions were not accepted.

It would therefore be natural for some of them now to be called upon to serve in the government. Would you be willing to do so? . . .

GENERAL KY: Nonetheless, I would object to the idea of the military going back into the government right away. People will say it is a military coup.

AMBASSADOR TAYLOR AND AMBASSADOR JOHNSON: (together) People will say it anyway . . .

AMBASSADOR TAYLOR: You have destroyed the Charter. The Chief of State will still have to prepare for elections. Nobody believes that the Chief of State has either the power or the ability to do this without the HNC or some other advisory body. If I were the Prime Minister, I would simply overlook the destruction of the HNC. But we are preserving the HNC itself. You need a legislative branch and you need this particular step in the formation of a government with National Assembly . . .

AMBASSADOR TAYLOR: It should be noted that Prime Minister Huong has not accepted the dissolution of the HNC . . .

GENERAL THIEU: What kind of concession does Huong want from us?

Ambassador Taylor again noted the need for the HNC function.

GENERAL KY: Perhaps it is better if we now let General Khanh and Prime Minister Huong talk.

GENERAL THIEU: After all, we did not arrest all the members of the HNC. Of nine members we detained only five. These people are not under arrest. They are simply under controlled residence . . .

AMBASSADOR TAYLOR: Our problem now, gentlemen, is to organize our work for the rest of the day. For one thing, the government will have to issue a communique.

GENERAL THIEU: We will still have a press conference this afternoon but only to say why we acted as we did.

AMBASSADOR TAYLOR: I have real troubles on the U.S. side. I don't know whether we will continue to support you after this. Why don't you tell your friends before you act? I regret the need for my blunt talk today but we have lots at stake . . .

AMBASSADOR TAYLOR: And was it really all that necessary to carry out the arrests that very night? Couldn't this have been put off a day or two? . . .

In taking a friendly leave, Ambassador Taylor said: You people have broken a lot of dishes and now we have to see how we can straighten out this mess.

381

Chapter 7

The Launching of the Ground War: March–July, 1965

—BY NEIL SHEEHAN

President Johnson decided on April 1, 1965, to use American ground troops for offensive action in South Vietnam because the Administration had discovered that its long-planned bombing of North Vietnam—which had just begun—was not going to stave off collapse in the South, the Pentagon's study of the Vietnam war discloses. He ordered that the decision be kept secret.

"The fact that this departure from a long-held policy had momentous implications was well recognized by the Administration leadership," the Pentagon analyst writes, alluding to the policy axiom since the Korean conflict that another land war in Asia should be avoided.

Although the President's decision was a "pivotal" change, the study declares, "Mr. Johnson was greatly concerned that the step be given as little prominence as possible."

The decision was embodied in National Security Action Memorandum 328, on April 6, which included the following paragraphs:

"5. The President approved an 18-20,000 man increase in U.S. military support forces to fill out existing units and supply needed logistic personnel.

"6. The President approved the deployment of two additional Marine Battalions and one Marine Air Squadron and associated headquarters and support elements.

"7. The President approved a change of mission for all Marine Battalions deployed to Vietnam to permit their more active use under conditions to be established and approved by the Secretary of Defense in consultation with the Secretary of State."

The paragraph stating the President's concern about publicity gave stringent orders in writing to members of the National Security Council:

"11. The President desires that with respect to the actions in paragraphs 5 through 7, premature publicity be avoided by all possible precautions. The actions themselves should be taken as rapidly as practicable, but in ways that should minimize any appearance of sudden changes in policy, and official statements on these troop movements will be made only with the direct approval of the Secretary of Defense, in consultation with the Secretary of State. The President's desire is that these movements and changes should be understood as being gradual and wholly consistent with existing policy." [See Document #98.]

The period of increasing ground-combat involvement is shown in the Pentagon papers to be the third major phase of President Johnson's commitment to South Vietnam. This period forms another section of the presentation of those papers by The New York Times.

In the spring of 1965, the study discloses, the Johnson Administration pinned its hopes on air assaults against the North to break the enemy's will and persuade Hanoi to stop the Vietcong insurgency in the South. The air assaults began on a sustained basis on March 2.

"Once set in motion, however, the bombing effort seemed to stiffen rather than soften Hanoi's backbone, as well as the willingness of Hanoi's allies, particularly the Soviet Union, to work toward compromise," the study continues.

"Official hopes were high that the Rolling Thunder program would rapidly convince Hanoi that it should agree to negotiate a settlement to the war in the South. After a month of bombing with no response from the North Vietnamese, optimism began to wane," the study remarks.

"The U.S. was presented essentially with two options: (1) to withdraw unilaterally from Vietnam leaving the South Vietnamese to fend for themselves, or (2) to commit ground forces in pursuit of its objectives. A third option, that of drastically increasing the scope and scale of the bombing, was rejected because of the concomitant high risk of inviting Chinese intervention."

And so within a month, the account continues, with the Administration recognizing that the bombing would not work quickly enough, the crucial decision was made to put the two

Highlights of the Period

Within a month of the start of Operation Rolling Thunder, the Pentagon study says, the Johnson Administration had made the first of the decisions that were to lead, in the next months, to American assumption of the major burden of the ground war in South Vietnam.

Here, in chronological order, are the highlights of this period of debate and decision:

MARCH, 1965

First "Rolling Thunder" air strike at ammunition depot and naval base. The two Marine battalions deployed in Vietnam.

APRIL, 1965

President approves 18,000-20,000-man increase in "military support forces" and "a change of mission" for marines "to permit their more active use. . . ." Memo notes his desire for "all possible precautions" against "premature publicity" and to "minimize any appearance of sudden changes in policy."

John T. McNaughton, Assistant Secretary of Defense for International Security Affairs, urges deployment of 173d Airborne Brigade also.

Ambassador Maxwell D. Taylor, calls this "hasty and ill-conceived."

Honolulu strategy meeting. Conferees agree to urge increase to 82,000 U.S. troops.

George W. Ball, Under Secretary of State, proposed United States "cut its losses" and withdraw instead, study says.

MAY, 1965

Vietcong "summer offensive" begins, analyst says. About 200 Marine casualties during April, May.

JUNE, 1965

Gen. William C. Westmoreland, commander in Vietnam, says United States must "reinforce our efforts . . . as rapidly as practical." Asks total of 44 battalions.

State Department announces that United States troops are "available for combat support."

First major ground action by United States forces northwest of Saigon.

Gen. Westmoreland, in reply to Joint Chiefs, makes "big pitch . . . for a free hand to maneuver the troops around . . . ," analyst says.

Ambassador Taylor "confirms the seriousness of the military situation" and "very tenuous hold" of new Government, study goes on.

General Westmoreland given authority to use U.S. forces in battle when necessary "to strengthen" South Vietnam forces.

Mr. Ball, analyst writes, opposes ground-troop increase. Says it gives "absolutely no assurance" of success, risks "costly and indeterminate struggle." Urges "base defense and reserve" strategy "while the stage was being set for withdrawal."

William Bundy, history says, urges President avoid "ultimatum aspects" of either Ball or Westmoreland proposal. Says United States troops should be held to supporting "reserve reaction" role.

JULY, 1965

President at first approves deployment of 34 battalions, about 100,000 men; 44 battalions finally agreed on; total 193,887 troops.

History says this decision "perceived as a threshold—entrance into Asian land war. . . ."

By year's end, history notes, United States forces in South Vietnam total 184,314.

Marine battalions already in South Vietnam on the offensive. The 3,500 marines had landed at Danang on March 8—bringing the total United States force in South Vietnam to 27,000—with their mission restricted to the static defense of the Danang airfield.

As a result of the President's wish to keep the shift of mission from defense to offense imperceptible to the public, the April 1, decision received no publicity "until it crept out almost by accident in a State Department release on 8 June," in the words of the Pentagon study.

The day before, the hastily improvised static security and enclave strategies of the spring were overtaken by a request from Gen. William C. Westmoreland, the American commander in Saigon, for nearly 200,000 troops. He wanted these forces, the Pentagon study relates, to hold off defeat long enough to make possible a further build-up of American troops.

"Swiftly and in an atmosphere of crisis," the study says, President Johnson gave his approval to General Westmoreland's request a little more than a month later, in mid-July. And once again, the study adds Mr. Johnson concealed his decision.

New Warnings of Failure

Before the opening of the air war in the spring warnings were sounded high in the Administration that it would not succeed. Now there were warnings that a ground war in the South might prove fruitless. The warnings came not only from Under Secretary of State George W. Ball, long known as a dissenter on Vietnam, but also from John A. McCone, Director of Central Intelligence, who felt the actions planned were not strong enough.

On April 2 Mr. McCone circulated a memorandum within the National Security Council asserting that unless the United States was willing to bomb the North "with minimum restraint" to break Hanoi's will, it was unwise to commit ground troops to battle.

"In effect," he said, "we will find ourselves mired down in combat in the jungle in a military effort that we cannot win and from which we will have extreme difficulty extracting ourselves." [See Document #97.]

It is not clear from the documentary record whether President Johnson read this particular memorandum, but the Pentagon study says Mr. McCone expressed these same views in a personal memorandum to the President on April 28.

In a separate intelligence estimate for the President on May 6, Vice Adm. William F. Rabon Jr., Mr. McCone's successor, indicated agreement with Mr. McCone.

Mr. Ball's dissent came from the opposite side. He believed that neither bombing the North nor fighting the guerrillas in the South nor any combination of the two offered a solution and said so in a memorandum circulated on June 28, the study reports.

"Convinced that the U.S. was pouring its resources down the drain in the wrong place," the account goes on, Mr. Ball proposed that the United States "cut its losses" and withdraw from South Vietnam.

"Ball was cold-blooded in his analysis," the study continues, describing the memorandum. "He recognized that the U.S. would not be able to avoid losing face before its Asian allies if it staged some form of conference leading to withdrawal of U.S. forces. The losses would be of short-term duration, however, and the U.S. could emerge from this period of travail as a 'wiser and more mature nation.'"

On July 1, the analyst says, Mr. Ball reiterated his proposal for withdrawal in a memorandum to the President entitled "A Compromise Solution for South Vietnam." [See Document #103.]

But the President, the narrative continues, was now heeding the counsel of General Westmoreland to embark on a full-scale ground war. The study for this period concludes that Mr. Johnson and most of his Administration were in no mood for compromise on Vietnam.

As an indication of the Administration's mood during this period, the study cites "a marathon public-information campaign" conducted by Secretary of State Dean Rusk late in February and early in March as sustained bombing was getting under way.

Mr. Rusk, the study says, sought "to signal a seemingly reasonable but in fact quite tough U.S. position on negotiations, demanding that Hanoi 'stop doing what it is doing against its neighbors' before any negotiations could prove fruitful.

"Rusk's disinterest in negotiations at this time was in concert with the view of virtually all of the President's key advisers, that the path to peace was not then open," the Pentagon account continues. "Hanoi held sway over more than half of South Vietnam and could see the Saigon government crumbling before her very eyes. The balance of power at this time simply did not furnish the U.S. with a basis for bargaining and Hanoi had no reason to accede to the hard terms that the U.S. had in mind. Until military pressures on North Vietnam could tilt the balance of forces the other way, talk of negotiation could be little more than a hollow exercise."

The study also says that two of the President's major moves involving the bombing campaign in the spring of 1965 were designed, among other aims, to quiet critics and obtain public support for the air war by striking a position of compromise. But in fact, the account goes on, the moves masked publicly unstated conditions for peace that "were not 'compromise' terms, but more akin to a 'cease and desist' order that, from the D.R.V./VC point of view, was tantamount to a demand for their surrender." "D.R.V." denotes the Democratic Republic of Vietnam; "VC" the Vietcong.

In Mr. Johnson's first action, his speech at the Johns Hopkins University in Baltimore on April 7, he offered to negotiate "without posing any preconditions" and also held out what the study calls a "billion-dollar carrot" in the form of an economic-development program for the Mekong River Basin financed by the United States, in which North Vietnam might participate.

The second action was the unannounced five-day pause in bombing in May, during which the President called upon Hanoi to accept a "political solution" in the South. This "seemed to be aimed more at clearing the decks for a subsequent intensified resumption than it was at evoking a reciprocal act of deescalation by Hanoi," the study says. Admiral Raborn, in his May 6 memorandum, had suggested a pause for this purpose and as an opportunity for Hanoi "to make concessions with some grace."

The air attacks had begun Feb. 8 and Feb. 11 with reprisal raids, code-named Operations Flaming Dart I and II, announced as retaliation for Vietcong attacks on American installations at Pleiku and Quinhon.

In public Administration statements on the air assaults, the study goes on, President Johnson broadened "the reprisal concept as gradually and imperceptibly as possible" into sustained air raids against the North, in the same fashion that the analyst describes him blurring the shift from defensive to offensive action on the ground during the spring and summer of 1965.

The study declares that the two February strikes—unlike the Tonkin Gulf reprisals in August, 1964, which were tied directly to a North Vietnamese attack on American ships—were publicly associated with a "larger pattern of aggression" by North Vietnam. Flaming Dart II, for example, was characterized as "a generalized response to 'continued acts of aggression,'" the account notes.

"Although discussed publicly in very muted tones," it goes on, "the second Flaming Dart operation constituted a sharp break with past U.S. policy and set the stage for the continuing bombing program that was now to be launched in earnest."

In another section of the study, a Pentagon analyst remarks that "the change in ground rules . . . posed serious public-information and stage-managing problems for the President."

It was on Feb. 13, two days after this second reprisal, that Mr. Johnson ordered Operation Rolling Thunder. An important influence on his unpublicized decision was a memorandum from his special assistant for national security affairs, McGeorge Bundy, who was heading a fact-finding mission in Vietnam when the Vietcong attacked at Pleiku occurred on Feb. 7. With Mr. Bundy were Assistant Secretary of Defense John T. McNaughton and Deputy Assistant Secretary of State Leonard Unger.

"A policy of sustained reprisal against North Vietnam" was the strategy advocated by Mr. Bundy in his memorandum, drafted on the President's personal Boeing 707, Air Force One, while returning from Saigon the same day. [See Document #92.]

The memorandum explained that the justification for the air attacks against the North, and their intensity, would be keyed to the level of Vietcong activity in the South.

"We are convinced that the political values of reprisal require a continuous operation," Mr. Bundy wrote. "Episodic responses geared on a one-for-one basis to 'spectacular' outrages would lack the persuasive force of sustained pressure. More important still, they would leave it open to the Communists to avoid reprisals entirely by giving up only a small element of their own program. . . . It is the great merit of the proposed scheme that to stop it the Communists would have to stop enough of their activity in the South to permit the probable success of a determined pacification effort."

The analyst notes, however, that Mr. Bundy's memorandum was a "unique articulation of a rationale for the Rolling Thunder policy" because Mr. Bundy held out as the immediate benefit an opportunity to rally the anti-Communist elements in the South and achieve some political stability and progress in pacification. "Once such a policy is put in force," Mr. Bundy wrote, in summary conclusions to his memorandum," we shall be able to speak in Vietnam on many topics and in many ways, with growing force and effectiveness."

It was also plausible, he said, that bombing in the North, "even in a low key, would have a substantial depressing effect upon the morale of Vietcong cadres in South Vietnam."

Mr. Bundy, the study remarks, thus differed from most other proponents of bombing. These included Ambassador Maxwell D. Taylor, who despaired of improving the Saigon Government's effectiveness and who wanted bombing primarily as a will-breaking device "to inflict such pain or threat of pain upon the D.R.V. that it would be compelled to order a stand-down of Vietcong violence," in the study's words.

As several chapters of the Pentagon study show, a number of Administration strategists—particularly Walt W. Rostow, chairman of the State Department's Policy Planning Council—had assumed for years that "calculated doses" of American air power would accomplish this end.

Mr. Bundy, while not underrating the bombing's "impact on Hanoi" and its use "as a means of affecting the will of Hanoi," saw this as a "longer-range purpose."

The bombing might not work, Mr. Bundy acknowledged. "Yet measured against the costs of defeat in Vietnam," he wrote, "this program seems cheap. And even if it fails to turn the tide—as it may—the value of the effort seems to us to exceed its cost."

President Johnson informed Ambassador Taylor of his Rolling Thunder decision in a cablegram drafted in the White House and transmitted to Saigon late in the afternoon of Sunday, Feb. 13.

The cable told the Ambassador that "we will execute a program of measured and limited air action jointly with the GVN [the Government of Vietnam] against selected military targets in D.R.V., remaining south of the 19th Parallel until further notice."

"Our current expectation," the message added, "is that these attacks might come about once or twice a week and involve two or three targets on each day of operation." [See Document #93.]

Mr. Johnson said he hoped "to have appropriate GVN concurrence by Monday if possible. . . ."

The study recounts that "Ambassador Taylor received the news of the President's new program with enthusiasm. In his response, however, he explained the difficulties he faced in obtaining authentic GVN concurrence 'in the condition of virtual nongovernment' which existed in Saigon at that moment."

Gen. Nguyen Khanh, the nominal commander of the South Vietnamese armed forces, had ousted the civilian cabinet of Premier Tran Van Huong on Jan. 27. Led by Air Vice Marshall Nguyen Cao Ky, a group of young generals—the so-called Young Turks—were in turn intriguing against General Khanh.

(A footnote in the account of the first reprisal strikes, on Feb. 8, says that Marshal Ky, who led the South Vietnamese planes participating in the raid, caused "consternation" among American target controllers by dropping his bombs on the wrong targets. "In a last minute switch," the footnote says, Marshal Ky "dumped his flight's bomb loads on an unassigned target in the Vinhlinh area, in order, as he later explained, to avoid colliding with U.S.A.F aircraft which, he claimed, were striking his originally assigned target when his flight arrived over the target area." Adm. U.S. Grant Sharp, commander of United States forces in the Pacific, reported the incident to the Joint Chiefs.)

Referring to the political situation in Saigon, the account says: "This Alice-in-Wonderland atmosphere notwithstanding, Taylor was undaunted."

"It will be interesting to observe the effect of our proposal on the internal political situation here," the Ambassador cabled back to Mr. Johnson in Washington about the bombing. "I will use the occasion to emphasize that a dramatic change is occurring in U.S. policy, one highly favorable to GVN interests but demanding a parallel dramatic change of attitude on the part of the GVN. Now is the time to install the best possible Government as we are clearly approaching a climax in the next few months."

Ambassador Taylor apparently obtained what concurrence was possible and on Feb. 18 another cable went out from the State Department to London and eight United States Embassies in the Far East besides the one in Saigon. The message told the ambassadors of the forthcoming bombing campaign and instructed them to "inform head of government or State (as appropriate) of above in strictest confidence and report reactions." [See Document #95.]

Both McGeorge Bundy and Ambassador Taylor had recommended playing down publicity on the details of the raids. "Careful public statements of U.S.G. [United States Government], combined with fact of continuing air actions, are expected to make it clear that military action will continue while aggression continues," the cable said. "But focus of public attention will be kept as far as possible on D.R.V. aggression; not on joint GVN/US military operations.

The President had scheduled the first of the sustained raids, Rolling Thunder I, for Feb. 20. Five hours after the State Department transmitted that cable, a perennial Saigon plotter, Col. Pham Ngoc Thao, staged an unsuccessful "semi-coup" against General Khanh and "pandemonium reigned in Saigon," the study recounts. "Ambassador Taylor promptly recommended cancellation of the Feb. 20 air strikes and his recommendation was equally promptly accepted" by Washington, the Pentagon study says.

The State Department sent a cablegram to the various embassies rescinding the instructions to notify heads of government or state of the planned air war until further notice "in view of the disturbed situation in Saigon."

The situation there, the study says, remained "disturbed" for nearly a week while the Young Turks also sought to get rid of General Khanh.

"The latter made frantic but unsuccessful efforts to rally his supporters," the study says, and finally took off in his plane to avoid having to resign as commander in chief. "Literally running out of gas in Nhatrang shortly before dawn on Feb. 21, he submitted his resignation, claiming that a 'foreign hand' was behind the coup. No one, however, could be quite certain that Khanh might not 're-coup' once again, unless he were physically removed from the scene."

This took three more days to accomplish, and on Feb. 25 General Khanh finally went into permanent exile as an ambassador at large, with Ambassador Taylor seeing him off at the airport, "glassily polite," in the study's words. "It was only then that Taylor was able to issue, and Washington could accept, clearance for the long-postponed and frequently rescheduled first Rolling Thunder strike."

Less than three weeks earlier, in his memorandum to the President predicting that "a policy of sustained reprisal" might bring a better government in Saigon, McGeorge Bundy had said he did not agree with Ambassador Taylor that General Khanh "must somehow be removed from the . . . scene."

"We see no one else in sight with anything like his ability to combine military authority with some sense of politics," the account quotes Mr. Bundy as having written.

In the meantime two more Rolling Thunder strikes—II and III—had also been scheduled and then cancelled because, the study says, the South Vietnamese Air Force was on "coup alert," in Saigon.

During part of this period, air strikes against North Vietnam were also inhibited by a diplomatic initiative from the Soviet Union and Britain. They moved to reactivate their co-chairmanship of the 1954 Geneva conference on Indochina to consider the current Vietnam crisis. Secretary Rusk cabled Ambassador Taylor that the diplomatic initiative would not affect Washington's decision to begin the air war, merely its timing.

According to the Pentagon study, the Administration regarded the possibility of reviving the Geneva conference of 1954, which had ended the French Indochina War, "not as a potential negotiating opportunity, but as a convenient vehicle for public expression of a tough U.S. position."

But, the account adds, this "diplomatic gambit" had "languished" by the time General Khanh left Saigon, and the day of his departure Mr. Johnson scheduled a strike, Rolling Thunder IV, for Feb. 26.

The pilots had been standing by, for nearly a week, with the orders to execute a strike being canceled every 24 hours.

But the order to begin the raid was again canceled, a last time, by monsoon weather for four more days.

Rolling Thunder finally rolled on March 2, 1965, when F-100 Super Sabre and F-105 Thunderchief jets of the United States Air Force bombed an ammunition depot at Xombang while 19 propeller-driven A-1H fighter-bombers of South Vietnam struck the Quangkhe naval base.

The various arguments in the Administration over how the raids ought to be conducted, which had developed during the planning stages, were now revived in sharper form by the opening blow in the actual air war.

Secretary McNamara, whose attention to management of resources and cost-effectiveness is cited repeatedly by the study, was concerned about improving the military efficacy of the bombing even before the sustained air war got under way.

He had received bomb damage assessments on the two reprisal strikes in February, reporting that of 491 buildings attacked, only 47 had been destroyed and 22 damaged. The information "caused McNamara to fire off a rather blunt memorandum" to Gen. Earle G. Wheeler, Chairman of the Joint Chiefs of Staff, on Feb. 17, the account says.

"Although the four missions [flown during the two raids] left the operations at the targets relatively unimpaired, I am quite satisfied with the results," Mr. McNamara began. "Our primary objective, of course, was to communicate our political resolve. This I believe we did. Future communications or resolve, however, will carry a hollow ring unless we accomplish more military damage than we have to date. . . . Surely we cannot continue for months accomplishing no more with 267 sorties than we did on these four missions." A sortie is a flight by a single plane.

General Wheeler replied that measures were being taken to heighten the destructiveness of the strikes and said that one way to accomplish this was to give the operational commander on the scene "adequate latitude" to attack the target as he saw fit, rather than seeking to control the details from Washington.

One measure approved by the President on March 9 was the use of napalm in North Vietnam.

And the day before, the day that 3,500 marines came ashore at Danang to protect the airfield there, Ambassador Taylor had already expressed, in two cables to Washington, what the historian describes as "sharp annoyance" with the "unnecessarily timid and ambivalent" way in which the air war was being conducted.

No air strikes had been authorized by the President beyond the initial Rolling Thunder raids that began on March 2, and, according to the study, the Ambassador was irritated at "the long delays between strikes, the marginal weight of the attacks and the great ado about behind-the-scenes diplomatic feelers."

With the concurrence of General Westmoreland, Ambassador Taylor proposed "a more dynamic schedule of strikes, a several week program relentlessly marching north" beyond the 19th Parallel, which President Johnson had so far set as a limit, "to break the will of the D.R.V."

Ambassador Taylor cabled: "Current feverish diplomatic activity particularly by French and British" was interfering with the ability of the United States to "progressively turn the screws on D.R.V."

"It appears to me evident that to date D.R.V. leaders believe air strikes at present levels on their territory are meaningless and that we are more susceptible to international pressure for negotiations than they are," the Ambassador said. He cited as evidence a report from J. Blair Seaborn, the Canadian member of the International Control Commission, who, in Hanoi earlier that month, had performed one of the series of secret diplomatic missions for the United States.

Mr. Seaborn had been sent back to convey directly to the

Hanoi leaders an American policy statement on Vietnam that had been delivered to China on Feb. 24 through its embassy in Warsaw.

In essence, the Pentagon study reports, the policy statement said that while the United States was determined to take whatever measures were necessary to maintain South Vietnam, it "had no designs on the territory of North Vietnam, nor any desire to destroy the D.R.V."

The delivery of the message to the Chinese was apparently aimed at helping to stave off any Chinese intervention as a result of the forthcoming bombing campaign.

But the purpose in sending Mr. Seaborn back, the study makes clear, was to convey the obvious threat that Hanoi now faced "extensive future destruction of . . . military and economic investments" if it did not call off the Vietcong guerrillas and accept a separate, non-Communist South.

Premier Pham Van Dong of North Vietnam, who had seen Mr. Seaborn on two earlier visits, declined this time, and the Canadian had to settle for the chief North Vietnamese liaison officer for the commission, to whom he read Washington's statement.

The North Vietnamese officer, the account says, commented that the message "contained nothing new and that the North Vietnamese had already received a briefing on the Warsaw meeting" from the Chinese Communists.

This treatment led the Canadian to sense "a mood of confidence" among the Hanoi leaders, Ambassador Taylor told Washington in a cablegram, and Mr. Seaborn felt "that Hanoi has the impression that our air strikes are a limited attempt to improve our bargaining position and hence are no great cause for immediate concern."

"Our objective should be to induce in D.R.V. leadership an attitude favorable to U.S. objectives in as short a time as possible in order to avoid a build-up of international pressure to negotiate," the Ambassador said.

Therefore, he went on, it was necessary to "begin at once a progression of U.S. strikes north of 19th Parallel in a slow but steadily ascending movement" to dispel any illusions in Hanoi.

"If we tarry too long in the south [below the 19th Parallel], we will give Hanoi a weak and misleading signal which will work against our ultimate purpose," he said.

The next Rolling Thunder strikes, on March 14 and 15, were the heaviest of the air war so far, involving 100 American and 24 South Vietnamese planes against barracks and depots on Tiger Island off the North Vietnamese coast and the ammunition dump near Phuqui, 100 miles southwest of Hanoi.

For the first time, the planes used napalm against the North, a measure approved by Mr. Johnson on March 9 to achieve the more efficient destruction of the targets that Mr. McNamara was seeking and to give the pilots protection from antiaircraft batteries.

But the Ambassador regarded these, too, as an "isolated, stage-managed joint U.S./GVN operation," the Pentagon study says. He sent Washington another cable, saying that "through repeated delays we are failing to give the mounting crescendo to Rolling Thunder which is necessary to get the desired results."

Meanwhile, Admiral Sharp in Honolulu and the Joint Chiefs in Washington were quickly devising a number of other programs to broaden and intensify the air war now that it had begun.

On March 21, Admiral Sharp proposed a "radar busting day" to knock out the North Vietnamese early-warning system, and a program "to attrite harass and interdict the D.R.V. south" of the 20th Parallel by cutting lines of communication, "LOC" in official terminology.

The "LOC cut program" would choke off traffic along all roads and rail lines through southern North Vietnam by bombing strikes and would thus squeeze the flow of supplies into the South.

"All targets selected are extremely difficult or impossible to bypass," the admiral said in a cable to the Joint Chiefs. "LOC network cutting in this depth will degrade tonnage arrivals at the main 'funnels' and will develop a broad series of new targets such as backed-up convoys, offloaded matériel dumps and personnel staging areas at one or both sides of cuts."

These probable effects might in turn "force major D.R.V. log flow to seacarry and into surveillance and attack by our SVN [South Vietnamese] coastal sanitization forces," the admiral added.

In Washington at this time, the narrative goes on, the Joint Chiefs were engaged in an "interservice division" over potential ground-troop deployments to Vietnam and over the air war itself.

Gen. John P. McConnell, Chief of Staff of the Air Force adopted a "maverick position" and was arguing for a short and violent 28-day bombing campaign. All of the targets on the original 94-target list drawn up in May, 1964, from bridges to industries, would be progressively destroyed.

"He proposed beginning the air strikes in the southern part of North Vietnam and continuing at two- to six-day intervals until Hanoi was attacked," the study continues.

The raids would be along the lines of the mighty strikes, including the use of B-52 bombers, that the Joint Chiefs had proposed in retaliation for the Vietcong mortar attack in Beinhoa airfield on Nov. 1, 1964, the narrative says. General McConnell contended that his plan was consistent with previous bombing proposals by the Joint Chiefs.

The general abandoned his proposal, however, when the other members of the Joint Chiefs decided to incorporate Admiral Sharp's "LOC cut program" and some of General McConnell's individual target concepts into a bombing program of several weeks. They proposed this to Mr. McNamara on March 27.

This plan proposed an intense bombing campaign that would start on road and rail lines south of the 20th Parallel and then "march north" week by week to isolate North Vietnam from China gradually by cutting road and rail lines above Hanoi. In later phases upon which the Joint Chiefs had not yet fully decided, the port facilities were to be destroyed to isolate North Vietnam from the sea. Then industries outside populated areas would be attacked "leading up to a situation where the enemy will realize that the Hanoi and Haiphong areas will be the next logical targets in our continued air campaign."

But the President and Mr. McNamara declined to approve any multiweek program, the study relates. "They clearly preferred to retain continual personal control over attack concepts and individual target selection."

In mid-March, after a Presidential fact-finding trip to Vietnam by Gen. Harold K. Johnson, the Army Chief of Staff, the President did regularize the bombing campaign and relaxed some of the restrictions. Among the innovations was the selection of the targets in weekly packages with the precise timing of the individual attacks left to the commanders on the scene. Also, "the strikes were no longer to be specifically related to VC atrocities" and "publicity on the strikes was to be progressively reduced," the study says.

The President did not accept two recommendations from General Johnson relating to a possible ground war. They were to dispatch a division of American troops to South Vietnam to hold coastal enclaves or defend the Central Highlands in order to free Saigon Government forces for offensive action against the Vietcong. The second proposal was to create a four-division force of American and Southeast Asia Treaty

Organization troops, who, to interdict infiltration, would patrol both the demilitarized zone along the border separating North and South Vietnam and the Laotian border region.

Better organization for the air war meant that concepts such as Admiral Sharp's "LOC cut program" and his "radar busting" were now incorporated into the weekly target packages. But President Johnson and Secretary McNamara continued to select the targets and to communicate them to the Joint Chiefs—and thus, eventually, to the operating strike forces—in weekly Rolling Thunder planning messages issued by the Secretary of Defense.

Operation Rolling Thunder was thus being shifted from an exercise in air power "dominated by political and psychological considerations" to a "militarily more significant, sustained bombing program" aimed at destroying the capabilities of North Vietnam to support a war in the South.

But the shift also meant that "early hopes that Rolling Thunder could succeed by itself" in persuading Hanoi to call off the Vietcong were also waning.

"The underlying question that was being posed for the Administration at this time was well formulated," the study says, by Mr. McNaughton in a memorandum drafted on March 24 for Secretary McNamara in preparation for the April 1-2 National Security Council meetings.

"Can the situation inside SVN be bottomed out (a) without extreme measures against the DRV and/or (b) without deployment of large numbers of U.S. (and other) combat troops inside SVN?"

Mr. McNaughton's answer was "perhaps, but probably no." [See Document #96.]

General Westmoreland stated his conclusions in a half-inch-thick report labeled "Commander's Estimate of the situation in SVN." The document, "a classic Leavenworth-style analysis," the analyst remarks, referring to the Command and General Staff College, was completed in Saigon on March 26 and delivered to Washington in time for the April 1-2 strategy meeting.

The Saigon military commander and his staff had begun working on this voluminous report on March 13, the day after General Johnson left Vietnam with his ground war proposals of an American division to hold enclaves and a four-division American and SEATO force along the borders, the study notes.

General Westmoreland predicted that the bombing campaign against the North would not show tangible results until

June at the earliest, and that in the meantime the South Vietnamese Army needed American reinforcements to hold the line against growing Vietcong strength and to carry out an "orderly" expansion of its own ranks.

And, paraphrasing the report, the study says that the general warned that the Saigon troops, "although at the moment peforming fairly well, would not be able in the face of a VC summer offensive to hold in the South long enough for the bombing to become effective."

General Westmoreland asked for reinforcements equivalent to two American divisions, a total of about 70,000 troops, counting those already in Vietnam.

They included 17 maneuver battalions. The general proposed adding two more Marine battalion landing teams to the two battalions already at Danang in order to establish another base at the airfield at Phubai to the north; putting an Army brigade into the Bienhoa-Vungtau area near Saigon, and using two more Army battalions to garrison the central coastal ports of Quinhon and Nhatrang as logistics bases. These bases would sustain an army division that General Westmoreland proposed to send into active combat in the strategic central highlands inland to "defeat" the Vietcong who were seizing control there.

General Westmoreland said that he wanted the 17 battalions and their initial supporting elements in South Vietnam by June and indicated that more troops might be required thereafter if the bombing failed to achieve results.

The Saigon military commander and General Johnson were not alone in pressing for American ground combat troops to forestall a Vietcong victory, the study points out.

On March 20, the Joint Chiefs as a body had proposed sending two American divisions and one South Korean division to South Vietnam for offensive combat operations against the guerrillas.

Secretary McNamara, the Joint Chiefs and Ambassador Taylor all discussed the three-division proposal on March 29, the study relates, while the Ambassador was in Washington for the forthcoming White House strategy conference.

The Ambassador opposed the plan, the study says, because he felt the South Vietnamese might resent the presence of so many foreign troops—upwards of 100,000 men—and also because he believed there was still no military necessity for them.

The Joint Chiefs "had the qualified support of Mc-

Namara," however, the study continues, and was one of the topics discussed at the national security council meeting.

Thus, the study says, at the White House strategy session of April 1-2, "the principal concern of Administration policy makers at this time was with the prospect of major deployment of U.S. and third-country combat forces to SVN."

A memorandum written by McGeorge Bundy before the meeting, which set forth the key issues for discussion and decision by the President, "gave only the most superficial treatment to the complex matter of future air pressure policy," the Pentagon analyst remarks.

The morning that Ambassador Taylor left Saigon to attend the meeting, March 29, the Vietcong guerrillas blew up the American Embassy in Saigon in what the study calls "the boldest and most direct Communist action against the U.S. since the attacks at Pleiku and Quinhon which had precipitated the Flaming Dart reprisal airstrikes."

Admiral Sharp requested permission to launch a "spectacular" air raid on North Vietnam in retaliation, the narrative continues, but the "plea . . . did not fall on responsive ears" at the White House.

"At this point, the President preferred to maneuver quietly to help the nation get used to living with the Vietnam crisis. He played down any drama intrinsic in Taylor's arrival" and refused to permit a retaliation raid for the embassy bombing.

"After his first meeting with Taylor and other officials on March 31, the President responded to press inquiries concerning dramatic new developments by saying: "I know of no far-reaching strategy that is being suggested or promulgated."

"But the President was being less than candid," the study observes. "The proposals that were at that moment being promulgated, and on which he reached significant decision the following day, did involve a far-reaching strategy change: acceptance of the concept of U.S. troops engaged in offensive ground operations against Asian insurgents. This issue greatly overshadowed all other Vietnam questions then being reconsidered."

The analyst is referring to the President's decision at the White House strategy conference on April 1-2 to change the mission of the Marine battalions at Danang from defense to offense.

McGeorge Bundy embodied the decision in National Security Action Memorandum 328, which he drafted and signed on behalf of the President on April 6. The analyst says that this "pivotal document" followed almost "verbatim" the text of another memorandum that Mr. Bundy had written before the N.S.C. meeting to outline the proposals for discussion and decision by the President.

The Pentagon study notes that the actual landing of 3,500 marines at Danang the previous month had "caused surprisingly little outcry."

Secretary of State Rusk had explained on a television program the day before the marines came ashore that their mission was solely to provide security for the air base and "not to kill the Vietcong," in the words of the study. This initial mission for the marines was later to be referred to as the short-lived strategy of security that would apply only to this American troop movement into South Vietnam.

The President's decision to change their mission to offense now made the strategy of base security "a dead letter," the study says, when it was less than a month old.

At the April 1–2 meeting, Mr. Johnson had also decided to send ashore two more Marine battalions, which General Westmoreland had asked for in a separate request on March 17. Mr. Johnson further decided to increase support forces in South Vietnam by 18,000 to 20,000 men.

The President was "doubtless aware" of the general's additional request for the equivalent of two divisions, and of the Joint Chiefs' for three divisions, the Pentagon account says, but Mr. Johnson took no action on them.

"The initial steps in ground build-up appear to have been grudgingly taken," the study says, "indicating that the President . . . and his advisers recognized the tremendous inertial complications of ground troop deployments. Halting ground involvement was seen to be a manifestly greater problem than halting air or naval activity.

"It is pretty clear, then, that the President intended, after the early April N.S.C. meetings, to cautiously and carefully experiment with the U.S. forces in offensive roles," the analyst concludes.

National Security Action Memorandum 328 did not precisely define or limit the offensive role it authorized, and Ambassador Taylor, who had attended the National Security Council meeting during his visit to Washington, was not satisfied with the guidance he received from the State Department. Therefore, on his way back to Saigon on April 4, the Ambassador, formerly President John F. Kennedy's military adviser and Chairman of the Joint Chiefs, sent a cable from the Honolulu headquarters of the Commander of Pacific forces to the State Department, saying:

"I propose to describe the new mission to [Premier Pham Huy] Quat as the use of marines in a mobile counter-insurgency role in the vicinity of Danang for the improved protection of that base and also in a strike role as a reserve in support of ARVN operations anywhere within 50 miles of the base. This latter employment would follow acquisition of experience on local counter-insurgency missions."

Ambassador Taylor's 50-mile limit apparently became an accepted rule-of-thumb boundary for counterinsurgency strikes.

And so, the analyst sums up, with the promulgation of National Security Action Memorandum 328, "the strategy of security effectively becomes a dead letter on the first of April," and the strategy of enclave begins.

Confusion and Suspicion

There was some confusion, suspicion and controversy about the President's approval of an 18,000-20,000 increase in support troops, which, he explained, was meant "to fill out existing units and supply needed logistic personnel."

On April 21, Secretary McNamara told the President that 11,000 of these new men would augment various existing forces, while 7,000 were logistic troops to support "previously approved forces."

"It isn't entirely clear from the documents exactly what the President did have in mind for the support troop add-ons," the study comments. "What is clear, however, . . . was that the J.C.S. were continuing to plan for the earliest possible introduction of two to three divisions into RVN." The analyst cites a memorandum from Mr. McNamara to General Wheeler on April 6 as evidence of this planning.

Later, on May 5, the study continues, Assistant Secretary of Defense McNaughton would send a memorandum to Deputy Secretary of Defense Cyrus R. Vance, saying that "the J.C.S. misconstrued the [support] add-ons to mean logistic build-up for coastal enclaves and the possible later introduction of two to three divisions." (These were the divisions the Joint Chiefs had requested on March 20.)

The enclave strategy had as its object the involvement of

United States combat units at "relatively low risk." It proposed "that U.S. troops occupy coastal enclaves, accept full responsibility for enclave security, and be prepared to go to the rescue of the RVNF as far as 50 miles outside the enclave. . . . The intent was not to take the war to the enemy but rather to deny him certain critical areas," the study says.

To prove the viability of its "reserve reaction," the analyst goes on, the enclave strategy required testing, but the rules for committing United States troops under it had not been worked out by the time it was overtaken by events—a series of major military victories by the Vietcong in May and June that led to the adoption of the search and destroy strategy.

Search and destroy, the account says, was "articulated by Westmoreland and the J.C.S. in keeping with sound military principles garnered by men accustomed to winning. The basic idea . . . was the desire to take the war to the enemy, denying him freedom of movement anywhere in the country . . . and deal him the heaviest possible blows." In the meantime, the South Vietnamese Army "would be free to concentrate their efforts in populated areas."

From April 11 through April 14, the additional two Marine battalions were deployed at Hue-Phubai and at Danang, bringing the total maneuver battalions to four.

"The marines set about consolidating and developing their two coastal base areas, and, although they pushed their patrol perimeters out beyond their tactical wire and thereby conducted active rather than passive defense, they did not engage in any offensive operations in support of ARVN for the next few months," the study says.

At this point, the Defense Department, the Joint Chiefs and General Westmoreland collaborated—as it turned out, successfully—in what the study calls "a little cart-before-horsemanship." It involved the deployment to South Vietnam of the 173d Airborne Brigade, two battalions that were then situated on Okinawa in a reserve role.

General Westmoreland had had his eye on the 173d for some time. On March 26, in his "Commander's Estimate of the Situation," in which he requested the equivalent of two divisions, he also recommended that the 173d Airborne Brigade be deployed to the Bienhoa-Vungtau areas "to secure vital U.S. installations." This recommendation, like that for two divisions, was not acted upon by the National Security Council in the April 1-2 meeting.

On April 11, General Westmoreland cabled Admiral Sharp, the Pacific commander, that he understood from the National

Security Council's meetings and Ambassador Taylor's discussions in Washington at the beginning of the month that his requested divisions were not in prospect. But, he said, he still wanted the 173d Airborne Brigade.

This message, the study says, set in motion "a series of cables, proposals and false starts which indicated that Washington was well ahead of Saigon in its planning and in its anxiety."

The upshot of all this communication was that at a meeting in Honolulu of representatives of the Joint Chiefs and the Pacific command from April 10 to April 12, the deployment of the 173d Airborne Brigade was recommended. On April 14, the Joint Chiefs of Staff ordered the deployment to Bienhoa-Vungtau, and the replacement of the brigade by one from the United States.

"This decision to deploy the 173d apparently caught the Ambassador flatfooted," the study says, "for he had quite obviously not been privy to it."

On the day of the Joint Chiefs' decision, Ambassador Taylor cabled the State Department that "this [decision on the deploying the brigade] comes as a complete surprise in view of the understanding reached in Washington [during his visit] that we would experiment with the marines in a counterinsurgency role before bringing in other U.S. contingents." He asked that deployment of the brigade be held up until matters were sorted out.

However, the study notes, Ambassador Taylor "held the trump card" because the proposed action had to be cleared with Premier Quat, and the Ambassador told his superiors on April 17 that he did not intend to tell the Premier without clearer guidance explaining Washington's intentions. [See Document #99.]

"That Washington was determined, with the President's sanction, to go beyond what had been agreed to and formalized in NSAM 328 was manifested unmistakably in a cable under joint Defense/State auspices by Mr. McNaughton to the Ambassador on 15 April," the Pentagon study says.

In the cablegram, Mr. McNaughton said: "Highest authority [the President] believes the situation in South Vietnam has been deteriorating and that, in addition to actions against the North, something new must be added in the South to achieve victory." He then listed seven recommended actions, including the introduction of military-civil affairs personnel into the air effort and the deployment of the 173d Airborne Brigade to Bienhoa-Vungtau "as a security force for our installions and also to participate in counterinsurgency combat operations" according to General Westmoreland's plans.

Reacting to that cable on April 17, Ambassador Taylor protested to McGeorge Bundy in the White House against the introduction of military-civilian affairs personnel into the aid effort. The Ambassador's cablegram continued by saying that the McNaughton message "shows a far greater willingness to get into the ground war than I had discerned in Washington during my recent trip."

"Mac, can't we be better protected from our friends?" the Ambassador asked. "I know that everyone wants to help, but there's such a thing as killing with kindness."

Discussing the contretemps between the Pentagon and General Taylor, the study says: "The documents do not reveal just exactly when Presidential sanction was obtained for the expanded scope of the above [McNaughton] proposals. It is possible that [on the approval for deploying the brigade] the Ambassador may have caught the Defense Department and the J.C.S. in a little cart-before-horsemanship."

In any event, on April 15, the day after it had ordered the deployment of the brigade, the J.C.S. sent a memorandum to Secretary McNamara dealing with the Ambassador's objections and still insisting that the brigade was needed.

"Whether or not the J.C.S. wrote that memorandum with red faces," the study remarks, "the Secretary of Defense dates approval for final deployment of the 173d as of the 30th of April."

Pressure From Military

The strategy of base security having been ended by National Security Action Memorandum 328, a high-level meeting began in Honolulu on April 20 to "sanctify" and "structure", as the Pentagon analyst puts it, "an expanded enclave strategy."

Present at the meeting were Secretary of Defense McNamara; William Bundy, Assistant Secretary of State for Far Eastern Affairs; Assistant Secretary of Defense McNaughton; Ambassador Taylor; Admiral Sharp; General Wheeler and General Westmoreland.

"Some of these men had helped produce the current optimism in situation reports and cables," the Pentagon study says, "and yet the consensus of their meeting was that the then-present level of Vietcong activity was nothing but the lull before the storm.

"The situation which presented itself to the Honolulu conferees was in many ways the whole Vietnam problem in microcosm. What was needed to galvanize everyone to action was some sort of dramatic event within South Vietnam itself. Unfortunately, the very nature of the war precluded the abrupt collapse of a front or the loss of large chunks of territory in lightning strokes by the enemy. The enemy in this war was spreading his control and influence slowly and inexorably but without drama. The political infrastructure from which he derived his strength took years to create, and in most areas the expansion of control was hardly felt until it was a fait accompli."

Of the conferees, the study says, "by far the most dogged protagonist of the enclave strategy was Ambassador Taylor." It had already become apparent, however, and was to become manifestly clear at Honolulu, that the Ambassador was fighting a rear-guard action against both civilian and military officials in the Pentagon who were bent on expansion of U.S. forces in South Vietnam and an enlargement of their combat mission.

On March 18, in a message to Washington, Ambassador Taylor had suggested that if a division were sent to South Vietnam as had been proposed by the Army Chief of Staff, General Johnson, then consideration should be given to deploying it in either a highland or coastal enclave.

When he got no response, Ambassador Taylor sent another message on March 27, stating that if United States forces were to come, his preference was, as the study says, that they be used in a combination of defensive or offensive enclave plus reserve for an emergency, rather than in "territorial clear and hold" operations.

The Ambassador, the study notes, interpreted the pivotal National Security Action Memorandum as supporting his position, because in it the President seemed to make plain that he "wanted to experiment very carefully with a small amount of force before deciding whether or not to accept any kind of ground war commitment."

Therefore, the study says, "the Ambassador was surprised to discover that the marines [the two additional battalions that landed April 11-14] had come ashore with tanks, self-propelled artillery, and various other items of weighty equipment not 'appropriate for counterinsurgency operations.'"

In his April 17 cable to McGeorge Bundy, Ambassador

Taylor had also protested the "hasty and ill-conceived" proposals for the deployment of more forces with which he was being flooded.

"Thus was the Ambassador propelled into the conference of 20 April 1965, only one step ahead of the Washington juggernaut, which was itself fueled by encouragement from Westmoreland in Saigon," the study comments. "Taylor was not opposed to the U.S. build-up *per se,* but rather was concerned to move slowly with combat troop deployments . . . He was overtaken in Honolulu."

According to Mr. McNaughton's minutes, the conference in preliminary discussions on April 20 agreed that:

"(1) The D.R.V. was not likely to quit within the next six months; and in any case, they were more likely to give up because of VC failure in the South than because of bomb-induced 'pain' in the North. It could take up to two years to demonstrate VC failure.

"(2) The level of air activity through Rolling Thunder was about right. The U.S. did not, in Ambassador Taylor's words, want 'to kill the hostage.' Therefore, Hanoi and environs remained on the restricted list. It was recognized that air activity would not do the job alone.

"(3) Progress in the South would be slow, and great care should be taken to avoid dramatic defeat. The current lull in Vietcong activity was merely the quiet before a storm.

"(4) The victory strategy was to 'break the will of the D.R.V./VC by denying them victory.' Impotence would lead eventually to a political solution."

At the time of the Honolulu conference, the study notes, "the level of approved U.S. forces for Vietnam was 40,200," but 33,500 were actually in the country at that time.

"To accomplish the 'victory strategy' described above," the study continues, the conferees agreed that U.S. ground forces should be increased from 4 to 13 maneuver battalions and to 82,000 men. The United States, they agreed, should also seek to get additional troops from Australia and South Korea that would bring the so-called third-country strength to four maneuver battalions and 7,250 men.

Thus, the Honolulu conferees proposed raising the recommended United States-third country strength to 17 battalions.

The conferees also mentioned but did not recommend a possible later deployment of 11 U.S. and 6 South Korean battalions, which, when added to the approved totals, would bring the United States-third country combat capability to 34 battalions. In this later possible deployment was included an Army airmobile division.

Secretary McNamara forwarded the Honolulu recommendations to the President on April 21, together with a notation on possible later deployment of the airmobile division and the Third Marine Expeditionary Force.

On April 30 the Joint Chiefs presented a detailed program for deployment of some 48,000 American and 5,250 third-country soldiers. "Included were all the units mentioned in the Honolulu recommendations plus a healthy support package," the study says.

The Joint Chiefs said that these additional forces were "to bolster GVN forces during their continued build-up, secure bases and installations, conduct counterinsurgency combat operations in coordination with the RVNAF, and prepare for the later introduction of an airmobile division to the central plateau, the remainder of the third M.E.F. [the marine force] to the Danang area, and the remainder of a ROK [Republic of Korea] division to Quangngai."

From the thrust of this memorandum by the Joint Chiefs, the analyst comments, "it is apparent that the enclave strategy was no stopping place as far as the Chiefs were concerned. They continued to push hard for the earliest possible input of three full divisions of troops. They were still well ahead of the pack in that regard."

The Enemy Responds

The question of final Presidential approval of the 17-battalion recommendations now became academic as the enemy started attacks that provided the Pentagon and General Westmoreland with a battlefield rationale for their campaign to have American troops take over the major share of the ground war.

As the manpower debates continued in March and April, the study portrays the military situation: "The Vietcong were unusually inactive throughout March and April. There had been no major defeat of the enemy's forces and no signs of any major shift in strategy on his part. Hence it was assumed that he was merely pausing to regroup and to assess the effect of the changed American participation in the war embodied in air strikes and in the marines," the first two battalions deployed at Danang on March 8.

"There were, however, plenty of indications in the early spring of 1965 of what was to come," the study continues. . . . "From throughout the country came reports that Vietcong troops and cadres were moving into central Vietnam and into areas adjacent to the ring of provinces . . . around Saigon."

"Finally and most ominous of all," the study says, a memorandum by the Central Intelligence Agency and the Defense Intelligence Agency on April 21, 1965, "reflected the acceptance into the enemy order of battle of one regiment of the 325th PAVN [People's Army of Vietnam] division said to be located in Kontum province. The presence of this regular North Vietnamese unit, which had been first reported as early as February, was a sobering harbinger. . . ."

On May 11, when the Vietcong attacked Songbe, the capital of Phuoclong Province, using more than a regiment of troops, "the storm broke in earnest," the study says. The enemy overran the town and the American advisers' compound, causing heavy casualties. After holding the town for a day, the Vietcong withdrew, the study relates.

Later in May, in Quangngai Province in the northern part of South Vietnam, a battalion of Government troops—the Army of the Republic of Vietnam—was ambushed and overrun near Bagia, west of Quangngai. Reinforcements were also ambushed.

"The battle," the study says, "dragged on for several days and ended in total defeat for the ARVN. Two battalions were completely decimated. . . . From Bagia came a sense of urgency, at least among some of the senior U.S. officers who had been witness to the battle."

Then in June, two Vietcong regiments attacked an outpost at Dongxoai and when Government reinforcements were committed "piecemeal" they were "devoured by the enemy" the Pentagon study says.

"My mid-June, 1965," it asserts, "the Vietcong summer offensive was in full stride." By mid-July, the Vietcong were "systematically forcing the GVN to yield what little control it still exercised in rural areas outside the Mekong Delta."

On June 7, after the attack on Bagia, General Westmoreland sent a long message on the military situation and his needs to the Pacific Commander for relay to the Joint Chiefs.

"In pressing their campaign," the general said, "the Vietcong are capable of mounting regimental-size operations in all four ARVN corps areas, and at least battalion-sized attack in virtually all provinces. . . .

"ARVN forces on the other hand are already experiencing difficulty in coping with this increased VC capability. Desertion rates are inordinately high. Battle losses have been higher than expected; in fact, four ARVN battalions have been rendered ineffective by VC action in the I and II Corps zones. . . .

"Thus, the GVN/VC force ratios upon which we based our estimate of the situation in March have taken an adverse trend. You will recall that I recommended the deployment of a U.S. division in II Corps to cover the period of the RVNAF build-up and to weight the force ratios in that important area. We assumed at that time that the ARVN battalions would be brought to full strength by now and that the force build-up would proceed on schedule. Neither of these assumptions has materialized. . . .

"In order to cope with the situation outlined above, I see no course of action open to us except to reinforce our efforts in SVN with additional U.S. or third country forces as rapidly as is practical during the critical weeks ahead."

What General Westmoreland asked for added up to a total force of 44 battalions and the June 7 message became known as the "44-battalion request."

Just as intense internal debate was beginning on the request, there was a "credibility" flare-up deriving from President Johnson's injunction of secrecy on the change of missions for the marines authorized on April 1 in National Security Action Memorandum 328.

"The long official silence between the sanction for U.S. offensive operations contained in NSAM 328 and the final approval [in negotiations with Saigon] of the conditions under which U.S. troops could be committed was not without cost," the study asserts. "The President had admonished each of the N.S.C. members not to allow release of provisions of the NSAM, but the unduly long interregnum inevitably led to leaks." In addition, the marines had 200 casualties, including 18 killed, as they went about "tidying up," as the study puts it, their newly assigned area in April and May.

"The Commandant of the Marine Corps," the study continues, "raised the tempo of speculation by saying to the press during an inspection trip to Vietnam in April that the marines were not in Vietnam to 'sit on their dittyboxes'—and they were there to 'kill Vietcong.'

"An honest and superficially innocuous statement by Department of State Press Officer Robert McCloskey on 8 June to the effect that 'American forces would be available for combat support together with Vietnamese forces when and if necessary' produced an immediate response [in the press].

"The White House was hoisted by its own petard. In an attempt to quell the outcry, a statement was issued on the 9th of June which, because of its ambiguity, only served to exacerbate the situation and to widen what was being described as 'the credibility gap'."

The White House statement said: "There has been no change in the mission of United States ground combat units in Vietnam in recent days or weeks. The President has issued no order of any kind in this regard to General Westmoreland recently or at any other time. The primary mission of these troops is to secure and safeguard important military installations like the air base at Danang. They have the associated mission of . . . patrolling and securing actions in and near the areas thus safeguarded.

"If help is requested by the appropriate Vietnamese commander, General Westmoreland also has authority within the assigned mission to employ those troops in support of Vietnamese forces faced with aggressive attack when other effective reserves are not available and when, in his judgment, the general military situation urgently requires it."

Discussing this statement, the Pentagon analyst says: "The documents do not reveal whether or not the ground rules for engagement of U.S. forces had actually been worked out to everyone's satisfaction at the time of the White House statement. There is good indication that they had not." The analyst also notes that during the battles of Bagia and Dongxoai, the Government forces "were desperately in need of assistance," but that United States forces were not committed although the marines were available for Bagia and the 173d Airborne Brigade for Dongxoai.

The study reports that the first major ground action by United States forces took place northwest of Saigon from June 27 to June 30, and involved the 173d Airborne Brigade, an Australian battalion and South Vietnamese forces.

"The operation could by no stretch of definition have been described as a reserve reaction," the study says. "It was a search and destroy operation into Vietcong base areas. . . . The excursion was a direct result of the sanction given to General Westmoreland . . . [as a result of National Security Action Memorandum 328 and the enemy offensive] to 'commit U.S. troops to combat, independent of or in conjunction

411

with GVN forces in any situation in which the use of such troops is requested by an appropriate GVN commander and when in [General Westmoreland's] judgment, their use is necessary to strengthen the relative position of GVN forces'." The wording of this sanction came in a State Department message.

However, as the study notes, "At that juncture the 44-battalion debate was in full swing and the enclave strategy, as a means to limit the amount and use of U.S. combat force in Vietnam, was certainly overcome by events," and by "a much more ambitious strategy sanctioned by the President."

Recapitulating the situation just before the debate, the study gives this picture of deployment: At the beginning of June, the enclave strategy was in its first stages with Marine Corps forces at Phubai, Danang and Chulai, and Army forces in Vungtau. Other enclaves were under consideration. Approved for deployment—but not all arrived in South Vietnam yet— were approximately 70,000 troops in 13 maneuver battalions; with third-country forces the total came to 77,250 men and 17 maneuver battalions.

This was the situation when, on June 7, General Westmoreland asked for reinforcements "as rapidly as possible."

General Westmoreland's message, the Pentagon study says, "stirred up a veritable hornet's nest in Washington," because his request for large reinforcements and his proposed strategy to go on the offensive "did not contain any of the comfortable restrictions and safeguards which had been part of every strategy debated to date."

"In such a move," the study continues "the specter of U.S. involvement in a major Asian ground war was there for all to see."

Just as Ambassador Taylor had consistently resisted involvement of United States forces, the study says, so General Westmoreland had been equally determined to get the troops into the war and have "a free hand" in using them.

At the time of his message, the general had available in Vietnam seven Marine and 2 Army maneuver battalions, plus an Australian battalion. Now, he was asking for a total of 33 battalions, and if the 173d Airborne Brigade's two battalions— which were on temporary assignment—were added, the total came to 35. But in a subparagraph, General Westmoreland also identified nine other United States battalions that he might request at a later date. Thus the total of 44 battalions, and hence the name given the request. In the total was included an airmobile division of nine battalions to be formed later.

Admiral Sharp favored the request in a message to the Joint Chiefs on June 7, saying, "We will lose by staying in enclaves defending coastal areas."

The Joint Chiefs, the Pentagon analyst says, favored bolstering the United States troop commitment. As far back as March 20, the Joint Chiefs had advocated sending three divisions—two American and one Korean—with the objective of "destroying the Vietcong."

Now, the study states, General Westmoreland's request "altered drastically the role of the J.C.S. in the build-up debate.

"Up to that time," the study continues, "the J.C.S. had, if anything, been ahead of General Westmoreland in advocating allied forces for Vietnam. The 27 battalions of their three-division plan were in themselves more than Westmoreland ever requested until 7 June. After that date, the big push came from Westmoreland in Saigon, and the J.C.S. were caught in the middle between the latter and the powerful and strident opposition his latest request for forces had surfaced in Washington."

On June 11, the Joint Chiefs cabled Admiral Sharp that something less than General Westmoreland's request was close to approval, but they wanted to know, the study says, "where Westmoreland intended to put this force in Vietnam."

He replied on June 13 in detail and the study comments: "This message was extremely important, for in it [he] spelled out the concept of keeping U.S. forces away from the people. The search and destroy strategy for U.S. and third country forces which continues to this day and the primary focus of RVNAF no pacification both stem from that concept. In addition, Westmoreland made a big pitch in this cable for a free hand to maneuver the troops around inside the country. . . ."

Ambassador Taylor, in a report on June 17, "confirmed the seriousness of the military situation as reported by General Westmoreland and also pointed up the very tenuous hold the new government had on the country." This was the Government of President Nguyen Van Thieu and Premier Nguyen Cao Ky.

"This report apparently helped to remove the last obstacles to consideration of all of the forces mentioned in Westmoreland's request of 7 June," the analyst says.

On June 22, General Wheeler cabled General Westmoreland and asked if the 44 battalions were enough to convince the enemy forces that they could not win. General Westmoreland replied, the study says, "that there was no evidence the

VC/DRV would alter their plans regardless of what the U.S. did in the next six months."

"The 44-battalion force should, however, establish a favorable balance of power by the end of the year," the study quotes the general as having said. "If the U.S. was to seize the initiative from the enemy, then further forces would be required into 1966 and beyond. . . ."

On June 26, the general was given authority to commit U.S. forces to battle when he decided they were necessary "to strengthen the relative position of GVN forces."

"This was about as close to a free hand in managing the forces as General Westmoreland was likely to get," the analyst says. "The strategy was finished, and the debate from then on centered on how much force and to what end."

Divergent Views at Home

The opposition to General Westmoreland had "its day in court," late in June and early in July, the study says. The embassy in Saigon, "while recognizing the seriousness of the situation in South Vietnam, was less then sanguine about the prospects for success if large numbers of foreign troops were brought in."

Another critic of General Westmoreland's recommendations, the account reports, was Under Secretary of State Ball who was "convinced that the U.S. was pouring its resources down the drain in the wrong place."

"In Ball's view," the account continues, "there was absolutely no assurance that the U.S. could with the provision of more ground forces achieve its political objectives in Vietnam. Instead, the U.S. risked involving itself in a costly and indeterminate struggle. To further complicate matters, it would be equally impossible to achieve political objectives by expanding the bombing of the North. . . ." [See Document #103.]

Assistant Secretary William P. Bundy, the study says, "like so many others found himself in between Westmoreland and Ball."

In a memorandum to the President on July 1, Mr. Bundy gave his position, as summarized in the Pentagon study:

"The U.S. needed to avoid the ultimatum aspects of the 44 battalions and also the Ball withdrawal proposal. . . . The U.S. should adopt a policy which would allow it to hold on without risking disasters of scale if the war were lost despite deployment of the full 44 battalions. For the moment, according to Bundy, the U.S. should complete planned deployments to bring in-country forces to 18 maneuver battalions and 85,000 men. . . . The forces in Vietnam, which Bundy assumed would be enough to prevent collapse, would be restricted to reserve reaction in support of RVNAF. This would allow for some experimentation without taking over the war effort—a familiar theme."

As for Secretary McNamara's views, the study comments: "It is difficult to be precise about the position of the Secretary of Defense during the build-up debate because there is so little of him in the files."

"There are plenty of other indications in the files that the Secretary was very carefully and personally insuring that the Defense Establishment was ready to provide efficient and sufficient support to the fighting elements in Vietnam," the study continues. "From the records, the Secretary comes out much more clearly for good management than he does for any particular strategy."

The Secretary went to South Vietnam for a four-day inspection starting July 16. The study says that while he was in Saigon on July 17, he received a cable from Deputy Secretary of Defense Vance informing him that the President had decided to go ahead with the plan to deploy 34 battalions.

"The debate was over," the analyst says. "McNamara left Saigon bearing Westmoreland recommendations for an even greater increase in forces. . . ."

The study says 34 battalions. This is not entirely clear, because in his request General Westmoreland had asked for a total of 33, and if the battalions of the 173rd Airborne Brigade were added, the total would be 35. The explanation apparently is that when the Airmobile Division was finally organized, it had eight rather than nine battalions. The 34 battalions were, of course, to be supplied immediately. The nine others were to be requested later if needed.

The Pentagon analyst apparently did not have access to White House memoranda, so he is able to give only a sketchy account of Mr. Johnson's role. But he says: "There is no question that the key figure in the early 1965 buildup was the President."

On May 4, the President asked Congress for a $700-million supplemental appropriation "to meet mounting military requirements in Vietnam."

"Nor can I guarantee this will be the last request," he said in a message. "If our need expands I will turn again to the Congress. For we will do whatever must be done to insure the safety of South Vietnam from aggression. This is the firm and irrevocable commitment of our people and nation."

On July 28, the President held a press conference in which he said, "The lesson of history dictated that the U.S. commit its strength to resist aggression in South Vietnam."

As for the troop increases, the President said:

"I have asked the commanding general, General Westmoreland, what more he needs to meet this mounting aggression. He has told me. We will meet his needs.

"I have today ordered to Vietnam the Airmobile Division and certain other forces which will raise our fighting strength from 75,000 to 125,000 men almost immediately. Additional forces will be needed later, and they will be sent as requested.
. . .

"I have concluded that it is not essential to order Reserve units into service now."

During the questioning after the announcement, this exchange took place:

"Q. Mr. President, does the fact that you are sending additional forces to Vietnam imply any change in the existing policy of relying mainly on the South Vietnamese to carry out offensive operations and using American forces to guard installations and to act as emergency back-up?

"A. It does not imply any change in policy whatever. It does not imply change of objective."

On July 30, the Joint Chiefs approved 44 maneuver battalions for deployment, involving a total of 193,887 United States troops. By the end of the year, United States forces in South Vietnam numbered 184,314.

"The major participants in the decision knew the choices and understood the consequences," the study says in summation. The decision taken in mid-July to commit 44 battalions of troops to battle in South Vietnam "was perceived as a threshold—entrance into an Asian land war. The conflict was seen to be long, with further U.S. deployments to follow. The choice at that time was not whether or not to negotiate, it was not whether to hold on for a while or let go—the choice was viewed as winning or losing South Vietnam."

Accompanying this decision to give General Westmoreland enough troops to embark on the first phase of his search-and-destroy strategy "was a subtle change of emphasis," the study says, adding:

"Instead of simply denying the enemy victory and convincing him that he could not win, the thrust became defeating the enemy in the South. This was sanctioned implicitly as the only way to achieve the U.S. objective of a non-Communist South Vietnam.

"The acceptance of the search-and-destroy strategy . ,. left the U.S. commitment to Vietnam open-ended. The implications in terms of manpower and money are inescapable.

"Final acceptance of the desirability of inflicting defeat on the enemy rather than merely denying him victory opened the door to an indeterminate amount of additional force."

Precisely what President Johnson and Secretary of Defense McNamara expected their decisions of July to bring within the near term "is not clear," the study says, "but there are manifold indications that they were prepared for a long war."

KEY DOCUMENTS

Following are texts of key documents accompanying the Pentagon's study of the Vietnam war, covering the opening of the sustained bombing campaign against North Vietnam in the first half of 1965. Except where excerpting is indicated, the documents are printed verbatim, with only unmistakable typographical errors corrected.

90

Letter from Rostow Favoring Commitment of Troops by U.S.

Personal letter from Walt W. Rostow, chairman of the State Department's Policy Planning Council, to Secretary McNamara, Nov. 16, 1964, "Military Dispositions and Political Signals."

Following on our conversation of last night I am concerned that too much thought is being given to the actual damage we do in the North, not enough thought to the signal we wish to send.

The signal consists of three parts:

a) damage to the North is now to be inflicted because they are violating the 1954 and 1962 accords;

b) we are ready and able to go much further than our initial act of damage;

c) we are ready and able to meet any level of escalation they might mount in response, if they are so minded.

Four points follow.

1. I am convinced that we should not go forward into the next stage without a U.S. ground force commitment of some kind:

a. The withdrawal of those ground forces could be a critically important part of our diplomatic bargaining position. Ground forces can sit during a conference more easily than we can maintain a series of mounting air and naval pressures.

b. We must make clear that counter escalation by the Communists will run directly into U.S. strength on the ground; and, therefore the possibility of radically extending their position on the ground at the cost of air and naval damage alone, is ruled out.

c. There is a marginal possibility that in attacking the airfield they were thinking two moves ahead; namely, they might be planning a pre-emptive ground force response to an expected U.S. retaliation for the Bien Hoa attack.

2. The first critical military action against North Vietnam should be designed merely to install the principle that they will, from the present forward, be vulnerable to retaliatory attack in the north for continued violations for the 1954 and 1962 Accords. In other words, we would signal a shift from the principle involved in the Tonkin Gulf response. This means that the initial use of force in the north should be as limited and as unsanguinary as possible. It is the installation of the principle that we are initially interested in, not tit for tat.

3. But our force dispositions to accompany an initial retaliatory move against the north should send three further signals lucidly:

a. that we are putting in place a capacity subsequently to step up direct and naval pressure on the north, if that should be required;

b. that we are prepared to face down any form of escalation North Vietnam might mount on the ground; and

c. that we are putting forces into place to exact retaliation directly against Communist China, if Peiping should join in an escalatory response from Hanoi. The latter could take the form of increased aircraft on Formosa plus, perhaps, a carrier force sitting off China distinguished from the force in the South China Sea.

4. The launching of this track, almost certainly, will require the President to explain to our own people and to the world our intentions and objectives. This will also be perhaps the most persuasive form of communication with Ho and Mao. In addition, I am inclined to think the most direct communication we can mount (perhaps via Vientiane and Warsaw) is desirable, as opposed to the use of cut-outs. They should feel they now confront an LBJ who has made up his mind. Contrary to an anxiety expressed at an earlier stage, I believe it quite possible to communicate the limits as well as the seriousness of our intentions without raising seriously the fear in Hanoi that we intend at our initiative to land immediately in the Red River Delta, in China, or seek any other objective than the re-installation of the 1954 and 1962 Accords.

91

Memo from Rostow Advocating Ground Troops and Air Attacks

Memorandum from Mr. Rostow to Secretary Rusk, Nov. 23, 1964, "Some Observations as We Come to the Crunch in Southeast Asia."

I leave for Lima this Saturday for the CIAP and CIES meetings. I presume that in early December some major decisions on Southeast Asia will be made. I should, therefore, like to leave with you some observations on the situation. I have already communicated them to Bill Bundy.

1. We must begin by fastening our minds as sharply as we can around our appreciation of the view in Hanoi and Peiping of the Southeast Asia problem. I agree almost completely with SNIE 10-3-64 of October 9. Here are the critical passages:

"While they will seek to exploit and encourage the deteriorating situation in Saigon, they probably will avoid actions that would in their view unduly increase the chances of a major U.S. response against North Vietnam (DRV) or Communist China. We are almost certain that both Hanoi and Peiping are anxious not to become involved in the kind of war in which the great weight of superior U.S. weaponry could be brought against them. Even if Hanoi and Peiping estimated that the U.S. would not use nuclear weapons against them, they could not be sure of this. . . .

"In the face of new U.S. pressures against the DRV further actions by Hanoi and Peiping would be based to a considerable extent on their estimate of U.S. intentions, i.e., whether the U.S. was actually determined to increase its pressures as necessary. Their estimates on this point are probably uncertain, but we believe that fear of provoking severe measures by the U.S. would lead them to temper their responses with a good deal of caution. . . .

"If despite Communist efforts, the U.S. attacks continued, Hanoi's leaders would have to ask themselves whether it was not better to suspend their support of Viet Cong military action rather than suffer the destruction of their major military facilities and the industrial sector of their economy. In the belief that the tide has set almost irreversibly in their favor in South Vietnam, they might calculate that the Viet Cong could stop its military attacks for the time being and renew the insurrection successfully at a later date. Their judgment in this matter might be reinforced by the Chinese Communist concern over becoming involved in a conflict with U.S. air and naval power."

Our most basic problem is, therefore, how to persuade them that a continuation of their present policy will risk major destruction in North Viet Nam; that a preemptive move on the ground as a prelude to negotiation will be met by U.S. strength on the ground; and that Communist China will not be a sanctuary if it assists North Viet Nam in counter-escalation.

2. In terms of force dispositions, the critical moves are, I believe, these:

a. The introduction of some ground forces in South Viet Nam and, possibly, in the Laos corridor.

b. A minimal installation of the principle that from the present forward North Viet Nam will be vulnerable to retaliatory attacks for continued violation of the 1954-1962 Accords.

c. Perhaps most important of all, the introduction into the Pacific Theater of massive forces to deal with any escalatory response, including forces evidently aimed at China as well as North Viet Nam, should the Chinese Communists enter the game. I am increasingly confident that we can do this in ways which would be understood—and not dangerously misinterpreted—in Hanoi and Peiping.

3. But the movement of forces, and even bombing operations in the north, will not, in themselves, constitute a decisive signal. They will be searching, with enormous sensitivity, for the answer to the following question: Is the President of the United States deeply committed to reinstalling the 1954-1962 Accords; or is he putting on a demonstration of force that would save face for, essentially, a U.S. political defeat at a diplomatic conference? Here their judgment will depend not merely on our use of force and force dispositions but also on the posture of the President, including commitments he makes to our own people and before the world, and on our follow-through. The SNIE accurately catches the extent of their commitments and their hopes in South Viet Nam and Laos. They will not actually accept a setback until they are absolutely sure that we really mean it. They will be as searching in this matter as Khrushchev was before he abandoned the effort to break our hold on Berlin and as Khrushchev was in searching us out on the Turkish missiles before he finally dismantled and removed his missiles from Cuba. Initial rhetoric and military moves will not be enough to convince them.

4. Given the fundamental assessment in this SNIE, I have no doubt we have the capacity to achieve a reinstallation of the 1954-1962 Accords if we enter the exercise with the same determination and staying power that we entered the long test on Berlin and the short test on the Cuba missiles. But it will take that kind of Presidential commitment and staying power.

5. In this connection, the SNIE is quite sound in emphasizing that they will seek, if they are permitted, either to pretend to call off the war in South Viet Nam, without actually doing so; or to revive it again when the pressure is off. (We can see Castro doing this now in Venezuela.) The nature of guerrilla war, infiltration, etc., lends itself to this kind of ambiguous letdown and reacceleration. This places a high premium on our defining precisely what they have to do to remove the pressure from the north. It is because we may wish to maintain pressure for some time to insure their compliance that we should think hard about the installation of troops not merely in South Viet Nam south of the seventeenth parallel, but also in the infiltration corridor of Laos. The same consideration argues for a non-sanguinary but important pressure in the form of naval blockade which will be easier to maintain during a negotiation or quasi-negotiation phase than bombing operations.

6. The touchstones for compliance should include the following: the removal of Viet Minh troops from Laos; the cessation of

infiltration of South Viet Nam from the north; the turning off of the tactical radio network; and the overt statement on Hanoi radio that the Viet Cong should cease their operations and pursue their objectives in South Viet Nam by political means. On the latter point, even if contrary covert instructions are given, an overt statement would have important political and psychological impact.

7. As I said in my memorandum to the President of June 6, no one can be or should be dogmatic about how much of a war we still would have—and for how long—if the external element were thus radically reduced or eliminated. The odds are pretty good, in my view, that, if we do these things in this way, the war will either promptly stop or we will see the same kind of fragmentation of the Communist movement in South Viet Nam that we saw in Greece after the Yugoslav frontier was closed by the Tito-Stalin split. But we can't proceed on that assumption. We must try to gear this whole operation with the best counter-insurgency effort we can mount with our Vietnamese friends outside the country; and not withdraw U.S. forces from Viet Nam until the war is truly under control. (In this connection, I hope everyone concerned considers carefully RAND proposal of November 17, 1964, entitled "SIAT: Single Integrated Attack Team, A Concept for Offensive Military Operations in South Viet-Nam.")

8. I do not see how, if we adopt this line, we can avoid heightened pressures from our allies for either Chinese Communist entrance into the UN or for a UN offer to the Chinese Communists on some form of two-China basis. This will be livable for the President and the Administration if—but only if—we get a clean resolution of the Laos and South Viet Nam problems. The publication of a good Jordan Report will help pin our allies to the wall on a prior reinstallation of the 1954 and 1962 Accords.

9. Considering these observations as a whole, I suspect what I am really saying is that our assets, as I see them, are sufficient to see this thing through if we enter the exercise with adequate determination to succeed. I know well the anxieties and complications on our side of the line. But there may be a tendency to underestimate both the anxieties and complications on the other side and also to underestimate that limited but real margin of influence on the outcome which flows from the simple fact that at this stage of history we are the greatest power in the world—if we behave like it.

10. In the President's public exposition of his policy, I would now add something to the draft I did to accompany the June 6 memorandum to the President. I believe he should hold up a vision of an Asian community that goes beyond the Mekong passage in that draft. The vision, essentially, should hold out the hope that if the 1954 and 1962 Accords are reinstalled, these things are possible:

   a. peace;

   b. accelerated economic development;

   c. Asians taking a larger hand in their own destiny;

d. as much peaceful coexistence between Asian Communists and non-Communists as the Communists wish.

11. A scenario to launch this track might begin as follows:

A. A Presidential decision, communicated to but held by the Congressional leaders. Some leakage would not be unhelpful.

B. Immediate movement of relevant forces to the Pacific.

C. Immediate direct communication to Hanoi to give them a chance to back down before faced with our actions, including a clear statement of the limits of our objectives but our absolute commitment to them.

D. Should this first communication fail (as is likely) installation of our ground forces and naval blockade, plus first attack in North, to be accompanied by publication up-dated Jordan Report and Presidential speech.

92

McGeorge Bundy Memo to Johnson on "Sustained Reprisal" Policy

Annex A, "A Policy of Sustained Reprisal," to memorandum to President Lyndon B. Johnson from McGeorge Bundy, Presidential assistant for national security, Feb. 7, 1965.

I. INTRODUCTORY

We believe that the best available way of increasing our chance of success in Vietnam is the development and execution of a policy of *sustained reprisal* against North Vietnam—a policy in which air and naval action against the North is justified by and related to the whole Viet Cong campaign of violence and terror in the South.

While we believe that the risks of such a policy are acceptable, we emphasize that its costs are real. It implies significant U.S. air losses even if no full air war is joined, and it seems likely that it would eventually require an extensive and costly effort against the whole air defense system of North Vietnam. U.S. casualties would be higher—and more visible to American feelings—than those sustained in the struggle in South Vietnam.

Yet measured against the costs of defeat in Vietnam, this program seems cheap. And even if it fails to turn the tide—as it may—the value of the effort seems to us to exceed its cost.

II. OUTLINE OF THE POLICY

In partnership with the Government of Vietnam, we should develop and exercise the option to retaliate against *any* VC act of violence to persons or property.

2. In practice, we may wish at the outset to relate our reprisals to those acts of relatively high visibility such as the Pleiku incident. Later, we might retaliate against the assassination of a province chief, but not necessarily the murder of a hamlet official; we might retaliate against a grenade thrown into a crowded cafe in Saigon, but not necessarily to a shot fired into a small shop in the countryside.

3. Once a program of reprisals is clearly underway, it should not be necessary to connect each specific act against North Vietnam to a particular outrage in the South. It should be possible, for example, to publish weekly lists of outrages in the South and to have it clearly understood that these outrages are the cause of such action against the North as may be occurring in the current period. Such a more generalized pattern of reprisal would remove much of the difficulty involved in finding precisely matching targets in response to specific atrocities. Even in such a more general pattern, however, it would be important to insure that the general level of reprisal action remained in close correspondence with the level of outrages in the South. We must keep it clear at every stage both to Hanoi and to the world, that our reprisals will be reduced or stopped when outrages in the South are reduced or stopped—and that we are *not* attempting to destroy or conquer North Vietnam.

4. In the early stages of such a course, we should take the appropriate occasion to make clear our firm intent to undertake reprisals on any further acts, major or minor, that appear to us and the GVN as indicating Hanoi's support. We would announce that our two governments have been patient and forebearing in the hope that Hanoi would come to its senses without the necessity of our having to take further action; but the outrages continue and now we must react against those who are responsible; we will not provoke; we will not use our force indiscriminately; but we can no longer sit by in the face of repeated acts of terror and violence for which the DRV is responsible.

5. Having once made this announcement, we should execute our reprisal policy with as low a level of public noise as possible. It is to our interest that our acts should be seen—but we do not wish to boast about them in ways that make it hard for Hanoi to shift its ground. We should instead direct maximum attention to the continuing acts of violence which are the cause of our continuing reprisals.

6. This reprisal policy should begin at a low level. Its level of force and pressure should be increased only gradually—and as indicated above should be decreased if VC terror visibly decreased. The object would not be to "win" an air war against Hanoi, but rather to influence the course of the struggle in the South.

7. At the same time it should be recognized that in order to maintain the power of reprisal without risk of excessive loss, an "air war" may in fact be necessary. We should therefore be ready to develop a separate justification for energetic flak suppression

424

and if necessary for the destruction of Communist air power. The essence of such an explanation should be that these actions are intended solely to insure the effectiveness of a policy of reprisal, and in no sense represent any intent to wage offensive war against the North. These distinctions should not be difficult to develop.

8. It remains quite possible, however, that this reprisal policy would get us quickly into the level of military activity contemplated in the so-called Phase II of our December planning. It may even get us beyond this level with both Hanoi and Peiping, if there is Communist counter-action. We and the GVN should also be prepared for a spurt of VC terrorism, especially in urban areas, that would dwarf anything yet experienced. These are the risks of any action. They should be carefully reviewed—but we believe them to be acceptable.

9. We are convinced that the political values of reprisal require a *continuous* operation. Episodic responses geared on a one-for-one basis to "spectacular" outrages would lack the persuasive force of sustained pressure. More important still, they would leave it open to the Communists to avoid reprisals entirely by giving up only a small element of their own program. The Gulf of Tonkin affair produced a sharp upturn in morale in South Vietnam. When it remained an isolated episode, however, there was a severe relapse. It is the great merit of the proposed scheme that to stop it the Communists would have to stop enough of their activity in the South to permit the probable success of a determined pacification effort.

III. EXPECTED EFFECT OF SUSTAINED REPRISAL POLICY

1. We emphasize that our primary target in advocating a reprisal policy is the improvement of the situation in *South* Vietnam. Action against the North is usually urged as a means of affecting the will of Hanoi to direct and support the VC. We consider this an important but longer-range purpose. The immediate and critical targets are in the South—in the minds of the South Vietnamese and in the minds of the Viet Cong cadres.

2. Predictions of the effect of any given course of action upon the states of mind of people are difficult. It seems very clear that if the United States and the Government of Vietnam join in a policy of reprisal, there will be a sharp immediate increase in optimism in the South, among nearly all articulate groups. The Mission believes—and our own conversations confirm—that in all sectors of Vietnamese opinion there is a strong belief that the United States could do much more if it would, and that they are suspicious of our failure to use more of our obviously enormous power. At least in the short run, the reaction to reprisal policy would be very favorable.

3. This favorable reaction should offer opportunity for increased American influence in pressing for a more effective government—

at least in the short run. Joint reprisals would imply military planning in which the American role would necessarily be controlling, and this new relation should add to our bargaining power in other military efforts—and conceivably on a wider plane as well if a more stable government is formed. We have the whip hand in reprisals as we do not in other fields.

4. The Vietnamese increase in hope could well increase the readiness of Vietnamese factions themselves to join together in forming a more effective government.

5. We think it plausible that effective and sustained reprisals, even in a low key, would have a substantial depressing effect upon the morale of Viet Cong cadres in South Vietnam. This is the strong opinion of CIA Saigon. It is based upon reliable reports of the initial Viet Cong reaction to the Gulf of Tonkin episode, and also upon the solid general assessment that the determination of Hanoi and the apparent timidity of the mighty United States are both major items in Viet Cong confidence.

6. The long-run effect of reprisals in the South is far less clear. It may be that like other stimulants, the value of this one would decline over time. Indeed the risk of this result is large enough so that we ourselves believe that a very major effort all along the line should be made in South Vietnam to take full advantage of the immediate stimulus of reprisal policy in its early stages. Our object should be to use this new policy to effect a visible upward turn in pacification, in governmental effectiveness, in operations against the Viet Cong, and in the whole U.S./GVN relationship. It is changes in these areas that can have enduring long-term effects.

7. While emphasizing the importance of reprisals in the South, we do not exclude the impact on Hanoi. We believe, indeed, that it is of great importance that the level of reprisal be adjusted rapidly and visibly to both upward and downward shifts in the level of Viet Cong offenses. We want to keep before Hanoi the carrot of our desisting as well as the stick of continued pressure. We also need to conduct the application of force so that there is always a prospect of worse to come.

8. We cannot assert that a policy of sustained reprisal will succeed in changing the course of the contest in Vietnam. It may fail, and we cannot estimate the odds of success with any accuracy —they may be somewhere between 25% and 75%. What we can say is that even if it fails, the policy will be worth it. At a minimum it will damp down the charge that we did not do all that we could have done, and this charge will be important in many countries, including our own. Beyond that, a reprisal policy—to the extent that it demonstrates U.S. willingness to employ this new norm in counter-insurgency—will set a higher price for the future upon all adventures of guerrilla warfare, and it should therefore somewhat increase our ability to deter such adventures. We must recognize, however, that that ability will be gravely weakened if there is failure for any reason in Vietnam.

IV. PRESENT ACTION RECOMMENDATIONS

1. This general recommendation was developed in intensive discussions in the days just before the attacks on Pleiku. These attacks and our reaction to them have created an ideal opportunity for the prompt development and execution of sustained reprisals. Conversely, if no such policy is now developed, we face the grave danger that Pleiku, like the Gulf of Tonkin, may be a short-run stimulant and a long-term depressant. We therefore recommend that the necessary preparations be made for continuing reprisals. The major necessary steps to be taken appear to us to be the following:

(1) We should complete the evacuation of dependents.

(2) We should quietly start the necessary westward deployments of [word illegible] contingency forces.

(3) We should develop and refine a running catalogue of Viet Cong offenses which can be published regularly and related clearly to our own reprisals. Such a catalogue should perhaps build on the foundation of an initial White Paper.

(4) We should initiate joint planning with the GVN on both the civil and military level. Specifically, we should give a clear and strong signal to those now forming a government that we will be ready for this policy when they are.

(5) We should develop the necessary public and diplomatic statements to accompany the initiation and continuation of this program.

(6) We should insure that a reprisal program is matched by renewed public commitment to our family of programs in the South, so that the central importance of the southern struggle may never be neglected.

(7) We should plan quiet diplomatic communication of the precise meaning of what we are and are not doing, to Hanoi, to Peking and to Moscow.

(8) We should be prepared to defend and to justify this new policy by concentrating attention in every forum upon its cause—the aggression in the South.

(9) We should accept discussion on these terms in any forum, but we should *not* now accept the idea of negotiations of any sort except on the basis of a stand down of Viet Cong violence. A program of sustained reprisal, with its direct link to Hanoi's continuing aggressive actions in the South, will not involve us in nearly the level of international recrimination which would be precipitated by a go-North program which was not so connected. For this reason the international pressures for negotiation should be quite manageable.

93

White House Cable to Taylor on the Rolling Thunder Decision

Excerpts from cablegram from the State Department to Ambassador Taylor, Feb. 13, 1965, as provided in the body of the Pentagon study. The words in brackets are those of the study. The narrative says this message was drafted at the White House.

The President today approved the following program for immediate future actions in follow-up decisions he reported to you in Deptel 1653. [The first FLAMING DART reprisal decision.]

1. We will intensify by all available means the program of pacification within SVN.

2. We will execute a program of measured and limited air action jointly with GVN against selected military targets in DRV, remaining south of 19th parallel until further notice.

FYI. Our current expectation is that these attacks might come about once or twice a week and involve two or three targets on each day of operation. END FYI.

3. We will announce this policy of measured action in general terms and at the same time, we will go to UN Security Council to make clear case that aggressor is Hanoi. We will also make it plain that we are ready and eager for 'talks' to bring aggression to an end.

4. We believe that this 3-part program must be concerted with SVN, and we currently expect to announce it by Presidential statement directly after next authorized air action. We believe this action should take place as early as possible next week.

5. You are accordingly instructed to seek immediate GVN agreement on this program. You are authorized to emphasize our conviction that announcement of readiness to talk is stronger diplomatic position than awaiting inevitable summons to Security Council by third parties. We would hope to have appropriate GVN concurrence by Monday [Feb. 14th] if possible here.

In presenting above to GVN, you should draw fully, as you see fit, on following arguments:

a. We are determined to continue with military actions regardless of Security Council deliberations and any 'talks' or negotiations when [words illegible]. [Beginning of sentence illegible] that they cease [words illegible] and also the activity they are directing in the south.

b. We consider the UN Security Council initiative, following another strike, essential if we are to avoid being faced with really damaging initiatives by the USSR or perhaps by such powers as India, France, or even the UN.

c. At an early point in the UN Security Council initiative, we would expect to see calls for the DRV to appear in the UN. If they failed to appear, as in August, this will make doubly clear that it is they who are refusing to desist, and our position in pursuing military actions against the DRV would be strengthened. For some reason we would now hope GVN itself would appear at UN and work closely with U.S.

d. With or without Hanoi, we have every expectation that any 'talks' that may result from our Security Council initiative would in fact go on for many weeks or perhaps months and would above all focus constantly on the cessation of Hanoi's aggression as the precondition to any cessation of military action against the DRV. We further anticipate that any detailed discussions about any possible eventual form of agreement returning to the essentials of the 1954 Accords would be postponed and would be subordinated to the central issue. . . .

94

Draft by William Bundy on Results of Policy in '65

Draft paper by William Bundy, "Where Are We Heading?," Feb. 18, 1965. An attached note, dated June 25, says, "Later than November paper, and unfinished."

This memorandum examines possible developments and problems if the U.S. pursues the following policy with respect to South Viet-Nam:

a. Intensified pacification within South Viet-Nam. To meet the security problem, this might include a significant increase in present U.S. force strength.

b. A program of measured, limited, and spaced air attacks, jointly with the GVN, against the infiltration complex in the DRV. Such attacks would take place at the rate of about one a week, unless spectacular Viet Cong action dictated an immediate response out of sequence. The normal pattern of such attacks would comprise one GVN and one U.S. strike on each occasion, confined to targets south of the 19th parallel, with variations in severity depending on the tempo of VC action, but with a slow upward trend in severity as the weeks went by.

c. That the U.S. itself would take no initiative for talks, but would agree to cooperate in consultations—not a conference—undertaken by the UK and USSR as Co-Chairmen of the Geneva Conference. As an opening move, the British would request an expression of our views, and we would use this occasion to spell out our position fully, including our purposes and what we regard as essential to the restoration of peace. We would further present our case against the DRV in the form of a long written document to be sent to the President of the United Nations Security Council and to be circulated to members of the UN.

1. **Communist responses.**

a. Hanoi would almost certainly not feel itself under pressure at any early point to enter into fruitful negotiations or to call off its activity in any way. They would denounce the continued air attacks and seek to whip up maximum world opposition to them. Within South Viet-Nam, they might avoid spectacular actions, but would certainly continue a substantial pattern of activity along past lines, probably with emphasis on the kind of incidents we have seen this week, in which Communist agents stirred up a village "protest" against government air attacks, and against the U.S. Basically, they would see the situation in South Viet-Nam as likely to deteriorate further ("crumble", as they have put it), and would be expecting that at some point someone in the GVN will start secret talks with them behind our backs.

b. Communist China might supply additional air defense equipment to the DRV, but we do not believe they would engage in air operations from Communist China, at least up to the point where the MIGs in the DRV were engaged and we had found it necessary to attack Fukien or possibly—if the MIGs had been moved there—Vinh.

c. The Soviets would supply air defense equipment to the DRV and would continue to protest our air attacks in strong terms. However, we do not believe they would make any new commitment at this stage, and they would probably not do so even if the Chicoms became even more deeply involved—provided that were not ourselves attacking Communist China. At that point, the heat might get awfully great on them, and they would be in a very difficult position to continue actively working as Co-Chairman. However, their approach to the British on the Co-Chairmanship certainly suggests that they would find some relief in starting to act in that role, and might use it as a hedge against further involvement, perhaps pointing out to Hanoi that the Co-Chairman exercise serves to prevent us from taking extreme action and that Hanoi will get the same result in the end if a political track is operating and if, in fact, South Viet-Nam keeps crumbling. They might also argue to Hanoi that the existence of the political track tends to reduce the chances of the Chicoms having to become deeply involved—which we believe Hanoi does not want unless it is compelled to accept it.

2. **Within South Viet-Nam** the new government is a somewhat better one, but the cohesive effects of the strikes to date have at most helped things a bit. The latest MACV report indicates a deteriorating situation except in the extreme south, and it is unlikely that this can be arrested in any short period of time even if the government does hold together well and the military go about their business. We shall be very lucky to see a leveling off, much less any significant improvement, in the next two months. In short, we may have to hang on quite a long time before we can

hope to see an improving situation in South Viet-Nam—and this in turn is really the key to any negotiating position we could have at any time.

3. **On the political track** we believe the British will undertake their role with vigor, and that the Soviets will be more reserved. The Soviet can hardly hope to influence Hanoi much at this point, and they certainly have no leverage with Communist China. In the opening rounds, the Soviets will probably fire off some fairly sharp statements that the real key to the situation is for us to get out and to stop our attacks, and the opposing positions are so far apart that it is hard to see any useful movement for some time to come. We might well find the Soviets—or even the Canadians —sounding us out on whether we would stop our attacks in return for some moderation in VC activity. This is clearly unacceptable, and the very least we should hold out on is a verified cessation of infiltration (and radio silence) before we stop our attacks. Our stress on the cessation of infiltration may conceivably lead to the Indians coming forward to offer policing forces—a suggestion they have made before—and this would be a constructive move we could pick up. But, as noted above, Hanoi is most unlikely to trade on this basis for a long time to come.

4. In sum—the most likely prospect is for a prolonged period without major risks of escalation but equally without any give by Hanoi. If, contrary to our present judgment, the GVN should start to do better,

95

Cable to U.S. Envoys in Asia Announcing Sustained Bombing

Cablegram from State Department to heads of nine United States diplomatic missions in the Far East, Feb. 18, 1965, as provided in the body of the Pentagon study.

Policy on Viet-Nam adopted today calls for the following:

1. Joint program with GVN of continuing air and naval action against North Viet-Nam whenever and wherever necessary. Such action to be against selected military targets and to be limited and fitting and adequate as response to continuous aggression in South Viet-Nam directed in Hanoi. Air strikes will be jointly planned and agreed with GVN and carried out on joint basis.

2. Intensification by all available means of pacification program within South Viet-Nam, including every possible step to find and attack VC concentrations and headquarters within SVN by all conventional means available to GVN and U.S.

3. Early detailed presentation to nations of world and to public of documented case against DRV as aggressor. Forum and form

this presentation not yet decided, but we do not repeat not expe╎
to touch upon readiness for talks or negotiations at this time. W╎
are considering reaffirmation our objectives in some form in t╎
near future.

4. Careful public statements of USG, combined with fact ╎
continuing air action, are expected to make it clear that milita╎
action will continue while aggression continues. But focus ╎
public attention will be kept as far as possible on DRV aggre╎
sion; not on joint GVN-U.S. military operations. There will be ╎
comment of any sort on future actions except that all such actio╎
will be adequate and measured and fitting to aggression. (You w╎
have noted President's statement of yesterday, which we w╎
probably allow to stand.)

Addressees should inform head of government or State (╎
appropriate) of above in strictest confidence and report reaction╎
In the case of Canberra and Wellington [several words illegibl╎
subject to security considerations of each operation as it occu╎
as we did with respect to operations of February 7 and 11.

96

McNaughton Draft for McNamara on
"Proposed Course of Action"

*First draft of "Annex—Plan for Action for South Viet-
nam," appended to memorandum from John T. McNaughton, Assistant Secretary of Defense for International Security Affairs, for Secretary of Defense Robert S. McNamara,
March 24, 1965.*

1. **U.S. aims:**
70%—To avoid a humiliating U.S. defeat (to our reputatic╎
as a guarantor).
20%—To keep SVN (and the adjacent) territory from Chine╎
hands.
10%—To permit the people of SVN to enjoy a better, freer w╎
of life.
ALSO—To emerge from crisis without unacceptable taint fro╎
methods used.
NOT—to "help a friend," although it would be hard to stay ╎
if asked out.
2. **The situation:** The situation in general is bad and deteriora╎
ing. The VC have the initiative. Defeatism is gaining among t╎
rural population, somewhat in the cities, and even among t╎
soldiers—especially those with relatives in rural areas. The Ho╎
Tac area around Saigon is making little progress; the Delta sta╎
bad; the country has been severed in the north. GVN control ╎
shrinking to the enclaves, some burdened with refugees. ╎

Saigon we have a remission: Quat is giving hope on the civilian side, the Buddhists have calmed, and the split generals are in uneasy equilibrium.

3. **The preliminary question:** Can the situation inside SVN be bottomed out (a) without extreme measures against the DRV and/or (b) without deployment of large numbers of U.S. (and other) combat troops inside SVN? The answer is perhaps, but probably no.

4. **Ways GVN might collapse:**

(a) VC successes reduce GVN control to enclaves, causing:
(1) insurrection in the enclaved population,
(2) massive defections of ARVN soldiers and even units,
(3) aggravated dissension and impotence in Saigon,
(4) defeatism and reorientation by key GVN officials,
(5) entrance of left-wing elements into the government,
(6) emergence of a popular-front regime,
(7) request that U.S. leave,
(8) concessions to the VC, and
(9) accommodations to the DRV.

b) VC with DRV volunteers concentrate on I and II Corps,
(1) conquering principal GVN-held enclaves there,
(2) declaring Liberation Government
(3) joining the I & II Corps areas to the DRV, and
(4) pressing the course in (a) above for rest of SVN.

c) While in a temporary funk, GVN might throw in sponge:
(1) dealing under the table with VC,
(2) asking the U.S. to cease at least military aid,
(3) bringing left-wing elements into the government,
(4) leading to a popular-front regime, and
(5) ending in accommodations to the VC and DRV.

d) In a surge of anti-Americanism, GVN could ask the U.S. out and pursue course otherwise similar to (c) above.

5. **The "trilemma":** US policy appears to be drifting. This is because, while there is consensus that efforts inside SVN (para 6) will probably fail to prevent collapse, all three of the possible remedial courses of action have so far been rejected:

a. Will-breaking strikes on the North (para 7) are balked (1) by flash-point limits, (2) by doubts that the DRV will cave and (3) by doubts that the VC will obey a caving DRV. (Leaving strikes only a political and anti-infiltration nuisance.)

b. Large U.S. troop deployments. (para 9) are blocked by "French-defeat" and "Korea" syndromes, and Quat is queasy. (Troops could be net negatives, and be besieged.)

c. Exit by negotiations (para 9) is tainted by the humiliation likely to follow.

Effort inside South Vietnam: Progress inside SVN is our main aim. Great, imaginative efforts on the civilian political as well as military side must be made, bearing in mind that progress depends as much on GVN efforts and luck as on added U.S. efforts. While only a few of such efforts can pay off quickly

enough to affect the present ominous deterioration, some may, a
we are dealing here in small critical margins. Furthermore, su
investment is essential to provide a foundation for the longer ru

a. Improve spirit and effectiveness. (fill out further, drawi
from State memo to the President)

(1) Achieve governmental stability.
(2) Augment the psy-war program.
(3) Build a stronger pro-government infrastructure.
b. Improve physical security. (fill out)
c. Reduce infiltration. (fill out)

STRIKES ON THE NORTH (PROGRAM OF PROGRESSIVE MILITARY PRESSURE)

a. Purposes:
(1) to reduce DRV/VC activities by affecting DRV will.
(2) To improve the GVN/VC relative "balance of morale."
(3) To provide the U.S./GVN with a bargaining counter.
(4) To reduce DRV infiltration of men and materiel.
(5) To show the world the lengths to which U.S. will go for
friend.

b. Program: Each week, 1 or 2 "mission days" with 100-pla
high-damage U.S.-VNAF strikes each "day" against importa
targets, plus 3 armed recce missions—all moving upward
weight of effort, value of target or proximity to Hanoi and Chir

ALTERNATIVE ONE: 12-week DRV-wide program shunni
only "population" targets.

ALTERNATIVE TWO: 12-week program short of taking c
Phuc Yen (Hanoi) airfield.

c. Other actions:
(1) Blockade of DRV ports by VNAF/U.S.-dropped mines
by ships.
(2) South Vietnamese-implemented 34A MAROPS.
(3) Reconnaissance flights over Laos and the DRV.
(4) Daily BARREL ROLL armed recce strikes in Laos (p
T-28s).
(5) Four-a-week BARREL ROLL choke-point strikes in Laos
(6) U.S./VNAF air & naval strikes against VC ops and bas
in SVN.
(7) Westward deployment of U.S. forces.
(8) No de Soto patrols or naval bombardment of DRV
this time.

d. Red "flash points." There are events which we can expe
to imply substantial risk of escalation.
(1) Air strikes north of 17°. (This one already passed.)
(2) First U.S./VNAF confrontation with DRV MIGs.
(3) Strike on Phuc Yen MIG base near Hanoi.
(4) First strikes on Tonkin industrial/population targets.
(5) First strikes on Chinese railroad near China.
(6) First U.S./VNAF confrontation with Chicom MIGs.

(7) First hot pursuit of Chicom MIGs into China.

(8) First flak-suppression of Chicom or Soviet-manned SAM.

(9) Massive introduction of U.S. ground troops into SVN.

(10) U.S./ARVN occupation of DRV territory (e.g., Ile de Tigre).

(11) First Chi/Sov-U.S. confrontation or sinking in blockade.

e) Blue "flash points." China/DRV surely are sensitive to events which might cause *us* to escalate.

(1) All of the above "red" flash points.

(2) VC ground attack on Danang.

(3) Sinking of a U.S. naval vessel.

(4) Open deployment of DRV troops into South Vietnam.

(5) Deployment of Chinese troops into North Vietnam.

(6) Deployment of FROGs or SAMs in North Vietnam.

(7) DRV air attack on South Vietnam.

(8) Announcement of Liberation Government in I/II Corps area.

f. Major risks:

(1) Losses to DRV MIGs, and later possibly to SAMs.

(2) Increased VC activities, and possibly Liberation Government.

(3) Panic or other collapse of GVN from under us.

(4) World-wide revulsion against us (against strikes, blockades, etc.).

(5) Sympathetic fires over Berlin, Cyprus, Kashmir, Jordan waters.

(6) Escalation to conventional war with DRV, China (and USSR?)

(7) Escalation to the use of nuclear weapons.

g. Other Red moves:

(1) More jets to NVN with DRV or Chicom pilots.

(2) More AA (SAMs?) and radar gear (Soviet-manned?) to NVN.

(3) Increased air and ground forces in South China.

(4) Other "defensive" DRV retaliation (e.g., shoot-down of a U-2)

(5) PL land grabs in Laos.

(6) PL declaration of new government in Laos.

(7) Political drive for "neutralization" of Indo-China.

h. Escalation control. We can do three things to avoid escalation too-much or too fast:

(1) Stretch out. Retard the program (e.g., 1 not 2 fixed strikes a week).

(2) Circuit breaker. Abandon at least temporarily the theory that our strikes are intended to break D.R.V. will, and "plateau" them below the "Phuc Yen Airfield" flash point on one or the other of these tenable theories:

(a) That we strike as necessary to interdict infiltration.

(b) That our level of strikes is generally responsive to the level of VC/DRV activities in South Vietnam.

(3) Shunt. Plateau the air strikes per para (2) and divert th
energy into:

(a) A mine—and/or ship-blockade of DRV ports.

(b) Massive deployment of U.S. (and other?) troops into SV
(and Laos?):

(1) To man the "enclaves", releasing ARVN forces.

(2) To take over Pleiku, Kontum, Darlac provinces.

(3) To create a [word illegible] sea-Thailand infiltration wall.

i. Important miscellany:

(1) Program should appear to be relentless (i.e., possibility
employing "circuit-breakers" should be secret).

(2) Enemy should be kept aware of our limited objectives.

(3) Allies should be kept on board.

(4) USSR should be kept in passive role.

(5) Information program should preserve U.S. public suppor

PROGRAM OF LARGE U.S. GROUND EFFORT
IN SVN AND SEA

a. Purposes:

(1) To defeat the VC on the ground.

(2) To improve GVN/VC relative "morale balance."

(3) To improve U.S./GVN bargaining position.

(4) To show world lengths to which U.S. will go to fulfill com
mitments.

b. Program:

(1) Continue strike-North "crescendo" or "plateau" (para
above.)

(2) Add any "combat support" personnel needed by MAC
and (3) Deploy remainder of the III Marine Expeditionary For
to Danang; and (4) Deploy one U.S. (plus one Korean?) d
vision to defeat VC in Pleiku-Kontum-Darlac area, and/or (5
Deploy one U.S. (plus one Korean?) division to hold enclav
(Bien Hoa/Ton Son Nhut, Nha Trang, Qui Non, Pleiku); and/
(6) Deploy 3-5 U.S. divisions (with "international" elements
across Laos-SVN infiltration routes and at key SVN populatic
centers.

c. Advantages:

(1) Improve (at least initially) manpower ratio vs. the VC.

(2) Boost GVN morale and depress DRV/VC morale.

(3) Firm up U.S. commitment in eyes of all Reds, allies ar
neutrals.

(4) Deter (or even prevent) coups in the South.

d. Risks:

(1) Deployment will suck Chicom troops into DRV.

(2) Deployment will suck counter-balancing DRV/Chines
troops into SVN.

(3) Announcement of deployment will cause massive DRV
Chicom effort preemptively to occupy new SVN territory.

(4) U.S. losses will increase.

(5) Friction with GVN (and Koreans?) over command will arise.

(6) GVN will tend increasingly to "let the U.S. do it."

(7) Anti-U.S. "colonialist" mood may increase in and outside SVN.

(8) U.S. forces may be surrounded and trapped.

e. Important miscellany:

(1) There are no obvious circuit-breakers. Once U.S. troops are in, it will be difficult to withdraw them or to move them, say, to Thailand without admitting defeat.

(2) It will take massive deployments (many divisions) to improve the GVN/U.S.:VC ratio to the optimum 10+:1.

(3) In any event, our Project 22 planning with the Thais for defense of the Mekong towns must proceed apace.

EXIT BY NEGOTIATIONS

a. Bargaining counters.

(1) What DRV could give:

(a) Stop training and sending personnel to SVN/Laos.

(b) Stop sending arms and supplies into SVN/Laos.

(c) Stop directing military actions in into SVN/Laos.

(d) Order the VC/PL to stop their insurgencies.

(e) Stop propaganda broadcasts to South Vietnam.

(f) Remove VM forces and cadres from SVN and Laos.

(g) See that VC/PL stop incidents in SVN and Laos.

(h) See that VC/PL cease resistance.

(i) See that VC/PL turn in weapons and bases.

(j) See that VC/PL surrender for amnesty/expatriation.

(2) What GVN/U.S. could give:

(a) Stop (or not increase) air strikes on DRV.

(b) Remove (or not increase) U.S. troops in SVN.

(c) Rice supply to DRV.

(d) Assurance that U.S./GVN have no designs on NVN.

(e) Assurance that U.S./GVN will not demand public renunciation by the DRV of Communist goals.

(f) Assurance that "peaceful coexistence" (e.g., continuation of Red propaganda in SVN) is acceptable.

(g) Capitulation: Leftists in GVN, coalition government, and eventual incorporation of SVN into DRV.

b. Possible outcomes.

(1) Pacified non-Communist South Vietnam.

(2) "Laotian" solution, with areas of de facto VC dominion, a "government of national unity," and a Liberation Front ostensibly weaned from DRV control.

(3) Explicit partition of SVN, with each area under a separate government.

(4) A "semi-equilibrium"—a slow-motion war—with slowly shifting GVN-VC lines.

(5) Loss of SVN to the DRV.

c. Techniques to minimize impact of bad outcomes. If/when it is estimated that even the best U.S./GVN efforts mean failure ("flash" or defeat), it will be important to act to minimize the afterdamage to U.S. effectiveness and image by steps such as these:

(1) Publicize uniqueness of congenital impossibility of SVN case (e.g., Viet Minh held much of SVN in 1954, long sieve-like borders, unfavorable terrain, no national tradition, few administrators, mess left by French, competing factions, Red LOC advantage, late U.S. start, etc.).

(2) Take opportunity offered by next coup or GVN anti-U.S. tantrum to "ship out" (coupled with advance threat to do so if they fail to "shape up"?)

(3) Create diversionary "offensives" elsewhere in the world (e.g., to shore up Thailand, Philippines, Malaysia, India, Australia; to launch an "anti-poverty" program for underdeveloped areas).

(4) Enter multi-nation negotiations calculated to shift opinion and values.

d. Risks. With the physical situation and the trends as they are the fear is overwhelming that an exit negotiated now would result in humiliation for the U.S.

Evaluation: It is essential—however badly SEA may go over the next 1-3 years—that U.S. emerge as a "good doctor." We must have kept promises, been tough, taken risks, gotten bloodied, and hurt the enemy very badly. We must avoid harmful appearances which will affect judgments by, and provide pretexts to, other nations regarding how the U.S. will behave in future cases of particular interest to those nations—regarding U.S. policy, power, resolve and competence to deal with their problems. In this connection, the relevant audiences are the Communists (who must feel strong pressures), the South Vietnamese (whose morale must be buoyed), our allies (who must trust us as "underwriters") and the U.S. public (which must support our risk-taking with U.S. lives and prestige).

Urgency: If the strike-North program (para 7) is not altered, we will reach the MIG/Phuc Yen flash point in approximately one month. If the program is altered only to stretch out the crescendo: up to 3 months may be had before that flash point at the expense of a less persuasive squeeze. If the program is altered to "plateau" or dampen the strikes: much of their negotiating value will be lost. (Furthermore, there is now a hint of flexibility on the Red side: the Soviets are struggling to find a Gordian knot-cutter; the Chicoms may be wavering (Paris 5326

POSSIBLE COURSE

(1) Redouble efforts inside SVN (get better organized for it

(2) Prepare to deploy U.S. combat troops in phases, starting with one Army division at Pleiku and a Marine MEF at Danang

(3) Stretch out strike-North program, postponing Phuc Yen until June (exceed flash points only in specific retaliations).

(4) Initiate talks along the following lines, bearing in mind that formal partition, or even a "Laos" partition, is out in SVN; we must break the VC back or work out an accommodation.

PHASE ONE TALKS:

(A) When: Now, before an avoidable flash point.

(B) Who: U.S.-USSR, perhaps also U.S.-India. (Not with China or Liberation Front; not through UK or France or U Thant; keep alert to possibility that GVN officials are talking under the table.)

(C) How: With GVN consent, private, quiet (refuse formal talks).

(D) What:

(1) Offer to stop strikes on DRV and withhold deployment of large U.S. forces in trade for DRV stoppage of infiltration, communications to VC, and VC attacks, sabotage and terrorism, and for withdrawal of named units in SVN.

2. Compliance would be policed unilaterally. If as is likely, complete compliance by the DRV is not forthcoming, we would carry out occasional strikes.

(3) We make clear that we are not demanding cessation of Red propaganda nor a public renunciation by Hanoi of its doctrines.

(4) Regarding "defensive" VC attacks—i.e., VC defending VC-held areas from encroaching ARVN forces—we take the public position that ARVN forces must be free to operate throughout SVN, especially in areas where amnesty is offered (but in fact, discretion will be exercised).

(5) Terrorism and sabotage, however, must be dampened markedly throughout the country, and civilian administrators must be free to move and operate freely, certainly in so-called contested areas (and perhaps even in VC base areas).

PHASE TWO TALKS:

(A) When: At the end of Phase One.

(B) Who: All interested nations.

(C) How: Publicly in large conference.

(D) What:

(1) Offer to remove U.S. combat forces from South Vietnam in exchange for repatriation (or regroupment?) of DRV infiltrators and for erection of international machinery to verify the end of infiltration and communication.

(2) Offer to seek to determine the will of the people under international supervision, with an appropriate reflection of those who favor the VC.

(3) Any recognition of the Liberation Front would have to be accompanied by disarming the VC and at least avowed VC independence from DRV control.

PHASE THREE TALKS: Avoid any talks regarding the future of all of Southeast Asia. Thailand's future should not be up for discussion; and we have the 1954 and 1962 Geneva Accords covering the rest of the area.

c. Special Points:

(1) Play on DRV's fear of China.

(2) To show good will, suspend strikes on North for a few days if requested by Soviets during efforts to mediate.

(3) Have a contingency plan prepared to evacuate U.S. personnel in case a para-9-type situation arises.

(4) If the DRV will not "play" the above game, we must be prepared (a) to risk passing some flash points, in the Strike-North program. (b) to put more U.S. troops into SVN, and/or (c) to reconsider our minimum acceptable outcome.

97

McCone Memo to Top Officials on Effectiveness of Air War

Memorandum from John A. McCone, Director of Central Intelligence, to Secretary Rusk, Secretary McNamara, McGeorge Bundy and Ambassador Taylor, April 2, 1965, as provided in the body of the Pentagon's study. Paragraphs in italics are the study's paraphrase or explanation.

McCone did not inherently disagree with the change in the U.S. ground-force role, but felt that it was inconsistent with the decision to continue the air strike program at the feeble level at which it was then being conducted. McCone developed his argument as follows:

I have been giving thought to the paper that we discussed in yesterday's meeting, which unfortunately I had little time to study, and also to the decision made to change the mission of our ground forces in South Vietnam from one of advice and static defense to one of active combat operations against the Viet Cong guerrillas.

I feel that the latter decision is correct only if our air strikes against the North are sufficiently heavy and damaging really to hurt the North Vietnamese. The paper we examined yesterday does not anticipate the type of air operation against the North necessary to force the NVN to reappraise their policy. On the contrary, it states, "We should continue roughly the present slowly ascending tempo of ROLLING THUNDER operations——," and later, in outlining the types of targets, states, "The target systems should continue to avoid the effective GCI range of MIG's," and these conditions indicate restraints which will not be persuasive to the NVM and would probably be read as evidence of a U.S. desire to temporize.

I have reported that the strikes to date have not caused a change in the North Vietnamese policy of directing Viet Cong insurgency, infiltrating cadres and supplying material. If anything, the strikes to date have hardened their attitude.

I have now had a chance to examine the 12-week program referred to by General Wheeler and it is my personal opinion that this program is not sufficiently severe and [words illegible] the North Vietnamese to [words illegible] policy.

On the other hand, we must look with care to our position under a program of slowly ascending tempo of air strikes. With the passage of each day and each week, we can expect increasing pressure to stop the bombing. This will come from various elements of the American public, from the press, the United Nations and world opinion. Therefore time will run against us in this operation and I think the North Vietnamese are counting on this.

Therefore I think what we are doing is starting on a track which involves ground force operations, which, in all probability, will have limited effectiveness against guerrillas, although admittedly will restrain some VC advances. However, we can expect requirements for an ever-increasing commitment of U.S. personnel without materially improving the chances of victory. I support and agree with this decision but I must point out that in my judgment, forcing submission of the VC can only be brought about by a decision in Hanoi. Since the contemplated actions against the North are modest in scale, they will not impose unacceptable damage on it, nor will they threaten the DRV's vital interests. Hence, they will not present them with a situation with which they cannot live, though such actions will cause the DRV pain and inconvenience.

I believe our proposed track offers great danger of simply encouraging Chinese Communists and Soviet support of the DRV and VC cause, if for no other reason than the risk for both will be minimum. I envision that the reaction of the NVN and Chinese Communists will be to deliberately, carefully, and probably gradually, build up the Viet Cong capabilities by covert infiltration on North Vietnamese and, possibly, Chinese cadres and thus bring an ever-increasing pressure on our forces. In effect, we will find ourselves mired down in combat in the jungle in a military effort that we cannot win, and from which we will have extreme difficulty in extracting ourselves.

Therefore it is my judgment that if we are to change the mission of the ground forces, we must also change the ground rules of the strikes against North Vietnam. We must hit them harder, more frequently, and inflict greater damage. Instead of avoiding the MIG's, we must go in and take them out. A bridge here and there will not do the job. We must strike their airfields, their petroleum resources, power stations and their military compounds. This, in my opinion, must be done promptly and with minimum restraint.

If we are unwilling to take it this kind of a decision now, we must not take the actions concerning the mission of our ground forces for the reasons I have mentioned [words illegible].

98

April, '65, Order Increasing Ground Force and Shifting Mission

National Security Action Memorandum 328, April 6, 1965, signed by McGeorge Bundy and addressed to the Secretary of State, the Secretary of Defense and the Director of Central Intelligence.

On Thursday, April 1, The President made the following decisions with respect to Vietnam:

1. Subject to modifications in light of experience, to coordination and direction both in Saigon and in Washington, the President approved the 41-point program of non-military actions submitted by Ambassador Taylor in a memorandum dated March 31, 1965.

2. The President gave general approval to the recommendations submitted by Mr. Rowan in his report dated March 16, with the exception that the President withheld approval of any request for supplemental funds at this time—it is his decision that this program is to be energetically supported by all agencies and departments and by the reprogramming of available funds as necessary within USIA.

3. The President approved the urgent exploration of the 12 suggestions for covert and other actions submitted by the Director of Central Intelligence under date of March 31.

4. The President repeated his earlier approval of the 21-point program of military actions submitted by General Harold K. Johnson under date of March 14 and re-emphasized his desire that aircraft and helicopter reinforcements under this program be accelerated.

5. The President approved an 18-20,000 man increase in U.S. military support forces to fill out existing units and supply needed logistic personnel.

6. The President approved the deployment of two additional Marine Battalions and one Marine Air Squadron and associated headquarters and support elements.

7. The President approved a change of mission for all Marine Battalions deployed to Vietnam to permit their more active use under conditions to be established and approved by the Secretary of Defense in consultation with the Secretary of State.

8. The President approved the urgent exploration, with the Korean, Australian, and New Zealand Governments, of the possibility of rapid deployment of significant combat elements from their armed forces in parallel with the additional Marine deployment approved in paragraph 6.

9. Subject to continuing review, the President approved the following general framework of continuing action against North Vietnam and Laos:

We should continue roughly the present slowly ascending tempo of ROLLING THUNDER operations being prepared to add strikes in response to a higher rate of VC operations, or conceivably to slow the pace in the unlikely event VC slacked off sharply for what appeared to be more than a temporary operational lull.

The target systems should continue to avoid the effective GGI range of MIGs. We should continue to vary the types of targets, stepping up attacks on lines of communication in the near future, and possibly moving in a few weeks to attacks on the rail lines north and northeast of Hanoi.

Leaflet operations should be expanded to obtain maximum practicable psychological effect on North Vietnamese population.

Blockade or aerial mining of North Vietnamese ports need further study and should be considered for future operations. It would have major political complications, especially in relation to the Soviets and other third countries, but also offers many advantages.

Air operation in Laos, particularly route blocking operations in the Panhandle area, should be stepped up to the maximum remunerative rate.

10. Ambassador Taylor will promptly seek the reactions of the South Vietnamese Government to appropriate sections of this program and their approval as necessary, and in the event of disapproval or difficulty at that end, these decisions will be appropriately reconsidered. In any event, no action into Vietnam under paragraphs 6 and 7 above should take place without GVN approval or further Presidential authorization.

11. The President desires that with respect to the actions in paragraphs 5 through 7, premature publicity be avoided by all possible precautions. The actions themselves should be taken as rapidly as practicable, but in ways that should minimize any appearance of sudden changes in policy, and official statements on these troop movements will be made only with the direct approval of the Secretary of Defense, in consultation with the Secretary of State. The President's desire is that these movements and changes should be understood as being gradual and wholly consistent with existing policy.

99

Taylor Cable to Washington on Step-Up in Ground Forces

Cablegram April 17, 1965, from Ambassador Maxwell D. Taylor in Saigon to Secretary of State Dean Rusk, with a copy to the White House for the attention of McGeorge Bundy.

This message undertakes to summarize instructions which I have received over the last ten days with regard to the introduction of third-country combat forces and to discuss the preferred way of presenting the subject to the GVN.

As the result of the meeting of the President and his advisors on April 1 and the NSC meeting on the following day, I left Washington and returned to Saigon with the understanding that the reinforcement of the Marines already ashore by two additional BLT's and a F-4 squadron and the progressive introduction of IIAWPNPPP support forces were approved but that decision on the several proposals for bringing in more U.S. combat forces and their possible modes of employment was withheld in an offensive counterinsurgency role. State was to explore with the Korean, Australian and New Zealand govts the possibility of rapid deployment of significant combat elements in parallel with the Marine reinforcement.

Since arriving home, I have received the following instructions and have taken the indicated actions with respect to third-country combat forces.

April 6 and 8. Received GVN concurrence to introduction of the Marine reinforcements and to an expanded mission for all Marines in Danang-Phu Bai area.

April 8. Received Deptel 2229 directing approach to GVN, suggesting request to Australian govt for an infantry battalion for use in SVN. While awaiting a propitious moment to raise the matter, I received Deptel 2237 directing approach be delayed until further orders. Nothing further has been received since.

April 14. I learned by JCS 009012 to Cincpac of apparent decision to deploy 173rd airborne brigade immediately to Bien Hoa-Vung Tau. By Embtel 3373, delay in this deployment was urgently recommended but no reply has been received. However, Para 2 of Doc 152339 apparently makes reference to this project in terms which suggest that is something less than as an approved immediate action. In view of the uncertainty of its status, I have not broached the matter with Quat.

April 15. Received Deptel 2314 directing that embassy Saigon discuss with GVN introduction of Rok regimental combat team and suggest GVN request such a force Asap. Because of Quat's absence from Saigon, I have not been able to raise matter. As matter of fact, it should not be raised until we have a clear concept of employment.

April 16. I have just seen state-defense message Dod 152339 cited above which indicates a favorable attitude toward several possible uses of U.S. combat forces beyond the NSC decisions of April 2. I am told to discuss these and certain other non-military matters urgently with Quat. The substance of this cable will be addressed in a separate message. I can not raise these matters with Quat without further guidance.

Faced with this rapidly changing picture of Washington desires and intentions with regard to the introduction of third-country (as well as U.S.) combat forces, I badly need a clarification of our purposes and objectives. Before I can present our case to GVN, I have to know what that case is and why. It is not going to be easy to get ready concurrence for the large-scale introduction of foreign troops unless the need is clear and explicit.

Let me suggest the kind of instruction to the AMB which it would be most helpful to receive for use in presenting to GVN what I take to be a new policy of third-country participation in ground combat.

"The USG has completed a thorough review of the situation in SVN both in its national and international aspects and has reached certain important conclusions. It feels that in recent weeks there has been a somewhat favorable change in the overall situation as the result of the air attacks on DRV, the relatively small but numerous successes in the field against the VC and the encouraging progress of the Quat govt. However, it is becoming increasingly clear that, in all probability, the primary objective of the GVN and the USG of changing the will of the DRV to support the VC insurgency can not be attained in an acceptable time-frame by the methods presently employed. The air campaign in the North must be supplemented by signal successes against the VC on the South before we can hope to create that frame of mind in Hanoi which will lead to the decisions we seek.

"The JCS have reviewed the military resources which will be available in SVN by the end of 1965 and have concluded that even with an attainment of the highest feasible mobilization goals, ARVN will have insufficient forces to carry out the kind of successful campaign against the VC which is considered essential for the purposes discussed above. If the ground war is not to drag into 1966 and even beyond, they consider it necessary to reinforce GVN ground forces with about 23 battalion equivalents in addition to the forces now being recruited in SVN. Since these reinforcements can not be raised by the GVN, they must inevitably come from third-country sources.

"The USG accepts the validity of this reasoning of the JCS and offers its assistance to the GVN to raise these additional forces for the purpose of bringing the VC insurgency to an end in the shortest possible time. We are prepared to bring in additional U.S. ground forces provided we can get a reasonable degree of participation from other third countries. If the GVN will make urgent representations to them, we believe it entirely possible to obtain the following contributions; Korea, one regimental combat team; Australia, one infantry battalion; New Zealand, one battery and one company of tanks; PI, one battalion. If forces of the foregoing magnitude are forthcoming, the USG is prepared to provide the remainder of the combat reinforcements as well as the necessary logistic personnel to support the third-country contingents. Also it will use its good offices as desired in assisting the GVN approach to these govts.

"You (the Ambassador) will seek the concurrence of the GVN

to the foregoing program, recognizing that a large number of questions such as command relationships, concepts of employment and disposition of forces must be worked out subsequently." Armed with an instruction such as the foregoing, I would feel adequately equipped to initiate what may be a sharp debate with the GVN. I need something like this before taking up the pending troop matters with Quat.

100

Johnson's Message to Taylor on the May 10 Halt in Bombing

Message from President Johnson to Ambassador Taylor, May 10, 1965, as provided in the body of the Pentagon study.

I have learned from Bob McNamara that nearly all ROLLING THUNDER operations for this week can be completed by Wednesday noon, Washington time. This fact and the days of Buddha's birthday seem to me to provide an excellent opportunity for a pause in air attacks which might go into next week and which I could use to good effect with world opinion.

My plan is not to announce this brief pause but simply to call it privately to the attention of Moscow and Hanoi as soon as possible and tell them that we shall be watching closely to see whether they respond in any way. My current plan is to report publicly after the pause ends on what we have done.

Could you see Quat right away on Tuesday and see if you can persuade him to concur in this plan. I would like to associate him with me in this decision if possible, but I would accept a simple concurrence or even willingness not to oppose my decision. In general, I think it important that he and I should get together in such matters, but I have no desire to embarrass him if it is politically difficult for him to join actively in a pause over Buddha's birthday.

[Words illegible] noted your [words illegible] but do not yet have your appreciation of the political effect in Saigon of acting around Buddha's birthday. From my point of view it is a great advantage to use Buddha's birthday to mask the first days of the pause here, if it is at all possible in political terms for Quat. I assume we could undertake to enlist the Archbishop and the Nuncio in calming the Catholics.

You should understand that my purpose in this plan is to begin to clear a path either toward restoration of peace or toward increased military action, depending upon the reaction of the Communists. We have amply demonstrated our determination and our commitment in the last two months, and I now wish to gain some flexibility.

I know that this is a hard assignment on short notice, but there is no one who can bring it off better.

I have kept this plan in the tightest possible circle here and wish you to inform no one but Alexis Johnson. After I have your report of Quat's reaction I will make a final decision and it will be communicated promptly to senior officers concerned.

101

Rostow Memorandum on "Victory and Defeat in Guerrilla Wars"

Memorandum from Walt W. Rostow, chairman of the State Department's Policy Planning Council, for Secretary of State Rusk, "Victory and Defeat in Guerilla Wars: The Case of South Vietnam," May 20, 1965, as provided in the body of the Pentagon's study.

In the press, at least, there is a certain fuzziness about the possibility of clear-cut victory in South Viet-nam; and the President's statement that a military victory is impossible is open to misinterpretation.

1. Historically, guerrilla wars have generally been lost or won cleanly: Greece, China mainland, North Viet-Nam, Malaya, Philippines. Laos in 1954 was an exception, with two provinces granted the Communists and a de facto split imposed on the country.

2. In all the cases won by Free World forces, there was a phase when the guerrillas commanded a good part of the countryside and, indeed, placed Athens, Kuala Lumpur, and Manila under something close to siege. They failed to win because all the possible routes to guerrilla victory were closed and, in failing to win, they lost. They finally gave up in discouragement. The routes to victory are:

a) Mao Stage Three: going to all-out conventional war and winning as in China in 1947-49;

b) Political collapse and takeover: North Viet-Nam;

c) Political collapse and a coalition government in which the Communists get control over the security machinery; army and/or police. This has been an evident Viet Cong objective in this [rest illegible].

d) Converting the bargaining pressure generated by the guerrilla forces into a partial victory by splitting the country: Laos. Also, in a sense, North Viet-Nam in 1954 and the Irish Rebellion after the First World War.

3. If we succeed in blocking these four routes to victory, dis-

couraging the Communist force in the South, and making
continuance of the war sufficiently costly to the North there is
reason we cannot win as clear a victory in South Viet-Nam as
Greece, Malaya, and the Philippines. Unless political morale
Saigon collapses and the ARVN tends to break up, case c),
most realistic hope of the VC, should be avoidable. This dang
argues for more rather than less pressure on the North, wh
continuing the battle in the South in such a way as to make V
hopes of military and political progress wane.

4. The objective of the exercise is to convince Hanoi that
bargaining position is being reduced with the passage of time; f
even in the worst case for Hanoi, it wants some bargaining po
tion (rather than simply dropping the war) to get U.S. fore
radically reduced in South Viet-Nam and to get some minimu
face-saving formula for the VC.

5. I believe Hanoi understands its dilemma well. As of ea
February it saw a good chance of a quiet clean victory via ro
c). It now is staring at quite clear-cut defeat, with the rising U
strength and GVN morale in the South and rising costs in
North. That readjustment in prospects is painful; and they wo
in my view, accept its consequences unless they are convinc
time has ceased to be their friend, despite the full use of th
assets on the ground in South Viet-Nam, in political warfa
around the world, and in diplomacy.

6. Their last and best hope will be, of course, that if they e
the war and get us out, the political, social, and economic situ
tion in South Viet-Nam will deteriorate in such a way as to pern
Communist political takeover, with or without a revival of gu
rilla warfare. It is in this phase that we will have to consolida
with the South Vietnamese, a victory that is nearer our grasp th
we (but not Hanoi) may think.

102

Prime Minister Wilson's Warning to
Johnson on Petroleum Raids

*Excerpts from cablegram to President Johnson from
Prime Minister Harold Wilson of Britain, June 3, 1965, as
provided in the body of the Pentagon's study.*

I was most grateful to you for asking Bob McNamara
arrange the very full briefing about the two oil targets near Han
and Haiphong that Col. Rogers gave me yesterday. . . .

I know you will not feel that I am either unsympathetic
uncomprehending of the dilemma that this problem presents f
you. In particular, I wholly understand the deep concern you mu
feel at the need to do anything possible to reduce the losses

oung Americans in and over Vietnam; and Col. Rogers made it
lear to us what care has been taken to plan this operation so as
o keep civilian casualties to the minimum.

However, . . . I am bound to say that, as seen from here, the
ossible military benefits that may result from this bombing do
ot appear to outweigh the political disadvantages that would
eem the inevitable consequence. If you and the South Vietnamese
Government were conducting a declared war on the conventional
attern . . . this operation would clearly be necessary and right.
ut since you have made it abundantly clear—and you know how
much we have welcomed and supported this—that your purpose
s to achieve a negotiated settlement, and that you are not striving
or total military victory in the field, I remain convinced that the
ombing of these targets, without producing decisive military
dvantage, may only increase the difficulty of reaching an eventual
ettlement. . . .

The last thing I wish is to add to your difficulties, but, as I
varned you in my previous message, if this action is taken we
hall have to dissociate ourselves from it, and in doing so I should
ave to say that you had given me advance warning and that I
ad made my position clear to you. . . .

Nevertheless I want to repeat . . . that our reservations about
his operation will not affect our continuing support for your
olicy over Vietnam, as you and your people have made it clear
rom your Baltimore speech onwards. But, while this will remain
he Government's position, I know that the effect on public opinion
n this country—and I believe throughout Western Europe—is
ikely to be such as to reinforce the existing disquiet and criticism
hat we have to deal with.

103

George Ball Memo for Johnson on
"A Compromise Solution"

Memorandum, "A Compromise Solution in South Viet-
nam," from Under Secretary of State George W. Ball for
President Johnson, July 1, 1965.

(1) A Losing War: The South Vietnamese are losing the war
o the Viet Cong. No one can assure you that we can beat the
Viet Cong or even force them to the conference table on our
erms, no matter how many hundred thousand *white, foreign*
U.S.) troops we deploy.

No one has demonstrated that a white ground force of whatever
ize can win a guerrilla war—which is at the same time a civil
var between Asians—in jungle terrain in the midst of a population
hat refuses cooperation to the white forces (and the South Viet-

namese) and thus provides a great intelligence advantage to
other side. Three recent incidents vividly illustrate this po
(a) the sneak attack on the Da Nang Air Base which invol
penetration of a defense perimeter guarded by 9,000 Mari:
This raid was possible only because of the cooperation of the l:
inhabitants; (b) the B52 raid that failed to hit the Viet Cong v
had obviously been tipped off; (c) the search and destroy miss
of the 173rd Air Borne Brigade which spent three days look
for the Viet Cong, suffered 23 casualties, and never made con
with the enemy who had obviously gotten advance word of tl
assignment.

(2) The Question to Decide: Should we limit our liabilities
South Vietnam and try to find a way out with minimal long-te
costs?

The alternative—no matter what we may wish it to be—
almost certainly a protracted war involving an open-ended c
mitment of U.S. forces, mounting U.S. casualties, no assurance
a satisfactory solution, and a serious danger of escalation at
end of the road.

(3) Need for a Decision Now: So long as our forces
restricted to advising and assisting the South Vietnamese,
struggle will remain a civil war between Asian peoples. Once
deploy substantial numbers of troops in combat it will becom
war between the U.S. and a large part of the population of So
Vietnam, organized and directed from North Vietnam and bac
by the resources of both Moscow and Peiping.

The decision you face now, therefore, is crucial. Once la
numbers of U.S. troops are committed to direct combat, they
begin to take heavy casualties in a war they are ill-equipped
fight in a non-cooperative if not downright hostile countryside.

Once we suffer large casualties, we will have started a well-n
irreversible process. Our involvement will be so great that
cannot—without national humiliation—stop short of achieving
complete objectives. *Of the two possibilities I think humilia*
would be more likely than the achievement of our objective
even after we have paid terrible costs.

(4) Compromise Solution: Should we commit U.S. manpo
and prestige to a terrain so unfavorable as to give a very la
advantage to the enemy—or should we seek a compromise se
ment which achieves less than our stated objectives and thus
our losses while we still have the freedom of maneuver to do

(5) Costs of a Compromise Solution: The answer involve
judgment as to the cost to the U.S. of such a compromise se
ment in terms of our relations with the countries in the area
South Vietnam, the credibility of our commitments, and
prestige around the world. In my judgment, if we act before
commit substantial U.S. troops to combat in South Vietnam
can, by accepting some short-term costs, avoid what may well
a long-term catastrophe. I believe we tended grossly to exagge:

450

the costs involved in a compromise settlement. An appreciation of probable costs is contained in the attached memorandum.

(6) With these considerations in mind, I strongly urge the following program:

(a) Military Program

(1) Complete all deployments already announced—15 battalions—but decide not to go beyond a total of 72,000 men represented by this figure.

(2) Restrict the combat role of the American forces to the June 19 announcement, making it clear to General Westmoreland that this announcement is to be strictly construed.

(3) Continue bombing in the North but avoid the Hanoi-Haiphong area and any targets nearer to the Chinese border than those already struck.

(b) Political Program

(1) In any political approaches so far, we have been the prisoners of whatever South Vietnamese government that was momentarily in power. If we are ever to move toward a settlement, it will probably be because the South Vietnamese government pulls the rug out from under us and makes its own deal *or* because we go forward quietly without advance prearrangement with Saigon.

(2) So far we have not given the other side a reason to believe there is *any* flexibility in our negotiating approach. And the other side has been unwilling to accept what *in their terms* is complete capitulation.

(3) Now is the time to start some serious diplomatic feelers looking towards a solution based on some application of a self-determination principle.

(4) I would recommend approaching Hanoi rather than any of the other probable parties, the NLF—or Peiping. Hanoi is the only one that has given any signs of interest in discussion. Peiping has been rigidly opposed. Moscow has recommended that we negotiate with Hanoi. The NLF has been silent.

(5) There are several channels to the North Vietnamese but I think the best one is through their representative in Paris, Mai Van Bo. Initial feelers of Bo should be directed toward a discussion both of the four points we have put forward and the four points put forward by Hanoi as a basis for negotiation. We can accept all but one of Hanoi's four points, and hopefully we should be able to agree on some ground rules for serious negotiation—including no preconditions.

(6) If the initial feelers lead to further secret, exploratory talks, we can inject the concept of self-determination that would permit the Viet Cong some hope of achieving some of their political objectives through local elections or some other device.

(7) The contact on our side should be handled through a non-governmental cut-out (possibly a reliable newspaper man who can be repudiated).

(8) If progress can be made at this level a basis can be laid

for a multinational conference. At some point, obviously, th
government of South Vietnam will have to be brought on boar
but I would postpone this step until after a substantial feeling o
of Hanoi.

(7) Before moving to any formal conference we should b
prepared to agree once the conference is started:

(a) The U.S. will stand down its bombing of the North

(b) The South Vietnamese will initiate no offensive operation
in the South, and

(c) the DRV will stop terrorism and other aggressive actio
against the South.

(8) The negotiations at the conference should aim at inco
porating our understanding with Hanoi in the form of a mult
national agreement guaranteed by the U.S., the Soviet Union ar
possibly other parties, and providing for an international mech
nism to supervise its execution.

Probable Reactions to the Cutting of Our Losses in South Vietnam

We have tended to exaggerate the losses involved in a comple
settlement in South Vietnam. There are three aspects to the prol
lem that should be considered. First, the local effect of our actio
on nations in or near Southeast Asia. Second, the effect of ou
action on the credibility of our commitments around the worl
Third, the effect on our position of world leadership.

A. Free Asian Reactions to a Compromise Settlement in Sout
Vietnam Would Be Highly Parochial.

With each country interpreting the event primarily in terms c
(a) its own immediate interest, (b) its sense of vulnerability t
Communist invasion or insurgency, and (c) its confidence in th
integrity of our commitment to its own security based on evidenc
other than that provided by our actions in South Vietnam.

Within this framework the following groupings emerge:

(1) The Republic of China and Thailand: staunch allies whos
preference for extreme U.S. actions including a risk of war wit
Communist China sets them apart from all other Asian nation

(2) The Republic of Korea and the Philippines: equally staunc
allies whose support for strong U.S. action short of a war wit
Communist China would make post-settlement reassurance a pres
ing U.S. need;

(3) Japan: it would prefer wisdom to valor in an area remot
from its own interests where escalation could involve its Chines
or Eurasian neighbors or both;

(4) Laos: a friendly neutral dependent on a strong Thai-U.S
guarantee of support in the face of increased Vietnamese and Lac
pressures.

(5) Burma and Cambodia: suspicious neutrals whose fear c
antagonizing Communist China would increase their leanin
toward Peiping in a conviction that the U.S. presence is not lon
for Southeast Asia; and

(6) Indonesia: whose opportunistic marriage of convenience c

both Hanoi and Peiping would carry it further in its overt aggression against Malaysia, convinced that foreign imperialism is a fast fading entity in the region.

Japan

Government cooperation [words illegible] essential in making the following points to the Japanese people:

(1) U.S. support was given in full measure as shown by our casualties, our expenditures and our risk taking;

(2) The U.S. record in Korea shows the credibility of our commitment so far as Japan is concerned.

The government as such supports our strong posture in Vietnam but stops short of the idea of a war between the U.S. and China.

Thailand

Thai commitments to the struggle within Laos and South Vietnam are based upon a careful evaluation of the regional threat to Thailand's security. The Thais are confident they can contain any threats from Indochina alone. They know, however, they cannot withstand the massive power of Communist China without foreign assistance. Unfortunately, the Thai view of the war has seriously erred in fundamental respects. They believe American power can do anything, both militarily and in terms of shoring up the Saigon regime. They now assume that we really could take over in Saigon and win the war if we felt we had to. If we should fail to do so, the Thais would initially see it as a failure of U.S. will. Yet time is on our side, providing we employ it effectively. Thailand is an independent nation with a long national history, and unlike South Vietnam, an acute national consciousness. It has few domestic Communists and none of the instability that plague its neighbors, Burma and Malaysia. Its one danger area in the northeast is well in hand so far as preventive measures against insurgency are concerned. Securing the Mekong Valley will be critical in any long-run solution, whether by the partition of Laos with Thai-U.S. forces occuping the western half or by some [word illegible] arrangement. Providing we are willing to make the effort, Thailand can be a foundation of rock and not a bed of sand in which to base our political/military commitment to Southeast Asia.

—With the exception of the nations in Southeast Asia, a compromise settlement in South Vietnam should not have a major impact on the credibility of our commitments around the world . . . Chancellor Erhard has told us privately that the people of Berlin would be concerned by a compromise settlement of South Vietnam. But this was hardly an original thought, and I suspect he was telling us what he believed we would like to hear. After all, the confidence of the West Berliners will depend more on what they see on the spot than on [word illegible] news or events halfway around the world. In my observation, the principal anxiety of our NATO Allies is that we have become too preoccupied with an area which seems to them an irrelevance and may be tempted in neglect to our NATO responsibilities. Moreover, they have a

vested interest in an easier relationship between Washington an
Moscow. By and large, therefore, they will be inclined to regard
compromise solution in South Vietnam more as new evidence c
American maturity and judgment than of American loss of fac
. . . On balance, I believe we would more seriously undermine th
effectiveness of our world leadership by continuing the war an
deepening our involvement than by pursuing a carefully plotte
course toward a compromise solution. In spite of the number c
powers that have—in response to our pleading—given verbal suj
port from feeling of loyalty and dependence, we cannot ignore th
fact that the war is vastly unpopular and that our role in it
perceptively eroding the respect and confidence with which othe
nations regard us. We have not persuaded either our friends c
allies that our further involvement is essential to the defense c
freedom in the cold war. Moreover, the men we deploy in th
jungles of South Vietnam, the more we contribute to a growin
world anxiety and mistrust.

[Words illegible] the short run, of course, we could expect som
catcalls from the sidelines and some vindictive pleasure on th
part of Europeans jealous of American power. But that would, i
my view, be a transient phenomenon with which we could liv
without sustained anguish. Elsewhere around the world I woul
see few unhappy implications for the credibility of our commi
ments. No doubt the Communists will to gain propaganda valu
in Africa, but I cannot seriously believe that the Africans car
too much about what happens in Southeast Asia. Australia an
New Zealand are, of course, special cases since they feel lonely i
the far reaches of the Pacific. Yet even their concern is far greate
with Malaysia than with South Vietnam, and the degree of thei
anxiety would be conditioned largely by expressions of our suppoi
for Malaysia.

[Words illegible] Quite possibly President de Gaulle will mak
propaganda about perfidious Washington, yet even he will b
inhibited by his much-heralded disapproval of our activities i
South Vietnam.

South Korea—As for the rest of the Far East the only seriou
point of concern might be South Korea. But if we stop pressin
the Koreans for more troops to Vietnam (the Vietnamese sho
no desire for additional Asian forces since it affronts their sens
of pride) we may be able to cushion Korean reactions to a con
promise in South Vietnam by the provision of greater military an
economic assistance. In this regard, Japan can play a pivotal rol
now that it has achieved normal relations with South Korea.

104

McNaughton Memo to Goodpaster on "Forces Required to Win"

Excerpts from memorandum from Assistant Secretary McNaughton to Lieut. Gen. Andrew J. Goodpaster, assistant to the Chairman of the Joint Chiefs of Staff, July 2, 1965, "Forces Required to Win in South Vietnam," as provided in the body of the Pentagon's study.

Secretary McNamara this morning suggested that General Wheeler form a small group to address the question, "If we do everything we can, can we have assurance of winning in South Vietnam?" General Wheeler suggested that he would have you head up the group and that the group would be fairly small. Secretary McNamara indicated that he wanted your group to work with me and that I should send down a memorandum suggesting some of the questions that occurred to us. Here are our suggestions:

1. I do not think the question is whether the 44-battalion program (including 3d-country forces) is sufficient to do the job although the answer to that question should fall out of the study. Rather, I think we should think in terms of the 44-battalion build-up by the end of 1965, with added forces—as required and as our capabilities permit—in 1966. Furthermore, the study surely should look into the need for forces other than ground forces, such as air to be used one way or another in-country. I would hope that the study could produce a clear articulation of what our strategy is for winning the war in South Vietnam, tough as that articulation will be in view of the nature of the problem.

2. I would assume that the questions of calling up reserves and extending tours of duty are outside the scope of this study.

3. We must make some assumptions with respect to the number of VC. Also, we must make some assumptions with respect to what the infiltration of men and material will be especially if there is a build-up of U.S. forces in South Vietnam. I am quite concerned about the increasing probability that there are regular PAVN forces either in the II Corps area or in Laos directly across the border from II Corps. Furthermore, I am fearful that especially with the kind of build-up here envisioned, infiltration of even greater numbers of regular forces may occur. As a part of this general problem of enemy build-up, we must of course ask how much assistance the USSR and China can be expected to give to the VC. I suspect that the increased strength levels of the VC and the more "conventional" nature of the operations implied by larger force levels may imply that the often-repeated ratio of "10 to 1" may no longer apply. I sense that this may be the case in the future, but I have no reason to be sure. For example, if the

VC, even with larger forces engaged in more "conventional" type actions, are able to overrun towns and disappear into the jungles before we can bring the action troops to bear, we may still be faced with the old "ratio" problem.

4. I think we might avoid some spinning of wheels if we simply assumed that the GVN will not be able to increase its forces in the relevant time period. Indeed, from what Westy has reported about the battalions being chewed up and about their showing some signs of reluctance to engage in offensive operations, we might even have to ask the question whether we can expect them to maintain present levels of men—or more accurately, present levels of effectiveness.

5. With respect to 3d-country forces, Westy has equated the 9 ROK battalions with 9 U.S. battalions, saying that, if he did not get the former, he must have the latter. I do not know enough about ROK forces to know whether they are in all respects "equal to" U.S. forces (they may be better in some respects and not as good in others). For purposes of the study, it might save us time if we assumed that we would get no meaningful forces from anyone other than the ROKs during the relative time frame. (If the Australians decide to send another battalion or two, this should not alter the conclusions of the study significantly.) . . .

9. At the moment, I do not see how the study can avoid addressing the question as to how long our forces will have to remain in order to achieve a "win" and the extent to which the presence of those forces over a long period of time might, by itself, nullify the "win." If it turns out that the study cannot go into this matter without first getting heavily into the political side of the question, I think the study at least should note the problem in some meaningful way.

10. I believe that the study should go into specifics—e.g., the numbers and effectiveness and uses of the South Vietnamese forces, exactly where we would deploy ours and exactly what we would expect their mission to be, how we would go about opening up the roads and providing security for the towns as well as protecting our own assets there, the time frames in which things would be done, command relationships, etc. Also, I think we should find a way to indicate how badly the conclusions might be thrown off if we are wrong with respect to key assumptions or judgments. . . .

105

McNamara's Memo on July 20, 1965, on Increasing Allied Ground Force

Excerpts from memorandum from Secretary McNamara for President Johnson, drafted on July 1, 1965, and revised on July 20, as provided in the body of the Pentagon's study.

Paragraphs in italics are the study's paraphrase or explanation.

In a memorandum to the President drafted on 1 July and then revised on 20 July, immediately following his return from a week-long visit to Vietnam, he recommended an immediate decision to increase the U.S.-Third Country presence from the current 16 maneuver battalions (15 U.S., one Australian), and a change in the mission of these forces from one of providing support and reinforcement for the ARVN to one which soon became known as "search and destroy"—as McNamara put it, they were "by aggressive exploitation of superior military forces . . . to gain and hold the initiative . . . pressing the fight against VC-DRV main force units in South Vietnam to run them to ground and destroy them." . . .

His specific recommendations, he noted, were concurred in by General Wheeler and Ambassador-designate Lodge, who accompanied him on his trip to Vietnam, and by Ambassador Taylor, Ambassador Johnson, Admiral Sharp and General Westmoreland, with whom he conferred there. The rationale for his decisions was supplied by the CIA, whose assessment he quoted with approval in concluding that 1 July version of his memorandum. It stated:

Over the longer term we doubt if the Communists are likely to change their basic strategy in Vietnam (i.e., aggressive and steadily mounting insurgency) unless and until two conditions prevail: (1) they are forced to accept a situation in the war in the South which offers them no prospect of an early victory and no grounds for hope that they can simply outlast the U.S. and (2) North Vietnam itself is under continuing and increasingly damaging punitive attack. So long as the Communists think they scent the possibility of an early victory (which is probably now the case), we believe that they will persevere and accept extremely severe damage to the North. Conversely, if North Vietnam itself is not hurting, Hanoi's doctrinaire leaders will probably be ready to carry on the Southern struggle almost indefinitely. If, however, both of the conditions outlined above should be brought to pass, we believe Hanoi probably would, at least for a period of time, alter its basic strategy and course of action in South Vietnam.

McNamara's memorandum of 20 July did not include this quotation, although many of these points were made elsewhere in the paper. Instead, it concluded with an optimistic forecast:

The overall evaluation is that the course of action recommended in this memorandum—if the military and political moves are properly integrated and executed with continuing vigor and visible determination—stands a good chance of achieving an acceptable outcome within a reasonable time in Vietnam.

Never again while he was Secretary of Defense would McNamara make so optimistic a statement about Vietnam—except in public.

This concluding paragraph of McNamara's memorandum spoke

of political, as well as military, "vigor" and "determination." Earlier in the paper, under the heading "Expanded political moves," he had elaborated on this point, writing:

Together with the above military moves, we should take political initiatives in order to lay a groundwork for a favorable political settlement by clarifying our objectives and establishing channels of communications. At the same time as we are taking steps to turn the tide in South Vietnam, we would make quiet moves through diplomatic channels (a) to open a dialogue with Moscow and Hanoi, and perhaps the VC, looking first toward disabusing them of any misconceptions as to our goals and second toward laying the groundwork for a settlement when the time is ripe; (b) to keep the Soviet Union from deepening its military [sic] in the world until the time when settlement can be achieved; and (c) to cement support for U.S. policy by the U.S. public, allies and friends, and to keep international opposition at a manageable level. Our efforts may be unproductive until the tide begins to turn, but nevertheless they should be made.

Here was scarcely a program for drastic political action. McNamara's essentially procedural (as opposed to substantive) recommendations amounted to little more than saying that the United States should provide channels for the enemy's discreet and relatively facesaving surrender when he decided that the game had grown too costly. This was, in fact, what official Washington (again with the exception of Ball) meant in mid-1965 when it spoke of a "political settlement." (As McNamara noted in a footnote, even this went too far for Ambassador-designate Lodge, whose view was that "any further initiative by us now [before we are strong] would simply harden the Communist resolve not to stop fighting." In this view Ambassadors Taylor and Johnson concurred, except that they would maintain "discreet contacts with the Soviets.")

McNamara's concluding paragraph spoke of "an acceptable outcome." Previously in his paper he had listed "nine fundamental elements" of a favorable outcome. These were:

(a) VC stop attacks and drastically reduce incidents of terror and sabotage.

(b) DRV reduces infiltration to a trickle, with some reasonably reliable method of our obtaining confirmation of this fact.

(c) U.S./GVN stop bombing of North Vietnam.

(d) GVN stays independent (hopefully pro-U.S., but possibly genuinely neutral).

(e) GVN exercises governmental functions over substantially all of South Vietnam.

(f) Communists remain quiescent in Laos and Thailand.

(g) DRV withdraws PAVN forces and other North Vietnamese infiltrators (not regroupees) from South Vietnam.

(h) VC/NLF transform from a military to a purely political organization.

(i) U.S. combat forces (not advisors or AID) withdraw.

Chapter 8

The Buildup: July, 1965–
September, 1966

—BY FOX BUTTERFIELD

The Pentagon's secret study of the Vietnam war indicates that the rapid expansion of American forces in 1965 and 1966 occurred because "no one really foresaw what the troop needs in Vienam would be" and because the ability of the enemy forces "to build up their effort was consistently underrated."

"It would seem," the study asserts, that the American planners would have been "very sensitive to rates of infiltration and recruitment by the [Vietcong and North Vietnamese Army]; but very little analysis was, in fact, given to the implications of the capabilities of the VC/VNA in this regard."

As a result of the unanticipated enemy build-up, the Pentagon study discloses, Gen. William C. Westmoreland's troop requests jumped from a total of 175,000 men in June, 1965, to 275,000 that July, to 443,000 in December and then to 542,000 the following June. Neither the requests of the American commander in Vietnam nor President Lyndon B. Johnson's rapid approval of all but the last of them was made public.

At the same time, the study says, the Johnson Administration's continual expansion of the air war during 1965 and 1966 was based on a "colossal misjudgment" about the bombing's effect on Hanoi's will and capabilities.

In particular, the study discloses that the Administration's decision in 1966 to bomb North Vietnam's oil-storage facilities was made despite repeated warning from the Central Intelligence Agency that such action would not "cripple Communist military operations." Instead the study says, Washington apparently accepted the military's estimate that the bombing

Highlights of the Period

The United States military effort in Vietnam, according to the Pentagon study, continued to intensify—both on the ground and in the air—throughout 1965 and well into 1966, despite continuing evidence that this escalation was bringing "an acceptable outcome" no closer to realization.

Here, in chronological order, are highlights of this period:

JULY, 1965

John T. McNaughton, Assistant Secretary of Defense, defines "win" for U.S. as "demonstrating to the VC that they cannot win."

Secretary of Defense Robert S. McNamara, assured by special study group headed by Gen. Earle G. Wheeler, Chairman of Joint Chiefs, that "there appears to be no reason we cannot win if such is our will," approves request by Gen. William Westmoreland, U.S. military commander in Vietnam, for 100,000 more U.S. troops.

Mr. McNamara, in memo to President, says he thinks General Westmoreland's three-phase strategy plan "stands a good chance" of success, notes casualties will increase, suggests U.S. "killed-in-action might be in the vicinity of 500 a month by the end of the year . . . ."

Pentagon study notes U.S. strategy "did not take escalatory reactions into account."

NOVEMBER, 1965

General Westmoreland asks for 154,000 more men; this would bring total U.S. troops in Vietnam to 375,000, study says. General explains to Adm. U. S. Grant Sharp, U.S. commander in the Pacific, that Vietcong-North Vietnamese rate of troop build-up is expected to be "double that of U.S."

Mr. McNamara, in memo to President, recommends U.S. supply total of nearly 400,000 men by end of 1966, adds that this "will not guarantee success."

DECEMBER, 1965

General Westmoreland asks for total of 443,000 troops by end of 1966. Air war continues at rate of 1,500 sorties weekly.

JANUARY, 1966

General increases request to 459,000 men.

McNamara memorandum concedes that air war "has not successfully interdicted infiltration." Second memo warns, "We are in an escalating military stalemate." Includes coalition, neutralist "or even anti-U.S." Government as among outcomes U.S. should be able to accept. Still urges more troops, bombing.

MARCH, 1966

Secretary McNamara, after months of pressure from Joint Chiefs, recommends U.S. bomb petroleum, oil and lubricant supplies in North Vietnam. Admiral Sharp had predicted this would "bring the enemy to the conference table or cause the insurgency to wither."

APRIL, 1966

White House policy meetings to consider Vietnam options. George W. Ball, Under Secretary of State, urges "cutting our losses," concedes "no really attractive options open to us."

MAY, 1966

President decides to order P.O.L. air strikes. C.I.A. estimates this will not halt "infiltration of men and supplies."

JUNE, 1966

Oil strikes begin, hitting Haiphong, Hanoi storage sites.

JULY, 1966

By month's end, Defense Intelligence Agency estimates 70 per cent North Vietnam's original storage capacity destroyed.

AUGUST, 1966

Major storage sites destroyed; study calls flow of men and material to South "undiminished," notes North Vietnam's adaptability and resourcefulness" in switching to small, dispersed sites, almost impossible to bomb.

Joint Chiefs pass on new Westmoreland ground-troop request to Mr. McNamara: 542,588 total for 1967.

SEPTEMBER, 1966

Report to Secretary McNamara from study group says Operation Rolling Thunder "had no measurable direct effect" on Hanoi's capability in South Vietnam; concludes that "there is no firm basis for determining if there is any feasible level of effort that would achieve" U.S. air-war objectives.

Study group recommends building electronic barrier across Vienamese demilitarized zone.

would "bring the enemy to the conference table or cause the insurgency to wither from lack of support." But the flow of men and supplies to the South continued "undiminished."

The Pentagon study of this period of escalation in the air and on the ground also makes these disclosures:

• American military commanders were confident of victory. General Westmoreland, for example, told Washington in July, 1965, that by using his search-and-destroy strategy he could defeat the enemy "by the end of 1967." And the same month, the Joint Chiefs of Staff assured Secretary of Defense Robert S. McNamara that "there is no reason we cannot win if such is our will."

• High-level civilian authorities, including Secretary McNamara, began to have serious doubts about the effectiveness of both the air and ground war as early as the fall of 1965, but they continued to recommend escalation as the only acceptable policy, despite their doubts.

• A secret Defense Department seminar of 47 scientists—"the cream of the scholarly community in technical fields"—concluded in the summer of 1966 that the bombing of North Vietnam had had "no measurable effect" on Hanoi. The scientists recommended building an electronic barrier between North and South Vietnam as an alternative to the bombing. [See Document #117.]

The Pentagon account of this period of the war—from July, 1965, to the fall of 1966—forms another section in the series presented by The New York Times.

The study, ordered by Secretary McNamara in 1967 and prepared by a team of 30 to 40 officials and analysts to determine how the United States became involved in the war in Indochina, consists of 3,000 pages of analysis and 4,000 pages of supporting documents.

Open-Ended Strategy

When President Johnson decided in July, 1965, to accept General Westmoreland's request for 44 combat battalions and to endorse his search-and-destroy strategy, he "left the U.S. commitment to Vietnam open-ended," the study declares.

"Force levels for the search-and-destroy strategy had no empirical limits," it adds. "The amount of force required to defeat the enemy depended entirely on his response to the build-up and his willingness to continue the fight."

"The basic idea" underlying the search-and-destroy strategy, the study says, "was the desire to take the war to the enemy, denying him freedom of movement anywhere in the country . . . and deal him the heaviest possible blows." This concept replaced the static-defense and enclave strategies, which called for fewer American troops, and which had been tried briefly in the spring of 1965.

General Westmoreland intended his original allotment of 44 battalions to be only a stopgap measure, the account says. They would be used to blunt the enemy offensive that threatened to overwhelm the fragile Saigon Government, but more men would quickly be needed if the allies were to win.

To find out how much "additional force was required to seize the initiative from the enemy and to commence the win phase of the strategy," Secretary McNamara flew to Saigon on July 16, 1965, for a four-day visit. While he was there he received a cablegram notifying him that President Johnson had approved General Westmoreland's request for 44 battalions and the use of his search-and-destroy strategy.

According to the study, General Westmoreland then reported that he needed 24 additional American battalions, or 100,000 men, for the "win phase," which would begin in 1966.

He also outlined, as quoted in the study, his over-all strategy, based on a three-phase build-up:

"Phase I—The commitment of U.S./F.W.M.A. [United States/Free World Military Assistance] forces necessary to halt the losing trend by the end of 1965.

"Phase II—The resumption of the offensive by U.S./F.W.M.A. forces during the first half of 1966 in high-priority areas necessary to destroy enemy forces, and reinstitution of rural-construction activities.

"Phase III—If the enemy persisted, a period of a year to a year and a half following Phase II would be required for the defeat and destruction of the remaining enemy forces and base areas.

"Withdrawal of U.S./F.W.M.A. forces would commence following Phase III as the GVN [Government of Vietnam] became able to establish and maintain internal order and to defend its borders."

According to the Pentagon study, General Westmoreland's plan shows that "with enough force to seize the initiative from the VC sometime in 1966, General Westmoreland expected to take the offensive and, with appropriate additional reinforcements, to have defeated the enemy by the end of 1967."

Secretary McNamara was seriously concerned, the Pentagon account says, about whether the United States could "win" in Vietnam. He was worried lest the United States "become involved more deeply in a war which could not be brought to a satisfactory conclusion."

Thus while he was preparing for his July 16 trip to Saigon, the Secretary asked Gen. Earle G. Wheeler, Chairman of the Joint Chiefs of Staff, for an assessment of "the assurance the U.S. can have of winning in South Vietnam if we do everything we can."

General Wheeler's answer, prepared by a study group of officers and civilians in the Defense Department, was: "Within the bounds of reasonable assumptions—there appears to be no reason we cannot win if such is our will—and if that will is manifested in strategy and tactical operations."

According to a memorandum to the study group from Assistant Secretary of Defense John T. McNaughton, on the working definition of "win," it "means that we succeed in demonstrating to the VC that they cannot win."

This definition, the Pentagon analyst writes, "indicates the assumption upon which the conduct of the war was to rest—that the VC could be convinced in some meaningful sense that they were not going to win and that they would then rationally choose less violent methods of seeking their goals."

Secretary McNamara got this assurance, the study goes on, and, armed with it, he recommended on his return from Saigon on July 20 that President Johnson meet General Westmoreland's request for 100,000 additional troops.

"The over-all evaluation," Secretary McNamara wrote the President, "is that the course of action recommended in this memorandum stands a good chance of achieving an acceptable outcome within a reasonable time in Vietnam."

"U.S. and South Vietnamese casualties will increase, just how much cannot be predicted with confidence," the Secretary added, "but the U.S. killed-in-action might be in the vicinity of 500 a month by the end of the year . . . . United States public opinion will support the course of action because it is a sensible and courageous military-political program designed and likely to bring about a success in Vietnam."

The Pentagon account declares: "Never again while he was Secretary of Defense would McNamara make so optimistic a statement about Vietnam—except in public."

By November, 1965, the situation in South Vietnam had undergone important changes, the study says.

The Phase I deployment of American troops, which was now nearing its 175,000-man goal, had apparently stopped deterioration in the military situation.

But at the same time, the narrative relates, the enemy had unexpectedly built up strength much faster than the American command had foreseen.

Where there were estimated to be 48,550 Communist combat troops in South Vietnam in July, 1965, American intelligence officials believed by that November that there were 63,550. And the number of North Vietnamese regiments had increased during these months from one to eight, according to the intelligence officials.

"The implications of the build-up were made abundantly clear by the bloody fighting in the Iadrang Valley in mid-November," the study says. In this first big battle of the Vietnam war, units of the United States First Cavalry Division fought numerically superior North Vietnamese forces for several weeks in the western part of the Central Highlands, along the Cambodian border. More than 1,200 of the enemy were reportedly killed in the fighting, which also left more than 200 Americans dead.

The Pentagon study says that the carefully calculated American strategy, with its plans for the number of American troops required to win, "did not take escalatory reactions into account."

While the study does not deal with this subject at length, the public record shows that the Johnson Administration had repeatedly said during early 1965 that North Vietnam was infiltrating large quantities of men and supplies into the South.

In February, for example, the State Department published a white paper entitled "Aggression From the North," asserting that North Vietnam was responsible for the war in South Vietnam and that Hanoi had infiltrated more than 37,000 men.

The public record also shows that Secretary McNamara devoted a major part of a televised news conference on April 26, 1965, to a charge that North Vietnamese had stepped up their infiltration. "The intensification of infiltration," Mr. McNamara said, "has grown progressively more flagrant and more unconstrained."

Despite these frequent public statements about the build-up, in November, the Pentagon account says, General Westmoreland suddenly found it necessary to request a vast increase in troops for the Phase II part of his plan. The general said he would need 154,000 more men.

As the general explained his needs to Adm. U. S. Grant Sharp, commander of American forces in the Pacific, who was his immediate superior:

"The VC/PAVN build-up rate is predicated to be double that of U.S. Phase II forces. Whereas we will add an average of 7 maneuver battalions per quarter the enemy will add 15. This development has already reduced the November battalion-equivalent ratio from an anticipated 3.2 to 1, to 2.8 to 1, and it will be further reduced to 2.5 to 1 by the end of the year."

In response to General Westmoreland's request for 154,000 men, Secretary McNamara detoured on his way from a Paris meeting of the North Atlantic Treaty Organization and flew to Saigon.

On his return to Washington on Nov. 30, Secretary McNamara wrote a memorandum to President Johnson in which he began to reveal doubts about the ground war. While recommending that the United States send a total of nearly 400,000 men to Vietnam by the end of 1966, the next year, he warned:

"We should be aware that deployments of the kind I have recommended will not guarantee success. U.S. killed-in-action can be expected to reach 1,000 a month, and the odds are even that we will be faced in early 1967 with a 'no decision' at an even higher level. My over-all evaluation, nevertheless, is that the best chance of achieving our stated objectives lies in . . . the deployments mentioned above." [See Document #107.]

While Secretary McNamara and President Johnson were considering troop increases up to nearly 400,000 men—the number of Americans in South Vietnam was then 184,000—news accounts were speculating that the troop ceiling might go as high as 200,000. This was the figure used, for example, in The New York Times's dispatch on Mr. McNamara's visit to Saigon on Nov. 28.

The Pentagon study does not say what decision President Johnson reached on Mr. McNamara's Nov. 30 recommendation. But the analyst does say that on Dec. 13, in another memorandum, Mr. McNamara outlined for the President an approved troop deployment of 367,000 men for 1966 and 395,000 men for June 1967.

Then on Dec. 16, the study reveals, Secretary McNamara received another request from General Westmoreland, raising to 443,000 men the total he needed by the end of 1966. And on Jan. 28 the Secretary received a new request, this time increasing the total to 459,000 men.

Neither General Westmoreland's requests nor President Johnson's approvals were made public. At a news conference on Feb. 26, 1966, the President said, "We do not have on my desk at the moment any unfilled requests from General Westmoreland." There were 235,000 American soldiers in South Vietnam at the time.

The Pentagon narrative suggests two possible interpretations for the rapid ballooning of the number of troops required:

"It can be hypothesized, that from the outset of the American build-up, some military men felt that winning a meaningful victory in Vietnam would require something on the order of one million men.

"Knowing that this would be unacceptable politically, it may have seemed a better bargaining strategy to ask for increased deployments incrementally.

"An alternative explanation is that no one really foresaw what the troop needs in Vietnam would be and that the ability of the D.R.V./VC to build up their effort was consistently underrated.

"This explanation seems, with some exceptions, to be reasonable. The documents from the period around July 1965 seem to indicate that [General Westmoreland] had not given much thought to what he was going to do in the year or years after 1965."

Citing a document of General Westmoreland's Military Assistance Command in Vietnam, the study goes on: "The words of the MACV history of 1965 indicate something of this. 'The President's July 28 announcement that the U.S. would commit additional massive military forces in SVN necessitated an overall plan clarifying the missions and deployment of the various components. [The general's] concept of operations was prepared to fulfill this need.'"

"If this is a true reflection of what happened," the analyst says, "it would indicate the MACV's plan of what to do was derived from what would be available rather than the requirement for manpower being derived from any clearly thought out military plan."

In April, 1965, when President Johnson secretly changed the mission of the Marines at Danang from defense to offense and thus commited the United States to the ground war in Vietnam, the sustained bombing of North Vietnam was relegated to a secondary role, the Pentagon study declares. Discussing this bombing campaign, known as Operation Rolling Thunder, the study adds:

"Earlier expectations that bombing would constitute the primary means for the U.S. to turn the tide of the war had been overtaken by the President's decision to send in substantial U.S. ground forces. With this decision the main hope had shifted from inflicting pain in the North to proving, in the South, that NVN could not win a military victory there. Rolling Thunder was counted as useful and necessary, but in the prevailing view it was a supplement and not a substitute for efforts within SVN."

By the summer of 1965, Operation Rolling Thunder's scope and pattern of operation had also been determined, the narrative relates.

To emphasize American power, it goes on, the bombing of the North would proceed "in a slow, steady, deliberate manner, beginning with a few infiltration-associated targets in southern NVN and gradually moving northward with progressively more severe attacks on a wider variety of targets."

Because Operation Rolling Thunder was considered "comparatively risky and politically sensitive," all bombing strikes were carefully selected in Washington. Targets were chosen in weekly packages, the study says, and each target package "had to pass through a chain of approvals which included senior levels of O.S.D. [Office of the Secretary of Defense], the Department of State and the White House."

Attacks were also permitted against certain broad categories of targets, such as vehicles, locomotives and barges, which were defined in Washington. In this type of attack, known as armed reconnaissance, the final selection of a specific target was left to the pilot.

The number of sorties—individual flights by individual planes—was gradually increased, the account relates, from 900 a week during July to 1,500 a week in December, 1965. By the end of the year 55,000 sorties had been flown, nearly three-fourths of them on armed reconnaissance.

While the list of targets was also lengthened, Secretary McNamara continued to keep the Hanoi-Haiphong area and the Chinese border area off limits through the end of 1965.

The study reports that the original purpose of Rolling Thunder, "to break the will of North Vietnam," was changed during the summer of 1965 to cutting the flow of men and supplies from the North to the South.

This change in the Government's internal rationale, the

analyst writes, brought it in line with the publicly expressed rationale, which had always been an infiltration cutoff.

The rationale was changed, the study declares, because it was recognized that "as a venture in strategic persuasion the bombing had not worked."

In fact, intelligence estimates commissioned by Secretary McNamara showed that by the end of 1965 the bombing had had little effect on North Vietnam.

In November, 1965, the Defense Intelligence Agency told Mr. McNamara that while the "cumulative strains" resulting from the bombing had "reduced industrial performance" in North Vietnam, "the primarily rural nature of the area permits continued functioning of the subsistence economy."

And, the agency's estimate continued, "The air strikes do not appear to have altered Hanoi's determination to continue supporting the war in South Vietnam."

In the analyst's view, "The idea that destroying, or threatening to destroy, North Vietnam's industry would pressure Hanoi into calling it quits, seems, in retrospect, a colossal misjudgment." The analyst continues:

"NVN was an extremely poor target for air attack. The theory of either strategic or interdiction bombing assumed highly developed industrial nations producing large quantities of military goods to sustain mass armies engaged in intensive warfare. NVN, as U.S. intelligence agencies knew, was an agricultural country with a rudimentary transportation system and little industry of any kind.

"What intelligence agencies liked to call the 'modern industrial sector' of the economy was tiny even by Asian standards, producing only about 12 per cent of the G.N.P. of $1.6-billion in 1965. There were only a handful of 'major industrial facilities.' When NVN was first targeted, the J.C.S. found only eight industrial installations worth listing."

"NVN's limited industry made little contribution to its military capabilities," the account continues. "The great bulk of its military equipment, and all of the heavier and more sophisticated items, had to be imported. This was no particular problem, since both the U.S.S.R. and China were apparently more than glad to help.

"The NVN transportation system was austere and superficially looked very vulnerable to air attack, but it was inherently flexible and its capacity greatly exceeded the demands placed upon it.

"Supporting the war in the south was hardly a great strain on NVN's economy. The NVA/VC forces there did not constitute a large army. They did not fight as conventional division or field armies, with tanks and airplanes and field artillery; they did not need to be supplied by huge convoys of trucks, trains or ships. They fought and moved on foot, supplying themselves locally, in the main, and simply avoiding combat when supplies were low."

A Pause as Pressure

An important element in Secretary McNamara's program of pressure against North Vietnam, the study says, was a pause in the bombing. On July 20, 1965, Mr. McNamara wrote in a memorandum to the President:

"After the 44 U.S.-third-country battalions have been deployed and after some strong action has been taken in the program of bombing in the North, we could, as part of a diplomatic initiative, consider introducing a 6-8 week pause in the program of bombing the North."

He apparently felt, the Pentagon study says, that the previous pause—May 8 to May 13, 1965—had been too short and too hastily arranged to be effective. Hanoi was simply not given enough time to reply during the May pause, the study says. It also relates that President Johnson had viewed the pause "as a means of clearing the way for an increase in the tempo of the air war in the absence of a satisfactory response from Hanoi."

The Secretary of Defense repeated his proposal for a bombing pause several times during the fall of 1965, the account goes on. As he and Assistant Secretary of Defense McNaughton envisioned it, the pause would be used as a kind of "ratchet,"—which the analyst likens to "the device which raises the net on a tennis court, backing off tension between each phase of increasing it."

All the high officials who debated the pause in bombing assumed that it would be temporary, the study declares. "Throughout this discussion it was taken for granted that bombing would be resumed."

The officials, known in government circles as the "Vietnam principals," believed the bombing would be resumed, the narrative adds, because they knew that the conditions they had set for a permanent halt were tougher than Hanoi could accept.

In a confidential memorandum on Dec. 3, apparently intended only for Mr. McNamara, Assistant Secretary McNaughton outlined the conditions the United States should insist upon for a permanent halt:

"A. The D.R.V. stops infiltration and direction of the war.

"B. The D.R.V. moves convincingly toward withdrawal of infiltrators.

"C. The VC stops attacks, terror and sabotage.

"D. The VC stop significant interference with the GVN's exercise of governmental functions over substantially all of South Vietnam."

After noting these conditions, Mr. McNaughton wrote that they amounted to "capitulation by a Communist force that is far from beaten."

The Joint Chiefs as well as Secretary of State Dean Rusk opposed any halt in bombing, the study says, because they were concerned that a pause would ease the pressure on Hanoi. [See Document #106.]

They also feared that Hanoi might offer an opening of negotiations in exchange for a halt in bombing, without making any of the substantive concessions that Washington wanted, the study adds.

"The available materials do not reveal the President's response to these arguments," the narrative relates, "but it is clear from the continuing flow of papers that he delayed positively committing himself either for or against a pause until very shortly before the actual pause began."

The pause was to last 37 days, from Dec. 24, 1965, to Jan. 31, 1966.

Doubts Start to Emerge

The ineffectiveness of Rolling Thunder and General Westmoreland's mounting demand for troops soon began to create doubts among the "Vietnam principals," the Pentagon study says. During the pause in the bombing, both Mr. McNaughton and Secretary McNamara wrote lengthy memorandums outlining the change in their feelings.

In a paper titled "Some Observations About Bombing North Vietnam," dated Jan. 18, 1966 and quoted in the narrative, Mr. McNaughton asked: "Can the program be

expected to reduce (not just increase the cost of) D.R.V. ai●
to the South and hopefully put a ceiling on it?"

His own answer was no. "The program so far has not suc●
cessfully interdicted infiltration of men and material int●
South Vietnam," he wrote. "Despite our armed reconnaissanc●
efforts and strikes of railroads, roads, bridges, storage centers
training bases and other key links in their lines of communica
tions, it is estimated that they are capable of generating in th●
North and infiltrating to the South 4,500 men a month an●
between 50 and 300 tons a day depending on the season."

This, he noted, was enough to support a major effor
against the United States.

The next day Mr. McNaughton prepared another memo
randum, expanding on his first draft, in which he warned:
"We have in Vietnam the ingredients of an enormous miscalculation." [See Document #109.]

"The ARVN is tired, passive and accommodation-prone.
. . ." he wrote. "The PAVN/VC are effectively matching
our deployments . . . The bombing of the North may o●
may not be able effectively to interdict infiltration . . . Pacification is still stalled . . . The GVN political infrastructure is
moribund and weaker than the VC infrastructure . . . South
Vietnam is near the edge of serious infiltration and economic
chaos.

"We are in an escalating military stalemate."

"The present U.S. objective in Vietnam is to avoid humiliation," he wrote. "At each decision point we have gambled;
at each point, to avoid the damage to our effectiveness of defaulting on our commitment, we have upped the ante. We have
not defaulted, and the ante (and commitment) is now very
high." The words in parentheses were in the memorandum.

Mr. McNaughton suggested that Washington ought to consider settling for something short of a military victory.

"Some will say that we have defaulted if we end up . . .
with anything less than a Western-oriented, non-Communist,
independent government, exercising effective sovereignty over
all of South Vietnam," he wrote. "This is not so. As stated
above, the U.S. end is solely to preserve our reputation as a
guarantor."

He then outlined some outcomes that he felt the United
States should be able to accept:

"Coalition government including Communists.

"A free decision by the South to succumb to the VC or to
the North.

"A neutral (or even anti-U.S.) government in SVN.

"A live-and let-live 'reversion to 1959.' "

This presumably referred to the situation of low-level guerrilla warfare that prevailed in 1959, before either North Vietnam or the United States had committed major forces to the conflict.

Despite the pessimism of his analysis, the study adds, Mr. McNaughton went on to recommend "more effort for pacification, more push behind the Ky government, more battalions . . . and intensive interdiction bombing."

On Jan. 24, Secretary McNamara wrote a revised version of his Nov. 30, 1965, memorandum to President Johnson that, the study says, echoed much of his Assistant Secretary's pessimism.

While Mr. McNamara, too, recommended increasing the bombing strikes against North Vietnam, he could say only that "the increased program probably will not put a tight ceiling on the enemy's activities in South Vietnam."

And though he recommended raising the number of United States troops in Vietnam to more than 400,000 by the end of 1966, he told the President:

"Deployments of the kind we have recommended will not guarantee success. Our intelligence estimate is that the present Communist policy is to continue to prosecute the war vigorously in the South. They continue to believe that the war will be a long one, that time is their ally and that their own staying power is superior to ours.

"It follows, therefore, that the odds are about even that, even with the recommended deployments, we will be faced in early 1967 with a military standoff at a much higher level, with pacification still stalled, and with any prospect of military success marred by the chances of an active Chinese intervention and with the requirement for the deployment of still more U.S. forces."

The doubts among officials of the Johnson Administration grew further with a political crisis in the cities of Hue and Danang during the spring of 1966, the narrative relates, and at the White House a major debate was conducted on America's goals in Southeast Asia.

The South Vietnamese political crisis was touched off March 12, 1966, when Air Vice Marshal Nguyen Cao Ky, who was Premier, removed the powerful and semiautonomous commander of the I Corps, Gen. Nguyen Chanh Thi. Buddhist monks and students quickly joined demonstrations supporting General Thi and attacking the Ky regime.

The demonstrations stirred fears in Washington that Marshal Ky might be overthrown and replaced by a neutralist Buddhist government, the study recalls, and hurried meetings were called at the White House.

At the first of these meetings, on April 9, the study says, four policy papers were debated: George Carver, a senior C.I.A. analyst on Vietnam, argued for what was referred to as Option A—continuing as is; Leonard Unger, Deputy Assistant Secretary of State and head of the Interdepartmental Vietnam coordinating committee, presented Option B—continuing but pressing for a compromise settlement; Assistant Secretary of Defense McNaughton argued Option B-P—continuing but with a pessimistic outlook; and George W. Ball, the Under Secretary of State, took Option C—disengagement.

Mr. Ball asserted, as he had the previous June in a memorandum for the President, that "We should concentrate our attention on cutting our losses." The United States, he said, should "halt the deployment of additional forces, reduce the level of air attacks on the North, and maintain ground activity at the minimum level required to prevent the substantial improvement of the Vietcong position."

"Let us face the fact that there are no really attractive options open to us," Secretary Ball concluded in his policy paper, as quoted in the Pentagon study.

Other papers, including one by Walt W. Rostow, who had just replaced McGeorge Bundy as Presidential adviser on national security, were prepared and debated on April 12, 14 and 16.

A hint of Mr. McNaughton's state of mind during this period, the Pentagon study says, can be gathered from notes he had taken of a conversation with an official just back from Saigon. Mr. McNaughton's notes read:

"Place (VN) in unholy mess.

"We control next to no territory.

"Fears economic collapse.

"Militarily will be same place year from now.

"Pacification won't get off ground for a year."

At the April 16 meeting, William P. Bundy, Assistant Secretary of State for Far Eastern Affairs, presented a draft entitled "Basic Choices in Vietnam." He apparently favored the option of continuing along present lines, the narrative recounts, but he also said:

"As we look a year or two ahead, with a military program that would require major further budget costs—with all their implications for taxes and domestic programs—and with steady or probably rising casualties, the war could well be

come an albatross around the Administration's neck at least
equal to what Korea was for President Truman in 1952."

What new decisions these meetings produced is not clear
from the record, the Pentagon study says. The meetings ended
around April 20 with a lull in the South Vietnamese political
crisis.

The Fuel-Depot Issue

During the spring of 1966, the Pentagon study says, the
question of bombing North Vietnam's oil-storage tanks became a "major policy dispute."

"Before the question was settled," the account goes on,
"it had assumed the proportions of a strategic issue, fraught
with military danger and political risk, requiring thorough
examination and careful analysis."

The Joint Chiefs of Staff had advocated bombing North
Vietnam's oil tanks as early as the fall of 1965, the narrative
says, adding:

"The Joint Chiefs of Staff pressed throughout the autumn
and winter of 1965-66 for permission to expand the bombing
virtually into a program of strategic bombing aimed at all industrial and economic resources as well as at all interdiction
targets."

"The Chiefs did so, it may be added, despite the steady
stream of memoranda from the intelligence community consistently expressing skepticism that bombing of any conceivable sort (that is, any except bombing aimed primarily at the
destruction of North Vietnam's population) could either
persuade Hanoi to negotiate a settlement on U.S./GVN terms
or effectively limit Hanoi's ability to infiltrate men and supplies
into the South."

In a memorandum to Secretary McNamara on Nov. 10,
1965, the Chiefs asserted that the only reason the bombing
campaign had not worked thus far was because of the "self-
imposed restraints:"

"We shall continue to achieve only limited success in air
operation in D.R.V./Laos if required to operate within the
constraints presently imposed," the Joint Chiefs said. "The
establishment and observance of de facto sanctuaries within
the D.R.V., coupled with a denial of operations against the

most important military and war supporting targets, preclude attainment of the objectives of the air campaign."

The Joint Chiefs added: "Now required is an immediate and sharply accelerated program which will leave no doubt that the U.S. intends to win and achieve a level of destruction which they will not be able to overcome."

In a separate memorandum the same day, the Joint Chiefs said that an attack on North Vietnam's P.O.L.—petroleum, oil and lubricants, in military terminology—"would be more damaging to the D.R.V. capability to move war-supporting resources within country and along the infiltration routes to SVN than an attack against any other single target system."

"The flow of supplies would be greatly impeded," the Joint Chiefs said. And they contended that "recuperability of the D.R.V. P.O.L. system from the effects of an attack is very poor."

"It is not surprising that the J.C.S. singled out the P.O.L. target system for special attention," the Pentagon analyst says. "NVN had no oil fields or refineries, and had to import all of its petroleum products, in refined form. . . . Nearly all of it came from the Black Sea area of the U.S.S.R. and arrived by sea at Haiphong, the only port capable of conveniently receiving and handling bulk P.O.L. brought in by large tankers. From large tank farms at Haiphong with a capacity of about one-fourth of the annual imports, the P.O.L. was transported by road, rail and water to other large storage sites at Hanoi and elsewhere in the country. Ninety-seven per cent of the N.V.N. P.O.L. storage capacity was concentrated in 13 sites, 4 of which had already been hit. They were, of course, highly vulnerable to air attack."

In support of the Joint Chiefs' view, Adm. U. S. Grant Sharp, the commander of American forces in the Pacific, in a cablegram to the Joint Chiefs in January, 1966, made the evaluation that bombing North Vietnam's oil would "bring the enemy to the conference table or cause the insurgency to wither from lack of support." Admiral Sharp also wanted to close North Vietnam's ports, presumably by aerial mining.

But from the outset of the debate over bombing North Vietnam's oil tanks, the study discloses, the intelligence community had been skeptical that such bombing would have much effect on Hanoi.

Replying to a query from Secretary McNamara on what the effect of oil-tank bombing would be, the Central Intelligence Agency said in November, 1965: "It is unlikely that this loss would cripple the Communist military operations in the South, though it would certainly embarrass them."

"We do not believe," the agency's evaluation added, "that the attacks in themselves would lead to a major change of policy on the Communist side, either toward negotiations or toward enlarging the war."

"Present Communist policy is to continue to prosecute the war vigorously in the south," another agency estimate, on Dec. 3, 1965, said. It added:

"The Communists recognize that the U.S. reinforcements of 1965 signify a determination to avoid defeat. They expect more U.S. troops and probably anticipate that targets in the Hanoi-Haiphong area will come under air attack. Nevertheless, they remain unwilling to damp down the conflict or move toward negotiation. They expect a long war, but they continue to believe that time is their ally and that their own staying power is superior."

If the United States bombed all major targets in North Vietnam, Secretary McNamara asked, how would Hanoi react? The C.I.A. replied: "The D.R.V. would not decide to quit; PAVN infiltration southward would continue."

In March, 1966, after months of hesitation, Mr. McNamara accepted the Joint Chiefs' requests and recommended bombing North Vietnam's oil, the study relates. But President Johnson did not immediately go along with the Secretary's recommendation.

There were several reasons for the President's hesitation, the account goes on.

The continuing chaotic political situation in South Vietnam, with rumors of a change in government, made any further escalation seem unwise for the moment. There was also a widespread campaign by several world leaders during the spring to get Washington and Hanoi to the negotiating table. President Kwame Nkrumah of Ghana and Prime Minister Harold Wilson of Britain separately traveled to Moscow to try to start negotiations.

President Charles de Gaulle of France was in touch with President Ho Chi Minh in Hanoi, and Secretary General Thant of the United Nations appealed to both sides to come to the Security Council. President Johnson could not afford to escalate the war during these peace efforts, the Pentagon record says.

An important influence on President Johnson's thinking, the account goes on, was a memorandum he received from Mr. Rostow on May 6. Mr. Rostow, who as a major with the

Office of Strategic Services during World War II had helped plan the bombing of Germany, recalled in his memorandum the damage done to that country's war effort through th bombing of oil-storage facilities. He then asserted:

"With an understanding that simple analogies are danger ous, I nevertheless feel it is quite possible the military effect of systematic and sustained bombing of P.O.L. in North Viet nam may be more prompt and direct than conventional in telilgence analysis would suggest."

It was late in May when President Johnson decided to orde the oil bombing, the narrative says, and he apparently se June 10 as the target day. But his decision "was very closel held," the analyst writes, and not even Admiral Sharp o General Westmoreland was told.

The Central Intelligence Agency, in a last-minute evaluatio ordered by the "Vietnam principals," reiterated its skepticisn about the effects of oil-tank bombing.

"It is estimated," the agency's report said, "that the infiltra tion of men and supplies into SVN can be sustained."

The sequence of events was interrupted on June 7, th study relates, when Washington learned that a Canadia diplotmat, Chester A. Ronning, was on his way to Hanoi t test North Vietnam's attitude toward negotiations, a missio for which he had received State Department approval.

Secretary Rusk, who was traveling in Europe, cabled Presi dent Johnson to urge that the oil strikes be postponed until i could be learned what Mr. Ronning had found out.

"I am deeply disturbed," Mr. Rusk said in his cablegram "by general international revulsion, and perhaps a great dea at home if it becomes known that we took an action which sabotaged the Ronning mission to which we had given ou agreement. I recognize the agony of this problem for al concerned."

President Johnson, responding to Mr. Rusk's request suspended the oil raids, the study discloses. When Mr. Ron ning returned, Assistant Secretary Bundy flew to meet hin in Ottawa, but quickly reported that the Canadian had foun no opening or flexibility in the North Vietnamese position

While Mr. Ronning was in Hanoi, Secretary McNamar, had informed Admiral Sharp by cablegram of the high-leve consideration of oil attacks and told him:

"Final decision for or against will be influenced by exten they can be carried out without significant civilian casualties What preliminary steps to minimize would you recommen and if taken what number of casualties do you believe would result?"

Admiral Sharp "replied eagerly," the study declares, with a list of precautions: The strikes would be carried out only under favorable weather conditions, with experienced pilots fully briefed, and with especially selected weapons. He predicted that civilian casualties could be held "under 50."

With Mr. Ronning's return and Admiral Sharp's assurances, the stage was set for the oil-tank strikes.

On June 22, Washington [see Document #114] gave the execution message authorizing strikes on the oil targets in the Hanoi-Haiphong area. The Pentagon analyst terms the execution message "a remarkable document, attesting in detail to the political sensitivity of the strikes." The message said:

"Strikes to commence with initial attacks against Haiphong and Hanoi P.O.L. on same day if operationally feasible. . . . At Haiphong avoid damage to merchant shipping. No attacks authorized on craft unless U.S. aircraft are first fired on and then only if clearly North Vietnamese.

"Decision made after SecDef and C.J.C.S. [Chairman, Joint Chiefs of Staff] were assured every feasible step would be taken to minimize civilian casualties. . . . Take the following measures: maximum use of most experienced Rolling Thunder personnel, detailed briefing of pilots stressing need to avoid civilians, execute only when weather permits visual identification of targets and improved strike accuracy, select best axis of attack to avoid populated areas, maximum use of ECM [electronic countermeasurers] to hamper SAM [surface-to-air missiles] and AAA [antiaircraft artillery] fire control, in order to limit pilot distraction and improve accuracy, maximum use of weapons of high precision delivery consistent with mission objective, and limit SAM and AAA suppression [bombing] to sites located outside populated areas.

"Take special precautions to insure security. If weather or operational considerations delay initiation of strikes, do not initiate on Sunday, 26 June."

It is not clear, the Pentagon account says, why what it calls the "never on Sunday" order was issued.

Because of bad weather, it was June 29 before the oil strikes were finally begun, reportedly with great success. The Haiphong dock facility appeared about 80 per cent destroyed, the study says, and the Hanoi "tank farm" was apparently knocked out. Only one United States aircraft was lost to ground fire.

A report from the Seventh Air Force in Saigon called the

operation "the most significant, the most important strike of the war."

"Official Washington reacted with mild jubilation to the reported success of the P.O.L. strikes and took satisfaction in the relatively mild reaction of the international community to the escalation," the Pentagon analyst recounts. "Secretary McNamara described the execution of the raids as a 'superb professional job,' and sent a message of personal congratulations to the field commanders involved in the planning and execution of the attacks."

In early July, Mr. McNamara informed Admiral Sharp in a cablegram that the President wished the first priority in the air war to be given to the "strangulation" of North Vietnam's fuel system. And he ordered Admiral Sharp to develop a comprehensive plan to accomplish this.

Throughout the summer of 1966, Operation Rolling Thunder was concentrated on destroying oil-storage sites, the narrative relates. By the end of July, the Defense Intelligence Agency reported to Secretary McNamara that 70 per cent of North Vietnam's original storage capacity had been destroyed.

But "what became clearer and clearer as the summer wore on," the account discloses, "was that while we had destroyed a major portion of North Vietnam's storage capacity, she retained enough dispersed capacity, supplemented by continuing imports (increasingly in easily dispersable drums, not bulk) to meet her ongoing requirements."

In August, the study says, with the large storage sites already destroyed and the small, dispersed sites hard to find and bomb, "it was simply impractical and infeasible to attempt any further constriction of North Vietnam's P.O.L. storage capacity."

And, it adds, the flow of men and supplies from North Vietnam to the Vietcong continued "undiminished."

"It was clear," the study says, "that the P.O.L. strikes had been a failure. . . . There was no evidence that NVN had at any time been pinched for P.O.L. . . . The difficulties of switching to a much less vulnerable but perfectly workable storage and distrubution system, not an unbearable strain when the volume to be handled was not really very great, had been overestimated. Typically, also, N.V.N.'s adaptability and resourcefulness had been greatly underestimated."

"McNamara, for his part, made no effort to conceal his dissatisfaction and disappointment at the failure of the P.O.L. strikes," the study continues. "He pointed out to the Air

Force and the Navy the glaring discrepancy between the optimistic estimates of results their pre-strike P.O.L. studies had postulated and the actual failure of the raids to significantly decrease infiltration."

"The Secretary was already in the process of rethinking the role of the entire air campaign in the U.S. effort," the Pentagon study says. "He was painfully aware of its inability to pinch off the infiltration to the South and had seen no evidence of its ability to break Hanoi's will, demoralize its population or bring it to the negotiation table."

"The attack on North Vietnam's P.O.L. system," the study goes on, "was the last major escalation of the air war recommended by Secretary McNamara."

Troops, More Troops

Another important factor in Secretary McNamara's "disenchantment" during the summer of 1966, the Pentagon account declares, was General Westmoreland's continual requests for more troops.

In June Mr. McNamara approved a new deployment schedule specifically designed to meet General Westmoreland's requests. The new schedule, labeled Program 3, called for putting 391,000 American soldiers—79 battalions—into South Vietnam by the end of 1966 and 431,000 by June, 1967.

Because articles had begun to appear in the press that the Joint Chiefs were dissatisfied with the pace of the build-up in ground forces, the study relates, President Johnson and Mr. McNamara resorted to a bureaucratic "ploy" to insure that their new schedule met the Joint Chiefs' requests.

On June 28 the President wrote a formal directive to the Secretary of Defense:

"As you know, we have been moving our men to Vietnam on a schedule determined by General Westmoreland's requirements.

"As I have stated orally several times this year, I should like this schedule to be accelerated as much as possible so that General Westmoreland can feel assured that he has all the men he needs as soon as possible.

"Would you meet with the Joint Chiefs and give me at your earliest convenience an indication of what acceleration is possible for the balance of this year."

Secretary McNamara then passed this directive to the Joint Chiefs, who replied in a memorandum on July 7 that the new schedule did meet General Westmoreland's requirements. In turn, Mr. McNamara replied formally to the President that he was "happy to report" that the new deployments were satisfactory.

Thus, the study says, the President and Mr. McNamara gained a record that could be easily pulled out to show any critic that in fact they were meeting the military's requests.

But while President Johnson and Secretary McNamara were approving this schedule, General Westmoreland had already initiated a new request—for 111,588 men—which was passed through channels to the Joint Chiefs on June 18. The figure General Westmoreland said he would now need for 1967 was 542,588 troops.

On Aug. 5 the Joint Chiefs passed the new request to Secretary McNamara, expressing their view that the proposed increases were important and necessary.

Mr. McNamara replied the same day:

"As you know, it is our policy to provide the troops, weapons and supplies requested by General Westmoreland at the times he desires them, to the greatest possible degree.

"Nevertheless I desire and expect a detailed line-by-line analysis of these requirements to determine that each is truly essential to the carrying out of our war plan. We must send to Vietnam what is needed, but only what is needed." [See Document #115.]

When the Joint Chiefs completed their detailed study of the new requests in the fall, the study relates, Mr. McNamara was no longer ready to approve troop increases automatically. And in October, for the first time, he would turn General Westmoreland down.

The major reason General Westmoreland gave for needing more troops, the account discloses, is that during the summer of 1966 North Vietnamese infiltration again appeared to be increasing.

Throughout the summer and early fall, the narrative says, General Westmoreland sent a steady stream of cables to Admiral Sharp and General Wheeler warning about the enemy build-up. [See Document #116.]

A Secret Seminar

During the summer of 1966, while Secretary McNamara was pondering the failure of the oil-storage strikes and considering General Westmoreland's latest troop request, a secret seminar of leading scientists under Government sponsorship was studying the over-all results of Operation Rolling Thunder.

Their conclusions, the historian relates, would have a "dramatic impact" on Mr. McNamara and further contribute to his disenchantment. [See Document #117.]

The idea for a summer seminar of scientists and academic specialists to study technical aspects of the war had been suggested in March by Dr. George B. Kistiakowsky and Dr. Carl Kaysen of Harvard and Dr. Jerome B. Wiesner and Dr. Jerrold R. Zacharias of the Massachusetts Institute of Technology.

Dr. Kistiakowsky had been special assistant for science and technology under President Dwight D. Eisenhower and Dr. Wiesner had held that post under President Kennedy. Dr. Kaysen had been a Kennedy aide for national security.

Secretary McNamara liked the idea, the study says, and sent Dr. Zacharias a letter on April 16 formally requesting that he and the others arrange the summer study on "technical possibilities in relation to our military operations in Vietnam."

The Secretary specifically instructed Mr. McNaughton, who was to oversee the project, that the scientists should look into the feasibility of "a fence across the infiltration trails, warning systems, reconnaissance (especially night) methods, night vision devices, defoliation techniques and area-denial weapons."

The idea of constructing an anti-infiltration barrier across the demilitarized zone had first been suggested by Prof. Roger Fisher of the Harvard Law School in a memorandum to Mr. McNaughton in January, 1966, the narrative says.

The scientists—47 men representing "the cream of the scholarly community in technical fields," the narrative says— met in Wellesley, Mass., during June, July and August under the auspices of the Jason Division of the Institute for Defense Analyses.

The Jason Division, named for the leader of the Argonauts in Greek mythology, was used to conduct "ad hoc high-level studies using primarily non-I.D.A. scholars," the Pentagon study says. The scientists were given briefings by high officials from the Pentagon, the Central Intelligence Agency, the State Department and the White House, the study recounts, and they were provided with secret materials.

Their conclusions and recommendations, which were given to the Secretary of Defense at the beginning of September, had "a powerful and perhaps decisive influence in McNamara's mind," the Pentagon record says.

These were the recommendations, it goes on, of "a group of America's most distinguished scientists, men who had helped the Government produce many of its most advanced technical weapons systems since the end of the Second World War, men who were not identified with the vocal academic criticism of the Administration's Vietnam policy."

Their report evaluating the results of the Rolling Thunder campaign began:

"As of July, 1966, the U.S. bombing of North Vietnam had had no measurable direct effect on Hanoi's ability to mount and support military operations in the South at the current level."

They then pointed out the reasons that they felt North Vietnam could not be hurt by bombing: It was primarily a subsistence agricultural country with little industry and a primitive but flexible transport system, and most of its weapons and supplies came from abroad.

These factors, the scientists said, made it "quite unlikely" that an expanded bombing campaign would "prevent Hanoi from infiltrating men into the South at the present or a higher rate."

In conclusion, the Pentagon study says, the scientists addressed the assumption behind the bombing program—that damage inflicted on a country reduces its will to continue fighting. The scientists criticized this assumption, the study says, by denying that it is possible to measure the relationship.

"It must be concluded," the scientists said, "that there is currently no adequate basis for predicting the levels of U.S. military effort that would be required to achieve the stated objectives—indeed, there is no firm basis for determining if there is any feasible level of effort that would achieve these objectives."

As an alternative to bombing North Vietnam, the 47

scientists suggested that an elaborate electronic barrier, using recently developed devices, be built across the demilitarized zone.

The barrier would consist of two parts, the Pentagon report discloses: an anti-troop system made up of small mines (called gravel mines) to damage the enemy's feet and legs, and an anti-vehicle system composed of acoustic sensors that would direct aircraft to the target.

Most of the mines and sensors would be dropped by planes, but the system would have to be checked by ground troops.

The whole system would cost about $800-million a year, the scientists estimated, and would take a year to build.

Secretary McNamara "was apparently strongly and favorably impressed" by the scientists' ideas, the Pentagon study relates, and he immediately ordered Lieut. Gen. Alfred D. Starbird, an Army engineering expert, to begin research on the barrier.

On Oct. 10, 1966, the study reports, Secretary McNamara set out for Saigon to assess General Westmoreland's latest troop request. He had ordered General Starbird to precede him there to begin an investigation of conditions for the barrier.

Characterizing Mr. McNamara's attitudes toward the war, the Pentagon analyst says that the Secretary had gone from "hesitancy" in the winter of 1965 to "perplexity" in the spring of 1966 to "disenchantment" the following fall.

When he returned from his October trip to Saigon, the study relates, he would detail his feelings in two long memorandums to President Johnson and for the first time would recommend against filling a troop request from General Westmoreland.

KEY DOCUMENTS

Following are texts of key documents accompanying the Pentagon's study of the Vietnam war, covering the period late 1965 to the summer of 1966. Except where excerpting is specified, the documents are printed verbatim, with only unmistakable typographical errors corrected.

106

State Department Memorandum in November on Bombing Pause

Excerpts from memorandum, "Courses of Action in Vietnam," from the State Department, Nov. 9, 1965, as provided in the body of the Pentagon study. According to the study, the memorandum was speaking for Secretary of State Dean Rusk, and "a penciled note by [Assistant Secretary of Defense John T.] McNaughton indicates that Ambassador U. Alexis Johnson was the author."

. . . The purpose of—and Secretary McNamara's arguments for—such a pause are four:

(a) It would offer Hanoi and the Viet Cong a chance to move toward a solution if they should be so inclined, removing the psychological barrier of continued bombing and permitting the Soviets and others to bring moderating arguments to bear:

(b) It would demonstrate to domestic and international critics that we had indeed made every effort for a peaceful settlement before proceeding to intensified actions, notably the latter stages of the extrapolated Rolling Thunder program;

(c) It would probably tend to reduce the dangers of escalation after we had resumed the bombing, at least insofar as the Soviets were concerned;

(d) It would set the stage for another pause, perhaps in late 1966, which might produce a settlement.

Against these propositions, there are the following considerations arguing against a pause:

(a) In the absence of any indication from Hanoi as to what reciprocal action it might take, we could well find ourselves in the position of having played this very important card without receiving anything substantial in return. There are no indications that Hanoi is yet in a mood to agree to a settlement acceptable to us. The chance is, therefore, very slight that a pause at this time could lead to an acceptable settlement.

(b) A unilateral pause at this time would offer an excellent opportunity for Hanoi to interpose obstacles to our resumption of bombing and to demoralize South Vietnam by indefinitely dangling before us (and the world) the prospect of negotiations with no intent of reaching an acceptable settlement. It might also tempt the Soviet Union to make threats that would render very difficult a decision to resume bombing.

(c) In Saigon, obtaining South Vietnamese acquiescence to a pause would be difficult. It could adversely affect the Government's solidity. Any major falling out between the Government and the United States or any overturn in the Government's political structure could set us back very severly (sic).

(d) An additional factor is that undertaking the second course of action following a pause [i.e., "extrapolation" of ROLLING THUNDER] would give this course a much more dramatic character, both internationally and domestically, and would, in particular, present the Soviets with those difficult choices that we have heretofore been successful in avoiding.

On balance, the arguments against the pause are convincing to the Secretary of State, who recommends that it not be undertaken at the present time. The Secretary of State believes that a pause should be undertaken only when and if the chances were significantly greater than they now appear that Hanoi would respond by reciprocal actions leading in the direction of a peaceful settlement. He further believes that, from the standpoint of international and domestic opinion, a pause might become an overriding requirement only if we were about to reach the advanced stages of an extrapolated Rolling Thunder program involving extensive air operations in the Hanoi/Haiphong area. Since the Secretary of State believes that such advanced stages are not in themselves desirable until the tide in the South is more favorable, he does not feel that, even accepting the point of view of the Secretary of Defense, there is now any international requirement to consider a "Pause." . . .

107

Notes on McNamara Memorandum for Johnson after Vietnam Visit

Excerpts from notes accompanying the Pentagon study, from a memorandum for President Lyndon B. Johnson from Secretary McNamara, Nov. 30, 1965.

. . . The Ky "government of generals" is surviving, but not acquiring wide support or generating actions; pacification is thoroughly stalled, with no guarantee that security anywhere is permanent and no indications that able and willing leadership will emerge in the absence of that permanent security. (Prime Minister Ky estimates that his government controls only 25% of the population today and reports that his pacification chief hopes to increase that to 50% two years from now).

The dramatic recent changes in the situation are on the military side. They are the increased infiltration from the North and the increased willingness of the Communist forces to stand and fight, even in large-scale engagements. The Ia Drang River Campaign of early November is an example. The Communists appear to have decided to increase their forces in SVN both by heavy recruitment in the South (especially in the Delta) and by infiltration of regular NVN forces from the North. . . . The enemy can be expected to enlarge his present strength of 110 battalion equivalents to more than 150 battalion equivalents by the end of calendar 1966, when hopefully his losses can be made to equal his input.

As for the Communist ability to supply this force, it is estimated that, even taking account of interdiction of routes by air and sea, more than 200 tons of supplies a day can be infiltrated—more than enough, allowing for the extent to which the enemy lives off the land, to support the likely PAVN/VC force at the likely level of operations.

To meet this possible—and in my view likely—Communist buildup, the presently contemplated Phase I forces will not be enough (approx 220,000 Americans, almost all in place by end of 1965). Bearing in mind the nature of the war, the expected weighted combat force ratio of less than 2-to-1 will not be good enough. Nor will the originally contemplated Phase II addition of 28 more U.S. battalions (112,000 men) be enough; the combat force ratio, even with 32 new SVNse battalions, would still be little better than 2-to-1 at the end of 1966. The initiative which we have held since August would pass to the enemy; we would fall far short of what we expected to achieve in terms of population control and disruption of enemy bases and lines of communications. Indeed, it is estimated that with the contemplated Phase II addition of 28 U.S. battalions, we would be able only to hold our present geographical positions.

3. We have but two options, it seems to me. One is to go now for a compromise solution (something substantially less than the "favorable out once" I described in my memo of Nov. 3) and hold further deployments to a minimum. The other is to stick with our stated objectives and with the war, and provide what it takes in men and materiel. If it is decided not to move now toward a compromise, I recommend that the U.S. both send a substantial number of additional troops and very gradually intensify the bombing of NVN. Amb. Lodge, Wheeler, Sharp and Westmoreland concur in this prolonged course of action, although Wheeler

488

and Sharp would intensify the bombing of the North more quickly. (recommend up to 74 battalions by end-66: total to approx 400,000 by end-66. And it should be understood that further deployments (perhaps exceeding 200,000) may be needed in 1967. Bombing of NVN. . . . over a period of the next six months we gradually enlarge the target system in the northeast (Hanoi-Haiphong) quadrant until, at the end of the period, it includes "controlled" reconnaissance of lines of comm throughout the area, bombing of petroleum storage facilities and power plants, and mining of the harbors. (Left unstruck would be population targets, industrial plants, locks and dams).

4. Pause in bombing NVN. It is my belief that there should be a three- or four-week pause in the program of bombing the North before we either greatly increase our troop deployments to VN or intensify our strikes against the North. (My recommendation for a "pause" is not concurred in by Lodge, Wheeler or Sharp.) The reasons for this belief are, first, that we must lay a foundation in the minds of the American public and in world opinion for such an enlarged phase of the war and second, we should give NVN a face-saving chance to stop the aggression. I am not seriously concerned about the risk of alienating the SVNese, misleading Hanoi, or being "trapped" in a pause; if we take reasonable precautions, we can avoid these pitfalls. I am seriously concerned about embarking on a markedly higher level of war in VN without having tried, through a pause, to end the war or at least having made it clear to our people that we did our best to end it.

5. Evaluation. We should be aware that deployments of the kind I have recommended will not guarantee success. U.S. killed-in-action can be expected to reach 1000 a month, and the odds are even that we will be faced in early 1967 with a "no-decision" at an even higher level. My over-all evaluation, nevertheless, is that the best chance of achieving our stated objectives lies in a pause followed, if it fails, by the deployments mentioned above.

108

Notes from McNamara Memo on Course of War in 1966

Excerpts from notes accompanying the Pentagon study, from a memorandum for President Johnson from Secretary McNamara, "Military and Political Actions Recommended for South Vietnam," Dec. 7, 1965.

. . . We believe that, whether or not major new diplomatic initiatives are made, the U.S. must send a substantial number of additional forces to VN if we are to avoid being defeated there. (30 Nov program; concurred in by JCS)

IV. Prognosis assuming the recommended deployments

Deployments of the kind we have recommended will not guarantee success. Our intelligence estimate is that the present Communist policy is to continue to prosecute the war vigorously in the South. They continue to believe that the war will be a long one, that time is their ally, and that their own staying power is superior to ours. They recognize that the U.S. reinforcements of 1965 signify a determination to avoid defeat, and that more U.S. troops can be expected. Even though the Communists will continue to suffer heavily from GVN and U.S. ground and air action, we expect them, upon learning of any U.S. intentions to augment its forces, to boost their own commitment and to test U.S. capabilities and will to persevere at higher level of conflict and casualties (U.S. KIA with the recommended deployments can be expected to reach 1000 a month).

If the U.S. were willing to commit enough forces—perhaps 600,000 men or more—we could ultimately prevent the DRV/VC from sustaining the conflict at a significant level. When this point was reached, however, the question of Chinese intervention would become critical. (*We are generally agreed that the Chinese Communists will intervene with combat forces to prevent destruction of the Communist regime in the DRV. It is less clear whether they would intervene to prevent a DRV/VC defeat in the South.) The intelligence estimate is that the chances are a little better than even that, at this stage, Hanoi and Peiping would choose to reduce the effort in the South and try to salvage their resources for another day; but there is an almost equal chance that they would enlarge the war and bring in large numbers of Chinese forces (they have made certain preparations which could point in this direction).

It follows, therefore, that the odds are about even that, even with the recommended deployments, we will be faced in early 1967 with a military standoff at a much higher level, with pacification still stalled, and with any prospect of military success marred by the chances of an active Chinese intervention.

(memo of 24 jan 66: JCS believe that "the evaluation set forth in Par. 7 is on the pessimistic side in view of the constant and heavy military pressure which our forces in SEA will be capable of employing. While admittedly the following factors are to a degree imponderables, they believe that greater weight should be given to the following:

a. The cumulative effect of our air campaign against the DRV on morale and DRV capabilities to provide and move men and materiel from the DRV to SVN.

b. The effects of constant attack and harassment on the ground and from the air upon the growth of VC forces and on the morale and combat effectiveness of VC/PAVN forces.

c. The effect of destruction of VC base areas on the capabilities of VC/PAVN forces to sustain combat operations over an extended period of time.

490

d. The constancy of will of the Hanoi leaders to continue a struggle which they realize they cannot win in the face of progressively greater destruction of their country

109

Further McNaughton Memo on Factors in Bombing Decision

Excerpts from memorandum by Assistant Secretary of Defense McNaughton, "Some Paragraphs on Vietnam," third draft, Jan. 19, 1966, as provided in the body of the Pentagon study. Paragraphs in italics are the analysts' paraphrase or explanation.

McNaughton prepared a second memorandum complementing and partially modifying the one on bombing. It concerned the context for the decision. Opening with a paragraph which warned, "We . . . have in Vietnam the ingredients of an enormous miscalculation," it sketched the dark outlines of the Vietnamese scene:

. . . The ARVN is tired, passive and accommodation-prone . . . The PAVN/VC are effectively matching our deployments . . . The bombing of the North . . . may or may not be able effectively to interdict infiltration (partly because the PAVN/VC can simply refuse to do battle if supplies are short). . . . Pacification is stalled despite efforts and hopes. The GVN political infrastructure is moribund and weaker than the VC infrastructure among most of the rural population . . . South Vietnam is near the edge of serious inflation and economic chaos.

The situation might alter for the better, McNaughton conceded. "Attrition—save Chinese intervention—may push the DRV 'against the stops' by the end of 1966." Recent RAND motivation and morale studies showed VC spirit flagging and their grip on the peasantry growing looser. "The Ky government is coming along, not delivering its promised 'revolution' but making progress slowly and gaining experience and stature each week." Though McNaughton termed it "doubtful that a meaningful ceiling can be put on the infiltration," he said "there is no doubt that the cost of infiltration can . . . be made very high and that the flow of supplies can be reduced substantially below what it would otherwise be." Possibly bombing, combined with other pressures, could bring the DRV to consider terms after "a period of months, not of days or even weeks."

The central point of McNaughton's memorandum, following from its opening warning, was that the United States, too, should consider coming to terms. He wrote:

C. The present U.S. objective in Vietnam is to avoid humilia-

tion. The reasons why we *went into* Vietnam to the present depth are varied; but they are now largely academic. Why we have *not withdrawn* from Vietnam is, by all odds, *one* reason: (1) to preserve our reputation as a guarantor, and thus to preserve our effectiveness in the rest of the world. We have not hung on (2) to save a friend, or (3) to deny the Communists the added acres and heads (because the dominoes don't fall for that reason in this case), or even (4) to prove that "wars of national liberation" won't work (except as our reputation is involved). At each decision point we have gambled; at each point, to avoid the damage to our effectiveness of defaulting on our commitment, we have upped the ante. We have not defaulted, and the ante (and commitment) is now very high. It is important that we behave so as to protect our reputation. At the same time, since it is our *reputation* that is at stake, it is important that we not construe our obligation to be more than do the countries whose opinions of us *are* our reputation.

D. We are in an escalating military stalemate. There is an honest difference of judgment as to the success of the present military efforts in the South. There is no question that the U.S. deployments thwarted the VC hope to achieve a quick victory in 1965. But there is a serious question whether we are now defeating the VC/PAVN main forces and whether planned U.S. deployments will more than hold our position in the country. Population and area control has not changed significantly in the past year; and the best judgment is that, even with the Phase IIA deployments, we will probably be faced in early 1967 with a continued stalemate at a higher level of forces and casualties.

2. U.S. commitment to SVN. Some will say that we have defaulted if we end up, at any point in the relevant future, with anything less than a Western-oriented, non-Communist, independent government, exercising effective sovereignty over all of South Vietnam. This is not so. As stated above, the U.S. end is solely to preserve our reputation as a guarantor. It follows that the "softest" credible formulation of the U.S. commitment is the following:

a. DRV does not take over South Vietnam by force. This does not *necessarily* rule out:

b. A coalition government including Communists.

c. A free decision by the South to succumb to the VC or to the North.

d. A neutral (or even anti-U.S.) government in SVN.

e. A live-and-let-live "reversion to 1959." Furthermore, we must recognize that even if we fail to in achieving this "soft" formulation, we could over time come out with minimum damage:

f. If the reason was GVN gross wrongheadedness or apathy.

g. If victorious North Vietnam "went Titoist."

h. If the Communist take-over was fuzzy and very slow.

Current decisions, McNaughton argued, should reflect awareness that the U.S. commitment could be fulfilled with something con-

siderably short of victory. "It takes time to make hard decisions," he wrote, "It took us almost a year to take the decision to bomb North Vietnam; it took us weeks to decide on a pause; it could take us months (and could involve lopping some white as well as brown heads) to get us in position to go for a compromise. We should not expect the enemy's molasses to pour any faster than ours. And we should 'tip the pitchers' now if we want them to 'pour' a year from now."

But the strategy following from this analysis more or less corresponded over the short term to that recommended by the Saigon mission and the military commands: More effort for pacification, more push behind the Ky government, more battalions for MACV, and intensive interdiction bombing roughly as proposed by CINCPAC. The one change introduced in this memorandum, prepared only one day after the other, concerned North Vietnamese ports. Now McNaughton advised that the ports not be closed.

The argument which coupled McNaughton's political analysis with his strategic recommendations appeared at the end of the second memorandum:

The dilemma. We are in a dilemma. It is that the situation may be "polar." That is, it may be that while going for victory we have the strength for compromise, but if we go for compromise we have the strength only for defeat—this because a revealed lowering of sights from victory to compromise (a) will unhinge the GVN and (b) will give the DRV the "smell of blood." The situation therefore requires a thoroughly loyal and disciplined U.S. team in Washington and Saigon and great care in what is said and done. It also requires a willingness to escalate the war if the enemy miscalculates, misinterpreting our willingness to compromise as implying we are on the run. The risk is that it may be that the "coin must come up heads or tails, not on edge."

110

McNaughton Memo for McNamara on Anti-Infiltration Barrier Plan

Excerpts from a memorandum to Secretary of Defense McNamara, "A Barrier Strategy," as provided in the body of the Pentagon study. According to the narrative, the memorandum is unsigned but is by Assistant Secretary of Defense McNaughton, in whose handwriting the copy is marked "1/30/66" and "copy given to RSM 3/22/66." The study further says that the document is based on a draft memo of Jan. 3, 1966, "A Barrier Strategy," by Prof. Roger D. Fisher of Harvard Law School.

B. PRESENT MILITARY SITUATION IN NORTH VIETNAM.

1. Physical consequences of bombing

a. The DRV has suffered some physical hardship and pain, raising the cost to it of supporting the VC.

b. Best intelligence judgment is that:

(1) Bombing may or may not—by destruction or delay—have resulted in net reduction in the flow of men or supplies to the forces in the South;

(2) Bombing has failed to reduce the limit on the capacity of the DRV to aid the VC to a point below VC needs;

(3) Future bombing of North Vietnam cannot be expected physically to limit the military support given the VC by the DRV to a point below VC needs.

2. Influence consequences of bombing

a. There is no evidence that bombings have made it more likely the DRV will decide to back out of the war.

b. Nor is there evidence that bombings have resulted in an increased DRV resolve to continue the war to an eventual victory. [Fisher's draft had read "There is some evidence that bombings. . . ."]

C. FUTURE OF A BOMBING STRATEGY

Although bombings of North Vietnam improve GVN morale and provide a counter in eventual negotiations (should they take place) there is no evidence that they meaningfully reduce either the capacity or the will for the DRV to support the VC. The DRV knows that we cannot force them to stop by bombing and that we cannot, without an unacceptable risk of a major war with China or Russia or both, force them to stop by conquering them or "blotting them out." Knowing that if they are not influenced we cannot stop them, the DRV will remain difficult to influence. With continuing DRV support, victory in the South may remain forever beyond our reach.

Having made the case against the bombing, the memo then spelled out the case for an anti-infiltration barrier:

II. SUBSTANCE OF THE BARRIER PROPOSAL

A. That the U.S. and GVN adopt the concept of physically cutting off DRV support to the VC by an on-the-ground barrier across the Ho Chi Minh Trail in the general vicinity of the 17th Parallel and Route 9. To the extent necessary the barrier would run from the sea across Vietnam and Laos to the Mekong, a straightline distance of about 160 miles.

B. That in Laos an "interdiction and verification zone," perhaps 10 miles wide, be established and legitimated by such measures as leasing, international approval, compensation, etc.

C. That a major military and engineering effort be directed toward constructing a physical barrier of minefields, barbed wire, walls, ditches and military strong points flanked by a defoliated strip on each side.

D. That such bombing in Laos and North Vietnam as takes place be narrowly identified with interdiction and with the construction of the barrier by

1. Being within the 10-mile-wide interdiction zone in Laos, or

2. Being in support of the construction of the barrier, or

3. Being interdiction bombing pending the completion of the barrier.

E. That, of course, intensive interdiction continues at sea and from Cambodia.

(It might be stated that all bombings of North Vietnam will stop as soon as there is no infiltration and no opposition to the construction of the verification barrier.)

111

Johnson's Remarks to Officials of U.S. and Saigon at Honolulu

Excerpts from remarks by President Johnson to senior United States and South Vietnamese after the issuance of a joint communiqué at their Honolulu conference, Feb. 9, 1966, as provided in the body of the Pentagon study. The paragraph in italics is the study's explanation.

(The Vietnamese then thanked the Americans for the conference, and in turn some of the senior members of the American delegation—in order, Admiral Sharp, Leonard Marks, General Wheeler, Ambassador Lodge, Ambassador Harriman—made brief statements about the meaning of the conference. The President then made his final statement:

. . . Preserve this communiqué, because it is one we don't want to forget. It will be a kind of bible that we are going to follow. When we come back here 90 days from now, or six months from now, we are going to start out and make reference to the announcements that the President, the Chief of State and the Prime Minister made in paragraph 1, and what the leaders and advisors reviewed in paragraph 2. . . . You men who are responsible for these departments, you ministers, and the staffs associated with them in both governments, bear in mind we are going to give you an examination and the finals will be on just what you have done.

In paragraph 5; how have you built democracy in the rural areas? How much of it have you built, when and where? Give us dates, times, numbers.

In paragraph 2; larger outputs, more efficient production to improve credit, handicraft, light industry, rural electrification—are those just phrases, high-sounding words, or have you coonskins on the wall. . . .

Next is health and education, Mr. Gardner. We don't want to talk about it; we want to do something about it. "The President pledges he will dispatch teams of experts." Well, we better do something besides dispatching. They should get out there. We are going to train health personnel. How many? You don't want to be like the fellow who was playing poker and when he made a big bet they called him and said "what have you got?" He said "aces" and they asked "how many" and he said "one aces". . . .

Next is refugees. That is just as hot as a pistol in my country. You don't want me to raise a white flag and surrender so we have to do something about that. . . .

Growing military effectiveness: we have not gone in because we don't want to overshadow this meeting here with bombs, with mortars, with hand grenades, with "Masher" movements. I don't know who names your operations, but "Masher." I get kind of mashed myself. But we haven't gone into the details of growing military effectiveness for two or three reasons. One, we want to be able honestly and truthfully to say that this has not been a military build-up conference of the world here in Honolulu. We have been talking about building a society following the outlines of the Prime Minister's speech yesterday.

Second, this is not the place, with 100 people sitting around, to build a military effectiveness.

Third, I want to put it off as long as I can, having to make these crucial decisions. I enjoy this agony. . . . I don't want to come out of this meeting that we have come up here and added on X divisions and Y battalions or Z regiments or D dollars, because one good story about how many billions are going to be spent can bring us more inflation that we are talking about in Vietnam. We want to work those out in the quietness of the Cabinet Room after you have made your recommendations, General Wheeler, Admiral Sharp, when you come to us. . . .

112

Memo on Pentagon Meeting Following up Honolulu Session

Excerpts from memorandum by Richard C. Steadman, special assistant to Secretary of Defense McNamara, Feb. 9, 1966, summarizing a Pentagon meeting after the Honolulu talks. According to Mr. Steadman the participants included the Secretary, his deputies, the secretaries of each of the armed services and other Defense Department officials.

. . . **3. Southeast Asia Program Office.** It is essential that the Department of Defense has at all times a readily available and centralized bank of information with respect to the Southeast Asia build-up. To this end. Dr. Enthoven is to establish a Southeast Asia Program Office which is to be able to furnish Mr. McNamara and Mr. Vance all information that may be required with respect to Southeast Asia. Among other things, this unit is to be able to provide immediate information on what overseas units are being depleted in order to accommodate Southeast Asia needs. If there is any drawdown anywhere, Mr. McNamara wants to know it promptly. We must know the full price of what we are doing and propose to do.

Mr. McNamara suggested that each Service Secretary establish a similar Southeast Asia Program Unit to bring together and keep current data relating to that Service involving Southeast Asia, and that the Joint Staff might establish a similar set-up.

Mr. McNamara said that it was mandatory that the situation be brought under better control. For example, the Southeast Asia construction program was $1.2-billion in the FY 66 Supplement; yesterday at Honolulu the figure of $2.5-billion was raised. Yet there is only the vaguest information as to how these funds will be spent, where, on what, and by whom. This is part of the bigger problem that there is no proper system for the allocation of available resources in Vietnam. McGeorge Bundy is to help organize the country team to deal with this problem, including reconciling military and non-military demands.

4. Manpower Controls. Mr. McNamara designated Mr. Morris as the person to be responsible for the various manpower requirements. He is either to insure that the requirements are met or to let Mr. McNamara know if they are not being met. Mr. McNamara wants a written statement whenever we have been unable to do something that General Westmoreland says he needs for full combat effectiveness. (In this regard, General Westmoreland recognizes that it is not possible to have 100 percent combat effectiveness for all the 102 battalions. For example, there are not sufficient helicopter companies. Roughly, he estimates he will get 96 battalion combat effectiveness out of the 102 battalions.)

At this point there was a brief discussion concerning the use of U.S. troops for pacification purposes. Mr. Nitze indicated that in his view the Marines were doing this to some degree. The point was disputed. At any rate, Mr. McNamara said that the 102 combat battalions contemplated under Case 1 were not to be used for pacification but only for defense of base areas and offensive operations. Mr. McNamara outlined briefly the South Vietnamese Government's plan for pacification. It will affect some 235,000 people in the whole country. The major allocation of resources and personnel will be to four very limited areas, one of which is near Danang. There will also be a general program extending throughout the country involving some 900 hamlets.

5. Call-Up of Reserves. Mr. McNamara said that it was important that everyone understand why a Reserve call-up is receiving such careful study. There are at least two important considerations. First, the problem is a very complicated one and we do not yet have all the facts. Mr. Morris and others will amass the necessary data as soon as possible. Second, the political aspects of a Reserve call-up are extremely delicate. There are several strong bodies of opinion at work in the country. Look, for example, at the Fulbright Committee hearings. One school of thought, which underlies the Gavin thesis, is that this country is over-extended economically and that we cannot afford to do what we are doing. Another school of thought feels that we plain should not be there at all, whether or not we can afford it. A third school of thought is that although we are rightly there, the war is being mismanaged so that we are heading straight toward war with China. Furthermore, there is no question but that the economy of this country is beginning to run near or at its capacity with the resulting probability of a shortage of certain skills and materials. If this continues we may be facing wage and price controls, excess profits taxes, etc., all of which will add fuel to the fire of those who say we cannot afford this. With all these conflicting pressures it is a very difficult and delicate task for the Administration to mobilize and maintain the required support in this country to carry on the war properly. The point of all this is to emphasize that a call-up of the Reserves presents extremely serious problems in many areas and a decision cannot be made today.

General Johnson said he wished to add three additional considerations. First, a Reserve call-up might be an important factor in the reading of the North Vietnamese and the Chinese with respect to our determination to see this war through. Second, Reserve call-ups are traditionally a unifying factor. Third, as a larger problem, a hard, long-term look should be taken at the degree to which we as a government are becoming committed to a containment policy along all the enormous southern border of China. Mr. McNamara said he would ask for a JCS study of this last point and discussed it briefly.

During the course of the meeting, General Johnson also pointed out that with respect to overseas deployment, the Army is already shortchanging certain overseas areas so as to increase the training cadres in CONUS. He pointed out that because of the effect on the strategic reserve of deployments already made, the quality of new units will be lower than at present. He raised certain additional points affecting the Army. Mr. McNamara, Mr. Vance, Mr. Resor and General Johnson will discuss these problems further. . . .

113

Rostow's Memo on Bombing of Hanoi's Petroleum Facilities

Excerpt from memorandum from Walt W. Rostow, Presidential assistant for national security, to Secretary of State Rusk and Secretary of Defense McNamara, May 6, 1966, as provided in the body of the Pentagon study. Paragraphs in italics are the study's paraphrase or explanation.

Rostow developed his argument for striking the petroleum reserves on the basis of U.S. experience in the World War II attacks on German oil supplies and storage facilities. His reasoning was as follows:

From the moment that serious and systematic oil attacks started, front line single engine fighter strength and tank mobility were affected. The reason was this: It proved much more difficult, in the face of general oil shortage, to allocate from less important to more important uses than than the simple arithmetic of the problem would suggest. Oil moves in various logistical channels from central sources. When the central sources began to dry up the effects proved fairly prompt and widespread. What look like reserves statistically are rather inflexible commitments to logistical pipelines.

The same results might be expected from heavy and sustained attacks on the North Vietnamese oil reserves,

With an understanding that simple analogies are dangerous, I nevertheless feel it is quite possible the military effects of a systematic and sustained bombing of POL in North Vietnam may be more prompt and direct than conventional intelligence analysis would suggest.

I would underline, however, the adjectives "systematic and sustained." If we take this step we must cut clean through the POL system—and hold the cut—if we are looking for decisive results. . . .

114

Joint Chiefs' Order to Begin Bombing of Hanoi's Oil Facilities

Joint Chiefs of Staff's cablegram to Adm. U. S. Grant Sharp, commander in chief of Pacific forces, June 22, 1966, as provided in the body of the Pentagon study.

Strikes to commence with initial attacks against Haiphong and Hanoi POL on same day if operationally feasible. Make maximum effort to attain operational surprise. Do not conduct initiating attacks under marginal weather conditions but reschedule when weather assures success. Follow-on attacks authorized as operational and weather factors dictate.

At Haiphong, avoid damage to merchant shipping. No attacks authorized on craft unless U.S. aircraft are first fired on and then only if clearly North Vietnamese. Piers servicing target will not be attacked if tanker is berthed off end of pier.

Decision made after SecDef and CJCS were assured every feasible step would be taken to minimize civilian casualties would be small [sic]. If you do not believe you can accomplish objective while destroying targets and protecting crews, do not initiate program. Take the following measures; maximum use of most experienced ROLLING THUNDER personnel, detailed briefing of pilots stressing need to avoid civilians, execute only when weather permits visual identification of targets and improved strike accuracy, select best axis of attack to avoid populated areas, maximum use of ECM to hamper SAM and AAA fire control, in order to limit pilot distraction and improve accuracy, maximum use of weapons of high precision delivery consistent with mission objectives, and limit SAM and AAA suppression to sites located outside populated areas.

Take special precautions to insure security. If weather or operational considerations delay initiation of strikes, do not initiate on Sunday, 26 June.

115

August McNamara Memo to Chiefs Challenging Troop Request

Memorandum, "CINCPAC CY 1966 Adjusted Requirements & CY 1967" from Secretary McNamara to the Joint Chiefs of Staff Aug. 5, 1966, as provided in the body of the Pentagon study.

As you know, it is our policy to provide the troops, weapons, and supplies requested by General Westmoreland at the times he desires them, to the greatest possible degree. The latest revised CINCPAC requirements, submitted on 18 June 1966, subject as above, are to be accorded the same consideration: valid requirements for SVN and related tactical air forces in Thailand will be deployed on a schedule as close as possible to CINCPAC/COMUSMACV's requests.

Nevertheless, I desire and expect a detailed, line-by-line analysis of these requirements to determine that each is truly essential to the carrying out of our war plan. We must send to Vietnam what is needed, but only what is needed. Excessive deployments weaken our ability to win by undermining the economic structure of the RVN and by raising doubts concerning the soundness of our planning.

In the course of your review of the validity of the requirements, I would like you to consider the attached Deployment Issue Papers which were prepared by my staff. While there may be sound reasons for deploying the units questioned, the issues raised in these papers merit your detailed attention and specific reply. They probably do not cover all questionable units, particularly for proposed deployments for the PACOM area outside of SVN. I expect that you will want to query CINCPAC about these and other units for which you desire clarification.

I appreciate the time required to verify the requirements and determine our capability to meet them, but decisions must be made on a timely basis if units are to be readied and equipment and supplies procured. Therefore I would appreciate having your recommended deployment plan, including your comments on each of the Deployment Issue Papers, no later than 15 September 1965.

116

Cable from Westmoreland in August on Manpower Needs

Excerpts from cablegram from General Westmoreland to Gen. Earle G. Wheeler, Chairman of the Joint Chiefs of Staff, and Adm. U. S. Grant Sharp, commander in chief of Pacific forces, Aug. 10, 1966, as provided in the body of the Pentagon study.

These and other facts support earlier predictions and suggest that the enemy intends to continue a protracted war of attrition. We must not underestimate the enemy nor his determination.

The war can continue to escalate. Infiltration on enemy troops and supplies from NVN can increase and there is no assurance that this will not occur.

If, contrary to current indication, Hanoi decides not to escalate further, some modification of the forces which I have requested probably could be made. Under such circumstances, I conceive of a carefully balanced force that is designed to fight an extended war of attrition and sustainable without national mobilization.

I recognize the possibility that the enemy may not continue to follow the pattern of infiltration as projected. Accordingly, my staff is currently conducting a number of studies with the objective of placing this command and the RVN in a posture that will permit us to retain the initiative regardless of the course the enemy chooses to pursue. These include:

A. A study which considers possible courses of action by the enemy on our force posture and counteractions to maintain our superiority.

B. An analysis of our requirements to determine a balanced U.S. force that can be employed and sustained fully and effectively in combat on an indefinite basis without national mobilization.

C. A study to determine the evolutionary steps to be taken in designing an ultimate GVN security structure.

D. A study to determine the optimum RVNAF force structure which can be attained and supported in consideration of recent experience and our estimate of the manpower pool.

REF B [The CINCPAC submission] establishes and justifies minimal force requirements, emphasizing the requirement for a well balanced, sustainable force in SVN for an indefinite period. Consequently, at this point in time I cannot justify a reduction in requirements submitted.

117

Vietnam Bombing Evaluation by Institute for Defense Analyses

Excerpts from report by Institute for Defense Analyses, "The Effects of U.S. Bombing on North Vietnam's Ability to Support Military Operations in South Vietnam: Retrospect and Prospect," Aug. 29, 1966, as provided in the body of the Pentagon study. Paragraphs in italics are the study's paraphrase or explanation.

1. As of July 1966 the U.S. bombing of North Vietnam (NVN) had had no measurable direct effect on Hanoi's ability to mount and support military operations in the South at the current level.

Although the political constraints seem clearly to have reduced the effectiveness of the bombing program, its limited effect on Hanoi's ability to provide such support cannot be explained solely on that basis. The countermeasures introduced by Hanoi effectively reduced the impact of U.S. bombing. More fundamentally, however, North Vietnam has basically a subsistence agricultural economy that presents a difficult and unrewarding target system for air attack.

The economy supports operations in the South mainly by functioning as a logistic funnel and by providing a source of manpower. The industrial sector produces little of military value. Most of the essential military supplies that the VC/NVN forces in the South require from external sources are provided by the USSR and Communist China. Furthermore, the volume of such supplies is so low that only a small fraction of the capacity of North Vietnam's rather flexible transportation network is required to maintain the flow. The economy's relatively underemployed labor force also appears to provide an ample manpower reserve for internal military and economic needs including repair and reconstruction and for continued support of military operations in the South.

2. Since the initiation of the ROLLING THUNDER program the damage to facilities and equipment in North Vietnam has been more than offset by the increased flow of military and economic aid, largely from the USSR and Communist China.

The measurable costs of the damage sustained by North Vietnam are estimated by intelligence analysts to have reached approximately $86 million by 15 July 1966. In 1965 alone, the value of the military and economic aid that Hanoi received from the USSR and Communist China is estimated to have been on the order of $250-400 million, of which about $100-150 million was economic, and they have continued to provide aid, evidently at an increasing rate, during the current year. Most of it has been from the USSR, which had virtually cut off aid during the 1962-64 period. There can be little doubt, therefore, that Hanoi's Communist backers have assumed the economic costs to a degree that has significantly cushioned the impact of U.S. bombing.

3. The aspects of the basic situation that have enabled Hanoi to continue its support of military operations in the South and to neutralize the impact of U.S. bombing by passing the economic costs to other Communist countries are not likely to be altered by reducing the present geographic constraints, mining Haiphong and the principal harbors in North Vietnam, increasing the number of armed reconnaissance sorties and otherwise expanding the U.S. air offensive along the lines now contemplated in military recommendations and planning studies.

An expansion of the bombing program along such lines would make it more difficult and costly for Hanoi to move essential military supplies through North Vietnam to the VC/NVN forces in the South. The low volume of supplies required, the demonstrated effectiveness of the countermeasures already undertaken by Hanoi, the alternative options that the NVN transportation network provides and the level of aid the USSR and China seem prepared to provide, however, make it quite unlikely that Hanoi's capability to function as a logistic funnel would be seriously impaired. Our past experience also indicates that an intensified air campaign in NVN probably would not prevent Hanoi from infiltrating men into the South at the present or a higher rate, if it chooses. Furthermore there would appear to be no basis for assuming that the damage that could be inflicted by an intensified air offensive would impose such demands on the North Vietnamese labor force that Hanoi would be unable to continue and expand its recruitment and training of military forces for the insurgency in the South.

4. While conceptually it is reasonable to assume that some limit may be imposed on the scale of military activity that Hanoi

can maintain in the South by continuing the ROLLING THUNDER program at the present, or some higher level of effort, there appears to be no basis for defining that limit in concrete terms or, for concluding that the present scale of VC/NVN activities in the field have approached that limit.

The available evidence clearly indicates that Hanoi has been infiltrating military forces and supplies into South Vietnam at an accelerated rate during the current year. Intelligence estimates have concluded that North Vietnam is capable of substantially increasing its support.

5. The indirect effects of the bombing on the will of the North Vietnamese to continue fighting and on their leaders' appraisal of the prospective gains and costs of maintaining the present policy have not shown themselves in any tangible way. Furthermore, we have not discovered any basis for concluding that the indirect punitive effects of bombing will prove decisive in these respects.

It may be argued on a speculative basis that continued or increased bombing must eventually affect Hanoi's will to continue, particularly as a component of the total U.S. military pressures being exerted throughout Southeast Asia. However, it is not a conclusion that necessarily follows from the available evidence; given the character of North Vietnam's economy and society, the present and prospective low levels of casualties and the amount of aid available to Hanoi. It would appear to be equally logical to assume that the major influences on Hanoi's will to continue are most likely to be the course of the war in the South and the degree to which the USSR and China support the policy of continuing the war and that the punitive impact of U.S. bombing may have but a marginal effect in the broader context.

In the body of the report these summary formulations were elaborated in more detail. For instance, in assessing the military and economic effect of the bombing on North Vietnam's capacity to sustain the war, the report stated:

The economic and military damage sustained by Hanoi in the first year of the bombing was moderate and the cost could be (and was) passed along to Moscow and Peiping.

The major effect of the attack on North Vietnam was to force Hanoi to cope with disruption to normal activity, particularly in transportation and distribution. The bombing hurt most in its distruption of the roads and rail nets and in the very considerable repair effort which became necessary. The regime, however, was singularly successful in overcoming the effects of the U.S. interdiction effort.

Much of the damage was to installations that the North Vietnamese did not need to sustain the military effort. The regime made no attempt to restore storage facilities and little to repair damage to power stations, evidently because of the existence of adequate excess capacity and because the facilities were not of vital importance. For somewhat similar reasons, it made no major effort to restore military facilities, but merely abandoned barracks and dispersed materiel usually stored in depots.

The major essential restoration consisted of measures to keep traffic moving, to keep the railroad yards operating, to maintain communications, and to replace transport equipment and equipment for radar and SAM sites.

A little further on the report examined the political effects of the bombing on Hanoi's will to continue the war, the morale of the population, and the support of its allies.

The bombing through 1965 apparently had not had a major effect in shaping Hanoi's decision on whether or not to continue the war in Vietnam. The regime probably continued to base such decisions mainly on the course of the fighting in the South and appeared willing to suffer even stepped-up bombing so long as prospects of winning the South appeared to be reasonably good.

Evidence regarding the effect of the bombing on the morale of the North Vietnamese people suggests that the results were mixed. The bombing clearly strengthened popular support of the regime by engendering patriotic and nationalistic enthusiasm to resist the attacks. On the other hand, those more directly involved in the bombing underwent personal hardships and anxieties caused by the raids. Because the air strikes were directed away from urban areas, morale was probably damaged less by the direct bombing than by its indirect effects, such as evacuation of the urban population and the splitting of families.

Hanoi's political relations with its allies were in some respects strengthened by the bombing. The attacks had the effect of encouraging greater material and political support from the Soviet Union than might otherwise have been the case. While the Soviet aid complicated Hanoi's relationship with Peking, it reduced North Vietnam's dependence on China and thereby gave Hanoi more room for maneuver on its own behalf.

This report's concluding chapter was entitled "Observations" and contained some of the most lucid and penetrating analysis of air war produced to that date, or this! It began by reviewing the original objectives the bombing was initiated to achieve:

. . . Reducing the ability of North Vietnam to support the Communist insurgencies in South Vietnam and Laos, and . . . increasing progressively the pressure on NVN to the point where the regime would decide that it was too costly to continue directing and supporting the insurgency in the South.

After rehearsing the now familiar military failure of the bombing to halt the infiltration, the report crisply and succinctly outlined the bombing's failure to achieve the critical second objective—the psychological one:

. . . Initial plans and assessments for the ROLLING THUNDER program clearly tended to overestimate the persuasive and disruptive effects of the U.S. air strikes and, correspondingly, to underestimate the tenacity and recuperative capabilities of the North Vietnamese. This tendency, in turn, appears to reflect a general failure to appreciate the fact, well-documented in the historical and social scientific literature, that a direct, frontal attack on a society tends to strengthen the social fabric of the nation, to increase popular support of the existing government, to improve the determination of both the leadership and the populace to fight back, to induce a variety of protective measures that reduce the society's vulnerability to future attack, and to develop an increased capacity for quick repair and restoration of essential functions. The great variety of physical and social counter-measures that North Vietnam has taken in response to the bombing is now well documented in current intelligence reports, but the potential effectiveness of these counter-measures was not stressed in the early planning or intelligence studies.

Perhaps the most trenchant analysis of all, however, was reserved for last as the report attacked the fundamental weakness of the air war strategy—our inability to relate operations to objectives:

In general, current official thought about U.S. objectives in bombing NVN implicitly assumes two sets of causal relationships:

1. That by increasing the damage and destruction of resources in NVN, the U.S. is exerting pressure to cause the DRV to stop their support of the military operations in SVN and Laos; and

2. That the combined effect of the total military effort against NVN—including the U.S. air strikes in NVN and Laos, and the land, sea, and air operations in SVN—will ultimately cause the DRV to perceive that its probable losses accruing from the war have become greater than its possible gains and, on the basis of this net evaluation, the regime will stop its support of the war in the South.

These two sets of interrelationships are assumed in military planning, but it is not clear that they are systematically addressed in current intelligence estimates and assessments. Instead, the tendency is to encapsulate the bombing of NVN as one set of operations and the war in the South as another set of operations, and to evaluate each separately; and to tabulate and describe data on the physical, economic, and military effects of the bombing, but not to address specifically the relationship between such effects and the data relating to the ability and will of the DRV to continue its support of the war in the South.

The fragmented nature of current analyses and the lack of adequate methodology for assessing the net effects of a given set of military operations leaves a major gap between the quantifiable data on bomb damage effects, on the one hand, and policy judgments about the feasibility of achieving a given set of objectives, on the other. Bridging this gap still requires the exercise of broad political-military judgments that cannot be supported or rejected on the basis of systematic intelligence indicators. It must be concluded, therefore, that there is currently no adequate basis for predicting the levels of U.S. military effort that would be required to achieve the stated objectives—indeed, there is no firm basis for determining if there is *any* feasible level of effort that would achieve these objectives.

The critical impact of this study on the Secretary's thinking is revealed by the fact that many of its conclusions and much of its analysis would find its way into McNamara's October trip report to the President.

Having submitted a stinging condemnation of the bombing, the Study Group was under some obligation to offer constructive alternatives and this they did, seizing, not surprisingly, on the very idea McNamara had suggested—the anti-infiltration barrier. The product of their summer's work was a reasonably detailed proposal for a multi-system barrier across the DMZ and the Laotian panhandle that would make extensive use of recently innovated mines and sensors. The central portion of their recommendation follows:

The barrier would have two somewhat different parts, one designed against foot traffic and one against vehicles. The preferred location for the anti-foot-traffic barrier is in the region along the southern edge of the DMZ to the Laotian border and then north of Tchepone to the vicinity of Muong Sen, extending about 100 by 20 kilometers. This area is virtually unpopulated, and the terrain is quite rugged, containing mostly V-shaped valleys in which the opportunity for alternate trails appears lower than it is elsewhere in the system. The location of choice for the anti-vehicle part of the system is the area, about 100 by 40 kilometers, now covered by Operation Cricket. In this area the road network tends to be more constricted than elsewhere, and there appears to be a smaller area available for new roads. An alternative location for the anti-personnel system is north of the DMZ to the Laotian border and then north along the crest of the mountains dividing Laos from North Vietnam. It is less desirable economically and militarily because of its greater length, greater distance from U.S. bases, and greater proximity to potential North Vietnamese counter-efforts.

The air-supported barrier would, if necessary, be supplemented by a manned "fence" connecting the eastern end of the barrier to the sea.

The construction of the air-supported barrier could be initiated using currently available or nearly available components, with some necessary modifications, and could perhaps be installed by a year or so from go-ahead. However, we anticipate that the North Vietnamese would learn to cope with a barrier built this way after some period of time which we cannot estimate, but which we fear may be short. Weapons and sensors which can make a much more effective barrier, only some of which are now under development, are not likely to be available in less than 18 months to 2 years. Even these, it must be expected, will eventually be overcome by the North Vietnamese, so that further improvements in weaponry will be necessary. Thus we envisage a dynamic "battle of the barrier," in which the barrier is repeatedly improved and strengthened by the introduction of new components, and which will hopefully permit us to keep the North Vietnamese off balance by continually posing new problems for them. . . .

The anti-troop infiltration system (which would also function against supply porters) would operate as follows. There would be a constantly renewed mine field of non-sterilizing Gravel (and possibly button bomblets), distributed in patterns covering interconnected valleys and slopes (suitable for alternate trails) over the entire barrier region. The actual mined area would encompass the equivalent of a strip about 100 by 5 kilometers. There would also be a pattern of acoustic detectors to listen for mine explosions indicating an attempted penetration. The mine field is intended to deny opening of alternate routes for troop infiltrators and should be emplaced first. On the trails and bivouacs currently used, from which mines may—we tentatively assume—be cleared without great difficulty, a more dense pattern of sensors would be designed to locate groups of infiltrators. Air strikes using Gravel and SADEYES would then be called against these targets. The sensor patterns would be monitored 24 hours a day by patrol aircraft. The struck areas would be reseeded with new mines.

The anti-vehicle system would consist of acoustic detectors distributed every mile or so along all truckable roads in the interdicted area, monitored 24 hours a day by patrol aircraft, with vectored strike aircraft using SADEYE to respond to signals that trucks or truck convoys are moving. The patrol aircraft would distribute self-sterilizing Gravel over parts of the road net at dusk. The self-sterilizing feature is needed so that road-watching and mine-planting teams could be used in this area. Photo-reconnaissance aircraft would cover the entire area each few days to look for the development of new truckable roads, to see if the transport of supplies is being switched to porters, and to identify any other change in the infiltration system. It may also be desirable to use ground teams to plant larger anti-truck mines along the roads, as an interim measure pending the development of effective air-dropped anti-vehicle mines.

The cost of such a system (both parts) has been estimated to be about $800 million per year, of which by far the major fraction is spent for Gravel and SADEYES. The key requirements would be (all numbers are approximate because of assumptions which had to be made regarding degradation of system components in field use, and regarding the magnitude of infiltration): 20 million Gravel mines per month; possibly 25 million button bomblets per month . . .

Apart from the tactical counter-measures against the barrier itself, one has to consider strategic alternatives available to the North Vietnamese in case the barrier is successful. Among these are: a move into the Mekong Plain; infiltration from the sea either directly to SVN or through Cambodia; and movement down the Mekong from Thakhek (held by the Pathet Lao-North Vietnamese) into Cambodia.

Finally, it will be difficult for us to find out how effective the barrier is in the absence of clearly visible North Vietnamese responses, such as end runs through the Mekong plan. Because of supplies already stored in the pipeline, and because of the general shakiness of our quantitative estimates of either supply or troop infiltration, it is likely to be some time before the effect of even a wholly successful barrier becomes noticeable. A greatly stepped-up intelligence effort is called for, including continued road-watch activity in the areas of the motorcade roads, and patrol and reconnaissance activity south of the anti-personnel barrier.

Chapter 9

Secretary McNamara's Disenchantment: October, 1966–May, 1967

—By Hedrick Smith

The Pentagon's secret study of the Vietnam war discloses that Secretary of Defense Robert S. McNamara sought in October, 1966, to persuade President Lyndon B. Johnson to cut back the bombing of North Vietnam to seek a political settlement—17 months before Mr. Johnson made that move on March 31, 1968.

In May, 1967, the study reveals, Mr. McNamara went a step further and advocated that the Johnson Administration stop trying to guarantee a non-Communist South Vietnam and be willing to accept a coalition government in Saigon that included elements of the Vietcong.

What the study terms his "radical" proposal for scaling down American objectives in the war called for Saigon to negotiate with elements of the guerrilla movement not only for a political compromise but also for a cease-fire.

Mr. McNamara's disillusionment with the war has been reported previously, but the depth of his dissent from established policy is fully documented for the first time in the Pentagon study, which he commissioned on June 17, 1967.

The study details how this turnabout by Mr. McNamara— originally a leading advocate of the bombing policy and, in 1965, a confident believer that American intervention would bring the Vietcong insurgency under control—opened a deep policy rift in the Johnson Administration.

The study does not specifically say, however, that his break with established policy led President Johnson to nominate him on Nov. 28, 1967, as president of the World Bank and to replace him as Secretary of Defense.

But Mr. McNamara has previously revealed that in both

May and August of 1967 the subject of his possible departure from the Administration came up in talks with President Johnson, and the Pentagon study depicts both periods as critical points in the internal maneuvering on military strategy. In May Mr. McNamara was pressing his proposals to scale down the war, and in August President Johnson decided to expand the air war against the Secretary's advice.

The account of the Johnson Administration from late 1966 onward is that of a government wrestling with itself as the views of some senior policymakers changed under the pressures of protracted war.

Three identifiable camps are described: the McNamara group—the "disillusioned doves," as the analysts put it—trying to set limits on the war and then reduce it; the military faction, led by the Joint Chiefs of Staff and Gen. William C. Westmoreland, the commander in Vietnam, pressing for wider war; and President Johnson, as well as senior civilian officials at the White House and State Department, taking a middle position.

At each stage, the primary issues of debate were much the same: the size of American troop commitments; the effectiveness of the bombing of North Vietnam, which began on a sustained basis in March, 1965, and the proposed expansion of the air war and of the ground war in the South.

Beginning in late 1966, the study relates, President Johnson was being urged by the military leaders to step up the air war sharply and to consider allied invasions of Laos, Cambodia and even North Vietnam. Repeatedly the President was pressed to mobilize reserves to provide the manpower for a larger war.

The military leaders reacted to Secretary McNamara's proposals for a reduction of the air war with what the study calls "the stiffest kind of condemnation" and they "bombarded" him with rebuttals.

According to the study, Gen. Earle G. Wheeler, Chairman of the Joint Chiefs of Staff, warned on May 24, 1967, that halting the bombing north of the 20th Parallel would be "an aerial Dienbienphu"—a reference to the disastrous French military defeat in May, 1954, just before the negotiations that ended the French Indochina war.

The Joint Chiefs, the study relates, saw an "alarming pattern" in Mr. McNamara's over-all strategy—one, they declared, that would undermine the entire American war effort.

Their most vehement criticism was directed against the Secretary's memorandum to President Johnson on May 19,

---

Highlights of the Period

Starting late in 1966, the Pentagon study recounts, doubts about the effectiveness of American policy in Vietnam began to shred the unity of the Johnson Administration, with Secretary of Defense McNamara emerging as the leader of a group of "disillusioned doves."

Here are highlights of the months of doubt and debate:

OCTOBER, 1966

McNamara, returning from South Vietnam, tells President in memorandum that "pacification has if anything gone backward" and air war has not "either significantly affected infiltration or cracked the morale of Hanoi." Recommends limit or increase in forces, and consideration of halt in bombing, or shifting targets from Hanoi-Haiphong to infiltration routes, to "increase the credibility of our peace gestures."

Joint Chiefs, also in memorandum to President, oppose any cutback in bombing; propose "sharp knock," including strikes at locks, dams and rail yards. They say military situation has "improved substantially over the past year" and call bombing "a trump card."

NOVEMBER, 1966

McNamara gives Joint Chiefs new troop authorization: 469,000 by end of June, 1968, below military requests. Study comments that from now on "the judgment of the military . . . would be subject to question."

McNamara tells President there is "no evidence" that addition of more troops "would substantially change the situation," and that bombing "is yielding very small marginal returns" with "no significant impact" on war in the South.

JANUARY, 1967

Central Intelligence Agency study estimates 1965-1966 air-war casualties in North Vietnam to be 36,000—"about 80 per cent civilians"—making civilian-casualty total about 29,000.

FEBRUARY, 1967

President approves "spring air offensive" including attacks on power plants, mining of rivers, relaxation of restrictions on air raids near Hanoi and Haiphong.

MARCH, 1967

General Westmoreland asks 200,000 more troops, for a total U.S. force of 671,616.

APRIL, 1967

Joint Chiefs transmit Westmoreland troop request, call for mobilization of reserves, propose "an extension of the war" into Laos and Cambodia and possibly North Vietnam.

President asks Westmoreland if enemy cannot increase troop strength and adds: "If so, where does it all end?"

MAY, 1967

Assistant Secretary of State William Bundy opposes ground operations against North Vietnam as likely to provoke China; also warns—as does C.I.A.—of possible Soviet reaction to mining Haiphong.

Walt W. Rostow, in memo to President, urges cutback in bombing.

McNamara-McNaughton memo to President recommends cut-back to 20th Parallel, troop increase of only 30,000 and what study calls basically "a recommendation that we accept a compromise outcome" and "scaled-down goals." Study calls these "radical positions" under the circumstances.

1967. That paper gave a discouraging picture of the military situation and a pessimistic view of the American public's impatience with the war, and said:

"The time has come for us to eliminate the ambiguities from our minimum objectives—our commitments—in Vietnam. Specifically, two principles must be articulated, and policies and actions brought in line with them: (1) Our commitment is only to see that the people of South Vietnam are permitted to determine their own future. (2) This commitment ceases if the country ceases to help itself.

"It follows that no matter how much we might *hope* for some things, our *commitment* is *not:*

". . . To ensure that a particular person or group remains in power, nor that the power runs to every corner of the land (though we prefer certain types and we hope their writ will run throughout South Vietnam),

"To guarantee that the self-chosen government is non-Communist (though we believe and strongly hope it will be), and

"To insist that the independent South Vietnam remain separate from North Vietnam (though in the short-run, we would prefer it that way)." The material in italics and in parentheses is in the McNamara memorandum.

Specifically, the Secretary urged that in September, 1967, after the South Vietnamese presidential elections, the United States "move" the Saigon Government "to seek a political settlement with the non-Communist members of the NLF [National Liberation Front, or Vietcong]—to explore a cease-fire and to reach an accommodation with the non-Communist South Vietnamese who are under the VC banner; to accept them as members of an opposition political party, and if necessary, to accept their individual participation in the national government—in sum, a settlement to transform the members of the VC from military opponents to political opponents."

Mr. McNamara acknowledged that one obvious drawback would be "the alleged impact on the reputation of the United States and of its President," but argued that "the difficulties of this strategy are fewer and smaller than the difficulties of any other approach."

President Johnson, the study recounts, preferred the middle ground of piecemeal escalation—what the study calls "the slow squeeze"—to either the "sharp knock" advocated by the Joint Chiefs of Staff or the shift toward political and military accommodation favored by Mr. McNamara.

514

It is "not surprising," the Pentagon analysts remark, that the President did not adopt the McNamara approach in view of his need to keep "the military 'on board' in any new direction for the U.S. effort in Southeast Asia." This is evidently an allusion to reports at the time that some high-ranking officers were in the mood to threaten resignation if the McNamara policy was adopted.

Satisfying neither extreme, President Johnson "was in the uncomfortable position of being able to please neither his hawkish nor his dovish critics with his carefully modulated middle course," the study asserts.

During the prolonged internal debate, the Pentagon account discloses, such issues as stalemate in the ground war and civilian casualties of the air war were of much more concern to some policy makers than the Administration publicly acknowledged.

Press dispatches from Hanoi in late 1966 stimulated what the analysts call an "explosive debate" in public about civilian casualties. Privately, the analysts add, the Central Intelligence Agency produced a summary of the bombing in 1965 and 1966 that estimated that there had been nearly 29,000 civilian casualties in North Vietnam—a figure far higher than Hanoi itself had ever used.

The Pentagon study also discloses that early in 1967 the growing stalemate on the ground became a concern of high civilian officials—even, at times, of President Johnson himself.

On April 27, the study notes, the President met with General Westmoreland and General Wheeler, who urged him to grant General Westmoreland's request for 200,000 more troops—a request the two officers repeated nearly a year later—but Mr. Johnson was wary.

Their discussion was recorded in notes, found in Pentagon files and quoted in the study. [See Document #125.]

"When we add divisions, can't the enemy add divisions?" the President asked. "If so, where does it all end?"

When General Westmoreland conceded that the enemy was likely to match American reinforcements, President Johnson turned to the worry that Hanoi might ask Communist China for help.

"At what point," he asked, "does the enemy ask for volunteers?"

The only recorded reply from General Westmoreland was, "That is a good question."

The real ceiling on the American commitment, the analysts

suggest several times, was imposed primarily by President Johnson's refusal to be pushed by the military leaders into asking Congress to mobilize reserve forces—both former servicemen on inactive status and organized units of these servicemen.

Mobilization, the analysts assert, became the "political sound barrier" that President Johnson would not break.

A Pessimistic Report

For Mr. McNamara and his influential aide John T. McNaughton, Assistant Secretary of Defense for International Security Affairs, the first frontal challenge to the basic trend of policy came in October, 1966, and grew out of doubts that had been mounting for nearly a year.

As early as November, 1965—eight months after the American decision to intervene with ground forces—the Secretary of Defense warned President Johnson that the major new reinforcements he was approving could "not guarantee success." And in January, 1966, Mr. McNaughton, the third-ranking official in the Pentagon, voiced fear that the United States had become caught in "an escalating military stalemate."

In mid-October, Secretary McNamara returned disturbed from a trip to South Vietnam. He had been the intended target of a Vietcong assassination squad that was discovered only a few hours before his arrival in Saigon—a point to which he seemed to allude in his report to the President. "Full security exists nowhere," he said, "not even behind the U.S. Marines' lines and in Saigon [and] in the countryside, the enemy almost completely controls the night." [See Document #118.]

The Pentagon study notes that in this Oct. 14 memorandum, Mr. McNamara for the first time recommended cutting back sharply on military requests for reinforcements. Such requests had previously been given almost routine approval in Washington.

In September, 1966, Adm. U. S. Grant Sharp, commander in chief of forces in the Pacific, had pressed on behalf of General Westmoreland for an increase in the projected strength of American forces in South Vietnam from 445,000 to 570,000 by the end of 1967. Actual strength was 325,000 men, and still rising.

On Oct. 7, the Joint Chiefs of Staff urged what the Pentagon study calls "full-blown" mobilization of 688,500 Army, Navy, Air Force and Marine reservists to help provide more troops for Vietnam and also to build up the armed forces around the world.

In his Oct. 14 memorandum, Mr. McNamara told President Johnson that he was "a little less pessimistic" than he had been a year earlier because the allied military campaign had "blunted the Communist military initiative" and prevented a total collapse in Saigon. But he went on to say that this had not produced results in what he called "the 'end products'—broken enemy morale and political achievements" by the South Vietnamese Government.

Discussing Saigon's struggle to win the people's allegiance, Mr. McNamara showed none of the confidence of high American officials in the early sixties that the mere introduction of Americans would revitalize the South Vietnamese civilian and military leadership.

"The discouraging truth," he said, "is that, as was the case in 1961 and 1963 and 1965, we have not found the formula, the catalyst, for training and inspiring them into effective action."

Summing up the crucial drive to extend Government control in the countryside, he said:

"Pacification has if anything gone backward. As compared with two, or four, years ago, enemy full-time regional forces and part-time guerrilla forces are larger; attacks, terrorism and sabotage have increased in scope and intensity; more railroads are closed and highways cut; the rice crop expected to come to market is smaller; we control little, if any, more of the population. . . . In essence, we find ourselves . . . no better, and if anything worse off."

"Nor," he said, turning to the air war, "has the Rolling Thunder program of bombing the North either significantly affected the infiltration or cracked the morale of Hanoi."

The essence of Mr. McNamara's recommendations was that the United States should be "girding, openly, for a longer war" rather than pursuing what the Pentagon study terms General Westmoreland's "meatgrinder" strategy of trying to kill enemy troops more rapidly than they could be replaced either by new recruits or by infiltration from North Vietnam.

In his memorandum, the Secretary put forward his program:

- "Limit the increase in U.S. forces" in 1967 to a total of 470,000 men—25,000 more than planned, and 100,000 fewer than requested by the military.

- "Install a barrier" to infiltration just south of the demilitarized zone astride the two Vietnams' border and jutting across the Ho Chi Minh Trail complex of enemy supply lines in the mountainous panhandle of Laos. The electronic barrier would cost roughly $1-billion.

- "Stabilize the Rolling Thunder program against the North" at the current monthly level of 12,000 sorties—individual flights by planes—because "to bomb the North sufficiently to make a radical impact upon Hanoi's political, economic and social structure, would require an effort which we could make but which would not be stomached either by our own people or by world opinion; and it would involve a serious risk of drawing us into open war with China."

- "Pursue a vigorous pacification program" that would require "drastic reform" in the approach of South Vietnamese civilian, police and military officials to insure that they "will 'stay' in the [contested] area, . . . behave themselves decently and . . . show some respect for the people."

- "Take steps to increase the credibility of our peace gestures in the minds of the enemy" through both political and military moves.

Among these moves, he proposed that "we should consider" a decision to "stop bombing all of North Vietnam" or, alternatively, to "shift the weight-of-effort away from 'zones 6A and 6B'—zones including Hanoi and Haiphong and areas north of those two cities to the Chinese border" and concentrate the air war instead "on the infiltration routes in Zones 1 and 2 (the southern end of North Vietnam, including the Mugia Pas), in Laos and in South Vietnam." The parenthetical material is Mr. McNamara's.

Politically, he suggested consideration of efforts to "try to split the VC off from Hanoi" and to "develop a realistic plan providing a role for the VC in negotiations, postwar life and government of the nation."

Joint Chiefs Demur

The public position of the Johnson Administration opposed negotiating with the Vietcong or recognizing them. A proosal for political compromise from Senator Robert F. Kennedy on Feb. 19, 1966—that the Vietcong should be admitted to a share of power and responsibility" in Saigon—had been quickly denounced by Vice President Hubert H. Humphrey. That, Mr. Humphrey said, would be like putting "a fox in a chicken coop; soon there wouldn't be any chickens left."

Mr. McNamara was skeptical that any approach would work rapidly. "The prognosis is bad that the war can be brought to a satisfactory conclusion within the next two years," he told President Johnson in his memorandum. "The large-unit operations probably will not do it; negotiations probably will not do it."

There are no indications that other agencies of government were called upon to comment formally, although the McNamara report did receive general endorsement from Under Secretary of State Nicholas deB. Katzenbach, who had gone with the Secretary of Defense to Saigon. A note at the end of Mr. McNamara's paper stated: "Mr. Katzenbach and I have discussed many of its main conclusions and recommendations—in general, but not in particulars, it expresses his views as well as my own."

The reaction of the Joint Chiefs of Staff to Mr. McNamara's proposals of Oct. 14, the Pentagon study reports, was "predictably rapid—and violent." Obviously forewarned, the Joint Chiefs had their own memorandum ready on the same day for Mr. McNamara and the President. [See Document #119.]

Their paper, quoted at length in the Pentagon study, agreed that a long war was likely but took issue with Mr. McNamara's guarded assessment of the military situation, which, in their eyes, had "improved substantially over the past year." They were especially concerned that the McNamara paper did not take into account what they called the "adverse impact over time of continued bloody defeats on the morale of VC/ N.V.A. [Vietcong/North Vietnamese Army] forces and the determination of their political and military leaders."

The Joint Chiefs objected to Mr. McNamara's suggestion of a halt or a cutback in bombing to stimulate negotiations. The bombing, they argued, was a "trump card" that should not be surrendered without an equivalent return, such as "an end to the NVN aggression in SVN." Rather than cutting back or leveling off, they advocated a "sharp knock" against North Vietnamese military assets and war-supporting facilities.

Whatever the "political merits" of slowly increasing the pressure, they said:

"We deprived ourselves of the military effects of earl weight of effort and shock, and gave to the enemy time t adjust to our slow quantitative and qualitative increase o pressure. This is not to say that it is now too late to deriv military benefits from more effective and extensive use of ou air and naval superiority."

What the Joint Chiefs recommended in their Oct. 1 memorandum—and what they largely succeeded in gettin President Johnson to approve, though only step by step—wa a bombing program that would have these effects:

"Decrease the Hanoi and Haiphong sanctuary areas, au thorize attacks against the steel plant [at Thainguyen] th Hanoi rail yards, the thermal power plants, selected area within Haiphong port and other ports, selected locks an dams controlling water LOCs [lines of communications— canals and rivers] SAM [surface-to-air missile] support fa cilities within residual Hanoi and Haiphong sanctuaries, an P.O.L. [petroleum-oil-lubricants storeage] at Haiphong, Hagia (Phucyen) and Canthon (Kep)."

The Joint Chiefs commented that Mr. McNamara's pro posal for total American troop strength of 470,000 men wa "substantially less" than the earlier recommendations of Gen eral Westmoreland and Admiral Sharp. On Nov. 4, the study recounts, they recommended a build-up to 493,969 men by the end of 1967 and eventually to 555,741. They also dis cussed their preferred strategy, which involved the lifting of political restraints:

"The concept describes preparation for operations that have not as yet been authorized, such as mining ports, naval quarantine, spoiling attacks and raids against the enemy in Cambodia and Laos, and certain special operations."

But at a conference of the allied powers in Manila on Oct. 23 to 25 came an indication that General Westmoreland had sensed that, as the Pentagon study puts it, "McNamara and Johnson were not politically and militarily enchanted with a costly major force increase at that time, nor with cross-border and air operations which ran grave political risks."

The general's talks with President Johnson on these issues "remain a mystery," the Pentagon study says. But twice the general sought out Assistant Secretary McNaughton, who re ported to Mr. McNamara on Oct. 26 that General Westmore land had trimmed his requests to 480,000 men by the end of 1967 and 500,000 by the end of 1968.

According to Mr. McNaughton's report, cited in the study, General Westmoreland said that those forces would be enough

ven if infiltration went on at a high level" but that he
anted a contingency force of roughly two divisions on reserve
the Pacific. This could range between 50,000 and 75,000
en.

The time for decision came virtually on the eve of the
ov. 8 Congressional election. Although the war was not a
ntral issue in most districts, the Pentagon account says,
resident Johnson had obtained at the Manila meeting a state-
ent on ultimate allied withdrawal that would favorably im-
ess American voters.

The final Manila communiqé, issued on Oct. 25, pledged
at allied forces would be withdrawn from Vietnam "not
ter than six months after" the other side "withdraws its
rces to the North, and ceases infiltration, and as the level
violence thus subsides."

According to Mr. McNaughton's notes, "the President was
etermined to get the language in, including the reference to
ix months' (opposed by State, supported by me)."

Three days before the election, Secretary McNamara said
a news conference at Johnson City, Tex., that the Ameri-
an troop commitment to South Vietnam would grow in
967 at a rate "substantially less" than the 200,000 men added
1966.

The Pentagon study says that the troop decision had been
ade in a meeting with the President that morning after
eeks of detailed studies and arguments, but Mr. McNamara
ould give no figure to reporters. When they questioned him,
e replied: "I couldn't give you an estimate. We don't have
etailed plans."

Nor did the Secretary give any indication of the discourage-
ent with the war that had characterized his confidential re-
ort to the President on Oct. 14. Instead, he dwelt upon allied
uccess in preventing the Communist take-over that had been
xpected a year before. Whereas in private Mr. McNamara
ad talked about the build-up of enemy forces and the Ameri-
an inability to energize the Saigon Government, in public he
ited prisoner interrogations that suggested that enemy morale
as sagging.

The troop build-up decision was formally communicated
the Joint Chiefs on Nov. 11. Mr. McNamara told them,
e Pentagon study recounts, that the new goal would be
69,000 men in the field by June 30, 1968—not only fewer
en than General Westmoreland's revised figures at Manila
ut an even slower build-up than Mr. McNamara himself
ad foreseen in mid-October.

The Pentagon study asserts that the significance of the 1966 troop debate was that for the first time the President essentially said "no" to General Westmoreland. Moreover, Secretary McNamara, in his October memorandum, had generated alternative strategies to those put forward by the military commander. "From this time on," the Pentagon study comments, "the judgment of the military as to how the war should be fought and what was needed would be subject to question."

On Nov. 17, Mr. McNamara went a step further and challenged General Westmoreland's strategy of attrition. In a paper to the President, Mr. McNamara reported Pentagon calculations that previous American reinforcements had not brought sharp enough increases in enemy casualties to justify further heavy reinforcements. [See Document #120.]

Pentagon efficiency specialists showed, Mr. McNamara said, that from 1965 to 1966 "enemy losses increased by 115 per week during a period in which friendly strength increased by 166,000, an increase of about 70 losses per 100,000 of friendly strength. . . . We have no evidence that more troops than the 470,000 I am recommending would substantially change the situation."

"Moreover," he went on, "It is possible that our attrition estimates substantially overstate actual VC/NVA losses. For example, the VC/NVA apparently lose only about one-sixth as many weapons as people, suggesting the possibility that many of the killed are unarmed porters or bystanders."

He made a similar report on the air war. "At the scale we are now operating, I believe our bombing is yielding very small marginal returns, not worth the cost in pilot lives and aircraft," Mr. McNamara said. "In spite of an interdiction campaign costing at least $250-million per month at current levels, no significant impact on the war in South Vietnam is evident."

But President Johnson did not accept Mr. McNamara's earlier suggestions for a cutback in the bombing. The study reveals that the Secretary's pessimism about the war was not shared by such White House officials as Walt W. Rostow and Robert W. Komer, both special assistants to the President.

The one change in the air war that the President approved, the study shows, was an increase in B-52 sorties from 60 to 800 monthly, effective in February, 1967, as urged by Admiral Sharp and the Joint Chiefs of Staff.

By the turn of the year, the air war had become the main point of controversy. Public dissent over the bombing was ising. Dispatches from Hanoi by Harrison E. Salisbury, assistant managing editor of The New York Times, generated an "explosive debate about the bombing," the Pentagon study adds.

"His dispatches carried added sting," the study explains, because he was in North Vietnam as the bombing moved in close to Hanoi. On Dec. 25, 1966, Mr. Salisbury reported from Namdinh that the air campaign had killed 89 persons and wounded 405 others. Press reports from Washington quoted officials as expressing irritation and contending that Mr. Salisbury was exaggerating the damage to civilian areas.

But soon, the Government's own intelligence specialists were privately estimating that civilian casualties in North Vietnam were far more numerous than indicated in the dispatches of Mr. Salisbury or of William C. Braggs, editor of The Miami News, who went later to Hanoi.

In January, 1967, the Pentagon account discloses, the Central Intelligence Agency produced a study estimating that military and civilian casualties of the air war in North Vietnam had risen from 13,000 in 1965 to 23,000 or 24,000 in 1966—"about 80 per cent civilians." In all, that meant nearly 29,000 civilian casualties in an air war that was to expand in the next 15 months.

The study reports that the total number of individual flights against North Vietnam in Operation Rolling Thunder rose from 55,000 in 1965 to 148,000 in 1966, total bomb tonnage rose from 33,000 to 128,000, the number of aircraft lost rose from 171 to 318, and direct operational costs rose from $460-million to $1.2-billion. But, paraphrasing the C.I.A. analysis, the Pentagon study comments that the bombing in 1966 "accomplished little more than in 1965."

According to the account, the major result of the raids close to Hanoi on Dec. 2, 4, 13 and 14—all inside a previously established 30-mile sanctuary around the capital—"was to undercut what appeared to be a peace feeler from Hanoi."

The Pentagon version of this diplomatic maneuver, code-named Marigold by the State Department, is reportedly included in the diplomatic section of the study, the one part not obtained by The New York Times. The authors of other sections relied on press accounts and on the book "The Secret Search for Peace" by David Kraslow and Stuart H. Loory of The Los Angeles Times.

The study recounts that the Polish member of the International Control Commission for Vietnam tried to arrange for talks between American and North Vietnamese representatives in early December, 1966, in Warsaw.

"When the attacks were launched inadvertently against Hanoi in December," the Pentagon study comments, "the attempt to start talks ran into difficulty. A belated attempt to mollify Norh Vietnam's bruised ego failed and formal talks did not materialize." This is an allusion to President Johnson's decision to restore part of the bomb-free sanctuary around Hanoi. The analyst does not explain why he considered the raids inadvertent.

Recapitulating the public furor over the bombing, the study comments that 1966 "drew to a close on a sour note for the President."

"He had just two months before resisted pressure from the military for a major escalation of the war in the North and adopted the restrained approach of the Secretary of Defense," the study continues, "only to have a few inadvertent raids within the Hanoi periphery mushroom into a significant loss of world opinion support."

Pressure for Wider War

As 1967 began, the study asserts, the stage was set for "a running battle" inside the Johnson Administration " between the advocates of a greatly expanded air campaign against North Vietnam, one that might genuinely be called 'strategic,' and the disillusioned doves who urged relaxation, if not complete suspension, of the bombing in the interests of greater effectiveness and the possibilities for peace."

"The 'hawks,' of course, were primarily the military," the study continues, "but in wartime their power and influence with an incumbent administration is disproportionate. McNamara, supported quantitatively by John McNaughton . . . led the attempt to deescalate the bombing. Treading the uncertain middle ground at different times in the debate were William P. Bundy [Assistant Secretary of State for Far Eastern Affairs], Air Force Secretary Harold Brown and, most importantly, the President himself. Buffeted from right to left, he determinedly tried to pursue the temperate course, escalating gradually in the late spring but levelling off again in the summer."

With the exception of a diplomatic interlude during the

oliday truce at Tet, the Lunar New Year celebration in arly February, the pressures for widening the war were un-elenting, according to the Pentagon account.

Mr. Rostow, the President's special assistant for national ecurity, said in a memorandum on Dec. 12, for example, at he found the allied military position "greatly improved" in 1966 and pictured a dominant—even potentially victori-us—position by the end of 1967.

In Congress, the study also notes, the military received sup-ort from Senator John C. Stennis, chairman of the influential enate Preparedness Subcommittee. On Jan. 18, the Missis-ippi Democrat declared that General Westmoreland's troop equests should be met, "even if it should require mobiliza-on or partial mobilization."

In Saigon, General Westmoreland was pressing Washing-on to speed the troop shipments already promised. In sup-ort of his requests, the study notes, General Westmoreland escribed the growth of enemy forces as of Jan. 2:

". . . 9 division headquarters, 34 regimental headquarters, 52 combat battalions, 34 combat support battalions, 196 eparate companies, and 70 separate platoons totaling some 28,600, plus at least 112,800 militia and at least 39,175 olitical cadre . . . (a) strength increase of some 42,000 uring 1966 despite known losses."

For the allies, he explained, this posed the danger that in ny of the three military regions north of Saigon, "the enemy an attack at any time selected targets . . . in up to division trength" of roughly 10,000 men.

Diplomatic activity reached a peak during Tet, Feb. 8 to 2, as the United States halted the bombing. In London, rime Minister Harold Wilson, acting on President Johnson's ehalf, met with the Soviet Premier, Aleksei N. Kosygin, in n effort to get the bombing stopped permanently and peace alks started.

Then, on Feb. 13, after a pause of nearly six days, the ombing of North Vietnam was resumed. Mr. Johnson said e had based his decision on what he termed the unparalleled nagnitude of the North Vietnamese supply effort.

Excerpts from Mr. Wilson's memoirs, "The Labor Govern-ment, 1964-70: A Personal Record," published two months go in The Sunday Times of London and Life magazine, lamed President Johnson for the collapse of the talks, charg-ng that at the last moment he had changed his terms for a ombing halt by demanding a cessation of enemy infiltration s a precondition.

By Mr. Wilson's account, this was a "total reversal" of the offer Washington first authorized him to pass through Mr Kosygin to Hanoi: a secret agreement under which the bombing would be stopped first, infiltration second and the American troop build-up third.

The sections of the Pentagon study available to The New York Times provide no insight into why Mr. Johnson's position changed suddenly.

The study makes it clear, however, that the collapse of the diplomatic efforts was a turning point, for shortly afterward President Johnson began approving additional targets in North Vietnam for attack.

"The President perceived the [air] strikes as necessary in the psychological test of wills between the two sides to punish the North," the study adds, "in spite of the near consensus opinion of his [civilian] advisers that no level of damage or destruction that we were willing to inflict was likely to destroy Hanoi's determination to continue to struggle."

President Johnson approved what the Pentagon account calls the "spring air offensive" in the following phases:

• On Feb. 22, for attacks on five urban thermal power plants, excluding those in Hanoi and Haiphong, and on the Thainguyen steel plant; for mining of rivers and estuaries and conducting naval barrages against the coastline up to the 20th Parallel.

• On March 22, the two Haiphong thermal power plants

• On April 8, by relaxing the previous restrictions on raids around Hanoi and Haiphong, for raids against Kep airfield the power transformer near the center of the city; for attacks on petroleum storage facilities, an ammunition dump and cement plant in Haiphong.

• On May 2, for a raid on the thermal power plant a mile north of the center of Hanoi.

By early May these raids, the Pentagon study relates, had become a focus of controversy among Presidential advisers General Wheeler sent the President a memorandum on May 5, justifying the raids on such targets as power plants with this assertion:

"The objective of our attacks on the thermal electric power system in North Vietnam was not . . . to turn the lights off in major population centres, but . . . to deprive the enemy of a basic power source needed to operate certain war supporting facilities and industries."

In rebuttal to this was the position of McGeorge Bundy As President Johnson's assistant for national security until he left the government on Feb. 28, 1966, Mr. Bundy had been one of the foremost original advocates of the air war against North Vietnam. But in a personal letter to President Johnson, evidently received by the White House on May 4, Mr. Bundy termed the "strategic bombing" of North Vietnam "both unproductive and unwise," especially the raids on the power plants. [See Document #126.]

"The lights have not stayed off in Haiphong," he said, "and even if they had, electric lights are in no sense essential to the Communist war effort."

Mr. Bundy emphasized that he was "very far indeed from suggesting that it would make sense now to stop the bombing of the North altogether" because that would be "to give the Communists something for nothing." But as for the power plants, he commented: "We are attacking them, I fear, mainly because we have 'run out' of other targets. Is it a very good reason?"

The 200,000 Request

The main catalyst for the sharp debate in the Johnson Administration in the spring of 1967, however, was not the air war but General Westmoreland's request for 200,000 more troops.

According to the Pentagon account, General Westmoreland first notified the Joint Chiefs of Staff on March 18 of his additional troop needs and then, at their suggestion, submitted a more detailed request on March 26. He spoke with concern about the large enemy build-ups in sanctuaries in Laos, Cambodia and parts of South Vietnam as well as about the threat posed by large North Vietnamese forces just north of the DMZ.

"The minimum essential force" needed to contain the enemy threat and maintain the "tactical initiative," as he put it in his March 18 message, was two and one-third divisions —roughly 100,000 men—"as soon as possible but not later than 1 July 1968." For an "optimum force," he said he needed four and two-thirds divisions in all—201,250 more troops—to boost the ultimate strength of American forces in Vietnam to 671,616 men. [See Document #122.]

The reinforcements, General Westmoreland asserted, would enable him to destroy or neutralize enemy main forces "more quickly" and deny the enemy long established "safe havens" in South Vietnam.

In some regions, however, his picture sounded less hopeful. In the northernmost portion of South Vietnam, and in the Central Highlands along the Laotian border, he wanted more troops largely "to contain the infiltration" of North Vietnamese forces from Cambodia, Laos and North Vietnam.

One point that quickly aroused controversy in Washington, the Pentagon study notes, was General Westmoreland's argument that the American build-up would "obviate the requirement for a major expansion" of South Vietnamese forces. This, the authors report, "prompted many who disagreed with the basic increases to ask why the U.S. should meet such expanded troop requirements when the Government of South Vietnam would neither mobilize its manpower nor effectively employ it according to U.S. wishes."

The Joint Chiefs transmitted General Westmoreland's main troop requests to Secretary McNamara on April 20 with their endorsement. "Once again," the Pentagon analyst notes, the Joint Chiefs "confronted the Johnson Administration with a difficult decision on whether to escalate or level off the U.S. effort."

"What they proposed," the study says, paraphrasing their April 29 memorandum to Secretary McNamara, "was the mobilization of the reserves, a major new troop commitment in the South, an extension of the war into the VC/NVA sanctuaries (Laos, Cambodia and possibly North Vietnam), the mining of North Vietnamese ports and a solid commitment in manpower and resources to a military victory. The recommendation not unsurprisingly touched off a searching reappraisal of the course of U.S. strategy in the war."

The Joint Chiefs spoke for mobilization despite President Johnson's previous opposition to such a move.

Without a reserve call-up, the Joint Chiefs told Mr. McNamara, the Army could provide only one and one-third of the four and two-thirds divisions that General Westmoreland wanted by July, 1968, and a second division could probably not be provided until late in 1969. "A reserve call-up and collateral actions," they asserted, "would enable the services to provide the major combat forces required."

General Westmoreland and General Wheeler put the military case before President Johnson on April 27 when, according to the Pentagon account, ostensibly to deliver a speech, General Westmoreland returned to the United States.

According to unsigned "Notes on Discussions With the

President," which the writers of the Pentagon study found in the files of Assistant Secretary of Defense McNaughton and attributed to him, General Westmoreland told President Johnson that if he did not get the first 100,000 men, "it will be nip and tuck to oppose the reinforcements the enemy is capable of providing," though he acknowledged this would not risk defeat. The second 100,000 troops, he said, were needed to push the allied strategy to success. [See Document #125.]

That was the point at which President Johnson, worried about enemy infiltration, asked, "When we add divisions, can't the enemy add divisions? If so, where does it all end?"

General Westmoreland replied that the Vietcong and North Vietnamese now had 285,000 troops, or roughly eight divisions, in South Vietnam and had "the capability of deploying 12 divisions. . . . If we add 2½ divisions, it is likely the enemy will react by adding troops."

Later, according to the notes, the general warned of prolonged fighting. He predicted that "unless the will of the enemy is broken or unless there was an unraveling of the VC infrastructure the war could go on for five years." Reinforcements would shorten the time—"with a force level of 565,000, the war could well go on for three years," General Westmoreland said. "With a second increment of 2 1/3 divisions leading to a total of 665,000 men, it could go on for two years."

General Wheeler, presumably citing other reasons for a reserve call-up, voiced his concern that the United States might face military threats elsewhere—in South Korea or in the form of Soviet pressure on Berlin.

In Indochina, he went on, the Joint Chiefs of Staff were deeply concerned about the North Vietnamese build-up in Cambodia and Laos and felt that American troops "may be forced to move against these units." Beyond that, he was quoted as putting forward the idea of possible invasion of North Vietnam: "We may wish to take offensive action against the D.R.V. with ground troops."

Picking up that theme, General Westmoreland told the President that he had an operational plan that "envisioned an elite South Vietnamese division conducting ground operations in Laos against D.R.V. bases and routes under cover of U.S. artillery and air support." In time, he foresaw "the eventual development of Laos as a major battlefield," as the analysts put it.

According to the Pentagon account, General Westmoreland also told President Johnson "that he possessed contingency plans to move into Cambodia in the Chu Pong area, again using South Vietnamese forces but this time accompanied by U.S. advisers."

Turning to the air war, General Wheeler argued that it was time to consider action "to deny the North Vietnamese use of the ports" because otherwise the American air strategy was "about to reach the point of target saturation—when all worthwhile fixed targets except the ports had been struck."

The Pentagon study says that President Johnson concluded this discussion by asking: "What if we do not add the 2-1/3 divisions?" General Wheeler was quoted as replying that the allied military momentum would die and in some areas the enemy would recapture the initiative, meaning a longer war but not that the allies would lose. General Westmoreland's reply, if any, was not recorded.

The President then reportedly urged his commanders to "make certain we are getting value received from the South Vietnamese troops."

The cleavage between the military and civilian views in the Johnson Administration emerged at once.

On April 24 Under Secretary of State Katzenbach, acting in Secretary Rusk's absence, ordered an interagency review of two major options that in effect set out the two opposing views:

• Course A—providing General Westmoreland with 200,-000 more troops and, as the analysts put it, "possible . . . intensification of military actions outside South Vietnam including invasion of North Vietnam, Laos and Cambodia."

• Course B—confining troop increases, in Mr. Katzenbach's words, to "those that could be generated without calling up the reserves." Coupled with this, the various agencies should consider "a cessation . . . of bombing North Vietnamese areas north of 20 degrees (or, if it looked sufficiently important to maximize an attractive settlement opportunity, cessation of bombing in all of North Vietnam.)"

The resistance of high civilian officials to the military proposals was virtually unanimous, according to the Pentagon study, though the position of Secretary of State Dean Rusk is not described. The three most sensitive issues were the reserve call-up, attacks on the port of Haiphong, and allied ground offensives into Laos, Cambodia or North Vietnam.

At the State Department, Assistant Secretary Bundy, in a memorandum on May 1 to Under Secretary Katzenbach, came out "totally against" ground operations against North Vietnam, asserting that the odds were 75 to 25 that it would provoke Chinese Communist intervention. He was also "strongly opposed" to sending a South Vietnamese division into Laos.

Except for allowing attacks on the Hanoi power station, Mr. Bundy was against further expansion of the air war, especially the mining of Haiphong so long as the Soviet Union refrained from sending combat weapons through the port. Both Mr. Bundy and the C.I.A., in a special intelligence estimate in early May, warned of the dangers of Soviet counteraction if the port was attacked, according to the Pentagon account.

The mobilization required to provide large troop reinforcements for the ground war, Mr. Bundy contended, would entail "a truly major debate in Congress." With signs of rising domestic dissent over the war, he advised that "we should not get into such a debate this summer."

The Assistant Secretary felt the "real key factors" were the political development in the South leading up to presidential elections in September. The internal political turmoil in Communist China, he suggested, was an important and potentially helpful factor because of the worry it caused in Hanoi.

In the Pentagon, resistance to the Westmoreland-Wheeler strategy came from another angle. The systems-analysis section, headed by Assistant Secretary of Defense Alain C. Enthoven, produced a series of papers late in April and early in May arguing that, contrary to General Westmoreland's expectations, American troop increases did not produce correspondingly sharp increases in enemy losses.

"On the most optimistic basis, 200,000 more Americans would raise [the enemy's] weekly losses to about 3,700, or about 400 a week more than they could stand." Dr. Enthoven told Secretary McNamara in a memoradum on May 4. "In theory we'd then wipe them out in 10 years." [See Document #127.]

A major effort to oppose the military stategy and to limit the air war was building in Secretary McNamara's office. The moving force, the Pentagon study shows; was Assistant Secretary McNaughton, who eventually wrote key portions of Mr. McNamara's controversial May 19 memorandum.

Roughly two years before, Mr. McNaughton had been an advocate of the "progressive squeeze" on Hanoi through air power. But by October, 1966, he was so doubtful of its effectiveness that he helped Secretary McNamara draft the first suggestion for a cutback in the air war and for political compromise.

Now, in May, 1967, the Pentagon account relates, both he and the Secretary of Defense were preparing for a more vigorous argument. First, on May 5, Mr. McNaughton sent Mr. McNamara a paper intended for inclusion in a memorandum from the Secretary to President Johnson, known as a Draft Presidential Memorandum—D.P.M.—because it not only stated the Secretary's views but also was intended to become a policy document for the President's signature.

The core of Mr. McNaughton's paper was a recommendation that "all of the sorties allocated to the Rolling Thunder program be concentarted on the lines of communications—the 'funnel' through which men and supplies to the south must flow—between 17-20 degrees, reserving the option and intention to strike (in the 20-23 degree area) as necessary to keep the enemy's investment in defense and in repair crews high throughout the country."

The proposed cutback of the air war, he said, was to reduce American pilot and aircraft losses over heavily defended Hanoi and Haiphong and not primarily to get North Vietnam to negotiate. No favorable response should be expected, Mr. McNaughton said, but "to optimize the chances" for such a response he proposed this scenario:

"To inform the Soviets quietly (on May 15) that within a few (5) days the policy would be implemented, stating no time limits and making no promise not to return to the Red River Basin to attack targets . . . and then to make an unhuckstered shift as predicted on May 20."

Without what he called "an ultimatum-like time limit," Mr. McNaughton suggested that North Vietnam "might be in a better posture to react favorably than has been the case in the past." The American public should be told, he said, that the bombing was being concentrated on the southern infiltration routes to "increase the efficiency of our interdiction effort" and because "major northern military targets have been destroyed."

According to the Pentagon account, the McNaughton paper, combined with other Defense Department proposals on the ground war, was read by Secretary McNamara at a White House meeting on May 8, although it is not clear whether Mr. McNamara also signed it and sent it to President Johnson.

Its significance, the Pentagon study reveals, is that for the first time a specific recommendation was put before President Johnson urging a cutback on the bombing to the 20th Parallel. That went a step further than the McNamara memorandum of Oct. 14, 1966 which urged the President "to consider" narrowing the bombing campaign as a possible step toward negotiations.

Several other papers went before President Johnson on May 8, according to the Pentagon account. They included one, recommending a bombing cutback, by Mr. Rostow, described in the study as a "strong bombing advocate" long in favor of attacks on the "North Vietnamese industrial target system."

Mr. Rostow's memorandum, quoted at length in the Pentagon study, rejected proposals for mining North Vietnamese harbors and bombing port facilities lest these steps lead to a "radical increase in Hanoi's dependence on Communist China" and increase United States tensions with the Soviet Union and China. [See Document #128.]

He was considerably more positive than Mr. McNaughton on the results of the strategic bombing campaign, but urged that the bombing be concentrated on the supply routes in southern North Vietnam supplemented by "the most economical and careful attack on the Hanoi power station" and by "keeping open the . . . option" of bombing the Hanoi-Haiphong area in the future.

A more equivocal position, the Pentagon study discloses, was taken by Assistant Secretary of State Bundy. His paper, completed on May 8, favored tactics that would "concentrate heavily on the supply routes" but would also "include a significant number of restrikes" north of the 20th Parallel. Without restrikes, he argued, "it would almost certainly be asked why we had ever hit the targets in the first place." Moreover, it would keep Hanoi and Moscow "at least a little bit on edge."

But he was opposed to hitting such new and "sensitive targets" as the Hanoi power station, the Red River bridge at Hanoi and Phucyen airfield, 13 miles outside the city.

The Pentagon study comments that "this significant convergence of opinion on bombing strategy in the next phase among key Presidential advisers could not have gone unnoticed in the May 8 meeting." The account notes that a new effort began after the session to combine the various views in one paper largely drafted by Mr. McNaughton for Secretary McNamara and finally submitted to the President on May 19.

Even before the White House meeting, Mr. McNaughton was uneasy about the over-all Pentagon position, especially the willingness to provide General Westmoreland with considerable reinforcements. The Pentagon study does not say who drafted the portions of the May 5 memorandum on the ground war or precisely what was proposed, although it reports that Secretary McNamara had been told that 66,000 more soldiers could be provided without calling up the reserves. Later the figure rose to 84,000.

In a note to Secretary McNamara on May 6, Mr. McNaughton indicated that the May 5 memorandum proposed giving General Westmoreland 80,000 more men. Excerpts from that note vividly portray Mr. McNaughton's unhappiness about this course of action:

"I am afraid there is a fatal flaw in the strategy in the [May 5] draft. It is that the strategy falls into the trap that has ensnared us for the past three years. It actually *gives* the troops while only *praying* for their proper use and for constructive diplomatic action." (The emphasis was Mr. McNaughton's.)

"Limiting the present decision to an 80,000 add-on," he continued, "does the very important business of postponing the issue of a reserve call-up (and all of its horrible baggage), but postpone is all that it does—probably to a worse time, 1968. Providing the 80,000 troops is tantamount to acceding to the whole Westmoreland-Sharp request. This being the case, they will 'accept' the 80,000. But six months from now, in will come messages like the '470,000-570,000' messages, saying that the requirement remains at 201,000 (or more). Since no pressure will have been put on anyone, the military war will have gone on as before and no diplomatic progress will have been made.

"It follows that the 'philosophy' of the war should be fought out now so everyone will not be proceeding on their own major premises, and getting us in deeper and deeper; at the very least, the President should give General Westmoreland his limit (as President Truman did to General MacArthur). That is, if General Westmoreland is to get 550,000 men, he should be told, 'That will be all, and we mean it.' " (The parentheses were Mr. McNaughton's.)

The note to Secretary McNamara, the study reveals, expressed uneasiness about the breadth and intensity of public unrest and dissatisfaction with the war. As a man whose 18-year-old son was about to enter college, the study notes, Mr. McNaughton was especially sensitive to the unpopularity of the war among the young.

"A feeling is widely and strongly held that 'the Establishment' is out of its mind," he wrote. "The feeling is that we are trying to impose some U.S. image on distant peoples we cannot understand (any more than we can the younger generaon here at home), and we are carrying the thing to absurd lengths.

"Related to this feeling is the increased polarization that is taking place in the United States with seeds of the worst split in our people in more than a century. . . ."

A major assault on Administration policy drew near. In early May, the Pentagon study recounts, there were three C.I.A. intelligence papers "to reinforce the views" of civilian opponents of the bombing.

One report concluded that 27 months of American bombing "have had remarkably little effect on Hanoi's over-all strategy in prosecuting the war, on its confident view of long-term Communist prospects, and on its political tactics regarding negotiations." A second, issued on May 12, characterized the mood in North Vietnam after prolonged bombing as one of "resolute stoicism with a considerable reservoir of endurance still untapped."

The third said that as of April, the American air campaign had "significantly eroded the capacities of North Vietnam's industrial and military bases. These losses, however, have not meaningfully degraded North Vietnam's material ability to continue the war in South Vietnam."

New Trend of Policy

The climax for what the study calls the "disillusioned doves" came in Secretary McNamara's May 19 memorandum to President Johnson, which marshaled the arguments against the strategy of widening the war and sharpened the case for curtailing the air war.

What gave the May 19 "draft Presidential memorandum" a new and radical thrust, the analysts observe, were its political recommendations, reflecting Mr. McNaughton's earlier point about the need to argue out "the philosophy of the war."

The May 19 paper not only recommended a cutback of the bombing to the 20th Parallel and only 30,000 more troops for General Westmoreland, but also advocated a considerably more limited over-all American objective in Vietnam that, in the words of the Pentagon study, "amounted to . . . a recommendation that we accept a compromise outcome." [See Document #129.]

As Mr. McNamara and Mr. McNaughton put it in th[e] memorandum. "Our commitment is only to see that the peopl[e] of South Vietnam are permitted to determine their ow[n] future. . . . This commitment ceases if the country cease[s] to help itself."

However much the United States might "strongly hope[d] for a non-Communist government that would remain separat[e] from North Vietnam, they said, "our commitment is not" t[o] guarantee and insist on those conditions.

"Nor do we have an obligation to pour in effort out o[f] proportion to the effort contributed by the people of Sout[h] Vietnam or in the face of coups, corruption, apathy or othe[r] indications of Saigon's failure to cooperate satisfactorily wit[h] us," the writers declared.

The United States was committed, they went on, "to stop[-] ping or offsetting the effect of North Vietnam's application o[f] force in the South, which denies the people of the South th[e] ability to determine their own future."

The Pentagon study underscores the significance of M[r.] McNamara's break with policy. The paper, it says, "pointedl[y] rejected the high blown formulations of U.S. objectives i[n] NSAM 288 ('an independent non-Communist South Vietnam[,]' 'defeat the Vietcong,' etc.), and came forcefully to grips wit[h] the old dilemma of the U.S. involvement dating from th[e] Kennedy era: only limited means to achieve excessive ends."

The reference was to National Security Action Memoran[-] dum 288, issued on March 17, 1964, which had since provide[d] the basic doctrine for Johnson Administration policy.

The emphasis in the "scaled-down" set of goals pu[t] forward by the McNamara-McNaughton memorandum. th[e] analysts observed, was on South Vietnamese self-determina[-] tion, which envisioned an eventual "full-spectrum govern[-] ment."

At several points the Pentagon study emphasizes the shar[p] departure that this represented from established policy. "Le[t] there be no mistake," the study comments, "these wer[e] radical positions for a senior U.S. policy official within th[e] Johnson Administration to take. They would bring the bitte[r] condemnation of the [Joint] Chiefs and were scarcely de[-] signed to flatter the President on the success of his efforts t[o] date."

In addition to advancing its own views, the McNamara[-] McNaughton paper developed the counterarguments agains[t] the military option of large reinforcements and a wider wa[r]

mphasizing the increasing popular discontent with the war
mong the American public.

The memorandum acknowledged that a cutback on the
ombing "will cause psychological problems" for allied officers
nd troops "who will not be able to understand why we should
vithhold punishment from the enemy."

However, the paper added: "We should not bomb for
unitive reasons if it serves no other purpose. . . . It costs
American lives; it creates a backfire of revulsion and oppo-
ition by killing civilians; it creates serious risks; it may harden
ie enemy."

The paper also pointed out that the bombing in the Hanoi
nd Haiphong regions took an extremely high toll in American
ilots' lives. On May 5, Mr. McNaughton commented that the
oss rate over Hanoi-Haiphong was six times as great as over
ie rest of North Vietnam. Now, on May 19, the McNamara-
IcNaughton paper noted that the campaign against these
eavily defended areas lost "one pilot in every 40 sorties."
t predicted that if the bombing was held below the 20th
arallel, these losses would be cut "by more than 50 per
ent."

Their arguments against granting General Westmoreland
ie scale of reinforcements that he had requested were cen-
:red on what the Pentagon analysts refer to as the growing
:ar that such forces would engender "irresistible pressures"
or carrying the battle beyond the borders of South Vietnam.

The mobilization of reserves to provide the necessary man-
ower, according to the McNamara-McNaughton paper,
ould almost certainly stimulate a "bitter Congressional de-
ate."

"Cries would go up—much louder than they have already—
 'take the wraps off the men in the field,' " their memoran-
um asserted. It foresaw pressures not only for ground opera-
ons against Laos, Cambodia and North Vietnam, but also,
t some point, for proposals to use tactical nuclear arms and
acteriological and chemical weapons if the Chinese entered
ie war "or if U.S. losses were running high."

"Dilemma of President"

Secretary McNamara showed his paper to President Johnson
n May 19, the day it was completed, the study says. Although

the analyst provides no documentary record of Mr. Johnson's reaction, he comments that it was "not surprising" that the President "did not promptly endorse the McNamara recommendations as he had on occasions in the past."

"This time," the study continues, "he faced a situation where the Chiefs were in ardent opposition to anything other than a significant escalation of the war wth a call-up of reserves. This put them in direct opposition to McNamara and his aide and created a genuine policy dilemma for the President."

In any event, the study says, Secretary McNamara quickly got the message intended by the President's inaction. On May 20, Mr. McNamara—"perhaps reflecting a cool Presidential reaction,"—ordered a new study of bombing alternatives.

The Joint Chiefs of Staff needed no spur. Within four days they had submitted three memorandums, renewing earlier recommendations for more than 200,000 new troops and for air attacks to "shoulder out" foreign shipping from Haiphong and to mine the harbors and approaches, as well as raids on eight major airfields and on roads and railways leading to China. "It may ultimately become necessary," they said, to send American troops into Cambodia and Laos and take "limited ground action in North Vietnam."

Their sharpest rebuttal to Mr. McNamara, however, came on May 31 in a paper contending that the "drastic changes in American policy advocated by the Secretary "would undermine and no longer provide a complete rationale for our presence in South Vietnam or much of our efforts over the past two years."

Moreover, the parts of this paper quoted in the Pentagon narrative asserted that the McNamara-McNaughton memorandum "fails to appreciate the full implications for the free world of failure" in Vietnam.

On the issue of public support for the war, the Joint Chiefs said they were "unable to find due cause for the degree of pessimism expressed" in the McNamara paper. They asserted their belief "that the American people, when well informed about the issues at stake, expect their Government to uphold its commitments."

Addressing the specific proposal for a bombing cutback, the Joint Chiefs were doubtful that such a step would induce Hanoi to move toward negotiations. They contended it would "most likely have the opposite effect" and "only result in the strengthening of the enemy's resolve to continue the war."

In conclusion, the military leaders urged that the Mc

Namara proposals "not be forwarded to the President" because they represented such a divergence from past policy that they were not worthy of consideration. The Chiefs were unaware that Mr. Johnson had seen the paper 12 days before.

In other agencies, the Pentagon study relates, official viewpoints fell between the two extremes and the debate floundered toward a compromise on the issues of tactics, without any shift in war aims.

Under Secretary of State Katzenbach, for example, proposed on June 8, according to the study, that the United States add 30,000 ground troops "in small increments over the next 18 months" and "concentrate bombing on lines of communication throughout" North Vietnam but shifting away from strategic targets around Hanoi and Haiphong. The American political objective, he said, should be to leave behind a stable democratic government in Saigon by persuading Hanoi to end the war and by neutralizing the Vietcong threat internally.

In the Pentagon, Mr. McNaughton found mixed views on the air war and summarized them for Mr. McNamara in another memorandum on June 12. The findings, cited in the study, were that Cyrus R. Vance, Deputy Secretary of Defense; Paul H. Nitze, Secretary of the Navy; and Mr. McNaughton favored the cutback in bombing; the Joint Chiefs renewed their case for escalation; and Secretary Brown of the Air Force recommended adding a few targets to the present list.

The Pentagon study says it is unclear whether this paper was formally presented to President Johnson who, in any case, was preoccupied in June, 1967, with the six-day Arab-Israeli war and with preparations for his meeting with Premier Kosygin at Glassboro, N.J.

Secretary McNamara's primary attention remained on the unresolved troop issue. According to the Pentagon account, he went to Saigon from July 7 to July 12 under President Johnson's instructions "to review the matter with General Westmoreland and reach an agreement on a figure well below the 200,000 [Westmoreland] had requested in March."

On Mr. McNamara's final evening in Saigon, the Pentagon account says, the two men agreed on a 55,000-man increase, to a total of 525,000 troops. President Johnson approved the compromise, far closer to Mr. McNamara's position than General Westmoreland's, and announced it in a tax message on Aug. 4.

But in a series of decisions on the air war during July and August, the President adopted a course that differed markedly from the strategy of de-escalation that Secretary McNamara had urged on him.

His first decision, in mid-July, added only a few fixed targets, but in the next two months he approved all but about a dozen of the 57 targets the Chiefs of Staff wanted. On July 20, the Pentagon study reports, he added 16 targets, including a previously forbidden airfield, a rail yard, two bridges and 12 barracks and supply areas, all within the restricted circles around Hanoi and Haiphong.

The day before the authorization of Rolling Thunder 57—each number signaling an extension of the air war—Secretary McNamara lost perhaps his closest adviser and staunchest ally. On July 19, Mr. McNaughton and his wife, Sarah, and their 11-year-old son Theodore were killed in a plane collision over North Carolina.

By late July, the study continues, the frustrations of the military commanders over the restraints imposed upon them had prompted the Senate Preparedness Subcommittee to schedule hearings on the conduct of the air war. Although conducted in secret, the hearings gave the public its first real knowledge of the policy division between Secretary McNamara and the Joint Chiefs over bombing.

"The subcommittee unquestionably set out to defeat Mr. McNamara," the analyst comments. "Its members. Senators Stennis. Symington, Jackson, Cannon, Byrd, Smith, Thurmond and Miller, were known for their hard-line views and military sympathies. . . . They viewed the restraints on bombing as irrational, the shackling of a major instrument which could help win victory."

Such powerful Congressional backing for the air war, the study observes, "must have forced a recalculation on the President."

The study finds it "surely no coincidence" that on Aug. 9, the day the Stennis hearings opened, President Johnson authorized "an additional 16 fixed targets and an expansion of armed reconnaissance."

"Significantly," the study continues, "six of the targets were within the sacred 10-mile Hanoi inner circle . . . . Nine targets were located in the northeast rail line in the China buffer zone [formerly a proscribed zone], the closest one eight miles from the border. . . . The tenth was a naval base, also within the China buffer zone."

The raids began promptly, the study recounts, and more targets were approved shortly afterward. The prohibited zone around Hanoi was restored from Aug. 24 to Sept. 4 to permit a follow-up to what the study calls "a particularly delicate set of contacts with North Vietnam." The military sections of the Pentagon study give no details, but published reports have identified this as a secret effort to test Hanoi on what became known later as the San Antonio formula.

It was made public by President Johnson in a speech on Sept. 29 at San Antonio, Tex., when he offered to halt the bombing provided that action would lead to prompt and productive negotiations, on the assumption that the North Vietnamese would "not take advantage" of the halt militarily. Hanoi rejected these terms as imposing conditions on a halt in bombing.

For months the secret diplomatic probing went on fruitlessly while the air war widened slowly—although still short of the desires of the Joint Chiefs. Not until March, 1968—a few days after Secretary McNamara had left the Government—did his proposal for a reduction of the bombing to the 20th Parallel re-emerge and open the way toward negotiations in Paris in May.

KEY DOCUMENTS

Following are texts of key documents accompanying the Pentagon's study of the Vietnam war, covering the period late 1966 to mid-1967, in which Secretary of Defense Robert S. McNamara began to express disillusionment with the effectiveness of the war effort. Except where excerpting is specified, the documents are printed verbatim, with only unmistakable typographical errors corrected.

118

McNamara Memo of Oct. 14, 1966, Opposing Increase in War Effort

Draft memorandum for President Lyndon B. Johnson, "Actions Recommended for Vietnam," from Secretary of Defense Robert S. McNamara, Oct. 14, 1966.

1. Evaluation of the situation. In the report of my last trip to Vietnam almost a year ago, I stated that the odds were about even that, even with the then-recommended deployments, we would be faced in early 1967 with a military stand-off at a much higher level of conflict and with "pacification" still stalled. I am a little less pessimistic now in one respect. We have done somewhat better militarily than I anticipated. We have by and large blunted the communist military initiative—any military victory in South Vietnam the Viet Cong may have had in mind 18 months ago has been thwarted by our emergency deployments and actions. And our program of bombing the North has exacted a price.

My concern continues, however, in other respects. This is because I see no reasonable way to bring the war to an end soon. Enemy morale has not broken—he apparently has adjusted to our stopping his drive for military victory and has adopted a strategy of keeping us busy and waiting us out (a strategy of attriting our national will). He knows that we have not been, and he believes we probably will not be, able to translate our military successes into the "end products"—broken enemy morale and political achievements by the GVN.

The one thing demonstrably going for us in Vietnam over the

542

past year has been the large number of enemy killed-in-action resulting from the big military operations. Allowing for possible exaggeration in reports, the enemy must be taking losses—deaths in and after battle—at the rate of more than 60,000 a year. The infiltration routes would seem to be one-way trails to death for the North Vietnamese. Yet there is no sign of an impending break in enemy morale and it appears that he can more than replace his losses by infiltration from North Vietnam and recruitment in South Vietnam.

Pacification is a bad disappointment. We have good grounds to be pleased by the recent elections, by Ky's 16 months in power, and by the faint signs of development of national political institutions and of a legitimate civil government. But none of this has translated itself into political achievements at Province level or below. Pacification has if anything gone backward. As compared with two, or four, years ago, enemy full-time regional forces and part-time guerrilla forces are larger; attacks, terrorism and sabotage have increased in scope and intensity; more railroads are closed and highways cut; the rice crop expected to come to market is smaller; we control little, if any, more of the population; the VC political infrastructure thrives in most of the country, continuing to give the enemy his enormous intelligence advantage; full security exists nowhere (now even behind the U.S. Marines' lines and in Saigon); in the countryside, the enemy almost completely controls the night.

Nor has the ROLLING THUNDER program of bombing the North either significantly affected infiltration or cracked the morale of Hanoi. There is agreement in the intelligence community on these facts (see the attached Appendix).

In essence, we find ourselves—from the point of view of the important war (for the complicity of the people)—no better, and if anything worse off. This important war must be fought and won by the Vietnamese themselves. We have known this from the beginning. But the discouraging truth is that, as was the case in 1961 and 1963 and 1965, we have not found the formula, the catalyst, for training and inspiring them into effective action.

2. Recommended actions. In such an unpromising state of affairs, what should we do? We must continue to press the enemy militarily; we must make demonstrable progress in pacification; at the same time, we must add a new ingredient forced on us by the facts. Specifically, we must improve our position by getting ourselves into a military posture that we credibly would maintain indefinitely—a posture that makes trying to "wait us out" less attractive. I recommend a five-pronged course of action to achieve those ends.

a. Stabilize U.S. force-levels in Vietnam. It is my judgment that, barring a dramatic change in the war, we should limit the increase in U.S. forces in SVN in 1967 to 70,000 men and we should level off at the total of 470,000 which such an increase would provide.* It is my view that this is enough to punish the enemy at the large-unit operations level and to keep the enemy's main forces from interrupting pacification. I believe also that even many more than 470,000 would not kill the enemy off in such numbers as to break their morale so long as they think they can wait us out. It is possible that such a 40 percent increase over our present level of 325,000 will break the enemy's morale in the short term; but if it does not, we must, I believe, be prepared for and have underway a long-term program premised on more than breaking the morale of main force units. A stabilized U.S. force level would be part of such a long-term program. It would put us in a position where negotiations would be more likely to be productive, but if they were not we could pursue the all-important pacification task with proper attention and resources and without the spectre of apparently endless escalation of U.S. deployments.

b. Install a barrier. A portion of the 470,000 troops—perhaps 10,000 to 20,000—should be devoted to the construction and maintenance of an infiltration barrier. Such a barrier would lie near the 17th parallel—would run from the sea, across the neck of South Vietnam (choking off the new infiltration routes through the DMZ) and across the trails in Laos. This interdiction system (at an approximate cost of $1 billion) would comprise to the east a ground barrier of fences, wire, sensors, artillery, aircraft and mobile troops; and to the west—mainly in Laos—an interdiction zone covered by air-laid mines and bombing attacks pinpointed by air-laid acoustic sensors.

The barrier may not be fully effective at first, but I believe that it can be effective in time and that even the threat of its becoming effective can substantially change to our advantage the character of the war. It would hinder enemy efforts, would permit more efficient use of the limited number of friendly troops, and would be persuasive evidence both that our sole aim is to protect the South from the North and that we intend to see the job through.

c. Stabilize the ROLLING THUNDER program against the North. Attack sorties in North Vietnam have risen from about 4,000 per month at the end of last year to 6,000 per month in the first quarter of this year and 12,000 per month at present. Most of our 50 percent increase of deployed attack-capable aircraft has been absorbed in the attacks on North Vietnam. In North Vietnam, almost 84,000 attack sorties have been flown (about 25 percent against fixed targets), 45 percent during the past seven months.

Despite these efforts, it now appears that the North Vietnamese-Laotian road network will remain adequate to meet the requirements of the Communist forces in South Vietnam—this is so even

---

*Admiral Sharp has recommended a 12/31/67 strength of 570,000. However, I believe both he and General Westmoreland recognize that the danger of inflation will probably force an end 1967 deployment limit of about 470,000.

if its capacity could be reduced by one-third and if combat activities were to be doubled. North Vietnam's serious need for trucks, spare parts and petroleum probably can, despite air attacks, be met by imports. The petroleum requirement for trucks involved in the infiltration movement, for example, has not been enough to present significant supply problems, and the effects of the attacks on the petroleum distribution system, while they have not yet been fully assessed, are not expected to cripple the flow of essential supplies. Furthermore, it is clear that, to bomb the North sufficiently to make a radical impact upon Hanoi's political, economic and social structure, would require an effort which we could make but which would not be stomached either by our own people or by world opinion; and it would involve a serious risk of drawing us into open war with China.

The North Vietnamese are paying a price. They have been forced to assign some 300,000 personnel to the lines of communication in order to maintain the critical flow of personnel and material to the South. Now that the lines of communication have been manned, however, it is doubtful that either a large increase or decrease in our interdiction sorties would substantially change the cost to the enemy of maintaining the roads, railroads, and waterways or affect whether they are operational. It follows that the marginal sorties—probably the marginal 1,000 or even 5,000 sorties—per month against the lines of communication no longer have a significant impact on the war. (See the attached excerpts from intelligence estimates.)

When this marginal inutility of added sorties against North Vietnam and Laos is compared with the crew and aircraft losses implicit in the activity (four men and aircraft and $20 million per 1,000 sorties), I recommend, as a minimum, against increasing the level of bombing of North Vietnam and against increasing the intensity of operations by changing the areas or kinds of targets struck.

Under these conditions, the bombing program would continue the pressure and would remain available as a bargaining counter to get talks started (or to trade off in talks). But, as in the case of a stabilized level of U.S. ground forces, the stabilization of ROLLING THUNDER would remove the prospect of ever escalating bombing as a factor complicating our political posture and distracting from the main job of pacification in South Vietnam.

At the proper time, as discussed on pages 6-7 below, I believe we should consider terminating bombing in all of North Vietnam, or at least in the Northeast zones, for an indefinite period in connection with covert moves toward peace.

d. Pursue a vigorous pacification program. As mentioned above, the pacification (Revolutionary Development) program has been and is thoroughly stalled. The large-unit operations war, which we know best how to fight and where we have had our successes, is largely irrelevant to pacification as long as we do not lose it.

By and large, the people in rural areas believe that the GVN when it comes will not stay but that the VC will; that cooperations with the GVN will be punished by the VC; that the GVN is really indifferent to the people's welfare; that the low-level GVN are tools of the local rich; and that the GVN is ridden with corruption.

Success in pacification depends on the interrelated functions of providing physical security, destroying the VC apparatus, motivating the people to cooperate and establishing responsive local government. An obviously necessary but not sufficient requirement for success of the Revolutionary Development cadre and police is vigorously conducted and adequately prolonged clearing operations by military troops, who will "stay" in the area, who behave themselves decently and who show some respect for the people.

This elemental requirement of pacification has been missing.

In almost no contested area designated for pacification in recent years have ARVN forces actually "cleared and stayed" to a point where cadre teams, if available, could have stayed overnight in hamlets and survived, let alone accomplish their mission. VC units of company and even battalion size remain in operation, and they are more than large enough to overrun anything the local security forces can put up.

Now that the threat of a Communist main-force military victory has been thwarted by our emergency efforts, we must allocate far more attention and a portion of the regular military forces (at least half of the ARVN and perhaps a portion of the U.S. forces) to the task of providing an active and permanent security screen behind which the Revolutionary Development teams and police can operate and behind which the political struggle with the VC infrastructure can take place.

The U.S. cannot do this pacification security job for the Vietnamese. All we can do is "Massage the heart." For one reason, it is known that we do not intend to stay; if our efforts worked at all, it would merely postpone the eventual confrontation of the VC and GVN infrastructures. The GVN must do the job; and I am convinced that drastic reform is needed if the GVN is going to be able to do it.

The first essential reform is in the attitude of GVN officials. They are generally apathetic, and there is corruption high and low. Often appointments, promotions, and draft deferments must be bought; and kickbacks on salaries are common. Cadre at the bottom can be no better than the system above them.

The second needed reform is in the attitude and conduct of the ARVN. The image of the government cannot improve unless and until the ARVN improves markedly. They do not understand the importance (or respectability) of pacification nor the importance to pacification of proper, disciplined conduct. Promotions, assignments and awards are often not made on merit, but rather on the basis of having a diploma, friends or relatives, or because of bribery. The ARVN is weak in dedication, direction and discipline.

Not enough ARVN are devoted to area and population security, and when the ARVN does attempt to support pacification, their actions do not last long enough; their tactics are bad despite U.S. prodding (no aggressive small-unit saturation patrolling, hamlet searches, quick-reaction contact, or offensive night ambushes); they do not make good use of intelligence; and their leadership and discipline are bad.

Furthermore, it is my conviction that a part of the problem undoubtedly lies in bad management on the American as well as the GVN side. Here split responsibility—or "no responsibility"—has resulted in too little hard pressure on the GVN to do its job and no really solid or realistic planning with respect to the whole effort. We must deal with this management problem and deal with it effectively.

One solution would be to consolidate all U.S. activities which are primarily part of the civilian pacification program and all persons engaged in such activities, providing a clear assignment of responsibility and a unified command under a civilian relieved of all other duties.** Under this approach, there would be a carefully delineated division of responsibility between the civilian-in-charge and an element of COMUSMACV under a senior officer, who would give the subject of planning for and providing hamlet security the highest priority in attention and resources. Success will depend on the men selected for the jobs on both sides (they must be among the highest rank and most competent administrators in the U.S. Government), on complete cooperation among the U.S. elements, and on the extent to which the South Vietnamese can be shocked out of their present pattern of behavior. The first work of this reorganized U.S. pacification organization should be to produce within 60 days a realistic and detailed plan for the coming year.

From the political and public-relations viewpoint, this solution is preferable—if it works. But we cannot tolerate continued failure. If it fails after a fair trial, the only alternative in my view is to place the entire pacification program—civilian and military—under General Westmoreland. This alternative would result in the establishment of a Deputy COMUSMACV for Pacification who would be in command of all pacification staffs in Saigon and of all pacification staffs and activities in the field; one person in each corps, province and district would be responsible for the U.S. effort.

(It should be noted that progress in pacification, more than anything else, will persuade the enemy to negotiate or withdraw.)

c. Press for Negotiations. I am not optimistic that Hanoi or the VC will respond to peace overtures now (explaining my recommendations above that we get into a level-off posture for the long

---

**If this task is assigned to Ambassador Porter, another individual must be sent immediately to Saigon to serve as Ambassador Lodge's deputy.

pull). The ends sought by the two sides appear to be irreconcilable and the relative power balance is not in their view unfavorable to them. But three things can be done, I believe, to increase the prospects:

(1) Take steps to increase the credibility of our peace gestures in the minds of the enemy. There is considerable evidence both in private statements by the Communists and in the reports of competent Western officials who have talked with them that charges of U.S. bad faith are not solely propagandistic, but reflect deeply held beliefs. Analyses of Communists' statements and actions indicate that they firmly believe that American leadership really does not want the fighting to stop, and, that we are intent on winning a military victory in Vietnam and on maintaining our presence there through a puppet regime supported by U.S. military bases.

As a way of projective U.S. bona fides, I believe that we should consider two possibilities with respect to our bombing program against the North, to be undertaken, if at all, at a time very carefully selected with a view to maximizing the chances of influencing the enemy and world opinion and to minimizing the chances that failure would strengthen the hand of the "hawks" at home: First, without fanfare, conditions, or avowal, whether the stand-down was permanent or temporary, stop bombing all of North Vietnam. It is generally thought that Hanoi will not agree to negotiations until they can claim that the bombing has stopped unconditionally. We should see what develops, retaining freedom to resume the bombing if nothing useful was forthcoming.

Alternatively, we could shift the weight-of-effort away from "Zones 6A and 6B"—zones including Hanoi and Haiphong and areas north of those two cities to the Chinese border. This alternative has some attraction in that it provides the North Vietnamese a "face saver" if only problems of "face" are holding up Hanoi peace gestures; it would narrow the bombing down directly to the objectionable infiltration (supporting the logic of a stop-infiltration/full-pause deal); and it would reduce the international heat on the U.S. Here, too, bombing of the Northeast could be resumed at any time, or "spot" attacks could be made there from time to time to keep North Vietnam off balance and to require her to pay almost the full cost by maintaining her repair crews in place. The sorties diverted from Zones 6A and 6B could be concentrated on infiltration routes in Zones 1 and 2 (the southern end of North Vietnam, including the Mu Gia Pass), in Laos and in South Vietnam.***

***Any limitation on the bombing of North Vietnam will cause serious psychological problems among the men who are risking their lives to help achieve our political objectives; among their commanders up to and including the JCS; and among those of our people who cannot understand why we should withhold punishment from the enemy. General Westmoreland, as do the JCS, strongly believes in the military value of the bombing program. Further, Westmoreland reports that the morale of his Air Force personnel may already be showing signs of erosion—an erosion resulting from current operational restrictions.

To the same end of improving our credibility, we should seek ways—through words and deeds—to make believable our intention to withdraw our forces once the North Vietnamese aggression against the South stops. In particular, we should avoid any implication that we will stay in South Vietnam with bases or to guarantee any particular outcome to a solely South Vietnamese struggle.

(2) Try to split the VC off from Hanoi. The intelligence estimate is that evidence is overwhelming that the North Vietnamese dominate and control the National Front and the Viet Cong. Nevertheless, I think we should continue and enlarge efforts to contact the VC/NLF and to probe ways to split members or sections off the VC/NLF organization.

(3) Press contacts with North Vietnam, the Soviet Union and other parties who might contribute toward a settlement.

(4) Develop a realistic plan providing a role for the VC in negotiations, postwar life, and government of the nation. An amnesty offer and proposals for national reconciliation would be steps in the right direction and should be parts of the plan. It is important that this plan be one which will appear reasonable, if not at first to Hanoi and the VC, at least to world opinion.

3. The prognosis. The prognosis is bad that the war can be brought to a satisfactory conclusion within the next two years. The large-unit operations probably will not do it; negotiations probably will not do it. *While we should continue to pursue both of these routes in trying for a solution in the short run, we should recognize that success from them is a mere possibility, not a probability.*

The solution lies in girding, openly, for a longer war and in taking actions immediately which will in 12 to 18 months give clear evidence that the continuing costs and risks to the American people are acceptably limited, that the formula for success has been found, and that the end of the war is merely a matter of time. All of my recommendations will contribute to this strategy, but the one most difficult to implement is perhaps the most important one—enlivening the pacification program. The odds are less than even for this task, if only because we have failed consistently since 1961 to make a dent in the problem. But, because the 1967 trend of pacification will, I believe, be the main talisman of ultimate U.S. success or failure in Vietnam, extraordinary imagination and effort should go into changing the stripes of that problem.

President Thieu and Prime Minister Ky are thinking along similar lines. They told me that they do not expect the Enemy to negotiate or to modify his program in less than two years. Rather, they expect that enemy to continue to expand and to increase his activity. They expressed agreement with us that the key to success is pacification and that so far pacification has failed. They agree that we need clarification of GVN and U.S. roles and that the bulk of the ARVN should be shifted to pacification. Ky will, between January and July 1967, shift all ARVN infantry divisions to that role. And he is giving Thang, a good Revolutionary Development director, added powers. Thieu and Ky see this as part of a two-year (1967–68) schedule, in which offensive operations against enemy main force units are continued, carried on primarily by the U.S. and other Free-World forces. At the end of the two-year period, they believe the enemy may be willing to negotiate or to retreat from his current course of action.

Note: Neither the Secretary of State nor the JCS have yet had an opportunity to express their views on this report. Mr. Katzenbach and I have discussed many of its main conclusions and recommendations—in general, but not in all particulars, it expresses his views as well as my own.

APPENDIX

Extracts from CIA/DIA Report "An Appraisal of the Bombing of North Vietnam through 12 September 1966."

1. There is no evidence yet of any shortage of POL in North Vietnam and stocks on hand, with recent imports, have been adequate to sustain necessary operations.

2. Air strikes against all modes of transportation in North Vietnam and during the past month, but there is no evidence of serious transport problems in the movement of supplies to or within North Vietnam.

3. There is no evidence yet that the air strikes have significantly weakened popular morale.

4. Air strikes continue to depress economic growth and have been responsible for the abandonment of some plans for economic development, but essential economic activities continue.

Extracts from a March 16, 1966 CIA Report "An Analysis of the ROLLING THUNDER Air Offensive against North Vietnam."

1. Although the movement of men and supplies in North Vietnam has been hampered and made somewhat more costly (by our bombing), the Communists have been able to increase the flow of supplies and manpower to South Vietnam.

2. Hanoi's determination (despite our bombing) to continue its policy of supporting the insurgency in the South appears as firm as ever.

3. Air attacks almost certainly cannot bring about a meaningful reduction in the current level at which essential supplies and men flow into South Vietnam.

Bomb Damage Assessment in the North by the Institute for Defense Analyses' "Summer Study Group."

What surprised us (in our assessment of the effect of bombing North Vietnam) was the extent of agreement among various intelligence agencies on the effects of past operations and probable effects of continued and expanded Rolling Thunder. The conclusions of our group, to which we all subscribe, are therefore merely sharpened conclusions of numerous Intelligence summaries. They are that Rolling Thunder does not limit the present logistic flow into SVN because NVN is neither the source of supplies nor the choke-point on the supply routes from China and USSR. Although an expansion of Rolling Thunder by closing Haiphong harbor, eliminating electric power plants and totally destroying railroads, will at least indirectly impose further privations on the populace of NVN and make the logistic support of VC costlier to maintain, such expansion will not really change the basic assessment. This follows because NVN has demonstrated excellent ability to improvise transportation, and because the primitive nature of their economy is such that Rolling Thunder can affect directly only a small fraction of the population. There is very little hope that the Ho Chi Minh Government will lose control of population because of Rolling Thunder. The lessons of the Korean War are very relevant in these respects. Moreover, foreign economic aid to NVN is large compared to the damage we inflict, and growing. Probably the government of NVN has assurances that the USSR and/or China will assist the rebuilding of its economy after the war, and hence its concern about the damage being inflicted may be moderated by long-range favorable expectations.

Specifically:

1. As of July 1966 the U.S. bombing of North Vietnam had had no measurable direct affect on Hanoi's ability to mount and support military operations in the South at the current level.

2. Since the initiation of the Rolling Thunder program the damage to facilities and equipment in North Vietnam has been more than offset by the increased flow of military and economic aid, largely from the USSR and Communist China.

3. The aspects of the basic situation that have enabled Hanoi to continue its support of military operations in the South and to neutralize the impact of U.S. bombing by passing the economic costs to other Communist countries are not likely to be altered by reducing the present geographic constraints, mining Haiphong and the principal harbors in North Vietnam, increasing the number of armed reconnaissance sorties and otherwise expanding the U.S. air offensive along the lines now contemplated in military recommendations and planning studies.

4. While conceptually it is reasonable to assume that some limit may be imposed on the scale of military activity that Hanoi can maintain in the South by continuing the Rolling Thunder program at the present, or some higher level of effort, there appears to be no basis for defining that limit in concrete terms, or for concluding that the present scale of VC/NVN activities in the field have approached that limit.

5. The indirect effects of the bombing on the will of the North Vietnamese to continue fighting and on their leaders' appraisal of the prospective gains and costs of maintaining the present policy have not shown themselves in any tangible way. Furthermore, we have not discovered any basis for concluding that the indirect punitive effects of bombing will prove decisive in these respects.

119

Joint Chiefs' Memo Disputing McNamara View on Bombing

Excerpts from Joint Chiefs of Staff memorandum, signed by Gen. Earle G. Wheeler, Chairman, to Secretary of Defense McNamara, Oct. 14, 1966, as provided in the body of the Pentagon study.

The Joint Chiefs of Staff do not concur in your recommendation that there should be no increase in level of bombing effort and no modification in areas and targets subject to air attack. They believe our air campaign against NVN to be an integral and indispensable part of over all war effort. To be effective, the air campaign should be conducted with only those minimum constraints necessary to avoid indiscriminate killing of population. . .

The Joint Chiefs of Staff do not concur with your proposal that, as a carrot to induce negotiations, we should suspend or reduce our bombing campaign against NVN. Our experiences with pauses in bombing and resumption have not been happy ones. Additionally, the Joint Chiefs of Staff believe that the likelihood of the war being settled by negotiation is small, and that, far from inducing negotiations, another bombing pause will be regarded by North Vietnamese leaders, and our Allies, as renewed evidence of lack of U.S. determination to press the war to a successful conclusion. The bombing campaign is one of the two trump cards in the hands of the President (the other being the presence of U.S. troops in SVN). It should not be given up without an end to the NVN aggression in SVN. . . .

The Joint Chiefs of Staff believe that the war has reached a stage at which decisions taken over the next sixty days can determine the outcome of the war and, consequently, can affect the overall security interests of the United States for years to come. Therefore, they wish to provide to you and to the President their unequivocal views on two salient aspects of the war situation: the search for peace and military pressures on NVN.

a. The frequent, broadly-based public offers made by the President to settle the war by peaceful means on a generous basis which would take from NVN nothing it now has, have been admirable. Certainly, no one—American or foreigner—except those who are determined not to be convinced, can doubt the sincerity, the generosity, the altruism of U.S. actions and objectives. In the opinion of the Joint Chiefs of Staff the time has come when further overt actions and offers on our part are not only nonproductive, they are counter-productive. A logical case can be made that the American people, our Allies, and our enemies alike are increasingly uncertain as to our resolution to pursue the war to a successful conclusion. The Joint Chiefs of Staff advocate the following:

(1) A statement by the President during the Manila Conference of his unswerving determination to carry on the war until NVN aggression against SVN shall cease;

(2) Continued covert exploration of all avenues leading to a peaceful settlement of the war; and

(3) Continued alertness to detect and react appropriately to withdrawal of North Vietnamese troops from SVN and cessation of support to the VC.

B. In JCSM-955-64, dated 14 November 1964, and in JCSM-962-64, dated 23 November 1964, the Joint Chiefs of Staff provided their views as to the military pressures which should be brought to bear on NVN. In summary, they recommended a "sharp knock" on NVN military assets and war-supporting facilities rather than the campaign of slowly increasing pressure which was adopted. Whatever the political merits of the latter course, we deprived ourselves of the military effects of early weight of effort and shock, and gave to the enemy time to adjust to our slow quantitative and qualitative increase of pressure. This is not to say that it is now too late to derive military benefits from more effective and extensive use of our air and naval superiority. The Joint Chiefs of Staff recommend:

(1) Approval of their ROLLING THUNDER 52 program, which is a step toward meeting the requirement for improved target systems. This program would decrease the Hanoi and Haiphong sanctuary areas, authorize attacks against the steel plant, the Hanoi rail yards, the thermal power plants, selected areas within Haiphong port and other ports, selected locks and dams controlling water LOC's, SAM support facilities within the residual Hanoi and Haiphong sanctuaries, and POL at Haiphong, Hai Gia (Phuc Yen) and Can Thon (Kep).

(2) Use of naval surface forces to interdict North Vietnamese coastal waterborne traffic and appropriate land LOCs and to attack other coastal military targets such as radar and AAA sites.

. . . The Joint Chiefs of Staff request that their views as set forth above be provided to the President.

120

McNamara Draft Memorandum for Johnson in November, '66

Excerpts from draft memorandum for President Johnson from Secretary McNamara, dated Nov. 17, 1966, and headed "Recommended FY67 Southeast Asia Supplemental Appropriation," as provided in the body of the Pentagon study.

A substantial air interdiction campaign is clearly necessary and worthwhile. In addition to putting a ceiling on the size of the force that can be supported, it yields three significant military effects. First, it effectively harasses and delays truck movements down through the southern panhandles of NVN and Laos, though it has no effect on troops infiltrating on foot over trails that are virtually invisible from the air. Our experience shows that day-time armed reconnaissance above some minimum sortie rate makes it prohibitively expensive to the enemy to attempt daylight movement of vehicles, and so forces him to night movement. Second, destruction of bridges and cratering of roads forces the enemy to deploy repair crews, equipment, and porters to repair or bypass the damage. Third, attacks on vehicles, parks, and rest camps destroy some vehicles with their cargoes and inflict casualties. Moreover, our bombing campaign may produce a beneficial effect on U.S. and SVN morale by making NVN pay a price for its enemy [sic]. But at the scale we are now operating, I believe our bombing is yielding very small marginal returns, not worth the cost in pilot lives and aircraft.

The first effect, that of forcing the enemy into a system of night movement, occurs at a lower frequency of armed reconnaissance sorties than the level of the past several months. The enemy was already moving at night in 1965, before the sorties rate had reached half the current level; further sorties have no further effect on the enemy's overall operating system. The second effect, that of forcing the enemy to deploy repair crews, equipment, and porters, is also largely brought about by a comparatively low interdiction effort. Our interdiction campaign in 1965 and early this year forced NVN to assign roughly 300,000 additional personnel to LOCs; there is no indication that recent sortie increases have caused further increases in the number of these personnel. Once the enemy system can repair road cuts and damaged bridges in a few hours, as it has demonstrated it can, additional sorties may work this system harder but are unlikely to cause a significant increase in its costs. Only the third effect, the destruction of vehicles and their cargoes, continues to increase in about the same proportion as the number of armed reconnaissance sorties, but without noticeable impact on VC/NVA operations. The overall capability of the NVN transport system to move supplies within NVN apparently improved in September in spite of 12,200 attack sorties.

In a summary paragraph, the draft memo made the entire case against the bombings:

The increased damage to targets is not producing noticeable results. No serious shortage of POL in North Vietnam is evident, and stocks on hand, with recent imports, have been adequate to sustain necessary operations. No serious transport problem in the movement of supplies to or within North Vietnam is evident; most transportation routes appear to be open, and there has recently been a major logistical build-up in the area of the DMZ. The raids have disrupted the civil populace and caused isolated food shortages, but have not significantly weakened popular morale.

Air strikes continue to depress economic growth and have been responsible for abandonment of some plans for economic development, but essential economic activities continue. The increasing amounts of physical damage sustained by North Vietnamese are in large measure compensated by aid received from other Communist countries. Thus, in spite of an interdiction campaign costing at least $250 million per month at current levels, no significant impact on the war in South Vietnam is evident. The monetary value of damage to NVN since the start of bombing in February 1965 is estimated at about $140 million through October 10, 1966.

121

Komer Report to Johnson after February Trip to Vietnam

Excerpts from memorandum to President Johnson from Robert W. Komer, his special assistant, Feb. 28, 1967, as provided in the body of the Pentagon study. Paragraphs in italics are the study's paraphrase or explanation.

After almost a year full-time in Vietnam, and six trips there, I felt able to learn a good deal more from my 11 days in-country, 13-23 February. I return more optimistic than ever before. The cumulative change since my first visit last April is dramatic, if not yet visibly demonstrable in all respects. Indeed, I'll reaffirm even more vigorously my prognosis of last November which would be achieved in 1967 on almost every front in Vietnam.

He firmly believed that in time we would just overwhelm the VC in SVN:

Wastefully, expensively, but nonetheless indisputably, we are winning the war in the South. Few of our programs—civil or military—are very efficient, but we are grinding the enemy down by sheer weight and mass. And the cumulative impact of all we have set in motion is beginning to tell. Pacification still lags the most, yet even it is moving forward.

Finally, and contrary to all military reports, he saw some let-up in the pressures for additional resources:

Indeed my broad feeling, with due allowance for over-simplification, is that our side now has in presently programmed levels all the men, money and other resources needed to achieve success. . . .

122

Westmoreland's March 18 Memo on Increase in Forces

Excerpts from cablegram from Gen. William C. Westmoreland, commander of United States forces in Vietnam, to Pacific command, March 18, 1967, as provided in the body of the Pentagon study. Paragraphs in italics are the study's paraphrase or explanation.

On 18 March, General Westmoreland submitted his analysis of current MACV force requirements projected through FY 68. This request was to furnish the base line for all further force deployment calculations during the Program 5 period. In preface to his specific request, COMUSMACV reviewed his earlier CY 67 requirement which asked for 124 maneuver battalions with their necessary combat and combat service support, a total strength of 555,741. This figure was the maximum figure requested during the Program 4 deliberations. The approved Program 4 package included only 470,336 and was considerably below the MACV request, a fact which led to the series of reclamas described in Section II. Westmoreland related that MACVCINCPAC had not strongly objected earlier to the 470,000 man ceiling because of adverse piaster impact and the realities of service capabilities, but, subsequent reassessment of the situation had indicated clearly to him that the Program 4 force, although enabling U.S. force to gain the initiative did not "permit sustained operations of the scope and intensity required to avoid an unreasonably protracted war."

As the cable continued, the American commander in Vietnam briefly restated his earlier assessment of enemy trends: That the enemy had increased his force structure appreciably and was now confronting Free World Military Forces with large bodies of troops in and above the DMZ, in the Laotian and Cambodian sanctuaries and certain areas wtihin SVN. In light of this new appraisal, he had establised an early requirement for an additional 2⅓ divisions which he proposed be accommodated by restructuring the original 555,741-man force package proposed during Program 4. This force was required "as soon as possible but not later than 1 July 1968." Part of the reasoning was that this in effect constituted no more than a 6-month "extension" of the CY 67 program and as such would permit shifting force programming from a Calendar Year to a Fiscal Year basis, a shift long needed in COMUSMACV's estimation to make force programming for Vietnam compatible with other programs and to provide essential lead time in the procurement of hardware. Westmoreland then looked further ahead, noting:

. . . It is entirely possible that additional forces, over and above the immediate requirement for 2⅓ Divisions, will materialize. Present planning, which will undergo continued refinement, suggests an additional 2⅓ division equivalents whose availability is seen as extending beyond FY 68.

Then as if to take the edge off his request, COMUSMACV turned attention to two programs which were becoming increasingly attractive to American decision-makers. These were development of an improved RVNAF and an increase in the other Free World Military Forces committed to the war in Vietnam. He commented that despite the force ceiling on RVNAF currently in effect some selective increase in Vietnamese capabilities was required, such as creation of a suitable base for establishing a constabulary, an organization vital to the success of the Revolutionary Development program. Westmoreland stated that it was the position of his headquarters that provision for any and all Free World Military Forces was welcomed as "additive reinforcements," but they would be treated as additions only, thereby having no effect upon U.S. force computations.

The concept of operations under which the new forces he requested were to be employed varied little in its essential aspects from that outlined in MACV's February "Assessment of the Military Situation and Concept of Operations," which had reached Washington but a week earlier. However, the new cable integrated the new forces as part of the MACV operational forces. Westmoreland reviewed the period just past then turned to the future:

... our operations were primarily holding actions characterized by border surveillance, reconnaissance to locate enemy forces, and spoiling attacks to disrupt the enemy offensive. As a result of our buildup and successes, we were able to plan and initiate a general offensive. We now have gained the tactical initiative, and are conducting continuous small and occasional large-scale offensive operations to decimate the enemy forces; to destroy enemy base areas and disrupt his infrastructure; to interdict his land and water LOC's and to convince him, through the vigor of our offensive and accompanying psychological operations, that he faces inevitable defeat.

Military success alone will not achieve the U.S. objectives in Vietnam. Political, economic and psychological victory is equally important, and support of Revolutionary Development program is mandatory. The basic precept for the role of the military in support of Revolutionary Development is to provide a secure environment for the population so that the civil aspects of RD can progress.

He then detailed corps by corps the two troop request requirements labeling them the "optimum force" [4⅔ Divs] and the "minimum essential force" [2⅓ Divs]:

B. FORCE REQUIREMENTS FY 68

(1) The MACV objectives for 1967 were based on the assumption that the CY 67 force requirements would be approved and provided expeditiously within the capabilities of the services. How-

ever, with the implementation of Program Four, it was recognized that our accomplishments might fall short of our objectives. With the additional forces cited above, we would have had the capability to extend offensive operations into an exploitation phase designed to take advantage of our successes.

(2) With requisite forces, we shall be able to complete more quickly the destruction or neutralization of the enemy main forces and bases and, by continued presence, deny to him those areas in RVN long considered safe havens. As the enemy main forces are destroyed or broken up, increasingly greater efforts can be devoted to rooting out and destroying the VC guerrilla and communist infrastructure. Moreover, increased assistance can be provided the RVNAF in support of its effort to provide the required level of security for the expanding areas undergoing Revolutionary Development.

(3) Optimum Force. The optimum force required implement the concept of operations and to exploit success is considered 4⅔ divisions or the equivalent; 10 tactical fighter squadrons with one additional base; and the full mobile riverine force. The order of magnitude estimate is 201,250 spaces in addition to the 1967 ceiling of 470,366 for a total of 671,616.

(A) In I Corps, the situation is the most critical with respect to existing and potential force ratios. As a minimum, a division plus a regiment is required for Quang Tri Province as a containment force. The latter has been justified previously in another plan. Employment of this force in the containment role would release the units now engaged there for expansion of the DaNang, Hue-Phu Bai and Chu Lai TAOR's as well as increase security and control along the corps northern coastal areas. One of the most critical areas in RVN today is Quang Ngai Province even if a major operation were conducted in this area during 1967, the relief would be no more than temporary. A force is needed in the province to maintain continuous pressure on the enemy to eliminate his forces and numerous base areas, and to remove his control over the large population and food reserves. The sustained employment of a division of 10 battalions is mandatory in Quang Ngai Province if desired results are to be realized. Employment of this force would provide security for the vital coastal areas, facilitate opening and securing Route 1 and the railroad and, perhaps equally important, relieve pressure on northern Binh Dinh Province.

(b) In II Corps, the task is two fold: destroy the enemy main and guerrilla forces in the coastal areas; and contain the infiltration of NVA forces from Cambodia and Laos. Continual expansion both north and south of the present capital coastal TAOR's opening and securing Route 1 and the railroad, securing Route 20 from Dalat south to the III Corps boundary, destruction of enemy forces in Pleiku and Kontum Provinces, and containment of enemy forces in the Cambodian and Laotian sanctuaries are all tasks to be accomplished given the large area in II Corps and the continuous enemy threat, an optimum force augmentation of four separate brigades is required to execute effectively an exploitation of our successes. An infantry brigade is needed in northern Binh Dinh Province to expand security along the coastal area and to facilitate operations in Quang Ngai Province to the north. A mechanized brigade in the western highlands will assist in offensive and containment operations in the Pleiku-Kontum area. An infantry brigade in the region of Nam Me Thout is needed to conduct operations against enemy forces and bases there and to add security to this portion of II Corps now manned with limited ARVN forces, and finally, a mechanized brigade is needed in Binh Thuan Province to neutralize the enemy forces and bases in the southern coastal area, and to open and secure highway 1 and the national railroad to the III Corps boundary.

(c) In III Corps, operations to destroy VC/NVA forces and bases in the northwestern & central parts of the corps area and to intensify the campaign against the enemy's infrastructure are being conducted. These operations are to be completed by intensive efforts to open and secure the principal land and water LOC's throughout the Corps Zone. However, deployment of the U.S. 9th Div to IV Corps will create a gap in the forces available in III Corps to operate against seen significant base areas in Phuoc Tuy, Bin Tuy, and Long Lhanh Provinces. These areas constitute the home base of the still formidable 5th VC Division. This unit must be destroyed, its bases neutralized and Route 1 and the national railroad opened and secured. Other critical locales that will require considerable effort are War Zone D and Phuoc Long area in which the VC 7th Division is believed to be located. With the forces operating currently in III Corps, substantial progress can be made, but to exploit effectively our successes an addition of one division, preferably air mobile is required. By basing this division in Bien Hoa province just north of the RSSZ, it would be in position to conduct operations against the 5th Div, and War Zone D, as well as to reinforce the U.S. 9th Div in Delta operations as required.

(d) In IV Corps, with deployment of the U.S. 9th Div to the Corps area and with increasing success of ARVN operations there, the situation will be greatly improved. Primary emphasis will be given to destroying VC main and guerrilla units and their bases, to intensifying operations to extend GVN control, to stopping the flow of food stuffs and materials to the enemy through Cambodia, and to assisting in the flow of goods to GVN outlets in Saigon. In addition emphasis will be accorded the opening and securing of principal water and land LOC's which are the key to all operations in the Delta. It is noteworthy on this score, that effectiveness of forces available is hampered severely by an inadequate mobile riverine force. In IV Corps, the essential requirement is to flesh out the mobile riverine force with three APB's (Barracks Ships) one ARL (repair ship), and two RAS (river assault squadrons).

(4) The Minimum Essential Force necessary to exploit success

of the current offensive and to retain effective control of expanding areas being cleaned of enemy influence is 2⅓ divisions with a total of 21 maneuver battalions. One division, with nine infantry battalions—each with 4 rifle companies—and an ACR of three squadrons are required. The other division of nine maneuver battalions, each battalion organized with four rifle companies is required in Quang Ngai Province. Four tactical fighter squadrons, each generating 113 sorties per month per identified maneuver battalion, are required. Two squadrons will be stationed at Phu Cat and two at Tuy Hoa. One C-130 or equivalent type squadron can provide adequate airlift and is justified on the basis of current planning factors: This SQD would be based at Cam Ranh Bay. A minimum essential logistic base can be provided by selective augmentation of NSA Danang, and by provision for lift capability equivalent to eight LST's in addition to two LST's identified previously for the containment force in Quang Tri Province. Two nondivisional Army combat engineer battalions and four Army construction battalions will be required to support divisional engineering effort to augment two navy construction battalions that previously have been identified with the containment force in Quang Tri Province.

(b) Effectiveness of the U.S. 9th Division's operations in IV Corps will be degraded unacceptably without adequate mobility on the waterways. For this reason, addition of two river assault squadrons with their associated support is deemed essential. The Mekong Delta Mobile Riverine Force originally was tailored and justified as a four RAS level. This requirement still is valid. The primary media of transport in the Delta are air and water. Air mobility is recognized as critical to success of operations in the area, but the size of offensive operations that can be mounted is limited by the inherent physical limitations of airborne vehicles. Accordingly, any sizeable offensive operation such as those visualized for the U.S. 9th Division must utilize the 300km of waterways in the Delta to exploit tactical mobility. Maintenance of LOC's and population control in the areas secured by the division's operations, along with extension of the interdiction effort, necessitates expansion of the game warden operation. Fifty PBR's can provide this capability based on experience factors accrued thus far. . . .

123

March 28 Westmoreland Cable to Joint Chiefs on Troop Needs

Excerpts from cablegram from General Westmoreland to the Joint Chiefs of Staff, "MACV FY-68 Force Requirements," March 28, 1967, as provided in the body of the

Pentagon study. Paragraphs in italics are the study's paraphrase or explanation.

On 26 March COMUSMACV submitted to the CINCPAC Requirements Task Group a detailed troop listing for the 2⅓ division "minimum essential force." Other than providing a detailed list of TO&E's and unit small strengths, the document provides little of interest. It did stipulate that the northern portion of the minimum essential force would be directed toward an expanded infiltration interdiction mission and that the southern portion of the force would pursue "presently prescribed operations."

In a follow-up message to the Task Requirements Group on the 28th of March COMUSMACV again commented on the restrictive aspects of Program 4. This in turn was picked up and amplified by CINCPAC in a message to the JCS on the same day. CINCPAC pointed out that as of 9 March 1967 Program 4 was 38,241 spaces short of full implementation and that this figure included spaces for five battalions or their equivalents which could not be considered for trade-off purposes. All of these spaces, especially the battalion equivalents, were significant elements when considered within the perspective of MACV's operational requirements and could not be deleted without seriously impairing MACV capability to achieve its objectives. In light of this shortfall in Program 4 CINCPAC requested that the JCS reconsider its earlier proposal that a 4th rifle company be added to all U.S. Army infantry battalions in Vietnam. The logic behind such a raise in program ceiling which would increase materially the combat power and effectiveness of the infantry without increasing unit overhead was irrefutable in CINCPAC's eyes. CINCPAC proposed that the addition of the rifle companies, a total of 8,821 men, be added to the Program 4 ceiling for a total of 479,231 of all services. The space requirements for the 2⅓ division minimum essential force reflected in the COMUSMACV request would then be added on to the adjusted Program 4 total of 479,000. However, in the event that any or all of the spaces reflected in that 479,000 were not approved or that the package itself would be reduced, the Pacific Commander predicted grave curtailment in MACV operations and a danger that the operational objectives set for the force requirements initially would not be achieved.

By 28 March the JCS through the CINCPAC group had the detailed justification and planning calculations for the COMUSMACV 67 force requirements in hand. MACV had added little that was new in the way of strategic concept other than to reaffirm their intention to concentrate on certain priority areas in each corps tactical zone. Priority areas themselves were selected because they seemed best suited to achieve destruction or neutralization of enemy main forces and bases—persistently prime MACV goals. Despite this strong declaration of intent MACV hedged by noting that "the enemy will be struck wherever he presents a lucrative target." Forces would also be maintained by MACV

561

outside the priority areas to contain the enemy in his out of country sanctuaries. In this connection, the planners anticipated that there would be large scale offensive operations continuously conducted during FY 68 to detect and destroy infiltration or invasion forces in the DMZ-Highland Border regions.

If the forces outlined under the optimum force request were granted priority was to be accorded to the expansion of secure areas. The RVNAF would be given the primary responsibility of providing military support of Revolutionary Development activities and Revolutionary Development operations would be intensified throughout the country as the pacified areas were expanded, MACV explained that such increased demands on the RVNAF would establish a concomitant demand for additional U.S. force resources to fill the operational void resulting from the intensified Revolutionary Development orientation of the RVNAF. The long message also broke ou the minimum essential and optimum package forces by service and by total troops as shown in the table below.

	STRENGTH (2⅓ Div Min essential Force)	STRENGTH (2⅓ Div Addition for optimum force package)	STRENGTH (Total Optimum Force)
Army	69,359	100,527*	169,886
Navy	5,739	8,023	13,762
Air Force	5,368	9,891	15,259
Marines	110	0	110
TOTAL	80,576	118,441	119,017

The total optimum force end strength was 678,248 arrived at by adding the approved Program 4 strength of 470,000 to the earlier MACV reclama of 8,821 (see page 68 this section) and the "optimum force" additive of 199,017. The justification for additional forces broken out by corps tactical zones were essentially the same as those presented in the original MACV request on 18 March. However, the later document prepared at PACOM Hqs on the 28th reflected the increased concern with the enemy threat developing in the I Corps tactical zone. Concerning this threat, COMUSMACV wrote:

. . . In I Corps tactical zone, the bulk of the population and the food producing regions are within 15 miles of the coast. In the northern part of the zone, multiple NVA Divisions possess the capability to move south of the DMZ. Additionally, there is constant enemy activity in much of the coastal area. The topography of I Corps lends itself to the establishment and maintenance of enemy base areas in the remote, sparsely populated regions. The enemy has operated for years virtually unmolested throughout

---

*Includes 5,547 spaces required to incorporate MACV Study recommendations.

most of Quang Ngai Province because friendly forces could not be diverted from other important tasks.

There are several important tasks which must be performed in I Corps. Security of bases and key population centers must be maintained. The area under GVN control must be extended by expanding existing TAOR's, and by opening and securing major LOC's, particularly Route 1. The enemy must be contained in his sanctuaries, and denied use of infiltration and invasion routes. Enemy main forces and bases must be sought out and destroyed. Surveillance and reconnaissance in force throughout the CTZ must complement the tasks discussed above.

The deployment of a division and an armored cavalry regiment to Quang Tri Province, south of the DMZ, would make it possible for Marine Corps units now conducting containment operations to secure and expand tactical areas of responsibility (TAOR's).

The RVNAF and U.S./FWMAF will intensify operations against organized enemy forces and base areas in and near the populated and food producing areas of the coastal plains thus denying them access to population and food resources.

Clearing and securing operations will be pursued to facilitate the expansion of the secured areas, the ultimate goal being to connect the Hue-Phu Bai, Danang, and Chu Lai TAOR's. The following major LOC's will be opened and secured: Route 9, from Route 1 to Thon San Lam; and Route 1 and the railroad throughout the entire length of I CTZ, including the spur to the An Hoa industrial complex.

One of the most critical areas in the RVN today is Quang Ngai Province. A division is required there to maintain continuous pressure on the enemy, to eliminate his forces and numerous base areas, and to remove his control over large population and food resources.

Sustained employment of a division in Quang Ngai would obviate the necessity to use other forces to meet a critical requirement. The division would provide security for the coastal area, facilitate opening and securing Route 1 and the railroad, and relieve some of the pressure on northern Binh Dinh Province. Of particular significance is the support which would be provided to the RVNAF in securing the important Mo Duc Area with its dense population and three annual rice crops. Additionally, deployment of the division as discussed above would allow III MAF to expand its clearing and securing operations into the heavily populated Tam Ky area north of the Chu Lai TAOR. Long term security must be provided for both of these areas so that Revolutionary Development can progress.

Failure to provide two and one-third divisions for I CTZ would result in the diversion of existing forces from other tasks to deny and defeat infiltration or invasion. Security in support of Revolutionary Development could not be increased to the desired degree in the coastal area, the major LOC's could not be opened throughout the CTZ, and the enemy would be able to continue operating virtually unmolested throughout the key Quang Ngai Province.

It is emphasized that the relationship of the two and one-third division force requirement for I Corps to that of Practice Nine is coincidental. This force is the minimum essential required to support operations planned for FY 68 without reference to Practice Nine.

The next most dangerous situation appeared to be that in II Corps, a diverse geographical area which included major population centers along the coastal plains as well as sizeable population centers and military bases on the western plateau such as Binh Dinh, Anke, Kontum, and Pleiku. Here the enemy, orienting himself on the population, presented a different problem which, in the words of General Westmoreland, required "a high degree of mobility and flexibility in U.S./FWMAF/RVNAF." As he analyzed the corps tactical situation, Westmoreland re-emphasized what he had already said about containing the large enemy military forces at the boundaries of the sanctuaries:

Enemy forces in the Pleiku and Kontum areas must be destroyed, and infiltration from Cambodia and Laos must be contained. Forces in-country will continue to make progress in areas of current deployment. Those programmed for deployment will augment this effort. However, there are gaps, as discussed below, that must be filled before success can be exploited and minimum essential security can be provided within the II Corps area.

Large enemy forces remaining in heavily populated Binh Dinh Province must be destroyed. Security must be established and maintained in the northern portion of the province, particularly along the coastal area, so that Revolutionary Development can progress. These security forces also will facilitate the conduct of operations in Quang Ngai Province.

Inadequacy of forces in the border areas is a significant weakness in II Corps. Reinforcement of units in the western highlands is needed to assist in the conduct of offensive and containment operations. With the large enemy forces located in border sanctuaries, II Corps is faced constantly with the possible requirement to divert critical resources from priority tasks to counter large scale intrusion.

The most pressing military objective in III Corps area was to expand security radically from the Saigon-Cholon area. MACV planned to accomplish this primarily by standard clearing and security operations featuring an intensified campaign conducted to root out the VC infrastructure. In conjunction with this, continuous pressure presumably in the form of search and destroy operations would be applied to the enemy in War Zones C and D, the Iron Triangle, and the base area clusters in the Phuoc Long area. Denial of these areas to the enemy would provide a protective shield behind which the Revolutionary Development programs could operate. However, deployment of the U.S. 9th Division to the 4th Corps area would create a gap in the forces available in

III Corps and seriously degrade the capability to provide this shield. The possible repositioning of the assets existing within III Corps to either I CTZ in the north or the 9th Division relocation just to the south just mentioned could also seriously limit the offensive capabilities in the northern and central portion of III Corps. Accordingly, COMUSMACV expressed an urgent requirement for an additional division for III Corps. This unit would be positioned just north of the Rung Sat operation zone and would assist in maintaining the protective shield around Saigon-Cholon. Revolutionary Development operations would then be able to proceed unhindered and operations against the VC 5th Division could be reinforced if required.

Throughout the force requirement justifications, one is immediately struck by the implicit ordering of the priorities for assignment of forces and missions. It is quite clear that the "minimum essential force" which COMUSMACV requested was intended to be employed against VC/NVA main force units in a containment role in the border areas and a destruction-disruption mode in I CTZ as well as the base areas within the country itself. Those forces over and above the "minimum essential," so labelled the "optimum force," were those intended to take up the slack in the RD "shield" role. MACV, probably rightly, calculated that not even minimal gains such as were forthcoming in the under-manned RD program would be possible unless the VC/NVA main force operations could be stymied and kept from directly assaulting the "shields."

124

Joint Chiefs' April 20 Report to McNamara on Troop Needs

Excerpts from Joint Chiefs of Staff Memorandum 218-67 to Secretary of Defense McNamara, April 20, 1967, as provided in the body of the Pentagon study. Paragraphs in italics are the study's paraphrase or explanation.

On 20 April, the JCS, in JCSM-218-67, formally reported to the Secretary of Defense that MACV required additional forces to achieve the objectives they considered the U.S. was pursuing in Vietnam. The JCS announcement came as little surprise to the Secretary of Defense since as early as 23 March he had seen the original message in which COMUSMACV had outlined the minimum essential and optimum force requirements.

JCSM 218-67 reaffirmed the basic objectives and strategic concepts contained in JCSM 702-66 dated 4 November 1966. Briefly, these entailed a national objective of attaining a stable and inde-

pendent non-communist government in South Vietnam and a four-fold military contribution toward achieving the objectives of:

(a) Making it as difficult and costly as possible for the NVA to continue effective support of the VC and to cause North Vietnam to cease direction of the VC insurgency.

(b) To defeat the VC/NVA and force the withdrawal of NVA forces.

(c) Extend government dominion, direction and control.

(d) To deter Chinese Communists from direct intervention in SEA.

The JCS listed three general areas of military effort that they felt should be pursued in the war:

(1) Operations against the Viet Cong/North Vietnamese Army (VC/NVA) forces in SVN while concurrently assisting the South Vietnamese Government in their nation-building efforts.

(2) Operations to obstruct and reduce the flow of men and materials from North Vietnam (NV) to SVN.

(3) Operations to obstruct and reduce imports of war-sustaining materials into NVN.

They continued by assessing the achievements of the U.S. and allies in these three areas:

In the first area, the United States and its allies have achieved considerable success in operations against VC/NVA forces. However, sufficient friendly forces have not been made available to bring that degree of pressure to bear on the enemy throughout SVN which would be beyond his ability to accommodate and which would provide the secure environment essential to sustained progress in Revolutionary Development. The current reinforcement of I CTZ by diversion of forces from II to III CTZs reduces the existing pressure in those areas and inevitably will cause a loss of momentum that must be restored at the earliest practicable date.

In the second area, U.S. efforts have achieved appreciable success. Greater success could be realized if an expanded system of targets were made available.

In the third area, relatively little effort has been permitted. This failure to obstruct and reduce imports of war-sustaining materials into NVN has affected unfavorably the desired degree of success of operations in the other areas.

The Joint Chiefs strongly recommended not only the approval of additional forces to provide an increased level of effort in SVN but that action be taken to reduce and obstruct the enemy capability to import the material support required to sustain the war effort. They argued that the cumulative effect of all these operations, in South Vietnam, in North Vietnam and against the enemy's strategic lines of communication would hasten the successful conclusion of the war and would most likely reduce the overall ultimate force requirements. Their rationale for the 1968 forces was summarized as follows:

The FY 1968 force for SVN is primarily needed to offset the

nemy's increased posture in the vicinity of the DMZ and to improve the environment for Revolutionary Development in I and V CTZs. To achieve the secure environment for lasting progress n SVN, additional military forces must be provided in order to 1) destroy the enemy main force, (2) locate and destroy district nd provincial guerrilla forces, and (3) provide security for the opulation. The increased effort required to offset VC/NVA main orces' pressure is diminishing the military capability to provide a ecure environment to villages and hamlets. Diversion of forces rom within SVN and the employment of elements of CINCPAC's eserve are temporary measures at the expense of high-priority rograms in other parts of SVN. Thus, if sufficient units are to be available to provide both direct and indirect support to Revolutionary Development throughout SVN, added forces must be deployed.

The three-TFS force for Thailand and the additional Navy forces in the South China Sea and the Gulf of Tonkin are required to bring increased pressures to bear on NVN.

125

Notes on Johnson Discussion with Wheeler and Westmoreland

Excerpts from the Pentagon study describing a conversation on April 27, 1967, between President Johnson and Generals Wheeler and Westmoreland. The narrative says the conversation was reported in notes by John T. McNaughton, Assistant Secretary of Defense for International Security Affairs. Italicized emphasis and words in parentheses are those of the Pentagon study.

Westmoreland was quoted as saying that without the 2⅓ additional divisions which he had requested "we will not be in danger of being defeated but it will be nip and tuck to oppose the reinforcements the enemy is capable of providing. In the final analysis we are fighting a war of attrition in Southeast Asia."

Westmoreland predicted that the next step if we were to pursue our present strategy to fruition would probably be the second addition of 2⅓ divisions or approximately another 100,000 men. Throughout the conversations he repeated his assessment that the war would not be lost but that progress would certainly be slowed down. To him this was "not an encouraging outlook but a realistic one." When asked about the influence of increased infiltration upon his operations the general replied that as he saw it "this war is action and counteraction. Anytime we take an action we expect a reaction. The President replied: "When we add divisions can't the enemy add divisions? If so, where does it all end?" Westmoreland answered: "The VC and DRV strength in SVN now total 285,000 men. It appears that last month we reached the crossover point *in areas excluding the two northern provinces.*" (Emphasis added.) "Attritions will be greater than additions to the force. . . . The enemy has 8 divisions in South Vietnam. He has the capability of deploying 12 divisions although he would have difficulty supporting all of these. He would be hard pressed to support more than 12 divisions. If we add 2½ divisions, it is likely the enemy will react by adding troops." The President then asked "At what point does the enemy ask for volunteers?" Westmoreland's only reply was, "That is a good question."

COMUSMACV briefly analyzed the strategy under the present program of 470,000 men for the President. He explained his concept of a "meatgrinder" where we would kill large numbers of the enemy but in the end do little better than hold our own, with the shortage of troops still restricting MACV to a fire brigade technique—chasing after enemy main force units when and where it could find them. He then predicted that "unless the will of the enemy is broken or unless there was an unraveling of the VC infrastructure the war could go on for 5 years. If our forces were increased that period could be reduced although not necessarily in proportion to increases in strength, since factors other than increase in strength had to be considered. For instance, a non professional force, such as that which would result from fulfilling the requirement for 100,000 additional men by calling reserves would cause some degradation of normal leadership and effectiveness. Westmoreland concluded by estimating that with a force level of 565,000 men, *the war could well go on for three years. With a second increment of 2⅓ divisions leading to a total of 665,000 men, it could go on for two years.*

General Wheeler . . . listed three matters . . . which were bothering the JCS. These were:

(a) DRV troop activity in Cambodia. U.S. troops may be forced to move against these units in Cambodia.

(b) DRV troop activity in Laos. U.S. troops may be forced to move against these units.

(c) Possible invasion of North Vietnam. We may wish to take offensive action against the DRV with ground troops.

The bombing which had always attracted considerable JCS attention was in Wheeler's estimation about to reach the point of target saturation—when all worthwhile fixed targets except the ports had been struck. Once this saturation level was reached the decision-makers would be impelled to address the requirement to deny to the North Vietnamese use of the ports. He summarized the JCS position saying that the JCS firmly believed that the President must review the contingencies which they faced, the troops required to meet them and additional punitive action against DRV. Westmoreland parenthetically added that he was "frankly dismayed at even the thought of stopping the bombing program." . . .

The President closed the meeting by asking: "What if we do

t add the 2⅓ divisions?" General Wheeler replied first, observ-
g that the momentum would die; in some areas the enemy
uld recapture the initiative, an important but hardly disastrous
velopment, meaning that we wouldn't lose the war but it would
a longer one. He added that:

"Of the 2⅓ divisions, I would add one division on the DMZ to
lieve the Marines to work with ARVN on pacification; and I
uld put one division east of Saigon to relieve the 9th Division
deploy to the Delta to increase the effectiveness of the three
od ARVN divisions now there; the brigade I would send to
uang Ngai to make there the progress in the next year that we
ave made in Binh Dinh in the past year."

The President reacted by saying:

"We should make certain we are getting value received from the
uth Vietnamese troops. Check the dischargees to determine
hether we could make use of them by forming additional units,
y mating them with US troops, as is done in Korea, or in other
ays."

There is no record of General Westmoreland's reply, if any. . . .

126

McGeorge Bundy's Memorandum to
Johnson in May on Bombing

*Excerpts from memorandum for President Johnson from
McGeorge Bundy, headed "Memorandum on Vietnam
Policy," as provided in the body of the Pentagon study.
According to the study, the document bore no date but a
copy was marked in pencil "rec'd 5-4-67 12n." Paragraphs
in italics are the study's paraphrase or explanation.*

Since the Communist turndown of our latest offers in February,
here has been an intensification of bombing in the North, and
ress reports suggest that there will be further pressure for more
ttacks on targets heretofore immune. There is also obvious pres-
ure from the military for further reinforcements in the South,
lthough General Westmoreland has been a model of discipline in
is public pronouncements. One may guess, therefore, that the
resident will soon be confronted with requests for 100,000-
00,000 more troops and for authority to close the harbor in
Haiphong. Such recommendations are inevitable, in the framework
f strictly military analysis. It is the thesis of this paper that in
he main they should be rejected, and that as a matter of high
ational policy there should be a publicly stated ceiling to the
evel of American participation in Vietnam, as long as there is no
urther marked escalation on the enemy side.

There are two major reasons for this recommendation: the

situation in Vietnam and the situation in the United States. As [to] Vietnam, it seems very doubtful that further intensifications [of] bombing in the North or major increases in U.S. troops in t[he] South are really a good way of bringing the war to a satisfacto[ry] conclusion. As to the United States, it seems clear that uncertain[ty] about the future size of the war is now having destructive effec[t] on the national will.

Unlike the vocal critics of the Administrations, Mac Bundy w[as] not opposed to the bombing per se, merely to any further extensio[n] of it since he felt such action would be counter-productive. B[e] cause his views carry such weight, his arguments against extendi[ng] the bombing are reproduced below in full:

On the ineffectiveness of the bombing as a means to end t[he] war, I think the evidence is plain—though I would defer to expe[rt] estimators. Ho Chi Minh and his colleagues simply are not goi[ng] to change their policy on the basis of losses from the air in Nor[th] Vietnam. No intelligence estimate that I have seen in the last tw[o] years has ever claimed that the bombing would have this effec[t.] The President never claimed that it would. The notion that th[is] was its purpose has been limited to one school of thought and h[as] never been the official Government position, whatever critics ma[y] assert.

I am very far indeed from suggesting that it would make sens[e] now to stop the bombing of the North altogether. The argumen[t] for that course seems to me wholly unpersuasive at the presen[t.] To stop the bombing today would be to give the Communist[s] something for nothing, and in a very short time all the doves i[n] this country and around the world would be asking for som[e] further unilateral concessions. (Doves and hawks are alike in thei[r] insatiable appetites; we can't really keep the hawks happy by smal[l] increases in effort—they come right back for more.)

The real justification for the bombing, from the start, has bee[n] double—its value for Southern morale at a moment of grea[t] danger, and its relation to Northern infiltration. The first reaso[n] has disappeared but the second remains entirely legitimate. Tac[-] tical bombing of communications and of troop concentrations— and of airfields as necessary—seems to me sensible and practica[l.] It is strategic bombing that seems both unproductive and unwis[e.] It is true, of course, that all careful bombing does some damag[e] to the enemy. But the net effect of this damage upon the militar[y] capability of a primitive country is almost sure to be slight. (Th[e] lights have not stayed off in Haiphong, and even if they had, elec[-] tric lights are in no sense essential to the Communist war effort.[)] And against this distinctly marginal impact we have to weigh th[e] fact that strategic bombing does tend to divide the U.S., to dis[-] tract us all from the real struggle in the South, and to accentuat[e] the unease and distemper which surround the war in Vietnam[,] both at home and abroad. It is true that careful polls show ma[-] jority support for the bombing, but I believe this support rest[s] upon an erroneous belief in its effectiveness as a means to end th[e]

ar. Moreover, I think those against extension of the bombing
re more passionate on balance than those who favor it. Finally,
ere is certainly a point at which such bombing does increase the
sk of conflict with China or the Soviet Union, and I am sure
ere is no majority for that. In particular, I think it clear that the
ase against going after Haiphong Harbor is so strong that a
ajority would back the Government in rejecting that course.

So I think that with careful explanation there would be more
pproval than disapproval of an announced policy restricting the
ombing closely to activities that support the war in the South.
General Westmoreland's speech to the Congress made this tie-in,
ut attacks on power plants really do not fit the picture very well.
We are attacking them, I fear, mainly because we have "run out"
f other targets. Is it a very good reason? Can anyone demon-
trate that such targets have been rewarding? Remembering the
laims made for attacks on [rest illegible].

*In a similar fashion Bundy developed his arguments against a
major increase in U.S. troop strength in the South and urged the
President not to take any new initiatives for the present. But the
appeal of Bundy's analysis for the President must surely have
been its finale in which Bundy, acutely aware of the President's
political sensitivities, cast his arguments in the context of the forthcoming 1968 Presidential elections. Here is how he presented the
case:*

There is one further argument against major escalation in 1967
and 1968 which is worth stating separately, because on the surface
it seems cynically political. It is that Hanoi is going to do everything it possibly can to keep its position intact until after our
1968 elections. Given their history, they are *bound* to hold out for
a possible U.S. shift in 1969—that's what they did against the
French, and they got most of what they wanted when Mendes
took power. Having held on so long this time, and having nothing
much left to lose—compared to the chance of victory—they are
bound to keep on fighting. Since only atomic bombs could really
knock them out (an invasion of North Vietnam would not do it
in two years, and is of course ruled out on other grounds), they
have it in their power to "prove" that military escalation does not
bring peace—at least over the next two years. They will surely do
just that. However much they may be hurting, they are not going
to do us any favors before November 1968. (And since this was
drafted, they have been publicly advised by Walter Lippmann to
wait for the Republicans—as if they needed the advice and as if
it was his place to give it!)

It follows that escalation will not bring visible victory over
Hanoi before the election. Therefore the election will have to be
fought by the Administration on other grounds. I think those
other grounds are clear and important, and that they will be
obscured if our policy is thought to be one of increasing—and
ineffective—military pressure.

If we assume that the war will still be going on in November

1968, and that Hanoi will not give us the pleasure of consenting to negotiations sometime before then what we must plan to offer as a defense of Administration policy is not victory over Hanoi but growing success—and self reliance—in the South. This we can do, with luck, and on this side of the parallel, the Vietnamese authorities should be prepared to help us out (though of course the VC will do their damndest against us.) Large parts of Westy's speech (if not quite all of it) were wholly consistent with this line of argument. . . .

If we can avoid escalation-that-does-not-seem-to-work, we can focus attention on the great and central achievement of these last two years: on the defeat we have prevented. The fact that South Vietnam has not been lost and is not going to be lost is a fact of truly massive importance in the history of Asia, the Pacific and the U.S. An articulate minority of "Eastern intellectuals" (like Bill Fulbright) may not believe in what they call the domino theory, but most Americans (along with nearly all Asians) know better. Under this administration the United States has already saved the hope of freedom for hundreds of millions—in this sense the largest part of the job is done. This critically important achievement is obscured by seeming to act as if we have to do much more lest we fail.

127

May 4 Memo on Force Levels by Systems-Analysis Chief

Memorandum for Secretary McNamara, "Force Levels and Enemy Attrition," from Alain C. Enthoven, Assistant Secretary of Defense for Systems Analysis, May 4, 1967, as provided in the body of the Pentagon study.

Although MACV has admitted to you that the VC/NVA forces can refuse to fight when they want to, this fact has played no role in MACV's analysis of strategy and force requirements. (For example, in his October 1965 briefing, General DePuy said, "The more often we succeed at (search and destroy operations) the less often will the VC stand and fight.") Because enemy attrition plays such a central role in MACV's thinking, and because the enemy's degree of control over the pace of the action determines how well he can control his attrition, we have taken a hard look at the facts on the enemy's tactical initiative. From reliable, detailed accounts of 56 platoon-sized and larger fire-fights in 1966 we have classified these fights according to how they developed. The first four categories in the table all represent cases in which the enemy willingly and knowingly stood and fought in a pitched battle; these categories include 47 (84%) of the 56 battles. The rst three categories, enemy ambushes and assaults on our forces, ave 66% of the cases; these three plus category 4a, comprising ιe cases where the enemy has the advantage of surprise, have 8% of the cases.

The results are independently confirmed from two sources. 'irst, the ARCOV study, which analyzed a different set of battles ι late 1965 and early 1966, found that 46% of the fights begin s enemy ambushes and that the enemy starts the fight in 88% ιf the cases; moreover, it found that 63% of the infantry targets ncountered were personnel in trenches or bunkers. Second, we ave analyzed the After-Action Reports submitted to MACV by he line commanders in the field; although generally vague and ncomplete in their descriptions of what happened, they broadly onfirm the drift of the above numbers.

These results imply that the size of the force we deploy has ittle effect on the rate of attrition of enemy forces. This concluion should scarcely surprise you in view of the trend of enemy osses in 1966 and in view of the obvious sensitivity of mouth-tonouth enemy losses to his known strategic initiatives. What is urprising to me is that MACV has ignored this type of informaion in discussing force levels. I recommend that you inject this actor into the discussion.

128

Rostow Memorandum of May 6 on the Bombing Program

Excerpts from a memorandum by Walt W. Rostow, Presidential assistant for national security, to Secretary of State Dean Rusk, Deputy Secretary of Defense Cyrus Vance, Under Secretary of State Nicholas deB. Katzenbach, Assistant Secretary of Defense John T. McNaughton, Assistant Secretary of State William P. Bundy and Richard Helms, Director of Central Intelligence, dated May 6, 1967, and headed "U.S. Strategy in Vietnam," as provided in the body of the Pentagon study. Paragraphs in italics are the study's paraphrase or explanation.

*Rostow's paper began by reviewing what the U.S. was attempt*ng to do in the war: frustrate a Communist take-over "by defeat*ng their main force units; attacking the guerrilla infrastructure; *nd building a South Vietnamese governmental and security struc*ure. . . ." The purpose of the air war in the North was defined*s "To hasten the decision in Hanoi to abandon the aggression*. .," for which we specifically sought:*
    (i) to limit and harass infiltration; and
    (ii) to impose on the North sufficient military and civil cost

to make them decide to get out of the war earlier rather than later.

Sensitive to the criticisms of the bombing, Rostow tried to dispose of certain of their arguments:

We have never held the view that bombing could stop infiltration. We have never held the view that bombing of the Hanoi-Haiphong area alone would lead them to abandon the effort in the South. We have never held the view that bombing Hanoi-Haiphong would directly cut back infiltration. We have held the view that the degree of military and civilian cost felt in the North and the diversion of resources to deal with our bombing could contribute marginally—and perhaps significantly—to the timing of a decision to end the war. But it was no substitute for making progress in the South.

Rostow argued that while there were policy decisions to be made about the war in the South, particularly with respect to new force levels, there existed no real disagreement with the Administration as to our general strategy on the ground. Where contention did exist was in the matter of the air war. Here there were three broad strategies that could be pursued. Rostow offered a lengthy analysis of the three options . . .

A. CLOSING THE TOP OF THE FUNNEL

Under this strategy we would mine the major harbors and perhaps, bomb port facilities and even consider blockade. In addition, we would attack systematically the rail lines between Hanoi and mainland China. At the moment the total import capacity into North Viet Nam is about 17,200 tons per day. Even with expanded import requirement due to the food shortage, imports are, in fact, coming in at about 5700 tons per day. It is possible with a concerted and determined effort that we could cut back import capacity somewhat below the level of requirements; but this is not sure. On the other hand, it would require a difficult and sustained effort by North Viet Nam and its allies to prevent a reduction in total imports below requirements if we did all these things.

The costs would be these:

—The Soviet Union would have to permit a radical increase in Hanoi's dependence upon Communist China, or introduce minesweepers, etc., to keep its supplies coming into Hanoi by sea;

—The Chinese Communists would probably introduce many more engineering and anti-aircraft forces along the roads and rail lines between Hanoi and China in order to keep the supplies moving;

—To maintain its prestige, in case it could not or would not open up Hanoi-Haiphong in the face of mines, the Soviet Union might contemplate creating a Berlin crisis. With respect to a Berlin crisis, they would have to weigh the possible split between the U.S. and its Western European allies under this pressure against damage to the atmosphere of detente in Europe which is working in favor of the French Communist Party and providing the Soviet Union with generally enlarged influence in Western Europe.

I myself do not believe that the Soviet Union would go to war with us over Viet Nam unless we sought to occupy North Viet Nam; and, even then, a military response from Moscow would not be certain.

With respect to Communist China, it always has the option of invading Laos and Thailand; but this would not be a rational response to naval and air operations designed to strangle Hanoi. A war throughout Southeast Asia would not help Hanoi; although I do believe Communist China would fight us if we invaded the northern part of North Viet Nam.

One can always take the view that, given the turmoil inside Communist China, an irrational act by Peiping is possible. And such irrationality cannot be ruled out.

I conclude that if we try to close the top of the funnel, tension between ourselves and the Soviet Union and Communist China would increase; if we were very determined, we could impose additional burdens on Hanoi and its allies; we might cut capacity below requirements; and the outcome is less likely to be a general war than more likely.

B. ATTACKING WHAT IS INSIDE THE FUNNEL

This is what we have been doing in the Hanoi-Haiphong area for some weeks. I do not agree with the view that the attacks on Hanoi-Haiphong have no bearing on the war in the South. They divert massive amounts of resources, energies, and attention to keeping the civil and military establishment going. They impose general economic, political, and psychological difficulties on the North which have been complicated this year by a bad harvest and food shortages. I do not believe that they "harden the will of the North." In my judgment, up to this point, our bombing of the North has been a painful additional cost they have thus far been willing to bear to pursue their efforts in the South.

On the other hand:

—There is no direct, immediate connection between bombing the Hanoi-Haiphong area and the battle in the South;

—If we complete the attack on electric power by taking out the Hanoi station—which constitutes about 80% of the electric power supply of the country now operating—we will have hit most of the targets whose destruction imposes serious military-civil costs on the North.

—With respect to risk, it is unclear whether Soviet warnings about our bombing Hanoi-Haiphong represent decisions already taken or decisions which might be taken if we persist in banging away in that area.

It is my judgment that the Soviet reaction will continue to be addressed to the problem imposed on Hanoi by us; that is, they might introduce Soviet pilots as they did in the Korean War; they might bring ground-to-ground missiles into North Viet Nam with the object of attacking our vessels at sea and our airfields in the Danang area.

I do not believe that the continuation of attacks at about the level we have been conducting them in the Hanoi-Haiphong area will lead to pressure on Berlin or a general war with the Soviet Union. In fact, carefully read, what the Soviets have been trying to signal is: Keep away from our ships; we may counter-escalate to some degree; but we do not want a nuclear confrontation over Viet Nam.

C. CONCENTRATION IN ROUTE PACKAGES 1 AND 2

The advantage of concentrating virtually all our attacks in this area are three:

—We would cut our loss rate in pilots and planes;

—We would somewhat improve our harassment of infiltration of South Viet Nam;

—We would diminish the risks of counter-escalatory action by the Soviet Union and Communist China, as compared with courses A and B.

He rejected course A as incurring too many risks with too little return . . . Here is how he formulated his conclusions:

With respect to Course B I believe we have achieved greater results in increasing the pressure on Hanoi and raising the cost of their continuing to conduct the aggression in the South than some of my most respected colleagues would agree. I do not believe we should lightly abandon what we have accomplished; and specifically, I believe we should mount the most economical and careful attack on the Hanoi power station our air tacticians can devise. Moreover, I believe we should keep open the option of coming back to the Hanoi-Haiphong area, depending upon what we learn of their repair operations; and what Moscow's and Peiping's reactions are; especially when we understand better what effects we have and have not achieved thus far.

I believe the Soviet Union may well have taken certain counter-steps addressed to the more effective protection of the Hanoi-Haiphong area and may have decided—or could shortly decide—to introduce into North Viet Nam some surface-to-surface missiles.

With respect to option C, I believe we should, while keeping open the B option, concentrate our attacks to the maximum in Route Packages 1 and 2; and, in conducting Hanoi-Haiphong attacks, we should do so only when the targets make sense. I do not expect dramatic results from increasing the weight of attack in Route Packages 1 and 2; but I believe we are wasting a good many pilots in the Hanoi-Haiphong area without commensurate results. The major objectives of maintaining the B option can be achieved at lower cost.

129

Secretary McNamara's Position of May 19 on Bombing and Troops

Excerpts from draft memorandum for the President from the office of Secretary of Defense McNamara dated May 19, 1967, and headed "Future Actions in Vietnam." Text, provided in the body of the Pentagon study, is labeled "first rough draft—data and estimates have not been checked." Paragraphs in italics are the study's paraphrase or explanation.

By the 19th of May the opinions of McNamara and his key aides with respect to the bombing and Westy's troop requests had crystalized sufficiently that another Draft Presidential Memorandum was written. It was entitled, "Future Actions in Vietnam," and was a comprehensive treatment of all aspects of the war— military, political, and diplomatic. It opened with an appraisal of the situation covering both North and South Vietnam, the U.S. domestic scene and international opinion. The estimate of the situation in North Vietnam hewed very close to the opinions of the intelligence community already referred to. Here is how the analysis proceeded:

C. NORTH VIETNAM

Hanoi's attitude towards negotiations has never been soft nor open-minded. Any concession on their part would involve an enormous loss of face. Whether or not the Polish and Burchett-Kosygin initiatives had much substance to them, it is clear that Hanoi's attitude currently is hard and rigid. They seem uninterested in a political settlement and determined to match U.S. military expansion of the conflict. This change probably reflects these factors: (1) increased assurances of help from the Soviets received during Pham Van Dong's April trip to Moscow; (2) arrangements providing for the unhindered passage of materiel from the Soviet Union through China; and (3) a decision to wait for the results of the U.S. elections in 1968. Hanoi appears to have concluded that she cannot secure her objectives at the conference table and has reaffirmed her strategy of seeking to erode our ability to remain in the South. The Hanoi leadership has apparently decided that it has no choice but to submit to the increased bombing. There continues to be no sign that the bombing has reduced Hanoi's will to resist or her ability to ship the necessary supplies south. Hanoi shows no signs of ending the large war and advising the VC to melt into the jungles. The North Vietnamese believe they are right; they consider the Ky regime to be puppets; they believe the world is with them and that the American public will not have staying power against them. Thus, although they may have factions in the regime favoring different approaches, they believe that, in the long run, they are stronger than we are for the purpose. They probably do not want to make significant concessions, and could not do so without serious loss of face.

When added to the continuing difficulties in bringing the war in the South under control, the unchecked erosion of U.S. public support for the war, and the smoldering international disquiet about the need and purpose of such U.S. intervention, it is not hard to understand the DPM's statement that, "This memorandum is written at a time when there appears to be no attractive course of action." Nevertheless, 'alternatives' was precisely what the DPM had been written to suggest. These were introduced with a recapitulation of where we stood militarily and what the Chiefs were recommending. With respect to the war in the North, the DPM states:

Against North Vietnam, an expansion of the bombing program (ROLLING THUNDER 56) was approved mid-April. Before it was approved, General Wheeler said, "The bombing campaign is reaching the point where we will have struck all worthwhile fixed targets except the ports. At this time we will have to address the requirement to deny the DRV the use of the ports." With its approval, excluding the port areas, no major military targets remain to be struck in the North. All that remains are minor targets, restrikes of certain major targets, and armed reconnaissance of the lines of communication (LOCs)—and, under new principles, mining the harbors, bombing dikes and locks, and invading North Vietnam with land armies. These new military moves against North Vietnam, together with land movements into Laos and Cambodia, are now under consideration by the Joint Chiefs of Staff.

The broad alternative courses of action it considered were two:

Course A. Grant the request and intensify military actions outside the South—especially against the North. Add a minimum of 200,000 men—100,000 (2⅓ division plus 5 tactical air squadrons) would be deployed in FY 1968, another 100,000 (2⅓ divisions and 8 tactical air squadrons) in FY 1969, and possibly more later to fulfill the JCS ultimate requirement for Vietnam and associated world-wide contingencies. Accompanying these force increases (as spelled out below) would be greatly intensified military actions outside South Vietnam—including in Laos and Cambodia but especially against the North.

Course B. Limit force increases to no more than 30,000; avoid extending the ground conflict beyond the borders of South Vietnam; and concentrate the bombing on the infiltration routes south of 20°. Unless the military situation worsens dramatically, add no more than 9 battalions of the approved program of 87 battalions. This course would result in a level of no more than 500,000 men (instead of the currently planned 470,000) on December 31, 1968. (See Attachment IV for details). A part of this course would be a termination of bombing in the Red River basin unless military necessity required it, and a concentration of all sorties in North Vietnam on the infiltration routes in the neck of North Vietnam, between 17° and 20°.

. . . This was the way the DPM developed the analysis of the war segment of course of action A:

BOMBING PURPOSES AND PAYOFFS

Our bombing of North Vietnam was designed to serve three purposes:
—(1) To retaliate and to lift the morals [sic] of the people in the South who were being attacked by agents of the North.
—(2) To add to the pressure on Hanoi to end the war.
—(3) To reduce the flow and/or to increase the cost of infiltrating men and material from North to South.

We cannot ignore that a limitation on bombing will cause serious psychological problems among the men, officers and commanders, who will not be able to understand why we should withhold punishment from the enemy. General Westmoreland said that he is "frankly dismayed at even the thought of stopping the bombing program." But this reason for attacking North Vietnam must be scrutinized carefully. We should not bomb for punitive reasons if it serves no other purpose—especially if analysis shows that the actions may be counterproductive. It costs American lives; it creates a backfire of revulsion and opposition by killing civilians; it creates serious risks; it may harden the enemy.

With respect to added pressure on the North, it is becoming apparent that Hanoi may already have "written off" all assets and lives that might be destroyed by U.S. military actions short of occupation of annihilation [sic]. They can and will hold out at least so long as a prospect of winning the "war of attrition" in the South exists. And our best judgment is that a Hanoi prerequisite to negotiations is significant retrenchment (if not complete stoppage of U.S. military actions against them—at the least, a cessation of bombing. In this connection, Consul-General Rice (Hong Kong 7581, 5/1/67) said that, in his opinion, we cannot by bombing reach the critical level of pain in North Vietnam and that, "below that level, pain only increases the will to fight." Sir Robert Thompson said to Mr. Vance on April 28 that our bombing, particularly in the Red River Delta, "is unifying North Vietnam."

With respect to interdiction of men and materiel, it now appears that no combination of actions against the North short of destruction of the regime or occupation of North Vietnamese territory will physically reduce the flow of men and materiel below the relatively small amount needed by enemy forces to continue the war in the South. Our effort can and does have severe disruptive effects, which Hanoi can and does plan on and prestock against. Our efforts physically to cut the flow meaningfully by actions in North Vietnam therefore largely fail and, in failing, transmute attempted interdiction into pain, or pressure on the North (the factor discussed in the paragraph next above.) The lowest "ceiling" on infiltration can probably be achieved by concentration on the North Vietnamese "funnel" south of 20° and on the Trail in Laos.

But what if the above analyses are wrong? Why not escalate the bombing and mine the harbors (and perhaps occupy southern North Vietnam)—on the gamble that it would constrict the flow, meaningfully limiting enemy action in the South, and that it would bend Hanoi? The answer is that the costs and risks of the actions must be considered.

The primary costs of course are U.S. lives: The air campaign against heavily defended areas costs us one pilot in every 40 sorties. In addition, an important but hard-to-measure cost is domestic and world opinion: There may be a limit beyond which many Americans and much of the world will not permit the United States to go. The picture of the world's greatest superpower killing or seriously injuring 1,000 non-combatants a week, while trying to pound a tiny backward nation into submission on an issue whose merits are hotly disputed, is not a pretty one. It could conceivably produce a costly distortion in the American national consciousness and in the world image of the United States—especially if the damage to North Vietnam is complete enough to be "successful."

The most important risk, however, is the likely Soviet, Chinese and North Vietnamese reaction to intensified US air attacks, harbor-mining, and ground actions against North Vietnam.

LIKELY COMMUNIST REACTIONS

At the present time, no actions—except air strikes and artillery fire necessary to quiet hostile batteries across the border—are allowed against *Cambodian* territory. In Laos, we average 5,000 attack sorties a month against the infiltration routes and base areas, we fire artillery from South Vietnam against targets in Laos, and we will be providing 3-man leadership for each of 20 12-man U.S.-Vietnamese Special Forces teams that operate to a depth of 20 kilometers into Laos. Against North Vietnam, we average 8,000 or more attack sorties a month against all worthwhile fixed and LOC targets; we use artillery against ground targets across the DMZ; we fire from naval vessels at targets ashore and afloat up to 19°; and we mine their inland waterways, estuaries . . . up to 20°.

Intensified air attacks against the same types of targets, we would anticipate, would lead to no great change in the policies and reactions of the Communist powers beyond the furnishing of some new equipment and manpower. China, for example, has not reacted to our striking MIG fields in North Vietnam, and we do not expect them to, although there are some signs of greater Chinese participation in North Vietnamese air defense.

Mining the harbors would be much more serious. It would place Moscow in a particularly galling dilemma as to how to preserve the Soviet position and prestige in such a disadvantageous place. The Soviets might, but probably would not, force a confrontation in Southeast Asia—where even with minesweepers they would be at as great a military disadvantage as we were when they blocked the corridor to Berlin in 1961, but where their vital interest, unlike ours in Berlin (and in Cuba), is not so clearly at stake. Moscow in this case should be expected to send volunteers, including pilots, to North Vietnam; to provide some new and better weapons and equipment; to consider some action in Korea, Turkey, Iran, the Middle East or, most likely, Berlin, where the Soviets can control the degree of crisis better; and to show across-the-board hostility toward the U.S. (interrupting any ongoing conversations on ABMs, non-proliferation, etc.). China could be expected to seize upon the harbor-mining as the opportunity to reduce Soviet political influence in Hanoi and to discredit the USSR if the Soviets took no military action to open the ports. Peking might read the harbor-mining as indicating that the U.S. was going to apply military pressure until North Vietnam capitulated, and that this meant an eventual invasion. If so, China might decide to intervene in the war with combat troops and air power, to which we would eventually have to respond by bombing Chinese airfields and perhaps other targets as well. Hanoi would tighten belts, refuse to talk, and persevere—as it could without too much difficulty. North Vietnam would of course be fully dependent for supplies on China's will, and Soviet influence in Hanoi would therefore be reduced. (Ambassador Sullivan feels very strongly that it would be a serious mistake, by our actions against the port, to tip Hanoi away from Moscow and toward Peking.)

To U.S. ground actions in North Vietnam, we would expect China to respond by entering the war with both ground and air forces. The Soviet Union could be expected in these circumstances to take all actions listed above under the lesser provocations and to generate a serious confrontation with the United States at one or more places of her own choosing.

The arguments against Course A were summed up in a final paragraph:

Those are the likely costs and risks of COURSE A. They are, we believe, both unacceptable and unnecessary. Ground action in North Vietnam, because of its escalatory potential, is clearly unwise despite the open invitation and temptation posed by enemy troops operating freely back and forth across the DMZ.

Yet we believe that, short of threatening and perhaps toppling the Hanoi regime itself, pressure against the North will, if anything, harden Hanoi's unwillingness to talk and her settlement terms if she does. China, we believe, will oppose settlement throughout. We believe that there is a chance that the Soviets, at the brink, will exert efforts to bring about peace; but we believe also that intensified bombing and harbor-mining, even if coupled with political pressure from Moscow, will neither bring Hanoi to negotiate nor affect North Vietnam's terms.

With Course A rejected, the DPM turned to consideration of the levelling-off proposals of Course B. The analysis of the de-escalated bombing program of this option proceeded in this manner:

The bombing program that would be a part of this strategy is, basically, a program of concentration of effort on the infiltration routes near the south of North Vietnam. The major infiltration-related targets in the Red River basin having been destroyed, such interdiction is now best served by concentration of all effort in the southern neck of North Vietnam. All of the sorties would be flown in the area between 17° and 20°. This shift, despite possible increases in anti-aircraft capability in the area, should reduce the pilot and aircraft loss rates by more than 50 per cent. The shift will, if anything, be of positive military value to General Westmoreland while taking some steam out of the popular effort in the North.

The above shift of bombing strategy, now that almost all major targets have been struck in the Red River basin, can to military advantage be made at any time. It should not be done for the sole purpose of getting Hanoi to negotiate, although that might be a bonus effect. To maximize the chances of getting that bonus effect, the optimum scenario would probably be (1) to inform the Soviets quietly that within a few days the shift would take place, stating no time limits but making no promises to return to the Red River basin to attack targets which later acquire military importance (any deal with Hanoi is likely to be midwifed by Moscow); (2) to make the shift as predicted, without fanfare; and (3) to explain publicly, when the shift had become obvious, that the northern targets had been destroyed, and that that had been militarily important, and that there would be no need to return to the northern areas unless military necessity dictated it. The shift should not be huckstered. Moscow would almost certainly pass its information on to Hanoi, and might urge Hanoi to seize the opportunity to de-escalate the war by talks or otherwise Hanoi, not having been asked a question by us and having no ultimatum-like time limit, would be in a better posture to answer favorably than has been the case in the past. The military side of the shift is sound, however, whether or not the diplomatic spill-over is successful.

In a section dealing with diplomatic and political considerations, the DPM outlined the political view of the significance of the struggle as seen by the U.S. and by Hanoi. It then developed a conception of large U.S. interests in Asia around the necessity of containing China. This larger interest required settling the Vietnam war into perspective as only one of three fronts that required U.S. attention (the other two being Japan-Korea and India-Pakistan). In the overall view, the DPM argued, long-run trends in Asia appeared favorable to our interests:

The fact is that the trends in Asia today are running mostly for, not against, our interests (witness Indonesia and the Chinese confusion); there is no reason to be pessimistic about our ability over the next decade or two to fashion alliances and combinations (involving especially Japan and India) sufficient to keep China from encroaching too far. To the extent that our original intervention and our existing actions in Vietnam were motivated by the perceived need to draw the line against Chinese expansionism in Asia, our objective has already been attained, and COURSE B will suffice to consolidate it!

With this perspective in mind the DPM went on to reconsider and restate U.S. objectives in the Vietnam contest under the heading "Commitment and Hopes Distinguished":

The time has come for us to eliminate the ambiguities from our minimum objectives—our commitments—in Vietnam. Specifically, two principles must be articulated, and policies and actions brought in line with them: (1) Our commitment is only to see that the people of South Vietnam are permitted to determine their own future. (2) This commitment ceases if the country ceases to help itself.

It follows that no matter how much we might *hope* for some things, our *commitment* is *not*:

—to expel from South Vietnam regroupees, who are South Vietnamese (thought we do not like them),

—to ensure that a particular person or group remains in power, nor that the power runs to every corner of the land (though we prefer certain types and we hope their writ will run throughout South Vietnam),

—to guarantee that the self-chosen government is non-Communist (though we believe and strongly hope it will be), and

—to insist that the independent South Vietnam remain separate from North Vietnam (though in the short-run, we would prefer it that way).

(Nor do we have an obligation to pour in effort out of proportion to the effort contributed by the people of South Vietnam or in the face of coups, corruption, apathy or other indications of Saigon failure to cooperate effectively with us.)

We *are* committed to stopping or off setting the effect of North Vietnam's application of force in the South, which denies the people of the South the ability to determine their own future. Even here, however, the line is hard to draw. Propaganda and political advice by Hanoi (or by Washington) is presumably not barred; nor is economic aid or economic advisors. Less clear is the rule to apply to military advisors and war materiel supplied to the contesting factions.

The importance of nailing down and understanding the implications of our limited objectives cannot be overemphasized. It relates intimately to strategy against the North, to troop requirements and missions in the South, to handling of the Saigon government, to settlement terms, and to US domestic and international opinion as to the justification and the success of our efforts on behalf of Vietnam.

This articulation of American purposes and commitments in Vietnam pointedly rejected the high blown formulations of U.S. objectives in NSAM 88 ["an independent non-communist South Vietnam," "defeat the Viet Cong," etc.], and came forcefully to grips with the old dilemma of the U.S. involvement dating from the Kennedy era: only limited means to achieve excessive ends. Indeed, in the following section of specific recommendations, the DPM urged the President to, "issue a NSAM nailing down U.S. policy as described herein." The emphasis in this scaled down set of goals, clearly reflecting the frustrations of failure, was South Vietnamese self-determination. The DPM even went so far as to suggest that, "the South will be in position, albeit imperfect, to start the business of producing a full-spectrum government in South Vietnam." What this amounted to was a recommendation that we accept a compromise outcome. Let there be no mistake these were radical positions for a senior U.S. policy official within the Johnson Administration to take. They would bring the bitter condemnation of the Chiefs and were scarcely designed to flatter the President on the success of his efforts to date. That they represented a more realistic mating of U.S. strategic objectives and capabilities is another matter.

The scenario for the unfolding of the recommendations in the DPM went like this:

(4) **June:** Concentrate the bombing of North Vietnam on physical interdiction of men and materiel. This would mean terminating, except where the interdiction objective clearly dictates otherwise, all bombing north of 20° and improving interdiction as much as possible in the infiltration "funnel" south of 20° by concentration of sorties and by an all-out effort to improve detection devices, denial weapons, and interdiction tactics.

(5) **July:** Avoid the explosive Congressional debate and U.S. Reserve call-up implicit in the Westmoreland troop request. Decide that, unless the military situation worsens dramatically, U.S. deployments will be limited to Program 4-plus (which according to General Westmoreland, will not put us in danger of being defeated, but will mean slow progress in the South). Associated with this decision are decisions not to use large numbers of U.S. troops in the Delta and not to use large numbers of them in grassroots pacification work.

(6) **September:** Move the newly elected Saigon government well beyond its National Reconciliation program to seek a political

584

settlement with the non-Communist members of the NLF—to explore a cease-fire and to reach an accommodation with the non-Communist South Vietnamese who are under the VC banner; to accept them as members of an opposition political party, and, if necessary, to accept their individual participation in the national government—in sum, a settlement to transform the members of the VC from military opponents to political opponents.

(7) October: Explain the situation to the Canadians, Indians, British, UN and others, as well as nations now contributing forces, requesting them to contribute border forces to help make the inside-South Vietnam accommodation possible, and—consistent with our desire neither to occupy nor to have bases in Vietnam—offering to remove later an equivalent number of U.S. forces. (This initiative is worth taking despite its slim chance of success.)

Having made the case for de-escalation and compromise, the DPM ended on a note of candor with a clear statement of its disadvantages and problems:

The difficulties with this approach are neither few nor small: There will be those who disagree with the circumscription of the U.S. commitment (indeed, at one time or another, one U.S. voice or another has told the Vietnamese, third countries, the U.S. Congress, and the public of "goals" or "objectives" that go beyond the above bare-bones statement of our "commitment"); some will insist that pressure, enough pressure, on the North can pay off or that we will have yielded a blue chip without exacting a price in exchange for our concentrating on interdiction; many will argue that denial of the larger number of troops will prolong the war, risk losing it and increase the casualties of the Americans who are there; some will insist that this course reveals weakness to which Moscow will react with relief, contempt and reduced willingness to help, and to which Hanoi will react by increased demands and truculence; others will point to the difficulty of carrying the Koreans, Filipinos, Australians and New Zealanders with us; and there will be those who point out the possibility that the changed U.S. tone may cause a "rush for the exits" in Thailand, in Laos and especially inside South Vietnam, perhaps threatening cohesion of the government, morale of the army, and loss of support among the people. Not least will be the alleged impact on the reputation of the United States and of its President. Nevertheless, the difficulties of this strategy are fewer and smaller than the difficulties of any other approach.

130

William Bundy's May 30 Memo on Reasons for U.S. Involvement

Excerpts from memorandum from Assistant Secretary of State Bundy, circulated at State and Defense Departments, May 30, 1967, as provided in the body of the Pentagon study. Paragraphs in italics are the study's paraphrase or explanation.

William Bundy at State drafted comments on the DPM on May 30 and circulated them at State and Defense. In his rambling and sometimes contradictory memo, Bundy dealt mainly with the nature and scope of the U.S. commitment—as expressed in the DPM and as he saw it. He avoided any detailed analysis of the two military options and focused his attention on the strategic reasons for American involvement; the objectives we were after; and the terms under which we could consider closing down the operation. His memo began with his contention that:

The gut point can almost be summed up in a pair of sentences. If we can get a reasonably solid GVN political structure and GVN performance at all levels, favorable trends could become really marked over the next 18 months, the war will be won for practical purposes at some point, and the resulting peace will be secured. On the other hand, if we do not get these results from the GVN and the South Vietnamese people, no amount of U.S. effort will achieve our basic objective in South Viet-Nam— a return to the essential provisions of the Geneva Accords of 1954 and a reasonably stable peace for many years based on these Accords.

It is the view of the central importance of the South that dominates the remainder of Bundy's memo. But his own thinking was far from clear about how the U.S. should react to a South Vietnamese failure for at the end of it he wrote:

None of the above decides one other question clearly implicit in the DOD draft. What happens if "the country ceases to help itself." If this happens in the literal sense, if South Viet-Nam performs so badly that it simply is not going to be able to govern itself or to resist the slightest internal pressure, then we would agree that we can do nothing to prevent this. But the real underlying question is to what extent we tolerate imperfection, even gross imperfection, by the South Vietnamese while they are still under the present grinding pressure from Hanoi and the NLF.

This is a tough question. What do we do if there is a military coup this summer and the elections are aborted? There would then be tremendous pressure at home and in Europe to the effect that this negated what we were fighting for, and that we should pull out.

But against such pressure we must reckon that the stakes in Asia will remain. After all, the military rule, even in peacetime, in Thailand, Indonesia, and Burma. Are we to walk away from the South Vietnamese, at least as a matter of principle, simply because they failed in what was always conceded to be a courageous and extremely difficult effort to became a true democracy during a guerrilla war?

Bundy took pointed issue with DPM's reformulation of U.S. objectives. Starting with the DPM's discussion of U.S. larger interests in Asia, Bundy argued that:

In Asian eyes, the struggle is a test case, and indeed much more black-and-white than even we ourselves see it. The Asian view bears little resemblance to the breast-beating in Europe or at home. Asians would quite literally be appalled—and this includes India—if we were to pull out from Viet-Nam or if we were to settle for an illusory peace that produced Hanoi control over all Viet-Nam in short order.

In short, our effort in Viet-Nam in the past two years has not only prevented the catastrophe that would otherwise have unfolded but has laid a foundation for a progress that now appears truly possible and of the greatest historical significance.

Having disposed of what he saw as a misinterpretation of Asian sentiment and U.S. interests there, Bundy now turned to the DPM's attempt to minimize the U.S. commitment in Vietnam. He opposed the DPM language because in his view it dealt too heavily with our military commitment to get NVA off the South Vietnamese back, and not enough with the equally important commitment, to assure that "the political board in South Vietnam is not tilted to the advantage of the NLF." Bundy's conception of the U.S. commitment was twofold:

—To prevent any imposed political role for the NLF in South Vietnamese political life, and specifically the coalition demanded by point 3 of Hanoi's Four Points, or indeed any NLF part in government or political life that is not safe and acceptable voluntarily to the South Vietnamese Government and people.

—To insist in our negotiating position that "regroupees," that is, people originally native to South Viet-Nam who went North in 1954 and returned from 1959 onward, should be expelled as a matter of principle in the settlement. Alternatively, such people could remain in South Viet-Nam if, but only if, the South Vietnamese Government itself was prepared to receive them back under a reconciliation concept, which would provide in essence that they must be prepared to accept peaceful political activity under the Constitution (as the reconciliation appeal now does). This latter appears to be the position of the South Vietnamese Government, which—as Tran Van Do has just stated in Geneva—argues that those sympathetic to the Northern system of government should go North, while those prepared to accept the Southern system of government may stay in the South. Legally, the first alternative is sound, in that Southerners who went North in 1954 became for all legal and practical purposes Northern citizens and demonstrated their allegiance. But if the South Vietnamese prefer the second alternative, it is in fact exactly comparable to the regroupment provisions of the 1954 Accords, and can legally be sustained. But in either case the point is that the South Vietnamese are not obliged to accept as citizens people whose total pattern of conduct shows that they would seek to overthrow the structure of government by force and violence.

The remainder of Bundy's comments were addressed to importance of this last point. The U.S. could not consider withdrawing its forces until not only the North Vietnamese troops but also the regroupees had returned to the North. Nowhere in his comments does he specifically touch on the merits of the two military options, but his arguments all seem to support the tougher of the two choices (his earlier support of restricting the bombing thus seems paradoxical). He was, it is clear, less concerned with immediate specific decisions on a military phase of the war than with the long term consequences of this major readjustment of American sights in Southeast Asia.

Chapter 10

The Tet Offensive and the Turnaround

—BY E. W. KENWORTHY

Amid the shock and turmoil of the Tet offensive in February, 1968, the Pentagon study of the Vietnam war discloses, the Joint Chiefs of Staff and Gen. William C. Westmoreland sought to force President Lyndon B. Johnson a long way toward national mobilization in an effort to win victory in Vietnam.

But, the study shows, this pressure by the Joint Chiefs of the commanding general in the field set off a last, bitter policy debate in the Administration that culminated in the opposite of the military's desires.

For the first time, the study explains, President Johnson squarely faced the prospect that he had sought adamantly to avoid during three years of steadily widening war: "A full-scale call-up of reserves" and "putting the country economically on a semiwar footing." And, the Pentagon study goes on, Mr. Johnson confronted this prospect "at a time of great domestic dissent, disatisfaction and disillusionment about both the purposes and the conduct of the war."

Finally the President relieved General Westmoreland of his command in late February, and on March 31, 1968, exactly two months after the opening blows of the Vietcong and North Vietnamese offensive at Tet, Mr. Johnson announced his decision to limit the American operation in Vietnam. He cut back the bombing of North Vietnam to the 20th Parallel and sent to South Vietnam a token troop increase: one-tenth of the 206,000 men his generals had requested to achieve "victory."

Having announced these steps as a hopeful prelude to a

Highlights of the Period

JANUARY-FEBRUARY, 1968

Enemy, on Tet holiday Jan. 31, strikes at U.S. Embassy, attacks scores of important towns and all major cities. Joint Chiefs urge bombing closer to centers of Hanoi and Haiphong; President Johnson refuses. Chiefs' Chairman, Wheeler, asks Westmoreland to specify troop needs. Westmoreland, advised repeatedly that a division and a half is available, requests force that size.

Chiefs—trying to force Johnson into mobilization, study says—insist reserve call-up must precede any deployment; but McNamara approves 10,500-man Vietnam deployment without call-up.

Late February, Wheeler visits Saigon, finds enemy holds initiative, says Westmoreland needs 206,756 more men.

Clifford, now Secretary-designate, convenes high-level working group for full policy review. Initial draft policy memorandum finds Saigon forces ineffective, enemy likely to match any escalation; urges static "population-security" strategy "to buy time" for Vietnamese to take over their defense; opposes extension of bombing as "unproductive or worse."

MARCH, 1968

C.I.A. study, bolstering advocates of de-escalation among working group, finds enemy can withstand war of attrition regardless of U.S. troop increases in next 10 months.

Clifford working group debates drafters' memorandum; develops consensus against completely abandoning initiative. Intense battle rages between military and advocates of de-escalation. Wheeler argues for extension of bombing; Assistant Defense Secretary Warnke argues against.

Revised draft, by Warnke and Assistant Secretary Goulding, goes to White House: asks 22,000 more men for Vietnam; favors deferring decision on further deployments; asks reserve call-up; no new peace initiatives; states that planners are unable to reach consensus on wider bombing.

Westmoreland welcomes the 22,000 but reasserts 206,756 request.

On March 5, Clifford asks Wheeler opinion on Rusk draft favoring halt in bombing of most of North Vietnam; study "infers" Clifford favors plan; Air Force Secretary Brown presses for bombing step-up, offers three optional plans for it.

On March 10, Westmoreland's "206,000" request becomes public in The New York Times, sets off brisk debate.

Senator Eugene J. McCarthy, peace candidate, edges out President Johnson in New Hampshire Democratic primary.

On March 13, President decides on 30,000-man Vietnam increase, with reserve call-up of 98,451.

Robert F. Kennedy joins Presidential contest.

On March 22, Westmoreland is recalled to be Army Chief of Staff—a signal, study says, that President would rule out major escalation. Abrams, later named successor, secretly visits White House.

"Wise Men"—council of present and former high officials—meets March 25-26 at President's request and advises de-escalation.

March 31: "I shall not seek, and I will not accept, the nomination of my party." President cuts bombing back to 20th Parallel.

APRIL, 1968

On April 3, North Vietnam agrees to talks.

negotiated settlement of the war, the President, citing a wish to ease the "partisan division" racking the country, said he would not seek re-election.

The enemy offensive during Tet, the Lunar New Year, began on Jan. 31 with an attack on the United States Embassy in Saigon; for a day enemy guerrillas held the embassy compound. The attacks spread rapidly to almost all the cities and major towns of South Vietnam. Hue, the ancient capital of central Vietnam, was captured and not retaken until Feb. 24 in the last days of the offensive.

On Feb. 2, three days after the initial assault, President Johnson summoned White House reporters to the Cabinet Room. The enemy attack, he said, had been "anticipated, prepared for and met." Militarily, the enemy had suffered "a complete failure." As for a "psychological victory," the enemy's second objective, the President said that "when the American people know the facts," they would see that here, too, the enemy had failed.

In reply to questions, the President said that General Westmoreland had been given "every single thing" he "believed that he needed at this time," and that therefore no change was contemplated in the planned level of 525,000 American soldiers nor was there likely to be "any change of great consequence" in strategy.

The Pentagon study, however, says that the offensive took the White House and the Joint Chiefs "by surprise, and its strength, length and intensity prolonged this shock."

For the President, the study makes plain, the shock and disappointment were particularly severe, because throughout much of 1967 he had discounted "negative analyses" of United States strategy by the Central Intelligence Agency and the Pentagon offices of International Security Affairs and Systems Analysis. Instead, the study says, Mr. Johnson had seized upon the "optimistic reports" from General Westmoreland to counteract what many Pentagon civilians sensed was a growing public disillusionment with the war.

As an example of an unheeded warning, the Pentagon analyst cites at length a bombing study by the Government-subsidized Institute for Defense Analyses that was submitted to Secretary McNamara in mid-December, 1967. In this study—on which Mr. McNamara was to draw heavily in his farewell statement on defense posture to the Senate Armed Services Committee on Feb. 1—the institute said that the bombing of North Vietnam had had "no measurable effect on Hanoi's ability to mount and support military operations in the South" and had "not discernibly weakened" Hanoi's will to support the insurgency.

As an example of the reports that the President did heed, the analyst cites the year-end assessment of General Westmoreland, which was deliverde on Jan. 27, four days before the Tet offensive. The general said:

"Interdiction of the enemy's logistics train in Laos and NVN [North Vietnam] by our indispensable air efforts has imposed significant difficulties on him. In many areas the enemy has been driven away from the population centers; in others he has been compelled to disperse and evade contact, thus nullifying much of his potential. The year ended with the enemy increasingly resorting to desperation tactics in attempting to achieve military/psychological victory; and he has experienced only failure in these attempts."

New Troop Needs

A far different assessment came on Feb. 12, with the Tet offensive at its height. General Westmoreland reported then to the Joint Chiefs and Secretary McNamara that, as of Feb. 11, the enemy had attacked "34 provincial towns, 64 district towns and all of the autonomous cities." This, the general said, the enemy had been able to do while committing "only 20 to 35 per cent of his North Vietnamese forces . . . employed as gap fillers were VC [Viet-cong] strength was apparently not adequate to carry out his initial thrust on the cities and towns."

The first formal reaction of the Joint Chiefs to the offensive came on Feb. 3 when they asked Mr. McNamara to reduce the radius of the zone in which bombing was prohibited in Hanoi and in the port of Haiphong. In Hanoi, they sought to cut the radius from 10 nautical miles from the city's center to 3, and in Haiphong from 4 nautical miles to 1.5, thus enlarging the outer "restricted" zones in which bombing of selected targets was permitted upon Presidential approval. The Joint Chiefs also asked that blanket authority be given to air commanders to bomb in these outer zones.

The Joint Chiefs said in their memorandum that this extension was necessary to reduce "the enemy capability for waging war in the South"—a reason that the Pentagon analyst dismisses as "a *nonsequitur*," in view of "the evident ineffectiveness of the bombing in preventing the offensive."

Paul C. Warnke, who had succeeded the late John T. McNaughton as Assistant Secretary of Defense for International Security Affairs, opposed the request on the ground that enlargement of the zones would allow strikes on "only a couple of fixed targets not previously authorized." The President did not approve the request.

In any event, the Pentagon analyst notes, the primary focus of Washington's reaction to the Tet offensive was inevitably centered on General Westmoreland's possible troop requirements. At this point, however, the Pentagon study does not take account of several messages between Gen. Earle G. Wheeler, Chairman of the Joint Chiefs, and General Westmoreland. These messages, which have been quoted verbatim by Marvin Kalb and Elie Abel in their 1971 book "Roots of Involvement," throw considerable light on what was to become a matter of contention; whether the President and General Wheeler pressed General Westmoreland to ask for more troops or whether, as Mr. Johnson was to insist, the President merely asked for General Westmoreland's "recommendations."

In the first of these cablegrams, on Feb. 3, four days after the offensive began, General Wheeler said: "The President asks me if there is any reinforcement or help that we can give you."

General Westmoreland had not replied by Feb. 8, and General Wheeler, according to the book, sent a second cablegram then that did not mention the President: "Query: Do you need reinforcement? Our capabilities are limited. We can provide 82d Airborne Division and about one-half a Marine Corps division, both loaded with Vietnam veterans. However, if you consider reinforcements imperative, you should not be bound by earlier agreements. United States Government is not prepared to accept defeat in Vietnam. In summary, if you need more troops, ask for them."

"Earlier agreements" referred to the authorized level of 525,000 troops in 1968, of whom about 500,000 had reached South Vietnam.

That same day General Westmoreland replied, requesting the proffered units and asking, according to the Kalb-Abel book, that the President authorize an amphibious assault by the marines into North Vietnam as a diversionary move. The next day, Feb. 9, he followed up with this message:

"Needless to say, I would welcome reinforcements at

594

any time they can be made available. A. To put me in a stronger position to contain the enemy's major campaign in the DMZ-Quangtri-Thuathien area and to go on the offensive as soon as his attack is spent. B. To permit me to carry out my campaign plans despite enemy's reinforcements from North Vietnam, which have influenced my deployment plans. C. To offset the weakened [South] Vietnamese forcs resulting from casualties and Tet desertions. Realistically, we must assume that it will take them at least six weeks to regain the military posture of several weeks ago. . . . D. To take advantage of the enemy's weakened posture by taking the offensive against him."

General Wheeler responded: ". . . It occurs to me that the deployment of the 82d Airborne Division and marine elements might be desirable earlier than April to assist in defense and pursuit operations. . . . Please understand that I am not trying to sell you on the deployment of additional forces which in any event I cannot guarantee. . . . However, my sensing is that the critical phase of the war is upon us, and I do not believe that you should refrain from asking for what you believe is required under the circumstances."

At this point the Pentagon study turns to the issue of troop levels. On Feb. 9, it says, Mr. McNamara asked the Joint Chiefs to furnish plans for General Westmoreland's emergency reinforcement. The study says that on Feb. 12, after extensive communication with General Westmoreland, the Joint Chiefs submitted to the Secretary three plans, all of which they said would leave the strategic reserve in the United States so thin as to seriously compromise the nation's worldwide commitments.

Therefore, the Joint Chiefs recommended in their memorandum that "a decision to deploy reinforcements to Vietnam be deferred at this time," but that preparatory "measures be taken now" for possible later deployment of the 82d Airborne Division and two-thirds of a Marine division air wing team.

The Pentagon study says: "The tactic the Chiefs were using was clear: by refusing to scrape the bottom of the barrel any further for Vietnam, they hoped to force the President to 'bite the bullet' on the call-up of the reserves— a step they had long thought essential, and that they were determined would not now be avoided."

Despite the Joint Chiefs' recommendation against deployments without calling up the reserves, the next day, Feb. 13, Secretary McNamara approved immediate emergency deployment of 10,500 men—a brigade of the 82d Airborne and a Marine regimental landing team—above the 525,000 ceiling.

The Joint Chiefs reacted immediately by sending the Secretary a memorandum recommending a call-up of reserves to replace and sustain the new deployment—32,000 Army reservists, 12,000 marines and 2,300 Navy men, a total of 46,300 former servicemen.

Mr. McNamara's action and the Joint Chiefs' response were only a foretaste of the struggle to come as a result of the Tet offensive, the Pentagon study says, since General Westmoreland was preparing to raise his sights with the full support of the Joint Chiefs.

On Feb. 14, President Johnson went to Fort Bragg, N. C., to say good-by to the brigade of the 82d Airborne going to South Vietnam. The Pentagon narrative recalls the scene:

"The experience proved for him to be one of the most profoundly moving and troubling of the entire Vietnam war. The men, many of whom had only recently returned from Vietnam, were grim. They were not young men going off to adventure but seasoned veterans returning to an ugly conflict from which they knew some would not return. The film clips of the President shaking hands with the solemn but determined paratroopers on the ramps of their aircraft revealed a deeply troubled leader. He was confronting the men he was asking to make the sacrifice and they displayed no enthusiasm. It may well be that the dramatic decisions of the succeeding month and a half that reversed the direction of American policy in the war had their genesis in those troubled handshakes."

"A Fork in the Road"

In late February, the President sent General Wheeler to Saigon to consult with General Westmoreland on precisely how many more men he wanted. General Wheeler returned on Feb. 28 and immediately delivered a written report to the President. The report began by saying that General Westmoreland had frustrated the enemy's objective of provoking a general uprising. But it went on to say that the offensive had been "a very near thing" for the allies and then ranged in bleak fashion over the situation in Vietnam:

Despite 40,000 killed, at least 3,000 captured and perhaps 5,000 disabled or dead of wounds, the North Vietnamese and the Vietcong now had the initiative. They were "operating with relative freedom in the countryside" and had driven the Saigon Government forces back into a "defensive posture around towns and cities." The pacification program "in many places . . . has been set back badly." To hold the northernmost provinces, General Westmoreland had been forced to send half of his American maneuver battalions there, "stripping the rest of the country of adequate reserves" and robbing himself of "an offensive capability. [See Document #132.]

"Under these circumstances," General Wheeler warned, "we must be prepared to accept some reverses."

However, once the enemy offensive is decisively defeated, General Wheeler said, "the situation over all will be greatly improved over the pre-Tet condition." But to accomplish this and to "regain the initiative through offensive operations," General Westmoreland would require more men.

The 500,000 soldiers then in South Vietnam and the 25,000 others who had been approved for eventual deployment under the ceiling established in the summer of 1967 were now "inadequate in numbers," General Wheeler said.

"To contend with, and defeat the new enemy threat," he continued, General Westmoreland "has stated requirements for forces over the 525,00 ceiling. . . . The add-on requested totals 206,756 spaces for a new proposed ceiling of 731,756." All of the additional 206,756 soldiers were to be in the war zone by the end of 1968. General Westmoreland wanted roughly half of them, the study notes, as early as May 1.

"Principal forces included in the add-on are three division equivalents, 15 tactical fighter squadrons and augmentation for current Navy programs," General Wheeler explained.

To provide this many troops by the end of the year, the President would have had to call up from civilian life 280,000 military reservists to replenish the strategic reserve in the United States and to sustain the units newly sent to Vietnam.

"A fork in the road had been reached," the Pentagon study comments. "Now the alternatives stood out in stark reality. To accept and meet General Wheeler's request for troops would mean a total U.S. military commitment to SVN [South Vietnam]—an Americanization of the war, a call-up of reserve forces, vastly increased expenditures. To deny the request for troops, or to attempt to again cut it to a size which could be sustained by the thinly stretched active forces, would just as surely signify that an upper limit to the U.S. military commitment in SVN had been reached."

The issue was immediately joined at the highest level of the Pentagon.

Clark M. Clifford, an old friend and adviser of President Johnson and an unwavering supporter of his Vietnam policy, had been designated to succeed Mr. McNamara as Secretary of Defense. He was not to be sworn in until March 1, but had begun to work at his job many days earlier. On Feb. 28, when the Wheeler-Westmoreland report was delivered, the President asked Mr. Clifford to gather a senior group of advisers for a complete review of United States policy in Vietnam.

The next day, Mr. Clifford convened what came to be known as the Clifford Group. The principals were Mr. McNamara; Gen. Maxwell D. Taylor, President Johnson's personal military adviser, as he had been President Kennedy's; Paul H. Nitze, Deputy Secretary of Defense; Henry H. Fowler, Secretary of the Treasury; Nicholas deB. Katzenbach, Under Secretary of State; Walt W. Rostow, the President's adviser on national security; Richard Helms, Director of Central Intelligence; William P. Bundy, Assistant Secretary of State for Far Eastern Affairs; Mr. Warnke, the head of the Pentagon's politico-military policy office, International Security Affairs, and Philip C. Habib, Mr. Bundy's deputy.

At the first meeting of the group, the Pentagon Study says, Mr. Clifford said that the real problem was "not whether we should send 200,000 additional troops to Vietnam," but whether if "we follow the present course in SVN, could it ever prove successful even if vastly more than 200,000 troops were sent?"

Mr. Clifford stipulated that the various papers he assigned on United States strategy should consider four options, ranging from granting General Westmoreland's full request to sending him no additional troops.

"The work [of drafting papers] became so intensive," the study states, "that it was carried out in teams within . . . International Security Affairs."

The dominant voice in the consideration of alternatives was the civilian hierarchy in the Pentagon. And the most influential force there, according to the study, was Mr. Warnke, whose young civilian assistants, including Morton H. Halperin and Richard C. Steadman, had become disenchanted with Vietnam policy since 1967 and were now among the leading dissenters in the Administration. The posi-

tion of the dissenters was strengthened by intelligence estimates from the C.I.A., which submitted papers to the
working group.

The most important of these, submitted on March 1,
suggested strongly that the most likely prospect for the future
—under any course of proposed action—was more stalemate.
These, as quoted in the Pentagon study, were the answers
it gave to questions by Mr. Clifford:

> Q. What is the likely course of events in South
> Vietnam over the next 10 months, assuming no
> change in U.S. policy or force levels?
> A. . . . It is manifestly impossible for the Com-
> munists to drive U.S. forces out of the country. It is
> equally out of the question for U.S./GVN forces to
> clear South Vietnam of Communist forces.
> Q. What is the likely N.V.A./VC [North Vietna-
> mese Army/Vietcong] strategy over the next 10
> months if U.S. forces are increased by 50,000,
> by 100,000 or by 200,000?
> A. We would expect the Communists to continue
> the war. They still have resources available in North
> Vietnam and within South Vietnam to increase their
> troop strength. . . . Over a 10-month period the Com-
> munists would probably be able to introduce sufficient
> new units into the South to offset the U.S. maneuver
> battalion increments of the various force levels given
> above.
> Q. What is the Communist attitude toward negotia-
> tions: in particular how would Hanoi deal with an
> unconditional cessation of U.S. bombing of NVN and
> what would be its terms for a settlement?
> A. The Communists probably still expect the war
> to end eventually in some form of negotiations . . .
> they are not likely to give any serious considerations
> to negotiations until this campaign has progressed far
> enough for its results to be fairly clear.

If the United States ceased the bombing of North
Vietnam in the near future, the C.I.A. believed, Hanoi would
probably respond to an offer to negotiate, although the
intelligence agency warned that the North Vietnamese would
not modify their terms for a final settlement or stop fighting
in the South.

"In any talks, Communist terms would involve the

establishment of a new 'coalition' government," the C.I.A.
said, "which would in fact, if not in appearance, be under
the domination of the Communists. Secondly, they would
insist on a guaranteed withdrawal of U.S. forces within some
precisely defined period. . . ."

General Taylor wrote a long memorandum that went not
only to the Clifford Group but also directly to the White
House. The general was opposed to any basic change in
policy.

"We should consider changing the objective which we
have been pursuing consistently since 1954 only for the most
cogent reasons," he wrote. "There is clearly nothing to recommend trying to do more than we are now doing at such
great cost. To undertake to do less is to accept needlessly a
serious defeat for which we would pay dearly in terms of
our worldwide position of leadership, of the political stability
of Southeast Asia and of the credibility of our pledges to
friends and allies."

General Taylor recommended against any initiative for
negotiations that might involve a halt in bombing. To this
end he proposed the withdrawal of the so-called San Antonio
formula, enunciated by President Johnson the previous
September, under which the United States would stop the
bombing of North Vietnam if Hanoi promised "prompt and
productive" talks and agreed to "not take advantage" of a
bombing cessation in a military way. The general argued
against "any thought of reducing the bombing."

Although he did not advocate any specific reinforcements
for General Westmoreland, General Taylor recommended a
build-up of the strategic reserve in the United States, thereby
by aligning himself with the Joint Chiefs.

The Pentagon's Office of Systems Analysis, headed by
Dr. Alain C. Enthoven, said in a paper that "the offensive
appears to have killed the [pacification] program once and
for all." In another paper, Assistant Secretary of Defense
Enthoven painted what the study calls "a bleak picture of
American failure in Vietnam."

"While we have raised the price to NVN of aggression and
support of the VC," the paper said, "it shows no lack of
capability or will to match each new U.S. escalation. Our
strategy of 'attrition' has not worked. Adding 206,000 more
U.S. men to a force of 525,000, gaining only 27 additional
maneuver battalions and 270 tactical fighters at an added
cost to the U.S. of $10-billion per year raises the question
of who is making it costly for whom. . . .

"We know that despite a massive influx of 500,000 U.S. troops, 1.2 million tons of bombs a year, 400,000 attack sorties per year, 200,000 enemy K.I.A. [killed in action] in three years, 20,000 U.S. K.I.A., etc., our control of the countryside and the defense of the urban areas is now essentially at pre-August 1965 levels. We have achieved stalemate at a high commitment. A new strategy must be sought."

The paper concluded that a shift to a military strategy of having the United States forces protect population centers in South Vietnam, rather than ranging the countryside on search-and-destroy operations, would, if unchallenged by the enemy, stabilize American casualty rates.

The Battle at Home

By the end of the first meeting on Feb. 29, the Clifford Group had produced an initial draft memorandum for the President. It began with a pessimistic appraisal, expressing doubt that the South Vietnamese Army "as currently led, motivated and influenced at the top," would buckle down to the job of pacifiying the countryside, or that the Saigon Government "will rise to the challenge" and "move toward a government of national union."

"Even with the 200,000 additional troops" requested by General Westmoreland, the draft memorandum said, "we will not be in a position to drive the enemy from SVN or to destroy his forces," since Hanoi had always been able to maintain from its reserve a ratio of one combat battalion to 1.5 American combat battalions. A North Vietnamese combat battalion has some 300 men and an American combat battalion has about 700 men.

If further escalation occurred, the draft went on, "it will be difficult to convince critics that we are not simply destroying South Vietnam in order to 'save' it and that we genuinely want peace talks." It added: "This growing disaffection accompanied, as it certainly will be, by increased defiance of the draft and growing unrest in the cities because of the belief that we are neglecting domestic problems, runs great risks of provoking a domestic crisis of unprecedented proportions."

The memorandum concluded that the United States presence in South Vietnam should be used "to buy the time" during which the South Vietnamese Army and Government "can develop effective capability." Therefore, the Clifford Group said, General Westmoreland should be told that his mission was to provide security to populated areas—along what the memorandum called "the demographic frontier." He should also be told that he was not to wage a war of attrition against enemy forces or seek to drive them out of the country.

This initial draft was discussed with military leaders in Mr. Clifford's office on March 1. The meeting started an intense battle that went on for the next three weeks, the study says.

"General Wheeler . . . was appalled at the apparent repudiations of American military policy in South Vietnam contained in the I.S.A. draft memorandum," the analyst writes. "He detected two 'fatal' flaws in the population-security strategy" similar to the flaws found by the military in the defensive "enclave strategy" that some had advocated in 1966.

The flaws, the Pentagon account says, were that "the proposed strategy would mean increased fighting in or close to the population centers and, hence, would result in increased civilian casualties," and that "by adopting a posture of static defense, we would allow the enemy an increased capability of massing near population centers, especially north of Saigon."

At a formal meeting on March 3, Mr. Warnke read the initial draft of the memorandum to the entire Clifford Group. "The ensuing discussion," the study says, "apparently produced a consensus that abandoning the initiative completely as the draft memo seemed to imply could leave allied forces and the South Vietnamese cities themselves more, not less, vulnerable."

There was also a sharp division on the bombing of North Vietnam. The initial draft recommended no bombing above present levels, and opposed proposals by the military to bomb closer to the centers of Hanoi and Haiphong as "likely to be unproductive or worse."

At the March 3 meeting, General Wheeler advocated an extension of the bombing again, rather than a cutback, while Mr. Warnke fought against expansion of the air war, the study asserts.

Finally, Mr. Warnke and Phil G. Goulding, Assistant Secretary of Defense for Public Affairs, were directed to write a new draft that would deal only with the troop issue, recommending a modest increase; call for "a study" of new strategic guidance to General Westmoreland, advise against a new initiative on negotiations and acknowledge the split on the air war.

The new paper, a draft Presidential memorandum intended for Mr. Johnson's approval as doctrine, was completed the next day, March 4. "Gone was any discussion of grand strategy," the study says. As it finally went to the White House, the memorandum made these recommendations:

• Deployment of 22,000 more troops, of whom 60 per cent would be combat soldiers.

• Reservation of a decision to deploy the remaining 185,000 men requested by General Westmoreland, contingent upon a week-by-week examination of the situation.

• Approval of a reserve call-up of approximately 262,000 men, increased draft calls and extension of terms of service.

• No new peace initiative.

• A general decision on bombing policy, which the Clifford Group had not been able to reach. "Here," the memorandum said, "your advisers are divided: a. General Wheeler and others would advocate a substantial extension of targets and authority in and near Hanoi and Haiphong, mining of Haiphong, and naval gunfire up to a Chinese buffer zone; b. Others would advocate a seasonal step-up through the spring, but without these added elements."

The analyst notes that both sides of the bombing argument in the memorandum were "devoted to various kinds of escalation."

"The proposal that was eventually to be adopted [by the President at the end of March], namely cutting back the bombing to the panhandle only, was not even mentioned, nor does it appear in any of the other drafts or papers related to the Clifford Group's work," the study notes. The Chairman of the Joint Chiefs and Secretary Clifford, the account emphasizes, "differed only on the extent to which the bombing campaign against North Vietnam should be intensified."

The study speculates at this point on why a cutback in bombing to the 20th Parallel was not mentioned in any of these documents.

The omission may be "misleading," the narrative says, since the cutback "apparently was one of the principal ideas being discussed and considered in the forums at various levels."

"It is hard to second-guess the motivation of a Secretary

of Defense," the study continues, "but, since it is widely believed that Clifford personally advocated this idea to the President, he may well have decided that . . . to have raised the idea of constricting the bombing below the 19th or 20th Parallel in the memo to the President would have generalized the knowledge of such a suggestion and invited its sharp, full and formal criticism by the J.C.S. and other opponents of a bombing halt. Whatever Clifford's reasons, the memo did not contain the proposal that was to be the main focus of the continuing debates in March and would eventually be endorsed by the President."

"Faced with a fork in the road of our Vietnam policy," the study concludes, "the working group failed to seize the opportunity to change directions. Indeed, they seemed to recommend that we continue rather haltingly down the same road, meanwhile consulting the map more frequently and in greater detail to insure that we were still on the right road."

The President asked that the memorandum be sent to General Westmoreland for his views, since the recommendations, as the analyst says, "were a long way down the road in meeting [his] request."

In his reply on March 8 the general welcomed the additional 22,000 men proposed as a first increment, but told Mr. Johnson in a cablegram that he stuck by his request for the full 206,756-man reinforcement by the end of 1968.

Mounting Pressure

The documentary record for the final rounds of the internal policy debate now "becomes sparse," the Pentagon study remarks, because the discussion was "carried forward on a personal basis by the officials involved, primarily, the Secretary of Defense and the Secretary of State."

"The decision, however," the account goes on, "had been placed squarely on the shoulders of the President. . . . The memorandum had recommended 'a little bit more of the same' to stabilize the military situation, plus a level of mobilization in order to be prepared to meet any further deterioration in the ground situation. . . .

"But many political events in the first few weeks of March, 1968, gave strong indications that the country was becoming increasingly divided over and disenchanted with the current

Vietnam strategy, and would no longer settle for 'more of the same.' "

The internal maneuvering revolved around the cutback in the bombing, first proposed, without result, by Secretary McNamara in October, 1966.

"The first appearance of the idea in the documents in March," the study says, came in a circuitous and seemingly casual way from Secretary of State Dean Rusk, who, as far as the record shows, had given no support to a cutback in bombing when it was proposed in 1967.

But now in a note to General Wheeler on March 5, Secretary Clifford wrote that he was "transmitting for the latter's exclusive 'information' a proposed 'statement' drafted by Secretary Rusk," the study says.

"The statement, which was given only the status of a 'suggestion' and therefore needed to be closely held," the study continues, "announced the suspension of the bombing of North Vietnam except 'in the area associated with the battle zone.' It was presumably intended for Presidential delivery.

"Attached to the draft statement, which shows Rusk himself as the draftee, was a list of explanatory reasons and conditions for its adoption. Rusk noted that bad weather in northern North Vietnam in the next few months would severely hamper operations around Hanoi and Haiphong in any event and the proposal did not, therefore, constitute a serious degradation of our military position. It was to be understood that in the event of any major enemy initiative in the South, either against Khesanh or the cities, the bombing would be resumed.

"Further, Rusk did not want a major diplomatic effort mounted to start peace talks. He preferred to let the action speak for itself and await Hanoi's reaction.

"Finally, he noted that the area still open to bombing would include everything up to and including Vinh (just below 19 degrees) and there would be no limitations on attacks in that zone."

Mr. Rusk was thus suggesting the 19th Parallel as the cutoff point for bombing. Both the 19th and the 20th Parallels had figured in the discussions in 1967.

"Clifford's views of the proposal and its explanation do not appear in his note," the study remarks. "It can be inferred, however, that he endorsed the idea. In any case, by the middle of March the question of a partial bombing halt became the dominant air-war alternative under consideration in meetings at State and Defense. It is possible that the President had already indicated to Clifford and Rusk enough approval of the idea to have focused the further deliberative effort of his key advisers on it."

Aware that a Presidential decision was in the making, the advocates of all-out bombing pressed their views. On March 4, Dr. Harold Brown, the Secretary of the Air Force, sent to Deputy Secretary of Defense Nitze a memorandum setting forth three options for a step-up. The first was intensification of the bombing of "remaining important targets" in North Vietnam, and "neutralization of the port of Haiphong by bombing and mining." The second was intensification of air raids in the "adjoining panhandle areas" of Laos and North Vietnam. The third involved increased air attacks in the South as a substitute for additional ground forces.

Mr. Brown made plain his preference for the first option, which he said would "permit bombing of military targets without the present scrupulous concern for collateral civilian damage and casualties." His objective was "to erode the will of the population by exposing a wider area of NVN to casualties and destruction."

In evaluating the effect of such a campaign, however, Mr. Brown "was forced to admit," the study says, that it would not "be likely to reduce NVN capability in SVN substantially below the 1967 level," and that North Vietnam would probably "be willing to undergo these hardships."

The study comments that Dr. Brown's proposals, while indicating military thinking, "were never considered as major proposals within the inner circle of Presidential advisers."

Among other major advisers, the analyst reports, Under Secretary of State Katzenbach opposed a partial suspension of the bombing "because he felt that a bombing halt was a trump card that could be only used once and should not be wasted when the prospects for a positive North Vietnamese response on negotiations seemed so poor. He reportedly hoped to convince the President to call a complete halt to the air war later in the spring when prospects for peace looked better and when the threat to [the Marine outpost at] Khesanh had been eliminated."

Mr. Rostow, the analyst continues, apparently resisted all suggestions for a restriction of the bombing, preferring to keep the pressure on the North Vietnamese for a response to the San Antonio formula."

Public pressure now began to mount on the President as speculation grew that he was considering further escalation in Vietnam.

On March 7, Senate debate on civil rights was interrupted as several prominent Senators demanded that Congress be consulted before any decision was made on troop increases.

On March 10, The New York Times published the first report, from Washington, about General Westmoreland's request for 206,000 troops. "The President was reportedly furious at this leak," the Pentagon study says. The publication of the troop-request figure provided a "focus" for political debate and intensified the "sense of [public] dissatisfaction," the study adds.

The next day, Secretary Rusk appeared before the Senate Foreign Relations committee, ostensibly to testify on foreign aid. But the televised hearings turned into a two-day grilling of the Secretary on Vietnam policy. He confirmed that an "A to Z" policy review was being held, but refused to discuss possible troop increases. He said it would "not be right for me to speculate about numbers of possibilities while the President is consulting his advisers."

Not long after the conclusion of the second day's hearings, the returns from the Democratic primary in New Hampshire began coming in. Senator Eugene J. McCarthy of Minnesota —the Pentagon historian terms him an "upstart challenger" for the Presidency—who had campaigned against President Johnson's war policy and demanded a halt to the bombing, was only narrowly beaten by Mr. Johnson. In fact, when the write-in vote was finally tabulated, Mr. McCarthy had a slight plurality over the President.

In one of the study's few discussions of domestic politics, the analyst declares: "It was clear that Lyndon Johnson, the master politician, had been successfully challenged, not by an attractive and appealing vote-getter, but by a candidate who had been able to mobilize and focus all the discontent and disillusionment about the war."

At a White House meeting on March 13, the President decided that, in addition to the 10,500-man emergency reinforcement already made, 30,000 more soldiers should be deployed to South Vietnam, an increase over the 22,000 men recommended by the Clifford Group. There would be two reserve call-ups to meet and sustain these deployments, one in March and one in May. The first would support the 30,000 deployment; the second would reconstitute the strategic reserve at seven active Army divisions.

Secretary of the Army Stanley R. Resor demurred, arguing that no reserve call-up had been provided to sustain the 10,500 deployed by Secretary McNamara in February. He urged that 13,500 more be called up for this purpose. This plan was approved by the President.

The troop deployment plan agreed upon brought the new ceiling to 579,000 men. To meet these requirements and fill out the strategic reserve, there would be a total reserve call-up of 98,451 men.

But in the fast-moving pace of the internal struggle over Vietnam policy, even this plan would soon be abandoned. "The President was troubled," the study declares. "In public he continued to indicate firmness and resoluteness, but press leaks and continued public criticism continued to compound his problem."

On March 16, Senator Robert F. Kennedy announced that he would seek the Democratic nomination for the Presidency.

On March 17, The New York Times, in a dispatch from Washington that the Pentagon study terms "again amazingly accurate," reported that the President would approve sending 35,000 to 50,000 more men to South Vietnam during the next six months.

The next day, in the House of Representatives, 139 members—98 Republicans and 41 Democrats—sponsored a resolution calling for an immediate Congressional review of policy in Southeast Asia.

That same day, in a speech at the convention of the National Farmers Union in Minneapolis, President Johnson said that Hanoi was seeking to "win something in Washington that they can't win in Hue, in the I Corps or in Khesanh." He pledged not to "tuck our tail and violate our commitments."

"Those of you who think that you can save lives by moving the battlefield in from the mountains to the cities where the people live have another think coming," he said.

Despite this explosion against his critics, there were indications—some public, some known only to insiders—that the President was weighing what the critics had been saying and was also pondering the mood of the country.

On March 20, for example, he had a meeting—now a matter of public record but not dealt with in the Pentagon study—with Arthur J. Goldberg in the White House. Only five days earlier, Mr. Goldberg, the United States representative at the United Nations, had sent a memorandum to Mr. Johnson recommending a halt in the bombing. It had infuriated the President. The next day, at a meeting with his advisers, Mr. Johnson was quoted by the press as having said: "Let's get one thing clear. I'm telling you now I am not going to stop the bombing. Now is there anybody here who doesn't understand that?"

But now he asked Mr. Goldberg to go through his arguments once more, and when Mr. Goldberg had finished, the President asked him to join a meeting on March 25 of his Senior Informal Advisory Group—familiarly known in Washington as the Wise Men.

Then suddenly, on March 22, the President recalled General Westmoreland and announced that he would become Chief of Staff of the Army. The transfer of General Westmoreland, the Pentagon analyst says, was a signal that the President had decided against any major escalation of the ground war.

On March 25, Gen. Creighton W. Abrams, General Westmoreland's deputy, flew to Washington unannounced. The next day he and the President were closeted, and—the Pentagon study speculates—"Mr. Johnson probably informed him of his intentions, both with respect to force augmentations and the bombing restraint, and his intention to designate Abrams" as General Westmoreland's successor.

Precisely when the President decided to reduce the bombing, the Pentagon study does not say. But it inclines to the view that, if he was still wavering at this time, the decisive advice was given by the Wise Men, who assembled in Washington on March 25 and 26.

The members of the Senior Informal Advisory Group had served in high Government posts or had been Presidential advisers during the last 20 years. They gathered at the State Department on March 25, six days before the President was due to address the nation on television.

Those present were Dean Acheson, Secretary of State under President Harry S. Truman; George W. Ball, Under Secretary of State in the Kennedy and Johnson Administrations, now in private business; General of the Army Omar N. Bradley, World War II commander and later Chairman of the Joint Chiefs; McGeorge Bundy, special assistant for national security under Presidents Kennedy and Johnson, now president of the Ford Foundation; Arthur H. Dean, lawyer and negotiator of the armstice in Korea, and Douglas Dillon, banker, Under Secretary of State under President Eisenhower and Secretary of the Treasury under Presidents Kennedy and Johnson.

Also present were Associate Justice Abe Fortas of the Supreme Court; Mr. Goldberg; Henry Cabot Lodge, twice Ambassador to South Vietnam and former representative at the United Nations; John J. McCloy, High Commissioner in West Germany under President Truman; Robert D. Murphy, a top-ranking career diplomat, now in private business; General Taylor; Gen. Matthew B. Ridgway, retired commander in the Korean war, and Cyrus R. Vance, former Deputy Secretary of Defense and trouble shooter for President Johnson.

With the exception of Mr. Ball and Mr. Goldberg, all had been accounted hawks. Only the previous fall, with Mr. Clifford then a participant, they had approved the President's escalation of the air war.

The Pentagon study does not give a version of the discussions over the two days, but simply reprints verbatim the first public account of the meetings, by Stuart H. Loory of The Los Angeles Times, published late in May, which the study says "has been generally considered to be a reliable account."

That dispatch told how the turnabout on the war by most of the Wise Men left the President "deeply shaken."

Nor does the Pentagon account relate the story—now well known—of how the drafts of the President's March 31 speech, at the hands of Harry C. McPherson, who had become a doubter of war policy, grew progressively less hawkish almost up to the hour when Mr. Johnson spoke on television.

What is new in the Pentagon account is a cablegram from the State Department that was sent the night before the speech to the United States Ambassadors in Australia, New Zealand, Thailand, Laos, the Philippines and South Korea. It instructed them to inform the heads of governments in those countries that the President's speech would include announcement of a bombing cutback.

The cablegram also instructed the ambassadors to "make clear that Hanoi is most likely to denounce the project and thus free our hand after a short period." [See Document #134.]

The analyst comments that it is "significant" that the cablegram reflected Secretary Rusk's draft statement on March 5.

"It is important to note that the Administration did not expect the bombing restraint to produce a positive Hanoi reply," the study comments. "The fact that the President was willing to go beyond the San Antonio formula and curtail the air raids at a time when few responsible advisers were suggesting that such action would produce peace talks is strong evidence of the major shift in thinking that took place in Washington about the war and the bombing after Tet, 1968."

In his speech, the President did not specifically set the bombing limit at the 20th Parallel. This had been altered in a final draft. Instead, he said:

"Tonight I have ordered our aircraft and our naval vessels to make no attacks on North Vietnam, except in the area north of the demilitarized zone where the continuing enemy build-up directly threatens allied forward positions and where the movements of their troops and supplies are clearly related to that threat.

"The area in which we are stopping our attacks includes almost 90 per cent of North Vietnam's population, and most of its territory. Thus there will be no attacks around the principal populated areas, or in the food-producing areas of North Vietnam."

In the excitement over the bombing restrictions and his astonishing epilogue—"I shall not seek, and I will not accept the nomination of my party"—little attention was paid to his announcement of a token troop increase—13,500 support troops for the 10,500 February emergency contingent. Only those privy to the internal debate would realize that the President had reversed his decision of two weeks earlier to send 30,000 more men.

"None of the some 200,000 troops requested by General Westmoreland on 27 February were to be deployed," the Pentagon study says, underscoring the turn that policy had taken.

Contrary to the expectations of the policy makers, Hanoi responded positively to the offer of negotiations. On April 3, President Johnson announced that North Vietnam had declared readiness for its representatives to meet with those of the United States.

In an epilogue to the narrative of the events of February and March, the study sums up the lesson of the Tet offensive, which, the analyst believes, imposed itself finally upon President Johnson and led him to accept the view of those civilian advisers and the intelligence community that he had so long resisted in his search for "victory." The analyst writes:

"In March of 1968, the choice had become clear cut. The price for military victory had increased vastly, and there was no assurance that it would not grow again in the future. There were also strong indications that large and growing elements of the American public had begun to believe the cost had already reached unacceptable levels and would strongly protest a large increase in that cost.

"The political reality which faced President Johnson was

that 'more of the same' in South Vietnam, with an increased commitment of American lives and money and its consequent impact on the country, accompanied by no guarantee of military victory in the near future, had become unacceptable to these elements of the American public. The optimistic military reports of progress in the war no longer rang true after the shock of the Tet offensive.

"Thus, the President's decision to seek a new strategy and a new road to peace was based upon two major considerations:

"(1) The conviction of his principal civilian advisers, particularly Secretary of Defense Clifford, that the troops requested by General Westmoreland would not make a military victory any more likely; and

"(2) A deeply felt conviction of the need to restore unity to the American nation."

KEY DOCUMENTS

Following are texts of key documents accompanying the Pentagon's study of the Vietnam war, covering the period in early 1968 surrounding the Vietcong's Tet offensive. Except where excerpting is specified, the documents are printed verbatim, with only unmistakable typographical errors corrected.

131

Adm. Sharp's Progress Report on War at End of 1967

Excerpts from cablegram from Adm. U. S. Grant Sharp, commander in chief of Pacific forces, to the Joint Chiefs of Staff, dated Jan. 1, 1968, and headed "Year-End Wrap-Up Cable," as provided in the body of the Pentagon study. Paragraphs in italics are the study's paraphrase or explanation.

Admiral Sharp outlined three objectives which the air campaign was seeking to achieve: disruption of the flow of external assistance into North Vietnam, curtailment of the flow of supplies from North Vietnam into Laos and South Vietnam, and destruction "in depth" of North Vietnamese resources that contributed to the support of the war. Acknowledging that the flow of fraternal communist aid into the North had grown every year of the war, CINCPAC noted the stepped up effort in 1967 to neutralize this assistance by logistically isolating its primary port of entry—Haiphong. The net results, he felt, had been encouraging:

The overall effect of our effort to reduce external assistance has resulted not only in destruction and damage to the transportation systems and goods being transported thereon but has created additional management, distribution and manpower problems. In addition, the attacks have created a bottleneck at Haiphong where inability effectively to move goods inland from the port has resulted in congestion on the docks and a slowdown in offloading ships as they arrive. By October, road and rail interdictions had reduced the transportation clearance capacity at Haiphong to about 2700 short tons per day. An average of 4400 short tons per day had arrived in Haiphong during the year.

The assault against the continuing traffic of men and material through North Vietnam toward Laos and South Vietnam, however, had produced only marginal results. Success here was measured in the totals of destroyed transport, not the constriction of the flow of personnel and goods.

Although men and material needed for the level of combat now prevailing in South Vietnam continue to flow despite our attacks on LOCs, we have made it very costly to the enemy in terms of material, manpower, management, and distribution. From 1 January through 15 December 1967, 122,960 attack sorties were flown in Rolling Thunder route packages I through V and in Laos, SEA Dragon offensive operations involved 1,384 ship-days on station and contributed materially in reducing enemy seaborne infiltration in southern NVN and in the vicinity of the DMZ. Attacks against the NVN transport system during the past 12 months resulted in destruction of carriers, cargo carried, and personnel casualties. Air attacks throughout North Vietnam and Laos destroyed or damaged 5,261 motor vehicles, 2,475 railroad rolling stock, and 11,425 watercraft from 1 January through 20 December 1967. SEA DRAGON accounted for another 1,473 WBLC destroyed or damaged from 1 January–30 November. There were destroyed rail-lines, bridges, ferries, railroad yards and shops, storage areas, and truck parks. Some 3,685 land targets were struck by Sea Dragon forces, including the destruction or damage of 303 coastal defense and radar sites. Through external assistance, the enemy has been able to replace or rehabilitate many of the items damaged or destroyed, and transport inventories are roughly at the same level they were at the beginning of the year. Nevertheless, construction problems have caused interruptions in the flow of men and supplies, caused a great loss of work-hours, and restricted movement particularly during daylight hours.

The admission that transport inventories were the same at year's end as when it began must have been a painful one indeed for CINCPAC in view of the enormous cost of the air campaign against the transport system in money, aircraft, and lives. As a consolation for this signal failure, CINCPAC pointed to the extensive diversion of civilian manpower to war related activities as a result of the bombing.

A primary effect of our efforts to impede movement of the enemy has been to force Hanoi to engage from 500,000 to 600,000 civilians in full-time and part-time war-related activities, in particular for air defense and repair of the LOCs. This diversion of manpower from other pursuits, particularly from the agricultural sector, has caused a drawdown on manpower. The estimated lower food production yields, coupled with an increase in food imports in 1967 (some six times that of 1966), indicate that agriculture is having great difficulty in adjusting to this changed composition of the work force. The cost and difficulties of the war to Hanoi have sharply increased, and only through the willingness of other communist countries to provide maximum replacement of goods and material has NVN managed to sustain its war effort.

To these manpower diversions CINCPAC added the cost to North Vietnam in 1967 of the destruction of vital resources—the third of his air war objectives:

C. Destroying vital resources:

Air attacks were authorized and executed by target systems for the first time in 1967, although the attacks were limited to specific targets within each system. A total of 9,740 sorties was flown against targets on the ROLLING THUNDER target list from 1 January–15 December 1967. The campaign against the power system resulted in reduction of power generating capability to approximately 15 percent of original capacity. Successful strikes against the Thau Nguyen iron and steel plant and the Haiphong cement plant resulted in practically total destruction of these two installations. NVN adjustments to these losses have had to be made by relying on additional imports from China, the USSR or the Eastern European countries. The requirement for additional imports reduces available shipping space for war supporting supplies and adds to the congestion at the ports. Interruptions in raw material supplies and the requirement to turn to less efficient means of power and distribution has degraded overall production.

Economic losses to North Vietnam amounted to more than $130 million dollars in 1967, representing over one-half of the total economic losses since the war began.

132

Wheeler's '68 Report to Johnson after the Tet Offensive

Excerpts from memorandum from Gen. Earle G. Wheeler to President Johnson, dated Feb. 27, 1968, and headed "Report of Chairman, J.C.S., on Situation in Vietnam and MACV Requirements."

1. The Chairman, JCS and party visited SVN on 23, 24 and 25 February. This report summarizes the impressions and facts developed through conversations and briefings at MACV and with senior commanders throughout the country.

2. SUMMARY

—The current situation in Vietnam is still developing and fraught with opportunities as well as dangers.

—There is no question in the mind of MACV that the enemy went all out for a general offensive and general uprising and ap-

parently believed that he would succeed in bringing the wa
to an early successful conclusion.

—The enemy failed to achieve his initial objective but is con
tinuing his effort. Although many of his units were badly hur
the judgement is that he has the will and the capability to con
tinue.

—Enemy losses have been heavy; he has failed to achieve hi
prime objectives of mass uprisings and capture of a large numbe
of the capital cities and towns. Morale in enemy units which wer
badly mauled or where the men were oversold the idea of
decisive victory at TET probably has suffered severely. How
ever, with replacements, his indoctrination system would seen
capable of maintaining morale at a generally adequate leve
His determination appears to be unshaken.

—The enemy is operating with relative freedom in the country
side, probably recruiting heavily and no doubt infiltrating NV
units and personnel. His recovery is likely to be rapid; his sup
plies are adequate; and he is trying to maintain the momentur
of his winter-spring offensive.

—The structure of the GVN held up but its effectiveness ha
suffered.

—The RVNAF held up against the initial assault with gratify
ing, and in a way, surprising strength and fortitude. However
RVNAF is now in a defensive posture around towns and citie
and there is concern about how well they will bear up unde
sustained pressure.

—The initial attack nearly succeeded in a dozen places, an
defeat in those places was only averted by the timely reaction o
U.S. forces. In short, it was a very near thing.

—There is no doubt that the RD Program has suffered a sever
set back.

—RVNAF was not badly hurt physically—they should recove
strength and equipment rather quickly (equipment in 2-3 month
—strength in 3-6 months). Their problems are more psychologica
than physical.

—U.S. forces have lost none of their pre-TET capability.

—MACV has three principal problems. First, logistic suppor
north of Danang is marginal owing to weather, enemy interdiction
and harassment and the massive deployment of U.S. forces int
the DMZ/Hue area. Opening Route 1 will alleviate this problem
but takes a substantial troop commitment. Second, the defensiv
posture of ARVN is permitting the VC to make rapid inroad
in the formerly pacified countryside. ARVN, in its own words, i
in a dilemma as it cannot afford another enemy thrust into th
cities and towns and yet if it remains in a defensive postur
against this contingency, the countryside goes by default. MAC
is forced to devote much of its troop strength to this problem
Third MACV has been forced to deploy 50% of all U.S. maneuve
battalions into I Corps, to meet the threat there, while strippin
the rest of the country of adequate reserves. If the enemy syn

616

hronizes an attack against Khe Sanh/Hue-Quang Tri with an offensive in the Highlands and around Saigon while keeping the pressure on throughout the remainder of the country, MACV will be hard pressed to meet adequately all threats. Under these circumstances, we must be prepared to accept some reverses.

—For these reasons, General Westmoreland has asked for a 3 division-15 tactical fighter squadron force. This force would provide him with a theater reserve and an offensive capability which he does not now have.

3. THE SITUATION AS IT STANDS TODAY:

a. Enemy capabilities.

(1) The enemy has been hurt badly in the populated lowlands, is practically intact elsewhere. He committed over 67,000 combat maneuver forces plus perhaps 25% or 17,000 more impressed men and boys, for a total of about 84,000. He lost 40,000 killed, at least 3,000 captured, and perhaps 5,000 disabled or died of wounds. He had peaked his force total to about 240,000 just before TET, by hard recruiting, infiltration, civilian impressment, and drawdowns on service and guerrilla personnel. So he has lost about one fifth of his total strength. About two-thirds of his trained, organized unit strength can continue offensive action. He is probably infiltrating and recruiting heavily in the countryside while allied forces are securing the urban areas. (Discussions of strengths and recruiting are in paragraphs 1, 2 and 3 of Enclosure (1)). The enemy has adequate munitions, stockpiled in-country and available through the DMZ, Laos, and Cambodia, to support major attacks and countrywide pressure; food procurement may be a problem. (Discussion is in paragraph 6 Enclosure (1)). Besides strength losses, the enemy now has morale and training problems which currently limit combat effectiveness of VC guerrilla, main and local forces. (Discussions of forces are in paragraphs 2, 5, Enclosure (1)).

(a) I Corps Tactical Zone: Strong enemy forces in the northern two provinces threaten Quanq Tri and Hue cities, and U.S. positions at the DMZ. Two NVA divisions threaten Khe Sanh. Eight enemy battalion equivalents are in the Danang-Hoi An area. Enemy losses in I CTZ have been heavy, with about 13,000 killed; some NVA as well as VC units have been hurt badly. However, NVA replacements in the DMZ area can offset these losses fairly quickly. The enemy has an increased artillery capability at the DMZ, plus some tanks and possibly even a limited air threat in I CTZ.

(b) II Corps Tactical Zone: The 1st NVA Division went virtually unscathed during TET offensive, and represents a strong threat in the western highlands. Seven combat battalion equivalents threaten Dak To. Elsewhere in the highlands, NVA units have been hurt and VC units chopped up badly. On the coast, the 3rd NVA Division had already taken heavy losses just prior to the

617

offensive. The 5th NVA Division, also located on the coast, is no[t] in good shape. Local force strength is about 13,000 killed; som[e] NVA as well as coastal II CTZ had dwindled long before the offen[sive]. The enemy's strength in II CTZ is in the highlands wher[e] enemy troops are fresh and supply lines short.

(c) III CTZ: Most of the enemy's units were used in the TET effort, and suffered substantial losses. Probably the only maj[or] unit to escape heavy losses was the 7th NVA Division. Howeve[r] present dispositions give the enemy the continuing capability [of] attacking in the Saigon area with 10 to 11 combat effective bat[talion] talion equivalents. His increased movement southward of suppor[t]ing arms and infiltration of supplies has further developed h[is] capacity for attacks by fire.

(d) IV Corps Tactical Zone: All enemy forces were committe[d] in IV Corps, but losses per total strength were the lightest in th[e] country. The enemy continues to be capable of investing or at[tacking] tacking cities throughout the area.

(2) New weapons or tactics:

We may see heavier rockets and tube artillery, additional armo[r] and the use of aircraft, particularly in the I CTZ. The only ne[w] tactic in view is infiltration and investment of cities to creat[e] chaos, to demoralize the people, to discredit the governmen[t] and to tie allied forces to urban security.

b. RVNAF Capabilities:

(1) Current Status of RVNAF:

(a) Strength

—As of 31 Dec RVNAF strength was 643,116 (Regula[r] Forces—342,951; RF—151,376; and PF—148,789)

Date	Auth	PFD	% of Strength
31 Dec.	112,435	96,667	86
10 Feb	112,435	77,000	68.5
15 Feb.	112,435	83,935	74.7

. . . (d) The redeployment of forces has caused major reloca[tions] tions of support forces, logistical activities and supplies.

(e) The short range solutions to the four major areas liste[d] above were: (a) Emergency replacement of major equipmen[t] items and ammunition from the CONUS and (b) day-to-day emer[gency] gency actions and relocation of resources within the theater. I[n] summary, the logistics system in Vietnam has provided adequat[e] support throughout the TET offensive.

d. GVN Strength and Effectiveness:

(1) Psychological—the people in South Vietnam were handed [a] psychological blow, particularly in the urban areas where the feel[ing] ing of security had been strong. There is a fear of further attacks[.]

(2) The structure of the Government was not shattered an[d] continues to function but at greatly reduced effectiveness.

(3) In many places, the RD program has been set back badl[y.] In other places the program was untouched in the initial stag[e]

f the offensive. MACV reports that of the 555 RD cadre groups, 78 remain in hamlets, 245 are in district and province towns on ecurity duty, while 32 are unaccounted for. It is not clear as to vhen, or even whether, it will be possible to return to the RD orogram in its earlier form. As long as the VC prowl the country-ide it will be impossible, in many places, even to tell exactly vhat has happened to the program.

(4) Refugees—An additional 470,000 refugees were generated during the offensive. A breakdown of refugees is at Enclosure (7). The problem of caring for refugees is part of the larger problem of reconstruction in the cities and towns. It is anticipated that he care and reestablishment of the 250,000 persons or 50,000 family units who have lost their homes will require from GVN sources the expenditure of 500 million piasters for their temporary care and resettlement plus an estimated 30,000 metric tons of rice. From U.S. sources, there is a requirement to supply aluminum and cement for 40,000 refugee families being reestablished under the Ministry of Social Welfare and Refugee self-help program. Additionally, the GVN/Public Works City Rebuilding Plan will require the provision of 400,000 double sheets of aluminum, plus 20,000 tons [words illegible].

4. WHAT DOES THE FUTURE HOLD

a. Probable enemy strategy. (Reference paragraph 7b, En-closure (1). We see the enemy pursuing a reinforced offensive to enlarge his control throughout the country and keep pressures on the government and allies. We expect him to maintain strong threats in the DMZ area, at Khe Sanh, in the highlands, and at Saigon, and to attack in force when conditions seem favorable. He is likely to try to gain control of the country's northern provinces. He will continue efforts to encircle cities and province capitals to isolate and disrupt normal activities, and infiltrate them to create chaos. He will seek maximum attrition of RVNAF elements. Against U.S. forces, he will emphasize attacks by fire on airfields and installations, using assaults and ambushes selectively. His central objective continues to be the destruction of the Government of SVN and its armed forces. As a minimum he hopes to seize sufficient territory and gain control of enough people to support establishment of the groups and committees he proposes for participation in an NLF dominated government.

b. MACV Strategy:

(1) MACV believes that the central thrust of our strategy now must be to defeat the enemy offensive and that if this is done well, the situation overall will be greatly improved over the pre-TET condition.

(2) MACV accepts the fact that its first priority must be the security of Government of Vietnam in Saigon and provincial capitals. MACV describes its objectives as:

—First, to counter the enemy offensive and to destroy or ejec the NVA invasion force in the north.

—Second, to restore security in the cities and towns.

—Third, to restore security in the heavily populated areas o the countryside.

—Fourth, to regain the initiative through offensive operations.

c. Tasks:

(1) Security of Cities and Government. MACV recognizes tha U.S. forces will be required to reinforce and support RVNAF in th security of cities, towns and government structure. At this time 10 U.S. batallions are operating in the environs of Saigon. It i clear that this task will absorb a substantial portion of U.S. forces

(2) Security in the Countryside. To a large extent the VC now control the countryside. Most of the 54 battalions formerly provid ing security for pacification are now defending district or provinc towns. MACV estimates that U.S. forces will be required in a num ber of places to assist and encourage the Vietnamese Army to leave the cities and towns and reenter the country. This i especially true in the Delta.

(3) Defense of the borders, the DMZ and northern provinces MACV considers that it must meet the enemy threat in I Corps Tactical Zone and has already deployed there slightly over 50% of all U.S. maneuver battalions. U.S. forces have been thinned out in the highlands, notwithstanding an expected enemy offensive in the early future.

(4) Offensive Operations. Coupling the increased requiremen for the defense of the cities and subsequent reentry into the rural areas, and the heavy requirement for defense of the I Corps Zone, MACV does not have adequate forces at this time to re sume the offensive in the remainder of the country, nor does it have adequate reserves against the contingency of simultaneous large-scale enemy offensive action throughout the country.

5. FORCE REQUIREMENTS

A. Forces currently assigned to MACV, plus the residual Pro gram Fives forces yet to be delivered, are inadequate in numbers to carry out the strategy and to accomplish the tasks described above in the proper priority. To contend with, and defeat, the new enemy threat, MACV has stated requirements for forces over the 525,000 ceiling imposed by Program Five. The add-on re quested totals 206,756 spaces for a new proposed ceiling of 731,756, with all forces being deployed into country by the end of CY 68. Principal forces included in the add-on are three division equivalents, 15 tactical fighter squadrons and augmenta tion for current Navy programs. MACV desires that these addi tional forces be delivered in three packages as follows:

(1) Immediate Increment, Priority One: To be deployed by 1 May 68. Major elements include one brigade of the 5th Mech-

anized Division with a mix of one infantry, one armored and one mechanized battalion; the Fifth Marine Division (less RLT-26); one armored cavalry regiment; eight tactical fighter squadrons; and a groupment of Navy units to augment on going programs.

(2) Immediate Increment, Priority Two: To be deployed as soon as possible but prior to 1 Sep 68. Major elements include the remainder of the 5th Mechanized Division, and four tactical fighter squadrons. It is desirable that the ROK Light Division be deployed within this time frame.

(3) Follow-on Increment: To be deployed by the end of CY 68. Major elements include one infantry division, three tactical fighter squadrons, and units to further augment Navy Programs.

b. Enclosure (9) treats MACV's force requirements for CY 68 to include troop lists, and service strengths for each of the three packages which comprise the total MACV request.

c. Those aspects of MACV's CY 68 force requirements recommendations meriting particular consideration are:

(1) Civilianization. Approximately 150,000 Vietnamese and troop contributing nations' civilians are currently employed by MACV components. Program Five contains provisions to replace 12,545 military spaces by civilians during CY 68. MACV is experiencing difficulties with the civilian program because of curfew impositions, disrupted transportation, fear, movement of military units which include civilians, strikes, and prospective mobilization [rest illegible].

133

Orientation Memo for Clifford Telling How Targets Are Chosen

Excerpts from memorandum from Assistant Secretary of Defense Paul C. Warnke to Clark M. Clifford, newly appointed Secretary of Defense, March 5, 1968, as provided in the body of the Pentagon study.

Twice a month the Joint Staff has been revising the Rolling Thunder Target List for the bombing of North Vietnam. The revisions are forwarded to my office and reconciled with the prior list. This reconciliation summary is then forwarded to your office. . . .

Every Tuesday and Friday the Joint Staff has been sending me a current list of the authorized targets on the target list which have not been struck or restruck since returning to a recommended status. After our review, this list also is sent to your office. . . .

In the normal course of events, new recommendations by the Chairman of the Joint Chiefs of Staff for targets lying within the 10 and 4 mile prohibited circles around Hanoi and Haiphong, respectively, or in the Chinese Buffer Zone have been submitted both to the Secretary of Defense's office and to my office in ISA. ISA would then ensure that the State Department had sufficient information to make its recommendation on the new proposal. ISA also submitted its evaluation of the proposal to your office. On occasions the Chairman would hand-carry the new bombing proposals directly to the Secretary of Defense for his approval. Under those circumstances, the Secretary, if he were not thoroughly familiar with the substance of the proposal, would call ISA for an evaluation. State Department and White House approval also were required before the Chairman's office could authorize the new strikes.

134

Cable to Envoys in Asia on Day of Johnson's De-escalation Speech

Excerpts from cablegram from State Department to United States Ambassadors in Australia, New Zealand, Thailand, Laos, the Philippines and South Korea, March 31, 1968, as provided in the body of the Pentagon study. The message announced provisions of the major speech President Lyndon B. Johnson was to make hours later. Paragraphs in italics are the study's paraphrase or explana-ation.

a. Major stress on importance of GVN and ARVN increased effectiveness with our equipment and other support as first priority in our own actions.

b. 13,500 support forces to be called up at once in order to round out the 10,500 combat units sent in February.

c. Replenishment of strategic reserve by calling up 48,500 additional reserves, stating that these would be designed to strategic reserve.

d. Related tax increases and budget cuts already largely needed for non-Vietnam reasons.

3. In addition, after similar consultation and concurrence, President proposes to announce that bombing will be restricted to targets most directly engaged in battlefield area and that this meant that there would be no bombing north of the 20th parallel. Announcement would leave open how Hanoi might respond, and would be open-ended as to time. However, it would indicate that Hanoi's response could be helpful in determining whether we were justified in assumption that Hanoi would not take advantage if we stopping bombing altogether. Thus, it would to this extent foreshadow possibility of full bombing stoppage at a later point.

This cable offered the Ambassadors some additional rationale for this new policy for their discretionary use in conversations with their respective heads of government. This rationale represents the only available statement by the Administration of some of its underlying reasons and purposes for and expectations from this policy decision.

a. You should call attention to force increases that would be announced at the same time and would make clear our continued resolve. Also our top priority to re-equipping ARVN forces.

b. You should make clear that Hanoi is most likely to denounce the project and thus free our hand after a short period. Nonetheless, we might wish to continue the limitation even after a formal denunciation, in order to reinforce its sincerity and put the monkey firmly on Hanoi's back for whatever follows. Of course, any major military change could compel full-scale resumption at any time.

c. With or without denunciation, Hanoi might well feel limited in conducting any major offensives at least in the northern areas. If they did so, this could ease the pressure where it is most potentially serious. If they did not, then this would give us a clear field for whatever actions were then required.

d. In view of weather limitations, bombing north of the 20th parallel will in any event be limited at least for the next four weeks or so—which we tentatively envisage as a maximum testing period in any event. Hence, we are not giving up anything really serious in this time frame. Moreover, air power now used north of 20th can probably be used in Laos (where no policy change planned) and in SVN.

e. Insofar as our announcement foreshadows any possibility of a complete bombing stoppage, in the event Hanoi really exercises reciprocal restraints, we regard this as unlikely. But in any case, the period of demonstrated restraint would probably have to continue for a period of several weeks, and we would have time to appraise the situation and to consult carefully with them before we undertook any such action.

Glossary

AA: Air America; or antiaircraft

AAA: antiaircraft artillery

ABM: antiballistic missile

AFB: Air Force Base

AID: Agency for International Development

Airops: air operations

AMB: ambassador

ARVN: Army of the Republic of (South) Vietnam

ASA: (U.S.) Army Security Agency

ASAP: as soon as possible

ASW: antisubmarine warfare

Ball: George W. Ball, Under Secretary of State, 1961–66

Bao Dat: Emperor of Vietnam, 1932–55

BAR: Browning automatic rifle

Barrel Roll: Code name for operation, U.S. air strikes against Laotian infiltration routes and facilities

Bidault: Georges Bidault, French Minister of Foreign Affairs, 1953–54

Bienhoa: airfield near Saigon, attacked by Vietcong October 31, 1964

B–57: name of U.S. bomber

black radio: in psychological warfare, broadcasts by one side that are disguised as broadcasts for the other

BLT: battalion landing team

Blue Springs: apparently a covert operation not further identified in study of the documents

Bohlen: Charles E. Bohlen, Ambassador to France, 1962–68

Bonnet: Henri Bonnet, French Ambassador to U.S., 1944–55

bonze: Buddhist monk

Box Top: apparently a code name for a covert operation not further identified in the documents

BPP: Border Patrol Police

Bundy, McGeorge: (See biography)

Bundy, William P.: (See biography)

Buu: Tran Quoc Buu, leader of Vietnamese Confederation of Labor under Diem

Can: Ngo Dinh Can, brother of Ngo Dinh Diem

Can Lao: semisecret South Vietnamese party organized by Ngo Dinh Nhu and Ngo Dinh Can

CAP: combat air patrol; prefix used to designate White House cablegrams sent through CIA channel

CAS: code name for Central Intelligence Agency; not otherwise explained in the documents

CAT: Civil Air Transport, airline based on Taiwan

CHICOM: Chinese Communist

CHINAT: Chinese Nationalist

CHMAAG: Chief, Military Assistance Advisory Group

CI: counterinsurgency

CIAP: Inter-American Committee for the Alliance for Progress

CINCPAC: Commander in Chief, Pacific

CIO: Central Intelligence Organizations (South Vietnam)

CJCS: Chairman, Joint Chiefs of Staff

Collins: General J. Lawton Collins, Presidential representative in South Vietnam, 1954–55

COMUSMACV: Commander, U.S. Military Assistance Command, Vietnam

COS: chief of station, CIA

country team: council of senior

U.S. officials in South Vietnam, including ambassador, commander of American forces, CIA chief, and others

CTZ: corps tactical zone

CY: calendar year

Deptel: (State) Department telegram

DePuy: Lieutenant General William E. DePuy, U.S. Military Assistance Command, Vietnam, 1964–66

De Soto patrols: U.S. destroyer patrols in Tonkin Gulf

DIA: Defense Intelligence Agency

Diem, Ngo Dinh: (See biography)

Dinh: Major General Ton That Dinh, military governor of Saigon, 1963

DMZ: Demilitarized Zone

Dobrynin: Anatoly F. Dobrynin, USSR Ambassador to the U.S., 1961–

Doc: document

DOD: Department of Defense

Don: Major General Tran Van Don, Chief of Staff, South Vietnamese armed forces, 1963; Defense Minister 1963–64; Deputy Commander in Chief, 1964

Dong, Pham Van: (See biography)

DPM: draft presidential memo

DRV: Democratic Republic of (North) Vietnam

Duan, Le: (See biography)

Dulles: Allen W. Dulles, director of Central Intelligence, 1953–61; or John Foster Dulles, Secretary of State, 1952–59

Durbrow: Elbridge Durbrow, U.S. Ambassador to Saigon, 1957–61

E and E: escape and evasion

ECM: electronic countermeasures

EDC: European Defense Community

Eden: Anthony Eden, Earl of Avon, Deputy Prime Minister and Secretary of State for Foreign Affairs, UK, 1951–55; Prime Minister, 1955–57

Ely: General Paul Ely, French commander in Indochina, 1954–55

Embtel: U.S. embassy telegram

EPTEL: apparently a typographical error for Deptel or Septel, q.v.

FAL: Lao armed forces

FAR: Royal Armed Forces (of Laos)

Farmgate: clandestine U.S. Air Force strike unit in Vietnam (1964)

FEC: French Expeditionary Corps

Felt: Admiral Harry D. Felt, Commander in Chief, Pacific, 1958–64

Flaming Dart: code name of operations, reprisals for attacks on U.S. installations

FOA: Foreign Operations Administration

Forrestal, Michael V.: (See biography)

Fulbright: J. W. Fulbright, chairman, Senate Foreign Relations Committee; U.S. Senator (D.–Ark.), 1945–

FWMA: Free World Military Assistance

FWMAF: Free World Military Assistance Force

FY: fiscal year

FYI: for your information

Gardner: John W. Gardner, Secretary of Health, Education and Welfare, 1965–68

Giap: General Vo Nguyen Giap, Commander in Chief of Vietminh Army at time of defeat of French at Dienbienphu (1954)

Gilpatric: Roswell L. Gilpatric, Deputy Secretary of Defense, 1961–64

GNP: gross national product

G–3: U.S. Army General Staff branch handling plans and operations

GVN: Government of (South) Vietnam

Hardnose: code name, apparently for covert project, not otherwise identified in the documents

Harkins, Paul D.: (See biography)

Harriman: W. Averell Harriman, Assistant, then Under Secretary of State, 1961–65; Ambassador at Large, 1965–68

Marops: maritime operations

Mau: Vu Van Mau, Foreign Minister, South Vietnam till fall of Diem (1963)

McCone: John A. McCone, director of Central Intelligence, 1961–65

McNamara: Robert S. McNamara, Secretary of Defense, 1961–68

McNaughton, John T.: (See biography)

MDAP: Mutual Defense Assistance Program

Mecklin: John M. Mecklin, public affairs officer, U.S. Embassy, Saigon, 1962–64

MEF: Marine Expeditionary Force

Mendès: Pierre Mendès-France, Premier of France, 1954–55

Minh: General Duong Van Minh ("Big Minh"), head of government, South Vietnam, 1963–64

Molotov: V. M. Molotov, Soviet Minister for Foreign Affairs, 1953–56

Morgan: Thomas E. Morgan, chairman, House Foreign Affairs Committee, 1954–

NATO: North Atlantic Treaty Organization

Navarre: General Henri Navarre, Commander in Chief, French forces in Indochina, 1953–54

NFLSV: National Front for the Liberation of South Vietnam

Ngo family: family of Ngo Dinh Diem and Ngo Dinh Nhu

Nhu, Madame: wife of Ngo Dinh Nhu

Nhu, Ngo Dinh: (See biography)

NIE: National Intelligence Estimate

Nitze: Paul H. Nitze, Secretary of the Navy, Deputy Secretary of Defense

NLF: National Liberation Front

Nolting: Frederick E. ("Fritz") Nolting, U.S. Ambassador in Saigon, 1961–63

Norstad: General Lauris Norstad, air deputy, SHAPE, 1953–56; commander, SHAPE, 1956–63

NSA: National Security Agency

NSAM: National Security Agency memorandum

NSC: National Security Council

NVA: North Vietnamese Army

NVN: North Vietnam

OB: Operation Brotherhood

OEEC: Organization for European Economic Cooperation

Opcon: Operations Control

Oplan: operation plan

ops: operations

OSD: Office of the Secretary of Defense

PACOM: Pacific Command

Para: paragraph

PARU: Police Aerial Resupply Unit

PAVN: People's Army of (North) Vietnam

PB: Planning Board

PBR: river patrol boat

PDJ: Plaine des Jarres

PF: Popular Forces

PI: Philippine Islands

Pierce Arrow: code name for U.S. reprisal bombing of North Vietnam after the Tonkin Gulf incidents

PL: Pathet Lao

Pleven: René Pleven, French Minister of National Defense, 1953, 1954

POL: petroleum, oil, lubricants

POLAD: political adviser (to Commander in Chief, Pacific)

Porter: William J. Porter, U.S. Deputy Ambassador (with rank of Ambassador) in Saigon, 1965–67

psyops: psychological operations

PTF: fast patrol boat

Quang: Trich Tri Quang, South Vietnamese Buddhist leader

Quat: Phan Huy Quat, head of government, South Vietnam, 1965

Queen Bee: code name for an allied operation not otherwise identified in the documents

QTE: quote

Radford: Admiral Arthur W. Radford, chairman, Joint Chiefs of Staff, 1953–57

RAS: river assault squadron

RD: Revolutionary Development; or Rural Development

RECCE: reconnaissance

REF: reference, meaning "the document referred to"

Reftel: in reference to your telegram, or telegram referred to

Resor: Stanley R. Resor, Secretary of the Army, 1965–

RF: Regional Forces

Rice: Edward E. Rice, U.S. Consul General in Hong Kong, 1963–67

RLAF: Royal Laotian Air Force

RLG: Royal Laotian Government

RLT: regimental landing team

ROK: Republic of (South) Korea

Rolling Thunder: code name of operation, sustained bombing of North Vietnam

Rostow: Walt W. Rostow, Presidential assistant for national security, 1961; chairman, State Department Policy Planning Council, 1961–66

rpt: repeat

RSM: Robert S. McNamara

RSSZ: Rungsat Special Zone

RTA: Royal Thai Army

RT–28: name of U.S. aircraft

Rusk: Dean Rusk, Secretary of State, 1961–69

RVN: Republic of (South) Vietnam

RVNAF: Republic of (South) Vietnam Air Force or armed forces

RVNF: Republic of (South) Vietnam forces

SAC: Strategic Air Command

SAM: surface-to-air missile

SAR: search and rescue

Sarit: Field Marshal Sarit Thanarat, Prime Minister of Thailand, 1958–63

SEA: Southeast Asia

Seaborn, J. Blair: (See biography)

SEATO: Southeast Asia Treaty Organization

Sec Def: Secretary of Defense

Septel: separate telegram

Sharp, U. S. Grant: (See biography)

Sihanouk: Prince Norodom Sihanouk, head of state, Cambodia, 1960–70

SMM: Saigon Military Mission

SNIE: Special National Intelligence Estimate

Souvanna: Prince Souvanna

Phouma, Prime Minister of Laos, 1951–

Stassen: Harold Stassen, Governor of Minnesota, 1938–45; director, Foreign Operations Administration, 1953–55

State: State Department

STC: Security Training Center

Stilwell: Lieutenant General Richard G. Stilwell, assistant to Chief of Staff, Operations, Military Assistance Command, Vietnam, 1963–64

SVN: South Vietnam

SVNese: South Vietnamese

TAOR: tactical area of responsibility

Taylor, Maxwell D.: (See biography)

TERM: Temporary Equipment Recovery Mission

Tet: lunar new year; 1968 offensive during Tet

TF: task force

Thang: General Nguyen Ngoc Thang, director, Revolutionary Development, South Vietnam

Thao: Colonel Pham Ngoc Thao (executed 1965 for part in attempted South Vietnamese coups, 1964–65)

Thieu: Lieutenant General Nguyen Van Thieu, President of South Vietnam, 1967–

34–A: operation plan, 1964, covering covert ground, air and sea raids against North Vietnam

Tho: Nguyen Ngoc Tho, head of government, South Vietnam, 1963–64

Thuan: Nguyen Dinh Thuan, holder of high positions in Diem government, South Vietnam

TO&E: table of organization and equipment

Triangle: code name for an allied operation not otherwise identified in the documents

TRIM: Training Relations and Instruction Mission

Trueheart: William C. Trueheart, deputy to Ambassador Nolting, 1961–63

T–28: name of U.S. fighter-bomber

UK: United Kingdom

Unger: Leonard Unger, U.S. Ambassador to Laos, 1962–64;

Deputy Assistant Secretary of State, 1965–67

UNO: United Nations Organization

UNQTE: unquote

USAF: United States Air Force

USG: United States Government

USIA: United States Information Agency

USIB: United States Intelligence Board

USIS: United States Information Service

USOM: United States Operations Mission (U.S. economic aid apparatus in Saigon)

UW: unconventional warfare

Vance: Cyrus R. Vance, Deputy Secretary of Defense, 1964–67; troubleshooter for President Johnson, 1967–69

VC: Vietcong

VM: Vietminh

VN: Vietnam

VNAF: (South) Vietnamese Air Force or armed forces

VNese: Vietnamese

VNSF: (South) Vietnamese Special Forces

VOA: Voice of America

Westmoreland, William C.: (See biography)

Westy: see Westmoreland

Wheeler, Earle G.: (See biography)

white radio: in psychological warfare, broadcasts openly attributed to the side transmitting them

Williams: Lieutenant General Samuel T. Williams, U.S. military adviser in South Vietnam, 1955–60

Wilson: Charles E. Wilson, Secretary of Defense, 1953–57

W/T: walkie-talkie

Yankee Team: phase of the Indochina bombing operation

YT: see Yankee Team

Biographies of Key Figures in the Vietnam Study

McGEORGE BUNDY

Special assistant to Presidents Kennedy and Johnson for national security affairs, 1961-66 . . . since 1966, president of the Ford Foundation. Born Boston March 30, 1919 . . . graduated from Yale, 1940, majoring in classics and mathematics . . . ran as a Republican for seat on Boston City Council, 1941 . . . served as aide to Adm. Alan G. Kirk, World War II . . . foreign-policy adviser to Thomas E. Dewey, Republican Presidential candidate, 1948 . . . joined Harvard faculty, 1949 . . . became dean of Faculty of Arts and Sciences, 1953 . . . named by President Kennedy to White House post . . . often described as principal architect of U.S. Vietnam policy . . . was recalled briefly by President Johnson during the Arab-Israeli crisis in summer of 1967 . . . often seen as a potential Secretary of State . . . just as visible—and controversial—as foundation head as when directing foreign policy from White House basement office . . . now lives in New York.

WILLIAM PUTNAM BUNDY

From 1951 to end of Johnson Administration, "the other Bundy" held sensitive positions in government departments, from the Central Intelligence Agency to State Department . . . now a senior research associate at Center for International Studies of Massachusetts Institute of Technology and will assume editorship of Foreign Affairs, the quarterly, after October, 1972. Born in Washington, Sept. 24, 1917 . . . earned, bachelor's degree from Yale, 1939; master's from Harvard, 1940; law degree from Harvard, 1947 . . . married to a daughter of Dean Acheson, former Secretary of State . . . practiced law, Washington, 1947-51 . . . a Democrat . . . with the C.I.A., 1951-61 . . . served consecutively as Assistant and Deputy Secretary of Defense for International Security Affairs, 1961-64 . . . Assistant Secretary of State for East Asian and Pacific Affairs, 1964-69 . . . always, compared with younger brother McGeorge, an anonymous figure . . . lives in Cambridge, Mass.

NGO DINH DIEM

Premier, South Vietnam, 1954-55; President, 1955-63; until death during overthrow Nov. 1, 1963. Born Quangbinh, near Hue, Jan. 3, 1901 . . . graduated from School of Administration, Hue . . entered civil service . . . rose to district administrator . . . Minister of Interior in Cabinet of Emperor Bao Dai, 1933 . . . resigned on learning Government was controlled by French . . . declared subversive by French in 1942, he fled to Saigon, 1944 . . refused Japanese offer to head puppet government, March, 1945 . . . refused offer to work with Hanoi regime, 1945 . . . began seeking some autonomy for Vietnam . . . fled country, 1950 . . during exile, 1951-52, lived at Maryknoll Seminary, Lakewood, N. J., 1951-52 . . returned Saigon as Premier in Bao Dai Government, 1954 . . . elected President in referendum making Vietnam a republic, 1955 . . . won second five-year term 1961 . . . survived several coup attempts . . . shot to death after accepting safe-conduct offer.

PHAM VAN DONG

Led Vietminh delegation to Geneva, 1954; in North Vietnam hierarchy thereafter and Premier since 1955 . . . born Quangngai, coastal region in South, 1906 . . . entered University of Hanoi, 1925 . . . led student strike, fled to China . . . joined Vietnamese political émigrés, including Ho Chi Minh, in Canton . . . sent back to Vietnam by Ho Chi Minh on secret mission . . . arrested, imprisoned on island of Poulo Condore, 1929-36 . . . worked to establish Communist movement in North and South . . . fled to south China, 1939 . . . with Ho Chi Minh and Vo Nguyen Giap, founded Vietminh, 1941; finance minister, 1945, in first Ho Chi Minh government . . . named chief negotiator with French at Fontainebleau, 1946 . . . premier, 1949 . . . guerrilla commander in Quangngai, 1951 . . . chief Geneva negotiator, 1954 . . . regarded as "the best nephew" of "Uncle" Ho Chi Minh called "my other self" by Ho . . . formulator of North Vietnam's "four points" for peace . . . sophisticated, articulate, a skilled diplomat.

LE DUAN

Vietcong organizer, nineteen-fifties; Secretary, Lao Dong (Communist) party Central Committee for the Southern Region 1956; Secretary General Lao Dong party, 1959; since 1960, First Secretary of party . . . born into peasant family, Quangtri province in central Vietnam, 1908 . . . worked as secretary with railways, Hanoi . . . given 20-year prison term for subversive activities, 1930 . . . released 1936, resumed political work for Indochinese Communist Party . . . given 10-year sentence, 1940 . . . released on Vietminh take-over 1945 . . . led guerrillas against French in South starting 1946 . . . commissioner at Vietminh's military headquarters in South, 1952 . . . rose in party, named First Secretary, September, 1960 . . . led Hanoi delegation to 1967 50th-anniversary celebrations in Moscow . . . since Ho Chi Minh's death, has emerged as "first among equals" in collective leadership . . . has sponsored popular economic reforms . . . advocates "protracted war" strategy . . . said to be self-effacing, pragmatic . . .

MICHAEL VINCENT FORRESTAL

White House specialist on Vietnam 1962-65 . . . in private law practice New York now . . . newly elected chairman of board, Metropolitan Opera Guild. Born Nov. 26, 1927, in New York . . . graduated from Phillips Exeter Academy . . . studies at Princeton interrupted to serve on staff of W. Averell Harriman at Paris headquarters of Economic Cooperation Administration, 1948-50 . . . his father, late James V. Forrestal, was the first Secretary of Defense . . . received law degree from Harvard, 1953 and practiced in New York till 1960 . . . returned to firm of Shearman & Sterling, where he is partner, in 1965 . . . as Kennedy and Johnson aide, served on National Security Council . . . in July 1964, appointed chairman White House interdepartmental Vietnam coordinating committee . . . accompanied Mrs. John F. Kennedy on 1967 visit to Cambodia . . . early supporter of the late Sen. Robert F. Kennedy's Presidential bid . . . member Council on Foreign Relations . . . lives in New York.

PAUL DONAL HARKINS

United States commander, Vietnam, 1962-64; now adviser to American Security Council, private "research" group, Boston. Born Boston, May 15, 1904 . . . graduated U.S. Military Academy, 1929 . . . deputy chief of staff, Western Task Force, North African invasion, 1942 . . . deputy chief of staff, Third Army then 15th Army . . . a protégé of Gen. George S. Patton Jr. . . . commandant of cadets, West Point, 1948-51 . . . chief of staff, Eighth Army, Korea, 1951-53 . . . commander, 45th and 24th Infantry Divisions, Korea, December, 1953-54 . . . Pentagon service, 1954-57 . . . deputy commander, chief of staff U.S. Army Forces, Pacific, 1960-62 . . . first commander, Military Assistance Command, Saigon, 1962-64 . . . consistently optimistic in his assessment of war . . . strong support of Ngo Dinh Diem . . . has said "biggest" U.S. mistake in Vietnam "was when we stopped backing Diem" . . . during his tenure, had sharp differences with Ambassador Henry Cabot Lodge . . . retired 1964 . . . moved to Dallas, 1965.

ROGER HILSMAN JR.

Director of State Department bureau of intelligence and research, 1961-63, Assistant Secretary of State for Far Eastern Affairs, 1963-64; now since 1964, professor of government, Columbia University. Born Waco, Tex., Nov. 23, 1919 . . . graduated U.S. Military Academy, 1943 . . . master's degree, Yale, 1950 . . . Ph.D., Yale, 1951 . . . served with Merrill's Marauders, Burma, 1944 . . . commanded O.S.S. guerilla group, Burma, 1944-45 . . . assistant chief Far East Intelligence, O.S.S., Washington, 1945-46 . . . assistant to executive officer, C.I.A., 1946-47 . . . State Department, NATO affairs, 1950-53 . . . Center for International Studies, Princeton, 1953-55 . . . deputy director, Legis-

ative Reference Service, Library of Congress, Washington, 1956-
8 . . . research associate, Washington Center for Foreign Policy
Research, international-affairs lecturer, Johns Hopkins School of
Advanced International Studies, 1957-61 . . . director, Bureau of
Intelligence and Research, State Department, 1961-63 . . . Assistant
Secretary of State, 1963-64 . . . resigned, 1964 . . . author of
"To Move a Nation," 1967, others . . . said after resignation he
thought U.S. could not win "a total victory" in South Vietnam
. . . now lives New York City, and Lyme, Conn.

NGUYEN KHANH

South Vietnam's Premier—on and off—from February, 1964,
through Mid-February, 1965 . . . since 1968 in exile in Paris.
Born in Travinh, South Vietnam, Nov. 8, 1927 . . . educated
military academy at Dalat, 1950, also in France, at U.S. Staff
College, Fort Leavenworth, Kan. . . . fought as guerrilla against
French . . . sent to Saigon on mission . . . joined French colonial
forces . . . paratrooper, reached rank of major . . . helped foil
1960 coup against Ngo Dinh Diem . . . stayed on sidelines during
1963 coup . . . ousted Gen. Duong Van Minh Jan. 30, 1964 . . .
in August, assumed dictatorial powers . . . forced out . . . remained
Army chief . . . led coup against incumbent . . . survived coup
attempt February . . . is deposed as commander in chief by
military . . . sent abroad as roving ambassador . . . a Buddhist,
but not popular with Buddhists . . . short, jaunty, goateed . . .
liked to wear paratrooper's red beret . . . fond of saying; "I am
a fighter."

VICTOR HAROLD KRULAK

Pentagon counterinsurgency expert, 1961-64 since July, 1968,
president of Copley News Service, San Diego, Calif. . . . born
Denver, Jan. 7, 1913 . . . graduate of Annapolis, 1934 . . . nick-
named "the Brute" because of short stature, unbrutish appearance
. . . served with Fleet Marine Corps, 1935-39 . . . battalion and
regimental commander, World War II . . . chief of staff, First
Marine Division, Korean conflict . . . commanding general, Marine
Corps Recruit Depot, San Diego . . . special assistant to director,
Joint Staff Counterinsurgency and Special Activities Office, Joint
Chiefs of Staff, 1961-64 . . . commanding general, Fleet Marine
Force, Pacific, 1964 till May, 1968, when he retired as lieutenant
general . . . known as corps theoretician and leading strategic
planner, had been considered prime contender for commandant
in late 1967 . . . awarded Navy Cross, Legion of Merit, Bronze
Star, Vietnam's Medal of Merit and Cross of Gallantry, among
others . . . living in San Diego.

EDWARD LANSDALE

United States Air Force officer, 1947-63; political adviser, South
Vietnam, 1954-56; special assistant to Ambassador Henry Cabot
Lodge, 1965-68. Born Detroit, Feb. 6, 1908 . . . studied at Univer-
sity of California, Los Angeles . . . in late nineteen-forties, was

adviser to President Ramon Magsaysay of Philippines . . . helped put down Communist-led Hukbalahap rebellion there . . . developed basic concept that Communist revolution best opposed by democratic revolution . . . went to South Vietnam, as Central Intelligence Agency operative, 1954 . . . helped establish Ngo Dinh Diem regime . . . believed to be model for "Colonel Hillandale" in the novel "The Ugly American" and for "Pyle" in "The Quiet American" . . . urged creation of Vietnam counterinsurgency force instead of conventional army . . . reassigned to Pentagon 1956 . . . reportedly helped develop Special Forces . . . retired 1963 with rank of major general . . . returned Saigon, 1965, as special assistant for pacification under Mr. Lodge . . . his known activities included supervising "rural reconstruction" . . . serving as liaison between embassy and Vietnamese . . . well known but mysterious . . . described as irreplaceable . . . reticent about his own role . . . returned United States 1968 . . . in private life still does magazine writing on Vietnam and counterinsurgency . . . lives in Alexandria, Va.

HENRY CABOT LODGE

Ambassador to South Vietnam, 1963-64 and 1965-67 . . . now since June, 1970, President Nixon's special envoy to the Vatican . . . born July 5, 1902, Nahant, Mass. . . . graduated from Harvard, 1924 . . . worked for The Boston Transcript and The New York Herald Tribune . . . two terms in Massachusetts Legislature 1933-36 . . . defeated James M. Curley for Senate seat, 1936 . . . took leave of absence to serve in Army during World War II . . . won re-election, then resigned from Senate to return to Army duty . . . won Bronze Star, Croix de Guerre, others . . . elected to Senate again, 1946 . . . influential in persuading Eisenhower to seek Presidency and served as his campaign manager . . . lost Senate seat, 1952, to John F. Kennedy . . . appointed U.S. representative at the U.N., 1953 . . . G.O.P. vice-presidential candidate 1960 . . . U.S. Ambassador, Saigon, August, 1963-July 1964, 1965-67 . . . chief U.S. negotiator, Paris peace talks 1969 . . . Ambassador at Large, 1967-68 . . . Ambassador to Germany, 1968-69 . . . chief U.S. negotiator, Paris peace talks January-December, 1969.

JOHN T. McNAUGHTON

Mr. McNaughton a close and trusted associate of Secretary of Defense Robert S. McNamara from 1961 to 1967, and his wife and their younger son died in plane collision near Asheville, N.C., July 19, 1967, a week before he was to be sworn in as Secretary of Navy. Born Nov. 21, 1921, in Bicknell, Ind. . . . graduated from DePauw University, 1942 . . . served four years in Navy during World War II . . . graduated from Harvard Law School 1948 . . . studied at Oxford as Rhodes scholar, working with European Cooperation Administration in Paris during vacation . . . also wrote for Pekin (Ill.) Times, owned by father . . . two years as editor of that paper . . . returned to Harvard as assistant professor, 1953, professor, 1956 . . . chosen by Mr. McNamara in 1961 to serve as Deputy Assistant Secretary for International Security Affairs . . . general counsel to Defense Department, 1962 . . . Assistant Secretary of Defense for International Security Affairs, 1964-67, heading Pentagon's foreign-affairs planning staff.

NGO DINH NHU

Headed secret apparatus of Ngo Dinh Diem Government, 1954-63 until his death during overthrow of Diem, his brother, on Nov. 1. Born about 1911 near Hue into distinguished Roman Catholic family . . . one of five brothers in Ngo family . . . was chief archivist. Indochina library, early forties . . . married, 1943 . . . separated from family during war . . . he and wife organized support for return from exile of Ngo Dinh Diem . . . Nhu ran a newspaper, developed philosophy of "personalism"—blend of religions and autocracy—that was said to be pervasive influence on Diem's rule . . . when Diem assumed power, Nhu became known as an "Oriental Richelieu" . . . controlled secret police . . . he and wife were said to be strong anti-Buddhist influence on Diem . . . Mr. Nhu was quiet, persuasive . . . Nhus prime target for discontent that led to overthrow of Diem regime . . . Mr. Nhu shot to death with brother as they were leaving the country under safe-conduct.

JAMES BLAIR SEABORN

Served as secret envoy to Hanoi for United States Government in 1964 while Canada's representative on International Control Commission; now Assistant Deputy Minister in Canadian Consumer Affairs Department. Born 1924 . . . received bachelor's and master's degrees in political economics from University of Toronto . . . served in Canadian Embassy in The Hague, then as First Secretary at Paris embassy, 1957-59 . . . as Counselor in Moscow embassy, 1959-62 . . . in 1962-64 in Ottawa as the head of Eastern European section of Department of External Affairs . . . Canadian Commissioner, International Commission for Supervision and Control, Vietnam, 1964-65 . . . returned to Department of External Affairs as head of Eastern European section, 1966-67, then as head Far Eastern section, 1967-70 . . . lived in Ottawa.

ULYSSES S. GRANT SHARP JR.

Commander in chief, Pacific forces 1964-68; since 1968, business consultant. Born Fort Benton, Mont., April 2, 1906 . . . graduated from United States Naval Academy, 1927 . . . destroyer commander, Casablanca landings and Pacific, World War II . . . fleet planning officer for Inchon invasion, Korean war . . . promoted to admiral, 1963 . . . succeeded Adm. Harry D. Felt as commander in chief, all U.S. forces, Pacific, 1964 . . . urged U.S. to "increase our pressures" on North Vietnam, 1967 . . . said bombing limitation "would just prolong the war," 1968 . . . retired July, 1968 . . . succeeded by Adm. John S. McCain . . . awarded two Silver Stars, two Bronze Stars among others . . . a Rotarian, eager golfer . . . lives in San Diego.

MAXWELL DAVENPORT TAYLOR

Chairman of the Joint Chiefs of Staff, 1962-64; United States Ambassador to South Vietnam, 1964-65; special consultant to the President, 1965-69 . . . now on the board of the Institute for Defense Analyses, chairman of Foreign Intelligence Advisory Board. Born Keytesville, Mo., Aug. 26, 1901 . . . graduated from United States Military Academy, 1922 . . . Command and General Staff School, 1933 . . . Army War College, 1940 . . . taught French, Spanish, at West Point . . . assistant military attaché, Pekin, 1937 . . . commander 101st Airborne Division, World War II . . . took part invasions Normally, Holland . . . Superintendent United States Military Academy, 1945-49 . . . United States Commander, Berlin, 1950 Commander of Eighth Army, Korea, 1953 Army Chief of Staff, 1955 . . . resigned 1959 in 'limited war' strategy dispute . . . recalled as adviser by President Kennedy 1961 . . . was influential in both Kennedy, Johnson Administrations . . . scholarly, much-decorated . . . now living in Chevy Chase, Md.

WILLIAM CHILDS WESTMORELAND

U.S. military commander, Vietnam, 1964-68; since then, Army Chief of Staff. Born Spartanburg County, S. C., March 26, 1914 . . . studied at The Citadel, South Carolina military college . . . graduated from U.S. Military Academy, 1936 . . . Harvard University Advanced Management Program, 1954 . . . first combat experience leading artillery battalion, Casablanca landing, 1942 . . . saw action in Tunisia and Sicily . . . landed on Utah Beach, Normandy, D-Day, with Ninth Infantry Division . . . commander Sixth Infantry Regiment, Germany, 1945 . . . chief of staff, 82d Airborne Division, 1947-50 . . . instructor, Command and General Staff College and Army War College, 1950-52 . . . commanded 187th Airborne combat team, South Korea . . . 1956, promoted to major general, youngest in the Army . . . commander, 101st Airborne Division, 1958-60 . . . superintendent, U.S. Military Academy, 1960-63 . . . once said: "Command is getting people to go the way you want them to go—enthusiastically . . . succeeded Gen. Paul D. Harkins as head of U.S. Military Assistance Command, Vietnam, June 20, 1964 . . . replaced on July 2, 1968, by Gen. Creighton W. Abrams Jr. . . . considered a consistent optimist about progress in Vietnam . . . occasionally rumored under consideration as political candidate . . . a former Eagle Scout enthusiastic about Boy Scouts, a member-at-large of group's national council . . . decorations include Distinguished Service Medal, Bronze Star, Thailand's Most Exalted Order of the White Elephant, Vietnam's Chuong My medal . . . starts day at Pentagon at 8 A.M. precisely.

EARLE GILMORE WHEELER

Chairman of Joint Chiefs of Staff, 1964-70; since 1970, retired to his West Virginia farm. Born Jan. 13, 1908, Washington . . graduated U.S. Military Academy, 1932 . . . joined National

Guard at new division in U.S. . . . director, joint staff, 1960-62 . . . assigned to brief John Kennedy weekly on military candidate during 1960 Presidential campaign . . . Protégé of Maxwell D. Taylor, whom he succeeded as Chairman of J.C.S., 1964 . . . sole service chief to support McNamara endorsement of test-ban treaty, 1963 . . . on Vietnam war, once told interviewer "If we just keep up the pressure those little guys will crack" . . . held top post longer than anyone else, under two Presidents, three Defense Secretaries . . . retired with disability because of heart ailment . . . now living on 180-acre farm, Martinsburg, W. Va.

Index of Key Documents

Chapter 4   The Overthrow of Ngo Dinh Diem: May-November, 1963

Chapter 5 The Covert War and Tonkin Gulf: February-August, 1964

Chapter 6   The Consensus to Bomb North Vietnam: August, 1964-February, 1965

Chapter 7   The Launching of the Ground War: March-July, 1965

Chapter 8   The Buildup: July, 1965-September, 1966

Appendix 1

EDITORIALS FROM THE NEW YORK TIMES

The Vietnam Documents

In an unprecedented example of censorship, the Attorney General of the United States has temporarily succeeded in preventing *The New York Times* from continuing to publish documentary and other material taken from a secret Pentagon study of the decisions affecting American participation in the Vietnam War.

Through a temporary restraining order issued by a Federal District judge yesterday, we are prevented from publishing, at least through the end of the week, any new chapters in this massive documentary history of American involvement in the war. But *The Times* will continue to fight to the fullest possible extent of the law what we believe to be an unconstitutional prior restraint imposed by the Attorney General.

What was the reason that impelled *The Times* to publish this material in the first place? The basic reason is, as was stated in our original reply to Mr. Mitchell, that we believe "that it is in the interest of the people of this country to be informed. . . ." A fundamental responsibility of the press in this democracy is to publish information that helps the people of the United States to understand the processes of their own government, especially when those processes have been clouded over in a hazy veil of public dissimulation and even deception.

As a newspaper that takes seriously its obligation and its responsibilities to the public, we believe that, once this material fell into our hands, it was not only in the interests of the American people to publish it but, even more emphatically, it would have been an abnegation of responsibility and a renunciation of our obligations under the First Amendment not to have published it. Obviously, *The Times* would not have made this decision if there had been any reason to believe that publication would have endangered the life of a single American soldier or in any way threatened the security of our country or the peace of the world.

The documents in question belong to history. They refer to the development of American interest and participation in Indochina from the post-World War II period up to mid-1968, which is now almost three years ago. Their publication could not conceivably damage American security interests, much less the lives of Americans or Indochinese. We therefore felt it incumbent to take on ourselves the responsibility for their publication, and in doing so raise once again the question of the Government's propensity for over-classification and mis-classification of documents that by any reasonable scale of values have long since belonged in the public domain.

We publish the documents and related running account not to prove any debater's point about the origins and development of American participation in the war, not to place the finger of blame on any individuals, civilian or military, but to present to the American public a history—admittedly incomplete—of decision-making at the highest levels of government on one of the most vital issues that has ever effected "our lives, our fortunes and our sacred honor"—an issue on which the American people and their duly elected representatives in Congress have been largely curtailed off from the truth.

It is the effort to expose and elucidate that truth that is the very essence of freedom of the press.

—June 16, 1971

Decision for Freedom

District Judge Murray L. Gurfein's decision yesterday denying the Government's plea for a preliminary injunction to bar this newspaper from publishing articles about a secret Pentagon study of the Vietnam war marks a significant victory for press freedom in the United States and for the right of the American people to be informed about the operations of their Government.

"A cantankerous press, an obstinate press, an ubiquitous press, must be suffered by those in authority in order to preserve the even greater values of freedom of expression and the right of the people to know," Judge Gurfein declared. "These are troubled times. There is no greater safety valve for discontent and cynicism about the affairs of government than freedom of expression in any form."

After hearing the Government's arguments in a lengthy secret session, the District Judge agreed with this newspaper's contention that publication of the articles and documents did not endanger national security. "Without revealing the content of the testimony," he said, "suffice it to say that no cogent reasons were advanced as to why these documents except in the general framework of embarrassment . . . would vitally affect the security of the nation."

The case now goes to the Appeals Court which we hope will speedily clear the way for resumed publication of the articles and documents based on the Pentagon study. By any definition of democratic government and freedom of the press, the public is entitled to the information contained in this history, which in fact is indispensable to an understanding of the evolution of American policy in Vietnam.

—June 20, 1971

The Vietnam Papers

On Nov. 25, 1964, some three weeks after President Johnson's election, *The Times* observed editorially that "another Vietnam reassessment is under way . . . [and] if there is to be a new policy now, if an Asian war is to be converted into an American war, the country has a right to insist that it be told what has changed so profoundly in the last two months to justify it." The country was not told.

Six months later, after repeated demands for "a straightforward explanation" of what was clearly becoming a major land war on the continent of Asia, this newspaper noted that "there is still no official explanation offered for a move that fundamentally alters the character of the American involvement in Vietnam" and pleaded "for the President to take the country into his confidence. . . ."

These comments illustrate how Congress and the American people were kept in the dark about fundamental policy decisions affecting the very life of this democracy during the most critical period of the war. The conviction even then that the Government was not being frank with the American people has been fully confirmed by the massive Pentagon history and documentation which *The Times* began to publish last week—until the Government undertook to censor it.

The running commentary and documents that did appear in this newspaper before the Government moved to block them throw a clear spotlight on the decision-making process during the period up to and including the major escalation of the Vietnam War in 1964 and 1965. The multi-volume study on which *The Times'* account was based shows beyond cavil how the decisions affecting American participation in and conduct of the war were planned and executed while their far-reaching political effect and profound significance, fully appreciated at the top reaches of government, were either deliberately distorted or withheld altogether from the public.

Even more important, the papers as published thus far suggest that almost no one in the upper ranks of the Administration during this crucial period six and seven years ago was probing into the basic political issue on which the military operation depended: Was the Saigon Government's control of South Vietnam of such vital, long-range interest to the United States that it warranted an open-ended American military involvement—or was this really an unexamined conclusion that had already become an article of faith? Nearly every official concerned was discussing the tactics and strategy of the war, how to handle it, how to win it, how to come out of it, what plans to make under various contingencies. These were important matters indeed and the officials in question would not have been doing their duty if they had failed to consider them. They should not be faulted for this; nor was it in any way improper to have planned for every conceivable military eventuality.

But the missing factor was discussion or argumentation over the *raison d'être* of the war and the rationale for continuing massive American involvement in it. It seems to have been accepted without question by virtually everyone in the top ranks, except Under Secretary of State George Ball, that the interests of the United States did indeed lie, at almost any cost and overriding almost any risk, in military victory for the South Vietnamese Government even to the point of major American participation in a war on the land mass of Southeast Asia.

This was the premise, this the context, and this the fateful error. If, as the principal officers of the Government saw the country being drawn into such a war, a full and frank debate and discussion in Congress and outside had been undertaken, it is quite possible that events would have moved in a different way. No one will ever know, for this "open covenant, openly arrived at" between American Government and American people never materialized.

This, then, is what the Vietnam Papers prove—not venality, not evil motivation, but rather an arrogant disregard for the Congress, for the public and for the inherent obligation of the responsibilities of leadership in a democratic society. The papers are not only part of the historical record; they are an essential part of that record. They are highly classified documents and so is the analytical study on which *The Times* running commentary was based. But they carry the story of Vietnam no farther than 1968—now three years ago; they in no way affect current plans, operations or policy; and there seems no longer any justification for these papers—along with many others in governmental files—to bear the kind of classification that keeps them from general public access. Overclassification and misclassification of documents is at best a normal reflection of governmental inertia; but, as here, it is often used to conceal governmental error.

The material was not published by *The Times* for purposes of recrimination or to establish scapegoats or to heap blame on any individual in civilian or military ranks. It was published because the American public has a right to have it and because, when it came into the hands of *The Times*, it was its function as a free and uncensored medium of information to make it public. This same principle held for *The Washington Post* when it too obtained some of the papers. To have acted otherwise would have been to default on a newspaper's basic obligation to the American people under the First Amendment, which is precisely the point that Federal District Judge Murray Gurfein suggested in his memorable decision in this newspaper's favor last Saturday.

And yet the Government of the United States, in an action unprecedented in modern American history, sought and is continuing to seek to silence both *The New York Times* and *The Washington Post*, claiming that "irreparable injury" to the national security would be caused by publication of further chapters in the Vietnam study. The fact is that "irreparable injury" has been done to the

Government itself, not because of anything that has been published but, quite the contrary, because of the extraordinary action the Government took to thwart and subvert in this manner the constitutional principle of freedom of the press which is the very essence of American democracy. Judge Gurfein's decision— whether or not it is sustained on appeal—surely represents a landmark in the endless struggle of free men and free institutions against the unwarranted exercise of governmental authority.

—June 21, 1971

"An Enlightened People"

The historic decision of the Supreme Court in the case of the United States Government vs. *The New York Times* and *The Washington Post* is a ringing victory for freedom under law. By lifting the restraining order that had prevented this and other newspapers from publishing the hitherto secret Pentagon Papers, the nation's highest tribunal strongly reaffirmed the guarantee of the people's right to know, implicit in the First Amendment to the Constitution of the United States.

This was the essence of what *The New York Times* and other newspapers were fighting for and this is the essence of the Court's majority opinions. The basic question, which goes to the very core of the American political system, involved the weighing by the Court of the First Amendment's guarantee of freedom against the Government's power to restrict that freedom in the name of national security. The Supreme Court did not hold that the First Amendment gave an absolute right to publish anything under all circumstances. Nor did *The Times* seek that right. What *The Times* sought, and what the Court upheld, was the right to publish these particular documents at this particular time without prior Governmental restraint.

The crux of the problem lay indeed in this question of prior restraint. For the first time in the history of the United States, the Federal Government had sought through the courts to prevent publication of material that it maintained would do "irreparable injury" to the national security if spread before the public. *The Times,* supported in this instance by the overwhelming majority of the American press, held on the contrary that it was in the national interest to publish this information, which was of historic rather than current operational nature.

If the documents had involved troop movements, ship sailings, imminent military plans, the case might have been quite different; and in fact *The Times* would not have endeavored to publish such material. But this was not the case; the documents and accompanying analysis are historic, in no instance going beyond 1968, and incapable in 1971 of harming the life of a single human being or interfering with any current military operation. The majority of the Court clearly recognized that embarrassment of

648

public officials in the past—or even in the present—is insufficient reason to overturn what Justice White described as "the concededly extraordinary protection against prior restraint under our constitutional system."

So far as the Government's classification of the material is concerned, it is quite true, as some of our critics have observed, that "no one elected *The Times*" to declassify it. But it is also true, as the Court implicitly recognizes, that the public interest is not served by classification and retention in secret form of vast amounts of information, 99.5 per cent of which a retired senior civil servant recently testified "could not be prejudicial to the defense interests of the nation."

Out of this case should surely come a total revision of governmental procedures and practice in the entire area of classification of documents. Everyone who has ever had anything to do with such documents knows that for many years the classification procedures have been hopelessly muddled by inertia, timidity and sometimes even stupidity and venality.

Beyond all this, one may hope that the entire exercise will induce the present Administration to re-examine its own attitudes toward secrecy, suppression and restriction of the liberties of free man in a free society. The issue the Supreme Court decided yesterday touched the heart of this republic; and we fully realize that this is not so much a victory for any particular newspaper as it is for the basic principles of freedom on which the American form of government rests. This is really the profound message of yesterday's decision, in which this newspaper rejoices with humility and with the consciousness that the freedom thus reaffirmed carries with it, as always, the reciprocal obligation to present the truth to the American public so far as it can be determined. That is, in fact, why the Pentagon material had to be published. It is only with the fullest possible understanding of the facts and of the background of any policy decision that the American people can be expected to play the role required of them in this democracy.

It would be well for the present Administration, in the light of yesterday's decision, to reconsider with far more care and understanding than it has in the past, the fundamental importance of individual freedoms—including especially freedom of speech, of the press, of assembly—to the life of the American democracy. "Without an informed and free press," as Justice Stewart said, "there cannot be an enlightened people."

—July 1, 1971

The Court's Decision

The decision of the Supreme Court allowing The Times and other newspapers to continue to publish hitherto secret Pentagon documents on the Vietnam war is in our view less important as

649

a victory for the press than as a striking confirmation of the vitality of the American democratic form of government.

Despite the potentially far-reaching significance of doubts and reservations expressed in the confusing welter of individual opinions—each of the nine Justices wrote his own—the outcome of this case is a landmark for the press in its centuries-old battle against the efforts of Governmental authority to impose prior restraints. But we believe its real meaning goes deeper than that, in the context of the present time and place. We believe that its more profound significance lies in the implicit but inescapable conclusion that the American people have a presumptive right to be informed of the political decisions of their Government and that when the Government has been devious with the people, it will find no constitutional sanction for its efforts to enforce concealment by censorship.

For this is the essential justification of The Times' grave decision to take on itself the responsibility of publishing the Pentagon papers. It was a decision not taken lightly; but The Times felt that the documents, all dating from 1968 or earlier, belonged to the American people, were now part of history, could in no sense damage current military operations or threaten a single life, and formed an essential element in an understanding by the American people of the event that has affected them more deeply than any other in this generation, the Vietnam war.

The decision had to be made whether or not the embarrassment to individuals, or even to governments, outweighed the value to the American public of knowing something about the decision-making process that led into the war and its subsequent escalation. Furthermore, it was evident that Governmental documents have been so generally overclassified and misclassified for so many years that the mere fact of labeling bore no necessary relationship to the national security. An intensive review of classification procedures is sure to be one beneficial result of this affair.

But there will be other results. We hope that the great lesson to have been learned from publication of the Pentagon papers is that the American Government must play square with the electorate. We hope that this Administration and those to come will realize that the major decisions have to be discussed frankly and openly and courageously; and that the essence of good government as of practical politics is, in Adlai Stevenson's phrase, to "talk sense to the American people."

The Pentagon papers demonstrate the failure of successive Administrations to carry out this policy in respect to Vietnam. We do not think it is a question of personal morality, but rather of private attitudes. We do not think that the respective officials involved made recommendations or took decisions that they did not conscientiously believe to be in the public interest. As an early opponent of the escalation of American military force in Vietnam, this newspaper has never attacked the motives of those leaders, but we have criticized and we continue to criticize their wisdom, their sense of values and their failure fully to apprise the people and Congress of the implications of decisions taken in secret.

Even if these decisions, now being revealed in the Pentagon papers, had been generally understood by the public at the time, we are not at all sure that in the climate of those days, the results would have been any different. Given the fear of Communist penetration and aggression throughout the '50's and most of the '60's, it is quite likely that the American public would have supported the basic rationale on escalation even if the respective Administrations had been as forthcoming as democratic procedures demanded.

The fact remains that out of the publication of this material, the American people emerge the gainers. They have gained in knowledge of the past, which should serve them well in the future. They have gained in an understanding of their rights under the Constitution. And they have gained in the perennial effort of free men to control their government rather than vice versa.

Appendix 2

SUPREME COURT DECISION

Following is the text of the decision released on June 30, 1971 by the United States Supreme Court upholding The New York Times and The Washington Post against an effort by the Federal Government to halt publication of articles and documents based on the Pentagon study of the Vietnam war and the texts of the concurring and dissenting opinions:

Decision

Per curiam.

We granted certiorari in these cases in which the United States seeks to enjoin The New York Times and The Washington Post from publishing the contents of a classified study entitled "History of U.S. Decision-Making Process on Viet Nam Policy." —U.S.—(1971).

"Any system of prior restraints of expression comes to this court bearing a heavy presumption against its constitutional validity." Bantam Books, Inc. v. Sullivan, 372 U.S. 58, 70 (1963); see also Near v. Minnesota, 283 U.S. 697 (1931). The Government "thus carries a heavy burden of showing justification for the enforcement of such a restraint." Organization for a Better Austin v. Keefe—U.S.—(1971). The District Court for the Southern District of New York in The New York Times case and the District Court for the District of Columbia and the Court of Appeals for the District of Columbia Circuit in The Washington Post case held that the Government had not met that burden.

We agree.

The judgment of the Court of Appeals for the District of Columbia Circuit is therefore affirmed. The order of the Court of Appeals for the Second Circuit is reversed and the case is remanded with directions to enter a judgment affirming the judgment of the District Court for the Southern District of New York. The stays entered June 25, 1971, by the court are vacated. The mandates shall issue forthwith.

So ordered.

Concurring Opinions

MR. JUSTICE DOUGLAS, *with whom* MR. JUSTICE BLACK *joins, concurring.*

While I join the opinion of the Court I believe it necessary to express my views more fully.

It should be noted at the onset that the First Amendment provides that "Congress shall make no law . . . abridging the freedom of speech or of the press." That leaves, in my view, no room for governmental restraint on the press.

There is, moreover, no statute barring the publication by the press of the material which The Times and Post seek to use. 18 U.S.C. Section 793 (e) provides that "whoever having unauthorized possession of, access to, or control over any document, writing, . . . or information relating to the national defense which information the possessor has reason to believe could be used to the injury of the United States or to the advantage of any foreign nation, willfully communicates . . . the same to any person not entitled to receive it . . . shall be fined not more than $10,000 or imprisoned not more than 10 years or both."

The Government suggests that the word "communicates" is broad enough to encompass publication.

There are eight sections in the chapter on espionage and censorship, sections 792-799. In three of those eight, "publish" is specifically mentioned: Section 794 (b) provides, "Whoever in time of war, with the intent that the same shall be communicated to the enemy, collects records, publishes, or communicates . . . [the disposition of armed forces]."

Section 797 prohibits "reproduces, publishes, sells, or gives away" photos of defense installations.

Section 798 relating to cryptography prohibits: "communicates, furnishes, transmits, or otherwise makes available . . . or publishes." Thus it is apparent that Congress was capable of and did distinguish between publishing and communication in the various sections of the Espionage Act.

The other evidence that Section 793 does not apply to the press is a rejected version of Section 793. That version read: "During any national emergency resulting from a war to which the U.S. is a party or from threat of such a war, the President may, by proclamation, prohibit the publishing or communicating of, or the attempting to publish or communicate, any information relating to the national defense, which in his judgment is of such character that it is or might be useful to the enemy." During the debates in the Senate the First Amendment was specifically cited and that provision was defeated. 55 Cong. Rec. 2166.

Judge Gurfein's holding in The Times case that this act does not apply to this case was therefore pre-eminently sound. Moreover, the act of Sept. 23, 1950, in amending 18 U.S.C. Section 793, states in Section 1 (b) that:

"Nothing in this act shall be construed to authorize, require, or establish military or civilian censorship or in any way to limit or infringe upon freedom of the press or of speech as guaranteed by the Constitution of the United States and no regulation shall be promulgated hereunder having that effect." 64 Stat. 987.

Thus Congress has been faithful to the command of the First Amendment in this area.

So any power that the Government possesses must come from its "inherent power."

The power to wage war is "the power to wage war successfully." See Hirabayashi v. United States, 320 U.S. 81, 93. But the war power stems from a declaration of war. The Constitution by Article I, Section 8, gives Congress, not the President, power "to declare war." Nowhere are Presidential wars authorized. We need not decide therefore what leveling effect the war power of Congress might have.

These disclosures may have a serious impact. But that is no basis for sanctioning a previous restraint on the press. As stated by Chief Justice Hughes in Near v. Minnesota, 283 U.S 697, 719-720:

". . . While reckless assaults upon public men, and efforts to bring obloquy upon those who are endeavoring faithfully to discharge official duties, exert a baleful influence and deserve the severest condemnation in public opinion, it cannot be said that this abuse is greater, and it is believed to be less, than that which characterized the period in which our institutions took shape. Meanwhile, the administration of Government has become more complex, the opportunities for malfeasance and corruption have multiplied, crime has grown to most serious proportions, and the danger of its protection by unfaithful officials and of the impairment of the fundamental security of life and property by criminal alliances and official neglect, emphasizes the primary need of a vigilant and courageous press, especially in great cities. The fact that the liberty of the press may be abused by miscreant purveyors of scandal does not make any the less necessary the immunity of the press from previous restraint in dealing with official misconduct."

As we stated only the other day in Organization for a Better Austin v. Keefe,—U.S.—, "any prior restraint on expression comes to this court with a 'heavy presumption' against its constitutional validity."

The Government says that it has inherent powers to go into court and obtain an injunction to protect that national interest, which in this case is alleged to be national security.

Near v. Minnesota, 283 U.S. 697, repudiated that expansive doctrine in no uncertain terms.

The dominant purpose of the First Amendment was to prohibit the widespread practice of governmental suppression of embarrassing information. It is common knowledge that the First Amendment was adopted against the widespread use of the

654

common law of seditious libel to punish the dissemination of material that is embarrassing to the powers-that-be. See Emerson, "The System of Free Expressions," C. XIII (1941). The present cases will, I think, go down in history as the most dramatic illustration of that principle. A debate of large proportions goes on in the nation over our posture in Vietnam. That debate antedated the disclosure of the contents of the present documents. The latter are highly relevant to the debate in progress.

Secrecy in government is fundamentally antidemocratic, perpetuating bureaucratic errors. Open debate and discussion of public issues are vital to our national health. On public questions there should be "open and robust debate." New York Times, Inc. v. Sullivan, 376 U.S. 254, 269-270.

I would affirm the judgment of the Court of Appeals in The Post case, vacate the stay of the Court of Appeals in The Times case and direct that it affirm the District Court.

The stays in these cases that have been in effect for more than a week constitute a flouting of the principles of the First Amendment as interpreted in Near v. Minnesota.

MR. JUSTICE BRENNAN, *concurring.*

I

I write separately in these cases only to emphasize what should be apparent: that our judgment in the present cases may not be taken to indicate the propriety, in the future, of issuing temporary stays and restraining orders to block the publication of material sought to be suppressed by the Government. So far as I can determine, never before has the United States sought to enjoin a newspaper from publishing information in its possession. The relative novelty of the questions presented, the necessary haste with which decisions were reached, the magnitude of the interests asserted, and the fact that all the parties have concentrated their arguments upon the question whether permanent restraints were proper may have justified at least some of the restraints heretofore imposed in these cases. Certainly it is difficult to fault the several courts below for seeking to assure that the issues here involved were preserved for ultimate review by this Court. But even if it be assumed that some of the interim restraints were proper in the two cases before us, that assumption has no bearing upon the propriety of similar judicial action in the future. To begin with, there has now been ample time for reflection and judgment; whatever values there may be in the preservation of novel questions for appellate review may not support any restraints in the future. More important, the First Amendment stands as an absolute bar to the imposition of judicial restraints in circumstances of the kind presented by these cases.

II

The error which has pervaded these cases from the outset was the granting of any injunctive relief whatsoever, interim or otherwise. The entire thrust of the Government's claim throughout these cases has been that publication of the material sought to be enjoined "could," or "might" or "may" prejudice the national interest in various ways. But the First Amendment tolerates absolutely no prior judicial restraints of the press predicated upon surmise or conjecture that untoward consequences may result. Our cases, it is true, have indicated that there is a single, extremely narrow class of cases in which the First Amendment's ban on prior judicial restraint may be overridden. Our cases have thus far indicated that such cases may arise only when the nation "is at war," Schenck v. United States, 249 U.S. 47. 52 (1919), during which times "no one would question but that a government might prevent actual obstruction to its recruiting service or the publication of the sailing dates of transports or the number and location of troops." Near v. Minnesota, 283 U.S. 697, 716 (1931). Even if the present world situation were assumed to be tantamount to a time of war, or if the power of presently available armaments would justify even in peacetime the suppression of information that would set in motion a nuclear holocaust, in neither of these actions has the Government presented or even alleged that publication of items from or based upon the material at issue would cause the happening of an event of that nature. "The chief purpose of [the First Amendment's] guarantee [is] to prevent previous restraints upon publication." Near v. Minnesota, supra, at 713. Thus, only governmental allegation and proof that publication must inevitably, directly and immediately cause the occurrence of an event kindred to imperiling the safety of a transport already at sea can support even the issuance of an interim restraining order. In no event may mere conclusions be sufficient: for if the executive branch seeks judicial aid in preventing publication, it must inevitably submit the basis upon which that aid is sought to scrutiny by the judiciary. And, therefore, every restraint issued in this case, whatever its form, has violated the First Amendment—and none the less so because that restraint was justified as necessary to afford the Court an opportunity to examine the claim more thoroughly. Unless and until the Government has clearly made out its case, the First Amendment commands that no injunction may issue.

MR. JUSTICE STEWART, *with whom* MR. JUSTICE WHITE *joins, concurring.*

In the governmental structure created by our Constitution, the executive is endowed with enormous power in the two related areas of national defense and international relations. This power, largely unchecked by the legislative and judicial branches, has been pressed to the very hilt since the advent of the nuclear missile age. For better or for worse, the simple fact is that a President of the United States possesses vastly greater constitutional independence in these two vital areas of power than does, say, a prime minister of a country with a parliamentary form of government.

In the absence of the governmental checks and balances present in other areas of our national life, the only effective restraint upon executive policy and power in the areas of national defense and international affairs may lie in an enlightened citizenry—in an informed and critical public opinion which alone can here protect the values of democratic government. For this reason, it is perhaps here that a press that is alert, aware, and free most vitally serves the basic purpose of the First Amendment. For without an informed and free press there cannot be an enlightened people.

Yet it is elementary that the successful conduct of international diplomacy and the maintenance of an effective national defense require both confidentiality and secrecy. Other nations can hardly deal with this nation in an atmosphere of mutual trust unless they can be assured that their confidences will be kept. And within our own executive departments, the development of considered and intelligent international policies would be impossible if those charged with their formulation could not communicate with each other freely, frankly and in confidence. In the area of basic national defense the frequent need for absolute secrecy is, of course, self-evident.

I think there can be but one answer to this dilemma, if dilemma it be. The responsibility must be where the power is. If the Constitution gives the executive a large degree of unshared power in the conduct of foreign affairs and the maintenance of our national defense, then under the Constitution the executive must have the largely unshared duty to determine and preserve the degree of internal security necessary to exercise that power successfully. It is an awesome responsibility, requiring judgment and wisdom of a high order. I should suppose that moral, political and practical considerations would dictate that a very first principle of that wisdom would be an insistence upon avoiding secrecy for its own sake.

For when everything is classified, then nothing is classified, and the system becomes one to be disregarded by the cynical or the careless, and to be manipulated by those intent on self-protection or self-promotion. I should suppose in short, that the hallmark of a truly effective international security system would be the maximum possible disclosure, recognizing that secrecy can best be preserved only when credibility is truly maintained. But be that as it may, it is clear to me that it is the constitutional duty of the executive—as a matter of sovereign prerogative and not as a matter of law as the courts know law—through the promulgation and enforcement of executive regulations, to protect the confidentiality necessary to carry out its responsibilities in the fields of international relations and national defense.

This is not to say that Congress and the courts have no role to play. Undoubtedly Congress has the power to enact specific and appropriate criminal laws to protect Government property and preserve Government secrets. Congress has passed such laws, and several of them are of very colorable relevance to the apparent circumstances of these cases, and if a criminal prosecution is instituted, it will be the responsibility of the courts to decide the applicability of the criminal law under which the charge is brought. Moreover, if Congress should pass a specific law authorizing civil proceedings in this field, the courts would likewise have the duty to decide the constitutionality of such a law as well as its applicability to the facts proved.

But in the cases before us we are asked neither to construe specific regulations nor to apply specific laws. We are asked, instead, to perform a function that the Constitution gave to the executive, not the judiciary. We are asked, quite simply, to prevent the publication by two newspapers of material that the executive branch insists should not, in the national interest, be published. I am convinced that the executive is correct with respect to some of the documents involved. But I cannot say that disclosure of any of them will surely result in direct, immediate and irreparable damage to our nation or its people. That being so, there can under the First Amendment be but one judicial resolution of the issues before us.

I join the judgments of the court.

MR. JUSTICE MARSHALL, *concurring*.

The Government contends that the only issue in this case is whether in a suit by the United States, "the First Amendment bars a court from prohibiting a newspaper from publishing material whose disclosure would pose a grave and immediate danger to the security of the United States." Brief of the Government, at 6. With all due respect, I believe the ultimate issue in this case is even more basic than the one posed by the Solicitor General. The issue is whether this Court or the Congress has the power to make law.

In this case there is no problem concerning the President's power to classify information as "secret" or "top secret." Congress has specifically recognized Presidential authority, which has been formally exercised in Executive Order 10501, to classify documents and information. See, e.g., 18 U.S.C. Section 798; 50 U.S.C. Section 783. Nor is there any issue here regarding the President's power as Chief Executive and Commander in Chief to protect national security by disciplining employes who disclose information and by taking precautions to prevent leaks.

The problem here is whether in this particular case the executive branch has authority to invoke the equity jurisdiction of the courts to protect what it believes to be the national interest. See In Re Debs, 158 U.S. 564, 584 (1895). The Government argues that in addition to the inherent power of any government to protect itself, the President's power to conduct foreign affairs and his position as Commander in Chief give him authority to impose censorship on the press to protect his ability to deal effectively with foreign nations and to conduct the military affairs of the country. Of course, it is beyond cavil that the President has broad powers by virtue of his primary responsibility for the conduct of our foreign affairs and his position as Commander in Chief. Chicago & Southern Air Lines, Inc., v. Waterman Corp., 333 U.S. 103 (1948); Hirabayashi v. United States, 320 U.S. 81, 93 (1943); United States v. Curtiss-Wright Export Co., 299 U.S. 304 (1936). And in some situations it may be that under whatever inherent powers the Government may have, as well as the implicit authority derived from the President's mandate to conduct foreign affairs and to act as Commander in Chief there is a basis for the invocation of the equity jurisdiction of this Court as an aid to prevent the publication of material damaging to "national security," however that term may be defined.

It would, however, be utterly inconsistent with the concept of separation of power for this Court to use its power of contempt to prevent behavior that Congress has specifically declined to prohibit. There would be a similar damage to the basic concept of these co-equal branches of government if when the executive has adequate authority granted by Congress to protect "national security," it can choose instead to invoke the contempt power of a court to enjoin the threatened conduct. The Constitution provides that Congress shall make laws, the President execute laws, and courts interpret law. Youngstown Sheet & Tube Co. v. Sawyer, 343 U.S. 579 (1952). It did not provide for government by injunction, in which the courts and the executive can "make law" without regard to the action of Congress. It may be more convenient for the executive if it need only convince a judge to prohibit conduct rather than to ask the Congress to pass a law, and it may be more convenient to enforce a contempt order than seek a criminal conviction in a jury trial. Moreover, it may be considered politically wise to get a court to share the responsibility for arresting those who the executive has probably cause to believe are violating the law. But convenience and political considerations of the moment do not justify a basic departure from the principles of our system of government.

In this case we are not faced with a situation where Congress has failed to provide the executive with broad power to protect the nation from disclosure of damaging state secrets. Congress has on several occasions given extensive consideration to the problem of protecting the military and strategic secrets of the United States. This consideration has resulted in the enactment of statutes making it a crime to receive, disclose, communicate, withhold and publish certain documents, photographs, instruments, appliances and information. The bulk of these statutes are found in Chapter 37 of U.S.C., Title 18, entitled "Espionage and Censorship." In that chapter, Congress has provided penalties ranging from a $10,000 fine to death for violating the various statutes.

Thus it would seem that in order for this Court to issue an injunction it would require a showing that such an injunction would enhance the already existing power of the Government to act. See Bennett v. Laman, 277 N. Y. 368, 14 N. E. 2d 439 (1938). It is a traditional axiom of equity that a court of equity will not do a useless thing just as it is a traditional axiom that equity will not enjoin the commission of a crime. See Z. Chaffe & E. Re, Equity 935-954 (5th ed. 1967); H. Joyce, injunctions sections 58-60A (1909). Here there has been no attempt to make such a showing. The Solicitor General does not even mention in his brief whether the Government considers there to be probable cause to believe a crime has been committed or whether there is a conspiracy to commit future crimes.

If the Government had attempted to show that there was no effective remedy under traditional criminal law, it would have had to show that there is no arguably applicable statute. Of course, at this stage this Court could not and cannot determine whether there has been a violation of a particular statute nor decide the constitutionality of any statute. Whether a good-faith prosecution could have been instituted under any statute could, however, be determined.

At least one of the many statutes in this area seems relevant to this case. Congress has provided in 18 U.S.C. Section 793 (e) that whoever "having unauthorized possession of, access to, or control over any document, writing, code book, signal book . . . or note relating to the national defense, or information relating to the national defense which information the possessor has reason to believe could be used to the injury of the United States or to the advantage of any foreign nation, willfully communicates, delivers, transmits . . . the same to any person not entitled to receive it, or willfully retains the same and fails to deliver it to the officer or employe of the United States entitled to receive it . . . shall be fined not more than $10,000 or imprisoned not more than 10 years, or both." 18 U.S.C. Section 793 (e). Congress has also made it a crime to conspire to commit any of the offenses listed in 18 U.S.C. Section 793 (e).

It is true that Judge Gurfein found that Congress had not made it a crime to publish the items and material specified in Section 793 (e): He found that the words "communicates, delivers, transmits . . ." did not refer to publication of newspaper stories. And that view has some support in the legislative history and conforms with the past practice of using the statute only to prosecute those charged with ordinary espionage. But see 103 Cong. Rec. 10449 (remarks of Senator Humphrey). Judge Gurfein's view of the statute is not, however, the only plausible construction that could be given. See my brother White's concurring opinion.

Even if it is determined that the Government could not in

660

ood faith bring criminal prosecutions against The New York Times and The Washington Post, it is clear that Congress has specifically rejected passing legislation that would have clearly given the President the power he seeks here and made the current activity of the newspapers unlawful. When Congress specifically declines to make conduct unlawful it is not for this Court to redecide those issues—to overrule Congress. See Youngstown Sheet & Tube v. Sawyer, 345 U.S. 579 (1952).

On at least two occasions Congress has refused to enact legislation that would have made the conduct engaged in here unlawful and given the President the power that he seeks in this case. In 1917 during the debate over the original Espionage Act, still the basic provisions of Section 793, Congress rejected a proposal to give the President in time of war or threat of war authority to directly prohibit by proclamation the publication of information relating to national defense that might be useful to the enemy. The proposal provided that:

"During any national emergency resulting from a war to which the United States is a party, or from threat of such a war, the President may, by proclamation, prohibit the publishing or communicating of, or the attempting to publish or communicate any information relating to the national defense which, in his judgment, is of such character that it is or might be useful to the enemy. Whoever violates any such prohibition shall be punished by a fine of not more than $10,000 or by imprisonment for not more than 10 years, or both: provided, that nothing in this section shall be construed to limit or restrict any discussion, comment or criticism of the acts or policies of the Government or its representatives or the publication of the same." 55 Cong. Rec. 1763.

Congress rejected this proposal after war against Germany had been declared even though many believed that the threat of security leaks and espionage were serious. The executive has not gone to Congress and requested that the decision to provide such power be reconsidered. Instead, the executive comes to this Court and asks that it be granted the power Congress refused to give.

In 1957 the United States Commission on Government Security found that "airplane journals, scientific periodicals and even the daily newspaper have featured articles containing information and other data which should have been deleted in whole or in part for security reasons." In response to this problem the commission, which was chaired by Senator Cotton, proposed that "Congress enact legislation making it a crime for any person willfully to disclose without proper authorization, for any purpose whatever, information classified 'secret' or 'top secret,' knowing, or having reasonable grounds to believe, such information to have been so classified." Report of Commission on Government Security 619-620 (1957). After substantial floor discussion on the proposal, it was rejected. See 103 Cong. Rec. 10447-

10450. If the proposal that Senator Cotton championed on the floor had been enacted, the publication of the documents here would certainly have been a crime. Congress refused, however, to make it a crime. The Government is here asking this Court to remake that decision. This court has no such power.

Either the Government has the power under statutory grant to use traditional criminal law to protect the country or, if there is no basis for arguing that Congress has made the activity a crime, it is plain that Congress has specifically refused to grant the authority the Government seeks from this Court. In either case this court does not have authority to grant the requested relief. It is not for this Court to fling itself into every breach perceived by some Government official, nor is it for this Court to take on itself the burden of enacting law, especially law that Congress has refused to pass.

I believe that the judgment of the United States Court of Appeals for the District of Columbia should be affirmed and the judgment of the United States Court of Appeals for the Second Circuit should be reversed insofar as it remands the case for further hearings.

MR. JUSTICE BLACK, *with whom* MR. JUSTICE DOUGLAS *joins, concurring.*

I adhere to the view that the Government's case against The Washington Post should have been dismissed and that the injunction against The New York Times should have been vacated without oral argument when the cases were first presented to this Court. I believe that every moment's continuance of the injunctions against these newspapers amounts to a flagrant, indefensible and continuing violation of the First Amendment. Furthermore, after oral arguments, I agree completely that we must affirm the judgment of the Court of Appeals for the District of Columbia and reverse the judgment of the Court of Appeals for the Second Circuit for the reasons stated by my brothers Douglas and Brennan. In my view it is unfortunate that some of my brethren are apparently willing to hold that the publication of news may sometimes be enjoined. Such a holding would make a shambles of the First Amendment.

Our Government was launched in 1789 with the adoption of the Constitution. The Bill of Rights, including the First Amendment, followed in 1791. Now, for the first time in the 182 years since the founding of the Republic, the Federal courts are asked to hold that the First Amendment does not mean what it says, but rather means that the Government can halt the publication of current news of vital importance to the people of this country.

In seeking injunctions against these newspapers and in its presentation to the court, the executive branch seems to have forgotten the essential purpose and history of the First Amendment. When the Constitution was adopted, many people strongly opposed it because the document contained no bill of rights to safeguard certain basic freedoms. They especially feared that the new powers granted to a central government might be interpreted to permit the government to curtail freedom of religion, press, assembly and speech. In response to an overwhelming public clamor, James Madison offered a series of amendments to satisfy citizens that these great liberties would remain safe and beyond the power of government to abridge. Madison proposed what later became the First Amendment in three parts, two of which are set out below, and one of which proclaimed: "The people shall not be deprived or abridged of their right to speak, to write, or to publish their sentiments; and the freedom of the press, as one of the great bulwarks of liberty, shall be inviolable." The amendments were offered to curtail and restrict the general powers granted to the executive, legislative and judicial branches two years before in the original Constitution. The Bill of Rights changed the original Constitution into a new charter under which no branch of government could abridge the people's freedoms of press, speech, religion and assembly.

Yet the Solicitor General argues and some members of the Court appear to agree that the general powers of the Government adopted in the original Constitution should be interpreted to limit and restrict the specific and emphatic guarantees of the Bill of Rights adopted later. I can imagine no greater perversion of history. Madison and the other framers of the First Amendment, able men that they were, wrote in language they earnestly believed could never be misunderstood: "Congress shall make no law . . . abridging the freedom of the press." Both the history and language of the First Amendment support the view that the press must be left free to publish news, whatever the source, without censorship, injunctions or prior restraints.

In the First Amendment the Founding Fathers gave the free press the protection it must have to fulfill its essential role in our democracy. The press was to serve the governed, not the governors. The Government's power to censor the press was abolished so that the press would remain forever free to censure the Government. The press was protected so that it could bare the secrets of government and inform the people. Only a free and unrestrained press can effectively expose deception in government. And paramount among the responsibilities of a free press is the duty to prevent any part of the Government from deceiving the people and sending them off to distant lands to die of foreign fevers and foreign shot and shell. In my view, far from deserving condemnation for their courageous reporting, The New York Times, The Washington Post and other newspapers should be commended for serving the purpose that the Founding Fathers saw so clearly. In revealing the workings of government that led to the Vietnam war, the newspapers nobly did precisely that which the founders hoped and trusted they would do.

The Government's case here is based on premises entirely different from those that guided the framers of the First Amendment. The Solicitor General has carefully and emphatically stated:

"Now, Mr. Justice [Black], your construction of . . . [the First Amendment] is well known, and I certainly respect it. You say that no law means no law, and that should be obvious. I can only say, Mr. Justice, that to me it is equally obvious that 'no law,' and I would seek to persuade the Court that that is true . . . [t]here are other parts of the Constitution that grant power and responsibilities to the executive end . . . the First Amendment was not intended to make it impossible for the executive to function or to protect the security of the United States."

And the Government argues in its brief that in spite of the First Amendment, "the authority of the executive department to protect the nation against publication of information whose disclosure would endanger the national security stems from two interrelated sources: The constitutional power of the President over the conduct of foreign affairs and his authority as Commander in Chief."

In other words, we are asked to hold that despite the First Amendment's emphatic command, the executive branch, the Congress and the judiciary can make laws enjoining publication of current news and abridging freedom of the press in the name of "national security." The Government does not even attempt to rely on act of Congress. Instead it makes the bold and dangerously far-reaching contention that the courts should take it upon themselves to "make" a law abridging freedom of the press in the name of equity, Presidential power and national security, even when the representatives of the people in Congress have adhered to the command of the First Amendment and refused to make such a law. See concurring opinion of Mr. Justice Douglas, Post.

To find that the President has "inherent power" to halt the publication of news by resort to the courts would wipe out the First Amendment and destroy the fundamental liberty and security of the very people the Government hopes to make "secure." No one can read the history of the adoption of the First Amendment without being convinced beyond any doubt that it was injunctions like those sought here that Madison and his collaborators intended to outlaw in this nation for all time.

The word "security" is a broad, vague generality whose contours should not be invoked to abrogate the fundamental law embodied in the First Amendment. The guarding of military and diplomatic secrets at the expense of informed representative government provides no real security for our Republic.

The framers of the First Amendment, fully aware of both the need to defend a new nation and the abuses of the English and colonial Governments, sought to give this new society strength and security by providing that freedom of speech, press, religion and assembly should not be abridged. This thought was eloquently expressed in 1937 by Mr. Chief Justice Hughes—great man and great Chief Justice that he was—when the Court held a man could not be punished for attending a meeting run by Communists.

"The greater the importance of safeguarding the community from incitements to the overthrow of our institutions by force and violence, the more imperative is the need to preserve inviolate the constitutional rights of free speech, free press and free assembly in order to maintain the opportunity for free political discussion, to the end that government may be responsive to the will of the people and that changes, if desired, may be obtained by peaceful means. Therein lies the security of the Republic, the very foundation of constitutional government."

MR. JUSTICE WHITE, with whom MR. JUSTICE STEWART joins, concurring.

I concur in today's judgments, but only because of the concededly extraordinary protection against prior restraints enjoyed by the press under our constitutional system. I do not say that in no circumstances would the First Amendment permit an injunction against publishing information about Government plans or operations. Nor, after examining the materials the Government characterizes as the most sensitive and destructive, can I deny that revelation of these documents will do substantial damage to public interests. Indeed, I am confident that their disclosure will have that result. But I nevertheless agree that the United States has not satisfied the very heavy burden which it must meet to warrant an injunction against publication in these cases, at least in the absence of express and appropriately limited Congressional authorization for prior restraints in circumstances such as these.

The Government's position is simply stated: The responsibility of the executive for the conduct of the foreign affairs and for the security of the nation is so basic that the President is entitled to an injunction against publication of a newspaper story whenever he can convince a court that the information to be revealed threatens "grave and irreparable" injury to the public interest; and the injunction should issue whether or not the material to be published is classified, whether or not publication would be lawful under relevant criminal statutes enacted by Congress and regardless of the circumstances by which the newspaper came into possession of the information.

At least in the absence of legislation by Congress, based on its own investigations and findings, I am quite unable to agree that the inherent powers of the executive and the courts reach so far as to authorize remedies having such sweeping potential for inhibiting publications by the press. Much of the difficulty inheres in the "grave and irreparable danger" standard suggested by the United States. If the United States were to have judgment under such a standard in these cases, our decision would be of little guidance to other courts in other cases, for the material at issue here would not be available from the Court's opinion or from public records, nor would it be published by the press. Indeed, even today where we hold that the United States has not met its burden, the material remains sealed in court records and it is properly not discussed in today's opinions. Moreover, because the material poses substantial dangers to national interests and because of the hazards of criminal sanctions, a responsible press may choose never to publish the more sensitive materials. To sustain the Government in these cases would start the courts down a long and hazardous road that I am not willing to travel, at least without Congressional guidance and direction.

It is not easy to reject the proposition urged by the United States and to deny relief on its good-faith claims in these cases that publication will work serious damage to the country. But that discomfiture is considerably dispelled by the infrequency of prior restraint cases. Normally, publication will occur and the damage be done before the Government has either opportunity or grounds for suppression. So here, publication has already begun and a substantial part of the threatened damage has already occurred. The fact of a massive breakdown in security is known, access to the documents by many unauthorized people is undeniable and efficacy of equitable relief against these or other newspapers to avert anticipated damage is doubtful at best.

What is more, terminating the ban on publication of the relatively few sensitive documents the Government now seeks to suppress does not mean that the law either requires or invites newspapers or others to publish them or that they will be immune from criminal action if they do. Prior restraints require an unusually heavy justification under the First Amendment; but failure by the Government to justify prior restraints does not measure its constitutional entitlement to a conviction for criminal publication. That the Government mistakenly chose to proceed by injunction does not mean that it could not successfully proceed in another way.

When the Espionage Act was under consideration in 1917, Congress eliminated from the bill a provision that would have given the President broad powers in time of war to proscribe, under threat of criminal penalty, the publication of various categories of information related to the national defense. Congress at that time was unwilling to clothe the President with such far-reaching powers to monitor the press, and those opposed to this part of the legislation assumed that a necessary concomitant of such power was the power to "filter out the news to the people through some man." 55 Cong. Rec. 2008 (1917) (remarks of Senator Ashurst). However, these same members of Congress appeared to have little doubt that newspapers would be subject to criminal prosecution if they insisted on publishing information of the type Congress had itself determined should not be revealed. Senator Ashurst, for example, was quite sure that the editor of such a newspaper "should be punished if he did publish information as to the movement of the fleet, the troops, the aircraft, the location of powder factories, the location of defense works and all that sort of thing." 55 Cong. Rec. 2009 (1917).

The Criminal Code contains numerous provisions potentially relevant to these cases. Section 797 makes it a crime to publish certain photographs or drawings of military installations. Section 798, also in precise language, proscribes knowing and willful publications of any classified information concerning the cryptographic systems or communication intelligence activities of the United States as well as any information obtained from communication intelligence operations. If any of the material here at issue is of this nature, the newspapers are presumably now on full notice of the position of the United States and must face the consequences if they publish. I would have no difficulty in sustaining convictions under these sections on facts that would not justify the intervention of equity and the imposition of a prior restraint.

The same would be true under those sections of the Criminal Code casting a wider net to protect the national defense. Section 798 (e) makes it a criminal act for any unauthorized possessor of a document "relating to national defense" either (1) willfully to communicate or cause to be communicated that document to any person not entitled to receive it or (2) willfully to retain the document and fail to deliver it to an officer of the United States entitled to receive it. The subsection was added in 1950 because pre-existing law provided no penalty for the unauthorized possessor unless demand for the documents was made. "The dangers surrounding the unauthorized possession of such items are self-evident, and it is deemed advisable to require their surrender in such a case, regardless of demand, especially since their unauthorized possession may be unknown to the authorities who would otherwise make the demand." S. Rep. No. 2369, 81st Cong., 2d Sess., 9 (1950). Of course, in the cases before us, the unpublished documents have been demanded by the United States and their import has been made known at least to counsel for the newspapers involved. In Gorin v. United States, 312 U.S. 19, 28 (1941), the words "national defense" as used in a predecessor of Sec. 793 were held by a unanimous court to have "a well-understood connotation"—a "generic concept of broad connotations, referring to the military and naval establishments and the related activities of national preparedness" —and to be "sufficiently definite to apprise the public of prohibited activities" and to be "consonant with due process. 312 U.S., at 28. Also, as construed by the Court in Gorin, information "connected with the national defense" is obviously not limited to that threatening "grave and irreparable" injury to the United States.

It is thus clear that Congress has addressed itself to the problems of protecting the security of the country and the national defense from unauthorized disclosure of potentially damaging information. Cf. Youngstown Sheet & Tube Co. v. Sawyer, 343 U.S. 579, 585-586 (1952): see also id., at 593-628 (Frankfurter, J., concurring). It has not, however, authorized the injunctive remedy against threatened publication. It has apparently been satisfied to rely on criminal sanctions and their deterrent effect on the responsible as well as the irresponsible press. I am not, of course, saying that either of these newspapers has yet committed a crime or that either would commit a crime if they published all the material now in their possession. That matter must await resolution in the context of a criminal proceeding if one is instituted by the United States. In that event, the issue of guilt or innocence would be determined by procedures and standards quite different from those that have purported to govern these injunctive proceedings.

Dissents

Mr. Chief Justice Burger, *dissenting*.

So clear are the constitutional limitations on prior restraint against expression, that from the time of Near v. Minnesota, 283 U.S. 697 (1931), until recently in Organization for a Better Austin v. Keefe, (1971), we have had little occasion to be concerned with cases involving prior restraints against news reporting on matters of public interest. There is, therefore, little variation among the members of the Court in terms of resistance to prior restraints against publication. Adherence of this basic constitutional principle, however, does not make this case a simple one. In this case, the imperative of a free and unfettered press comes into collision with another imperative, the effective functioning of a complex modern government, and specifically the effective exercise of certain constitutional powers of the executive. Only those who view the First Amendment as an absolute in all circumstances—a view I respect, but reject—can find such a case as this to be simple or easy.

This case is not simple for another and more immediate reason. We do not know the facts of the case. No District Judge knew all the facts. No Court of Appeals Judge knew all the facts. No member of this Court knows all the facts.

Why are we in this posture, in which only those judges to whom the First Amendment is absolute and permits of no restraint in any circumstances or for any reason, are really in a position to act?

I suggest we are in this posture because these cases have been conducted in unseemly haste. Mr. Justice Harlan covers the chronology of events demonstrating the hectic pressures under which these cases have been processed and I need not restate them. The prompt setting of these cases reflects our universal abhorrence of prior restraint. But prompt judicial action does not mean unjudicial haste.

Here, moreover, the frenetic haste is due in large part to the manner in which The Times proceeded from the date it obtained the purloined documents. It seems reasonably clear now that the haste precluded reasonable and deliberate judicial treatment of these cases and was not warranted. The precipitous action of this court aborting a trial not yet completed is not the kind of judicial conduct which ought to attend the disposition of a great issue.

The newspapers make a derivative claim under the First Amendment: they denominate this right as the public right to know; by implication, The Times asserts a sole trusteeship of that right by virtue of its journalistic "scoop." The right is asserted as an absolute. Of course, the First Amendment right itself is not an absolute, as Justice Holmes so long ago pointed out in his aphorism concerning the right to shout of fire in a crowded theater. There are other exceptions, some of which Chief Justice Hughes mentioned by way of example in Near v. Minnesota. There are no doubt other exceptions no one has had occasion to describe or discuss. Conceivably such exceptions may be lurking in these cases and would have been flushed had they been properly considered in the trial courts, free from unwarranted deadlines and frenetic pressures.

A great issue of this kind should be tried in a judicial atmosphere conducive to thoughtful, reflective deliberation, especially when haste, in terms of hours, is unwarranted in light of the long period The Times, by its own choice, deferred publication.

It is not disputed that The Times has had unauthorized possession of the documents for three to four months, during which it has had its expert analysts studying them, presumably digesting them and preparing the material for publication. During all of this time, The Times, presumably in its capacity as trustee of the public's "right to know," has held up publication for purposes it considered proper and thus public knowledge was delayed. No doubt this was for a good reason; the analysis of 7,000 pages of complex material drawn from a vastly greater volume of material would inevitably take time and the writing of good news stories takes time.

But why should the United States Government, from whom this information was illegally acquired by someone, along with all the counsel, trial judges, and appellate judges be placed under needless pressure? After these months of deferral, the alleged right to know has somehow and suddenly become a right that must be vindicated instanter.

669

Would it have been unreasonable, since the newspaper could anticipate the Government's objections to release of secret material, to give the Government an opportunity to review the entire collection and determine whether agreement could be reached on publication? Stolen or not, if security was not in fact jeopardized, much of the material could no doubt have been declassified, since it spans a period ending in 1968.

With such an approach—one that great newspapers have in the past practiced and stated editorially to be the duty of honorable press—the newspapers and Government might well have narrowed the area of disagreement as to what was and was not publishable, leaving the remainder to be resolved in orderly litigation if necessary. To me it is hardly believable that a newspaper long regarded as a great institution in American life would fail to perform one of the basic and simple duties of every citizen with respect to the discovery or possession of stolen property or secret Government documents. That duty, I had thought—perhaps naively—was to report forthwith, to responsible public officers. This duty rests on taxi drivers, justices and The New York Times. The course followed by The Times, whether so calculated or not, removed any possibility of orderly litigation of the issues. If the action of the judges up to now has been correct, that result is sheer happenstance.

Our grant of the writ before final judgment in The Times case aborted the trial in the District Court before it had made a complete record pursuant to the mandate of the Court of Appeals, Second Circuit.

The consequences of all this melancholy series of events is that we literally do not know what we are acting on. As I see it we have been forced to deal with litigation concerning rights of great magnitude without an adequate record, and surely without time for adequate treatment either in the prior proceedings or in this court. It is interesting to note that counsel in oral argument before this Court were frequently unable to respond to questions on factual points. Not surprisingly they pointed out that they had been working literally "around the clock" and simply were unable to review the documents that give rise to these cases and were not familiar with them. This Court is in no better posture. I agree with Mr. Justice Harlan and Mr. Justice Blackmun but I am not prepared to reach the merits.

I would affirm the Court of Appeals for the Second Circuit and allow the District Court to complete the trial aborted by our grant of certiorari, meanwhile preserving the status quo in The Post case. I would direct that the District Court on remand give priority to The Times case to the exclusion of all other business of that court but I would not set arbitrary deadlines.

I should add that I am in general agreement with much of what Mr. Justice White has expressed with respect to penal

670

sanctions concerning communication or retention of documents or information relating to the national defense.

We all crave speedier judicial processes, but when judges are pressured as in these cases the result is a parody of the judicial process.

MR. JUSTICE HARLAN, *with whom the* CHIEF JUSTICE *and* MR. JUSTICE BLACKMUN *join, dissenting.*

These cases forcefully call to mind the wise admonition of Mr. Justice Holmes, dissenting in Northern Securities Co. v. United States, 193 U.S. 197, 400-401 (1904):

"Great cases like hard cases make bad law. For great cases are called great, not by reason of their real importance in shaping the law of the future, but because of some accident of immediate overwhelming interest which appeals to the feelings and distorts the judgment. These immediate interests exercise a kind of hydraulic pressure which makes what previously was clear seem doubtful, and before which even well settled principles of law will bend."

With all respect, I consider that the Court has been almost irresponsibly feverish in dealing with these cases.

Both the Court of Appeals for the Second Circuit and the Court of Appeals for the District of Columbia Circuit rendered judgment on June 23. The New York Times's petition for certiorari, its motion for accelerated consideration thereof, and its application for interim relief were filed in this Court on June 24 at about 11 A.M. The application of the United States for interim relief in The Post case was also filed here on June 24, at about 7:15 P.M. This Court's order setting a hearing before us on June 26 at 11 A.M., a course which I joined only to avoid the possibility of even more peremptory action by the Court, was issued less than 24 hours before. The record in The Post case was filed with the clerk shortly before 1 P.M. on June 25; the record in The Times case did not arrive until 7 or 8 o'clock that same night. The briefs of the parties were received less than two hours before argument on June 26.

This frenzied train of events took place in the name of the presumption against prior restraints created by the First Amendment. Due regard for the extraordinarily important and difficult questions involved in these litigations should have led the Court to shun such a precipitate timetable. In order to decide the merits of these cases properly, some or all of the following questions should have been faced:

1. Whether the Attorney General is authorized to bring these suits in the name of the United States. Compare In Re Debs, 158 U.S. 564 (1895), with Youngstown Sheet & Tube Co. v. Sawyer, 343 U.S. 479 (1952). This question involves as well the construction and validity of a singularly opaque statute—the Espionage Act, 18 U.S.C. Section 793 (e).

2. Whether the First Amendment permits the Federal Courts

to enjoin publication of stories which would present a serious threat to national security. See Near v. Minnesota, 283 U.S. 697, 716 (1931) (dictum).

3. Whether the threat to publish highly secret documents is of itself a sufficient implication of national security to justify an injunction on the theory that regardless of the contents of the documents harm enough results simply from the demonstration of such a breach of secrecy.

4. Whether the unauthorized disclosure of any of these particular documents would seriously impair the national security.

5. What weight should be given to the opinion of high officers in the executive branch of the Government with respect to questions 3 and 4.

6. Whether the newspapers are entitled to retain and use the documents notwithstanding the seemingly uncontested facts that the documents, or the original of which they are duplicates, were purloined from the Government's possession and that the newspapers received them with the knowledge that they had been feloniously acquired. Cf. Liberty Lobby, Inc., v. Pearson, 390 F. 2d 489 (CADC 1968).

7. Whether the threatened harm to the national security or the Government's possessory interest in the documents justifies the issuance of an injunction against publication in light of—

A. The strong First Amendment policy against prior restraints on publication;

B. The doctrine against enjoining conduct in violation of criminal statutes; and

C. The extent to which the materials at issue have apparently already been otherwise disseminated.

These are difficult questions of fact, of law and of judgment; the potential consequences of erroneous decision are enormous. The time which has been available to us, to the lower courts and to the parties has been wholly inadequate for giving these cases the kind of consideration they deserve. It is a reflection on the stability of the judicial process that these great issues— as important as any that have arisen during my time on the Court—should have been decided under the pressures engendered by the torrent of publicity that has attended these litigations from their inception.

Forced as I am to reach the merits of these cases, I dissent from the opinion and judgments of the Court. Within the severe limitations imposed by the time constraints under which I have been required to operate, I can only state my reasons in telescoped form, even though in different circumstances I would have felt constrained to deal with the cases in the fuller sweep indicated above.

It is a sufficient basis for affirming the Court of Appeals for the Second Circuit in The Times litigation to observe that its order must rest on the conclusion that because of the time elements the Government had not been given an adequate opportunity to present its case to the District Court. At the least this conclusion was not an abuse of discretion.

In The Post litigation the Government had more time to prepare; this was apparently the basis for the refusal of the Court of Appeals for the District of Columbia Circuit on re-hearing to conform its judgment to that of the Second Circuit. But I think there is another and more fundamental reason why this judgment cannot stand—a reason which also furnishes an additional ground for not reinstating the judgment of the District Court in The Times litigation, set aside by the Court of Appeals. It is plain to me that the scope of the judicial function in passing upon the activities of the executive branch of the Government in the field of foreign affairs is very narrowly restricted. This view is, I think, dictated by the concept of separation of powers upon which our constitutional system rests.

In a speech on the floor of the House of Representatives, Chief Justice John Marshall, then a member of that body, stated:

"The President is the sole organ of the nation in its external relations, and its sole representative with foreign nations." Annals, 6th Cong., Col. 613 (1800).

From that time, shortly after the founding of the nation, to this, there has been no substantial challenge to this description of the scope of executive power. See United States v. Curtiss-Wright Export Corp., 299 U.S. 304, 319-321 (1936), collecting authorities.

From this constitutional primacy in the field of foreign affairs, it seems to me that certain conclusions necessarily follow. Some of these were stated concisely by President Washington, declining the request of the House of Representatives for the papers leading up to the negotiation of the Jay Treaty:

"The nature of foreign negotiations requires caution, and their success must often depend on secrecy; and even when brought to a conclusion a full disclosure of all the measures, demands, or eventual concessions which may have been proposed or contemplated would be extremely impolitic; for this might have a pernicious influence on future negotiations, or produce immediate inconveniences, perhaps danger and mischief, in relation to other powers." J. Richardson, "Messages and Papers of the Presidents" 194-195 (1899).

The power to evaluate the "pernicious influence" of premature disclosure is not, however, lodged in the executive alone. I agree that, in performance of its duty to protect the values of the First Amendment against political pressures, the judiciary must review the initial executive determination to the point of satisfying itself that the subject matter of the dispute does lie within the proper compass of the President's foreign relations power. Constitutional considerations forbid "a complete abandonment of judicial control." Cf. United States v. Reynolds, 345 U.S. 1, 8 (1953). Moreover, the judiciary may properly insist that the determination that disclosure of the subject matter would irreparably impair the national security be made by the head of the executive department concerned—here the Secretary of State or the Secretary of Defense—after actual personal consideration by that office. This safeguard is required in the analogous area of executive claims of privilege for secrets of state. See United States v. Reynolds, supra, at 8 and N. 20; Duncan v. Cammell, Laird & Co., (1942) A. C. 624, 638 (House of Lords).

But in my judgment the judiciary may not properly go beyond these two inquiries and redetermine for itself the probable impact of disclosure on the national security.

"The very nature of executive decisions as to foreign policy is political, not judicial. Such decisions are wholly confided by our Constitution to the political departments of the Government, executive and legislative. They are delicate, complex, and involve large elements of prophecy. They are and should be undertaken only by those directly responsible to the people whose welfare they advance or imperil. They are decisions of a kind for which the judiciary has neither aptitude, facilities nor responsibility and which has long been held to belong in the domain of political power not subject to judicial intrusion or inquiry." Chicago & Southern Air Lines v. Waterman Steamship Corp., 333 U.S. 103, 111 (1948) (Jackson, J.).

Even if there is some room for the judiciary to override the executive determination, it is plain that the scope of review must be exceedingly narrow. I can see no indication in the opinions of either the District Court or the Court of Appeals in The Post litigation that the conclusions of the executive were given even the deference owing to an administrative agency, much less that owing to a co-equal constitutional prerogative.

Accordingly, I would vacate the judgment of the Court of Appeals for the District of Columbia Circuit on this ground and remand the case for further proceedings in the District Court. Before the commencement of such further proceedings, due opportunity should be afforded the Government for procuring from the Secretary of State or the Secretary of Defense or both an expression of their views on the issue of national security. The ensuing review by the District Court should be in accordance with the views expressed in this opinion. And for the reasons stated above I would affirm the judgment of the Court of Appeals for the Second Circuit.

Pending further hearings in each case conducted under the appropriate ground rules, I would continue the restraints on publication. I cannot believe that the doctrine prohibiting prior restraints reaches to the point of preventing courts from maintaining the status quo long enough to act responsibly in matters of such national importance as those involved here.

MR. JUSTICE BLACKMUN.

I join Mr. Justice Harlan in his dissent. I also am in substantial accord with much that Mr. Justice White says, by way of admonition, in the latter part of his opinion.

At this point the focus is on only the comparatively few documents specified by the Government as critical. So far as the other material—vast in amount—is concerned, let it be published and published forthwith if the newspapers, once the strain is gone and the sensationalism is eased, still feel the urge so to do.

But we are concerned here with the few documents specified from the 47 volumes. Almost 70 years ago Mr. Justice Holmes, dissenting in a celebrated case, observed:

"Great cases like hard cases make bad law. For great cases are called great, not by reason of their real importance in shaping the law of the future, but because of some accident of immediate overwhelming interest which appeals to the feelings and distorts the judgment. These immediate interests exercise a kind of hydraulic pressure. . . ." Northern Securities Co. v. United States, 193 U.S. 197, 400-401 (1904).

The present cases, if not great, are at least unusual in their posture and implications, and the Holmes observation certainly has pertinent application.

The New York Times clandestinely devoted a period of three months examining the 47 volumes that came into its unauthorized possession. Once it had begun publication of material from those volumes, the New York case now before us emerged. It immediately assumed, and ever since has maintained, a frenetic pace and character. Seemingly, once publication started, the material could not be made public fast enough. Seemingly, from then on, every deferral or delay, by restraint or otherwise, was abhorrent and was to be deemed violative of the First Amendment and of the public's "right immediately to know." Yet that newspaper stood before us at oral argument and professed criticism of the Government for not lodging its protest earlier than by a Monday telegram following the initial Sunday publication.

The District of Columbia case is much the same.

Two Federal District Courts, two United States Courts of Appeals, and this Court—within a period of less than three weeks from inception until today—have been pressed into hurried decision of profound constitutional issues on inadequately developed and largely assumed facts without the careful deliberation that, hopefully, should characterize the American judicial process. There has been much writing about the law and little knowledge and less digestion of the facts. In the New York case the judges, both trial and appellate, had not yet examined the basic material when the case was brought here. In the District of Columbia case, little more was done, and what was accomplished in this respect was only on required remand, with The Washington Post, on the excuse that it was trying to protect its source of information, initially refusing to reveal what material it actually possessed, and with the District Court forced to make assumptions as to that possession.

With such respect as may be due to the contrary view, this in my opinion, is not the way to try a lawsuit of this magnitud and asserted importance. It is not the way for Federal Court to adjudicate, and to be required to adjudicate, issues that allegedl concern the nation's vital welfare. The country would be non the worse off were the cases tried quickly, to be sure, but i the customary and properly deliberative manner. The most recen of the material, it is said, dates no later than 1968, alread about three years ago, and The Times itself took three month to formulate its plan of procedure and, thus, deprived its publi for that period.

The First Amendment, after all, is only one part of an entire Constitution. Article II of the great document vests in the executive branch primary power over the conduct of foreign affairs and places in that branch the responsibility for the nation's safety.

Each provision of the Constitution is important, and I canno subscribe to a doctrine of unlimited absolutism for the First Amendment at the cost of downgrading other provisions.

First Amendment absolutism has never commanded a majority of this Court. See, for example, Near v. Minnesota, 283 U.S 697, 708 (1931), and Schenck v. United States, 249 U.S. 47, 52 (1919). What is needed here is a weighing, upon properly developed standards, of the broad right of the press to print and of the very narrow right of the Government to prevent. Such standards are not yet developed. The parties here are in disagreement as to what those standards should be. But even the newspapers concede that there are situations where restraint is in order and is constitutional. Mr. Justice Holmes gave us a suggestion when he said in Schenck:

"It is a question of proximity and degree. When a nation is at war many things that might be said in time of peace are such a hindrance to its effort that their utterance will not be endured so long as men fight and that no court could regard them as protected by any constitutional right." 249 U.S., at 52.

I therefore would remand these cases to be developed expeditiously, of course, but on a schedule permitting the orderly presentation of evidence from both sides, with the use of discovery, if necessary, as authorized by the rules, and with the preparation of briefs, oral argument and court opinions of a quality better than has been seen to this point. In making this last statement, I criticize no lawyer or judge. I know from past personal experience the agony of time pressure in the preparation of litigation. But these cases and the issues involved and the courts, including this one, deserve better than has been produced thus far.

It may well be that if these cases were allowed to develop as they should be developed, and to be tried as lawyers should try them and as courts should hear them, free of pressure and

676

nic and sensationalism, other light would be shed on the
tuation and contrary considerations, for me, might prevail.
ut that is not the present posture of the litigation.

The Court, however, decides the cases today the other way.
therefore add one final comment.

I strongly urge, and sincerely hope, that these two newspapers
ill be fully aware of their ultimate responsibilities to the
nited States of America. Judge Wilkey, dissenting in the Dis-
ict of Columbia case, after a review of only the affidavits be-
re this Court (the basic papers had not then been made
ailable by either party), concluded that there were a number
f examples of documents that, if in the possession of The
ost, and if published, "could clearly result in great harm to
e nation," and he defined "harm" to mean "the death of sol-
ers, and destruction of alliances, the greatly increased difficulty
f negotiation with our enemies, the inability of our diplomats
 negotiate. . . ." I, for one, have now been able to give at
ast some cursory study not only to the affidavits, but to the
aterial itself. I regret to say that from this examination I fear
at Judge Wilkey's statements have possible foundation. I there-
re share his concern. I hope that damage already has not
en done.

If, however, damage has been done, and if, with the Court's
ction today, these newspapers proceed to publish the critical
ocuments and there results therefrom "the death of soldiers,
e destruction of alliances, the greatly increased difficulty of
egotiation with our enemies, the inability of our diplomats to
egotiate," to which list I might add the factors of prolonga-
on of the war and of further delay in the freeing of United
tates prisoners, then the nation's people will know where the
sponsibility for these sad consequences rests.